COMMITMENT TO CULTURE

ART PATRONAGE IN EUROPE
ITS SIGNIFICANCE FOR AMERICA

Austria
Italy
Switzerland
France
West Germany
The Netherlands
Belgium
Luxembourg
England

COMMITMENT TO CULTURE

BY FREDERICK DORIAN

UNIVERSITY OF PITTSBURGH PRESS

Library of Congress Catalog Card No. 64–12488

To My Dear Wife

ACKNOWLEDGEMENTS

This study was made possible by a grant of the A. W. Mellon Educational and Charitable Foundation. The grant enabled me to conduct the inquiry in Europe and to take sabbatical leave from my teaching assignments to complete the manuscript.

I am deeply indebted to Mr. Adolph W. Schmidt, President of the A. W. Mellon Educational and Charitable Foundation, a man in the forefront of the cultural scene, for his generous encouragement of this research.

Mr. Philip S. Broughton, Secretary of the Foundation, has with kindness and patience seen this study through its various phases from the early drafts to final publication. His congenial attitude and comprehension of problems inherent in this project were decisive factors in its growth.

* * * * *

Warm words of gratitude are addressed to Mr. and Mrs. Leland Hazard for their friendly and sustained interest in my work. I was fortunate to have the counsel of Professor Hazard who is internationally known for his exemplary service to cultural causes and whose progressive thinking is an inspiration within the community.

I gratefully acknowledge the interest in this research shown by Dr. John Christian Warner, President of Carnegie Institute of Technology.

I would like to thank Mr. Norman Rice, Dean of the College of Fine Arts at Carnegie Institute of Technology, for his sympathetic understanding and help in various matters pertaining to the preparation of this study.

It is in the very nature of this project that I am indebted to many people and organizations in Europe. Without their cooperation, this book could never have materialized.

The United States Information Agency, the American Embassies and Consulates abroad cooperated in establishing contacts with European government offices and administrations of the art organizations covered in this study. Many of the officials were generous with their time and energy, making available pertinent information and documents relative to the inquiry. Permission to print and/or reprint facts and statistics is herewith gratefully acknowledged.

Many productive hours were spent with friends and colleagues reading the manuscript and discussing the issues involved. Virgil Thomson with his expert knowledge of both the European and American art scene was always stimulating with knowledgeable conversation and advice.

The counsel of Gladys Schmitt, the distinguished writer, and of Simon Goldfield was most beneficial. Over the years I have conferred with these friends on various aspects of my book and have greatly profited from this association. I am likewise grateful to Dr. Yale David Koskoff for his penetrating analysis of my findings and conclusions. Dr. Arnold Walter of the University of Toronto offered valuable criticism and suggestions. My colleague Mr. Dale R. Tuttle read the proofs of the book. It is a pleasure to acknowledge his counsel and painstaking attention to detail. Mr. John S. Edwards, manager of the Pittsburgh Symphony Orchestra, advised me in matters concerning support of the Orchestra.

I should like to acknowledge the assistance of some of my former students at Carnegie Institute of Technology: particularly Patricia Hummel and Frank Traficante. They aided me in various ways: reading chapters in drafts or proofs, checking data, and other work incidental to the completion of the book.

I am also appreciative of the help of Irene Millen, head of the Music Division at Carnegie Library of Pittsburgh, and Nancy Chalfant, Fine Arts Librarian at the Hunt Library of Carnegie Institute of Technology.

My friends and helpers are responsible for much that may be good in this study, but not for its shortcomings.

I must finally express my gratitude to Professor Agnes L. Starrett who had the burden of all editorial work. From the vantage point of her expert knowledge, she has been invaluable in the preparation of the manuscript for print. And her kind and perceptive cooperation proved to be a most felicitous experience.

The picture of the author on the book jacket was taken by Herbert K. Barnett.

The jacket was designed by Howard Warner.

CONTENTS

TABLES

PROLOGUE

I. American Paradox

The art scene in the United States reveals a puzzling and painful paradox.

Numerous aspects of art life in the United States can be interpreted with optimism. The creative achievement of American artists has earned world-wide respect and recognition. Public appreciation of the arts has grown from coast to coast. Schools, radio, television, the press, and popular magazines have spread interest in the arts among those who seldom, if ever before, participated in the artistic experience. New art centers have been completed and are functioning for the benefit of the people. The Lincoln Center for the Performing Arts in New York City dwarfs in magnitude of design and generosity of sponsorship all other projects of its kind.

Reports of a "cultural explosion" are flooding the country. But the simplified concept of the nation-wide "cultural boom" has developed into a cliché which in stereotyped repetition obscures rather than clarifies the state of the American art scene. For there is another side to its picture.

As the public interest in art and the national income attain an all-time high, the stability and security of many of our cultural institutions are precarious. In spite of all signs of progress and promise, some of our most important art organizations are not assured of continued existence. This is particularly true of institutions devoted to the performing arts, which are a chief concern of this study.

Several chains of events have dramatized the urgency of a proper solution of our problem. A sequence of crises ominously preceded the recent seasons of some of our foremost art organizations — the Metropolitan Opera, the New York Philharmonic, and the Philadelphia Orchestra. They were seriously threatened with the cancellation of their seasons for 1961-62. As this book goes to press, however, great strides forward are being made to secure more satisfactory contracts for these and other major orchestras of the nation.

The American theater is in a precarious state. A recent study[1] diagnoses the decline of the legitimate theater on the basis of irrefutable fact: in 1931 there were 66 playhouses in New York City; by 1960 this number had been halved; there were 264 productions in 1928 and only 57 in 1960. During this same period, spanning an entire generation, the attendance has declined from 12,300,000 to 8,100,000 — a decline of more than one-third. This happened in spite of the notable increase in population and the 365 per cent rise in personal income. Members of the Dramatists Guild, characterizing the situation as "the worst economic crisis the theater has ever had," in May 1961, voted overwhelmingly in favor of royalty cuts "to help alleviate the economic plight of the theater."

In short, the problem of art support is unsolved in the United States. The actual need for support is admitted. How to meet the need is still our problem. The United States, as a matter of fact, is the only large progressive nation in Western civilization without a systematic subsidy of the performing arts.

The reason for the insecurity of the performing arts is familiar: private art patronage — America's long accepted pattern — has carried, almost alone, the overwhelming burden of the growing costs of our national art life. Only in sporadic instances has the public purse been opened to aid the performing arts. We are now confronted with the question of whether the paternalistic sponsors, whose wealth for more than a century has yielded munificent contributions to American art, will be able to continue to assume the ever-mounting responsibilities. It is true foundations have become increasingly generous to the humanities, especially in educational institutions, but the share allocated to the performing arts is unimpressive compared with that granted other beneficiaries.[2]

II. Antithetical Attitudes

The methods of art support in America are in sharp contrast with those of Europe. European art patronage is an ancient tradition and the experience of centuries. The history of art support in Europe proves how a cultural legacy creates simultaneously the enjoyment of and need for a full art life and the means for its continuous fulfillment. As a result of a process spanning many centuries, there prevails in contemporary Europe a secure support of the performing arts, both west and east of the Iron Curtain.

The Europeans have adopted the principle of government patronage. Whatever the form of government — monarchy or republic — European countries have traditionally managed to make large funds available for their theaters, operas, and concert organizations. The sums required are voted by federal and provincial parliaments or by municipal councils, and the allocations are administered by governmental departments.

European patronage is perpetual. It has flourished in times of peace. It has survived social upheavals and wars. At all times official recognition has surrounded the arts with an aura of prestige and public importance. And Europeans are constantly extending the scope of a patronage which is their heritage of thousands of years.

The United States is a young country, and art patronage has been in private hands since its inception. Yet the possibility of government assistance to the arts has not been overlooked or objected to, even in government circles. In fact, members of both the Democratic and Republican parties have introduced bills to direct government aid to the arts.* Some of these proposals center around the provision to establish a "Federal Advisory Council on the Arts to assist in the growth and development of the fine arts in the nation's capital and elsewhere in the United States." Others aim at a "program of grants to states for the development of projects in the arts." All proposals have in common the principle of governmental encouragement and assistance to the arts. At this writing, however, Congress has acted on few of these bills.

The late President Kennedy set forward proposals for an Advisory Council on the Arts to consist of twenty to thirty private citizens "recognized for their knowledge and experience in the arts." Their main task will be to make recommendations to the President and provide him with vital suggestions for cultivating the art life of the nation.

There are widespread claims that our country is not ready for legislation in favor of public art subsidy. The chief objections are twofold. First, we are told that the United States cannot afford governmental aid to the arts. Second, there is fear of federal controls; centralization and bureaucracy, so it is argued, might render the most noble intentions ineffective. There is distrust of a closer relationship between art and politics. Curiously, however, our government has not hesitated to take a direct and active part in promoting American art abroad. The arts are considered a valuable tool of foreign policy, a dialectic form of defense in the cold war. But on the domestic front our government traditionally abstains from assisting the arts.**

The differences in the basic attitudes toward patronage — governmental aloofness in the United States, governmental participation in Europe — are deeply rooted in history and cultural traditions.

III. Aim of the Study

This book analyzes the nature and form of European art patronage, past and present. Such a task may be considered an end in itself — research to establish a record that is part of the story of civilization. But there is this added and specific objective: to find out what we can learn from the European patterns. Can certain methods applied to art support across the Atlantic be successfully transplanted to America? We believe they can. Despite all obvious disparities between art life in the Old

*Cf. concluding Chapter for list of proposed legislation.

**A noteworthy exception occurred in 1935 when the government inaugurated the Works Progress Administration with a special department devoted to the arts.

World and in the New World there are strong analogies: they have grown out of various practical as well as ideological premises which uphold freedom of expression. Furthermore, the moral and aesthetic values inherent in great works of art are identical all over the world; they do not change with geography and climate.

Art patronage, like art itself, is subject to organic growth. As this study intends to show, the organic conditions by which the arts flourish in a favorable environment can be created and fostered by the will to culture. The arts thrive, not haphazardly in any environment, but through conditions created within specific environments. Through an analysis of the conditions the following survey of the vast complex of European art patronage can provide some useful answers to corresponding problems in the United States.

The study covers the field of the performing arts in Europe west of the Iron Curtain; it does not aim at all-inclusiveness but concentrates on countries that offer the most time-tested and characteristic solutions of our problems. The choice of countries in no way suggests lack of respect for the cultural achievements and art patronage of Europe's nations not included in this study. Neither does this book mean to glorify the European ways; its aim has been to consider objectively both the negative and the positive aspects.

The nine countries surveyed in the following chapters claim a tradition of art patronage which can be traced to the Middle Ages and, in certain cases, even to antiquity. Their governments* hold a highly advanced attitude toward the support of the performing arts, even though the forms of government are not the same. Four are monarchies (Belgium, England, Holland, Luxembourg) and five republics (Austria, France, Italy, Switzerland, West Germany). At the same time, the patterns of patronage in these nations differ from one another in vital aspects. Thus our survey provides a panorama of many roads leading to the solution of the problems under study. The following chapters, then, are intended as a storehouse of information. It is an obvious advantage that we can use the European scene as a testing ground. There we can observe, almost in laboratory fashion, the connections between all possible forms of organized patronage and their benefits to the people.

We should be aware, however, that full art support is accorded priority not only in the West. The Soviet countries, Russia and her satellites, do not differ from the Western democracies in the principle of governmental subsidization of the arts; they disagree in their definition of the

*In Europe the term "state" is used interchangeably with "nation" or "country." State, then, is also the sovereign government of an entire nation, collectively rather than one of the separate states forming a nation (as in the United States).

role of art in society. The democratic belief in the fundamental free values of all art clashes with the totalitarian concept that upholds art and artist as tools of the political state.

IV. The Inquiry, its Method and Perspective

Music and drama live through interpretation. It is in performance that the vitality and success of the musical and dramatic arts are directly tested and measured. In performance the creator, the interpreter, and the audience form a specific interrelationship, a triad of the art experience. The support of performance is one of the patron's crucial responsibilities to artist as well as to society.

Inevitably, the performing arts make greater demands on support than do the visual arts. Performances in the theater or on the concert stage are costly, often prohibitively so. Their deficits are common knowledge. The large ensembles in the production of musical or dramatic works call for extensive preparation and organization. The highly specialized nature of these ensembles requires trained and skilled teams working within art institutes that must be skillfully administered, properly housed, and equipped with expensive technical machinery. Most of these organizations can never become self-supporting. The opera, the drama, the ballet, the symphony orchestra, the chamber music group — all require adequate support if they are to function on a high artistic level. This is so in America, or in Europe, or anywhere else on the globe — regardless of political environment and of the kind of controls within which such performing organizations must exist.

The special circumstances surrounding art support in Europe prompted the method of inquiry for this study. The basic research took the form of interviewing government officials on federal, provincial, and municipal levels, conferring with administrators, artistic directors, and various personnel of art organizations. Documents were examined to establish the authentic readings of parliamentary laws, of royal decrees and statutes of all kinds pertaining to the detailed premises and execution of official sponsorship. Where private patronage still assists the arts, special note of this method has been made. Tax support is examined and European art patronage is evaluated from the viewpoint of the governmental donors as well as of the people who are the beneficiaries.

As the following chapter will show, European methods for the most part work well. And there is much to be learned from the multiformity of solutions. But Europe has also witnessed lethal experiments with the arts. In three major instances the Old World has demonstrated the effects of dictatorships on art life. The usurpation of the arts by the

Fascists, the Nazis, and the Communists reminds us of the blessings of democratic solutions. This report does not overlook the totalitarian traps west of the Iron Curtain, where under the pretense of "total patronage," death attacked the arts from ambush.

The patterns of European art patronage are the logical outgrowth of European history. And so, understanding of the chief problems of this study is not possible without some understanding of European traditions and governments. Political, economic, and psychological factors have contributed directly to the development of European art life in all of its diversity. Research in the arts and humanities — even when restricted to so specialized a field as art patronage — must recognize the interrelationship of these components. Everywhere art support appears as a cause and as a consequence of a will to culture; creative ingenuity inspires sponsorship and sponsorship stimulates creative work.

Thus we become aware that the problem of patronage is more than facts and figures. It is inherently an issue of human relations and the result of human motivation on all of its levels. It is determined by values and standards, and it represents choice on the part of an individual, of a group, of a country.

Obviously all statistics pertaining to art support are in continual change. But the fluctuation of budgets and expenditures is of minor significance in comparison with the persistence of patronage which the facts and figures unequivocally uphold.

This study is always mindful of motivation. What made kings and aristocrats become munificent patrons of the arts? Why did the people themselves maintain this patronage when monarchies fell and were succeeded by republics? Why did they finally extend art subsidies to their present scope? History holds the key to the answers to these questions. Heritage and tradition have provided Europeans with sufficient motivation to help the arts on an extensive scale. But to us in the United States this entire complex of causalities is of more than historical interest. For we are faced with the troublesome barrier of insufficient motivation in regard to national and communal art support. And the unsatisfactory state of art subsidy can be reduced, in its final analysis, to this simple fact: we still do not sufficiently care to aid the performing arts in a manner worthy of our nation's greatness, of our cultural mission, and of our proud claim to leadership in a free world. This attitude can be changed; there are already many clear indications that it is changing.

The study of cultural conditions which prompt Europeans to revere and aid the arts generously is as worthy of our attention as the actual financial support. Hence the following chapters are not merely concerned with a report of what is happening on the art scene today, but with how this happened throughout the centuries and why it still is happening with such marked success. Inevitably the search leads to the borders of psychology and historical philosophy. The framework of this volume permitted only occasional development of historical detail. It is the broad historical perspective which is essential for our conclusions.

The great deeds of patronage, history shows, have originated where specific environments have been favorable to the arts. The study of art support cannot be separated from the study of inherent ideologies, of people living within the framework of agelong traditions that shape their thinking. The psychology of nations is still a young science. We still have much to learn about the citizen side of the individual. And we must try to explore the psychological climate in which the arts and their patronage grow best.

Art patronage is a living process. As the title of this book implies, it is only through a *commitment to culture* that a nation can achieve a rich and flourishing art life. The principal theme of this book is the continuous and generous art patronage which has pervaded Europe's cultural history throughout the ages. This theme is a thread woven into the texture of the study. Each chapter, concentrating on premises and procedures of art support in an individual country, is in essence a variation of the central thematic emphasis.

The first chapter discusses art patronage in Austria. Vienna, her two thousand-year-old capital, appears, in terms of cultural geography, as the last undivided fortress of Western civilization. Once the center of the great Habsburg empire, Vienna is today ominously close to the Iron Curtain and the anxiously guarded frontier between the Eastern and the Western worlds.

In succeeding chapters the panorama of European patronage unfolds westward, country by country. And finally, with the chapter on England it reaches the nation which in language and history, in tradition of parliamentary democracy and, before all, in the various manifestations of art life, appears closest to us in the United States.

The concluding part of the book is addressed to America. Art patronage is a prime force of civilization, west and east of the Atlantic. And in its broadest sense, the problem of art support concerns every American; for a free art life — its creative strength as well as its full enjoyment — is allied with the basic concepts of genuine democracy. It is bound up, as European history has shown so dramatically and fatefully, with the cause of personal liberty and spiritual leadership in the free world.

AUSTRIA

I. Wellsprings of Culture

Bulwark of the Performing Arts

Art patronage is not an isolated phenomenon; it is conditioned in every phase of its growth by the state of general culture. An attempt to trace the advance of civilization in any country faces the difficult question where to begin. In a study of Austria this problem is particularly complex.

"Oesterreich" — the very concept of Austria as an independent nation — assumed its meaning through slow historic developments. Even in the limited territory which comprises modern Austria there prevails amazing stratification of ancient cultures.

The soil of Austria has nurtured art life since time immemorial. It was the prehistoric home of one of the oldest civilizations. In the Alpine lake region near Salzburg lies Hallstatt, a town known today primarily for its pictorial charm. Even in prehistoric times Hallstatt was a cultural center of paramount significance. Archeology has adopted the topographical name Hallstatt to designate an era of prehistoric civilization; "Hallstatt Period" marks the First Iron Age in Central and Western Europe.

Inquiry into Austria's culture might begin with a later and crucial phase of its history, a millennium after the Iron Age, when Austria had become a Roman colony, whose center, Vindobona, is now known as Vienna. Vienna has kept the first syllable of its Latin name, Vin; Wien is the Germanized spelling for Vienna. Marcus Aurelius, Roman Emperor and philosopher, died in Vindobona in 180 A.D.

Or inquiry could begin after the tribal migrations, with the great missionary movement that was fostered by many monasteries throughout Austria, when the monks became the torch carriers of a new Western culture. The Benedictine monastery in Salzburg founded a library as early as 700 A.D., and for centuries to come the libraries in the abbeys and cloisters of Austria remained primary sources of learning and scholarship. As in other Western countries, so in Austria, worship was the cradle of art patronage. Within their long historical evolution the performing arts first served the liturgy, and their support came from the Church.

Along with the service to the Church, the arts appear as an enrichment of various Austrian court residences, and as adornment of life on the aristocratic estates, until finally, the performing arts interpret a people's culture where both the government and private patrons share their support. This triple role of patronage, exercised over many centuries, has created specific traditions of art support that have remained Austria's revered heritage to this very day. But despite the changes in patronage, the tradition of art support through the centuries maintains a remarkable continuity.

The long heritage is apparent in many ways. The performing arts seldom prosper alone; they prosper concurrently with all manifestations of education and the sister arts. This is evident in the history of Church patronage, where music, morality plays, and the ornamentation of holy places went hand in hand. It is evident in the cultural achievements of the Habsburg dynasty, which began modestly in the thirteenth century, grew into hegemony over the Holy Roman Empire, and ended with the collapse of the Austrian-Hungarian monarchy at the end of World War I. In 1365 Rudolph IV founded the University of Vienna, which still bears the name Rudolphina. With the reign of Maximilian I (1493-1519) Austria already had reached an early summit of imperial art patronage.

But the chronicle of Austria is by no means only one of peace and the civilizing offerings of peace. On the contrary, it is a tempestuous history, replete with civil strife and international warfare of untold cruelty. In defiance of the fiercest threats from Asiatic hordes in the Middle Ages and of the civil rebellions and partitionings of later times, Austria has stood, until today, an outpost of Western civilization.

Austria is a land of music and of the theater. It has not produced painters of world stature as have Italy, Spain, and The Netherlands. Nor have Austria's poets made an impact on world literature to a degree comparable to those of England, France, or Germany. Austria's composers, however, are without peer. And the temples of art built by her architects still stand as monuments of noble imagination, of impeccable taste, and of refined elegance.

During the Baroque era, Austria engaged in a munificent patronage of the performing arts. Since the sixteenth century Vienna has been the capital of a large empire. That remarkable "Baroque emperor," Leopold I (1658-1705), envisioned Vienna as a resplendent art center. His successors, Joseph I, Karl VI, and Maria Theresia, maintained Vienna as a cultural mirror of the West. Austrian art life, during this period following the repelled attacks from the East, became an eloquent testimony of a painfully won liberty. Brilliant men of every European land were invited by the emperors to work in the cities of Austria so that the nation might be enriched by their artistry, knowledge, and wisdom. And so they came: composers and poets from Italy; architects and scientists from Germany and France; painters from the Low Countries; and a legion of hard-working artisans from Bohemia, Hungary, Poland, Bosnia, and other distant dominions of the Habsburg empire.

Contributions of artists from many lands transformed the nation into what it has never ceased to be: a bulwark of the performing arts, and a showplace of Baroque architecture inspired by the melody and rhythm of a beautiful landscape. Austria's cities form a continuous stage of impressive palaces, gardens, and monuments on squares that seem to be outdoor festival halls, and the Baroque scenery blends curiously well with the medieval substructure of the cities. Ancient towns grew around the Gothic churches that are among the oldest and most characteristic in the world, for instance Vienna's St. Stephan, with its heaven-seeking spiral which survived, in the center of utter destruction, even the aerial attack of World War II.

Thus, in Austria the arts unify, affirm, and inspire the environment in which they have flourished.

II. Ecclesiastical and Imperial Patronage

Austria's splendid art patronage, to be sure, was partly designed to reflect the imperial idea, to represent its grandeur, and to instill admiration of its patron, the Court.

How could the Habsburgs afford patronage on such a scale? What was the economic state of the monarchy? The answer leads to a paradox. At the most crucial time of extravagant sponsorship Austria was a world power in decline. The brilliant era of Charles V (1500-1558) had spent itself. This most sovereign ruler of the Habsburg dynasty had controlled the vast Holy Roman Empire of the German Nation and had governed Europe from the Atlantic and Mediterranean to the Carpathian Mountains and the Balkans. But by the eighteenth century the European balance of power had changed and the Catholic Habsburgs were losing their grip over the Protestant north. Abandoning Spain altogether, they withdrew to Austria. Vienna, then the largest German-speaking city (population, 250,000), had become the permanent Habsburg residence. The emperors imported much of the Spanish *grandezza* and court etiquette into the relaxed and amiable environment of the Danubian city. Wars and political entanglements had been costly. The Austrian monarchy was fast losing its fabulous wealth. Under the circumstances, economy and caution might have been the watchword of the rulers; but thrift was against their temperament. Lavish art patronage continued. And the people of Austria were receptive, for they had a strong affinity with the performing arts.

The Catholic Church (to which most of the population belongs) had begun early to sponsor music and drama on a semi-liturgical basis. The religious orders of Benedictines and Jesuits produced allegorical plays within their monasteries. By the sixteenth century these biblical plays had become well entrenched. They evoked apocalyptic visions and scenes from the New Testament in accordance with the church calendar. Eventually even musical plays found their way into monasteries. In the Upper Austrian abbey of Lambach, the old theater can still be seen in its original state.

During the seventeenth century, too, Baroque concepts of style, impressively manifest in the architecture of many of the country's churches, penetrated the musical part of the service. In 1628, at the solemn inauguration of the Cathedral of Salzburg, the *Festival Mass* by Orazio Benevoli (1602-1672) was performed. The spacious dimensions of the Cathedral, with its twelve balconies and its organ below the high dome, suggested to the composer the typical Baroque structure of his score. His music calls for two mixed choruses of eight parts each. These vocal forces were placed on the twelve individual balconies and accompanied by a thirty-four part orchestra and the three organs of the Cathedral. The trumpets gave the brass choir its festive color. This inaugural *Mass* for the Salzburg Cathedral set a new pattern of church concerts, which developed into a firmly established tradition.

Church and Court excelled in performances that were as brilliant as they were artistically significant. It would be wrong to interpret the munificence of Habsburg emperors merely as an external gesture, as a means of self-glorification. Many of the Habsburgs were truly cultivated people. Their artistic talent and love for the arts was beyond doubt. Some of them were creative. We have insight into their musical talent through their published compositions,[1] which show professional standards and devotion to serious music.

Leopold I (1658-1705) was the most talented of these imperial composers. He has no less than nine sacred oratorios to his credit; among these is the moving *Sacrificio Abramo*, completed two years after his ascension to the throne. In the imperial quarters Leopold kept a harpsichord in every room.

In subsequent generations the Habsburgs took more than a passing interest in the performing arts. Love and respect for the arts, particularly for music, was passed on as a spiritual heirloom in the imperial family. Some of the most extraordinary musicians served as court composers or music teachers for the children of the court. Among them were Caldara, Cesti, Fux, Gluck, Mozart, Paisiello, Salieri, Wagenseil. These were the musicians who set the tone and standards of the royal students. Thus the contact of the court with art was not haphazard and the purpose was not sheer entertainment. There was an empathy with the artistic experience itself, an attempt to come to grips with art and to learn its craft.

On many occasions members of the imperial court took an active part in the art life. Every official event was an opportunity for performance in the grand manner. Operas and plays were commissioned for all major celebrations. They were produced with the splendor and largess that was typical of court spectacles during the seventeenth and eighteenth centuries. They gave fresh meaning to the term *Baroque* and its style of representation.

In 1668 the wedding of Emperor Leopold I and the Princess Maria Theresia of Spain was celebrated in Vienna by the première of the opera *Il Pomo d'Oro*, composed by the court conductor, Marcantonio Cesti. The performance was turned into a fabulous show: five thousand people on the square near the court garden watched one thousand actors, singers, and dancers on a specially built stage. Like most operas of this era, the score of *Il Pomo d'Oro* contained one scene composed by the Emperor himself.

Court Theaters for the People

Leopold's successor, Joseph I, built a large opera house in Vienna in the initial year of his reign (1705), and he increased the court orchestra to 107 players. During his reign, in 1708, the Theater am Kärnthner-Thor was built. While the municipality had an important share in this enterprise, the Emperor paid for the building out of his own purse.

Karl VI, successor to his brother Joseph I, was an enthusiastic musician. At his summer palace in Laxenburg, he directed a performance of the opera *Elisa* by his scholarly court composer, J. J. Fux. "It is a pity your Majesty did not become a *Kapellmeister*," Fux complimented his sovereign employer. "I am doing quite all right, as it is," Karl VI replied with a touch of his Viennese humor.

In 1739, Maria Theresia, celebrating the birthday of her father, Karl VI, appeared as the prima donna of an Italian opera. The future Empress maintained a lifelong interest in the musical theater. After the death of her father she found herself in difficult financial circumstances; but she decided: "The theaters must continue. Without them, life is not worth living!" She underwrote the support of the theaters to the extent of 150,000 gulden, an enormous figure for the time and the state of Austria's economy.

On March 22, 1760, Maria Theresia established a permanent commission to organize and unify the educational system in the German-speaking parts of her nation, and in 1774, she made education compulsory in Austria.

This partnership of art patronage and education is a typical alliance which we shall encounter repeatedly throughout this study: where there is genuine concern with art, there is also a heightened recognition of the needs of education.

A new, truly modern dimension was added to art patronage during the reign of Maria Theresia's oldest son, Joseph II,* one of the most enlightened monarchs in European history. As a staunch disciple of Rousseau, Reason and Enlightenment were his guideposts. Joseph II was the unique combination of a revolutionary and an emperor. He abolished all remnants of tyrannical government. He set up an equitable basis for taxation, established religious tolerance, and inaugurated what might be considered a modern concept of freedom of the press. He founded many and various institutions, coordinating the health and spiritual welfare of the people. He built Vienna's great hospital from which the university clinics developed. His love of art expressed itself in a flare for organization, in sponsorship, and in productive initiative. His most personal contributions to the nation were the Burgtheater and the National Library.

On April 8, 1776, the "National Theater next to the Burg" opened its doors to the people. The Burgtheater, as it is called to this day, is the second oldest national theater in Europe. (The Comédie Française in Paris preceded it.)** The first manager of the newly founded stage was the Emperor himself. He was passionately devoted to this task. He decided on the repertory and engaged the actors. Even warfare did not dampen his preoccupation with the theater; he carried on his managerial activities from the front by way of special messengers. In 1778 Joseph asked the members of the Court theaters to submit in writing suggestions (eine schriftliche Erinnerung) for improving the management and artistic direction of their organizations. A committee of five members, the so-called *Regie*, was entrusted with the fate of the theaters. In the year 1779 the Emperor proclaimed the Theater Gesetz, the law of the theater, which raised their sponsorship to a national cause.

The new reforms were expensive. During the carnival season alone the deficit of the court theaters amounted to 60,000 florins. It is difficult, of course, to evaluate the purchasing power of such a sum in modern terms. The generous Emperor was worried about the possibility of having to curtail the theater budget, yet the stages retained priority within the new framework of the modern state Joseph envisioned.

At this time the Emperor replaced the title Court Theater with that of National Theater. It was a significant step. The theater was to be the property of the common people as distinguished from the court or

*Emperor from 1780 to 1790; in 1765 Joseph became co-regent with his mother; he succeeded Maria Theresia to the throne in 1780.

**Cf. Chapter on France.

any privileged class. The theaters were intended as a gift to the nation. But they remained Emperor Joseph's pride and joy. "I wonder what you will think of our theaters?" was his favorite question to the many officials and distinguished visitors who came to Vienna to study the reforms and structural organizations of his modern state.

Certain artistic policies inaugurated by Emperor Joseph are observed to this day in the Burgtheater. Among them is one of the theater's unwritten laws, the so-called *curtain prohibition.* It implies that no member of the permanent ensemble can be singled out for public acclaim during a performance. When the Emperor formulated in 1778 the organizational statute for the National Theater, he was vitally concerned with the unbroken and uninterrupted representation of masterworks. He would not tolerate any histrionic antics or claques or public outbursts. Such purism was appropriate, he thought, in a theater which he envisioned as the leading stage for the German language. The Burgtheater holds a place of honor to this day, and an uncompromising attitude toward integrity of performance has been a contributing factor.

Emperor Joseph II saw in the serious stage a principal instrument of education and enlightenment, and this idea determined the repertory in the new National Theater. He insisted that the plays and operas performed should always be works of unquestioned artistic merit. He was interested neither in audience appeal for its own sake, nor in the receipts at the box office as a measuring rod for success. He did not capitulate to the treasurer's complaint that the attendance of certain important, although unpopular, works was disappointing. "They will come eventually," Joseph said. "An Emperor can wait."

III. Aristocratic Sponsorship Haydn, Mozart, Beethoven

In the broad scope of their art life and significant artistic achievement, some of Austria's aristocratic residences compared well with the imperial court in Vienna.

Among the most munificent sponsors in the eighteenth century were the princes Anton and Nicholas Eszterházy, who achieved immortality as the patrons of Haydn.[2] The court opera, orchestra, and chamber ensemble at Eszterháza had a busy schedule. Normally, the schedule included two operas and two formal concerts weekly. The playing of chamber music was informal, and Prince Nicholas himself often participated. The opera productions were considered model performances. Empress Maria Theresia claimed, "One had to go to Eszterháza to hear opera well given."

Haydn spent three decades in the service of the Princes Eszterházy. It is worthy of note that one of the greatest composers to enjoy continuous patronage was the one who was freest from any control by his employer. Haydn's creative liberty of action emerges as the ideal formula for all patronage in a free society and at all times. We can assess the nature of the princely patronage from Haydn's words:

> My Prince was always satisfied with my works; I not only had the encouragement of constant approval, but as conductor of an orchestra, I could make experiments, observe what produced an effect and what weakened it, and was thus in a position to improve, alter, make additions or omissions, and be as bold as I pleased; I was cut off from the world; there was no one to confuse or torment me, and I was forced to become original.

Mozart was not as fortunate as Haydn in obtaining a similarly secure and creatively rewarding appointment. It is true that as a young man Mozart became Hofkapellist and concertmaster of the orchestra maintained by the Archbishop of Salzburg. By joining this organization in his native town Mozart seemed to be embarking on an auspicious career as a performer. But the Archbishop Hieronymous Count Colloredo, the last ecclesiastical sovereign (Landesfürst) of Salzburg, was a tyrannical ruler. And in 1776 Mozart's tenure in Salzburg came to an unpleasant end. He went abroad, but returned to his native Salzburg. He spent the last decade of his life in Vienna (1781-1791). Mozart never learned to conform; in the cosmopolitan capital he again failed to make the kind of adjustments that might have endeared him to the various powerful patrons he met. His correspondence with family and friends gives us much insight into his democratic disdain of aristocrats, in both the ecclesiastical and secular domains. It was partly due to this inability to come to lasting terms with some of his potential sponsors that Mozart's life remained a tragic struggle.

The Salzburg Court Music had been a long-established institution. Founded as early as 1591, it represented in Mozart's time a significant example of a fine orchestra maintained by a prince of the Church. Support by the clerical and the secular aristocracy remained a decisive factor in Austria's art life. In cities like Salzburg and in rural regions like Eszterháza, the common people depended on whatever share in the art life these aristocratic patrons cared to offer them, for many events were still reserved for the privileged guests of the patrons.

The French revolution of 1789 frightened some aristocrats — even outside of France — into a drastic curtailment of their roles as art patrons. Insecurity and instability besieged Europe's upper classes. But many of the titled landowners continued to sponsor the performing arts on a modest scale. The maintenance of their musical ensembles was made possible by the double duty of their employees: they were hired as servants and musical performers.

In this sense, we understand the kind of advertising that appeared in 1789, in the *Wiener Zeitung* (*Vienna Journal*):

> Wanted, for a house of the gentry, a manservant who knows how to play the violin well, and to accompany difficult clavier sonatas.

Such diversified requirements in one person were not unusual in the eighteenth century; often musicians were held to be in the same social category as domestic servants.

An Artist Immortalizes his Patrons

The Napoleonic wars threw Europe into chaos. Temporary defeat brought indignity to the Austrian dynasty. In 1806, Emperor Franz I abdicated as the ruler of the Holy Roman Empire. Vienna was chosen the seat of the fateful Congress of 1814, called for the purpose of redistributing the disturbed balance of continental power. The crucial diplomatic meeting restored world prestige to the Austrian capital.

The performances of Beethoven's *Fidelio* tower above the multitude of artistic events offered during these decisive times. The opera extols two fundamental ideals of mankind: liberty and sacrifice. It was a logical choice of the management of the Kärnthnerthor Theater for the auspicious year.

An account of Beethoven's behavior toward his various patrons would warrant a full length study in itself. The psychodynamics of these relationships ranged, in their ambivalence, from extreme attachment and friendship to downright hostility. The roster of Beethoven's sponsors includes members of the imperial family and of the high Austrian as well as the foreign nobility. There are more than fifty dedications of his works; and many of these are indirect acknowledgements of financial support.

In Beethoven's time private sponsorship of individual artists was practiced widely in Austrian society and had become a matter of great prestige to the sponsor himself. In this sense the patron needed the artist as much as the artist needed the patron. Social standing, originally determined by rank and title only, was now measured by nobility of another kind: by the degree of contribution to the art life in the community. It would be infamous to question the generous motivation and lofty idealism of most patrons; however, sponsoring of the arts was viewed by some as another chance to climb the ladder to higher social status and to rise above competing aristocrats. Before long the bourgeoisie began to imitate these patterns to gain prestige.

by the trusted advisors of the Emperor, space had to be found for new buildings to house the arts. The project to raze the walls was opposed violently by conservative Austrians, who begged the Emperor to veto what they denounced as shocking vandalism.

Franz Joseph stood firm. A circular avenue was constructed around the city and appropriately called *The Ring*. This wide and handsome tree-lined boulevard, bordering on a chain of neighboring gardens, became the site of public palaces, many of them devoted to the performing arts. The building program was of extraordinary scope, intended to enrich the nation with a veritable forum of "Temples of Art"; its realization dramatized the idea that a city itself could become a work of art. There originated, either directly on the Ring or in close proximity, two new Court theaters, the Opera and the Burgtheater; two museums of art and natural history; the new University; the "Grecian" Parliament; the neo-Gothic city hall, the Palace of Justice; the Academy of Fine Arts; the Musikverein; and the Künstlerhaus. All were built during this remarkable era when a congested city of stone became a garden city with many festive halls and educational institutions.

Vienna was the art metropolis of Europe, and the Opera was its shrine. The Emperor wanted the new building to be the most beautiful ever to house a lyrical theater, a "Temple of the Muses," and although he was a rather frugal man, he did not ask the architects for bids. The commission was to be given to the architect with the most beautiful design, regardless of its cost. In 1857 ground was broken on the Ring for the prize-winning project by the team of architects Eduard van der Nüll and August Siccard von Siccardsburg. The new Court Opera, completed in 1869, developed into an international center of dramatic music; Mozart's *Don Giovanni* was the opening performance; soon, Verdi and Wagner came as guest conductors.

The strongest leadership and moral impulse of Austrian art life within the first decade of the twentieth century stemmed from the director of the Court Opera, Gustav Mahler, who transformed this theater into an art institute with performances regarded all over the world as models of music-dramatic fulfillment. The Emperor supported faithfully Mahler's daring reforms. Mahler's authority as director of opera was almost absolute.[5] There were no financial pressures. Interferences were not tolerated. Unity between score and stage had been the creative aim of such masters as Gluck, Weber, or Wagner. But it was Mahler who succeeded in blending all aspects of production — music, drama, decor, costumes, and lighting — in an opera theater with constantly changing repertory.

The new Burgtheater (opened in 1888) became a worthy *pendant* to the Opera. It attained the prestige of the first theater of the German language, offering a variety of great plays each season, and continuing the tradition inaugurated by its founder, Joseph II. To this day the generous governmental subsidization of the Burgtheater is motivated by its cultural mission: to preserve the refinement of the German language, the ensemble idea of the theater, and the repertory system — on the highest possible level.

V. The Republic

Effects of World War I

Franz Joseph's long life of eighty-six years ended in 1916, in the middle of World War I. Fighting on the front lines did not disrupt the art life in the hinterland. Theaters and concerts continued in the Austrian cities; but works by poets or composers of enemy nations were avoided. On November 12, 1918, two years after Franz Joseph's death, Austria changed from a monarchy to a republic.

Prior to World War I, fifty-two million people lived in the multinational empire of Austria-Hungary. The monarchy of Franz Joseph I had stretched from the Russian border in the north to the Italian in the south; from its long German frontier deep down to the Balkans; from the high Alps at the Swiss border to the lowlands of the Hungarian steppes. And Austria reached to the Adriatic Sea, with Trieste as a port of call to every continent of the globe.

After the disintegration of the Habsburg monarchy, the republic of Austria counted not quite 7,000,000 inhabitants. Austria became a small inland nation with an area of 32,375 square miles, about the size of Maine. The Austrians had to reconcile themselves to the fact that they now lived in a small, economically weak and politically insecure state, with a capital once designed to be the economic and political center of a large empire. People were hungry. Misery had befallen the defeated country. Public morale was at its lowest ebb.

In this situation crucial decisions concerning art support had to be made by the government. Its attitude was positive. Art life had to go on, perhaps more than ever. There could be no vacuum. The will of the people asserted itself: now, especially, they needed the arts. And the government provided them with their operas, theaters, and concerts. In shabby clothes, ill-fed people walked through ill-lit streets or came in overcrowded streetcars to hear, in unheated halls, chamber and orchestral music, operas, and oratorios. The music of the masters never sounded more pure than when food and clothing were ersatz, when racketeers usurped business, and finance and inflation curtailed the buying power of the population. And so the new Republic of Austria assumed full responsibility for the art life of its people. The Court Opera became the State Opera; the Hofburg Theater became the Burgtheater. The department in charge of imperial art sponsorship, which had been the Oberst Hofmeisteramt (i.e., the office of the controller of the imperial household) was now taken over by the Ministry of Education. Only titles were changed; there was never a question of discontinuing function. The arts were treated as public utilities and necessities. One of the first appropriations of the new government — the largest within the total art budget — went to the State Opera, and the best available artists were put in charge. Beginning with the season 1919-20, Richard Strauss assumed the post of codirector of the opera.

The postwar years were years of highly charged intellectual climate. Sigmund Freud was practising in Vienna. Arthur Schnitzler, Hugo von Hofmannsthal, Stefan Zweig, and Peter Altenberg were writing plays, novels, poems. The great social critic Karl Kraus gave the written word new moral strength in his periodical, *Die Fackel* (*The Torch*). Vienna was the home of the painters Oskar Kokoschka and Egon Schiele. The architect Adolf Loos introduced the American-inspired concept "form follows function" to central Europe. Otto Wagner, likewise, brought new Western ideas to architectural projects in the Baroque capital. Vienna was enriched by the presence of the composers Arnold Schoenberg, Anton Webern, and Alban Berg.

Catastrophe of Anschluss

The twenties were soon to turn into an era of inflation which played havoc with all economic aspects of public and private life. The new token of Austrian standard currency, the so-called *Gold Krone* (gold crown), was worth millions in paper bills almost overnight. And soon *one* million in paper was not enough to buy a loaf of bread. Inevitably, the economic chaos and the consequent political confusion led to catastrophic events.

In the early thirties a cultural provincialism slowly crept over Austria. Some of the great artists, scientists, and scholars left the country for a more stimulating and congenial environment. There was a last flickering of the old glory in the opera and concert when Toscanini came to Austria for long stretches of the season. He and Bruno Walter transformed the Salzburg Festival into a truly global affair. The Salzburg theater still profited from the foundation laid by Max Reinhardt. Eugene Ormandy came to conduct the Bruckner Festival in Linz. But these were holidays on a volcano.

The year 1938 marked the *Anschluss*, Hitler's annexation of Austria. During the ensuing World War II, the Austrian theaters, for the first time in their long history, suffered a complete shutdown of all activities, as ordered by Goebbels, the Nazi Minister for Enlightenment and Propaganda. Austria had become part of the European race for self-destruction. By the end of the war, many of the nation's beautiful landmarks were destroyed. The Opera and Burgtheater were burnt-out shells.

Bipartisan Art Support

Today, Austria's political structure presents, once more, a nation where two main parties prevail. Not the World Wars, not even the Nazi horrors, have essentially shaken this balance.[6] To arrive at a workable coalition of bipartisan government, the ministries and portfolios are traditionally distributed between the two main parties, and the administration of Austria's art program is strictly bipartisan. Austrians describe this kind of government by the term *Proporz*. This implies a system of proportioning the power between the nation's two principal political parties. It is customary to assign all pivotal positions in Austrian government to two men: one representing the "Black" or Clerical Party (Österreichische Volkpartei) i.e., Austrian People's Party, the other the "Red Party" (Sozial Demokraten). As one would expect, the socialists are concentrated in the cities; the clericals in the rural districts. The bipartisan plan is this: if the minister is a socialist, his deputy will be a member of the clerical party, or vice versa. This system has worked well in the patronage of the performing arts — as evidenced by uncontestable results.

The Ministry of Education — which is the fountainhead of art patronage — has repeatedly been entrusted to a learned member of the clerical party, often to a man from the provinces. The city hall of Vienna, by contrast, is traditionally under control of the social democrats, who take a very active part in the support of the performing arts in the capital. In other Austrian cities analogous conditions prevail.

On all federal issues, which are of wide scope in the Austrian art program, patronage is directed by compromise. It speaks well for the political maturity of the government that a bipartisan team can act as a unit to guide Austria's cultural institutions. Whatever the party affiliations, the political beliefs do not perceptively interfere with artistic policies in the state theaters, in the principal concert organizations, or in the provincial operas and playhouses. Yet in such areas as censorship ideological differences assert themselves.

The Art Senate

The Ministry of Education is the federal department in charge of subsidies. But supreme within all cultural organization is the Art Senate (Kunst Senat) to which the Minister appoints some of the best available experts in their respective fields. (For instance, some members of the senate have received the Austrian State Prize, which is given annually in each of the arts.) The Minister habitually consults with this group on all artistic matters, and appointments go to competent men. If a crucial position is to be filled, the initial suggestions are submitted to the head of the proper department by the official "Referent" (who is always appointed on the strength of his long experience and his record of integrity). The head of the department examines the suggestions and takes them up with the section chief (the deputy to the Minister). By the time the recommendation finally reaches the desk of the Minister, checks and counterchecks have been made in every possible way through official as well as private channels. Finally, the Minister consults with the Art Senate. It is at this top level that the final decision is made. The name of each candidate thus passes through a veritable sieve of official scrutiny. Such a selective procedure offers promise that the choice is a wise one. The Minister of Education has every reason to seek the best solution. His decision must stand the test of public opinion, of a free and knowledgeable press, and of that large segment of its readers who are vitally concerned with artistic quality of performance in the nation's art life. The public debate on art in the press, in magazines and journals, and over the air is sharp and unsparing. In the most decisive issues, such as the appointment of the Director of the State Opera or the Burgtheater, no consideration is paid to local circumstances or to favorite sons. The best is demanded and is obtained.

Grants and Deficits

The federal budget, of course, is a matter of public record. Everyone has access to it; it is available in print and published in condensed form by the press; and so it is open to all forms of criticism.

The sums allocated as subsidies of the performing arts represent maximum estimates. The largest and most generous subsidies are traditionally accorded to the Bundestheater, i.e., the federal theaters, which are at present under the control of the Bundestheaterverwaltung. Yet the theaters are slated to be supervised in the future by a high official in the Ministry of Education.

Table I indicates the operational plan of the state theaters for the fiscal year of 1961, and it shows their overall budget for the same period.

TABLE I

Austrian Federal Theaters

1. Operational Plan 1961

	Type of Performances	*Planned Performances*	*Employees*
Burgtheater	Drama	300	658
Akademietheater		300	
Staatsoper	Opera and Ballet	300	994*
Volksoper		315	558
	Total	1,215	2,305 (plus an administrative personnel of 95)

*During the season 1960-61, the Vienna State Opera staged 325 performances which were attended by 680,371 persons. The opera employed 747 people, among them 54 male singers, 43 female singers, 125 orchestra members, 75 members of the ballet, and 104 members of the chorus. 95 per cent of the seating capacity was sold. Of the 57 works which were performed, Verdi led with seven operas, followed by Mozart, Wagner, and Puccini with five each.

2. Budget 1961

	Expenses (in millions of schillings)*	*Income*	*Deficit*
Burgtheater / Akademietheater	51	18	33
Staatsoper	110	35	75
Volksoper	53	12	41
Miscellaneous	5		
	219	65	

The deficit equals the federal subvention of 154,000,000 schillings, i.e., the Federal Republic pays approximately $6,160,000 to the State Theaters in Vienna.

*Exchange: $1.00 = .25 schillings (June 1963).

At present four stages have the status of federal theaters:* two musical theaters, namely the State Opera and the People's Opera (Volksoper), and two playhouses, the Burgtheater and the Akademietheater (which functions, in a more intimate frame, as an extension of the Burgtheater).

Of the current subventions allocated to these organizations, the Opera receives 55 per cent, the Burgtheater (including the Akademietheater), 25 per cent, and the Volksoper, 20 per cent. These figures are approximations; the federal government keeps the allocations flexible. Included in these sums are the annuities (pensions) for the retired personnel, an item which at present amounts to almost $1,000,000 annually.

*In Austria the term *Bund* and *Staat* are used interchangeably. Hence, the federal theater or *Bundestheater* are often referred to as State Theaters. The Vienna Opera is officially called State Opera.

The quoted subvention of approximately $6,000,000 for the state theaters alone is a considerable portion of the total national budget. Proudly the Austrian authorities call attention to the fact that this art subsidy exceeds the *total* budget of the federal government for its foreign service!

The allocations are very generous, not only in terms of Austrian, but of international standards as well. The Austrian federal theaters receive, in fact, a higher subsidy than comparable art institutes in much richer and larger countries. Only the governmental subventions of La Scala in Milan and the Opéra in Paris can be compared to the support of the Vienna State Opera.

Even the Volksoper (the People's Opera), which is a kind of opéra comique, is well subsidized, as Table I shows. The Volksoper is located on the "*Gürtel*," Vienna's outer belt, which separates the ancient inner city from the somewhat suburban districts at the foothills of the Vienna Woods. The very site of the theater suggests a different public as well as a different repertory. But not only in spirit are the State Opera and the People's Opera separate organizations. Each has its own orchestra and its own choir; the solo personnel is independently engaged, and so are the artistic directors and their administrative staffs. The same workshops, however, supply both stages with all materials, such as scenery and costumes. A close relationship unites the representative playhouse, the Burgtheater, with the small Akademietheater. The municipality of Vienna recently made a special contribution of 5,000,000 schillings toward the reconstruction of the Volksoper.

Subsidies to the Austrian State Theaters are the difference between expenditures and income. The federal government offers its theaters what is referred to as *Ausfallshaftung*, i.e., a guarantee for any possible deficit. If the actual deficit exceeds the estimated one, the government grants an additional subvention. A budget is submitted by each individual organization; it is carefully evaluated by the Minister of Education prior to its discussion in Parliament. But the subvention must be voted upon in Parliament.

Usually the allocation is granted without opposition, but exceptions are on record. A few years ago, the government — as a result of an economy drive — did not grant a sufficient subvention to the State Theaters. This provoked a dramatic response from the Austrians. They staged an impressive demonstration on The Ring, marching from the Opera to Parliament. The parade was spearheaded by the most popular actors and singers of the country. There followed a cordon of distinguished citizens, university professors, famous representatives of the arts and sciences (Nobel Prize winners among them). It was a march of protest, and it served its purpose. Parliament voted anew on the subsidies and granted the requested amount. Obviously, such a demonstration cannot occur every year, nor is it necessary. The elected representative of the people must be sensitive to the people's wishes and to a generously sponsored art program.

Occasionally the budget of the State Theaters has been overstepped, in spite of careful calculation by the management. The income of theaters, like that of comparable organizations, can be anticipated only as an estimate. Although the basic expenditures for the total personnel and maintenance are always known in advance, income is an uncertain factor. Management can hope for good box offices only by putting on first-rate productions. Yet experience teaches that there can be upsets to the most carefully estimated budgets. At times strikes have threatened the box office. At another time, civil war in nearby Hungary caused a reduction of 60 per cent in the general tourist traffic to Austria: all Vienna theaters were hard hit during this upheaval in Budapest, and the State Theaters, in particular, suffered substantial losses.

Of the total income of the federal theaters, approximately one-third is derived from ticket sales and other direct sources (such as fees for transmission of performances over radio and television). Consequently the "normal" deficit, which must be provided for in the budget, runs as high as two-thirds of the total expense. A good ticket for an opera seat, selling for 100 schillings (approximately $4.00), would have to cost 300 schillings ($12.00) to pay its appropriate share of the total expense of a performance.

Prior to the reconstruction of the badly damaged State Theater, the opera played in the venerable Theater an der Wien. But this historic hall soon proved inadequate. In 1960 the city of Vienna bought the building from private owners and brought the theater up to modern standards. On May 30, 1962, the Theater an der Wien reopened with a performance of *The Magic Flute*, the same opera with which the theater had originally been inaugurated, 171 years before. The ancient theater continues its tradition as the Vienna Festival Playhouse.

The Burgtheater, during the years following World War II, like the Opera, was forced to give its performances in a small house, the cabaret "Ronacher." As a result, the deficits of the State Theater were tremendous. But there was no thought of abandoning government subsidies. The government considers it vitally important, as previously emphasized, that its theaters during times of crisis should continue their cultural contributions to the people.

The Philharmonic

There is no direct subvention for the famous Vienna Philharmonic orchestra, and none is required. But the ensemble does double duty in the pit of the State Opera and during the summer is the principal orchestra of the Salzburg Festival. The State Opera engages the members of its orchestra independently. It numbers 125 players. The large number of performers permits the division of the orchestra into two active groups. Thus, it is possible to play opera in Vienna while the Philharmonic is on tour.

Since the Opera is an organization maintained by the federal government, its orchestra benefits from contracts given to all government employees. At retirement they receive an annuity of 70 per cent of their final salary. The average member of the orchestra earns $3,400 yearly in the Opera. He has an additional income from the concerts of the Philharmonic and from its extensive recordings. The value of the total income, of course, has to be measured in terms of purchasing power in Austria; many of the players own automobiles, definitely a luxury item for Austria.

The management of the Philharmonic is independent; the orchestra is a self-governing body. Its members boast, in fact, that theirs is the most democratic concert organization in the world. They elect their own chairman and executive committee by secret ballot. Every member of the orchestra is eligible for these posts. Most important — the players appoint their own conductor. This private management of the Philharmonic has at times caused, and still does cause, rather unusual situations which do not always add up to a glorious chapter in the chronicle of the orchestra. From the season 1898-99 to 1901, Gustav Mahler, then director of the Vienna Court Opera, served also as conductor of the (private) Philharmonic concerts. At the end of the season Mahler, whom the world recognized as one of the greatest conductors, made his acceptance for reappointment to the Philharmonic dependent upon a unanimous vote. The executive committee of the Philharmonic rejected his condition, and so Mahler resigned. The orchestra appointed Joseph Hellmesberger, the amiable ballet conductor of the Opera, to direct the Philharmonic concerts. To this day, the curious fact that the members of the Philharmonic can hire or fire their conductor — who may be their chief as director of the Opera — adds an ironic touch to an already complex picture. Be this as it may, it is a great advantage for the Vienna Opera and the Salzburg Festival to have such an extraordinary orchestra playing in the pit night after night.

The Cultural Penny

After the Second World War all Austrian theaters, except the State Theaters supported directly by the federal government, were in great financial difficulties. The general public simply could not afford to pay for tickets. In 1949 the situation reached a crisis. The government stepped in. A federal law was introduced and passed by Parliament on July 13, 1949, which became known as the *Kulturgroschen Gesetz*. This law of the Cultural Penny saved the private theaters from catastrophe.

The Kulturgroschen Gesetz levies a tax on each ticket for admission to a moving-picture theater. (It does not apply to the showing of educational films.) The Cultural Penny tax is flexible, adjusted to the size of the theater, its location, and special circumstances of performance. For each theater the amount is fixed by the Federal Ministry of Education, which reports to Parliament. The Ministry supervises the distribution of the Cultural Penny. The tax never amounts to more than 10 per cent of a single ticket; the minimum collected is 10 groschen (2.6 cents).

The income derived from the Cultural Penny is used to support the *private* theaters of Vienna, the festivals of Salzburg and Bregenz, the Vienna Festival Weeks, and the nonprofit theaters in the capitals of the Länder (federal provinces). No enterprise owned and exclusively administered by the Federal Republic qualifies for subsidies from the Kulturgroschen. Thus not even the State Theaters can draw from this source of income. In 1961, the Cultural Penny yielded 17,000,000 schillings ($680,000). The Cultural Penny assures the private theaters of continued existence.

The attendance figure for theatrical performances in Vienna was 3,300,000 during the season 1958-59, when the attendance at sports events was 2,200,000. These statistics reflect both the constantly growing interest of the population in serious art and a realistic policy of ticket prices.

Official patronage is directed to independent theaters, which are considered culturally important and therefore merit the Cultural Penny. Within such groups we find organizations of contrasting scope in widely different parts of the nation, some in large cities, some in distant towns.

VI. Vienna

Municipal Department for Art and Education

The city of Vienna sponsors an impressive variety of art projects. The municipal program aims to educate the population of 1,650,000 in broad cultural terms. To this end, the city has created the Municipal Department for Culture and People's Education, which supervises the libraries and museums of the city of Vienna and its important music and theater departments. Thousands of children are taught in the Kindersingschulen. The municipal administration for elementary schools has a comprehensive art program. School concerts were attended by 10,000 pupils in 1951-52, by 75,000 in 1953-54. Today, the number of regular listeners exceeds 100,000. Through the organization Musikalische Jugend the city makes it possible for all young people to attend the various concert cycles at greatly reduced prices. The total cost for a cycle of six first-rate orchestra concerts is only seventy-five cents. This nominal fee is made possible by a municipal subvention of about $50,000, set aside for this sole purpose.

In the summer of 1950 the city of Vienna began to give concerts in its large housing developments in the outer districts. The plan has grown into an important project, known under the title *Kunst ins Volk* (Art to the People). Experience has shown that many of the older citizens living in these settlements do not attend concerts in the inner city. By sending groups of performers to the largest of these settlements, where thousands of underprivileged people live, young and old have the opportunity to attend live concerts on their home grounds.

The municipality also sponsors frequent concerts in the arcades of the City Hall and in Vienna's numerous large old parks. It organizes repeat performances of all concerts given by the Society of Friends of Music. In all concerts specifically sponsored by the city of Vienna (such as in the court of the City Hall or the Belvedere Palace) at least one work of a living composer is performed. In worthy cases the city pays for the printing of new compositions. It also commissions new works.

The city maintains a conservatory (which is independent of both the State Academy of Music and the New Vienna Conservatory). The municipality offers various prizes, such as the Awards of the City of Vienna for talented youth, as well as stipends for gifted artists of mature age. The expenses paid by the city for music education in its own conservatory, in the public music schools, and in the special singing schools for children amount to approximately $500,000 annually.

In recent years the city has contributed to the support of nine private theaters with a combined seating capacity of 9,365. Besides the quoted concerts, dramatic performances are regularly arranged in the outer districts of the capital. Here a new public is being conquered for the theater. To date, 129 special performances have been attended by 58,707.

Subsidized Concert Organizations

In addition to the Philharmonic, Vienna is home to several other orchestras. The Vienna Symphony Orchestra, an internationally recognized organization, is supported by the municipality in collaboration with the federal government. Unlike the Philharmonic, the Vienna Symphony devotes much of its efforts to the performance of contemporary music. The organizational structure of the Vienna Symphony is that of a private society, to which both the republic and the city of Vienna make financial contributions, but without clearly defined obligations to cover the deficit. For 1963, the orchestra received a subsidy of 7,100,000 schillings ($284,000) derived from general taxes collected by the municipality of Vienna. The support represents a raise of 1,300,000 schillings over the preceding years. In addition, the municipality has made available a special travelling fund to underwrite the world-wide tours of the orchestra (including its trip to the United States, planned for 1964). The Vienna Symphony is the principal orchestra of the annual Summer Festival in Bregenz, provincial capital of Vorarlberg.

The city of Vienna and the federal government also subsidize the principal concert societies of the capital: the Society of Friends of Music and the Vienna Concert House Society.

Stadt Halle

In 1958, the city of Vienna opened its modern Stadt Halle, claimed to be the largest structure of its kind in Europe. Multipurpose in design, it is devoted to the arts and to sports. Located in one of Vienna's workers' districts, the hall was conceived to offer youth a huge and appealing recreation center to counteract the demoralizing influences of overcrowded, underprivileged urban quarters. The descriptive brochure and the speeches at its dedication in 1958 always placed culture first, sports second.

The large auditorium can be converted to a theater with a seating capacity of 5,619 plus standing room for 1,800 more. The hall is suited for concerts or cinema. For convention purposes, the main hall can be adjusted to a capacity of 17,000. In 1962 both the Vienna Philharmonic and the Vienna Symphony presented a cycle of orchestral concerts in the Stadt Halle. Works by Wagner and Verdi were offered in special performances for the young.

Festival Weeks

The municipality is the principal patron of the Wiener Festwochen (Vienna Festival Weeks), which take place annually in June and differ, in intent and scope, from most other European art festivals. This manifestation of cultural life in Vienna is not primarily geared to tourists who can afford to travel and attend Europe's festival circuit. The Vienna Festival addresses itself, before all, to the entire Austrian population. Tickets are modestly priced (in contrast to those for the Salzburg Festival).

Statistics show the ever-growing participation of the people from the workers' districts as well as from provincial towns and rural regions. The Festival is managed by an intendant appointed by the city council. The subsidy in 1960 was 6,000,000 schillings ($240,000). This subvention covered the deficit; all events were attended by capacity audiences.

The program presents a cross section of the best performances in theater and concert chosen from the preceding Vienna season. To these are added a limited number of new projects of special artistic interest.

Private Theaters

Vienna has several private theaters with a long and distinguished history. The most important of these is the Theater in der Josefstadt, for which Beethoven composed in 1822 his overture *Consecration of the House*. This theater, with a seating capacity of 785, is the largest privately owned stage in Vienna. It gave 491 performances for 332,700 people during the season 1959-60. The average attendance was 86 per cent of capacity; it rose to 91 per cent in 1962. The principal private patron of this venerable theater is a financial corporation, the Länder Bank, which guarantees more than one-third of the subvention. But in a typical year the Theater in der Josefstadt received from the government also a subvention of 4,000,000 schillings ($160,000), which is approximately one-tenth of the support accorded to the state-owned Burgtheater. The total budget for the Theater in der Josefstadt is 18,000,000 schillings ($720,000). There are 6,000 subscribers. About fifty actors are engaged with a three-year contract. The Theater in der Josefstadt offers avant garde repertory in the Kleines Theater im Konzerthaus, and frequently in another small hall.

The Volkstheater (People's Theater) is officially supported by the Gewerkschaftsbund (Collective of Workers' Unions), and the subvention is guaranteed by the Workers' Bank. How does patronage guaranteed by a political party affect artistic policy? Obviously, the management of the Volkstheater will not choose an antisocialistic play nor, by the same token, a pro-clerical one. The secretary of the Gewerkschaftsbund is always consulted on the repertory. The Volkstheater endeavors to offer an earnest fare and frequently chooses plays dealing with timely problems. Performances are about 80 per cent subscribed, which suffices to avoid a large deficit.

The Volkstheater is subsidized by the political Left. The Raimund Theater is supported by the political Right; it is, in fact, officially maintained by the Österreichische Volkspartei (Clerical Party). The repertory is a popular one. The Raimund Theater does not address itself exclusively to the urban population, but tries to promote interest for the stage in the farm belt surrounding the capital. The performances are normally sold out; party funds fully guarantee the operation.

In addition to these old-established stages, Vienna has a considerable number of small private theaters. These may be likened to the off-Broadway theater in New York. They, too, survive with the help of small subventions. An example is the Theater am Parkring, which is an outlet for young talent. The Kammeroper enjoys increasing governmental support. Its repertory consists of such noteworthy offerings as Mozart's early dramatic scores, and other works related in spirit and medium. Subsidies are also accorded to the Kammerspiele and the Tribuene. The latter is a very small stage, housed in a café opposite the Burgtheater.

Why does the government take an active interest in such small enterprises? The Tribuene may serve as an illustration. This theater operates on an experimental basis. Its purpose is to encourage young playwrights, actors, producers. The government official in charge of theatrical subsidies cannot afford to tell an unknown beginner, no matter how talented: "We will produce your play in the Burgtheater; we will risk expenses of 200,000 schillings." But the federal administrator of theatrical subsidies can say to a young author: "Here are a few thousand schillings for your first play. Let us try it out in the Tribuene!" Such a risk is reasonable, calculated for a modest production.

The federal government and the respective municipalities offer assistance to various theaters in small cities, such as the old resort of Baden or the industrial town of St. Pölten (both in Lower Austria). These theaters offer, in spite of their limitations, opera and serious drama as well as popular entertainment of operetta and light comedy. The theaters are eligible for support and the motivation of patronage is clear. Neither the size of the stage nor its locality are decisive, only the cultural scope and purpose. More than twenty private theaters fall, at present, into this category of subsidized stages.

VII. The Provinces

Winter Seasons and Summer Festivals

The Federal Republic of Austria has eight federal provinces called *Bundes Länder*. Not only their principal cities, but many of their small towns have long been distinguished by their indigenous art lives. The capitals possess handsome opera houses, prose theaters, and concert halls. During fall, winter, and spring these art institutes provide seasons that are stimulating in terms of the cultural needs of the native population. This does not imply, however, that the principal theaters and their orchestras do not occasionally attempt extraordinary productions — artistic ventures that are above the concept of the provincial as opposed to the more cosmopolitan taste. Five provincial capitals maintain orchestras which, in turn, serve in the respective resident theaters and are normally subsidized by city and province. These are the orchestras of Graz, Linz, Innsbruck, Salzburg, and Klagenfurt.

During the summer many towns and villages change into their festive garb. Austria has long been the land of festivals. Each of her provinces has long ago developed its own kind, in keeping with folkloristic traditions that blend harmoniously with the country's landscape and architecture. Today, most of these festivals are devoted to music and drama. One of them, the Salzburg Festival, has become an attraction of global scope. Other festivals emphasize folklore in mode and decor, aiming at the enjoyment of the native population, but they are pleasurable for foreign visitors, too.

Salzburg

Art has blended with nature to create on Salzburg soil a city that is unique in the world. There is something musical in the very patterns of the Austrian landscape. One does not have to recall that Mozart was born in Salzburg to recognize the musical sentiment of this environment. Nor does one have to see the city decorated with gay flags during the summer to recognize its festive spirit.

Architecture reflects the Salzburg scene. The early rulers envisioned their city for times of serenity: Salzburg was not, like most medieval German towns in the heart of Europe, built for defense in time of war and anxiously surrounded with confining belts of fortifying walls. Salzburg spreads open and free into the plains, the lake regions, and the mountain valleys of the poetic Salzkammergut. The inner city with its squares, Baroque fountains, and playful sculpture invites solemn processionals and outdoor performances of drama. The surrounding Lustschlösser, like the delightful Hellbrunn with its mechanical theater and water play, were designed as "castles of pleasure."

High above the town rises Hohensalzburg, the medieval mountain fortress, the only sign that the sovereigns of Salzburg could not entirely forget possible aggression from the outside. Looking down from this mountain castle we see the spirals of the Baroque cathedral and Salzburg's many churches rising above the town. We are reminded of the timeless.

This is the scene that inspired the annual Salzburg Festival, transforming the Austrian provincial city each summer into an international meeting place. The initiative of the poet Hugo von Hofmannsthal and the producer Max Reinhardt made the Festival a reality in 1920. But there had been an unbroken continuity of theater life in Salzburg since the mystery plays of the Middle Ages. During World War II good fortune spared Salzburg's inner city from destruction and the Festival district remained intact.

The Salzburg Festival opens during the last week of July and ends on the last day of August. Performances take place at a variety of places, in and out of doors. The square in front of the solemn cathedral accommodates the traditional production of *Everyman* (the medieval play in Hofmannsthal's adaptation). The old Festspielhaus is now linked with the spacious new opera house opened in 1960. Together, the two theaters form a close Festival district that reaches from the Toscanini Hof to the Siegmundsplatz. The district includes the Felsenreitschule (the riding school in the rocks), which is used for productions such as Beethoven's *Fidelio*. The Mozarteum[7] plays a vital and extensive part in the educational activities of the Festival, and also houses many of the concerts.

The new Festspielhaus is an opera theater with the most advanced equipment. By contrast to the modernity of the interior — the hall, the foyer, the social rooms, and before all the stage itself — the exterior of the new Festspielhaus has retained its Baroque architecture. The city planners felt bound to respect the stylistic character of this historic part of the old town. It would have been considered vandalism to disturb the architectural unity. And so, the most valuable structure in the district, the Baroque portal built by the great architect Fischer von Erlach on the Siegmunds Square, has remained in its original state. The enormous stage is cut out directly from the massive mountain rock of the Mönchsberg. The orchestral pit, corresponding to the proportions of the Vienna State Opera, accommodates 125 musicians. The smooth transfer of the performing apparatus from Vienna to Salzburg was a main consideration in the technical design of the new Festspielhaus.

The deficit of the Salzburg Festival is high, in spite of the fact that performances are sold out, usually far in advance, and that tickets are expensive even by international standards. But the financial aid accorded the Festival by government on all levels (federal, provincial, municipal) is interpreted as a sound investment. The great number of travelers who visit Salzburg has far-reaching effect on the economy of the country. Austria ranks third in Europe (behind France and Switzerland) as a tourist attraction, and the Salzburg Festival is known to be a strong factor in this appeal.

In recent years the annual allocation to the Salzburg Festival by the federal government was approximately 3,840,000 schillings ($153,600). In addition to this contribution, the Festival is supported by three other sources: the city of Salzburg, the province of Salzburg, and the Salzburg Office of Tourist Traffic. The sum total of these subventions makes the Salzburg Festival possible.

The administration of the Salzburg Festival is subdivided as follows:

1. The Kuratorium which makes all financial decisions. On its board are officials of the ministries of education and finance, as well as representatives of both the city and province of Salzburg.
2. The Artistic Direction of the Festival, which is autonomous and supervises the entire Festival program of opera, concert, and drama.
3. The Kunstrat (the Arts Council) which acts merely in a consulting capacity.

Admittedly, this administrative substructure does not lack a certain divergence of authority. As a result there have been internal crises in Salzburg. Yet the Festival is so deeply entrenched in the Austrian art life, and its technical basis so firmly established, that the popular success of the vast enterprise has never been affected.

In 1962 the 89 performances of the Salzburg Festival were attended by approximately 125,000 visitors. Thirty-one of these performances were transmitted by radio and television. The Summer Festival outshines the importance of Salzburg as a year-round art center.

The Landes Theater of Salzburg maintains a regular fall, winter, and spring season of opera, drama, ballet, and operetta. Its operation is independent of the Summer Festival. The Landes Theater is autonomous; it also offers open-air performances in nearby towns, such as St. Wolfgang. All departments of the Landes Theater offer standard repertory. (For further operational details, cf. Table II.)

Graz

Austria's second city is Graz, capital of the "greenland" of Styria. Emperors have reigned in this quaint town, where the elegance of Lombardian Renaissance and the serenity of the Austrian Baroque are curiously blended with the unsmiling drabness of nineteenth-century middle-class houses. Today, Graz has a population of 226,000. Its principal theaters are united under a composite name which indicates two mainsprings of their patronage: *Vereinigte Bühnen Stadt Graz — Land Steiermark* (United Stages, City of Graz, Province Styria). Although the Federal Republic is not represented in this title, it shares support with the city and the province. The theater offers drama, opera, operetta, and ballet, around the year.

The handsome opera house on The Ring gave in 1906 the Austrian première of *Salome* by Richard Strauss. The repertory of the season 1960-61 ranged from Mozart to Alban Berg. The theater's resident orchestra, which functions as a concert organization under the name *Graz Philharmonic*, claims the distinction of the first performance in 1895 of Bruckner's *Fifth Symphony*. The repertory of the Kammerspiele (housed in the Rittersaal) offers world drama from Calderon to Lessing, from Shaw to Anouilh.

After its regular season, Graz, like Vienna, celebrates an annual Summer Festival. The event, known as the *Grazer Sommerspiele*, lasts from the beginning of June to the second week of July, and its repertory comprises opera, concert, drama, operetta, and ballet. Parts of the program are very ambitious, for instance, the cycle "Opera of the Twentieth Century."[8] (For details of subsidization or operation and budget of the Graz theaters, cf. Table II.)

Linz

Until the fourth decade of the twentieth century, Linz — Upper Austria's capital — was a somewhat sleepy town of 45,000 inhabitants. Under the German occupation Linz was transformed into an industrial city of 190,000, and thus lost some of its quaint charm. But the city's spectacular location on the Danube, its ancient monastic buildings, and its two new modern theaters give Linz, 190 miles west of Vienna, independent distinction.

But Linz has long been a theatrical center. Five hundred years ago, Emperor Frederick III watched festival plays here in his palace. In 1608 the Jesuits founded a local theater. By 1677 opera was performed, with Emperor Leopold I attending. In 1752 the municipality sponsored a new but small theater near the embankment of the Danube. In 1772 the aristocracy decided to maintain the Redoutensaal as a theater. In 1803 the National Theater, later called the Landes Theater, was founded. In 1957 a modern building, the new Linz Opera house, was added to the obsolete Landes Theater. And the newly-built Kammerspiele is a charming intimate theater.

The support of these theaters is jointly guaranteed by the Bund, the province of Upper Austria, and the city of Linz. The contribution of the Republic is 25 per cent of the deficit. Province and city share the remaining 75 per cent. (For further details of budget and operation, cf. Table II.)

Innsbruck

Maximilian I, Emperor of the Holy Roman Empire from 1493 to 1519, called the mountainous province of Tyrol "the heart and shield of my Empire." The art-loving Habsburg sovereign frequently held court

TABLE II

*Theaters in Austrian Provinces**

1. Facilities and Operation

	Graz (Styria)	Salzburg (Salzburg)	Innsbruck (Tyrol)	Linz (Upper Austria)	Klagenfurt (Carinthia)
Ownership	Opera City Playhouse *Land* Building *Land* and City Equipment *Land* and City	Building City Equipment City and State**	Building City Equipment City and State**	Everything owned by *Land*	Theater City Building City Equipment City Playhouse *Land*
Number	2	1***	2	2	2
Capacity	Large hall 1400 Small hall 330	777	793 470	(prior to new 583 building) 400	879 304
Season	Opera: Sept. 8-July 8 Playhouse: Sept. 22 June 25	Sept. 9-June 23	Sept. 21-August 25	Sept. 15-June 30	Sept. 27-July 20
Type of Performance	Opera, operetta, ballet, and drama	Opera, operetta, and drama	Opera, operetta, ballet, musical comedy, and drama	Opera, operetta, ballet, and drama	Opera, operetta, musical comedy, and drama
Personnel (both opera and playhouse)					
Management	3	3	2	2	1
Performers	173	101	88	122	80
Opera (solo personnel)	26	8	12	25	10
Operetta (solo personnel)	9	14	5	24	9
Drama (solo personnel)	39	30	21	32	22
Ballet (solo personnel)	24	16	14	16	12
Choir (solo personnel)	48	20	23	33	21
Stage managers, assistants and prompters	10	6	6	7	7

*Season, 1958-59.

**According to Austrian terminology, *state* refers to federal government; *land* refers to province.

***Not counting the Festspiel Theaters.

	Graz	Salzburg	Innsbruck	Linz	Klagenfurt
Stage designers	3	1	1	3	2
Dramaturge	2	1	1	1	1
Conductors and coaches	12	5	5	6	5
Orchestra	96	37	49	64	37
Ushers	56	22	19	17	20
Administrative staff	24	8	10	16	9
Technical Personnel (both opera and playhouse)	134	58	52	93	60
Department heads	10	11	8	6	5
Stagehands	39	12	13	17	16
Electricians	7	3	3	5	4
Hairdressers	5	2	2	6	4
Carpenters	9	4	3	7	3
Painters	9	3	2	5	3
Costumers	18	8	6	19	6
Others	11	11	12	17	15
House personnel	26	4	3	11	4
Repertory					
Operas	25	7	7	8	9
Number of performances	144	92	85	81	69
Operettas	12	6	9	7	10
Number of performances	107	122	150	106	94
Drama	24	14	10	26	20
Number of performances	351	147	116	326	164
Ballet	1	1	—	2	5
Number of performances	10	7	—	17	5
Tours (number of places visited)	92	17	12	99	40
Visiting companies	18	5	18	30	9

TABLE II (continued)

Theaters in Austrian Provinces

2. Costs and Receipts in Austrian Schillings

	Graz	Salzburg	Innsbruck	Linz	Klagenfurt
Personnel	18,395,100	6,779,853	7,782,000	10,239,800	6,668,455
Operational Costs	3,706,400	1,792,700	2,604,000	2,102,500	1,560,284
Miscellaneous	911,000	150,000	—	657,000	—
Total Expenses	23,012,500	8,722,553	10,386,000	12,999,300	8,228,739
Total Income	5,724,600	3,272,553	3,360,000	2,800,000	2,367,900
Deficit	17,287,900	5,450,000	7,026,000	10,199,300	5,860,839
Coverage of Loss	State, *Land*, City	State, *Land*, City	State, *Land*, City	State, *Land*, City	State, *Land*, City
Statistics of Attendance Audience (local)	367,023	191,781	194,334	199,922	110,205
On Tour	35,222	——	3,197	53,252	——

in Innsbruck, Tyrol's capital. He employed Heinrich Isaak, one of the greatest masters of the Renaissance, as Court composer.

During four-and-one-half centuries there is an unbroken chronicle of theatrical history in Innsbruck. Biblical plays and carnival shows were performed by travelling groups. But in 1581 Archduke Ferdinand I built, as an annex to the old castle, the new Ballspielhaus, which in 1627 was transformed into an opera house. It eventually claimed distinction as the first permanent opera theater performing in the German language. As early as 1658, Innsbruck formed the Theater Society, which sent its ensemble over the high mountain passes as far as Switzerland for guest performances.

On October 5, 1786, Emperor Joseph II made an important decision. Hitherto, the reigning dynasty had paid entirely for the support of the provincial theater. From now on, an annual subsidy of 2,000 gulden was to be derived from a special tax on beer. When the thirsty Tyroleans complained, the Emperor replied: "For the enjoyment of his theater, the Innsbrucker must drink his beer a little more expensively. If he does not care to pay the extra penny, he will have no theater." We note this episode because it points to a remarkably progressive taxation in the eighteenth century.

The occupation of Tyrol by Napoleon's army in 1805 did not interrupt the art life of Innsbruck. On the contrary, on December 6, the commanding French general Marshall Ney personally urged "the ladies and gentlemen of the city to patronize wholeheartedly their theater." In 1885 the municipality of Innsbruck assumed the support of the playhouse. On October 1, 1921, the city decided to play the year around. Today, the Innsbruck theater is once more a Landes Theater, jointly supported by the province, the city, and the federal government. (For details of operation and budget, cf. Table II.)

Small Art Centers

Austria's other provincial capitals, such as Klagenfurt or Bregenz, maintain by comparison with Salzburg, Graz, or Linz a much more limited art program. Klagenfurt, Carinthia's first city, possesses an attractive theater in charming surroundings. Bregenz (Vorarlberg), Austria's medieval gateway to the west, is primarily noted for its summer festival. The producers take advantage of the spectacular location of the city on the large Lake Konstanz (Boden-See). The See Bühne, anchored in the lake itself, is the setting on warm summer nights for various theatrical productions (particularly of classical operettas). The artistically more valid part of the Bregenz Festival offers drama and symphony concerts at various places of the old town. The Vienna Symphony serves as the Festival orchestra. The recent seasons of the Kornmarkt Theater at Bregenz reveal an increasingly ambitious repertory.

The city of Eisenstadt (Burgenland) is known for its performances of Haydn, who was born in the nearby village of Rohrau and spent three decades of his mature life in this region on the estate of the Prince Eszterházy. Burgenland was also the home of Franz Liszt, who was born in the village of Raiding. Only since 1921 has Eisenstadt functioned as a provincial capital; this partly accounts for the lack of diversified activities in the performing arts. Ninety per cent of the Burgenland population, speaking either German, Hungarian, or Croatian, are farmers.

Support of the performing arts by the federal government is not limited to the capitals of Austria's provinces. As pointed out previously, special circumstances often warrant federal assistance in very small and remote places of the country. Thus the village stage of Mörbisch, also in Burgenland, receives a federal subsidy. Its closeness to the Iron Curtain gives the Mörbisch Theater special significance.

There is a new theater in the tiny village of Erl in the Tyrolean mountains. In June, 1959, Erl opened its festival playhouse, dedicated to religious drama. The cost of the theater was $250,000. Erl's own contribution of $40,000 toward the construction of the playhouse marks a creditable amount for the diminutive community with a total population of 945. Erl also receives financial aid for its theater from both federal and provincial sources.

The veteran Exelbühne of Tyrol, specializing in folk drama, is government supported.

Subsidies Increased

The latest available statistics on the operation of the provincial theaters in Austria indicate rising costs and, consequently, increases in the subvention on all levels. Thus, in 1962 the support for the Graz opera and playhouse consisted of:

Land (Styria)	10,000,000 schillings
City	8,500,000
Federal	3,556,000

In addition, the following allocations were accorded for the reconstruction of the Graz Schauspielhaus:

Federal	16,200,000 schillings
Land (Styria)	6,000,000
City	4,000,000

Subsidies were also granted to the Graz Summer Festival (900,000 schillings) and to the Musikverein of Styria (240,000 schillings).

In Linz the subvention granted by City and Land (Upper Austria) to opera and playhouse was increased to 14,000,000 schillings.

In Klagenfurt the increased support was as follows:

Land (Carinthia)	2,700,000 schillings
City	2,300,000
Federal	2,000,000

VIII. Radio and Television

Austrian radio and television are administered and produced by a company under government control. The ownership of this broadcasting company is shared by the federal and provincial governments.

The Austrian Broadcasting Company Ltd. is supervised by a board of trustees which, in turn, reflects the political proportions of the Austrian Parliament. One of the trustees is named director-general. In accordance with the bipartisan pattern at the root of Austria's public life, a codirector must be chosen. If the director-general (of either the radio or television network) belongs to the People's Party, the deputy will belong to the Socialist Party, and vice versa. Such bipartisan administration aims at a policy above individual group interests.

Austria interprets radio and television as cultural enterprises, hence, the broadcasting company falls under the jurisdiction of the federal Ministry of Education. The technical aspects, however, are supervised by the Ministry of Traffic. The Post Office (reporting to the Ministry of Traffic) collects the monthly license fees for both radio and television.

The Postal Service deducts approximately 20 per cent to defray its expenses. The total expenditures of radio and television for the fiscal year of 1961 were 410,000,000 schillings ($16,400,000). The combined income from license fees (for both radio and television) was 220,000,000 schillings ($8,880,000). The deficit, in this case 190,000,000 schillings ($7,410,000), is underwritten by the government. That there is a deficit at all is attributed chiefly to the low radio fee, which is only seven schillings per month (about twenty-eight cents). There are approximately 2,000,000 subscribers. An increase from seven to twelve schillings (28 to 48 cents) for each radio set has been proposed; Parliament has yet to approve the increase. The license fee for television is 50 schillings per month ($2.00).

The Austrian radio has seven stations, six of them in provincial capitals: Vienna (Lower Austria), Graz (Styria), Linz (Upper Austria), Salzburg (Salzburg), Innsbruck (Tyrol), Klagenfurt (Carinthia), and Dornbirn (Vorarlberg).[9] Of these stations, Radio Vienna is assigned 52 per cent of the total broadcasting time. Graz and Linz have 12 per cent each, and the other stations still less (in proportion to their respective populations). The long Alpine valleys of Austria, with the surrounding high mountain chains, cause difficulties of reception. But stronger transmitters are under construction and the entire country will eventually be covered by sufficiently powerful short waves.

Radio and television programs are adjusted to the pluralistic needs of the nation. Obviously, it is not possible to bring the taste of the entire population — the urban intelligentsia, the peasants in Austria's farm and mountain country, the workers in the mills and mines — under a common denominator. Various solutions try to cope with the requirements of such a heterogeneous audience.

There are three radio programs. The first program is exclusively regional. The second program is national. The third program is ultra-short-wave. There are no commercials on the second and third programs. Serious offerings are distributed over all three programs. This procedure is in contrast to that in other European countries (such as England or France), where all serious and educational fare is concentrated on the third program. The Austrian radio regularly broadcasts the best the nation has to offer in the performing arts: new productions of the state theaters, all Philharmonic concerts, the concerts of the Society of Friends of Music, the Summer Festivals of Salzburg and Vienna. Some of these events are also televised.

Austria's principal radio station, the Wiener Funkhaus, gives a series of free public concerts performed by the Rundfunk Orchestra of seventy-five players, directed by its staff or guest conductors. These concerts take place in the new auditorium of the Funkhaus. There are regular broadcasts of chamber and choral music. The series *Musica Nova* is devoted to contemporary composers.

Television developed in Austria during the country's occupation by the Allied forces following World War II. But television did not function in Austria as a public service until the last foreign soldier had left the country. One of the first telecasts was the solemn reopening of the Vienna State Opera in 1955.

Austrian television is still limited to one single channel. Sets are expensive for the average Austrian family. Yet the number of television subscribers increased in 1960 to 141,825, in 1961 to 250,000, in 1963 to 440,000. Half of the total number of sets is in Vienna. Telecasts generally begin at 6:30 P.M. and last until 10:30 P.M.; Sunday they begin at 5:00 P.M. and sometimes last until midnight.

Commercial advertising as a basic source of income is a controversial issue in Austria. Since July 1, 1961, however, commercials are shown with definite restriction on time and type. During the half hour from 7:00 P.M. to 7:30 P.M., spot advertising, separated by cartoons and shorts, is permitted. The advertisers pay for the ad-inserts an average of less than $1,000 per advertising minute. At the time being, this very limited advertising is the only commercial aspect on Austrian television.

The quality of programs is the result of the policy of the Austrian Broadcasting Company to draw on the rich resources of the theatrical and musical life of Vienna. There is a play with a prominent cast almost every evening. During the season the telecast of one opera a week is the rule.

Censorship

Censorship in Austria applies to the entire scope of the performing arts. Hence it applies to the cinema and to television, where the different viewpoints of Austria's two leading parties are sometimes hard to reconcile. For instance, the admission of juveniles to so-called "adult movies" causes general concern.

The Ministry of Education has appointed a special commission to supervise censorship in all of its aspects. On January 4, 1960, a decree was issued by the government requesting that only "films of value" be shown. Obviously the concept of value is a matter of interpretation.

The governmental decree demands that films "harmful to youth" be unequivocally eliminated. This classification applies to moving pictures that have "a deleterious effect on a young person's health, nerves, and spiritual development." It applies to pictures that "falsify true ethical and aesthetic concepts, to films that are brutal, dealing with criminal or sexual subjects, insulting the sense of decency, religious feeling, or basic civic virtues." In Vienna two commissions (the one appointed by the Federal Ministry of Education, the other by the Educational Department of the Municipality) sit independently in judgment. It can happen — and it has happened — that their verdicts do not coincide. This obviously causes confusion in the enforcement of the law, as Vienna is both the capital of the nation and an autonomous municipality. Attempts are under way to resolve this conflicting authority. Classification of films is adjusted according to the age of juveniles. Films are divided into three groups: those not to be shown to youngsters up to fourteen, those not to be shown to youth up to sixteen, and those not to be shown to youth up to eighteen. The film of Schiller's classical tragedy *Don Carlos* illustrates the flexibility of interpretation. This moving picture is an exact filmed reproduction of the Burgtheater's performance of Schiller's original drama. There are no adaptions, no revisions, no changes. The scenes between the tragic lovers, the Queen and Don

Carlos, passed both commissions which admitted the film for showing, even for juveniles, in spite of its relatively provocative content. The inherent artistic legitimacy of production convinced all censors that *Don Carlos* could be shown.

IX. The Youth Theaters

Tomorrow's Audience

In 1932 the organization Theater der Jugend was founded, to offer the best in theater to a public ranging from six to twenty-five years of age. Through the Theater of Youth, tickets for the professional stages are made available, and often the youth organization buys out the entire house at a reduced rate (usually at a reduction of 30 per cent). German and Austrian classics are included in the repertory, as are Shakespeare, Molière, Goldoni, Chekhov, Strindberg, and other great dramatists of world literature.

The support of the Theater der Jugend is generally considered one of the best investments for the future. In the initial season 20,000 youngsters attended performances; by 1962, the attendance figure had risen to 610,000. The young members literally fight for tickets, and at the present rate of supply, the demand can no longer be satisfied. In Vienna, a new hall devoted to youth is in the blueprint stage.

One might assume that this extraordinary demand for theater tickets is the result of organizational pressure. This is not so. In fact, the number of politically organized youth is amazingly small in Austria. According to latest statistics, only 12 to 15 per cent formally belong to any party unit. It is obvious, then, that the decades of systematic education have paid off: the vast majority of young people attend these performances of good theater spontaneously.

Thespian Carriage

The theatrical youth organizations are centered primarily in large cities, of which Austria has only a few. A great part of the nation's youth grows up in small towns and rural districts, or in the many long secluded valleys of the mountainous part of the country, where travel and communication are not easy. In this motorized age, cars are scarce and definitely a luxury in Austria. Even public transportation is expensive for many young people.

To this problem government again brings a solution. Wherever possible, the authorities arrange for special trains or buses to take the young audience to the theater in the cities. Where distances and other obstacles are considerable, the government brings good performances to the small communities in isolated valleys. The Thespian Carriage[10] of ancient Greece lives on in the Austrian countryside today, and it works well in its modernized form. The traveling theater visits the more distant regions, usually with a repertory of two or three classical pieces (tragedies alternating with comedies for two or three successive nights). The community that is host to the Thespian Carriage makes its visit a special event; in the local schools the teachers prepare their students for a proper appreciation of the scheduled plays.

The Thespian Carriage is not always manned by seasoned professionals. The most talented graduates of Austria's drama, opera, and ballet schools are often sent on these tours. This adds a special flavor to the theatrical enjoyment; the young audiences experience stimulating performances, acted and sung by people of their own age.

Everywhere the experience of theater serves an educational purpose; the plays offered in the theater are built into the school curriculum. For the young audiences they are assignments in art appreciation; for the drama and music students they function as workshop performances. In its overall aspect the Theater of Youth aims at education toward serious art and counteracts the pitfalls of superficial entertainment. Here the audience of the future is molded.

Vienna Student Theater

On Austrian soil the student theater has its roots in the centuries-old tradition of dramatic performances in monasteries, particularly of the Jesuits. This tradition was always kept alive in various forms throughout the country.

In March, 1961, the new Vienna Student Theater presented its opening performance as an ensemble of students playing for students. The essential difference between other typical school theaters and the Vienna Student Theater lies in the fact that it is exclusively administered by the students themselves, and decidedly progressive in its repertory. Its operation is completely nonprofit. And with its motto, *Maecenates voco*, the theater appeals to patrons everywhere. About one hundred students from all colleges of Vienna give their time, talent, and energy to create a dynamic theater that is in step with the contemporary stage. The accent falls on works which are neglected by the professional theater. Young unknown authors are given an opportunity to have their works performed. On Sunday afternoons the students present fairy tales for children. Opera has also been offered.

The antecedent of the Vienna Student Theater, the College Studio in the Kolingasse, was one of the original founders of the International Theater Week in Erlangen (Germany), which developed in the course of years into a representative meeting of European students. A large number of performers who belonged to the original College Studio have since become prominent in drama, opera, and cinema. Impressed by the serious effort and success of the Vienna Student Theater, the Austrian Ministry of Education is now ready to give support. We take note of this very modest enterprise in Austria's theater life only because of its potential. From humble beginnings a development of consequence has grown and can continue to grow.

X. Small Nation—Great Art Life

The Austrian art program imposes a heavy burden on the limited resources of the small nation. But in spite of this, the cultural responsibility of the Austrian government, federal, state, and local, has unwavering popular support. To quote a high officer in the federal Ministry of Education: "In regard to art, the government is here to spend money, not to take it in."

The underlying idea of Austrian patronage is one of realistic optimism. Not only are the great prestigious institutes generously aided and maintained, but small and seemingly unimportant art organizations are decidedly encouraged. There is a strong emphasis on youth and its ever-growing participation in the national art life. Workers' organizations play a decisive part in aiding the performing arts.

On all levels the government offers annual prizes, awards, and scholarships, which fall into two categories: prizes of encouragement for young artists who are clearly showing promise but have not yet achieved recognition; prizes given in acknowledgement of the lifework of already established artists.

Among the aged artists, those who have established a record of distinguished contributions to the nation are eligible for governmental annuities.* These pensions are modest, but they cover living expenses. At this writing there is a law before Parliament for protection of all artists against the financial hardships of illness and old age. This tentative legislation is referred to as "Artists Insurance Law." It is of vital importance, particularly to the considerable number of Austrian artists who have spent their professional years in self-employment and are, consequently, lacking the accumulated annuities which accrue from regular employment in organizational service.

The members of the various government-supported art organizations, like all other employees in the civil service, are employed on a yearly

*This group does not include artists in government service who at a retirement age are automatically pensioned as state employees.

basis, with tenure and full pension rights. The retirement insurance is very costly for the Austrian government. But the obligation to the aged artist has been accepted as an irrefutable responsibility by the Republic. There are other motivations for this official attitude. The government definitely wishes to offer talented youth every incentive to take up art as a profession. Today's youth is notoriously realistic, often extremely materialistic — in Austria no less than anywhere else in the postwar world. Young people will seek more lucrative professions if they see undue struggle and insecurity in the artist's life. Austria can ill afford the waste of talent; she cannot let her youth turn away from art as a profession. One of Austria's great assets is the image the world holds of her art life. It is an idealistic image. The government must make certain that the outlook for the artist is good, particularly for the gifted performer of tomorrow.

Austria's art program has a marked trend toward decentralization. This means strong support of art organizations in the provincial cities. It also means that by looking into countless small and modest groups — even on the amateur level — one might discover and encourage talent.

In her patronage of the performing arts, Austria is second to no other country. As indicated earlier, in detail, the state theaters alone receive annual subsidies exceeding 154,000,000 schillings ($6,160,000), and the Vienna Opera alone is supported with approximately $4,000,000. There always has been, and still is, an awareness on the part of government that the performing arts border on and fuse with the creative arts. Music and drama live through performance. Patronage of both categories of art — creative and performing — aims at the spiritual enrichment of life in the ancient nation.

Austria knows that long range and generous art support will prove as worthy an investment in the future as it has been in the past. In Austria there is a constant and urgent search for rediscovery of the mysterious roots of an age-old culture, which has again begun to find fresh life, and to blossom anew even after economic and social catastrophe.

ITALY

I. Archetypes of Patronage

Maecenas — Medici — Mussolini

The cultural phenomenon of art patronage has been nowhere else on the European continent more strikingly affirmed and more ominously challenged than on the soil of Italy. This ancient land has experienced both the most celebrated and potentially the most dangerous kinds of art sponsorship in the history of western Europe. Within two millennia one can observe prime examples of patronage which encouraged magnificent creative achievement or brought about the flagrant waste of all artistic forces. Centuries apart, and under decidedly different circumstances, three powerful and art-conscious men dominated the cultural life of their environment, their city, their nation, with imagination or destructive maneuver.

The three men — clearly representing archetypes of patronage — were Gaius Maecenas, Lorenzo de' Medici, and Benito Mussolini. Each established new forms of art sponsorship which in intent and realization are as meaningful today as they were in their respective eras — antiquity, Renaissance, and twentieth century.

Maecenas lived in ancient Rome. In several modern languages his Latin name lives on. Italians speak of "maecenatismo," the French of "le mécènat," the Germans of "Maezenatentum." These words are all synonyms for patronage on a grand scale.* Such continued use of his name shows the extent of acknowledgement which posterity has accorded to Gaius Maecenas.

The mere mention of the name Medici suggests the summit of princely patronage during the Florentine Renaissance. Much of what we admire in Florence today — the imaginative plan of the town on the banks of the Arno, the aristocratic wonders cut in stone, the noble palaces housing incomparable painting and sculpture — can be traced back to the vision of Lorenzo de' Medici, and to the continuous art sponsorship by the members of his family who preceded or followed him as sovereigns of the Florentine city-state.

Rome is Rome. Naples is Naples. But the Florence of the Medicis enshrined the glory of the Italian art world: here in the native town of Dante and Michelangelo the heart of Renaissance culture still beats. Lorenzo de' Medici, seemingly more than any patron in history, lifted the artist from his creative loneliness to productive work dedicated to

*Curiously, there is no English word — as in other European languages — to elevate the family name of Maecenas to a generic term.

the community. He liberated the artist from the usual sense of limitation and encouraged him to create masterworks.

The idea at the core of all true patronage — to free the artist for his work — was perverted to serfdom by Benito Mussolini. He led the arts, which had reached the summit on Italian soil, down in fast serpentines to the lowlands of Fascism, from which a direct road led to Hitler's apocalyptic onslaught and destruction of culture.

Gaius Maecenas, Lorenzo de' Medici, Benito Mussolini are all symbolic figures. They show us the possible options of patronage — of creative opportunities glorified or obliterated. We also recognize in the personal histories of the first two the highest reward attainable to a great patron: to share immortality with the creative artist he has sponsored.

Ancient Rome
First Minister of Culture

After two thousand years,* Gaius Maecenas is remembered as the patron of Virgil and Horace, the classical poets who honored Maecenas in enduring verse. But there are other circumstances, decisive ones, that make the figure of Maecenas so significant.

Maecenas appears as the first "minister of culture" on record. Emperor Augustus entrusted him with special administrative and budgetary responsibilities in cultural affairs. As the confidential counselor of the Emperor, Maecenas was in the position to sponsor the most gifted artists of his time in the interest of the state.

The era of Emperor Augustus was a propitious time for the blossoming of the humanities in Rome. His predecessor, Julius Caesar, had granted full citizenship to the teachers of liberal arts. Augustus, Caesar's grandnephew, continued an enlightened policy. By making Augustus recognize the importance of culture within the affairs of state Maecenas rendered his master a lasting service. Maecenas knew that the arts were more than embellishment of court life. He recognized their social value. He recognized in poetry a potential tool for the affirmation and even for the progress of the ideal state. In the sense of such ideology the Rome of Augustus recalls the Athens of Pericles. Greek philosophy, particularly of Plato and Aristotle, shines through the tenets of Gaius Maecenas. More than three centuries had passed since the Greek thinkers had formulated their epoch-making doctrines governing the role of art and education. The acceptance of these principles by Maecenas was most advanced for his Roman environment in the first century B.C.

*The birthday of Maecenas has not been established with certainty. He was probably born between 74 and 64 B.C. Arretium is given as his birthplace. He died in 8 B.C.

Maecenas was a discerning man of letters. He knew how to choose artists of stature, whose work could be directed toward ennobling the spirit of the community and of the entire nation. He was equipped in scholarship and dialectics to influence the aesthetics of the artists whom he sponsored.

The poetry of Virgil may serve as an example. There is a marked change in Virgil's outlook — a new and serious direction — on the road from the *Eclogues* to the *Georgics.* In the *Georgics* Virgil is no longer a poet dreaming of Utopia as in the *Eclogues.* In his later works Virgil is concerned with the reality of his country's needs. The good of the state depends on the attitude and behavior of the individual citizen and on his devotion to the cause of the Empire. It was Maecenas who guided Virgil on this way. "Without thy help and smile my thoughts attempt nothing of noble note," read Virgil's acknowledging lines of his indebtedness to his sponsor. And Virgil earned all favors shown him; he was useful to the state.[1] Virgil's talent lent veracity to the legend of the divine origin of Caesar, a veracity that intensified the Emperor's nimbus as a semisacred personage and confirmed his godly stature.

From the beginning of his creative pursuits Virgil enjoyed the friendship of Horace. Like Virgil, Horace contributed poetry that enhanced the glory of the Empire. His *Carmen Secularae* was chanted by a chorus of youth at the Roman games which the Emperor had inaugurated for the enjoyment of the people. Horace's verses helped the outdoor festival to its success at a time when the Romans were showing signs of restlessness with their government. Again it was Maecenas who had convinced Horace that his poetry could serve the cause of the state. In the first of his Odes (Book I) Horace eloquently praised his sponsor: "Maecenas, sprung from royal stock, my bulwark and my glory dearly cherished."

Maecenas, to be sure, was not the only major art patron in this era of Roman civilization. But he epitomizes an eminently revealing phase of classical art life. The Athenian principles, which employ the arts to serve the noble cause of the state, were given a fresh impulse by Maecenas. And the idea of this interaction became henceforth a leading motive in Italian history.

Christian Patronage

During the entire Middle Ages the Church's steady growth of authority in religion and politics was paralleled by its dominance in the arts. Ecclesiastical patronage brought the style of the art product into new and sharpest focus. Form and content were dogmatically prescribed whenever the Church commissioned works of art. The architecture of a dome and the structure of a score, the mode of representation in a painting or the expression of a piece of sculpture were predetermined by their religious purpose. The individual intent of the artist was unimportant; self-expression was undesirable; the maker of an art work was not considered "creative" and consequently often remained anonymous. And so, too often we have never learned the name of the man who built, composed, or painted a medieval masterpiece. The Middle Ages interpreted liturgical art as craft in the humble service of the Church.

Craft or art — whatever our retrospective interpretation — the Church Fathers employed with rare discernment the most formidable talent available to beautify the service. The glorification of God was expressed by noble music, heard in commanding cathedrals that had been built by great architects. Renowned sculptors and inspired painters decorated these structural masterpieces with imaginative and colorful representations of biblical scenes. And the distinguished composers of each era were frequently the conductors who were hired to complete the ceremonial of creed within the great ecclesiastical commonwealth of art. Sacred scores were sung *a cappella* by sensitive choirs, trained to master the intricacies of a highly polyphonic style. A praying community assembled in an aesthetically pure and exalted environment, where masterworks of visual art spoke even to the unlettered with pictorial eloquence. Not only in large cathedrals, but in innumerable small churches and chapels man's spirit was directed to divine prayer by works of art in settings of austere beauty and religious persuasion.

But only temporarily could the sponsoring hierarchy maintain its tight control over the performing and the visual arts. Man's persistent search for the meaning of life inaugurated epochal changes in philosophy and aesthetics underlying artistic creation. Corresponding changes in the patronage of art followed.

Florentine Renaissance — Climax of Secular Patronage

Of all Italian cities except Rome, Florence gradually emerged as the supreme model of urban culture. Ruled in an absolute monarchal manner by the Medicis, the fair Tuscan city on the banks of the Arno River witnessed during the Renaissance the rise of an art life which is almost incalculable in its imaginative variety and aesthetic consequence.

The ascent of the Medici family from uncertain beginnings to uncontested reign over Florence is in itself an absorbing story. There is no doubt that the Medicis represent the most colorful dynasty of art patrons in Western history. On the Piazza della Signoria in Florence, among the wonderful works of sculpture at the Loggia dei Lanza, stands the famous bronze statue of Perseus, triumphantly holding in his outstretched hand the head of Medusa. According to legend, the ancient hero Perseus, son of Zeus, was the ancestor of the Medicis. Benvenuto Cellini symbolized in this bronze statue the victory of the Medicis over Florence.

If Virgil's poetry pleaded in ancient Rome for trust in the Emperor's divine origin, Cellini's sculpture in Florence aimed equally at hero worship of his patrons, the Medicis. Whatever their real and probably humble origin, this family line of Renaissance Florence attained monarchal status, and whatever the political means to this end might have been, their patronage transformed the Tuscan capital into a veritable stronghold of culture. What we know today as the Uffizi and Pitti art galleries, their treasures second to none, were during the Renaissance the homes of the Medicis. The unique Ponte Vecchio, with its stores of jewelry and other fine works of goldsmiths and silversmiths, was built by the Medicis as a strategic bridge for their army. Whatever the Medicis touched — even purely functional structures — turned into works of art which beautified the city. As the bankers of the Popes, the Medicis over the subsequent generations of their rule returned their acquired power and wealth into creative channels. Cosimo de' Medici the Elder (1389-1464) and Lorenzo the Elder (1395-1440) founded the two branches of the family who concern us most as art patrons. Cosimo, the more active of the two, was the builder of churches as well as of palaces. He paid from his own purse for the first public library in Florence. He founded the Platonic Academy which was to become crucial in the development of Italian arts and letters. He was the patron of Brunelleschi and Donatello, of Fra Angelico and Fra Filippo Lippi.

Lorenzo de' Medici (called "the Magnificent," 1449-1492), grandson of Cosimo, was as lordly an art sponsor as the world has ever witnessed. No patron since Gaius Maecenas matched Lorenzo's intellectual stature, his dedicated searching for artists, and his finding of the very greatest. It was at Lorenzo's palace that Michelangelo first embarked on his work as a sculptor, among a host of illustrious artists who served Lorenzo's vast cultural enterprises. Lorenzo understood artists well; for steeped in the universal knowledge so typical of the Renaissance, Lorenzo was equally at home in all the arts. He personified the image the poet Novalis evoked of the ideal ruler: "a true prince is the artist of artists."[2]

But there is another side to Lorenzo de' Medici. His record was not free from blemishes. There were complaints that he sometimes confused his own bank account with that of the state. Others found that his morals were not as pure as his commitment to the two young men whom he trained within the walls of his palace for their future roles as Popes.[3]

One might attribute the conflicting facets of Lorenzo's personality to the ambivalent moral climate of the Renaissance. Lorenzo has also been interpreted as a "split personality," a man who was one day involved in rawest political deals and merciless intrigues, and on another day, in the noble pursuit of civic leadership. Modern psychology explains that such paradoxes in the character of an imaginative man may coexist without the "bad" preventing the "good" from expressing itself productively. And thus a life fraught with shocking and antisocial patterns of behavior, may at the same time yield vast contributions to society. We judge such a life primarily by what it has produced. For when the best elements in Lorenzo's personality merged, that of the visionary art sponsor and that of the generous sovereign, something extraordinary happened: the transformation of Florence into a microcosm of a cultural state. This could happen because Lorenzo knew that art on the highest level expressed something far greater than the power of his monarchy.

The Sacred and the Secular at Strife
The Council of Trent

The Renaissance brought to the fore a long-latent conflict within ecclesiastical art. Sharp discords between heterogeneous elements — the sacred and the secular — were painfully felt. The struggle was not new, nor was its cause. From a source as early as St. Augustine (354-430), and from numerous subsequent authorities, we learn that the Roman hierarchy had long viewed the lure of worldly art with suspicion. During the Middle Ages the conflict was kept under relative control by the Church. But in the sixteenth century the spread of secular expression forced the Church Fathers to take drastic action, if the very essence of ecclesiastical patronage was to be safeguarded. The spirit of the Church service was in jeopardy. Worldliness had infiltrated the creation of liturgical scores and even their interpretation. Composers adopted folk tunes, marches, dances — outright popular ditties — fashioning them into sacred hymns by simple devices.[4] But the community recognized the profane tunes even in religious guise; and often the new music appealed to the churchgoers more than the medieval austerity of conservative masses, litanies, and other forms of the sacred service. This marked a threat to the sanctity of music within the Roman Church. But another and even more serious challenge came from the outside.

On October 31, 1517, Martin Luther posted his ninety-five theses on the doors of the castle church of Wittenberg. Against the tidal current of a new creed, a revival of Catholicism became overdue. The arts were directly involved in this stormy religious issue. Luther was greatly concerned with Church music, and the scope of his reforms vigorously attacked vital aspects of the Roman liturgy.

The grave situation inspired the Counter Reformation to drastic action. The Council of Trent, meeting from 1545 to 1563, sought measures for a Catholic revival. The problems of Church music were studied by the committee of the Cardinals. On September 17, 1562, the Council decided[5] to ban from liturgy forever all worldly lure or profanity, direct or implied, in word or tone, within the vocal or instrumental medium, in order "to restore the House of God . . . . to a House of Prayer." The guideposts thus defined by the Council were only of a general religious and aesthetic nature. Their actual execution was left to the imagination and technical skill of the composers and conductors in the service of the Catholic Church. Perfect equilibrium between the intent of ecclesiastical patronage and its creative realization was achieved by Giovanni Pierluigi da Palestrina (1524-1594), the greatest master of sacred music in the sixteenth century. His *Missa Papae Marcelli* is rightly considered the model of great liturgical music.[6]

Universality of Sacred Art

Four centuries have passed since the Council of Trent redefined the nature of Catholic liturgical art and ordered intransigent directions for its authentic interpretation. The passing of time has not altered the view of the Church. On November 22, 1903, Pius X — continuing the line of music-loving Popes recorded by history as great reformers of liturgy — released another epochal decree, known as the *Motu Proprio*, which contains a synopsis of the general principles and the different categories of sacred music. The document explains the function of the liturgical text, the external form of sacred compositions, and the practice of church performance (such as the role of the singers, the organ, other instruments, and the like).

One of the most revealing aspects of the *Motu Proprio* is its insistence on *universality* of expression in any liturgical work. Here is a clue not only to the safeguarding of liturgy: the guideposts of universality shield all great art, both sacred and secular. Universality is the primary reason the great religious art works of the West can be appreciated the world over without denominational confinement. One does not have to be a Catholic to appreciate deeply Palestrina's *Missa Papae Marcelli* or Beethoven's *Missa Solemnis*. One does not have to be a Protestant to love the *St. Matthew Passion* of Bach, so movingly carried by Lutheran spirit. And the *Psalms* of the Jewish King David have belonged to the entire world for thousands of years. The main reason for their universal acceptance is the same in all of these religious works of art: they are imbued with the spirit of a supranational humanity.

The identical premise of universal expression is also at the core of secular art works which have become the property of the world. By contrast, styles nourished primarily from national sources will limit both the communicative power of art works and their message. By the same token, the enforced tailoring of art to merely fashionable measures has always proved deleterious. Thus the intent to gain favor with the masses by way of art styles that are today identified as "populism," or as "realism," necessarily weakens artistic integrity. We can observe this manipulation of art with variations, and under different names, with every dictatorship. Creative talent in all totalitarian countries has been wasted in the pursuit of such false goals. As we shall observe in detail, the dictator attacks art at its most vulnerable level — the level of standards.

II. Fascist Italy

Bloody Operetta

Benito Mussolini liked to think of himself as an artist. He was, at least so he thought, a violinist; and he never failed to stress his ties with music. He claimed Cesare Mussolini (composer, theorist, born in 1735) as an ancestor. Il Duce was a writer of sorts. He had been a newspaper editor. He published and produced a play on Napoleon called *One Hundred Days*, which dealt with the episode of the French Emperor's escape from the island of Elba. Benito Mussolini posed from the beginning of his reign as the great patron of the arts. When Mussolini set out to "unify" Italy by brutal force, the art life of the nation was usurped by his totalitarian schemes. It happened gradually. A comparison with Nazi methods* shows how relatively slow Mussolini was to interfere with and finally to obliterate the freedom of the performing arts.

In October, 1922, the Fascists obtained control of the country. No less than thirteen years later, in 1935, Mussolini laid down the laws which were henceforth to control all phases of Italian art life.

Why did Il Duce and his Fascist henchmen wait so long? Certainly not because of any consideration for the dignity of art and the liberty of artists. Various answers are suggested by the Italians themselves. Some argue that the whole business of Fascism was a large-scale show in itself, with Mussolini as chief producer. Those who have seen Italy in her full Fascist dress will not forget the strong impression of Mussolini's pageantry. Black-shirted groups marched through the old streets of the towns and villages of the nation singing the *Giovinezza*[7] from dawn to dusk and often all through the night. Bemedalled, sabre-rattling,

*Cf. Chapter on West Germany.

dapper young officers held forth on the Corso or in public squares, in theaters and cafés all over Italy. All official ceremony, in or out of doors, was staged in circus style. The circus itself became permanent. Following an ancient Roman prescription, Mussolini promised his plebeians "panem et circenses" (bread and plays).

When he tossed his empty boasting and vain pledges of the nation's future grandeur to the masses from the balcony of his Roman palace at the Piazza Venezia, it seemed to be a form of popular theater, though a bad one. Tens of thousands of his followers acted as a chorus — now responding with short reiterations, now chanting a speech-song, now singing in unison. The Nazis later learned this cheap stagecraft from the Fascists. Mussolini was a ham actor, but undeniably a successful one. When he appeared before the people to make a speech, he presented the popular image of the dictator. We do not know whether he identified himself with Caesar or Napoleon, the two dictators who were his obvious models, but he played a part in which traits of both predecessors were blended with his own braggadocio, on that enormous stage consisting of the entire Apennine peninsula and all of Italy's islands in the Mediterranean and the Adriatic. The Fascist symbol — an axe with a projected blade of a kind the ancient Roman magistrates carried as an emblem of authority — was plastered on every corner and stone of the nation, in every office and public building, in every cinema and store. The civilian wore it in his buttonhole. In a theater-struck nation the daily pageantry contributed immeasurably, at least in its initial years, to the hold of Fascism on the masses. For the Italians love performances, the bigger the better.

To the very gruesome end Mussolini's triumph and lament (in addition to his crimes against humanity) will always be remembered as a scenic representation. It was pompous histrionics when he marched on Rome accompanied by his early followers of all ages, frightening the weak little King Vittorio Emanuele III and his entourage of helpless ministers out of action. It was still grimmest theater when the curtain fell on the Milanese finale: when the Italians hung their butcher-dictator on a lamp post like a slaughtered swine, head downwards alongside his young and pretty mistress who had followed him into death. No television director could have imagined a more extravagant illustration of the ultimate penalty paid by the bad man for his evil deeds. But this last scene at least was *genuine* theater. It was produced by honest fury, long accumulated in the hearts and minds of Mussolini's victims throughout the twenty-three years of Fascist terror.

"Art after Work"

As time went on, Mussolini gradually turned his attention to the propaganda value of the performing arts, and finally designed for them a purposive framework within the gigantic machine of the Fascist party organization.

Some features of art support that have emerged from his reign merit study. He was the first to set up a national organization that would sponsor with absolute control "spectacles" throughout the entire peninsula, from the slopes of the Alps to the islands of Sardinia and Sicily. This organization set up by the Fascists proved to be usable in postwar years as the ground plan for Italy's national art support. In Mussolini's era the so-called *enti autonomi* of the Italian theater developed; it had been inaugurated by Arturo Toscanini at Milan's La Scala in 1921, the year before the Fascists marched on Rome.

Of various new organizations introduced by Mussolini, the Opera Nazionale Dopolavore (OND) is worthy of note. Its title has been freely translated as "national work for leisure time." Within this project, the government promised to turn the daily leisure hours after work into "healthy and simultaneously stimulating experiences in both entertainment and education, with the specific aim to ennoble the working people, physically, morally and intellectually."

No one will find fault with such aims. The blueprint of the OND reads well enough. And an objective evaluation must admit that the OND stimulated numerous activities and established new organizations that gave vigorous support to the performing arts. OND brought the lyrical and prose theater, as well as symphonic music, directly to the people. It concerned itself systematically with popular forms of art education. The national element was overstressed, as one would expect in a Fascist state, and all aspects of internationalism were suppressed. In each village folk customs and folk art were revived, particularly folk singing. Ancient Italian instruments were put to new use. Choirs and choir schools were established everywhere. Within a few years Italy could count on thousands of new performing groups. During 1932 alone there were more than 10,000 public concerts. The Banda Musicale, the traditional town band, was restored in every hamlet with the help of state money. These bands gave 760,000 public concerts in 1932, often with a program of operatic transcriptions surrounded by Fascist trash. The OND founded many string orchestras devoted to weekly performances of classical music. Wherever possible, performances of amateurs were encouraged. Talented graduates of music schools made their debuts in state-supported performances.

Experimental theaters and opera workshops sprang up in hundreds of communities. Here again, gifted amateurs were invited to participate. The great opera theaters (such as La Scala in Milan, Teatro dell'Opera in Rome, San Carlo in Naples, Teatro Massimo in Palermo) gave closed performances for members of the OND, either gratuitously or at nominal fees. The Thespian Carriage of Opera, known as "Carro di Tespi lirico," accommodated audiences of thousands in its enormous portable tent. This traveling opera company journeyed to the remote corners of Italy to give everybody live performances of opera with good singers.

There were, then, some commendable features in the program of the OND, some of them even worthy of imitation. What was obviously wrong with the OND was its political substructure, for which the arts were a mere cover, and which was used to diffuse Fascist propaganda into the last hamlet of the nation. Innumerable ways were used to infiltrate Italian art life and popular entertainment with political messages. The OND made it possible for members to buy radio sets at 50 per cent reduction, and their listening fees were cancelled altogether. This was a shrewd move. Millions who could now listen at home to *Aïda* or *The Barber of Seville* were also exposed to the speeches of Il Duce and the constant broadcasts of Fascist propaganda. The OND covered up the bad state of economics and the political misdeeds of Mussolini.

The Fascist Theater

Italy's legitimate theater remained in a dire state during the Fascistic regime. In 1934 Mussolini received an appeal, signed by a group of outstanding authors, to save the Italian theater from collapse. The document was inspired by Luigi Pirandello, Nobel Prize winning dramatist, who hoped to restore the Italian theater to its ancient dignity. But Pirandello's project was shelved. Mussolini distrusted the intellectual force inherent in good drama.

Pirandello had collaborated with the distinguished Venetian composer Francesco Malipiero in the opera *La Favola del Figlio Cambiato*. The work was first performed in Rome in 1934. It was a futile effort. Two days after its opening, Mussolini personally ordered the removal of the opera for reasons of "moral incongruity" in the story. (Censorship of the performing arts as well as of the press had become tantamount to Mussolini's sole judgment.) The blow did not prevent Pirandello, only one year later, from claiming Mussolini as "the glorious patron of the Italian theater, the greatest in the world."

Another prominent poet and dramatist of Mussolini's era, Gabriele d'Annunzio, turned out to be a full-fledged collaborator of Fascism. The ubiquitous and flamboyant d'Annunzio managed to play several leading roles in service of Mussolini — filling a variety of posts that were distributed among a number of different Nazis in Germany. D'Annunzio was poet-laureate to the Fascists, as was the aged Gerhart Hauptmann to the Nazis. He was the chief propaganda writer in Rome, as Goebbels was in Berlin. D'Annunzio lost one eye in combat and decorated himself, like Hermann Goering, his fellow flyer, with more orders than his uniform could hold. He coined, like Goebbels, phrases that became the Fascist slogans of his era. Hitler borrowed his war cries from Goebbels; Mussolini plagiarized d'Annunzio's demagogic calls to arms, such as the proverbial "mare nostrum" by which Il Duce claimed the entire Adriatic Sea as a property of his dream empire. The extravagant lip service of famous artists to the cause of Fascism was a crucial detail in the scheme of cultural politics. After all, artists such as Pirandello and d'Annunzio had enormous international prestige.

It is only fair to record, however, that some of Italy's best minds courageously resisted the lure of Fascism and withdrew into years of solitude and poverty. Some left their homeland forever. Some were murdered by Fascist gangs.

Futurism

Mussolini's attitude toward the creative expression of his time can best be described as haphazard and confused. Into the second decade of his era falls the renaissance of the trend that became known as "futurism," although the experiments of Filippo Marinetti, its principal exponent, far antedate the era of Fascism. In 1909 Marinetti had published his manifesto calling for a new art to cope with the machine age. "Pegasus, the winged horse of the Muses, should be retired," demanded Marinetti. The place of the mythological horse must be taken by the racing car, "rattling along like a machine gun, which is more beautiful than the Victory of Samothrace." In 1913 Marinetti's fellow futurist Luigi Russolo published "a table of noises for the futurist orchestra." Russolo listed six families of noises. Included in the first family are booms, thunderclaps, explosions, crashes, splashes, roars; in the second family are whistles, hisses, and snorts; in the third family are whispers, murmurs, mutterings, bustling noises, gurgles; in the fourth family are screams, screeches, rustlings, buzzes, cracklings, sounds obtained by friction, etc.

By 1914 Marinetti and Luigi Russolo created a scandal with a program of their futuristic music performed at the Teatro del Verme in Milan. They offered the public an ensemble of these noise instruments; but the Italians did not enjoy them. If futurism failed in the intervening years to make any legitimate impression on the art world, would Mussolini, with his shrewd concern for mass appeal, offer Marinetti and his associates the slightest chance of acceptance?

He did. Their kind of experimental noise-making was tolerated by Fascism. Mussolini simply could not resist the cheap flattery of the futurists and their "wholehearted" embrace of his regime. And so, in 1934, the August number of *Stile futurista*, the mouthpiece of this movement, brought the following exhortation:

> Italian musicians, be futurists! Rejuvenate the soul of your listeners by swift musical synthesis (not exceeding a minute), thunderously arousing the optimistic and active pride of living in the great Italy of Mussolini, which will henceforth be at the head of the Machine Age![8]

The pronouncement accomplished its purpose. And so, what would have been impossible in Germany — the strange bedfellowship of Fascism and futurism — was blessed in Italy. A place was reserved for Marinetti on Mussolini's noisy bandwagon.

Fascist Opera

In October, 1935, Mussolini, in a dastardly breach of international law, launched his treacherous attack against Abyssinia. The conquest of Ethiopia was celebrated in an opera named *Il deserto tentato*, for which the score was written by Alfredo Casella.

In the days following World War II, Casella had appeared, along with Malipiero, the most combative personality of Italian music. As early as 1917 Casella founded the Società Nazionale di Musica, the forerunner of the Italian section of the International Society for Contemporary Music. But the advent of Fascism marked the gradual downfall of this artist who had once set out so promisingly to bring cosmopolitanism into the threatening provincialism of his land. Glorifying Fascistic tyranny in his opera, Casella sacrificed the remnants of his artistic integrity. The role of this composer was as deplorable as it was typical of the effect on numerous talented artists who paid an infamous price for Mussolini's perverted patronage.

A climax of absurdity in musical performance was reached on the occasion of the ominous journey of Hitler to Mussolini in 1938. This visit fortified the Berlin-Rome axis in the year prior to the outbreak of World War II. A concert of a kind that Italy had not heard nor seen in her long history of flamboyant music-making was to celebrate the event. When maestro Gino Marinuzzi gave the downbeat, an orchestra of nine hundred began to play the Nazi hymn (the *Horst Wessel Lied*) followed by the Fascist *Giovinezza*. Forty-five military bands blared and one hundred eleven choruses, totalling ten thousand performers, joined in the monstrous singing and blowing.

In this kind of production there was at least a true element of musical Fascism, a bombastic, pompous organization of explosive roars and deafening powers of sound, designed to overwhelm Mussolini's apprentice, Hitler, who was already on the verge of becoming Mussolini's master.

Not every Italian conductor was as opportunistic as Gino Marinuzzi and scores of other Italian musicians. As in all of his political actions, Arturo Toscanini emerged from the severe test of behavior under Fascism a symbol of courage. His uncompromising democratic convictions had already caused a series of flare-ups; the maestro was bound to get into still greater trouble with the regime. On May 14, 1931, Toscanini mounted the podium to conduct a concert of symphonic music at Bologna. By that time the performance of the *Giovinezza* had become obligatory: the party song was to introduce all musical and theatrical performances as well as all public occasions. Ignoring this order, Toscanini opened his concert without playing the *Giovinezza*.

A Fascist hit the maestro in the face. Four days later, the official Syndicate of Artists and Musicians of Bologna denounced Toscanini as "absurd and unpatriotic." The episode is still remembered as a solitary instance of civil courage during an era of general cowardice, as a moral counterpoint to the attitude of many, many Italians and German artists collaborating with their Fascist "patrons." Toscanini left Italy and did not return to his homeland until after the liberation of his country at the end of World War II.

Pose of Patronage

In retrospect, the sponsorship of the performing arts under Fascism does not reveal a conclusive picture. At a time when Hitler had already embarked on his satanic drive to "purify" the racial culture of Nazi Germany, Mussolini was still trying various and conflicting courses to establish totalitarian methods of Fascist art control. Mussolini's support of the performing arts, in contrast to Hitler's, did not lack some achievement, as the development of the *enti autonomi* proves. What detracts even from this part of the program was the ugly role to which the arts were relegated — as in the badly camouflaged Fascistic propaganda of the OND. Mussolini's patronage, as the quoted "futuristic" episode shows, was full of grotesque contradictions and loopholes.

The lesson, then, to be learned from the Fascistic art experiment is this: Mussolini was well aware of the usefulness of the arts and of their impact on the people. If this had not been so, his totalitarian government would not have seized the arts so completely. He would not have supported the *enti autonomi* and the OND. But the Fascists usurped the performing arts. They promoted trash to official "art." They removed "provocative" works from the repertory. They commissioned only those artists who would extol Mussolini's state. They finally brutalized any artist who dared to speak up in protest.

Whatever the blurred picture of Fascist art life might hide, it is sufficiently clear to show that creative talent can prostitute itself to dictators, and it shows the obvious totalitarian maneuvers to use the arts to divert the people from the recognition of dangerous economic and political issues. Gradually, under Fascism the arts lost the last vestige of sovereignty. The oligarchy of a few commissars, handpicked by the dictator, was in control. It alone ordered the tune and laid down the laws for the kind of art that the artists might produce and that the people were permitted to hear and to see.

Mussolini's experiment preceded Hitler's by more than a decade. It finally limped behind the gigantic steam-rolling machine of the Nazis; when they finally overran Italy, they enforced the assimilation of the Italian laws to the German "Kultur Gesetz." But it was not until Propaganda Minister Goebbels imposed Teutonic "thoroughness" on the domestic art life of the Third Reich that one realized, compared to the Germans the Italians were easygoing amateurs.

III. Republican Italy

The New Republic

By 1945, after successful resistance to Fascists and Nazis, the allied armies had liberated all of Italy. The courage of the Italian partisan movement in the nation's fight for freedom has inspired many creative artists; it has become the theme for literary and dramatic works, and for moving pictures and television.

Italy has always been a country of extremes. World War II has shattered the economy. The postwar period has brought to focus serious antagonism on crucial public issues of which governmental art support is a part. Yet the highly realistic mind of the Italian has found workable formulas that enable the country's art life to continue. The Italians are accustomed to make concessions and even paradoxical compromises.

By 1946 Italians were ready to form a constituent assembly; but it was not until 1947 that they abolished the monarchy by national referendum. The members of the House of Savoy went into exile; but unlike other European dynasties to which they were related, the Italian rulers did not leave behind a notable record of personal art patronage.

The new Italian constitution may be compared with that of the French Fourth Republic. This is no coincidence: both constitutions were born following traumatic experiences with totalitarian tyranny. In 1948 free elections were held in Italy — the first in twenty-six years.

Today Italy is a Republic. Its government inherited Mussolini's centralized organization which, as we have seen, automatically incorporated control of the arts.

World War II caused on Italian soil a frightening amount of destruction which is still visible wherever major battles took place. Many historic sites — in Renaissance Florence and elsewhere — became the scenes of painful losses.[9] Millions of Italian citizens emerged from war in utter disillusionment, and millions, destitute to this day, are easy prey to propaganda from political extremes — the Left or the Right.

We cannot ignore the political picture of modern Italy in our appraisal of this nation's art program. For all citizens are called upon to vote on art support, whenever its various issues are decided in parliament by legislation.

In ironic contrast to the patent poverty of a large segment of the Italian people is their rich heritage: the treasures of the past. Traces of Italy's glorious history are everywhere, and new evidence of her ancient culture is being unearthed almost daily. Architectural wonders thousands of years old are spread over Italian soil and bear witness to a great civilization. Italy is like a gigantic museum, in- and out-of-doors, with many wonderful churches, galleries, palaces. In archeology Italy spends vast sums for continuous research in new excavations, as well as for the maintenance of historical landmarks of architecture and sculpture. In 1957 the government allocated 18,000,000 lire (approximately $29,000) to preserving the Colosseum. Continually, large sums will have to be spent for repairs of this most spectacular of all Roman ruins.

While a temperate climate has been a benign factor in protecting many of Italy's art treasures out-of-doors, they have been attacked from within by an almost uncontrollable army of termites. One million dollars has proved insufficient to combat the menace, even by modern methods of extermination. To be sure, there are costly problems of preservation in other countries. Yet none of the Mediterranean nations except France subsidizes cultural projects to a degree that compares even distantly with the expensive art program of the Italian government and its task of permanently shielding these shrines of a common Western heritage.

The Two Italys

Of the great industrial powers of the West, the new Republic of Italy — at least for the time being — is economically the weakest. World War II wiped out more than one-third of the nation's productive power. Of Italy's total population, approaching 51,000,000, nearly 5 per cent are unemployed. Millions of farmers and workers, although fully employed, receive inadequate wages. Many more find only part-time employment. From the point of view of living standards, there are actually two Italys — the north and the south (encompassing a combined area of 116,303 square miles). The economic contrasts are shocking. They pertain to everything: to shelter, food, clothing, to the opportunities of participating in the enjoyment of life.

The south is the poor part of Italy, as are Sicily, Sardinia, and other smaller Mediterranean and Adriatic islands united under the Italian flag. In the more prosperous north extreme contrasts are prevalent: wealth and poverty live in disturbing proximity. There are the old aristocracy and the splendor of their palaces. There are the *nouveau riche* and their intemperate display of wealth. Side by side with these affluent groups the Italian proletarian exists in unbelievably primitive housing, substandard and slumlike. Tourists sometimes find picturesque the narrow alleys, the colorful hanging wash waving in the wind, the street musicians, and the unaccountable number of children noisily playing in the streets. But poverty is not so attractive to those who live in it. Such an uneven distribution of national fortune is bound to cause tension. It is reflected in irreconcilable political thinking.

Rome is the seat of the Vatican. It is also the "reddest" capital of the West.[10] This fact dramatizes the extremes that are part of the local and national scene, affecting its equilibrium. As a result, there has been a steady sequence of governmental crises, and there are few signs of an immediate stabilization. The leading faction is that of the Christian Democrats. As they lack absolute majority, they always need support from other parties to achieve any kind of legislation that could be interpreted as the wish of the people. The parties left of center rank next in power.

Italy's art life is governmentally centralized; majority legislation is required for its support.

The religious element in art is of obvious importance to the Christian Democrats. Italian radio and television programs are frequently direct messengers of their belief. By contrast, the prose theaters in the urban centers are sometimes claimed to be the mouthpiece of the socialistic point of view.

In the patterns of art support there is a constant give and take. Decisions vary according to spheres of influence. The overall result has in recent years inclined to the liberal side. The Italians interpret this trend as the psychological consequence of their grim memories of Mussolini's tyranny. Even the ultraconservative wing, in exceptional cases, tends toward tolerance rather than toward the ill-reputed pitfalls of suppression. By the same token, the left wing sometimes votes for issues which on their face value would seem to preclude their agreement.

This national trend toward ideological toleration explains, in part, the political incongruities apparent in the fact that plays labeled "leftist" are commonly performed in government supported theaters in such cities as Milan, close to the largest Gothic cathedral on Italian soil, or at Rome, near St. Peter's, the mother church of Catholicism. But influences other than that interpreted as a reaction to Fascist tyranny abide as perpetual guardians of diversity in art; and the government cannot ignore these forces in its program of art support. For example, Milan and Rome are industrial centers with large working populations. They are also the homes of an intellectual elite. Further, they have a cosmopolitan public, including many foreigners. All of this accounts for the fact that there is in Milan and Rome an assertion of ideological independence, even in theaters enjoying the diverse patronage of the city, the province, and the national government.*

Fountainhead of National Art Support

The aftermath of World War II forced Italy into a complex reevaluation of all spiritual and cultural values. The political changes were fundamental. After having been united as a kingdom for eighty-five years, the nation had become a republic. After Fascistic dictatorship, Italy was now to enjoy the long-absent blessings of liberty. Today, she is a democracy like her neighbors France, Switzerland, and Austria.

The new Republican constitution of Italy was established in 1947. In the arts it spelled a return to free creative expression, which was bound to result in resumption of contact with the progressive artistic trends in the rest of free Europe from which Mussolini had systematically cut off Italy.

The principal art patron of modern Italy is the republican government. From its seat in Rome most of the nation's operas and theatrical companies, its radio and television networks, as well as all important concert organizations and conservatories, receive regular subsidies.

The responsibility of art patronage is written specifically into the Italian constitution. Article 9 refers to the provisions according to which "the Republic endeavors to promote the development of culture and to protect the historical and artistic heritage of the nation." To such ends, stated in the constitution merely in general terms, the Italian government permanently subsidizes large numbers of organizations in

*Analogous spheres of influence do not necessarily prevail in other European nations. Cf. chapters on Belgium or Austria, both overwhelmingly Catholic countries, for distribution of authority in the mass media.

the performing arts. To qualify for such financial aid, art institutes must fulfill carefully defined conditions.

The following pages review the evolutionary phases, which eventually led to the present state of governmental assistance to the performing arts in Italy.

Decree of 1946 and Revisions

The decree No. 538 of May 31, 1946, provided financial support from the government to a number of art institutes. A special commission was put in charge; its task was to examine the requests for subsidies, and to allocate moneys to those organizations which merited assistance.

Financial aid did not stem directly from the national budget. Its source was a yield of taxation on all public shows, sporting events, and betting games throughout Italy. Thus a characteristic procedure of public art support was established, by which one type of Spettacolo* subsidized another. Popular entertainment was called upon to support art on the high level. (King Vittorio Emanuele III was permitted to sign this order as a final gesture of royal patronage prior to his abdication and exile.) This kind of taxation corresponds in intent and procedure to the "Cultural Penny" of Austria. Decree No. 538 was revised several times. The changes were substantial. They concerned the amount of fiscal taxes from tickets and, consequently, the funds available for art subsidy. And the eligibility of organizations for governmental assistance came under close scrutiny.

A more recent law — No. 898 of July 31, 1956 — established that the 12 per cent derived from the direct dues of all entertainment was no longer to be taken from the entire assessment, but only from 85 per cent of it. Thus the legislation intended — with an actual reduction in the percentage rate — to maintain the fund approximately at the same level reached before. The above provisions of law, which expired on June 30, 1957, have been extended "sine die" and until the approval of a new law which will reorganize the entire segment pertaining to the theater. Subject to taxation as before are all places of entertainment such as theaters, ball grounds, race courses, boxing arenas, cinemas, and the like. The attendance figures of the "spectacles" obviously vary from one year to another. As the box office of theaters decreases the income of sport events may increase. This fluctuation is balanced by the distribution of the revenue.

*The word *Spettacolo* refers to various kinds of "spectacles" — the theater, opera, shows, amusements, public exhibitions, and sporting events.

IV. Categories of Subsidy

The governmental subventions of the performing arts fall into four main categories: for autonomous opera agencies known as *Enti Autonomi Lirici;* for provincial opera theaters and concert societies not included under *Enti Autonomi Lirici;* for Italian cultural events held in foreign countries; for various activities intended to promote theater and music in a more general way than those not included among the first three.

The new philosophy of art support is clear: Italy's operas are promoted to a cause of *national* concern. This terminates the exclusive relationship between specific cities or provinces and their theaters. Gradually, the support has been extended to art institutes beyond the field of opera. Article 7 of law 538 provides aid for the *enti autonomi* of the concert institutions of the Accademia di Santa Cecilia (in Rome), and of other musical and theatrical nonprofit institutions.

Autonomous Opera Agencies

Of all the legitimate art forms, opera is traditionally most congenial to the Italian temperament, and so opera receives the lion's share of all official subsidies.

The term *Enti Autonomi*, which plays so crucial a part in the modern structure of Italian art life, is officially translated, *autonomous agencies.** The Italian art institutes referred to by the classification *Enti Autonomi Lirici* (such as La Scala in Milan, San Carlo in Naples, or the Teatro dell'Opera in Rome) are independent state theaters which enjoy autonomy in all artistic matters. Yet their financial management is subject to governmental supervision.

Toscanini as Protagonist

The first theater which assumed legally the status of an *ente autonomo* was La Scala in Milan, Italy's principal opera house. The event falls into the era of Toscanini.[11] In 1921 the municipality of Milan invited the maestro to resume his post as director of La Scala. As a principal condition of his reacceptance, Toscanini requested that La Scala be placed upon a secure economic status guaranteed by law. Toscanini's sweeping demands were fulfilled, and thus a most auspicious period in the history of Italian theater began: a new pattern of patronage was established, the autonomous agency.

Two major transactions accompanied the first formation of La Scala into an *ente autonomo*. The city presented to its resident opera company

**Ente* means being, existence. *Ente autonomo*, then, refers to an autonomous organization. The word *ente* is often applied to offices or organizations performing some form of service for the welfare of the public, and without aim of profit.

the ground and buildings in which it is housed. With its rental problem solved, the theater still needed a subvention to cover the large cost of its productions. The box office receipts were very gratifying during Toscanini's reign, but the large deficit, which a first-rate lyrical theater inevitably incurs, still remained to be underwritten. The necessary additional income guaranteed La Scala was derived from the transfer of 2 per cent of fiscal taxes on all theatrical tickets sold within the province of Lombardy; the rebound of fiscal taxes and receipts collected from the *ente autonomo* of La Scala into its general fund. For the time being this arrangement proved satisfactory. The new agency received the official title, *Istituto Nazionale per l'arte lirico.* Significantly, the nation was now represented in the name of its most famous theater. It was administered by a commission of eight members; their chairman was nominated by the municipal council.

In due time other lyrical theaters followed the course of La Scala. In 1929, the *ente autonomo* of the Teatro dell'Opera in Rome was established, and in 1932, the Teatro Communale in Florence. The financial basis for the support of the opera theaters was the fiscal taxes from ticket receipts in the respective provinces: Milan depended on taxes from Lombardy; Florence, from Tuscany; etc. Each theater retained artistic independence. Each city is reserved the right to appoint, through the municipal council, the opera director.

Thirteen Subsidized Enti Autonomi

The number of subsidized autonomous agencies has reached thirteen. The republic subsidizes all of them on a regular basis.

Obvious guideposts for support are the size of personnel and artistic scope of the organization, the number of employees and performances, the nature and extent of repertory. The cultural significance of the city itself in which the opera is located is also decisive, and the artistic needs of its population are taken into account.

The *enti autonomi* are subdivided into opera theaters and concert organizations according to their size and scope of operation:

1. La Scala in Milan and Teatro dell'Opera in Rome each has an orchestra exceeding 100 permanent players and a chorus exceeding 100, a ballet of a minimum of 50, a minimum of 100 technicians, and two schools (chorus and ballet).

2. Teatro Communale in Florence and San Carlo in Naples have organizations of a more limited scope.

3. All other opera theaters which maintain performing forces and seasonal operations more limited than in Florence or Naples.

The number of performances and the governmental subsidies are indicated in Tables I and II.

The largest concert organizations of Italy (outside of the radio) are the orchestra of Santa Cecilia in Rome and the orchestras associated with the following opera theaters: La Scala in Milan, San Carlo in Naples, and Teatro Communale in Florence.

Some of the operas bear the title *Teatro Communale* (as for instance the opera companies in Florence, Bologna, or Genoa). This title implies that part of the supervision is entrusted to the municipal council and that the city assumes a decisive share of the support. Occasionally, the local subsidies are diversified still further. In addition to state, province, and city, some private banks or the local chamber of commerce and certain industrial syndicates offer regular contributions. The ratio of local subventions is high in Florence and Milan.

The following catalogue of agencies indicates the seasons of the theaters and the type of activities. In most cases the orchestra of the theater serves both in opera and concert. The order of this list follows the governmental memorandum of June 12, 1958 (signed by the President of the Council of Ministers), pertaining to the aid of theatrical and musical activities: Milan, Rome (opera), Florence, Naples, Palermo, Venice, Bologna, Genoa, Turin, Trieste, Verona, Rome (Santa Cecilia), Cagliari.

1. Milan: *Ente autonomo del Teatro alla Scala.* The opera season of this lyrical theater normally begins on the twenty-sixth of December and lasts until spring. Performances are in the large main hall or in La Piccola Scala (a new intimate 600-seat theater, which opened in December, 1955, inside the Scala building.) La Scala is also the seat of a concert series given by the opera orchestra, preceding and following the opera season.

2. Rome: *Ente autonomo del Teatro dell'Opera.* The winter opera season plays at the Opera House (formerly Teatro Costanzi). Plans for a new building are well advanced. Summer opera is held at the Baths of Caracalla.

3. Florence: *Ente autonomo del Teatro Communale.* There is an opera and concert season during the winter. The opera participates in the annual spring event of the Maggio Musicale.

4. Naples: *Ente autonomo del Teatro San Carlo.* The winter opera season is held at the Teatro San Carlo. Fall and spring concert seasons are held in the same theater. During the summer the opera moves to the Arena Flagrea.

5. Palermo: *Ente autonomo del Teatro Massimo.* The Teatro Massimo is the home of the spring opera season and of the winter concert season. During the fall popular opera is offered at the Politeama Garibaldi.

6. Venice: *Ente autonomo del Teatro La Fenice.* The winter opera season is presented at the Teatro La Fenice. A popular spring opera season is occasionally scheduled at the same theater. During the summer concerts are given in the courtyard of the Palazzo Ducale; in the autumn and spring, at the Teatro La Fenice.

7. Bologna: *Ente autonomo del Teatro Communale.* The opera season is in the fall at the Teatro Communale. Concerts are held in the theater during the winter and spring.

8. Genoa: *Ente autonomo del Teatro Communale dell'Opera.* Fall and spring opera seasons are traditionally scheduled at the Teatro Communale dell'Opera (formerly called Teatro Carlo Felice). The winter concert season takes place in the same theater.

9. Turin: *Ente autonomo del Teatro Regio.* Fall, winter, and spring opera seasons are offered at the Teatro Nuovo (the newly built home of the Teatro Regio) and at the Teatro Carignano. Popular symphony concerts are given at the University of Turin.

10. Trieste: *Ente autonomo del Teatro Communale G. Verdi.* Fall and winter opera seasons are at the Teatro Verdi; popular summer season of opera and operetta, at the San Giusto castle. Spring concerts are given at the Teatro Verdi.

11. Verona: *Ente autonomo Spettacoli lirici all'Arena.* The season is limited to outdoor summer opera in the ancient Roman Arena.

12. Rome: *Istituzione dei Concerti dell'Accademia Nazionale di Santa Cecilia.* The national capital is the seat of two independent *enti autonomi.* In addition to the Teatro dell'Opera, Rome is home to the ancient concert organization of the Academy of Santa Cecilia. Prior to the completion of a new auditorium, the fall and winter seasons of concerts have found temporary home in such places as the Teatro Argentina of the papal auditorium on the Via di Constellazione. Chamber music concerts are given at the Academy of Santa Cecilia during the winter. The season of summer symphony concerts is offered at the Basilica di Massenzio.

13. Cagliari: *Istituzione dei Concerti del Conservatorio Musicale di State G. Pierluigi Palestrina.* Opera is performed in this principal city of Sardinia at the Teatro Massimo. Symphony and chamber music concerts are given at the same theater and also at the conservatory of music.

Provincial Opera Theaters and Concert Societies (Not Included under Autonomous Agencies)

On February 20, 1948, decree No. 62 established a special fund derived from 6 per cent on the taxation yield on all public shows, sporting events, and betting games. This fund was to be appropriated in such a way that one-third was to be allocated to dramatic theaters and two-thirds to operas and concert societies exclusive of the autonomous agencies. In order to qualify for financial assistance the organizations had to establish their artistic worth. Between 1949 and 1957 the provisions of this decree were extended four times.*

From the two-thirds allocated to music, the following are entitled to receive subventions:

1. The opera seasons which are not organized by the more privileged autonomous opera agencies (as previously listed). This applies to the opera seasons planned and managed by individual communities, by theater deputations and cooperatives, by miscellaneous committees and institutes. Into this group fall, for example, the traditional opera seasons in such cities as Parma, Piacenza, Modena, Reggio Emilia, Brescia, Mantua, Novara, Bari, Catania, and Sassari.

2. The seasons devoted to symphony and chamber music concerts, organized annually by various nonprofit societies. But no part of this subvention is to be applied to the concert cycles which are offered by the autonomous opera agencies and performed by their affiliated orchestras. This is so because financial aid for these concerts is derived indirectly from the governmental subsidy allocated to the opera company of the performing orchestra.

3. Special events, such as the music festivals of the Biennale of Venice, of the Sagra Musicale Umbra, of the Settimana Musicale of Siena, of the Teatro della Novita at Bergamo, of the Teatro Lirico Sperimentale of Spoleto, and of the Associazione Lirica e Concertistica Italiana (an opera and concert association in Milan, founded to aid talented young singers in the initial phases of their careers).

Cultural Events in Foreign Countries

A fund for culturally significant performances outside of Italy by Italian artists or companies is obtained from the taxation yield of 2 per cent on the gross receipts of the Italian radio. The government and the RAI (Italian radio company) agreed on this procedure by the decree No. 180 of January 26, 1952.

*By the decrees of Law No. 959 of December 29, 1949; Law No. 175 of March 31, 1955; Law No. 898 of July 31, 1956; Law No. 1144 of December 3, 1957.

A special commission makes recommendations for dramatic and musical events held abroad, provided they merit subsidies from this fund. Among the projects that have benefited from such aid are the Italian opera seasons in North Africa (Cairo, Tunis, etc.), as well as in Europe (Toulouse, Madrid, Barcelona, Lisbon, London, Oslo etc.). Concert tours of Italian soloists and musical ensembles also are subsidized by this fund.

Activities Promoting Theater and Music in a General Way (Not Included in Other Categories)

This category concerns dramatic and musical performances, special and varied, particularly the development of young talent for the theater (such as the concert competitions in Naples, Bolzano, Vercelli and the special competitions for singers at Spoleto and Milan). Financial aid to composers of new operas is also included in this category.

The fund for this special project is obtained from the 6.17 per cent taxation yield derived from net subscription fees on radio broadcasts.* Here, too, the suggestions of a special commission decide the distribution of moneys.

TABLE I

The Enti Autonomi in a Typical Year[12]

Number of Performances

The work plans of the various opera and concert organizations that enjoy the status of autonomous agencies obviously fluctuate according to changing circumstances.

	Opera	*Concert*	*Total*
Milan	140	36	176
Rome (opera)	140	—	140
Florence (fall season and May festival)	40	30	70
Naples	95	16	111
Palermo	35	15	50
Venice	30	15	45
Bologna	30	15	45
Genoa	30	15	45
Turin	33	—	33
Verona	12	—	12
Rome (Santa Cecilia)	—	95	95
Cagliari	14	16	30
Total**	599	253	852

*The procedure is guided by the regulations of royal decree No. 1547 of June 16, 1938.
**The theater in Trieste was promoted to the status of Ente Autonomo at a later time.

TABLE II

Governmental Subvention

The following table shows the governmental subvention (in milliards of lire) and the specific percentage of the total governmental allocation to all *enti autonomi.*

	Performances	*Subvention*	*Per cent*
Milan	176	470	25.30
Rome (opera)	140	420	22.60
Florence	70	195	10.49
Naples	111	270	14.53
Palermo	50	65	3.50
Venice	45	55	2.96
Bologna	45	55	2.96
Genoa	45	55	2.96
Turin	33	55	2.96
Verona	12	36	1.95
Rome (Santa Cecilia)	95	150	8.07
Cagliari	30	32	1.72
		1,858	

$1 = 625 lire

V. Land of Opera

Social Forces

Fair Italy — her cities and her countryside, the whole of Italy — is a kind of opera. Many of the squares and streets look like perfect stage sets. Illusion and reality are one. Here one would not have to bring colorfully painted decor, cardboard columns, and movable wings to create theatrical scenery for performances out-of-doors. The landscape, seaside, churches, palaces, and fountains seem like perfect background for opera and drama. The temperament of the Italian, the *brio* of their dialogue, the dramatic discussions, suggest something of the tempo and dynamics of the musical theater.

The vast majority of Italians — poor and rich — are opera maniacs. If this were not so, the impoverished, notoriously frugal segment of the population could not, by any degree of imagination, be persuaded to vote for laws of art support through taxation. There would simply be no motivation for parliamentary action. But the average Italian loves opera and knows opera. A development of three-and-one-half centuries is at the root of his affection.

The cultural function of the performing arts in Italy has always been closely allied to the capacity of opera to attract large audiences. Soon after its inception, during the Florentine Renaissance, opera proved its strength as a social force of first order. Operatic music, like church music, has become a collective experience for the community. The ecclesiastical service unites the liturgical performers and the praying congregation in a spiritually unified group. Opera, in secular terms, forms a close bond between its interpreters and the audience. Eventually, opera emerged in Italy as the most important secular medium of the performing arts.

Competitive Demands

Public criticism of governmental patronage of opera pertains, before all, to the system of distributing funds. And so, with a passion commensurate to that evoked on the opera stage itself, like Manrico and Count di Luna in Verdi's *Trovatore* fighting for the love of Leonora, Italy's opera devotees struggle for their proper share of attention and support from their government.

Chief rivals for governmental patronage are the cities in which opera houses have long been established. As Table II, above, indicates, the lion's share of subsidies is allocated to Milan's La Scala, one of the three most highly endowed musical theaters in the world; the other two are the nationally supported principal operas in Paris and Vienna. But in Italy the inherent problems of allocation are not identical with those of France or Austria. For Italy has developed a considerable number of historically significant operatic centers. Florence and Venice, Naples and Rome, Mantua and Parma — these and other cities claim lasting acknowledgement of their role in the evolution of Italian opera. But some of these time-honored operatic centers are in towns that today have lost their former significance — both in terms of their economic strength and cultural impetus. Regardless of these handicaps, all of Italy's resident opera companies claim larger portions of governmental help.

There is the unbroken tradition and world prestige of La Scala; it commands large support for the high quality productions that, unchallenged, uphold the fame of La Scala as the nation's first opera. The Teatro dell'Opera in Rome, as the resident lyrical company of Italy's capital, is entitled to generous state support; it represents officially the nation itself (the opera performs on important official occasions). There is La Fenice, the beautiful opera house of Venice for which Verdi wrote two of his greatest masterpieces. But Venice is smaller than Milan or Rome, and La Fenice, a smaller theater, receives considerably less support. Venetians think this treatment unfair. And so over Italy dissatisfaction with the manner of distribution and amount of subsidy is widespread.

Dr. Antonio Ghiringhelli, superintendent of La Scala, has taken issue with the entire procedure of governmental patronage. Analyzing the problem in its various ramifications in his widely discussed study, *Appunti Sul Teatro Lirico*, he claims that governmental subsidies belong exclusively to opera theaters that bring fame and artistic distinction to the nation. He takes a dim view of theaters in smaller cities which are, for whatever reasons, no longer producing on a high artistic level. Subvention must be earned on the basis of present performance, he argues, and not on a past prestige or hopes for the future. Hence, he claims maximum support for La Scala.

This rationale is attacked by the proponents of an increasingly decentralized distribution of governmental patronage. They contend that Italy's traditional opera life can continue to blossom only by means of a complete nation-wide diffusion of funds; that curtailment of governmental subsidies to underprivileged theaters would create serious deprivations; and that, especially in poor regions or during times of economic stress, fulfillment of the people's cultural dependency upon their theaters can come only through direct government support. In brief, these are the dominant arguments opposed to those which urge the concentration of governmental funds in a few highly-esteemed opera houses.

The problem is a very complex one, and the republican government carries the heavy burden not only of raising the funds, but of shouldering the responsibility of their fair distribution.

* * * * *

The following review of some of Italy's most important operatic centers intends to convey a sense of their artistic heritage. It describes present operation of these theaters and the nature of their support.

Florence
Cradle of Opera

Opera was born in Florence around 1600.* This great musical innovation that proved of paramount consequence to art was, curiously enough, not an invention of musicians. Opera originated as a product of aesthetic speculation in an intellectual circle called *camerata*, which included philosophers, poets, painters, and composers who met in the Florentine palace of a generous patron, Count Bardi, for searching and provocative discussions on the state of the arts. Imbued with the spirit of the Renaissance, the comrades hoped to restore ancient tragedy in a new art form. Their conscious return to antiquity proved decisive for the future.

The Greek mode of interpretation, the performance of the poet's verses to the accompaniment of stringed instruments, guided the approach

*The score of what scholars consider the first opera, *Euridice* by Jacopo Peri (1597) is unfortunately lost.

of the Renaissance team of artists. Opera means penetration of drama with music. To make it possible to set a drama to music, one had to sacrifice certain elements of each component. Music had to abandon its absolute tonal sovereignty. And the poetry lost, when sung, some of its direct communication. But the invention of monody (the prevalence of one single voice unobtrusively accompanied) made it possible to blend, in the new art form, word and tone. And thus originated a new medium of lasting significance: *dramma per musica*, as opera was revealingly called.

Ancient myth, now told as drama with music, strongly affected the spectators. Within less than half a century opera spread from Florence to other Italian cities, which before long outshone Florence in creative contribution and beauty of production. Mantua and Venice were the principal places of the lifework of Claudio Monteverdi (1567-1643), the first great master of opera. The expressive power of his music overwhelmed the listeners. We learn that the audience broke out in tears when it heard the *Lamento* from Monteverdi's opera *Arianna*. This is the first instance on record of such emotional audience reaction to a work of the musical theater.

Meanwhile, the city of Florence competed, even after the end of the Medici reign, for a leading role in the performing arts. The year 1738, marking the ascendancy of Austria in Tuscany, brought another dynasty of discerning art patrons to northern Italy. In 1767, Peter Leopold,[13] Grand Duke of Tuscany, invited Christoph Willibald Gluck to come to Florence. Peter Leopold, son of Maria Theresia, had known the great master of opera in Vienna, and now asked him to produce his *Il prologo* in Florence. When Gluck's opera *Alceste* was published in the same year, the score contained an eloquent dedication to the Grand Duke. This preface became known as one of the most crucial records of music drama reforms. Gluck explained his intent:

> I was determined to abolish all those faults that had stolen into Italian opera through the unwarranted pride of singers and the foolish acquiescence of composers, that had made it tiresome and ludicrous, instead of the greatest and most impressive spectacle of modern times. I sought to restore music to its proper place — that of enhancing poetry by bringing out the sentiment and appeal of the situations, without interfering with the action, or impeding it with superfluous ornament.

Musical May

With all priority and subsequent achievement, Florence did not retain its role as a stronghold of the performing arts during the nineteenth and early twentieth centuries. But Florence has been staging a comeback.

A contributing factor, which has attracted international attention for the past few decades, is the May Festival of Florence: known as the *Maggio Musicale*, it has developed into an annual spring event lasting well into the summer.* It represents the confluence of various civic enterprises into one major effort. The steps preceding the festival are easily traced. A century ago, in May 1862, the Florentines opened a new opera house. They chose the month of May as the most appropriate time. Before long, the Teatro Politeama Fiorentino, as the opera was then called, had developed regular seasons.

In 1932 the government granted the privately managed opera company the status of an *ente autonomo*. The municipality of Florence decided to assume the support of the theater, and thus all remnants of private enterprise came to an end. Appropriately, the opera changed its name from Teatro Politeama to Teatro Communale, thus indicating the city as its principal patron. Repertory and productions proceeded along conventional lines. A new orientation resulted from the opera's association with the Maggio Musicale. This joint project became possible from the moment Florence possessed, in addition to its theater, a well-functioning opera company and a good orchestra. Now Florence could embark upon ambitious musical ventures.

The original plans called for a festival to be held every third year. After the first two years the success of the Maggio Musicale warranted extension of its activities; the festival became a biennial and by 1936, an annual. The initial programs were routine by Italian standards (concentrating on works by Verdi, Bellini, Donizetti, Rossini). There were fifteen operas and six dramatic performances, twenty-one symphony concerts, eighteen chamber music concerts. Thus the emphasis remained on music.

On May 24, 1961, the Florentines were ready to reopen their Teatro Communale, rebuilt and modernized. The theater now seats 2,100 in a hall well-suited for the performance of operas and concerts. Attending the auspicious première, the President of the Republic expressed the nation's hope that Florence may inaugurate a new era of opera at its very cradle.

The numerous events of the Maggio Musicale are now distributed at various sites on both banks of the Arno River. The festival program for 1961 included a new contemporary Italian opera: *The Merchant of Venice* by Mario Castelnuovo Tedesco (based on Shakespeare's play). A fair balance between old and new works must be the goal, if the renaissance of opera at its birthplace is to succeed.

*In 1961 the schedule of the Maggio Musicale was extended from May 4 to June 30.

Florence relies on diversified patronage for the support of its enterprises in the performing arts. The municipality is economically in a less advantageous situation than other Italian communities of comparable size and long-established cultural stature. There is no industry in Florence — only crafts, traditionally fine, which obviously have no mass market. The municipal income has fallen behind that of other large cities in the north such as Milan or Turin. In Florence private contributions for art support are solicited (in addition to the official subsidies from state and province). Several banks, the Florentine Chamber of Commerce, and a few syndicates are among the donors.

Florence maintains one of Italy's best orchestras, which enjoys, along with the Teatro Communale, the status of an *ente autonomo*. The regular activities of the orchestra include concerts in Florence as well as in other Italian cities. The Florentine ensemble is also the principal orchestra of the Sagre Musicale in Perugia (a festival of religious music held annually in this Umbrian town). During fall and early winter the orchestra plays in the regular Florentine opera season, in the pit of the Teatro Communale. A number of regular symphony concerts is always given. April is reserved for preparing the Maggio Musicale, which in turn keeps the orchestra busy until July. The month of August is vacation time, guaranteed with full salary to all orchestra members.[14]

Milan
La Scala, National Shrine

The air bombardment of August 16, 1943, destroyed La Scala, the great lyric theater which had stood for one hundred sixty-five years on its famous site in Milan, witnessing and weathering all preceding upheavals and warfare. But, during World War II, La Scala's tragic hour struck, annihilating the beautiful interior of the theater, although its old façade and terrace miraculously remained intact.

The first thing the Milanese decided to rebuild after the war was their opera house. No sooner were the Germans driven out than the mayor of Milan started plans for La Scala's reconstruction. In addition to American help from the Marshall Plan, private aid was forthcoming. One of the principal donors was appointed "extraordinary commissioner" of La Scala. The rapid reconstruction had a healthy influence on the people of Milan, who were disunited by war and internal discord.

In the intervening years Milan has regained its economic position as an oasis of affluence in Italy. Once again Lombardy's capital is productive and prosperous. The vitality of the metropolis in the fertile valley of the Po displays Italian *brio* at its best. One breathes here an air that is intellectual, artistically charged. Such a city is unthinkable without an important theatrical life. Milan has it, both in the lyrical and dramatic fields.

The steady growth of Milan into one of the world's principal operatic centers is unique. Other Italian cities, notably Naples, Rome, Florence, and Venice, nourished major schools of operatic composition on their soil. Not so Milan, which for many centuries was a stronghold of ecclesiastical music. As early as the fourth century St. Ambrose introduced the singing of hymns and psalms to Lombardy. The Church of Milan founded its Schola Cantorum, one of the first in the West to instill Christian music into the lives of the people. Due to such dogmatically liturgical orientation, Milan was slower than other northern cities to adopt the secular opera. And the Lombardian composers gifted in the secular field turned, for lack of patronage, to the purely instrumental medium. In spite of its retarded entrance, opera eventually became the favorite form of the theater for the Milanese. Their enthusiasm has never slackened, and finally in the perfection of lyrical performance La Scala achieved world fame. Milan became, from the nineteenth century on, the market place of music in Italy and the main seat of music publishing. In operatic prominence Milan surpassed Rome, even after the Eternal City had become the national capital, in 1871. The development is worthy of note. It proves that indigenous creativity is not the only condition for a city's growth to supremacy in the performing arts.

Empress Maria Theresia Founds La Scala

The rise of La Scala to its present height is associated with Habsburg patronage of opera. The founding patron of La Scala was the Austrian Empress Maria Theresia. One of her many titles included that of the Duchess of Milan, for the province of Lombardy was temporarily under Austrian rule. Having sponsored Vienna's extraordinary theatrical life, the art-loving Habsburg dynasty did not wish to limit its patronage to the residence in Vienna.

In July, 1776, the Empress commissioned the architect Giuseppe Piermarini to design an opera house for Milan which should be the largest and most modern of its kind in existence. When the new theater opened on August 3, 1778, the Milanese and many distinguished guests from other parts of Europe were delighted with the splendid opera that had risen on the site of the demolished church, Santa Maria della Scala. Part of this ecclesiastical name was retained for the new opera theater.

The opera *L'Europa reconosciuta* by Antonio Salieri was chosen for the opening. Salieri was court conductor in Vienna. The choice of his work stressed the union between the two opera houses; La Scala and the Vienna Court Opera remained temporarily under the same artistic administration. Archduke Ferdinand (son of Maria Theresia) and his wife, Maria Beatrice d'Este, were announced in the program as the princely patrons of the festive occasion. The Austrian Empress had instilled in her many children a deep respect for music and the theater. The results of this artistic education are, in fact, readily traced in the various courts of Europe to which marriage and political fate brought the sons and daughters of Maria Theresia as sovereigns.

This sidelight on the political history of Europe supports our understanding of historic patterns of patronage. Italy had long been divided into spheres of influence between the dynasties of the Austrian House of Habsburg and the Spanish Bourbons. In 1784, the treaty of Aix-la-Chapelle settled the War of Austrian Succession, and once more re-divided Italy. The Austrians retained the prize duchies of Milan and Tuscany. Yet Parma (along with a number of other towns) became a separate duchy under Prince Philip, son of Philip V of Spain. By marrying her daughter Maria Amalia to the young ruler of Parma, and another daughter, Maria Carolina, to Ferdinand of Naples, the Austrian Empress spread the Habsburg influence throughout Italy. In Florence, Maria Theresia's son Peter Leopold ruled as Grand Duke of Tuscany. But it was for the good of art. The presence of these Austrian princes and princesses, who had grown up in an intensely musical environment, always resulted in a rich art life. The courts in Milan and Florence, in Parma and Naples, excelled in the patronage of opera.

From its beginning under Austrian sponsorship to its present status as a national shrine La Scala underwent various fates. Yet the theater always remained a focal point of representation in Italy's history. Thus it was at La Scala where, in 1859, the liberation of Italy was celebrated with a solemn ceremony. Italy's King Vittorio Emanuele II and Emperor Napoleon II of France jointly appeared in the royal box on this gala evening when opera symbolized the dramatic turn of Italy's destiny. La Scala also celebrated the country's liberation in our time. When Arturo Toscanini returned on May 11, 1946, to the rebuilt opera house to conduct a concert of Italian masters, the world knew that the spirit of Italy was free once more.

Administration of La Scala

La Scala is a municipal theater. The mayor of Milan is the president of its board of directors. The general manager, called superintendent, is appointed by the board. The administration of the opera is typical of Italy's municipal art institutes that receive substantial governmental subsidies and enjoy the status of *enti autonomi*. The board of trustees represents a community-wide team. The directors are chosen from all organizations linked with the operation of the lyrical theater. The small executive committee of the *ente autonomo* of La Scala consists, in addition to the presiding mayor of Milan, of the superintendent of the opera and the general secretary.

The Board of La Scala

Members	*Representing*
6	the community at large
2	the syndicate of musicians
2	the Italian Association of Spectacles
2	the Federation of Spectacles
2	the provincial administration
2	the Chamber of Commerce
3	the Association of Friends of La Scala
2	the theater museum of La Scala
1	*Cassa di Risparmio* (Savings Bank) of Milan and Lombardy
6	controllers of accounts

Opera for Everybody

The basic policy of La Scala aims today at broadening the scope and size of its public. The performances of both opera and concerts in the theater are planned to raise the taste and standards of the people.

The following methods aim at increasing the participation of the public at large (particularly in segments of the population of Milan and the province of Lombardy that hitherto showed no or little interest in the lyrical theater)

1. Tickets for workers and students at the lowest possible prices; tickets are regularly distributed through the respective industrial and educational organizations. A minimum of forty performances per season are the so-called *serate per i lavoratori* (evenings for workers) at top prices of approximately one dollar.
2. Repetitions of all concerts on the basis of a popular subscription scheme (reserved for workers and students).
3. Collective subscriptions for syndicates and trade groups; here the tickets are likewise greatly reduced and available for all performances (exclusive of premières).
4. The maintenance of a general moderate price policy for seats in the galleries; the good seats cost 5,000 lire (eight dollars) for first and second performances.[15] Three dollars is an average ticket price for repeat performances.
5. Performances entirely reserved for syndicated organizations, student organizations, and various other cultural and scholarly groups.

Whatever the audience and whatever the ticket price, the same conductors and prominent singers appear for all occasions. All these procedures have been extremely successful. La Scala has become well integrated with the community.

Venice
First Public Opera Theater

On February 23, 1637, the Teatro San Cassiano in Venice opened its doors to the people. The event is a double landmark, in the general history of the theater and in the history of patronage.

First, anyone paying an admission fee was entitled to attend public opera performances. Second, a concession for the Teatro San Cassiano was granted to a few private entrepreneurs by the city. The opening production of *Andromeda* by Francesco Manelli (1595-1667) is the earliest manifestation of an opera performance backed by private capital. The composer, the librettist, and a group of their affluent friends produced this music drama at their own expense. At San Cassiano, then, occurred an important departure from preceding sponsorship. Hitherto opera was court opera; it was part of the festivities at royal or aristocratic residences. Now opera was on the way to becoming people's opera, for this new pattern of playing and supporting musical theater was eminently successful. No less than eight opera theaters came into existence in Venice prior to the nineteenth century. They performed close to four hundred works, mostly by Italian masters. But only one of these theaters was destined to gain lasting distinction. This was the Teatro La Fenice, to this day the theatrical pride of the Lagoon City.

La Fenice

The visitor to Venice who approaches this jewel case of a theater may reach his destination in a manner no other opera house in the world affords. He can arrive at the theater by gondola, gliding through the dark canals, and know the romance of nocturnal Venice before entering the glittering foyer. Or he may walk to the theater through the narrow streets over stepped bridges and finally arrive at the entrance of the theater with its brightly lit façade shining invitingly in the surrounding darkness. Whatever way he takes, the enchantment of Venice is a prelude to the musical offering in La Fenice. The Gothic and the Renaissance styles of the old houses and palaces on the way to the theater are fast forgotten inside of La Fenice. Here the elegant and playful world of the Italian Rococo prevails, with its graciously curving patterns and persuasive joyfulness. This cumulative experience of impressions — of the city, the approach, the façade, the foyer, and finally the hall itself — is probably the reason so many visitors agree that La Fenice is the most beautifully atmospheric opera house in the world.

La Fenice has been rebuilt several times since its opening in 1792. The theater reflects in architecture and decor the changes it has undergone. The historic significance of La Fenice is revealed also by a visit to the administrative office, which is really an unofficial museum, containing letters, memos, and pictures which are documents of operatic history. Verdi is the patron saint of La Fenice. The master composed for this theater two of his great works: *Rigoletto* (1851) and *La Traviata* (1853). But many other events preceding and following the era of Verdi integrate La Fenice forever into the chronicle of opera. To know this history is to understand the fierce pride the Venetians take in their opera house, and to appreciate their claim to higher allocations of governmental subsidies. Venetians feel that the noble traditions of their theater entitle it to a larger share of support from the government in Rome.

With all its romantic aura and singular background, La Fenice is by comparison with other leading Italian opera houses at a marked disadvantage. Venice is a much smaller city than metropolitan Rome, Milan, or Naples. There is little space for the development of industry because of the topographical limitations — the unique location of the city on the Adriatic lagoons and its diffusion of small suburbs over the islands. The population of Venice, generally, is not as affluent as that of the large competing operatic cities.

In 1959 the governmental allocation to La Fenice was 112,000,000 lire ($179,200). The same amount had been given in 1958. This represents a slight decrease from its high in 1954, when the subsidy was 172,000,000 lire ($275,200). The municipality of Venice (and a number of local groups) added 70,000,000 lire ($112,000) to the governmental grant. The annual minimum expenditure for La Fenice is 250,000,000 lire ($400,000). The deficit for the year 1957 was about 120,000,000 lire ($192,000). It was 100,000,000 lire ($160,000) in 1956 and 130,000,000 lire ($208,000) in 1958. The subsidy to La Fenice is considerably smaller than that accorded to the opera in Milan or Rome.

Like Florence, Venice maintains a permanent year-round orchestra. The instrumental ensemble serves in the pit of La Fenice; it also gives a series of symphony concerts. Expenses of the orchestra amount to 140,000,000 lire annually. But its engagements by other organizations add 30,000,000 lire to the general fund of La Fenice. The theater employs a chorus, which is engaged for the six months of the year in which operas are given. The cost of the chorus is 35,000,000 to 40,000,000 lire.

The direct income of La Fenice, derived from ticket sales, amounts to 1,750,000 lire for each performance of opera, and to 800,000 lire for each concert. The opera performances are nearly always sold by subscription. A mailing system of the *abbonamento* (the subscription) has proved successful for many years. Nearby provincial cities consider La Fenice their own theater. They buy their tickets by mail and always are assured of good seats during the entire season. The average price for a ticket on the first floor (pit) is $5.00, $1.50 for the large gallery, and 90 cents for the upper gallery.

The winter season of opera usually starts December 26 and lasts until the beginning of March. It is followed by a spring season of concerts, a popular opera season, and a season of ballet and drama. During the warm months the orchestra performances are in the stately courtyard of the Ducal Palace. The expenses for the administration and the overhead of La Fenice are kept on a modest level, usually about 20,000,000 lire annually. The administrative personnel totals only twelve members, including the director, the general secretary, and the press officer. The building of La Fenice is owned by the city of Venice, which acquired it in 1935 from the "Society of Box Owners." The municipality renovated the hall and the social rooms and it brought the stage installations up to modern standards.

Venice Biennale

The greatest asset of Venice on the contemporary art scene is the city's Biennale, dedicated to theater, music, the "figurative arts" (painting and sculpture), and the cinema. The Venetian exhibition of painting and sculpture, the Pittsburgh International, and the exhibition in São Paulo, Brazil are the three most important in the world today.

The festival of drama and music now takes place every year, but the exhibition of visual arts only every second year; hence the original name — Biennale — is still retained. For many years, the Biennale took place in September. In 1961 it was decided to move the festival up to April to avoid conflicts with other European art events in late summer and early fall.

The Biennale is committed to performances and exhibitions of works of true value — regardless of tendencies or schools. Yet the program in Venice is not to be a mere duplication of the activities at other festivals in Italy or abroad. Rather it is to be a touchstone of progress, a comparison of prevailing trends in both the Occident and Orient. Finally, the Biennale is to provide an evaluation of the most significant artistic efforts in Italy. The Biennale has the status of an *ente autonomo*. It is administered independently by a commission which is also responsible for the artistic part of the program and which has its seat in Rome, consistent with the centralistic organization of national Italian art life. The first president of the Biennale was the mayor of Venice, a college professor. Each of the four categories (music, theater, figurative arts, and cinema) is administered by an acknowledged expert who is in charge of the program. These four directors must be approved by the national Minister of Education.

The details of the programs are worked out in agreement with the participating nations. In 1959 the exhibition of the figurative arts represented thirty-five different countries. In all categories the invited nations themselves decide what art work to perform or to exhibit; the participants pay their own expenses. The Biennale merely offers for performance the exhibition halls and all utilities connected with the operation. To date, twenty-four countries have built their own pavilions. Italy has contributed a large pavilion for participants that have none of their own (such as Australia).

Subsidies for the Biennale

Republican Government	70 per cent (of the basic subvention)
Municipality of Venice	25 per cent
Province of Veneto	5 per cent

There are additional contributions from the tourist office of Venice, as well as from the provincial tourist office. Each of the four categories of the Biennale operates on a fixed budget which cannot be transferred from one category to another.

San Carlo
Background of Neapolitan Opera

Giuseppi Verdi was the first great artist of Italy to plead for national support of the principal opera houses of his country. He also proposed teamwork between the theaters and the resident conservatories of three key musical cities.

On March 15, 1876, the composer wrote to his friend Opprandino Arrivabene:

> [We are] completely agreed as to the orchestra and the permanent chorus, paid by the government and cities for the Italian theaters. Since 1861, I have suggested to Cavour* that the three leading Italian theaters (those of the capital, Milan, and Naples) should have choruses and orchestras maintained by the government. Free evening singing courses for all in return for a promise to put themselves at the disposal of the theater in these cities.
>
> Three conservatories in the above-named cities, with reciprocal obligations between theaters and conservatory. The program would have been feasible if Cavour had lived; with other ministers it is impossible. . . .[16]

Today Verdi's ideas have been realized to a degree that the master of opera could not have foreseen in the dawn of the *Risorgimento*, of Italy's national resurgence and subsequent unification as a kingdom. Not only have the operas of Milan, Rome, and Naples been nationalized,

*Camillo di Cavour, first prime minister of the United Kingdom of Italy.

but a number of less distinguished theaters throughout the country have come under governmental patronage. And the scope of subsidy, far exceeding Verdi's plan, today guarantees the total operation of these theaters.

After Milan's La Scala and Rome's Teatro dell'Opera, the historic opera house of Naples, Teatro di San Carlo, now ranks third for state subsidy. The Naples opera also enjoys the envied status of *ente autonomo*. The legendary capital of Italy's south — itself the scene of celebrated operas — has had great significance as a center of music drama since the seventeenth century. Governmental evaluation of San Carlo is based not only on present achievement of the opera theater, but on its distinguished historical record.

In 1648 Duke d'Onate, Viceroy of Spain, came to Naples to take charge of governmental affairs. The Duke was a patron of the new form of the musical theater. He had maintained his own opera company in Rome while he was Spanish Ambassador to the Vatican. Once in Naples, he lost no time renovating the Teatro di San Bartolomeo, the city's principal playhouse. By 1654 the Duke offered Neapolitans serious opera which had come, somewhat belatedly, to Italy's south. But opera could not have fallen on more fertile soil than the Mediterranean metropolis on the slope of Mt. Vesuvius. Before long Naples developed a regional school of opera composers who left their imprint on the art scene.[17]

The lasting gift of Naples to the musical theater was the comic opera. The first truly significant composer of this genre was Giovanni Battista Pergolesi (1710-1736). Having studied at the Conservatorio dei Poveri in Naples, Pergolesi, in his twenty-third year, completed his masterpiece, *La Serva Padrona*, a merry intermezzo which was inserted into the three act festival opera *Il Prigionier Superbo*. Neapolitans had been seeing their comedies with music in small theaters, but now they were to have a large opera house devoted to music drama. Today, the famous opera bears the name of its founder and enthusiastic patron, Charles III of Bourbon, King of Naples. The theater was inaugurated on St. Charles's Day, November 4, 1737. The royal sponsor exerted strict, almost puritanical supervision over the performances. The audience was not permitted to applaud or to ask for encores; only the sovereign enjoyed this privilege!

At this time the Teatro di San Carlo was supported by a subsidy of 3,200 ducats annually. In return, the opera's first impresario, the public notary Diego Tufarelli, was committed to produce each season a minimum of 70 performances with artists of established quality.

During the following decades support of the opera increased in Naples. The theater was completely remodeled and redecorated for the royal wedding of Ferdinand IV and the Archduchess Maria Carolina of Austria.[18] The traditional Habsburg patronage of opera further intensified the enthusiasm for music drama in the southern capital.

But the quality of patronage is not static. We learn that the standards of San Carlo as an art center were gradually threatened by a deterioration of the repertory and the deplorable conduct of the audience. Many Neapolitans discovered in the opera a convenient place for social entertainment. Fashionably dressed ladies and gentlemen in the boxes and stalls saw no particular reason why their animated conversation and flirtation should cease while the performance on the stage was in progress.

When Niccolò Jommelli, master of serious opera, returned to his hometown Naples in 1770 from his productive tenure as court composer in Stuttgart, he commented on the disillusioning state of the opera: ". . . in the theater a noisily chattering audience which tends to prefer a sort of morbid and pathetic music, an elaborately adorned virtuosity in which the notes and words of the singer are drowned. There is no convincing logical sequence in the action, no interest for the *recitatives* on which the development of the *aria* depends."

The time had arrived when sweeping reforms were to rescue the music drama from its creeping decadence. And the epochal reforms of Gluck were directly prompted by the contemporary state of Italian opera. The nineteenth century further improved the standards at San Carlo. Significant new works by Italian masters, notably Bellini, Donizetti, Rossini, and Verdi, fortified the opera from within.

The far-reaching upheavals in the political fate of Naples repeatedly interrupted the sources of the theater's support without, however, cancelling its continuity. While city and country changed governments, artistic activities went on at San Carlo. Eventually the municipality of Naples assumed the major share of subsidy. In 1927 the most crucial step in the support of San Carlo occurred when the theater was granted the status of *ente autonomo*. The blast of a bomb severely damaged the opera house in 1943. In 1944 the British military authorities requisitioned the theater. Soon after the armistice San Carlo resumed its contributions to the community. In 1947 the *ente autonomo* was resumed.

Presently, the lyric season of San Carlo lasts from December to May. It is followed by a series of symphonic and choral concerts in spring and in autumn, which are likewise supported within the framework of the *ente autonomo*. During the summer, performances take place out-of-doors, also at Pompeii, and occasionally on the island of Capri.

Home of Conservatories

Neapolitan opera was historically allied to its famous old conservatories. These schools, the first educational organizations of their kind, served in name and purpose as models for other conservatories over the world. In Naples they were founded by private patrons. Homeless orphans (of which Naples always had too many) were collected from the streets and slums, given food and shelter, and "conserved" in these institutions, where they were kept safe and sound. But the minds of these waifs had also to be nurtured, and music was foremost in the conservatory curriculum. The children sang, before all, for the liturgical service; but the more mature students were called upon to perform in the monastic mystery plays, and eventually they appeared in theatrical performances. In retrospect, we judge the significance of these Neapolitan conservatories by the catalogue of their students, faculties, and directors. Their list amounts to a roll call of important Italian composers of several eras.

There are four of these schools, all founded in the sixteenth century:

1. Conservatorio di Santa Maria di Loreto (1535). Durante, Provenzale, Scarlatti served here as *maestri*. Cimarosa was one of the students.

2. Conservatorio di Sant'Onofrio a Capuana (1576). Graduates of this school were Piccini and Jommelli.

3. Conservatorio della Pietà de'Turchini (1583). Paisiello and Fenaroli were the first directors.

4. Conservatorio de'Poveri di Gesù Cristo (1589). Paisiello and Pergolesi were among its students.

From the mutual relationship of these conservatories with the churches, theaters, and concert organizations, Naples grew into the musical center of Europe's south. And San Carlo proved to be, in almost every generation from the seventeenth century on, a springboard of indigenous creative talent.

Rome
Teatro dell'Opera

The Eternal City has not yet completed its first century as the capital of United Italy. In 1871 the ministries and parliament of the new kingdom were transferred to Rome. At this time, Italy's new secular capital still lacked an opera theater that could compare, in stateliness of appearance and artistic achievement, with La Scala of Milan, La Fenice of Venice, or San Carlo of Naples.

This does not imply that Roman opera life lagged behind that of other Italian cities, for Rome looks back to a significant and colorful operatic history. As earlier in Florence, the palaces of cultured aristocracy were the scenes of notable opera productions. Eventually private theaters were opened to the general public, such as the Teatro Capranica. But there was strong clerical opposition to opera and particularly to its ballets. They were rejected by the Vatican.

During the eighteenth century at least two theaters (Teatro delle Dame and Teatro Argentina) were regularly devoted to the performances of *opera seria*, but neither attained lasting national importance. When Rome finally rose to the new status of royal residence and national capital, the city found itself without a representative center for the performing arts. No official funds were found to remedy the situation.

The initiative and generosity of a single private donor gave to his city the much-needed opera house. This man was Domenico Costanzi. A life of ambition and shrewd speculation (particularly in building and real estate) had brought him wealth, and Costanzi decided to leave his city a lasting gift of cultural value — an opera house. On November 20, 1887, the opera *Semiramide* by Rossini inaugurated the new large theater, entirely paid for by Costanzi and named in his honor. The King and Queen were in the audience, and so witnessed how the cultural will of one Roman citizen had put official indifference and procrastination to shame.

In 1928, under the Fascist regime, the Teatro Costanzi abandoned the name of its sponsor. The municipality of Rome was assigned complete renovation of the building, which was to assume the title of Teatro Reale dell'Opera. Vittorio Emanuele III, in spite of Mussolini's usurpation of power, was still the figurehead of the Kingdom. The Regal Opera was reopened on February 27, 1928, with a performance of Arrigo Boito's *Nerone* (recalling the glory and decadence of ancient Rome). From this time on, opportunities of state representation through gala performances in the opera were frequent.

Today the Roman State Opera is under the management of a superintendent who receives his appointment from the General Direction of Spectacles. The artistic director decides all musical issues. Attached to the administration of the opera is the permanent Commissione di Lettura, constituted in July of 1951. The purpose of this authoritative body of readers is to advise the management on the acceptance of new works. The commission is not concerned with opera already included in the repertory of the theater. Here all decisions rest exclusively with the management.

The technical apparatus of the opera is large. The orchestra consists of 118 musicians (including the stage band); the chorus has 100 members (42 sopranos and altos; 58 tenors and basses). The ballet consists of 70 members (including apprentices). In 1928 a ballet school was created which has about 100 pupils. The opera gives approximately 110 performances per season in Rome and frequently goes on tours. In 1937 a summer season of opera was introduced at the Terme di Caracalla. These outdoor productions found great popular favor with Romans, and particularly with tourists. Here one can see Verdi's *Aïda*, performed with real camels and other exotic attractions in the victory processional of the second finale.

The repertory of the Roman State Opera has come under frequent criticism. The choice of works reflects primarily the tried and tested. Progressive voices argue that the resident opera company of a world capital should display a more advanced attitude, and could well afford a fair share of experimentation in view of the large government subvention. The recent appointment of a progressive artistic director, Massimo Bogianckino, promises a new and provocative repertory, beginning with the season 1963-64.

Accademia Nazionale di Santa Cecilia

In addition to the Teatro dell'Opera, another musical institute in Rome has been accorded the status of *ente autonomo:* the Accademia Nazionale di Santa Cecilia, one of the oldest permanent organizations devoted to the performance of music. The Academy traces its foundation to the year 1566. Originally suggested by Palestrina, it was canonically constituted by Pope Gregory XIII in 1584, and assumed then the lengthy name Congregazione dei Musici sotto l'invocazione della Beata Vergine e dei Santi Gregorio e Cecilia. Finally the name was shortened to Santa Cecilia; she is the patron saint of music and of the blind.

Papal patronage has maintained over the centuries other great musical institutions. The famous Cappella Sistina (founded by Pope Sixtus IV in 1471) and the Cappella Giulia (founded by Julius II in 1480) are both exclusively devoted to sacred performance. In contrast, the Accademia di Santa Cecilia did not eschew the performance of secular art, although it had originally attained its rights and privileges as a medium of liturgical music. But, over the subsequent generations the preoccupation with various forms of secular music brought great distinction to Santa Cecilia. A glance at the list of composers who conducted at the Academy bears witness to its continuous significance.[19]

On October 17, 1874, a royal decree brought about a decisive change in the patronage of the Academy. The once Papal organization was transformed into a royal institute, and King Vittorio Emanuele II ordered an adjustment of the title to Accademia Reale di Santa Cecilia. In 1876 the scope of Santa Cecilia was extended to that of an educational institution, again under the protectorate of the King. Known as the Liceo Musicale di Santa Cecilia, the school assumed lasting importance for Italy's art life. A library of vast historical dimensions was added.

Santa Cecilia did not remain the only regularly performing concert organization in Rome. During the nineteenth century the city had become the home of several other institutions, all dedicated to symphonic music.[20] With the steady rise of their audiences, the concerts given under the auspices of Santa Cecilia outgrew several halls. In 1908 the ancient equestrian circus at the Mausoleum of Augustus was remodeled and officially opened as a concert hall; it was demolished in 1936. From then until 1958, the orchestra of Santa Cecilia played in the Teatro Adriano and eventually in the Teatro Argentina. At the end of April, 1958, the concerts moved temporarily to the papal auditorium on the Via della Conciliazione, close to St. Peter's. A new hall with a capacity of 3,500 persons is being built; it will be known as Auditorio. The municipality of Rome and the Italian government (through the Ministry of Public Instruction) are co-sponsors of the project. The new hall will be on the Via Flamina and house also the administrative offices and the library of Santa Cecilia. During the summer regular concerts take place at the Basilica di Massenzio and at the Stadio di Domiziano.

A democratic organization supervises the business management of Santa Cecilia. Every year the general assembly meets to hold elections in conformity with its statutes. The executive committee consists of a president, two vice presidents, ten councilors, and three censors. The president is elected for three years; the councilors and censors, for two years, and they can succeed themselves in office.

VI. The Theater

On Ancient Soil

Like her opera, Italy's theater is distinguished by a resplendent past — a more distant past than that of Renaissance-born music drama. Monuments of a theatrical culture spanning several millennia are visible throughout the nation.

What is often referred to as the Golden Age of the Italian theater came relatively late: it followed the great period of the French theater by more than half a century. What Molière, Corneille, and Racine accomplished for France, such poets as Metastasio (1698-1782), Goldoni (1707-1793), and Alfieri (1749-1803) did for Italy; they shaped a national theatrical style out of indigenous dramatic traditions.

One of Italy's most lasting contributions to the world theater is the Commedia dell'arte; it is in essence a mode of performance where the comedians amuse their popular audiences with extemporaneous wit and every other conceivable kind of improvisation. The Commedia dell'arte of the sixteenth century, more than any form of Italy's theater, reveals its ancient heritage. Maccus, Bucco, and Pappus of ancient comedy are quite clearly the ancestors of the playful Arlecchino, friends of the whimsical Pulcinella in the Commedia dell'arte.

Folk Theater

In Italy there prevails a pronounced, historically established contrast between a theater for a sophisticated audience and a folk theater aiming at the enjoyment of the masses. This dualism persists today as it did during the Renaissance. An illustration of aristocratic fare in the sixteenth century is the pastoral drama (such as Torquato Tasso's *Aminta*, 1573), which for sophisticated spectators had little, if anything, in common with the Commedia dell'arte and its simple situations humorously depicting everyday life. For hundreds of years the Italian theater has most successfully functioned on these different levels. Appropriately, poets have employed different subject matter and different language to reach heterogeneous audiences.

Italy is a land of many dialects. Italian poetry and prose, growing from the ancient Latin mother tongue, have developed over the ages with considerable variety in the individual regions of the nation. In spite of the increasing unification of everyday speech through mass media and moving pictures, phonetic and grammatical differences of idiom strongly persist. The lack of a language common to all people causes obvious difficulties in the diffusion of the Italian theater. There are many differences of spoken Italian in the north and south. To be sure, such dissimilarities exist elsewhere, but they are more conspicuous in Italy. They affect the whole gamut of the spoken word and diction on the Italian stage and pose a particular problem for the establishment of a national theater in Italy.

The Florentine idiom is considered Italy's classical language. When spoken by cultivated people it has a refined flavor which has long been accepted as the ideal standard. Consequently, "Florentine Italian" has been promoted as the model speech of the serious Italian theater throughout the world.

By contrast the folk theater has its strongest hold in Naples. Here, in the capital of the south, an enthusiastic public fills to capacity the Teatro San Fernando of the Filippo brothers. The hilarious laughter of the popular audiences for Pulcinella and her delightful adventures is still an unfailing source of joy to the merry people of this Mediterranean port. The dialect remains untranslatable. Its idiomatic humor, born of the word-play itself, of earthy phrases and colloquial expressions, resists transplanting from the soil on which it has grown. But in spite of its limitations, the dialect theater of Naples will live on, at least in its own indigenous setting, where the people have been its faithful patrons for centuries.

Sophisticated Theater

The great literary accomplishments of nineteenth-century Italy, such as the lifework of Alessandro Manzoni, lie outside the realm of the stage. But Italian authors closer to our time have left their imprint on the international theater. Thus Pirandello's somewhat Freudian themes, and his novel techniques in such works as *Henry IV* or *Six Characters in Search of an Author*, have made inroads on the contemporary stage.

The present generation of Italian dramatists seeks little connection with the world of their predecessors. The topics of modern authors for better or worse are derived from the realities of the complex, often harsh life which has been imposed upon postwar Italy. The late Ugo Betti commented on this environment with sympathetic idealism tempered by melancholy resignation. Whatever the guideposts of other authors, the sum and substance of new Italian plays have not yet proved strong enough to lift the nation's theater from its languor.

But Italy has contributed to the world stage a specific style of dramatic performance: the type of virtuoso actor, gifted with a brilliant manner of immediate communication — in short an acting technique around which new schools developed at the beginning of our century. Eleanora Duse, Emma Gramatica, Ermete Zacconi are among those still remembered for their astonishing projection and incandescent individualism on Italy's stage or on tours abroad. In the final days of her life, Eleanora Duse observed, "The Italian theater will have to die, before it can be born again." Many of her compatriots accept this forecast by their unforgotten actress.

Today contemporary Italian theater is fighting for its existence. Some go so far as to claim that the serious prose theaters can survive only in Milan and Rome. The art-conscious and intellectual populations of these two metropolitan areas have proved ready to support a number of legitimate theaters, in addition to their flourishing opera houses.

Piccolo Teatro of Milan

After Mussolini's downfall progressive forces aimed at the reawakening of a free Italian stage. But these attempts had to contend with the postwar chaos. There were ambitious experiments; none of them attained lasting success.

It eventually fell to the Piccolo Teatro of Milan to give new direction to the Italian prose theater. The aim of this "Little Theater," as defined by its *spiritus rector*, Paolo Grassi, is to maintain the legitimate stage as a public utility, to offer drama with the needs of the various social strata of the urban population in mind.

The Piccolo Teatro is supported entirely by public funds. It has repeatedly proved its capacity to attract large and diversified audiences which fill the small house to capacity. The theater has 640 seats; the best seats cost approximately $3.00. The network of subscribers is constantly growing. The activities of the theater are effectively propagandized in the schools of Milan and Lombardy, in the syndicates, in the factories and offices, and in all organized professions.

The three principal sponsors supporting the remarkable efforts of the Little Theater are the national government (the Direction of Spectacles), the city of Milan, and the province of Lombardy. Their cooperation makes the Piccolo Teatro possible. It was essential to keep the scope of operation relatively small. For the lesson to be demonstrated here was — and still is — that other Italian communities could adopt tomorrow what Milan is doing so well today.

The management of the Piccolo Teatro enjoys freedom of action in terms of its artistic program. The theater has a staff of 175 persons. Eighty per cent of the actors are under contract for nine months. Efficiency and economy characterize all operations. The workshops for sets and costumes are used also by other companies; the theater has a stock of 3,000 costumes which it frequently rents out. A discriminating artistic policy reveals itself in the repertory. A check of 20 different productions lists 12 plays by Shakespeare. Otherwise there is a strong accent on Italian authors, both classical and modern — from Goldoni and Gozzi to Pirandello and Ugo Betti. Of non-Italian twentieth-century dramatists, the repertory includes Anouilh, Brecht, Bruckner, Camus, Sartre, Toller, and of Americans, Thornton Wilder and Tennessee Williams.

The codirectors of the Piccolo Teatro in a short time have promoted this playhouse to an art institute of undisputed consequence. Extended tours have acquainted many countries with the ideology and modern approach of the Piccolo Teatro in all aspects of production. Its artistic significance and impact on the contemporary art scene is in reverse proportion to its humble title — Little Theater.

Prose Theaters Major and Minor

The Italian government, burdened by its very costly patronage of the national opera theaters (*Enti Autonomi Lirici*) has so far not assumed a comparable responsibility for the prose theaters.

But in its decree of February 20, 1948, the government stated premises that would determine public aid for the prose theaters. A decade later, on July 23, 1958, a renewal of these qualifications was published.[21] According to this new decree, the national government is ready to subsidize permanent theaters (*teatri stabili*), provided they operate with high artistic standards and strictly without the aim of profit. To qualify for subventions the theatrical company must be affiliated with a communal administration. The theater must be of sufficient interest to its community; administrators of recognized standing must be in charge; the artistic directors must be of unquestioned distinction; the management, locally appointed, must be confirmed by the General Direction of Spectacles in Rome.

The theater applying for state subvention must have adequately furnished quarters. It must operate on a continuous basis. It must concentrate its activities within the periphery of its home region (except in special cases authorized by the government). The theater must have a complete artistic ensemble. The repertory must offer a valid cross section through the various categories of dramatic art. It must be inspired by genuine artistic criteria and broadly represent the national drama of Italy by at least 51 per cent of the total repertory. The government expects that this kind of artistic program will be supported by a substantial audience. The business management of the permanently state-supported theaters is under the surveillance of the national government, specifically of the General Director of Spectacles, who in turn is responsible to the Council of Ministers. Prior to receiving subventions the theater must submit its tentative budget with carefully planned details pertaining to the artistic program and its finances.

The permanent theaters are subdivided into two classes of major and minor companies. The difference is one of quantity: of the number of personnel and of the length of season. This classification is naturally reflected in the type of subsidy that the theater can command. But "major" or "minor" never refers to quality; this must never be in doubt with either of the two groups.

Major companies are defined as prose theaters with permanent ensembles of at least ten professional actors. Half of these must have had a minimum of two seasons of repertory experience in a major company.

The repertory of a major company must amount to a significant representation of Italian drama. The minimum duration of the season is six months, exclusive of rehearsal time.

Minor companies are defined as prose theaters that perform continually for a period of no less than three months. Like the major company, the minor company must cultivate an adequate amount of Italian repertory.

An allowance of 500,000 lire ($800) is paid to a major company for each premiére of an Italian author, provided his work is performed at least ten times during the season. A premium of 300,000 lire ($480) will be given for an additional novelty that has not yet been produced, either in the city (of the residing company), or in Rome, or in Milan. All the major companies receive support equivalent to 8 per cent of their intake for a maximum of 240 performances per year. Thus a ratio is established between the financial aid accorded to the theater and the participation of its public. This acts as a psychological incentive to the company as well as the community.

TABLE III

Italian Prose Theaters

In Regional Capitals*

	Performances	*Tickets Sold*	*Expenditures (in lire)*
Piedmont	140	98,122	54,706,095
Valle d'Aosta	—	—	—
Lombardy	1,413	429,437	416,332,059
Trentino-Alto Adige	21	6,393	4,285,680
Veneto	118	62,111	46,281,456
Friuli-Venezia Giulia	2	985	942,900
Territorio di Trieste	52	25,889	12,919,830
Liguria	243	88,761	64,170,260
Emilia-Romagna	125	78,766	61,383,358
Tuscany	125	63,799	51,675,000
Umbria	7	2,920	2,065,800
Marche	5	1,863	1,602,850
Lazio	959	282,547	280,426,626
Abruzzi-Molise	1	383	424,100
Campania	149	71,973	62,385,823
Puglia	26	12,128	12,412,400
Basilicata	—	—	—
Calabria	—	—	—
Sicily	16	7,057	9,312,800
Sardinia	9	6,599	6,759,782
Total	3,411	1,239,733	1,088,086,819

*Statistics pertain to the season 1956-57 (According to the official publications of the Italian Society of Authors and Editors).

The government has established 10 special awards for outstanding achievements by the state supported theaters: 2 prizes of 8,000,000 lire ($12,800), 3 of 6,000,000 lire ($9,600), 3 of 4,000,000 lire ($6,400), and 2 of 2,000,000 lire ($3,200). These prizes are given on recommendation of a committee of experts, which the government appoints. All companies are eligible, provided they have distinguished themselves by their productions, and win the joint consensus of connoisseurs, the general public, and the press.

TABLE IV

Italian Prose Theaters

In Total Provinces*

	Performances	*Tickets Sold*	*Expenditures (in lire)*
Piedmont	155	103,129	57,765,245
Valle d'Aosta	—	—	—
Lombardy	1,428	434,597	420,370,699
Trentino-Alto Adige	28	8,227	5,055,480
Veneto	134	67,477	48,391,556
Friuli-Venezia Giulia	2	985	942,900
Territorio di Trieste	52	25,889	12,919,830
Liguria	287	95,653	72,975,406
Emilia-Romagna	187	101,294	73,186,093
Tuscany	148	73,377	59,603,270
Umbria	7	2,920	2,065,800
Marche	18	6,263	4,149,100
Lazio	959	282,547	280,426,626
Abruzzi-Molise	1	383	424,100
Campania	155	76,477	67,583,823
Puglia	26	12,128	12,412,400
Basilicata	—	—	—
Calabria	—	—	—
Sicily	—	—	10,163,600
Sardinia	9	6,599	6,759,782
Total	3,596	1,297,945	1,135,195,710

**Ibid.*

Spoleto

The Festival of Two Worlds, held for the past four summers in the small hill town of Spoleto, represents a type of patronage unusual in its diversification. Its founder and director, Gian-Carlo Menotti, has explained the principal aim of the project as a presentation in Europe of the remarkable talent of young Americans in the performing as well as in the visual arts. Consequently, the Festival, annually scheduled in June, includes opera, drama, ballet, concerts, and exhibitions.

Spoleto has two theaters: the Teatro Nuovo, a typically Italian opera house seating 1,200, built in the nineteenth century, and an intimate seventeenth-century theater seating 300. The availability of these two theaters was one of the decisive factors in choosing this picturesque Umbrian town for the Festival.

The primary source of income supporting Spoleto is the United States, where foundations as well as private donors help subsidize the enterprise. But the Italian government, realizing the value of the Festival not only in terms of its obvious artistic merit, but also as a potential tourist attraction, has assumed a minimum guarantee (at present, $37,000). The diffusion of art support — where American and European, private and governmental sources join — is worthy of note. The expenditures for the Festival of 1961 left a deficit exceeding $28,000, which was met by Mr. Menotti himself.

The Communist mayor of Spoleto watches with enjoyment the growth of the Festival: it has given work to many of his citizens, brought distinction to the small impoverished city, and lifted it within a short time from regional obscurity into international limelight.

VII. Radio and Television

The Italian radio, to quote one of its high officials, was under Fascism "a galley with its slaves condemned to enthusiasm." Today, Radio Italiana (known as RAI), the company in charge of national broadcasting, is still under the surveillance of a highly centralized government. But the controlling government is a freely elected democratic body.

RAI, which has the status of an *ente autonomo*, reports to a parliamentary commission which, in turn, is controlled by the parliamentary majority. The program committee consists of representatives of both the radio company and the government, as well as a number of experts in the areas and media of performance covered by the official programs.

The relationship between state and RAI is defined by the agreement of December 15, 1952. It authorizes and describes the company's rights of transmitting radio broadcasts and telecasts throughout the nation. The contract was signed for twenty years, i.e., it is to remain in effect until the end of 1972.

Types of Program

As in other European countries, the program of the RAI is subdivided into three major groups. This division originated in 1953. The Third Program was inaugurated by the RAI as the consequence of the quoted agreement of December 15, 1952. Article 10 of this contract requested the establishment of three programs with the condition that one of these — the Third — would be of a decidedly cultural character. In a typical year musical programs comprise 48.4 per cent of the First (the so-called National Program), 37.3 per cent of the Second, 43.8 per cent of the Third. These musical programs are diversified: light music makes up almost one-third of the National (30.6 per cent) and also of the Second Program (30.7 per cent); classical music comprises 17.8 per cent of the National Program and 5.16 per cent of the Second Program. Serious music of all styles, including a large representation of contemporary music, is relegated to the Third Program.

TABLE V

Distribution of Non-Musical Programs in a Typical Year

Prose Readings	*Per Cent*	*Journalistic Service*	*Per Cent*
National Program	5.3	National Program	8.5
Second Program	23.1	Second Program	2.5
Third Program	15.2	Third Program	6.6
Information Service		*Special Cultural Broadcasts*	
National Program	16.4	National Program	17.9
Second Program	10.5	Second Program	19.5
Third Program	7.8	Third Program	26.6

Sports Bulletins	*Per Cent*
National Program	3.5
Second Program	2.1
Third Program	Not offered

The economic disparity of Italy is reflected in the number of radio sets owned in the different regions. As late as 1957, this inequality was still shocking. (See Table VI.)

The number of registered listeners had then reached the figure of 6,306,448.

TABLE VI

Regional Owned Radio Sets (1957)

In the Prosperous North	56.71
In the Center Regions	19.48
In the South	15.93
In the Islands	7.88

Table VII shows sets owned for every 100 persons in Italy and in four other European countries.

TABLE VII

Italy	12.82
France	22.05
West Germany	25.44
Holland	26.71
England	27.87

Today there is a proportionate increase iu these countries.

Italians in all parts of the country share a preference for the radio: it is definitely the most popular "spettacolo." Radio influences the taste of the people more than any other single factor of public life. More than half of Italy's adult population spends its free hours listening to the radio. This cannot be interpreted as an altogether "free" choice: for the radio simply represents the kind of entertainment that almost all of the Italian people can now afford. It is the most practical and cheapest, which makes all the differences in the poor south and on the islands, where the ownership of a radio is still something not to be taken for granted and where TV sets are a mark of luxury. And so the radio rather than TV functions as a principal medium of information.

The scope of serious music offered by RAI in "live performances" is substantial. There are four symphony orchestras employed full time by the stations in Rome, Milan, Turin, and Naples. The players receive contracts for the entire year with paid vacations. The radio orchestra of Naples, known as the Orchestra Scarlatti, is the smallest of these groups, an ensemble of fifty players only. Its engagement by RAI is typical of radio's role as a patron. In 1956 the Orchestra Scarlatti found itself in a financial crisis and was about to be abandoned. At this point, the radio adopted the ensemble.

The radio stations of Milan, Rome, and Turin permanently employ choruses. The singers enjoy the same security as the members of the orchestra. About 200 concerts of serious music are annually given by the 3 major networks. There are about 150 opera productions per year, at the average rate of 3 operas a week. The repertory is ambitious. (Such works as Berg's *Wozzeck* and *Lulu* have recently been broadcast.) In Milan, the public is invited to the regular concert series. Eventually, there will be free concerts also in the other cities with resident radio orchestras. Chamber music is frequently heard. A special series is devoted to young interpreters and young composers who are not yet generally known. Radio assumes the responsibility to sponsor them. In general the character of the repertory is international; not rarely the accent falls on the experimental.

Television came late to Italy. On July 20, 1949, the first television set arrived from the United States. The cardinal in the port city Genoa offered a benediction to be televised all over the nation. In 1950, at the initiation of the Holy Year, Radiodiffusion Télévision française presented Pope Pius XII with a television station. From this studio in the Vatican certain ecclesiastical functions are now telecast. Radio Televisione Italiana safeguards cultural programs. Table V has shown how special cultural broadcasts were distributed over Italy's three radio networks. Of television's two channels, the Second was originally chosen for the more cultural role. At present, however, both channels offer cultural programs as well as popular entertainment.

It is no surprise that Italians enjoy watching opera on their television screens. The demand for televised opera has become nation-wide, and the telecasts are good. Sixty operas have been performed between 1957 and 1960. The repertory proved all-inclusive, offering works from the early Baroque to contemporary music drama. Hopes are high that television will strengthen anew the interest in opera of every strata of the population. Optimists predict that once a television set is owned by each Italian family, a renewal of opera, and probably also of the legitimate theater, will arrive throughout the nation.

The number of owners of television sets is at present approaching 3,500,000. The figure is fast rising, particularly in the North. The annual license fee is approximately $22. The fee has been recently reduced to approximately $20 for both radio and television. Only one-fourth of this amount is allocated to the government; the Post Office supervises proceedings. Three-fourths of the fee is apportioned to Radio Televisione Italiana.

The First channel reaches the entire Apennine peninsula and all islands under the Italian flag. A very limited quantity of advertising is permitted; some of it surrounds the telecasts of evening news.

As are the radio broadcasts, the principal telecasts are sent from Italy's large stations in Rome and Milan and from Naples and Turin.

VIII. Issues Before Parliament
Prima Donnas, Copyright, Censorship

The atomic age and the ancient patriarchal life collide in today's Italy in many places and on many issues. The nation's art life is still a mixture of the progressive and the primitive.

As all major art institutes are state supported, parliament is in charge of their destinies. But the parliamentary decisions are not necessarily made along party lines. The difference between Italy and Europe's other nations, where analogous procedures prevail, is one of temperament — of the very passion with which issues concerning art are fought out — as well as of the often amazing nature of topics that reach parliament. Not only the major problems of governmental patronage are debated here, but curious incidents in Italy's art life come up for heated discussion and argument.

The antics of a prima donna at the opening night of the Roman opera season caused the President of Italy to walk out of the once-royal box of the theater. And the drama of a collapsing performance not only made giant-sized headlines on the front page of all papers and occupied news broadcasts, but the behavior and sudden indisposition of Madame Maria Callas soon became a grave issue of state. In parliament furious deputies wanted to know why the management of the government supported Teatro dell'Opera had failed to adopt measures to prevent such accidents; a second cast would have protected Italy from such a national disaster.

A case involving correctness and scholarship of opera performance finds its way to the chamber of the senate. In 1961 one of Italy's leading music publishing houses came under parliamentary fire. It was claimed that the firm had printed the scores of operatic masterworks with grave errors, and subsequently failed to rectify these mistakes in later editions (from the original manuscripts in its possession). Now the Italian government studies the entire complex of musical copyright and examines the possibility of legal changes. No issue pertaining to opera is taken lightly in Italy.

* * * * *

The fight for — or against — government censorship of performances in the prose theater and even opera, in cinema and, recently, in television, assumes in Italy a violence matched nowhere else in Western Europe, due to the nation's political extremes. The showing of the film *La Dolce Vita* caused bitter debate by the deputies. Members of the largest party, the Christian Democrats, inquired what protection the Secretary of Spectacles can offer "the God-abiding Italian people who are discredited in the entire world by such debased products of a pseudo-art." The *Osservatore Romano*, official newspaper of the Vatican, asserted that this film, named *The Sweet Life*, throws "the dignity of the Eternal City into dirt." The communistic paper, *Unita*, saw in this moving picture convincing proof of corruption in capitalistic society. Official Italy raged. Producers, actors, theater owners showing the film were challenged to duels or received outright threats that they would be murdered. But these are historic procedures; for this is the way Italians liked to settle differences of opinion during the Renaissance. Modern law enforcement has restored a relative sense of security, and performances continue unless prohibited by the police under governmental directive.

That these very orders not rarely confuse and bewilder the authorities charged with their execution is shown by the fate of the tragi-comedy *Arialda* by Giovanni Testori. In the fall of 1960 this play was removed from a Milan theater because it "offended the public morale." The play deals with a proletarian family and its complex-ridden children. The main characters are a spinster-seamstress, Arialda, and her handsome brother, Elio, who earns his living by friendships with men. When the attorney-general suppressed the performance of *Arialda* in Milan, a storm broke loose throughout the nation. At its Roman première the play had been given with the warning clause "not for juveniles under eighteen." Yet the Roman censor was still not satisfied; he brought the issue before the President of the Republic, who personally intervened, insisting on the elimination of all offensive passages.

Conflicting actions are caused by conflicting laws. The Italian government maintains a central office of censorship in Rome to decide which pieces are admitted for performance throughout the nation. Yet each city and province is autonomous; each arrives at its own verdict. Hence, the Milan censor was not only in the position to forbid the performances of *Arialda*, but to confiscate copies of the play in every bookstore of Lombardy. The actors were requested to turn in their scripts; the company that produced *Arialda* was disbanded. This started a chain reaction. The syndicate of Italian actors proposed a nation-wide strike. The society of critics signed a resolution against the infringement and arbitrariness of the Milan authorities. Parliament is now getting ready to reformulate national laws to clarify the issues of censorship and avoid similar dilemmas in the future.

In the spring of 1960 the state supported opera house San Carlo in Naples, scheduled the première of *le Martyre de St. Sebastièn* by Claude Debussy. The Archbishop of Naples strongly objected, primarily to the treatment of this sacred story in the text by Gabriele d'Annunzio, upon which Debussy had based his score. All writings of d'Annunzio are on the Vatican's *Index* of prohibited literature. The disapprobation of the Archbishop also pertained to the theatricality of the mystery play which was produced in the opera with stylistic traits of a ballet.

Lengthy conferences between the clergy, the municipality of Naples, and the management of San Carlo led to this compromise: Debussy's work was permitted to be given in the style of an oratorio, without action on the stage. Fragments from Wagner's *Parsifal* rounded out the musical offering in the theater at Easter time.

These examples from opera, prose theater, and cinema demonstrate the extent to which the wedges of control have been driven into the field of the performing arts, and the decisions which have been reached in test cases.

Unanimous Art Support

No matter how sharply divided the Italians are on certain issues of their art life, the nation remains agreed on the principle of art support as a public duty. Hence, in the debates before parliament the issue is not *whether* to aid the arts, but *how*. There is not a single responsible statesman who opposes the continuation of governmental subsidies, in spite of constant governmental crises. This is worthy of note, for it is the Republic that carries the overwhelming burden of assistance to the arts. It is true, there is some private patronage left in Italy, particularly among banks and syndicates. But this support is far from adequate. Donations are given as outright gifts to the community or nation. Italian laws grant no tax reductions for private contributions.

In contrast to other Western democracies (such as Austria or West Germany), Italy is not controlled by only two major factions. There are many political parties. A parliamentary majority has emerged which tends toward a "left of center" coalition. But whatever the changing political picture, there is nothing in Italian psychology to suggest serious curtailment of national art subsidy. On the contrary, increasing support of the performing arts is taken for granted, in spite of the urgent task of rehabilitating the impoverished south and numerous other pressing national assignments that can no longer be postponed. After the liberation from the Fascists, more than one-third of the country's total productive power was destroyed.

The Marshall Plan has helped Italy regain her impaired economic health. A new wave of prosperity is now approaching; but even in lean years, none of the parties has collectively objected to helping the arts. Criticism is concerned with the more equitable distribution of subsidies. As always, it is easier to demand better solutions than to supply a generally acceptable method for obtaining them. There exists no common denominator for the cultural needs of the Italian people. There are the peasants of the south, who still live their lives of utter simplicity, close to earth, as their ancestors lived for thousands of years. There is the urban society of the north, one of the most sophisticated and progressive to be found anywhere in the modern world. Obviously, no art program can appeal equally to these extremes.

But there is creative opportunity not to be missed: the government can, on appropriately different levels, educate all strata of the population toward the enjoyment of genuine art. The Italian administration is confident that this aim can be realized in a long-range program. Moreover, the performing arts can play a crucial role in the giant task of uniting the two Italys in one single organism of cultural vitality. It is hoped that the north, with its noble artistic past and present intellectual impulse, will join hands with the south to break down age-old social and cultural barriers. The modern media of performance are called upon to help in this cultural fusion, which would have been unattainable in an earlier era.

The government of the Italian republic seeks to meet justified criticism of its art support and to establish a reasonable and workable procedure for the benefit of its people. The art program must play its part in realizing Italy's second *risorgimento* — a revival of spiritual and economic strength — one century after the country's political forces joined to unify the nation as a kingdom.

The hard-tested country, so bitterly tried from within and from without, now has a democratic government, administrating art from a capital where the Forum Romanum — irresistibly beautiful even as a ruin — still stands as a symbol of ancient civilization. By its dedication to a program of generous art support, Italy's government gives assurance of its commitment to continuing its national heritage.

SWITZERLAND

I. Prosperity with Patina

Switzerland is the oldest democracy on the European continent. By a policy of continuous neutrality the Swiss Confederation has emerged as the only nation in the heart of Europe to avoid armed conflict, even during the cataclysm of the past two World Wars. Not since 1798, when Napoleon's army overran the small mountainous country, has there been major fighting on Swiss soil. The Vienna Congress guaranteed Switzerland's neutrality in 1815, and for nearly a century and a half, there has been no violation of this peaceful status. Whatever the moral merits of such complete aloofness from the apocalyptic struggles of opposing ideologies, the economic results of the long Swiss neutrality are immediately evident in the many signs of extreme prosperity throughout the country.

For generations the Swiss have had the opportunity, without crucial interruption or lasting damage, to build, to develop their cities and their industries, and to cultivate their land. Theirs is a different kind of prosperity from any we find in other countries of Western Europe. It is not reconstruction upon debris. It is not a new beginning. It is not the *Wirtschaftswunder*, the economic miracle that astonishes and almost bewilders the visitor in West Germany.

Swiss prosperity has the patina of age and all aspects of a continuous growth. It is the normal extension of an economic success that has developed since the Middle Ages, when the first trade routes, cutting through the Alps, linked Europe's north and south, west and east, by way of Switzerland. From Germany to Italy, from France to Austria, the early highways led over high mountain passes and through narrow valleys to Swiss settlements and villages. Aided by this unique geographical position, the economy of the country prospered from one century to another.

The Swiss have maintained their simple and dignified houses of worship, their strict schools, their precision plants and factories, their neat stores and often humble but spotless workshops. They give equal care to their theaters and concert halls, to their art museums and fine libraries. There is enough wealth to invest in all commodities and in all the good things of life.

Subsidies are distributed to the arts in a manner characteristic of the Swiss. We observe a patronage that differs from that in neighboring Austria, France, or Italy. The mainspring of Swiss art support is not the federal government. The principal aid stems primarily from the cantons, the municipalities, and the communities, which constitute the political units of the nation.

This pattern is deeply rooted in Swiss history. The Confederation grew from a free union of self-governing cantons. The territorial districts cover all of urban and rural Switzerland. The alliance of cantons is political in origin; their unity was "for common defense against a common foe." But the cantons are independent in their religious, cultural, and economic structure. Swiss thinking always stressed independence, in relation to other countries and in attitude toward their fellow citizens. This stimulated the coexistence of heterogeneous units within their own land, in spite of religious, ethnic, and linguistic differences. We find certain analogies to the United States in the centuries-long uncompromising democratic tradition of the Swiss, in their fierce upholding of the basic freedoms, in their predominantly capitalistic ideology, and in their stubborn adherence to private initiative.

Basic traits of a national psychology have been perceptible in Switzerland probably for a longer time than in any other continental country. There prevails in Switzerland an unbroken continuity of political ideas dating back to the thirteenth century. The "Bundesbrief" of 1291, in which the first cantons banded together, is the historical fountainhead of Swiss politics.

The Swiss struggle for liberty was zealously fought in the Middle Ages. Significantly, the historical myths of the Swiss have as their favorite subjects the fight against tyranny. Of the territorial powers which developed in the thirteenth century on Swiss soil, the Habsburgs assumed greatest importance. From its castle, the "Habichtsburg," near Basel, the Habsburg dynasty embarked on its road to world power. The expulsion of the Habsburg overlords is one of the favorite tales of the Swiss. Wilhelm Tell is their national hero, personifying this fight in the early fourteenth century. The story has found incomparable expression in Friedrich Schiller's classical drama *Wilhelm Tell* (1804).

What modern Switzerland regards as her basic civic law and her unshakable concept of federalistic democracy have directly grown through seven centuries. The patterns of Swiss art support are allied to historic events and principles. Swiss democracy, federalism, and regionalism cannot be understood apart from this causality; nor can Swiss art support.

In its network of many small and independent towns sponsoring indigenous art life, Switzerland is reminiscent of Germany. The greater segment of modern Switzerland was once part of the German Reich, specifically of the Dukedom of Schwaben. But on Swiss soil the decisive political issues became the rights of the burghers, the struggle for their independence, the rejection of privileges that elsewhere rested with the aristocratic ruler. And in the defense of their independence, mainly against threats of German sovereigns, the Swiss communities formed their Bünde. The first of these crucial alliances — Schwyz, Uri, and Unterwalden — set also the patterns for the regionalism and strict independence that characterize the Swiss way of life in our time. As late as the eighteenth century Switzerland had not yet become a uniform state. There were thirteen Orte, allied with each other through individual Bünde. But in 1815 the Congress of Vienna made it possible for the Swiss to have their own constitution, which stresses the sovereignty of the cantons. The constitution has been revised, but never rescinded, following various upheavals in the intervening years.

Role of Canton and City

As recently as 1848 the Swiss federal constitution was rewritten with the Constitution of the United States as model.*

The Swiss Congress is composed of two houses: the Ständerat, or conseil des états, corresponds to the American Senate. Each canton, large or small, sends two representatives to this body. The Nationalrat, or conseil national, is composed of representatives elected within the cantons in proportion to the population. There is one representative to every 24,000 inhabitants. (The population of Switzerland is 5,470,000.)

Bern, the capital of this Swiss Confederation, is the seat of the Federal Parliament. Three languages are recognized as official: the federal constitution of 1848, revised in 1874, acknowledges German, French, and Italian as national languages. All documents are trilingual; the three languages are on money bills; and all three are spoken in Parliament. Art support follows the tripartite pattern.

The Swiss Confederation is composed of twenty-two cantons, which correspond to the fifty states in our country. Just as the states, so the cantons are sovereign in carefully defined aspects of government.

Wherever there is cantonal art support, it is an adjunct to education. The cantons are in charge of the schools. The Swiss have always viewed public art support as closely related to education. And thus the cantons have for many years supported theaters and concert organizations in the cities which as provincial capitals are representative of cantonal culture.

The cantons embrace smaller units called Gemeinden (communities), which in Switzerland are the decisive political units of the nation.

In contrast to most other European countries, the Swiss Confederation does not assume a major responsibility in the patronage of the arts. As

*Both terms, *Confederation* and *Bund*, are used by the Swiss in reference to their federal government; the German word *Eidgenossenschaft* is applied synonymously with confederation.

already suggested, the primary responsibility of art patronage rests with the cantons and cities. This does not imply that the Bund excludes itself altogether: on the contrary, the central government in Bern sponsors specific enterprises on the basis of federal legality. This situation is clarified in Article III of the Swiss federal constitution, according to which the cantons are sovereign "to the extent to which the sovereignty is not expressly limited by the federal constitution." As a consequence, the cantons and/or the cities emerge as the primary sources of Swiss art patronage. For practical purposes, canton and city frequently coordinate their efforts. Numerous art institutions are subsidized jointly by their respective states and municipalities. All major issues of art support are decided by a public referendum as the legitimate expression of civic will.

Spiritual Defense

Ominous events preceding the outbreak of the Second World War prompted an official declaration from the Confederation. In October, 1922, Italy, the southern neighbor of Switzerland, was trapped in the yoke of Mussolini's Fascists. In January, 1933, the Nazi Reich, at Switzerland's northern border, increased the totalitarian menace. The circle of dictatorships around Switzerland almost enclosed the east. In March, 1938, Austria was usurped by Hitler. The Swiss Confederation was frightened by totalitarian tyranny. It was in view of this most serious threat that the government in Bern issued a federal decree on December 9, 1938. In this special message the National Council specifically referred to "the task of preserving Swiss culture" and examined "the possibilities of propagandizing the Swiss way of life."[1]

This charter is referred to as "The Spiritual Defense of the Country." It was a welcome federal "interference" at a dangerous time, when it would have been suicidal to let matters take their course. The threat from without created the postulate of public cultural patronage within the nation.

The December message of 1938 is unique in Swiss history. It aims at the mobilization of all cultural forces in the service of democratic freedom. The decree represents an important instance where a government assumed leadership in national art policy, calling for teamwork toward a common end. The December message is the *Magna Charta* of cultural care in Switzerland. But the call for a common front in times of stress did not basically alter the Swiss pattern of subsidizing the arts. It merely called for a concerted effort of all art organizations to emphasize anew the ideals of Swiss culture. The performing arts represented the natural forum where the spiritual climate of the nation was readily assessed.

II. Theaters Supported by Cantons and Cities

Swiss cantons and cities support their theaters with subsidies that are normally (but not always) proportionate to the size of their respective populations. In spite of this public patronage, the theme of private initiative still prevails in Swiss art life and often pertains to the theater and the concert. We are concerned here only with organizations that do not have financial profit as an aim. As a matter of principle, the Swiss authorities do not subsidize theaters which operate primarily as a business venture, regardless of their repertory.

On the other hand, the majority of Swiss municipal theaters cannot afford to devote themselves exclusively to purely cultural programs. Many of these stages admit the genre of musical comedy and the like into the general repertory. Only a substantial raise of the present subventions would enable these theaters to abandon the light fare which cannot be classified as "cultural."

The Swiss theaters play in German, French, and Italian, according to their geographical location. In cosmopolitan Zürich and a few other cities opera is often given in its original language. Each theater is governed by a board of trustees, which lays down the policies and engages the managers and the artistic directors (conductors, regisseurs, etc.). Occasionally the artistic director serves as general manager of the theater. The board of trustees functions on an honorary basis. One finds on these boards cultivated men of business and finance, college teachers, and civic-minded and artistically informed members of other professions.

Zürich Municipal Theater

The largest city of Switzerland is Zürich, with a population of 428,200. (Based on the census of 1961.) The Stadt Theater of Zürich (Municipal Theater), founded in 1891, receives subventions from the municipality of Zürich as well as from the canton of Zürich. (Frequently, a Swiss canton and its capital city bear the identical name.)

The Municipal Theater is managed by the Theater-Aktiengesellschaft (joint stock company) of Zürich. Of all the Swiss stages, the Zürich Stadt Theater is the only one devoted exclusively to music; the repertory is divided among opera, classical operetta, and ballet. The total personnel is 317 (artists and technicians). The general manager (intendant), according to European tradition, has often been a performing artist (at this writing, an opera regisseur). A business manager reports to the intendant. In addition to these chief administrators, the Municipal Theater has an artistic staff of 5 conductors, 5 stage directors, 3 stage designers, and 3 costume designers. Likewise engaged for at least one year (and not merely for a limited season) are the following: 1 choral director, 1 ballet master, 1 dramaturge, 6 assistant conductors (coaches), 2 inspectors, 40 solo singers, 22 dancers, 2 prompters. A staff of 15 serves in the offices of administration. There are 4 technical department heads supervising a staff of 44. The theater orchestra numbers 65; the chorus, 45. For certain opera performances it is necessary to augment the orchestra.[2]

The Municipal Theater gave in a typical season (1958-59) a total of 348 performances, attended by 331,245 people. One hundred per cent attendance was realized in 10 closed performances, also in 4 special performances for the city schools, and at 4 events of the series called "Introductory Evenings." Eight performances with prominent guests had 95 per cent attendance; 28 performances given for audiences from rural districts had 92 per cent; and 42 performances for elementary and high schools had 88 per cent. Fifteen gala performances averaged 79 per cent; 32 fairy tale performances, 79 per cent; and 4 charity performances, 77 per cent attendance.

Important Premières

Zürich has a tradition of distinguished operatic first performances. The world premières of *Lulu* (1937) by Alban Berg, and of *Mathis der Maler* (1938) by Hindemith took place in Zürich's Stadt Theater. A special grant was voted by the city fathers for the performance of Schoenberg's last opera, *Aron and Moses* (1957), and a staggering deficit was anticipated for this undertaking because of the high cost of the production, which involved an extraordinary number of rehearsals. The Swiss, known for their proverbial thrift, underwrote the première. They realized the cultural significance of the event. The investment paid off. The press prominently covered the performance in the papers of five continents, and the world learned of the progressive spirit of the city's art life.

The Zürich Stadt Theater seats 1,190. The hall and stage equipment have become obsolete. But at this writing, plans for the construction of a modern building are well under way, for the citizens have voted affirmatively on the new theater project. The positive ballot is remarkable in view of Zürich's large population of workers. After all, the Municipal Council did not propose to build the hall for workers' festivals which, according to widespread opinion, is much needed. The board asked for extensive financial support for the serious theater, for the opera, and for its uncompromising avant-garde repertory which is definitely above the grasp and interest of thousands who voted in favor of the theater's support. Statistics show that about 20 per cent of Zürich's population visit the

Stadt Theater at one time or another, but a much higher percentage voted for a new opera house. This is an encouraging sign of civic patronage.

The board of trustees of the Zürich theater has repeatedly applied for an increase of the municipal contribution. In 1962 the budget of the Stadt Theater amounted to $875,000; an additional $210,000 was requested. The present subsidy amounts to 1.4 per cent of the total municipal budget.[3] During the season 1961-62 the Zürich Opera earned 38 per cent of its expenses. By comparison with receipts of West German opera theaters, the Zürich income is very satisfactory. Düsseldorf and Wiesbaden earned during the same season 36 per cent, Munich 29 per cent, and Stuttgart 28 per cent of their respective operating costs.

In their argument for a raise of subvention, the trustees of the Zürich Opera emphasize that the demands of the public are rising, as radio and records set higher standards of performance. Again the question of subsidies, in traditional Swiss fashion, was decided by public referendum. On evenings preceding the voting, hundreds of students carrying torches paraded through the streets of the town to arouse the citizens to a positive ballot. The members of the Opera and its faithful audiences were not disappointed. On November 4, 1962, the citizens of Zürich voted affirmatively to raise the subsidy as requested.

Zürich also has a municipal Schauspielhaus (Playhouse), founded in 1926; it is a repertory theater of 1,050 seats. The major subvention stems from the city of Zürich, which allots 300,000 francs ($70,050) annually. Since 1938 the theater has been directed by the Neue Schauspielhaus Gesellschaft (New Playhouse Society). The total personnel is 104.

Table I shows income and expenses of the Zürich Municipal Theater for nine seasons between 1938 and 1958.[4] It also shows the percentage relationship of the theater's income to the public subsidy and to the operational deficit.

TABLE I

Zürich Municipal Theater (1938-1958)

(Figures are given in thousand francs.)*

Year	*Expenses*	*Actual Income*	%	*Public Subsidy*	%	*Deficit*	%
1938/39	1,739,1	1,126,5	64.7	495,4	28.5	117,2	6.8
1950/51	3,922,4	2,359,2	60.2	1,419,9	36.1	143,3	3.7
1951/52	3,879,9	2,289,4	59.0	1,530,8	39.4	59,7	1.6
1952/53	3,912,0	2,255,6	57.7	1,572,0	40.1	84,4	2.2
1953/54	4,004,5	2,323,3	58.1	1,582,0	39.4	99,2	2.5
1954/55	4,052,2	2,280,1	56.3	1,632,0	40.4	140,1	3.3
1955/56	4,485,6	2,339,4	52.1	2,075,0	46.1	71,2	1.8
1956/57	5,259,8	2,417,7	46.0	2,379,0	45.2	463,1	8.8
1957/58	4,886,3	2,203,7	45.1	2,379,0	48.7	303,6	6.2

*At this writing, 4.3 Swiss francs equal $1.00.

**Annual Reports, Rechenschaftsbericht des Verwaltungsrates der Theater Aktiengesellschaft, Zürich.

The number of performances in the Municipal Theater has increased throughout the years from 270 to an average of 350 annually. A further increase is technically not feasible. The present theater lacks a sufficient number of seats in the medium-priced category; about 20 per cent of the total capacity of 1,190 seats do not offer a good view of the stage. These and other problems will be solved in Zürich only by the new theater and its appropriately modern auditorium.

Current ticket prices for regular performances in the theater range from three to thirteen francs (70 cents to $3). They are raised for performances with prominent guest artists and for the June Festival. But this increase is not permitted to be excessive. To date it has not gone beyond 38 per cent. This is a crucial point: the municipality insists that the theater must remain accessible, at all times, to as broad a public as possible.[5]

TABLE II

Expenses of the Zürich Municipal Theater
Fiscal Year 1957-58

(Figures are given in thousand francs.)

		Totals
Salaries and Related Expenditures		
Soloists (ensemble and guests)	607	
Music directors (conductors, coaches, choir directors)	164	
Stage producer and dramaturge	64	
Prompter and stage inspector	43	
Chorus	378	
Ballet	211	
Miscellaneous	47	
		1,514
Orchestra		
Contribution to Tonhalle Orchestra	876	
Other orchestral costs	31	
		907
Stage and Hall		
Maintenance	315	
Decor	156	
Wardrobe	120,5	
Materials	58	
Electricians	73,5	
Hairdressers	42	
Cleaning	66,5	
Heating	25	
Employees in hall	66	
Costumers	32	
		954,5

Switzerland

Salaries		*Totals*
Management and Administration	213,5	213,5
Social Welfare		
Annuity	65	
Accident	50	
Illness	15	
Accident insurance	2	
Pension fund	95	
Miscellaneous	3	
		230
		3,819

Within the decade from 1951 to 1961 the total expenses of the Zürich Theater have increased one-third. The increases are caused partly by inflation, partly by the policy to raise artistic standards and the salaries of the performers. The inflation affects both: costs of production and salaries. Salaries amount to three-fourths of total expenses. (Table II.)

TABLE III

Selected Group of Municipal Theaters Switzerland, West Germany, Austria Expenses and Income (1956-57)

(Swiss figures given in thousand francs; Austrian and German in thousand marks.)

	Expenses	*Income* (derived from own activities)	*Income* (in % of expenses)
Switzerland			
Zürich	5,259,8	2,417,7	46
Basel	3,101,2	1,118,1	36
Bern	2,421,7	1,072,8	44
West Germany			
Düsseldorf	7,504,4	2,448,2	33
Frankfurt	7,921,7	2,489,7	31
Kassel	3,314,1	951,2	29
Mainz	2,365,5	702,9	30
München	7,963,2	2,108,2	26
Nürnberg	6,130,9	2,063,5	34
Stuttgart	6,663,0	3,573,0	52
Wiesbaden	4,442,7	1,514,3	34
Austria			
Graz	3,646,5	990,0	27
Linz	2,020,2	403,3	20

As Table III reveals, the financial operations of the Zürich Municipal Theater and of other Swiss stages fare well by comparison with those of theaters in West Germany and Austria. All of the theaters listed are subsidized by government on different levels. The benefits accrued from public patronage permit the maintenance of cultural programs. The comparison considers theaters of various scope in cities of various sizes within the three countries.

Tonhalle-Gesellschaft

The most important concert society in Zürich, known as the Tonhalle-Gesellschaft, is the parent organization of the Tonhalle Orchestra. Because of its size, the orchestra may perform in two sections simultaneously: in opera and in concert.

In a typical year the city of Zürich contributed 914,000 francs ($213,419) to the Tonhalle Society and, in addition, 132,000 francs ($30,821) for youth and popular concerts, a total of 1,046,000 francs ($244,240). The canton of Zürich contributed 350,000 francs ($80,955). There were also several private donors. A further source of income is the various engagements of the orchestra. In the Municipal Theater the orchestra earned 876,000 francs ($202,618); from various private societies there was further income of 67,277 francs ($15,561): a total of 943,277 francs ($218,179). The sale of tickets brought 395,424 francs ($91,363) — including subscription concerts and the June Festival. The sale of program books yielded 17,281 francs ($3,975). The grand total of all income, including interest, rental of musical materials, etc., was 2,826,567 francs ($653,784).

The total expenses for the concerts of the Tonhalle-Gesellschaft were 2,889,955 francs. The largest items of this budget were:

Salaries for orchestra and conductors	1,851,470 francs ($428,245)
Guest conductors and soloists	121,682 francs ($ 28,145)
Insurance, Social Security, Hospitalization	333,416 francs ($ 77,119)

Thus, the modest deficit of the Tonhalle Orchestra amounted to 63,388 francs ($14,801), which was met by public subvention.[6]

The Tonhalle Orchestra is permanently engaged by the Municipal Theater for performances of opera, classical operetta, and ballet. But the orchestra does not report to the administration of the Stadt Theater; the orchestra has its own functionaries. The relative independence of the orchestra has occasionally impaired the potential of the theater's artistic achievement.[7] Other organizational problems likewise result from procedures at the Zürich Opera. The governing board of the Municipal Theater does not always accept the expert judgment of the appointed Intendant.

Furthermore, for reasons previously analysed, all civic issues in Switzerland come before the people in the form of a plebescite. The major questions concerning the public support of the municipal theaters are no exception. Obviously, the preoccupation of a community with the fate of its publicly supported art institutes is most desirable. There must always be enlightenment through professional guidance; otherwise, an amateurish approach to public art life creates serious pitfalls.

* * * * *

The following pages briefly survey the operations of other municipal theaters of Switzerland.

*Basel**

Switzerland's second city in size, Basel, with a population of more than 200,000, is proud of its theatrical tradition. The Basel Stadt Theater was founded in 1834 and rebuilt in 1873 and 1909.

The theater has 1,150 seats. It is managed by the Genossenschaft des Stadt Theaters Basel. Subventions are allocated by both the city and the canton of Basel. The annual subsidy is 1,600,000 francs ($370,080). The repertory offers musical theater (opera, operetta, ballet) as well as drama. The personnel numbers 185.

Bern

The capital city of the Swiss federation, Bern, has a population of 161,300. The Stadt Theater receives a subvention of 1,000,000 francs ($230,000) from the city and canton of Bern. It is directed by the Theater Genossenschaft Bern. The hall, built in 1903, seats 1,000. The total personnel is 155.

Significantly, the federal government, with its seat in Bern, abstains from subsidizing even this principal theater of the Swiss capital. In addition to the Stadt Theater, three organizations in the performing arts receive subsidies from the canton of Bern through its Department of Education. These are Berner Orchesterverein, 55,000 francs; Kantonal Musikverein, 3,500 francs; Conservatory of Bern, 50,000 francs.

Geneva

The Grand Théâtre of Geneva, the chief city of French Switzerland, population 168,900, was founded in 1879. The theater burned down in 1951. During the following decade Geneva had to be satisfied with a substitute hall. On December 10, 1962, the theater was reopened with a performance of Verdi's *Don Carlo*. The cost of the modernized structure was 4,500,000 francs. The theater is administered by the Société Romande de Spectacles. There is an annual lyrical season. The munic-

*For further details on art support in Basel, Cf. P. 124 ff.

ipality of Geneva allocates a yearly grant of 800,000 francs. Included in this sum is the theater's share of 200,000 francs for the services of the orchestra.

Geneva has a playhouse known as Théâtre de la Comédie. The city owns the building, but the society administering the theater is private. The municipality offers the Comédie a yearly subvention of 170,000 francs ($39,221), which enables the management to maintain a repertory of high standards.

Lausanne

The Municipal Theater of Lausanne, the second city of French Switzerland, was built in 1931-1932. It is managed by a cooperative society. The subventions, allocated by this city of 118,900 and by the canton Vaud (of which Lausanne is the capital), amount to 315,000 francs ($72,859).

* * * * *

The remaining municipal theaters on this list belong to cities with a population of less than 80,000.

Lucerne

The Stadt Theater of Lucerne serves a community of 64,500. It was founded in 1839 and rebuilt in 1926. The theater, which seats 571, is supported by the municipality with a subvention of 500,000 francs ($115,650).

The municipality of Lucerne administers the theater. The required subvention is approximately 40 per cent of the total expenditures. The Stadt Theater is under the control of the municipal departments of schools and police. This curious alliance dates back to times when visiting theatrical troupes were anxiously watched by the police, because of widespread fear that the actors, like itinerant gypsies, might in some way disturb the moral life of the solid burghers of Lucerne.

In 1938, Arturo Toscanini with a group of patrons founded the Lucerne International Festival of Music. It has become one of Europe's most attractive summer musicals, scheduled from the middle of August through September 14.

St. Gallen

The Stadt Theater of St. Gallen (population 72,000) was rebuilt in 1857. There are 840 seats. The Stadt Theater-Aktiengesellschaft (joint stock company) is in charge of management. A subvention of 285,000 francs ($65,920) is allocated by the city and by the canton of St. Gallen. The management of the theater has requested a raise of the public subsidy from 410,000 francs ($94,833) to 530,000 francs ($122,589). Contrary to expectation the public referendum defeated the requested raise by a very close vote. The situation is complicated by the fact that the Konzertverein (the society forming the city's professional orchestra) is directly involved: the orchestra plays in the pit of the theater for its performances of opera, operetta, and ballet.

St. Gallen has a problem typical for all art-minded towns in the vicinity of a large city. Zürich can be reached from St. Gallen in less than one hour by train or car; here, in the nation's largest art center, first-rate performances in every medium are easily accessible for the visitors from nearby towns. The citizens of St. Gallen — a textile manufacturing center — wonder whether they should continue to assign priority to paying the deficit of their theater and orchestra, in preference to other urgent items within their community. Should one not look, they ask, for less costly and more practical solutions for the civic art life, perhaps by a more systematic program of importing performances of theater and drama? Nearby cities such as Konstanz, (Germany) or Bregenz (Austria) maintain art projects from which St. Gallen could profit, and there are organizations in Zürich, with which alliance is possible.

Art patrons of St. Gallen founded an action committee under the title "Save the Stadt Theater"; its campaign was conducted in a vigorous manner. Particularly convincing and effective was the committee's idea to include the young generation in various phases of this campaign. A march of pupils from the elementary schools through the old city was organized. The youngsters were silent, but carried large banners on which the citizens read this anxious question concerning the future of their theater and orchestra:

Theater und Konzertverein
Was wird deine Zukunft sein?

This verse, to be sure, is no serious competition for the poetry of Gottfried Keller or Hermann Hesse, but it is serving its purpose well enough.

Solothurn and Biel

The cooperative Städte-Bund Theater of the two towns Solothurn and Biel receives from these municipalities 254,983 francs. The population is 54,000 in Biel and 17,700 in Solothurn.

Special Subsidies

In addition to the municipal theaters regularly subsidized by cities and cantons, a small number of private Swiss theaters is occasionally aided on a more modest scale. Into this group belong the Komödie in Basel, the Atelier Theater in Bern, and the Comédie in Geneva.

A small subvention from city and canton is received by the Stadt Theater in Chur, which has a capacity of 400 and was opened in 1915.

During the summer, performances out-of-doors enjoy great popularity. There are numerous open-air theaters such as the Théâtre du Chateau in Lausanne, and the Sommer Theater in Winterthur. The Stadt Theater in St. Gallen plays during the summer months in the old resort town of Baden, which in turn contributes a small subvention to the St. Gallen budget. For all of these summer playhouses small subsidies usually suffice. The productions are on a small scale, and vacationers faithfully patronize the performances.

A special case is the Easter play in Lucerne. This festival represents a cherished tradition in Swiss folk theater, dating back to the sixteenth century; for this reason the Easter play is subsidized by the Confederation.

The federal government also contributes to the Theater Sammlung of Bern. The theatrical library contains historical material on the Swiss and foreign stages, suitable for reference and research. A private society owns the collection, but its maintenance is subsidized by the Bund.

III. Swiss Orchestras and Municipal Support

Since the fourteenth century the larger Swiss communities have employed small instrumental ensembles of woodwinds, brass, and drums, which have performed at official occasions. As early as 1385, the city of Basel maintained a band that played on holidays in public squares. Other cities followed suit. In the fifteenth century there was a Stadtpfeiferei in Bern, Zürich, Chur, and St. Gallen. These are antecedents of the regular concert life in modern Switzerland.

Side by side with the instrumental ensembles, choral groups developed all over the country. In 1842, the Eidgenössische Sängerverein was founded. Throughout the nineteenth century, musical activities were supported broadly in every field and medium, in church and school, in theater and concert. They were aided by the canton, the municipality, and the local Verein.

Today, the municipal theaters normally provide the economic foundation for resident orchestras. The double duty of the musicians in theater and concert offers them ample employment and there are opportunities for additional work during the summer months.

The following Swiss cities support full-sized professional orchestras the year-round: Basel, Bern, Geneva, Lucerne, St. Gallen, Winterthur, and Zürich. The organization and financial management of these organizations are private in each city. But canton and municipality normally help to defray expenses. Some of these orchestras regularly give concerts in neighboring communities. In the season 1960-61 the Swiss symphony orchestras gave approximately 250 concerts distributed over a territory of 23 communities.

Geneva: Growth of an Orchestra

The French part of Switzerland possesses the most distinguished orchestra of the nation. Its growth represents the lifework of one dedicated man. The Orchestre de la Suisse romande was envisioned, founded, and developed to its present level by Ernest Ansermet. For half a century the veteran conductor has given to a single community the kind of faithful service that is almost extinct in today's Europe, where prominent music directors are as roving as jet plane connections will permit.

In its early stage, the support of the Orchestre de la Suisse romande stemmed exclusively from private sources. In 1918, Ansermet organized a group of well-to-do citizens who were willing to underwrite the initial operation of a symphony orchestra in Geneva. About 350 people assumed the financial responsibility for the ensemble, which then consisted of 50 first-rate players carefully selected from all over Europe. There was no pressure to engage Swiss musicians, if they were not, in the conductor's judgment, fully qualified for the task. Today, a young generation of Swiss instrumentalists is ready to fill replacements. During the financial depression of the early thirties, when some of the Swiss patrons declared themselves unable to continue their pledges, a difficult period developed. Eventually Radio Geneva was able to assume the role of sponsor. By 1938, the network had raised 400,000 francs to cover the yearly deficit. In exchange for its support, the radio obtained the sole right of broadcasting the orchestra's concerts. There were then 84 players. Today, the strength of the orchestra has risen to 92, permitting an equal division into two groups of 46 players each. Thus, both groups can perform independently if two services of the orchestra are simultaneously needed (for instance, in the radio station and in the municipal theater).

The subsidy for the orchestra is now approaching 2,000,000 francs annually, which may be considered generous by European standards. The major shares of the subvention stem from the municipality (530,000 francs) and from Radio Geneva (540,000 francs). The orchestra gives most concerts at modest prices, and there are free concerts during the summer. An additional income (200,000 francs) is derived from the orchestra's association with Geneva's lyrical theater where 50 performances of opera are given annually. The canton of Geneva gives 370,000 francs; the city of Lausanne, 20,000 francs; the canton of Vaud, 35,000 francs. The Swiss Confederation pays for whatever service the orchestra is asked to perform on national occasions. There are private donors called Friends of the Orchestra.

Swiss cantons and municipalities do not always act jointly in their support of the performing arts. For instance, the city of Geneva and the canton of Geneva act independently. By contrast, the canton and the city of Basel, forming a "city-state," make collective contributions to cultural organizations.

The Orchestre de la Suisse romande serves not only the metropolitan area of Geneva, but the entire region of French Switzerland. As the distance from Lausanne to Geneva is only thirty minutes by train, frequent interchange of performances is feasible. The governing board of the orchestra is autonomous; it reports neither to the canton nor to the city. The musical director is in complete charge of artistic policy. On the foundation's board, which has 50 members, there are representatives of all institutions that employ the orchestra. This board supervises the orchestra's management.

In typical Swiss manner the home industry participates in some of the orchestra's performances. Thus after many hours of precise clock work, the Chorus of Watchmakers joins the Geneva orchestra at rehearsal, and copes here with equally exacting musical demands. The performance of Stravinsky's *Oedipus Rex*, as interpreted by the singing watchmakers and the Orchestre de la Suisse romande under Ansermet's direction, is commercially recorded. The Chorus of Teachers recorded with the same conductor and orchestra the biblical oratorio *King David* by Honegger.

The members of the orchestra have the status of civil servants and enjoy the corresponding privileges and security. At present, the average salary is about $4,000 annually. The municipality of Geneva sells a number of concerts to various syndicates, workers' unions, student groups. In these concerts young Swiss soloists are given a chance to perform.

Canton Basel-Stadt

In a typical pattern of Swiss government, a number of smaller communities near a single metropolitan area are united by a common administration and, consequently, also in the support of the arts. The canton Basel-Stadt is a case in point. The cultural department of this administration has a considerable budget for art and education. We quote a small section of the budget for the year 1958 in Table IV.

TABLE IV

Art and Education Budget of Canton Basel-Stadt (1958)

		Swiss Francs
Boys' Choir (Knabenmusik)		7,800
Art Society		90,000
Orchestra Society		908,300
Courses for Wind Instruments		8,000
Society for Wind Instruments		34,100
Society of the Basel Municipal Theater		
Subvention for general operation	1,765,000	
Guarantee of deficit	50,000	
Pension for members of the Stadt Theater	55,000	
Provision for inflationary increase	75,000	
State contribution toward additional pensions	40,000	
State contribution for salary increases	88,000	
		2,073,000
Society for Musicology		2,000
General Art Fund		80,000
Music Academy		125,000
Music Academy — salary increases		380,000
Musical Credit		15,000
Support of Plastic Arts		1,000
Society for Art and Musical Events		30,000

Basel Konzertverein

Since 1692 Basel has maintained a Collegium Musicum,* offering weekly chamber music for a closed circle of listeners. The eighteenth century brought no decisive development of public concerts in this Swiss city. But in 1826 a society was formed to give concerts in a new large hall, the Stadt-Casino. In 1855 the Kapellverein was founded for the specific purpose of sponsoring in Basel a competent professional orchestra. Soon sufficient funds were raised; the concerts could be attended only by subscribers and their guests. In the 1860's popular concerts were given on Sunday mornings in St. Martin's Church, with tickets available to the public at large. This led in 1876 to the formation of the Allgemeine Musikgesellschaft, which tried to achieve the organizational union of all hitherto isolated musical groups. There was sufficient participation to aid, for many years to come, an orchestra of 38 professional musicians, supplemented by 24 amateurs. After the First World War the Allgemeine Musikgesellschaft could no longer support itself on the basis of private initiative. Hence, the Baselers founded the Konzertverein, an orchestra society which received a modest annual subvention from the canton (30,000 francs).

*Cf. Chapter on West Germany for background of Collegium Musicum.

In subsequent years the orchestra so successfully asserted itself that canton and city decided on an adequate subsidization of the Konzertverein. The contribution for 1957-58 was 930,000 francs; earnings from rentals were 339,000 francs. The total income from all sources was 1,330,000 francs.*

The Basel orchestra is regularly engaged by the Allgemeine Musikgesellschaft for its symphony concerts, by the municipal theater, and by a variety of other music sponsoring groups. All of this adds up to a busy schedule for the orchestra of 71 members (1960). They have six weeks paid vacation during the summer, and all musicians have tenure and retire with adequate pensions. Originally, there was opposition to this kind of a contract. There were those who argued that a policy of permanent tenure might produce a feeling of over-security, that certain musicians would take advantage of their "safe" employment, that tenure would not encourage artistic ambition and performing quality. But experience has shown otherwise. The added security has promoted loyalty and steadiness in the members of the orchestra. There might have been an occasional exception, but the self-censorship of the musicians, who have an interest in maintaining their prestige and standards of workmanship, is a vigilant factor. No musician can shun his responsibilities in rehearsals and performance for long; the environmental pressures have proven to be an efficient corrective.[8]

Private Initiative

A remarkable example of private initiative in Swiss musical life is the Basel Chamber Orchestra. Founded in 1926 by the conductor Paul Sacher, the organization includes today a chamber chorus in addition to the instrumental ensemble. The works commissioned and first performed by the Basel group amount to a significant cross-section of modern music: the catalogue of premières, given over the years by the Basel Chamber Orchestra, includes works of Bartók, Honegger, Hindemith, Ibert, Krenek, Martin, Martinu, Richard Strauss, and Stravinsky. This small orchestra, which has attained international recognition, originated modestly as a workshop for young musicians. In the beginning, amateur performers were in the majority. Today their number is small, and limited to the chorus only.

Several years after the Chamber Orchestra was established, Paul Sacher founded the Schola Cantorum Basiliensis, a school with classes for both children and adults. Amateurs as well as professionals study singing and choral literature; the courses may lead to a diploma. In Zürich, a Collegium Musicum was reorganized,[9] modeled to a certain extent after the Basel Chamber Orchestra. In both cities small groups of civic-minded music lovers raised the necessary funds for the maintenance of these organizations.

Winterthur

The small industrial city of Winterthur (population 70,000) is proud of its outstanding art life. There is, before all, the Winterthur Orchestra, the creation of the late Werner Reinhart, head of an export and import firm. Jointly, with his brothers and a few other wealthy citizens, Werner Reinhart set out to give his town a distinguished artistic profile. He was an art patron who personally took charge of every small detail of the projects he generously sponsored. After his death the city of Winterthur paid Werner Reinhart the kind of tribute he would have hoped for: the municipality decided to subsidize the orchestra permanently.

TABLE V

Winterthur Orchestra Diversified Income (1958)

[Original single gift of Werner Reinhart 4,000,000 francs (approximately $1,000,000)]

Source	Amount	
Reichenberg Foundation	120,000	francs
Chamber of Industry and Commerce	70,000	
Subscriptions	50,000	
Membership	20,000	
Box Office	75,000	
Engagements of Orchestra	100,000	
City of Winterthur	150,000	
Canton of Zürich	30,000	
	615,000	francs

On an annual budget of about 600,000 francs, Winterthur offers a season of 10 subscription concerts in the City Hall, 20 free concerts (likewise in the City Hall), and a number of other scheduled events at various places, all within the city limits.

Winterthur is the seat of an active Music Society, a conservatory, two art galleries, and a folklore museum. Some of the material wealth of the town — the result of a community's close teamwork — is thus channeled back into cultural deeds. Another aspect of art life in this small Swiss city must not be overlooked. Winterthur is only twenty-five kilometres from Zürich. In America, we are only beginning to cultivate in small communities at the periphery of metropolitan centers some semblance of an indigenous art life. In Europe, cultural independence is an eminently characteristic pattern of patronage. And deep cultural roots are decisive in a nation's growth to creative sovereignty.

IV. Swiss Radio and Television

Support of Mass Media

Radio and television are officially under the control of the Swiss Confederation. Theoretically, the various networks are supervised by the Department of Railroads. Yet it is the Federal Department of Post, Telephone and Telegraph (PTT) that provides the radio stations with technical equipment and collects the fees from the listeners. All responsibility for the artistic part of the program falls to the Rundspruchgesellschaft (Radio Society), which is a private organization. This society is granted by the PTT a concession for the use of technical equipment. In return, the Rundspruchgesellschaft forwards to the PTT the greatest part of its revenues derived from listening fees. Every listener pays four francs (approximately $1.00) per year for each radio set. The population of Switzerland is 5,470,000.

Switzerland maintains three principal radio stations, which broadcast in the three main languages* of the Confederation: German, French, and Italian. These stations are Beromünster (German), Sottens (French), Monte Ceneri (Italian).

There are three studios in German-speaking Switzerland: Zürich, Bern, and Basel. There are studios in Geneva and Lausanne for French Switzerland and one in Lugano for Italian Switzerland. The programs of these studios are strongly representative of regional culture; this, as previously explained, is considered imperative in Switzerland. Each of the six studios receives one-sixth of the total national radio income to defray expenses of its operations.

Both Basel and Zürich have a fine record for their "Musical Hours." The Italian station of Monte Ceneri, outside of Lugano, is worthy of special note. Serving primarily the region of the Ticino, the network of Monte Ceneri has the same rights and income as the other Swiss stations; consequently Monte Ceneri can afford to employ a permanent orchestra of forty-two men. Indicative of its potential is the list of composers who have conducted here — among them Strauss, Stravinsky, Hindemith. The capital city of Ticino, Lugano, supports an annual spring festival with renowned guest performers. The considerable deficit is carried jointly by the radio, the city, and the Kursaal Gesellschaft, i.e., by the society in charge of the hall where the concerts take place. Monte Ceneri is building a new studio.

*A fourth language, known as Romansch and indigenous to the canton of Graubünden, is not spoken over any national network.

Television

Swiss television corresponds to radio in its trilingual services which originate in Zürich (German), Geneva (French), and Lugano (Italian), respectively. At present, Zürich telecasts the evening news in three languages, whereas other programs sent from the French or Italian station are sometimes exchanged nationally and heard in the regional language.

Swiss television is operated, like the radio, by the Rundspruchgesellschaft. The Confederation offers subsidies for the television program to cover that part of the expenses which cannot be defrayed by the income derived from licenses. To date, television has remained privately managed. But informed observers expect that the stations will eventually, like the radio, belong to the PTT. During its formative years the Confederation contributed considerable sums for technical experimentation. This experimental period, however, is now considered completed.

The license fee for each television set is $21 annually. The PTT receives one-third of this fee; two-thirds is assigned to defray the costs of producing and administering the programs. The number of television sets is approaching 400,000.

Financial aid to television and radio has come also from the Swiss Society of Newspaper Publishers, under the condition that no commercials be used on television. This works to the advantage of both parties: the papers remain the chief means of advertising, and television is not burdened by the interference of commercials.

In spite of this, plans are underway to sell spot announcements before and after certain weekday programs. But there are to be no sponsors; consequently there is no opportunity to influence the nature of programs.

The Association of Swiss Theaters, in February, 1957, signed a contract with the Swiss Rundspruchgesellschaft. The television section agreed to transmit each season a certain number of productions given by the Swiss theaters. These telecasts originate either directly in one of the studios or on the stage of the participating company. In a still more ambitious project, the Zürich Municipal Theater has staged a certain number of opera productions designed *a priori* for television purposes. The newly planned opera house of Zürich will be equipped with a complete television studio. This project will mark the first regular cooperation between opera and television.

In traditional Swiss fashion, television is supervised by regional and national boards. Representatives of government, the professions, industry, and labor make up the committees.

V. Pro Helvetia

On September 28, 1949, an organization was established to stimulate important aspects of Swiss culture. This foundation assumed the significant title, Pro Helvetia. The national government appointed a permanent commission to guide the policies of the foundation. This board consists of a maximum of twenty-five members, all prominent representatives of Swiss cultural life selected from the three principal ethnical parts of Switzerland (German, French, and Italian).

The basic aims of Pro Helvetia are officially stated as follows: preservation of the spiritual individuality of the country; sponsorship of Swiss cultural creativity based upon free productive forces in the cantons and in the different linguistic territories; sponsorship of mutual cultural exchange among the three different language groups of the nation; propaganda abroad for the understanding of Swiss political philosophy and cultural values.

The decision to administer Pro Helvetia by a government-controlled commission was by no means unopposed. But experience has proven that the role of the Confederation is voluntarily limited to the yearly subvention of 600,000 francs.[10] Consequently, the Parliamentary control is confined to an examination of spending according to the statutes of the foundation. Otherwise Parliament completely respects the independence of Pro Helvetia.

With such ideology of art patronage, cantons and local authorities continue to play the most decisive role. But private art support is probably stronger in Switzerland than anywhere else in Europe. One of the more obvious reasons for the survival of this individual pattern of sponsorship is the simple fact that Switzerland is a rich country where large individual fortunes still exist. Contributions to cultural causes, however, are not tax free.

A Conservative Democracy Supports Art

The knowledge of Swiss traditions guides our understanding of the ideology and structure of Swiss art patronage. It is, in essence, diversified sponsorship shared by cantonal, municipal, and private sources. As we have shown, the role of the Confederation is carefully defined and, for all practical purposes, is a very limited one. We may compare it to the part played by the Swiss federal government in education in that the Bund normally leaves all initiative to the cultural departments of the cantons and cities. This voluntary restriction is reflected by the fact that the Confederation subsidizes only one college (Hochschule) in the country, namely, the Technological Institute of Zürich. Repeatedly, plans to found a national Swiss university were promoted in various regions of the country. The project was always abandoned because of the deep-seated tradition in Swiss political thinking which insists on the sovereignty of cantons and municipalities. Hence, the principal universities of Switzerland remain without federal ties of any kind — in contrast to the schools of higher education in neighboring countries. But even where the Confederation is financially involved, it will not interfere with the independence and private character of supported institutions. In Switzerland there does not exist, as for instance in Austria, federal administration of state theaters; there is no Under-Secretary of Arts and Spectacles, as in Italy; there is no nationally supervised art program, as in France.

Switzerland is a conservative country. The Right and Center parties and a few independents make up the political majority. There is strong anticommunist sentiment. It may express itself in local decrees, prohibiting performances of artists from the Soviet Union or other communistic nations. Yet even in this issue, the independence of Swiss cantons and cities is reflected in curiously conflicting policies. Thus one can watch the Moscow Ballet or the Peiping Theater in Basel, in Lugano, or in the capital Bern, but not in Zürich, the nation's most cosmopolitan city with extensive industries and a large population of workers.

We have shown how the structure of Swiss democracy is built from the bottom up. It rises from the small village to towns and large cities, from the community to the canton, and from the canton to the Confederation. This order points precisely to the structural patterns along which Swiss art support functions. These historically conditioned strata of their patronage suit the temperament and outlook of the Swiss. They are convinced that their system of art subsidy is so well entrenched that even a change in political structure would not basically alter their traditional ways of aiding their art organizations. The Swiss see that their administrators and artistic directors are men of integrity. As a result, we observe in numerous communities of this democratic nation an uninterrupted and steadily progressing art life, which the Swiss regard with great pride, and which the rest of the world respects.

FRANCE

I. The Great Change
New Art Patronage for a New Age

The great nation which enriched Europe with a new concept of freedom also emerged from history as the pioneer of a new kind of art patronage. On July 14, 1789, when the people of Paris stormed the Bastille — the state prison that had become the sinister symbol of ruthless government — an ancient regal system broke down, seemingly forever. The French Revolution annihilated a social order which for ages had appeared firm and fixed. The people called a National Assembly to establish a revival of order along untried directions.

Inexperienced in holding the reins of government, the citizens of France gradually became heirs to the powerful controls and absolute privileges which had hitherto been the domain of the ruling Bourbons and the long line of their predecessors. At the same time the French people were the beneficiaries of priceless art treasures, of fabulous collections and magnificent palaces. And eventually they became the trustees and possessors of the orphaned court theaters.

What would all this mean in terms of art patronage? Many grave questions arose. What did the arts have to offer the people, who were now the masters of the land? As to the performing arts, was there any sense in continuing to sponsor the kind of drama and music that had delighted the court and its aristocratic guests in the luxurious surroundings of the palace and gardens in Versailles or the Palais Royal in Paris? A negative answer was a foregone conclusion. But there was a vacuum. One had to invent art forms which, at this crucial phase, could convey new messages of meaning to thousands of free people, among whom so many were uneducated and even illiterate. Their enjoyment of the arts needed guidance.

These turbulent years at the close of the eighteenth century were filled, for the first time in modern history, with frantic efforts to direct the arts toward hopefully envisioned political ends. Certain patterns that developed in these years from a new relationship between the performing arts and their sole patronage by the people were to serve as models in a distant future. History frequently repeated on European soil the drama of collapsing monarchies succeeded by peoples' democracies. Sometimes these transitions have been relatively controlled; at other times they have been violent and shamelessly indifferent to the values of human life. The arts have always reflected the social drama.

After the fall of the Bastille, France attempted a clear start in a new social organization. It was, before all, a task of fraternization and equalization of the citizenry, the like of which the Old World had never known before. Overnight, new patterns of living and planning had to be discovered.

A new way of life had to reinterpret the function of the arts. No longer serving as the enjoyment of the ruling court, the arts were now expected to speak to all, to teach as well as to entertain the people. Could such aims produce true works of art, or were old standards no longer important?

The story of post-Revolutionary art patronage answers these questions. First, however, it is best to assess the magnitude of the change by comparing the new era of art sponsorship following the Revolution with the old one that preceded it — during the reigns of the last three French kings, a total of one hundred forty-six years.

II. Grandeur of Patronage

Court of Louis XIV

The three pre-Revolution kings — Louis XIV, known as *Le Roi Soleil*, his great-grandson Louis XV, and the hapless King Louis XVI — were art sponsors of munificence. Comedy and tragedy, serious and comic opera, the concert and the ballet all were their immediate interest.

The long reign of Louis XIV (1643-1715) has been called with justification *L'Age d'Or;* it was the Golden Age of French art. In French annals no single chief of state, monarch or republican president, has a comparably brilliant record as art patron. Louis spared nothing toward the support of the arts. The significant French art of his era is court art par excellence, glorifying the King and his kingdom. The taste of the strongly narcissistic King, his likes and idiosyncracies, became the principal standards of evaluation. And so court art was pompous and elegant, worldly and brilliant. The courtiers, the wealthy aristocrats of France, and even the affluent bourgeoisie, eagerly imitated the gestures of regal grandeur. It was an advantage for the arts that their encouragement from the King was shared fully by the nobility.

The King's patronage was autocratic, but it was also phenomenally productive. The artistic results of court art are beyond reproach. Among the creative artists sponsored by Louis XIV, one enjoyed a special role, the painter Charles Le Brun (1619-1690). He was empowered with all important decisions regarding art life in Versailles and Paris. Le Brun responded shrewdly by directing the arts toward extraordinary encomiums of his sovereign. It was really Le Brun who helped to create what is known today as the *Style of Louis XIV*. Appointed First Painter of the King in 1662, Le Brun became the first artist of France to have dictatorial status. Modern aesthetics cannot accept Delacroix's evaluation of Le Brun as the greatest painter of France. But it seems that without Le Brun the remarkable court art of the Sun King could not have come to full fruition.

Versailles: Summit of Court Art

Louis XIV founded the great French institutions devoted to the performing arts: the Comédie Française, the Opéra, and the Opéra Comique. The King's patronage of Molière and Lully, of Racine and Corneille remains the most impressive aspect of his period — overshadowed as it was otherwise by questionable domestic and foreign policies. The King had a flare for the theater, and an obvious talent for acting. He played with a certain mastery the role in real life that he obviously envisioned for himself — that of Roi Soleil. Royal patronage was rooted in a search for self-identification. The King perpetuated his own image in countless manifestations of court art.

"L'état, c'est moi" ("I am the state") is the often-quoted, remarkably succinct definition by which Louis XIV epitomized in the shortest of phrases an enormous claim. Whatever its political implications, the Sun King was bound to search for a grandiose architectural representation of his monarchial absolutism. Versailles, the palace which the King built for himself twelve miles southwest of Paris, stands, indeed, as a lasting memorial to the pomp of court life in the Golden Age. But Versailles is not merely a palace. It is an early example of planning a residence with the environmental details of architecture and landscape incorporated in the original blueprint. Thus we see at Versailles, built by a team of court architects, the royal residence surrounded by spacious formal gardens and a net of avenues, squares, and parks, imaginatively supporting the overall ground plan of the King's dwellings. Approached by a wide expansive road through the town, the palace rises before one's eyes in all its resplendence — the monument of royal grandeur, the architectural evocation of the Golden Age.

The palace and its gardens became the envy of visiting monarchs and wealthy princes. Some of them tried to copy Versailles at their own residences. The palace of Prince Eszterházy, called the *Versailles of the East*, located at the Austrian-Hungarian border, was inspired by a visit of this nobleman to France. Also, the castle of Schönbrunn, the Habsburg summer residence of serene repose in Vienna's west end, was copied after the luxurious French model. Other European estates, too, show the Baroque influence of Versailles: here, with their continuous chain of balconies and terraces overlooking extensive formal gardens; there, with mirrored halls and long shining corridors decorated with Gobelins or large-sized paintings.

But most important, the style of court life at Versailles, its theaters, its festivities in- and out-of-doors, the munificence of French art patronage raised art standards all over the Continent.

Tragédie Classique

French drama blossomed at a decisive phase of European literature. When the inspired period of the Elizabethan theater in England began its decline, France was ready to assume hegemony in Europe's theater. The lasting contribution of the era of Louis XIV to the world stage is the Tragédie Classique. The triumvirate of French dramatists in the Golden Age consisted of Corneille (1606-1684), Molière (1622-1673), and Racine (1639-1699). In their works French drama adopted the Aristotelian principles of the three basic unities of time, place, and action.

Corneille turned from the writing of comedy on contemporary manners to full-fledged tragedy. His *Cid* is an heroic play of great consequence for future dramatic thought; it is the incarnation of flaming will power conquering all obstacles. The heroic theme was repeatedly varied in art works of later periods. But Louis XIV commissioned Corneille to write "machine plays," modeled after the technical resources of the Italian theater, stupefying tricks and gadgets for realistic and magical effects, and put the noted Italian engineer, Giacomo Torelli, in charge of stage machinery. For certain productions Le Brun painted the decorations. This begins the spectacular decor of French productions. The practice of enlisting the services of great painters for the theater still prevails in modern France.

Jean Racine won his first success as a young man. The poet accompanied with verse good and bad days in the life of his sovereign. For the wedding of Louis XIV, Racine contributed the ode *La Nymphe de la Seine*. The King's recovery from an illness (1663) inspired another ode. Both poems were handsomely compensated with 600 livres each. The reciprocal relationship between patron and poet must seem trivial as an exchange of verses for money. But what matters here is the quality of the artistic product. The King's choice of a court artist favored one of the great poets of the French language.

But art life in Versailles entailed other facets beyond such simple give and take. It was as fraught with intrigue as theater life is likely to be. Jealousy demanded a heavy toll; the entourage of the King tried to play politics with the artists and to use them for various schemes. Idolatry of the sovereign did not always guarantee success and protection. The artists at court competed with each other for status. At the Palais

Royal, Molière's troupe performed Racine's first drama, *La Thébaïde.* But Racine agreed to the performance of his play *Alexandre le Grand* by a rival company installed at the Hôtel de Bourgogne. This terminated the friendship of Molière and Racine; at the same time it promoted new rivalry between Racine and Corneille.

The Birth of Comédie Française Molière's Troupe du Roi

The one-and-a-half decades from 1658 to 1673, which mark the activities of Molière at court, are often viewed as the most decisive in French theatrical history. These were the years when comedy replaced tragedy. Molière's familiar works, with their penetrating social criticism hidden behind layers of humor, are a perennial gift of the French theater to the world stage.

Some credit for the sponsorship of Molière must be given to Prince de Conti, who helped the actor-playwright to a new start when he was released from debtors' prison and changed his name from Jean-Baptiste Poquelin to Molière, returning somewhat anonymously to Paris in 1658.

Molière's organization of a small theatrical company at this time is the embryonic stage of what was to become known as the *Comédie Française.* There were ten players when Molière first appeared before Louis XIV on October 24, 1658. Seven years later, in 1665, Molière's company was promoted to the status of the "troupe du roi," and was installed in the Palais Royal. The next eight years marked the summit of dramatic performance at court. Molière needed for the incidental music of his plays a collaborator with an innate sense of the theater. He found him in Jean-Baptiste Lully (1632-1687), a great composer who in his youth had immigrated to Paris from Florence.

In *Le Bourgeois gentilhomme* Molière and Lully jointly created a delightful comedy with music, deriding the *nouveau riche.* In *Les Précieuses ridicules* Molière went further and poked fun at the affected ladies at court. His ridicule of the clergy and of the professions (particularly physicians) was a calculated risk. Was the Sun King fully aware of all implications of Molière's satire, or was he too limited to understand the subtlety? Whatever the answer, his support of the playwright remained staunch to the very end.

The death of Molière on February 17, 1673, temporarily terminated this unique chapter of the French theater. But the King was determined that Molière's company should continue to perform, in spite of the loss of its guiding spirit. He ordered the fusion of Molière's troupe with the Théâtre du Marais; it was accomplished on June 23, 1673.

Seven years later, on August 25, 1680, Louis XIV issued another royal decree which formed one single company from the troupes installed in the Palais Royal and the Hôtel de Bourgogne. This is an historic date in the development of French theater: it marks the official birthday of the Comédie Française. A complete reorganization brought a more stable structure. There were now 28 comedians: 15 actors and 13 actresses, who represented the first permanent group associated with the theater. Later, a pension of 12,000 livres was guaranteed to each actor. This provision of August 24, 1682, might well represent the first instance of social security for members of the stage.

If Corneille, Racine, and Molière created the French theater by the strength of their genius, the Comédie Française as sponsored by Louis XIV gave it in the final decades of the seventeenth century its lasting organizational framework.

The company of actors had many homes before they were installed in the Jeu de Paume de l'Étoile (today known as the *rue de L'Ancienne Comédie*). Here this group of Royal Comedians permanently assumed the name that has come down to us with so much meaning; the Comédie Française remained in the same hall for eighty-one years.

In 1699 a company of players from Italy called *Comédie Italienne* decided to settle in Paris. The Comédie Française objected to this foreign competition and filed formal protest to the King. The episode marks an early example of xenophobia in the art world. But the King refused to grant the Comédie Française its claim to a monopoly based on priority and French birthright and permitted the Comédie Italienne to play in Paris. This was an intelligent decision and a remarkably antichauvinistic one. Ever since, the patronage of Italian art has remained a vital factor on French soil. As to the much feared competition, it worked in a manner unforeseen by the plaintiffs; for both parties — the Italians and the French — learned from each other, and Parisian theater life gradually assumed the cosmopolitan flavor which to this day is one of its most refreshing features.

Court Ballet

In 1661 Louis XIV appointed Jean-Baptiste Lully to the key position of Royal Composer of Instrumental Music. In 1662 his assignment was extended. Lully became Maitre de Musique de la Famille Royale. His diversified duties included the composition of scores for court ballet. Lully collaborated with Molière between the years 1664 and 1671 on the art form identified as the *Comédie-ballet*. He infused his scores for this genre with vocal music; some of these works clearly anticipate later developments in French opera.

Under the guidance of Lully the French court ballet achieved artistic definition and its claim to excellence — impeccable technique of the dancers. In a typical Latin sense, it was virtuoso dancing; court ballet had not yet developed a style of choreographic expressiveness.

Lully was equally successful in organizing orchestral performance. His string ensemble of 24 *Violons du Roi* became the finest in Europe. As its conductor, Lully introduced new playing techniques, insisting on unity of bowing to enforce a strict discipline of phrasing. The Sun King and his court were the first spectators to see an opera orchestra in performance, for Lully moved his instrumentalists from their hidden position backstage to a conspicuous placc in front of the stage.

Establishment of French Court Opera

The Chapter on Italy surveyed the origin of opera during the Florentine Renaissance. This new secular art form was introduced to France by an Italian-born patron, Cardinal Mazarin, who had known the enchantment of opera during his youth in Rome. The powerful statesman-priest persuaded Louis XIV to sponsor this newest musical development. As a result, the opera *La finta pazza* by Francesco Sacrati was produced in Paris on December 14, 1645; and during the Carnival season of the following year, the opera *Egisto* by Francesco Cavalli was heard. French artists became excited about the possibilities of the music-drama, and now wished to produce similar works composed in the French language and performed by a French company. The poet Pierre Perrin and the organist Robert Cambert collaborated in a "pastoral" for the musical stage. It was not a work of consequence, but it led to crucial developments.

On June 28, 1669, Louis XIV signed a decree authorizing Perrin to assume the headship of an organization devoted specifically to the performance of theatrical works with music, in Paris or elsewhere. But this was not yet a subsidized undertaking. Perrin merely obtained from the King the privilege of performing opera; and the enterprising poet ended up in debtors' prison. Thus he learned early what it means to finance opera: such a venture was, and still is, a poor risk for a private sponsor. On March 13, 1672, the King transferred the privilege of producing opera to Lully.

The title of the new lyrical theater was to be *L'Académie Royale de Musique*. The appellation *Académie* for an art institute was timely. Louis XIII and Louis XIV founded, in succession, the French Academy of Language and Literature (1635); the Royal Academy of Painting and Sculpture (1648); the Academy of the Dance (1662); the Academy of Belles-Lettres (1663); the French Academy at Rome (1665); the Academy of Science (1666); the Academy of Architecture (1671).

The repertory of the Académie Royale de Musique (later the *Opéra*) contained lyrical performances in French as well as in Italian. The first performance was *Les Fêtes de l'Amour et de Bacchus* (1672) composed and produced by Lully. The success of Lully's lyrical productions prompted Louis XIV, toward the end of his long reign, to establish a fund of 15,000 livres for the continuous maintenance of opera. He also granted 10,000 livres for pensions of the artists belonging to the Académie, and signed this progressive decree on January 11, 1713.

The very last year of the Sun King witnessed the foundation of another important lyrical stage. But it was essentially private sponsorship, initiated by Saint-Edme and Madame Baron, that organized a company to be called *Théâtre National de l'Opéra Comique.* We shall trace later the evolutionary phases of this institute destined to play a decisive role in the history of the musical stage.

Royal Concerts

The cultivated atmosphere of social gatherings at the royal court led to the patronage of regular concerts at Versailles. The eminent composer François Couperin (1668-1733), appointed Ordinaire de la Musique de la Chambre du Roi, organized and conducted these afternoon events. The *Concerts Royaux* (as Couperin specifically called the works performed at the palace) were intended as an homage to Louis XIV. As the composer himself explained: "The following pieces are rather different from the music I have previously written. They are not written for the harpsichord alone, but include the violin, flute, oboe, viol, and bassoon. I have composed these pieces for the command performances of chamber music given almost every Sunday of the year. They were performed by MM. Duval, Philidor, Alarius, Dubois; and I played the harpsichord. If they [the pieces] meet with as much approval from the public as they have from the late King, I could publish them in several complete volumes. I have arranged the music in order of their keys, and kept the name [*Concerts Royaux*] under which these concerts were known at Court in 1714 and 1715."

III. The Regency
Louis XV and Louis XVI

From 1715 to 1723 Philip of Orleans was ruler of France. This is the period known as the Regency; it bridges the reign of Louis XIV and that of his great-grandson, Louis XV.

The Court moved from Versailles to Paris. Prince Philip made his home in the Palais Royal. The boy-king, Louis XV, lived in the

Tuileries. Here he watched with youthful joy the royal ballet, and eventually performances of opera and drama. This interest in the theater remained with Louis XV throughout his mature years. As King he gave the Opéra a fine home in the Tuileries. In the serene environment of the Pavillon de Flore the Opéra was housed from 1764 to 1770. It moved into the Palais Royal in 1770, where it remained until 1821.

In Versailles, Louis XV added a small opera house to the palace. The opening celebrated the wedding of his grandson, the Dauphin and future King Louis XVI, to the Austrian Princess Marie Antoinette. The opera *Persée* by Lully was chosen for the festive occasion. In the design of the delightful, small Versailles theater, the architect Jacques-Ange Gabriel departed from the traditional rectangular ground plan. Instead, he conceived an intimate Opéra in oval shape, the interior decorated elegantly with golden balustrades and grilles, with fine wooden panels and fluted pillars.

The Fifth Republic has recently restored the Versailles Court Opéra to its past brilliance. The historic theater is, in fact, occasionally used for special performances.

The City of Paris Sponsors the Opéra

The most significant French master of Baroque opera was Jean-Philippe Rameau (1683-1764). Curiously, he had reached the age of fifty without attaining prestige beyond that of a distinguished theorist. Yet his first opera, *Hippolyte et Aricie* (1733), was received with deserved esteem. His subsequent works for the lyrical stage — *Les Indes galantes*, *Dardanus*, and *Castor et Pollux* — are today recognized as masterworks. Rameau had to endure much opposition. The era of Louis XIV, when the word of the royal sovereign was tantamount to undisputed patronage, was gone forever. As an opera composer, Rameau was ridiculed by the followers of Lully and became involuntarily involved in the fight of two opposing factions, French and Italian opera enthusiasts waging the "guerre des bouffons." In 1745, at the age of 62, Rameau was appointed Royal Composer of Chamber Music. In the same year his setting of Voltaire's *La Princesse de Navarre* was performed in Versailles.

The Versailles Opéra, to be sure, was merely a luxurious addition to the already existing Académie Royale de Musique, which had become the principal opera theater of Paris. The support and administration of this art institute were to undergo far-reaching changes.

In 1749 the city of Paris, for the first time in history, obtained the concession of the Académie Royale. Thus the municipality became involved gradually in the destiny of the most famous lyrical theater of France. The Opéra retained its official name, *Académie Royale de Musique*, which can still be read today on the ornate façade over its main entrance. By 1757 the city of Paris conceded the privilege of managing the opera to two associate directors. Ten years later the municipality decided to contribute a yearly subvention of 80,000 livres to the theater. This marks the first regular annual subvention on record to the Paris Opéra.

The administrators, appointed by the municipality, did not long remain solvent. They soon found out — as did Pierre Perrin a century earlier — that opera is a most expensive proposition. With all of its glamor, it does not pay its way. Understandably, the concessionaires became alarmed after the deficit ran up to 720,000 livres. This crisis brought a temporary end to municipal patronage of opera.

The royal purse was opened again. On March 17, 1780, King Louis XVI brought the art institute once more under the exclusive tutelage of the crown. Henceforth, the Paris Opéra was to experience good and bad times. But the continuity of its subsidy was never seriously challenged.

Opéra Comique

The opéra comique as one of the principal genres of the French musical theater traces its ancestry far back — at least to the so-called *sotie*, a satirical farce of the Middle Ages. There were other antecedents such as the allegorical satires and morality plays of the Renaissance.

Henry IV, the first king of the art-loving Bourbons, established, on May 9, 1596, the right of a small traveling troupe to play on a primitive stage at the Fair of St. Germain. The visitors presented a new kind of comedy with music which delighted popular audiences. These performances, simple as they were, anticipated certain characteristics of the later opéra comique. In St. Germain, however, competition and professional intrigue endangered the very existence of the traveling company. All fun, for the time being, was restricted to the platform of the Fair itself. The regular Comedians (the Parisian group installed at the Hôtel de Bourgogne) felt threatened in their position. They asked the prison officials of Paris to prosecute the itinerant performers for their encroachment. But the King upheld the rights of the visitors, provided their performances were "lawful and honorable, without offending any person's feelings." The travelers continued to perform "honorably." They did not hurt anyone's feelings, except those of their competitors. There followed many more attempts to manipulate the prevailing official rules, in order to obstruct the performances of the itinerants. One rule forbade them to sing; another to speak prose or verse. Soon, there were restrictions forbidding them to play pantomime. One wonders what the itinerants were permitted to do — in fact, how they were able to survive at all. But survive they did, because they created a genre of musical theater that was vital in itself.

In later phases of its evolution the new art form combined music and drama: a blend of brief arias alternated with spoken dialogues. The plays gave expression to simple feelings, to human and realistic situations which differed from those of the *opera seria* with its mythological themes and miraculous solutions.

Here was a musical theater close to the people. But in spite of this, the fate of the Opéra Comique was continuously shadowed by insecurity. Moving from place to place, its theater closed and reopened its doors several times. When King Louis XV saw to it that thc opéra comique was installed in a proper hall the company could perform with a professional orchestra, and give works by composers whose names still carry weight: Duri, Philidor, Monsigny.

In 1762 the King ordered the fusion of the Opéra Comique with an Italian troupe, which had enchanted Paris with its performances of *La Serva Padrona*, the comic masterpiece by the Neapolitan composer, G. B. Pergolesi. From this union of the two groups — the Comédie Italienne and the Opéra Comique—one single group emerged and was temporarily housed in the Hôtel de Bourgogne.

Associated Actors as Pensioners

The King's interest in opera by no means implied a decrease of his support of the legitimate theater. He favored the participation of the members of the Comédie Française in the administration.

In 1737, the *sociétaires*, as the senior actors were called, obtained the legal status of civil employees. At this time, an annuity of 1,000 livres was guaranteed to each member after twenty years of service; it was increased to 1,500 after thirty years. In exchange for these favorable conditions of employment, the Comédie Française was obliged to perform every night.

In 1759 the young actors called *aspirants* were invited to assist the senior actors in their administrative activities. The "associated actors" automatically became eligible for pensions. These are important steps on the road to stability and security for the personnel of the French theater.

Grandes Dames as Art Patrons
Marquise de Pompadour

The role of women as art patrons asserted itself relatively late on the European scene. Ancient civilization was predominantly masculine; art life was exclusively governed by men. Obviously, the Middle Ages was not a time of far-reaching ascent in the status of womanhood. But during the Renaissance aristocratic ladies began to make their influence felt on various cultural fronts. Their function in society was no longer carefully circumscribed. Their social importance grew in proportion to their talent, intellect, and humanistic education.

From northern Italy the emancipation of women spread fast to other parts of Europe. This development culminated in eighteenth-century France, where some *grandes dames* attained a social status even superior to that of men. Employing their varied attractions to best advantage, these ladies of the Bourbon era had come a long way in emancipation from French Catholic traditions.

The era of Louis XV witnessed a spectacular rise of women as powerful art patrons. It was not an entirely unmixed blessing when Jeanne Poisson, better known as the Marquise de Pompadour, the King's mistress, ruled court artists the way she ruled Louis XV and his ministers. The list of personalities included in her circle is an almost complete catalogue of contemporaries who were significant in their respective fields. In 1745 Voltaire was appointed Royal Historian through her influence.

There was little in the background of the Marquise to suggest her role as art patron and leading lady of court society. To quote Saint-Beuve: "She had been taught everything except morals, which would have stood in her way." Prussia's King Frederick the Great referred to her only as "Mademoiselle Poisson" ("Miss Fish"), implying that a fishwife was now ruling the Court of Louis XV. But in eighteenth-century France women frequently rose by virtue of their lack of virtue.

Emergence of the Salon

The new role of women as art patrons was accompanied by a related phenomenon, the "salon." The spectacle of the Marquise de Pompadour holding forth as the powerful hostess of social gatherings had its precedents as well as its consequences. It was soon imitated and multiplied: the drawing rooms of French nobility and of affluent bourgeoisie became the places where the careers of artists were made or thwarted. The salon became the *bourse*, the stock market to assess values and to confirm standards in judging art. Scientific and even philosophical ideas were aired in the salon. Sometimes the meetings and discussions in these drawing rooms resulted in actual policies of state.

It is difficult to pinpoint the emergence of the salon with historical precision. But the Marquise de Rambouillet deserves credit as a pioneer of this institution. She was the daughter of the French ambassador to the Vatican. She married and settled in Paris. Soon the finesse of her gatherings, as well as her social grace and talents, attracted aristocrats, artists, intellectuals, and politicians to her home. Corneille read his *Polyeucte* to her guests. The Marquise treated all with equality. This attitude was liberal; for the era of the Sun King it was daring. But the Marquise set out to prove that talent and accomplishment were equal to any birthright and inherited noble rank; the era of condescension — where the patron lorded over his protégé — was beginning to wane in France. The Marquise also played her part in the intellectual emancipation of women, encouraging them to participate in the exchange of ideas. She elevated the art of conversation to a new level of refinement and brilliance.

By the middle of the eighteenth century the maintenance of the salon was no longer the prerogative of the high aristocracy. An outstanding salon was maintained by Madame Geoffrin. While she was not received at court, her house on the rue Saint Honoré was visited by royalty, diplomats, artists, and scientists in search of sponsors for their projects. On Mondays, painters such as Boucher, Chardin, and Latour might meet prospective buyers and collectors at her parties. On Wednesdays, members of the *Encyclopédiste* movement met here with other literary figures. It was Madame Geoffrin who helped to finance the publication of the French *Encyclopédie*, one of the great intellectual enterprises of the century. Musicians — from the child Mozart on his first Paris visit to Rameau at the summit of his career — called on Madame Geoffrin in her *palais*, known as the *realm of rue Saint-Honoré.*

The Parisian salon did not lack its ridiculous aspects. Competition between powerful ladies flared high. The principal rival of Madame Geoffrin was the Marquise du Deffand, who received in the rue Saint Dominique. It was considered a grave act of disloyalty, punishable with loss of patronage, if one of her regular protégés crossed the borderline into the *realm of rue Saint-Honoré.* Madame Geoffrin was as vital a patroness as she was a vitriolic enemy. Many of the noted polemic writers of the time met in her house.

Before long, the sponsorship of artists became a tool in the hands of aggressive women striving for another rung on the social ladder. This adjunct to the art life of eighteenth-century France has to an astonishing extent survived to this very day and it has spread from France to other countries. Wherever it functions, it is a tragicomic sidelight on the artist's role in a free society that his fortune may depend on the way he is received and launched by the salon.

Marie Antoinette

Marquise de Pompadour, mistress of Louis XV, represents the usurped and illegitimate power of an upstart; but Marie Antoinette, last Queen of France, was an art patron by upbringing, inclination, and knowledge.

Under the reign of her husband, Louis XVI, the royal art institutes of France enjoyed great support. A hostile clique accused the Queen of squandering vast fortunes on what was derided as "court entertainment." Her participation in the theater, both as an actress and as a passionate observer, and her great love for music were the authentic heritage of the Austrian princess.

Marie Antoinette (1755-1793) was the ninth child of the Habsburg empress Maria Theresia. In Vienna, the great reformer of opera Gluck had been her music teacher. Her marriage to the Dauphin on May 16, 1770, was celebrated with the inauguration of the Versailles Opéra. In 1772 Gluck arrived in Paris, and his former pupil, then still the Dauphine, watched over his artistic fate in the capital. In 1774 (the year Marie Antoinette became Queen of France) Gluck's *Iphigénie en Aulide* was produced at the Paris Opéra. Marie Antoinette reported the event to her sister Marie Christine in a letter dated April, 1774: "A great triumph, my dear Christine! On the 19th [of April] we had the première of *Iphigénie:* I was enthralled by it. The people can no longer talk about anything else. Everyone is excited because of this event. . . . It is incredible, there are disagreement and quarrels, as though the issue were a religious one. At court, although I publicly expressed myself in favour of this inspired work, there are partisans and discussions of unusual liveliness. In the city it is still worse."

As an enthusiastic supporter of Gluck, the Queen's patronage of the lyrical theater centered on serious opera. Yet some interest in the Opéra Comique made itself felt indirectly. On January 26, 1789, Leonard Autié, hairdresser of the Queen, received permission to organize an opera company in the Théâtre de Monsieur, at the royal palace of the Tuileries. The repertory was to be diversified, reaching from French opéra comique to the Italian opera buffa. Giovanni Battista Viotti became the artistic director of this musical theater, and Luigi Cherubini its principal composer-conductor.

Meanwhile, Marie Antoinette had also been active on the legitimate stage. In 1779 she commissioned the architect Mique to build the charming theater on the palace grounds at Versailles. The Queen had chosen the small pavilion of the Petit Trianon as her favorite residence, particularly during the warm season. On August 19, 1784, Marie Antoinette played in this theater the leading role of Rosine in the comedy *Le Barbier de Seville* by Beaumarchais. The author of the comedy attended this performance.

Théâtre Français
The Marriage of Figaro

Patronage of the theater remained a prerogative of the royal family. In October, 1780, Monsieur, brother-in-law of Marie Antoinette, laid the ground stone for the new hall eventually known as *Salle Luxembourg.* The cost of the project, completed in 1782, was 2,000,000 francs. On the façade of the theater was written in large gold letters: "Théâtre Français." It contained 1,900 seats. The audience was permitted to sit in the *parterre* (i.e., the floor), which was a novelty for this prerevolutionary epoch.* The first seasons of the Théâtre Français were auspicious in many ways. We learn that the actors earned 75,000 livres in the initial month alone. This was considered a large income.

The third season of the Théâtre Français offered the première of a new comedy, *Le Mariage de Figaro* by Beaumarchais. The history-making event took place on April 27, 1784. The success was sensational. For five years the author had fought for the right to have his play performed, but the King was apprehensive. Was the text not "revolutionary," replete with social criticism? Did the play not try to show an overbearing aristocracy shallow in pleasures and heartless in their pursuits? It was true, Louis XIV had once tolerated Molière's satire, but times had changed. Louis XVI, by contrast, believed that he could not afford to patronize Beaumarchais' play, although its themes were treated in a feather-light manner and its conflicts were amiably resolved, avoiding frontal attack on authority.

But legalities and a set of circumstances finally forced the King to permit the performance of *Figaro.* It was an ironical spectacle when the aristocrats applauded the comedy and laughed at the mirror picture of their own manners. Members of the royal family, nobility and bourgeoisie alike, filled the theater every night that *Figaro* was given. The impact of these performances on the contemporary audiences was evaluated as elementary.

Twenty-one years after the première, Count Antoine Daru summarized its consequences in a speech before the French Academy (1805): "It was on this very day that the Revolution was made! The masses would not have dared to shake off their shackles which the powers had imposed on the entire nation. One applauded the satire because one wished to disdain authority."

Gustave Flaubert in his *Dictionary of Accepted Ideas* called *Le Mariage de Figaro* "another of the causes of the French Revolution."[1] These are eloquent tributes to the power of the theater.

*The prices were reduced to a more popular range, from one livre, ten sous to six livres (for orchestra and box seats).

IV. The Revolution

Patronage in Transition

Events following Bastille Day, July 14, 1789, brought infinite confusion to the world of art. There were both enthusiasm, and fear; there were attempts at new organizations, and chaos. It could not have been otherwise, considering the everchanging viewpoints within the revolutionary movement itself and the conflicting ideologies of its leaders.

Yet gradually, certain concepts of the purpose and function of art within a new society came to the fore. New ideas about interdependence between patronage and creative achievement developed. And there began a search for art forms that would be suitable for the festivities that the revolutionary movement inaugurated for the benefit of the people.

In the first phase of the revolution the royal edifice of patronage retained its basic structure. The great national theaters of France, as created by the Bourbons, continued to function and were well subsidized. Paris had five theaters. Three of them — the Comédie Française, the Académie Royale de Musique, and Opéra Comique — had attained great popular prestige.

The initial revolutionary years saw the artists of France strongly divided in their loyalties. Louis XVI was still king; for the time being he wielded some power. He was still the first patron of the nation. And so the artists, just as any other group of Frenchmen, followed the antagonistic trends of politics to the right or to the left.

The first test case of loyalty came soon. On November 4, 1789, the Théâtre Français gave the première of the tragedy *Charles IX* by Marie-Joseph Chénier. The play centers around the historic, infamous massacre of the Huguenots on St. Bartholomew's Eve, August 24, 1572. The superficial analogy in the play — a king involved in the slaughter of his citizens — sufficed to incite antiroyalist outbursts from the audience. The newly-installed mayor of Paris had tried to forbid the performance. But the National Assembly interceded, and the première took place as scheduled. *Charles IX* was not a good play; Parisians discovered significance, however, in its message. A young actor, François-Joseph Talma, appeared in the leading part. The senior members of the Théâtre Français, obviously encouraged by the King, demanded the dismissal of the revolutionary Talma from the company and the withdrawal of the play from the repertory.

Two different concepts of loyalty competed: faithfulness to Louis XVI as royal patron, or to the National Assembly as the new sponsor of public art life. For the time being, the issue was decided by the municipality of Paris, which ordered the reinstatement of Talma, closed the theater to forestall further riots, and eventually assumed full patronage of the King's theater.

Liberty of Theaters

In this transitional phase there still existed two fountainheads of official patronage and two companies of actors. But the decree of the Convention (January 13, 1791) officially proclaimed the liberty of the French theaters. From this time on, plays with direct or indirect praise of royalty were no longer tolerated on the French stages. Yet one could still read on advertising bills the announcement: "Theater of the Nation, Regular Comedians of the King." These royalists were under the leadership of the actor François-René Mollé. The revolutionary actors were guided by Talma, who installed his group in the Palais Royal. They announced the reopening for April 25, 1791, calling themselves *Théâtre Français de la rue de Richelieu.*

Both organizations wasted much effort on their mutual hostilities. But the trials of treason terminated the King's role as patron, and brought a temporary end to the royal status of the French stages. Talma's theater assumed a title bespeaking the epochal turn of events: *Théâtre de la Liberté et de l'Égalité.* The lengthy name was soon shortened to *Théâtre de la Nation.*

On September 21, 1792, royalty was officially abolished in France. At the time of the dreadful massacres, which had started early in that month, most of the royalist actors were arrested. As staunch supporters of the defunct monarchy, they were daring even on the stage: the actors alluded to the revolutionary leaders, particularly to Robespierre and Marat, with biting disdain. Considering the bloodthirstiness of the Revolutionary Tribunal, capital punishment for the royalists was an almost foregone conclusion. The unexpected happened. The little-known actor Labussie, serving as copyist of one of the revolutionary committees, showed unsuspected courage and also talent in his new role as a public defender. He saved the necks of his colleagues. Their theater, however, did not resume performances until years later.

The revolutionary upheavals that had caused so much distress to national playhouses did not affect the Opéra and the Opéra Comique to a comparable extent. The personnel of these lyrical theaters had been politically more neutral than their colleagues from the legitimate stage. And so most musicians were spared the ordeal of political trials.

In terms of support, the revolutionary government proved to be rather favorably disposed to the needs of the Opéra. On September 9, 1793, the regime of the Convention accorded to the lyrical theater the considerable monthly allowance of 30,000 francs, as well as a single payment of 100,000 francs to defray immediate needs.

But the Opéra had its opponents among powerful politicians. They denounced the lyrical theater as a useless leftover of royal luxury and ridiculed the ballet as shoddy court entertainment: the *plaisirs du roi* had no place on the stages of the people! But the dissenting voices ultimately failed to convince the government.

Music was still important. And the state of music throughout the nation was eventually to benefit from far-reaching educational reforms. In 1790 Mirabeau introduced to the National Assembly his plans for obligatory teaching of music in public schools. The National Assembly was ready to accept such proposals. At all out-of-door festivals various forms of music-making played an important part. The people sang collectively the hymns and chants of the Revolution; and so it made sense to incorporate music in the curricula of the schools.

La Marseillaise

The most famous musical piece of the revolutionary period is *La Marseillaise*, the spirited song which has become the national anthem of France. The composer Claude-Joseph Rouget de Lisle (1760-1836) wrote both words and music. He served as captain in the corps of engineers, then garrisoned in Strasbourg. The mayor of the Alsatian capital had sounded an appeal for a new marching tune for the army. Rouget de Lisle, an amateur composer, responded with the fiery hymn, "Allons, Enfans de la Patrie!"

Captain de Lisle played his new song for the Strasbourg mayor, who recognizing its quality, adopted it as the "War Song for the Army at the Rhine." The score was sent to Paris where Grétry confirmed its musical merit. As a result of this expert judgment, the republican government had 10,000 copies printed and distributed. This marks one of the first instances of a government-sponsored publication of music. The lasting name of the hymn is derived from the fact that the regiments, stationed in Marseille and marching north to Paris, enthusiastically adopted Rouget de Lisle's tune as their official song: it has been called *La Marseillaise* ever since. In Paris the song was heard on August 10, 1792 — the first anniversary of the day when the citizens of France were proclaimed "free" by law.

Festivals of Supreme Being
Interdependence of Art and Politics

The Jacobin republic lasted from August 1792 to July 1794. By the summer of 1793, the interdependence of art and politics entered a new, more clearly defined phase. The governmental edict of August 2, 1793, requested that the theaters, recognized by the Convention, produce a politically-geared repertory. This meant, before all, performing pieces glorifying the Revolution. Equally suitable were plays centering on popular heroes in different periods of history (for example, dramatic scripts extolling Gaius Gracchus, Brutus, or Wilhelm Tell).

Meanwhile Maximilien de Robespierre (1758-1794) had become the protagonist of the Republican government. He knew that he had to change the very thinking and feeling of the people, if his Jacobin State was to have a durable basis. A true leader, Robespierre hoped to bring the aspirations of Frenchmen to a higher level and to eliminate their vices — in short, to change their way of life. The Jacobin task was to give birth to a new religion and a changed society.

A new art was to play a major role in this Utopian program. The new religion was to replace various aspects of Catholicism predominant in France. A different calendar was introduced, eliminating the Saints' Days and the Sabbath. But Robespierre rejected extreme atheism. His plans were more moderate than those of his comrades. He wished to save the essence of religion by preserving the creed, the inherent belief in a Supreme Being. Robespierre's train of thought led to the inauguration of solemn public celebrations such as the Festival of the Supreme Being and the Festival of Reason. The first of these preserved the idea of monotheistic worship. But the second (the Festival of Reason) materialized in a manner which Robespierre did not foresee. The National Deputies, wearing red liberty caps, marched gravely to the venerable Cathedral of Notre Dame. They came to consecrate the church to the "Worship of Reason." A popular actress was triumphantly placed on the altar; she impersonated the "Goddess of Reason." While such ceremonies replaced the age-old rites of Christianity, both the government and the people played their officially prescribed parts during this atheistic pageant, in and out of the Cathedral.

The People Perform

A new type of performance came to the fore. The people were no longer passive spectators. They became activated as performers — at least in huge marching blocks. Their unison singing of hymns, their parading with symbols of the Revolution gave them a feeling of identification with the Republic and its higher cause. Soon, red flags, for the first time in history, became the symbol of the Revolution.

The festivals were conceived under allegorical titles, and their scenarios were accordingly written to cope with the huge productions on the squares and boulevards of Paris. In addition to the evocation of the "Supreme Being" and of "Reason," there were the festivals of "Life and Liberty," of the "Human Race," and of "Maternity." In contrast to these pageants glorifying positive aspects of human life, there were the allegories portraying "Human Sin." Thus cardboard symbols of "Civil Strife" were shown, only to be burned on a great pyre, accompanied by a chorus of condemnation. But when the figure of "Wisdom" took the place of "Civil Strife," the people grasped the meaning of this naive *quid pro quo*. They were expected to go home with a crucial lesson learned.

The Republican government was determined to sponsor these new forms of a "people's art" on a permanent basis. Like opera, these out-of-door festivals represented a blend of different media, of dramatic and musical elements. For these primitive performances the government demanded and obtained cooperation of the best artists. Incidental music was written by significant composers, such as Étienne-Nicolas Méhul and François-Joseph Gossec. No less a painter than Jacques-Louis David supervised the design of the gigantic stage and sets.

Jacques-Louis David
Arbiter of Art Life

The impact of the Revolution could not remain limited to the performing arts. In 1791 the Legislative Assembly cancelled all privileges and restrictions of the Royal Academy of Painting and Sculpture (founded in 1648). The new Republic permitted all artists to exhibit annually in public galleries.

The outstanding creative personality behind many of these changes was Jacques-Louis David (1748-1825). His biography shows the flexible career of the famous painter as a political artist. David became, in fact, not only the official painter for three successive regimes, but temporarily the arbiter of the entire French art life. Serving King Louis XVI and Count d'Artois (the future Charles X), David applied his versatile palette to such playful canvases as "Amours de Paris et Hélène." In September, 1792, David was elected to the Section du Muséum of the Convention, where he voted in January, 1793, for the death of his former sovereigns, Louis XVI and Marie Antoinette, sketching from a special window the doomed Queen enroute to the guillotine. David rose to the presidency of the Convention, became virtual dictator of the fine arts, and organized the Muséum of the Louvre. He was placed in charge of and decided on the organization, program, and style of the great Republican festivals (temporarily in collaboration with Robespierre).

In 1793 David organized the Commune des Arts which, in contrast to the dissolved Royal Academy, welcomed all French artists, regardless of their birth or social status. This foundation was the forerunner of the Société Populaire et Républicaine des Arts which stands as the prototype of all free democratic art organizations. After the coronation of Napoleon, David was appointed painter to the Emperor; his familiar portrait "Napoleon on Horseback" glorifies Bonaparte as he crosses the Alps into Italy, prior to the victorious Battle of Marengo in 1800.

Not since Le Brun, the art chief of the Sun King, was the official art life of the nation directed by the will of one single man. Le Brun helped to shape the aesthetics of the Golden Age; David defined the classical taste in the final phase of the Revolution and of the First Empire. David declared that harmony of form could be attained only by "the knowledge of the antique." "True beauty was untouched by changes of fashion because it was realized once for all by the Greeks and Romans."

The lonely moral giant of the Revolution was Georges-Jacques Danton (1759-1794). His educational role is remembered in his touching championship of the children of France and of legislation to assure their free schooling.

Danton became the victim of jealousies and bloody intrigues among revolutionary leaders. He finally preferred to be guillotined rather than to guillotine others. And so he died on the scaffold with Socratic dignity, without complex self-defense beyond explaining that he had tried to discipline the spirit of liberty, but never to weaken nor restrict it — not even in the avowed cause of liberty itself.

The greatness of Danton inspired several stage works, among them a masterpiece of the German stage, *Dantons Tod* by Georg Büchner, and of the French stage, *Danton* by Romain Rolland.

Republican Opera

In 1793 the Opéra Comique, which had become the most active theater of the nation, was officially taken over by the Republican government. How could opera fall into step with the new times? Intramural performances presented different kinds and, in many ways, more difficult problems of ideological identification than out-of-door pageantry attended by thousands of people. But opera has a story to tell. And the government, determined to encourage a "people's opera," commissioned the most skillful composers of France to produce music-dramatic scores, based on Revolutionary librettos.

In the stories of many operas written in the preceding era, the gods of ancient mythology appear as the helpers of man on earth. *Deus ex machina:* a benign god steps out of a cloud and miraculously assures the happy solution of human conflicts for which otherwise there would be no remedy. The Revolutionary artists, by contrast, wished to show how men could dispense with such wondrous formulas and attain their happiness on earth by struggle and determination. It was almost inevitable that the new political themes were oversimplified and rendered trivial in the subsequent attempts to teach uneducated audiences through the forum of the lyrical stage.

André Grétry's *La Rosière républicaine* (performed in 1794 at the Opéra) will serve as an example of how a real master tried to serve the absurdities of political propaganda. The libretto centers around two young lovers in a small French village. Their romance is set against the epochal background of their time as the waves of the Revolution reach their remote village. In keeping with the antireligious upheaval, Catholic saints are replaced by the Goddess of Reason and Virtue. When the doors of the village church are opened the young bride appears, representing Virtue. The priests are ready to join Revolutionaries. And even two nuns happily participate in the dance of the opera's finale.

In his score to this libretto Grétry characterizes the people by folkloristic songs, the Revolutionaries by their new hymns. The joyous reconciliation of all people is celebrated by earthy country dances.

The example of Grétry — the earnest attempt of a great musician to cope with the exigencies of revolutionary art — was rapidly multiplied throughout France. Most of his noted colleagues, Cherubini, Gossec, Le Sueur, or Méhul, made their craft available to the Republic. Other composers, such as Rodolphe Kreutzer and Pierre Gaveaux, were in great favor with the government. They could hardly cope with the demands and deadlines of their commissions.

National Publishing House and National Conservatory

On New Year's Day of 1794 Bernard Sarrette (1765-1858) suggested to the government the establishment of a national publishing house for music. It was to print and distribute valuable compositions appropriate for performance at festivals and ceremonies (such as hymns for the Fourteenth of July, tributes to liberty, etc.). Sarrette's petition was supported by a letter signed by 51 of the nation's most prominent musicians.

Within less than three weeks the revolutionary government put Sarrette's proposal into practice. Each of the newly-created districts of the Republic received, in advance, a subsidy of 33,000 livres to buy and distribute patriotic music. The first state publishing house for music on record had come into existence.

As early as 1792 Sarrette had founded a free school of music, where members of the military musical corps (of the National Guard) served as instructors. This school introduced a varied curriculum for vocal and instrumental performance. The school received the name *Institute National de Musique*; in 1795 its title was changed to *Conservatoire.* A milestone in the evolution of musical pedagogy was reached in France.

The Commission of Public Instruction

In the spring of 1794 the theaters of France came under the tutelage of the Commission of Public Instruction. This office decided which authors would be asked to write new works for the national theaters. The Commission suggested content and form of plays, operas, and outdoor ceremonies. It overhauled the old repertory and established the bureau of censorship. In short, the Commission of Public Instruction asserted totalitarian control over French art life. On April 26, 1794, the directors of the national theaters received this official admonition:

> We advise you, fellow citizens, in the name of the law as well as on your own personal responsibility, that you should eradicate the following titles without delay from all the plays, in verse or in prose, which you produce: Duke, Baron, Marquis, Count, Monsieur, Madame, etc. . . . These feudal titles stem from impure sources; they must no longer be allowed to contaminate the French theater.

These were minor changes. But tampering with the original script went much further. In classical plays admitted for production the red pencil of the state censor played havoc with the text. A considerable number of masterpieces were placed altogether on the Index of forbidden repertory. Among them were *Le Malade imaginaire* by Molière, *Andromaque*, *Britannicus*, *Phèdre* by Racine.

Summary of Revolutionary Patronage
First Proposal for Decentralization

The new Republican government proved to be wholeheartedly in favor of art subsidy. Not only did it have every intention to support all organization devoted to the performance of drama and music in Paris, but the Republic was ready to extend this patronage throughout the nation. The Jacobin Club requested that the Commission of Public Instruction of the National Convention "should organize theatrical activities in every French town of four thousand or more inhabitants. The pupils of the public schools and all older students should be instructed in music and the dramatic arts."*

This project marked a crucial departure from the complete indifference of the monarchy toward art support in the provinces. The very fact that towns of only 4,000 inhabitants were considered eligible for support of an indigenous art life is eloquent even by modern standards. At

*Obviously, population figures must always be interpreted in relation to specific periods in history.

the same time, the ideological purpose of the national art program was always kept in sight. As the Commission of Public Instruction demanded, only art works communicating the spirit of the Revolution should be performed in Paris or anywhere else throughout the nation.

Art for the People

The French Revolution searched for answers to the question: what can the arts do for the people? In theory this question is a simple and direct one. In practice it involves complex answers and shifting standards. Here is a problem that has lost nothing of its impact in modern times. Every democratic society must face it squarely, and solve the issue anew.

The goal of successive French governments was to make all the people participate in an art life attuned to the ideology of the new state. We know today that this was a Utopian aim. We also know why it failed. The revolutionary order to replace "useless" court art with a people's art remained a vague prescription, one that could not be filled overnight.

The aim of bringing art to all can be realized in any pluralistic society only on different levels, which must be adjusted to different needs and tastes of the people. There can be no common denominator in the appreciation and enjoyment of art. There never was and never will be. The wings of the artist's imagination are clipped by the axiomatic order of a government to produce art works consistent with the reality of an entirely political program and purpose.

But the art life of the revolutionary epoch merits study. For here is a total effort to include the arts in an overall governmental program. And the collaboration of the best artists of the nation was not merely commanded; it was, many times, spontaneous and sincere.

In France, at the end of the eighteenth century, the only patron of the artist was the people's government. It gave orders, extended commissions, and set their direction. It was up to the artist's skill and fantasy to fulfill the assignment — a difficult one, in spite of its primitiveness, or perhaps because of it. Some of the collaborating writers and composers, distinguished in their respective fields, were steeped in the aesthetics and sophistication of craftsmanship that had been taken for granted during the *ancien régime.* Furthermore, there were insufficient stylistic antecedents to guide the commissioned artist on his road to express revolutionary sentiment in valid art forms.

Trying to eliminate all traces of church art and court art, the Revolutionaries had to start almost from point zero. Obviously, playing theater and making music for the masses was an utterly different assignment. The artist now had to search for new content. He had to design simple frameworks and find a directly popular expression. It was easy for the government to demand these and other traits of a broadly popular style. It was difficult for the real artist to supply them, provided he wanted to maintain integrity and high standards of his métier. But there were, undeniably, new springboards for creative work. The events after 1789 produced numerous festive occasions. Huge open-air performances offered new possibilities for dramatic and musical productions. While many of these efforts were marked by crudity, they at least had the freshness of great popular emotion. And these were premises that the artist could legitimately utilize in his work. The French people enjoyed singing folk tunes, chanting in unison; they were fond of dancing in public squares; they loved all forms of pageantry. These predilections providing the stimulus in revolutionary hymns, chants, and collective mass performances were the seeds for a new popular style.

It was, before all, the very script of a play, the libretto of an opera, the text of a cantata or a hymn which could become direct carriers of ideological messages. And in full subordination to such texts, musical settings solved their assignments tentatively, though often primitively.

In 1789 only a very small segment of the French population was ready for the enjoyment of great art. Within the various media the people's appreciation of absolute music presented difficult problems. The symphony may serve as an example, because important revolutionary composers devoted much of their creative energy to this form. They attempted to adjust the level of symphonic communication to new audiences. Prior to the Revolution the symphony had been widely admired and enjoyed by aristocratic patrons who maintained court orchestras at their private estates. On the other hand, public concerts were no novelty in Paris; the Concert Spirituel, which performed in the Salle des Suisses of the Tuileries had been in existence since 1725.

French composers wrote symphonies after the fall of the Bastille, conscious of the fact that they now addressed another kind of public. The contemporary symphonies of Haydn (written for the court at Eszterháza, for the Paris Concerts de la Loge Olympique, or for the London Salomon series) are more intricate than those of the French composers because they were addressed to sophisticated audiences, long exposed to musical refinement.

The case of Francois-Joseph Gossec (1734-1829) is particularly revealing. The Belgian-born composer has more than thirty symphonies to his credit. This musician, who was to play such a paramount role on the revolutionary art scene, was originally a protégé of the aristocracy. His earlier works were steeped in the aesthetics of the *ancien régime*. As a composer-in-residence at the estate of Prince de Conde and Prince de Conti, Gossec composed classical chamber music and symphonies. His first symphony, in fact, was written five years prior to Haydn's first symphony (composed at the Bohemian estate of Lukavec under similar conditions of aristocratic sponsorship). But with the Revolution, the style of Gossec changed rapidly. Along with his fellow composers—notably, Le Sueur, Cherubini, and Méhul—Gossec transferred his skill to the service of his new patrons. And thus he helped to create the new "revolutionary style," particularly in his scores for the people's festivals. His ideologically-inspired scores (such as "The Fourteenth of July," "Tribute to Liberty," "Hymn to the Supreme Being") all aimed at an expression of patriotic grandiloquence. In the "Music for the Funeral of Mirabeau" (1791) Gossec achieved artistically legitimate effects. His *Te Deum*, written for a revolutionary festival, was performed by 1,200 singers and 300 wind instruments. There is little doubt that Berlioz inherited from the tone language of the Revolution the technique of scoring for very large forces.

The "Committed" Artist

The poets and the composers of the French Revolution were the first "committed" artists of modern times. They were engaged in the pursuit of an ideologically defined program. This was in all of its newness a bewildering task. The head-on clash of the new and old regimes shattered tradition.

But the new political formulas alone could not produce works of art. The circumscribed commissions of art works limited the creative pursuit to primitive levels of communication. It meant writing scripts and scenarios for the pomp and circumstance of a new kind of festival and ceremony. It meant composing bombastic music for grandstand effects, scoring military symphonies for public squares.

The Republic hoped to educate the masses gradually. And the best artists looked forward to the time when more liberal interpretation of their creative task would again permit more advanced modes of expression even within popular art. But this time never came. The monarchy returned. Lack of opportunity for organic growth prevented the development of aesthetically valid theater and music for a free democracy.

V. The Restoration and the Second Republic

Napoleon Bonaparte as Art Sponsor

The undistinguished government of the Directory, which was the chief executive body of France from 1795 to 1799, left an equally indifferent record of art patronage. When the Republican majority insisted on universal suffrage and the great national elections were being prepared, the government assigned to the Théâtre Français a new role —

that of election headquarters. But performances resumed in 1797 and the theater received then its famous name, *L'Odéon.*

Meanwhile history had set the stage for the most fateful man of the era, who was also to rank high in the annals of art patronage. Tired of the incompetent five Directors, France replaced them in 1799 with the commission of three Consuls. One of these was Napoleon Bonaparte. In the next one-and-a-half decades the destiny of Europe was forced by the political fantasies of this powerful soldier.

The image of Napoleon in his various roles is familiar: as hero and patriotic commander; as able administrator; as a fighter for freedom; and as freedom's suppressor. Whatever posterity's verdict on these many roles may be, Napoleon deserves also to be known as an imaginative patron of the arts. He realized that the theater was a perfect means to pay homage to the glory of France — the very cause with which, he claimed, he was so strongly identified. Napoleon's era did not produce masterworks comparable in quality to those of the Bourbon era, but it maintained and greatly strengthened the national framework for the performing arts. He made large funds available for the theaters, and one of his early administrative acts was to allot to the Opéra an annual subvention of 75,000 francs.

Napoleon's decrees of 1801 and 1804 reorganized to marked advantage the administration of the national theaters. In 1801 (still under the First Consulate) the rivalry between the two theaters devoted to the genre of comic opera finally led to their union. At this time, the company performing at the Théâtre Feydeau was fused with that playing at the Théâtre Favart.* Their new association became known under the generic title of *Théâtre National Opéra Comique* (which remains to this day the official name for this lyrical stage). The Salle Feydeau became its home; its status was to be permanently that of a national theater. Napoleon accorded the Opéra Comique a subvention of 50,000 francs and placed the theater under the control of a superintendent.

Parterre of Kings

The last Bourbon monarchs had allowed the Théâtre Français an annual subsidy of 12,000 francs. Napoleon multiplied this contribution to 100,000 francs. On May 30, 1799, the two hitherto independent companies of state-sponsored actors joined forces in the theater housed in the Salle Richelieu. One year later Napoleon requested that the building owned by the state be given gratuitously to the company of actors. From this time on annual benefits to the theater and to actors were gradually increased.

*In 1793 the Comédie Italienne, promoted to the national status of Opéra Comique, had assumed the name *Théâtre Favart.*

Under Napoleon's patronage the national theaters repeatedly embarked on tours. He was the first French commander-in-chief to realize the value of the theater as a morale booster and entertainment for the army. While still a general he had a company of state actors cross the Mediterranean to Africa, where they played for the soldiers engaged in the Egyptian campaign.

In proportion to the rising reputation of the French national theaters, requests for guest appearance from various quarters culminated in tours and performances abroad attended by royal audiences. In his *Parterre of Kings*, as he called it, Napoleon was proud to display the Théâtre Français and the mastery of its dramatic interpretations. He called this theater the "Glory of France." Napoleon could hardly have gone further to dramatize on the world stage of politics the significance of the performing arts. And in the Parterre of Kings he inaugurated a new concept: cultural exchange.

On April 17, 1804, one month before the Senatus Consultum conferred on him the title of Emperor, Napoleon laid the groundwork of the operational fusion which officially associated the Comédie Française with the Théâtre Français. Among the fifty articles of this lengthy and involved document, paragraph fifteen stresses the social security of the artists employed by the state theaters. The approach is progressive in its humaneness: "If one of the members of the theater suffers an accident or illness that makes continuation of service impossible, he (or she) is permanently entitled to a substantial part of the total pension."

In 1808 the Théâtre l'Odéon was given the name *Théâtre de l' Impératrice*. This was Napoleon's gallant gesture to his wife, at a time when the playhouse enjoyed its greatest popular success. But Josephine complained to Napoleon: "What a nuisance! One now has to cross the Seine to ride to the theater."

Moscow Decree

From the point of view of art patronage, the most important document of the Napoleonic Era is the so-called *Moscow Decree*. Bonaparte signed this order on behalf of the Comédie Française on October 15, 1812. It is astonishing that the Emperor, at the end of his Russian campaign, and actually facing military and political disaster, would in Moscow have been urgently concerned about cultural life in faraway Paris. But exactly at this time he put into reality definite policies in favor of the national theater of France. Surrounded by the Russian snow and cold, defeated with a loss of four-fifths of his army, Napoleon signed in the Russian metropolis this decree so characteristic of imperial sponsorship.

The Moscow Decree shows Napoleon's familiar gift for organization. It treats all essential problems of the theater. It defines the relationship of the government to art as well as the inner structure of the Comédie Française. It determines salaries of the artistic personnel. It is concerned with the educational aspects of the theater. To this very day, essential details in the operation of the French theater are guided by the Moscow Decree. No doubt the commoner who had risen from the rank of a cadet to that of emperor proved a sense of devotion to the arts that is comparable, and in certain aspects superior, to the patronage displayed by other centuries-old dynasties of Europe. Napoleon did not think of the arts as luxuries. Not even in times of catastrophe could they become targets of economy drives and curtailment. The arts were necessities to be preserved at all costs, even in times of disaster.

Napoleon's reign was succeeded by the Restoration (1814-1824). The Bourbon dynasty returned, and Louis XVIII ascended the French throne. This era marks the rise of many political factions. The multiparty system made the formation of government, and consequently of a parliamentary art policy, more complex. The support of the national theaters was charged to the civil list of expenditures.

Upon the death of Louis XVIII in 1824, his brother the Count of Artois became the French monarch. He assumed the name Charles X. The King favored traditional court opera and ballet of the prerevolutionary kind. Charles X maintained an attitude of largesse toward the support of the theaters, although expenses mounted constantly. The new extravagance of scenic spectacles was primarily responsible for growing deficits. In 1827 the Opéra alone added almost 1,000,000 francs to the costs of the art budget.

The decisive impulse of this era came from new quarters. In 1827 Victor Hugo (1802-1885) published the preface to his *Cromwell*, which became with its ardent argument a herald for the oncoming age. The entire generation of young French poets, Alexandre Dumas, George Sand, Alfred de Vigny, and others, heard his call: Victor Hugo emerged as the torchbearer of French romanticism. "The object of modern art is not beauty, but life," Hugo proclaimed; and he set out to show that the inherent principle of living art was dynamic, evolutionary. Several of Hugo's works, such as *Marion de Lorme*, were rejected by the royal censor. But the drama *Hernani** was produced at the Théâtre Français on February 25, 1830. The theme of the play is Castilian honor; but the drama does not lack an antimonarchial counterpoint. The year of *Hernani* is the last year of Charles X as the French ruler. The reactionary

*Hugo's drama *Hernani* was transformed, fourteen years later, into the libretto of Verdi's opera *Ernani*.

autocrat had the audacity to dissolve the legislature. His forms of censorship had become increasingly severe; not only the theater, but the press and all conceivable media of free expression, became its target.

The July Revolution was the answer to this, and the flag of the tricolor once more waved high from the towers of Notre Dame. Charles X went into exile.

July Monarchy

A younger Bourbon, the Duke of Orleans, came to the fore to play the paradoxical role of a revolutionary prince. As the King, he assumed the name Louis-Philippe I. He relinquished the established court at Versailles (to which his predecessors had ceremoniously returned), and again established the Palais Royal in Paris as the royal residence. Louis-Philippe changed the tone at court to that of semi-democratic informality. His government marks the first bourgeois rule within a large European kingdom.

During the so-called *July Monarchy* moneys for the support of the arts were always available. But this subsidy alone did not guarantee a healthy state of art life. Louis-Philippe offered France temporary prosperity, but little honor. Corruption was rampant within his government. Scandals involving ranking members of government and society shocked the nation.

These times are reflected in a magistral work of art — *La Comédie humaine* by Honoré de Balzac (1799-1850). In this gigantic novel of manners, Balzac immortalized his era, dominated by arrogant aristocrats and the *nouveau riche* — all claiming their rights based on birth, bank account, or both. Balzac evoked the France of the July Monarchy, the glamor as well as the misery of a godless world. His viewpoint is, by and large, that of a monarchist and of a son of the Church.

In November 1832, Hugo's drama *Le Roi s'amuse** (antimonarchial in its undertones, like *Hernani*) was first performed, but the royal censor banned the play on the second night. Three months later Hugo produced his *Lucrèce Borgia* at the Théâtre Porte St. Martin. The première, enthusiastically received, marks a departure: the Théâtre Français had lost its exclusive hold on the avant-garde.

Other stages gradually assumed the important mission of presenting new provocative drama.

**Le Roi s'amuse* became the basis for the libretto of Verdi's *Rigoletto* (1851).

Opéra Commercialized

In 1831 Dr. Louis Véron, a physician, was appointed general administrator of the Opéra. His own record of preliminary conferences with the royal ministry of Louis-Philippe has become a sociological document.[2]

A skillful management of the Opéra, Véron pleaded with the ministry, could be politically valuable for the royal government. Many foreign tourists would come to Paris, attracted by spectacular performances. The Opéra boxes would be occupied by an elegant, satisfied society. The ministry was convinced. It trusted Véron with the Opéra's directorship for six years at his own financial risk, but with annual subventions from the government.

An era of semiprivate patronage set in, with the managerial entrepreneur enjoying limited state subvention. Véron was in sole charge of the art institute. He engaged some of the best performers available. François-Antoine Habeneck, later admired by Richard Wagner, became principal conductor. Excellent singers were engaged. Jacques-François Halévy, the noted composer, served as chorus director. Véron had a flair for public relations; he did not overlook any method to popularize his theater. Box holders, for the first time, were admitted backstage, a welcome innovation, particularly on ballet evenings. Enthusiastic subscribers could pay homage to beauty in the hitherto jealously guarded seraglio of the *balleteuses*. The activities at the annual Opéra ball further extinguished the already dimmed borderlines between a national art institute and a *café dansant*.

Véron's first production — Meyerbeer's *Robert le Diable* — was a signal success. In due time the Opéra became the most widely discussed theater of Paris, of France — of Europe. After the première of Halévy's *La Juive*, a critical account commented on the new prominence of the theater: "If we do not watch out, the Opéra will become a power strong enough to throw its armies into the struggle for European balance."

It did not quite reach this stage, but the commercialized Opéra of Véron assumed various strategic roles in the life of the nation. The Opéra's record as an institute committed to French culture was less impressive. Véron gave no encouragement to Hector Berlioz, the most inspired French composer of the young generation, who was then working on his opera *Benvenuto Cellini*, and only after Véron was no longer in office was Berlioz honored with a performance of this remarkable work at the Paris Opéra.[3]

VI. The Second Empire and the Third Republic

Palais Garnier

The building of a new opera house in Paris had been long overdue. The new wave of prosperity in the middle of the nineteenth century favored the realization of this expensive project. No doubt, the nation needed a representative lyrical theater, where opera could be produced with the splendor and grandeur inherent in French tradition and where worthy performances of foreign opera could be heard and seen in an auspicious frame. A large stage was needed to present "modern" music-drama with newly developed techniques of production, romantic decor, and illusionary effects. The role of Paris as a world capital required a luxurious theater for the accessory purpose of national and diplomatic representation. France should not tag behind Italy, Austria, and Germany in the possession of a beautiful and brilliantly equipped opera theater. The Exhibition of 1855 focused global attention on the splendor of life in the French capital.

All seemed well, at least on the surface, with the regime of Louis Napoleon. This nephew of Napoleon Bonaparte, making demagogical use of the great family name, had maneuvered himself from the status of national president to French emperor. Whatever the real sentiments of the French middle and working classes, Paris now felt the effects of a prosperous era. An alert minority profited from the new high standards of living. There was the beginning of a new industrialization in France. There was a flow of gold from overseas, particularly from America and Australia, into the coffers of a new network of banks. All of this was advantageous for the continued support of the theater.

Napoleon III, as the Emperor now called himself, was quick to renew the long tradition of court festivities at his country estate at Compiègne. Shades of Versailles! For Napoleon III believed that there was still no better means of gaining imperial status in the mind of the world than through the splendor of art patronage. But for several years, plans for the new Opéra theater remained shelved.

A dramatic set of circumstances proved to be the necessary incentive. On January 14, 1858, the Italian anarchist Pierri, a follower of Félix Orsini, tried to assassinate Napoleon III. The fanatic jumped to the Emperor's equipage when it was just approaching the old Opéra in the narrow rue le Pelletier. Pierri threw his "infernal machine" against the carriage. The Emperor escaped without bodily injury, but with a major shock. The trauma removed his earlier reluctance to build the new Opéra. He called on the architects of France to submit designs to a jury. Instead of the dangerously cramped access to the theater on the rue le Pelletier, the new Opéra should stand freely on a spacious square and be approached by broad converging avenues. On September 29, 1860, Napoleon III signed the decree sponsoring the great project of the Paris Opéra as we know it today. Its costs were to be raised from national funds for the theater. It was to serve as an enterprise of public utility. From almost two hundred blueprints submitted for the new structure, the jury chose the sumptuous and beautifully representative design by Charles Garnier.

Work began in 1861. Progress was slow. When the Opéra was almost completed, war between Prussia and France broke out. Ironically, the first use of the large lyrical theater was for defense. The Opéra served as a post for the regular army and as a storehouse for war materials. Military balloons took off from the spacious roof when the German artillery encircled the capital.

Napoleon did not live to attend the gala opening. His empire had collapsed by the time the curtain went up for the première on January 5, 1875. President Mac-Mahon, his guests, and a brilliant audience attended the opening, which began with the Overture to *William Tell* by the Italian Rossini. The other numbers were works by French composers: selections from Auber's *La Muette de Portici*, two acts of *La Juive* by Halévy, a scene from Meyerbeer's *Les Huguenots*, and the ballet *La Source* by Delibes. Music of the two greatest French composers of the epoch — Berlioz and Bizet — was ignored.

The total cost of the new Opéra, including the price of the land, amounted to approximately 100,000,000 francs. It is estimated that a comparable theater built today in the nerve center of Paris would probably cost approximately $55,000,000.

The Thirteenth Hall

This handsome theater — the *Palais Garnier* as Parisians often call it in honor of its imaginative builder — was the thirteenth home of the Opéra since its founding on June 28, 1669, under Louis XIV. No superstition could prevent the French seeing thirteen as the luckiest number. And true enough, the Opéra escaped the cruel fate of its only rivals on the world scene of the lyrical theater — of Milan's La Scala and of Vienna's Staatsoper — both of the two great theaters which were terribly damaged during World War II. But the declaration of the French capital as an open city saved its Opéra, too.

In terms of patronage, the Opéra was equally fortunate in this thirteenth hall. Every successive national administration continued to support it.

During the Third Republic (1870-1940) the Opéra once again experienced a period of semiprivate sponsorship which lasted well into the twentieth century. On January 1, 1908, a new contract with a private management was signed. The deposit of a guarantee of 400,000 francs by the concessionaire-manager was required. But the government continued the customary pattern of support. In 1914 the wealthy industrialist Jacques Rouché assumed the leadership of the Opéra and a considerable part of the financial responsibility. A generous patron, Rouché, embarked on costly productions far beyond the governmental subsidy. As a result, he incurred heavy losses. But he felt the sacrifice worthwhile. While this era of diversified patronage was artistically a successful one, the financial setup could not possibly last. With increasing wages on the one hand, and new forms of taxation on the other, no individual donor, not even a group of patrons, could for any length of time sustain a lyrical institute of such magnitude as the Palais Garnier. Hence the French government had to assume the full support of the Opéra once more — permanently as it would seem — and to accord it the unqualified status of a national art institute.

Table I gives an indication of the subsidies allocated to the Opéra by successive governments from the First Consulate to the end of the Third Republic. The survey spans one and one-third centuries. Obviously it is difficult, if not impossible, to compare money values and buying power accurately over so long a time. None the less the survey serves a purpose: it shows the unbroken continuity of subvention. Whatever the type of government — monarchy, republic, or directory — and what-

TABLE I

Annual Subventions of the Opéra During Successive Regimes

		*Francs**
The Consulate	1802	600,000
The First Empire	1804	750,000
	1813	950,000
The Restoration	1815	950,000
	1824	966,000
July Monarchy	1830	810,000
Second Republic	1848	870,000
Second Empire	1851	820,000
Third Republic	1870	800,000
	1929	2,400,000
	1930	3,200,000
	1931	4,800,000
	1933	7,900,000
	1934	8,400,000
	1937	12,561,000
	1938	17,000,000

*If not specifically noted, all figures in this chapter are given in old francs (OF), the basic monetary unit of France until December 29, 1958, when a new franc (NF) of 100 times the value of the old franc was introduced. At that time the exchange was 4.93 new francs to one U. S. dollar.

ever the particular regime — Consulate, First Empire, Restoration, Second Republic, Second Empire or Third Republic — all had in common the unswerving patronage of the French theater. Each of the regimes listed in Table I gave annual subventions to the Opéra.

From 1870 to 1925, the subvention remained around 800,000 francs annually. The inflationary spiral necessitated a sudden rise and steady increase in the support of the Opéra.

By way of contrast and as further indication of continuing governmental patronage, the subvention of the Opéra in 1938 was equivalent to approximately $43,557 whereas, in 1961, an annual allocation of $4,321,800 was given to the Réunion des Théâtres Lyriques Nationaux (since January 14, 1939, both the Opéra and the Opéra Comique).*

Summit of the Opéra Comique

We have left the chronicle of the Opéra Comique at the time of its patronage by Napoleon Bonaparte. The period reaching approximately from the middle of the nineteenth century to the beginning of the twentieth century crowned the Opéra Comique with lasting laurels. This is the era when some of the *chef d'oeuvres* of the operatic repertory had their premières in this lyrical theater. The mere listing of the names of the scores and their composers brings into focus an amazingly large segment of operatic masterworks unsurpassed within their own genre. Among these premières at the Opéra Comique were (in chronological order) *Mignon* by Thomas (1866), *Carmen* by Bizet (1875), *Les Contes d'Hoffmann* by Offenbach (1881), *Manon* by Massenet (1884), *Louise* by Charpentier (1900), *Pelléas et Mêlisande* by Debussy (1902), *L'Heure espagnole* by Ravel (1911). Of twentieth-century compositions (in addition to those of Debussy and Ravel) works by Milhaud, de Falla, Ibert, Roussel, were first given at the Opéra Comique. By 1960 the Opéra Comique had performed within fifty years 401 works by 206 composers.

Many of these scores defy the etymological meaning which the term *opéra comique* suggests. The French call *opéra comique* any score for the musical theater in which some parts (or sections) are sung and other parts are spoken. By contrast, what is called *opéra* contains singing parts only (besides the instrumental parts of the accompaniment).

In other countries such a differentiation has often proved to be puzzling. For according to such terminology, Verdi's final work, the eminently humorous *Falstaff* (after Shakespeare's *The Merry Wives of Windsor*) is an opera — and not a *comic* opera — because the score offers only singing parts and has no spoken dialogue.

*The French franc continually fluctuates. Dollar values in this chapter approximate the exchange rate at time of subsidization.

On the other hand, Beethoven's deeply serious *Fidelio* would theoretically belong to the category of the comic opera: the score includes spoken dialogue. The traditional differentiation of genre and place of performance was challenged on November 10, 1959, when Bizet's *Carmen* was given for the first time in the Opéra. This spelled sheer madness to many French music lovers. Since its world première on March 3, 1875, *Carmen* was the most treasured possession of the Opéra Comique. But it was played there for the last time on June 3, 1959, the event marking performance 2,946 of *Carmen* at the Salle Favart (home of the Opéra Comique). The large stage of the Palais Garnier is now considered the appropriate forum for a new production of the music-drama with its many populous scenes out-of-doors. On the other hand, Verdi's *La Traviata* and Gounod's *Roméo et Juliette* moved from the Opéra to the Opéra Comique. The more intimate frame of the smaller theater seems more appropriate for these lyrical tragedies. Their transfer marks part of a new approach to production and repertory in the state-supported opera theaters.

End of Semiprivate Patronage

We have observed how France supported her national Opéra during certain periods by a formula blending private with governmental patronage. At such times, part of the financial risk was charged to a concessionaire, who was responsible for both the artistic and business management of the theater. Due to these circumstances (observed also in theatrical developments in other countries) the shaping of the artistic policy was bound to be influenced directly by commercial calculations. The concessionaires were inclined to choose a repertory promising sound monetary returns. The engagement of performers and many other problems of management would likewise be motivated by box office considerations.

The management of Jacques Rouché (as previously mentioned) was the notable exception: as general administrator of the Opéra, he generously opened his own purse to cover that part of the deficit not met by the government. But other concessionaires could neither afford a comparable liberality, nor were they motivated by ideals similar to those of Jacques Rouché.

Semiprivate patronage eventually created a paradox. It certainly made no sense spending government money aimed at the maintenance of high standards for an art institute that was run as a commercial enterprise. During the interim between the two World Wars it became increasingly clear that the national lyrical theaters could no longer prosper under semiprivate sponsorship.

Reunion of Lyrical Theaters

The search for new solutions finally led to the formation of the Réunion des Théâtres Lyriques Nationaux. This reorganization united both principal lyrical theaters of France, the Opéra and the Opéra Comique under one single administration and governmental supervision, completely subsidized by the government of the French Republic.

The Réunion became law with the decree of January 14, 1939. It was greeted with a flood of criticism from various quarters. Yet the step was really not as large as its opponents claimed. There had been analogous procedures foreshadowing the Réunion. Had the government not solved the tasks of managing national museums, such as the Louvre and the Museum of Modern Art, in a similar manner? The national libraries of France were likewise supported by a system of reunion as was the centralization of all great educational services of the nation, based on state subsidies. The reunion of the national lyrical theaters merely followed a successfully established pattern.

Most of the objections attacked the cost of the Réunion. The support of such a large organization by the government alone was obviously expensive. But the French state is not unduly concerned with the financial returns of its lyrical theaters. Deficits, often substantial ones, are expected, provided the artistic results justify the spending of tax money. The national treasury collects all receipts of the theaters and pays their expenses. In this more narrow sense, the Réunion does not receive any subsidy, for the government collects the income and pays whatever bills its theaters accrue.

In 1939 the government's initial contribution was relatively modest: 40,990,000 old francs ($98,417). In this same year, the tax on tickets for the national theater was cancelled. By 1947 the governmental subsidy had risen to 337,900,000 old francs ($811,297). But a small tax was reinstated to cope with the overall purpose of imposing a deduction on tickets of any kind for the national treasury. In 1958 governmental maintenance of the lyrical theaters had risen to 1,327,000,000 old francs ($3,186,127) and in 1961 to 1,800,000,000 old francs ($4,321,800).

At present, 1,400 people work full time for the Opéra and the Opéra Comique. This figure includes singers, orchestra members, ballet corps, choristers, artistic directors (such as conductors, regisseurs, choreographers, coaches), machinists, electricians, dressmakers, decorators, and many others.

The law of January 14, 1939, defines in its first paragraph the Réunion as a national, public organization founded under the authority of the Ministry of National Education. The Réunion is invested with civil authority and financial autonomy. It is entrusted with the artistic and financial direction of the Opéra and the Opéra Comique.

The decree of May 11, 1939, defines (under article VIII) the financial operation; the income of the Réunion is divided into ordinary and extraordinary receipts:

> The ordinary receipts comprise all direct income of the Opéra and Opéra Comique. This includes subsidies and all kinds of payments which have annual or permanent character (for instance, compensation derived from the Radiodiffusion Télévision Française, etc.). The extraordinary receipts comprise all income from sources that are not on a regular basis.

The entire personnel (artistic as well as technical) of the two opera theaters is protected by the general legislation of social security, accident insurance, and pensions (as directed by the *législation général du travail*). Pensions are available to singers and choristers at the age of fifty and after a minimum of twenty-five years of service; to members of the orchestra, at sixty and after twenty-five years of service. In the ballet corps, men at forty-five and women at forty (with a minimum of twenty years of service) are entitled to retirement pensions.

The amount of the pension is determined by the average salaries during three consecutive years of the highest pay received by an individual artist. There are pensions for invalids (because of accidents or illness) and for widows (who are eligible to receive 50 per cent of the old-age annuity of a deceased husband). There are temporary pensions for orphans up to the age of twenty-one. These always amount to 10 per cent of the retirement pension. The pension plan adds to the dignity of national patronage.

VII. The Fourth Republic

Paris *is* France. "Du temps de la Fronde Paris n'est encore que la plus grande ville de France; en 1789, il est déjà la France même."[4] This succinct observation of Alexis de Tocqueville was as true in the aftermath of World War II as it was in 1858, when the distinguished writer completed his penetrating study, *l'Ancien Régime et la Révolution.*

The concentration of administrative power of France in her capital is motivated by her history. Centuries ago a dynamic central authority became obligatory in a nation permanently exposed to war — waged by lusty neighbors with their incessantly repeated invasions. French rulers from Charlemagne to Louis XIV instinctively enforced extreme centralization of their government at their residences. Napoleon, himself an aggressive warrior, equally desired Paris to stand as a fortress of converged authority. From the First to the Fifth Republic nothing happened to alter this centrality of government.

Official French art life has always reflected this pattern of centralization in all of its branches. In the arts and letters Paris was not only the greatest city of France, it has been France itself since the days of the Bastille. Yet, during the past one-hundred-fifty years there have been attempts to establish new or strengthen old art centers in the provinces. Many of these projects resulted from private initiative. None had lasting success.

Decline of Theater in the Provinces

Prior to World War I the large provincial cities of France valiantly maintained rudiments of theatrical life. Some of them even had impressive theaters; some were home to a resident company (like the famous Grand-Théâtre in Bordeaux).

On most of these stages quality of performances rarely rose above the provincial level. The advents of the silent film, later of the moving pictures with sound track, and finally of television were steps toward the downfall of the legitimate theater in the French provinces. There was — and still is — the competition of sports, for which youth abandoned the local theater. Other causes hastened defeat of the resident companies and even discouraged visits of touring ensembles to the provinces. The basic interests of the provincial population are narrow in France as elsewhere, and not enough was done to enlighten the people culturally.

Whatever the specific reasons, only a few French cities continued to support their theaters. In the decades before World War II the total number of theater performances was halved in the French provinces. Between 1914 and 1937, 83 halls out of 150 closed their doors.

Various experiments tried to cope with this stagnation. During the season 1919-20 the traveling theater Fermin Gremiere performed Shakespeare's *Merchant of Venice* all over France. This touring company is the antecedent of a modern large-scale national project that has become known as *Dramatic Decentralization.*

Fighting Cultural Retreat

The venture of Fermin Gremiere failed. And while legitimate drama and opera were dying in the provinces, their cities became the market places for theatrical hucksters, importing from Paris worthless fare. The bourgeoisie of the provinces became easy prey for unscrupulous entrepreneurs. Vulgar farces and cheap musicals were pawned off on audiences who accepted the shoddy entertainment as genuine theater.

Something had to be done to stem this alarming cultural retreat in the provinces. Ever since the liberation of France in 1945, the General Direction of Arts and Letters (a section of the National Ministry of Education) had explored suitable methods to awaken the country from its apathy toward serious art. The Fourth Republic could no longer tolerate this; France had much to lose if her theater would not function as a direct form of popular culture.

The government decided to embark on a master plan to rehabilitate theatrical life in the provinces. This new national assignment known as *Dramatic Decentralization* became an extraordinary success.

Dramatic Centers

In the pursuit of this long-range plan, the national government set up a number of so-called *centres dramatiques*. These centers were established at five widely spaced, culturally strategic points throughout France. They are theatrical workshops, expected to grow into full-fledged, permanent playhouses. The centers are all subsidized by the government, yet in specifically defined forms of cooperation with the cities chosen as seats of these stages. (See Table II.)

TABLE II

Geographical Distribution of the Initial Dramatic Centers

Center	*Founded*	*City*
East (Intercommunal)	1947	Colmar, Haguenau, Metz, Mulhouse, Strasbourg
Central	1947	Saint-Étienne
Southwest	1949	Toulouse
West	1949	Rennes
Southeast	1952	Aix-en-Provence

In general, the activities of these dramatic strongholds are not limited to the city of residence; they distribute performances over as wide an area as feasible.

The governmental patronage of these centers is today interpreted as one of the crucial means of spreading culture on a national basis. The Chamber of Deputies has sanctioned this outlook, as shown by its voting record.

For the season 1956-57 the allocation of subsidies on the part of the national government and the municipalities is shown in Table III.

It is estimated that the combined national and municipal support covers approximately half the total cost of the expenditures incurred by the five dramatic centers. The balance is earned at the box office, in spite of the fact that ticket prices are kept very low (from 100 to 500 old francs).

TABLE III

Allocation of Subsidies by National Government and Municipalities (OF)

1956-57

	National Government	*Municipality*
East	47,000,000 ($112,847)	3,000,000 ($7,203)
Central	20,000,000 ($ 48,000)	3,000,000 ($7,203)
Southwest	18,000,000 ($ 43,218)	2,500,000 ($6,000)
West	17,000,000 ($ 40,817)	2,500,000 ($6,000)
Southeast	16,000,000 ($ 38,416)	2,000,000 ($4,808)

In 1958 the governmental subvention of these centers was approximately $260,000. But the support is expected to be greatly increased in the near future, and additional centers are being developed.

The resident workshops are not the only form of dramatic decentralization. The Thespian Carriage (which we have watched on its successful rides in other European countries) frequently makes its trips from Paris in all directions, particularly to regions still lacking dramatic centers. The French territories overseas were originally included in theatrical visits; recent events have interfered with these plans.

The following survey of some of the important dramatic centers and of their background will show how the legitimate theater has gained ground in towns and regions that were hitherto far removed from any serious preoccupation with the performing arts.

Saint-Étienne

The beginning of the Dramatic Center of Saint-Étienne curiously involves another city. In Grenoble, shortly after the liberation, a private company attempted to establish a permanent playhouse. Grenoble, a university city of 200,000 in the southeast of France, is remembered also as the birthplace of one of the country's great writers, Henri Stendhal. This seemed a good omen. But the *Comedians of Grenoble*, as the company called itself, failed in spite of the quality of its productions. Local co-operation was unsatisfactory.

But the Grenoble players, not discouraged, decided to make another attempt at a different place. In 1947 the Comedians migrated from Grenoble westward to the Département of Loire. Saint-Étienne, a hardened industrial city in the center of France, known for its coal mines and steel factories, placed at the disposal of the theatrical company a large storehouse belonging to the School of Mines. In acknowledgement of its new sponsors the company now changed its name to *Comedians of Saint-Étienne*. They dared to offer Molière's *Le Bourgeois gentilhomme* as their initial performance for an audience made up of miners, factory workers, merchants, and students. The reception was a victory for the classical play as well as for its production. As additional support came from the community, regular theatrical activities — such as rehearsals, building of stage sets, and the like — could be organized. The next step was to establish a series of regular performances. After a modest start (20 classical and 10 modern works) the Comedians of Saint-Étienne now average no less than 150 plays each season, representing a varied and valid repertory of French and foreign authors in this industrial city of 178,000. The perseverance of the actors paid off.

Toulouse

The city of Toulouse (population 270,000) is primarily known as a commercial and industrial center. In the years prior to the liberation it would hardly have occurred to anyone to visit this capital of the Department of Haute-Garonne for the sake of a theatrical experience. But on June 20, 1945, a dramatic workshop made up entirely of actors and technicians recruited from Toulouse began its activities. In spite of numerous handicaps the group courageously carried on. In January, 1949, the theatrical workshop attained official status: it became the Dramatic Center of the Southwest. The National Government, the city of Toulouse, and the Department of Haute-Garonne all agreed on a joint support of the Center.

The gradual awakening of the southern audience was, admittedly, a most difficult task in a region so long removed from serious art life. But it was not love's labor lost. Today, the Dramatic Center of the Southwest plays Shakespeare and contemporary French classics to capacity audiences. The box office receipts are turned into productive channels and are reinvested in more experimental productions.

By 1959 the Toulouse company had visited more than 100 cities in continental France as well as in North Africa. The warm reception of these tours in other communities has induced the municipality of Toulouse to vote an appreciable increase of its share of the subvention. The thrifty city fathers realize well the prestige value of the city's dramatic theater. No longer is Toulouse spoken of only as a coal mining and steel center; today Toulouse is also known for its good theater.

Rennes

On December 13, 1949, a young group of actors, calling themselves *Jeune Compagnie*, made a promising debut in the Grand Théâtre of Rennes, the medieval capital of Brittany. The company quickly established itself with a series of well-rehearsed performances. Today this group is a permanent ensemble and it has been promoted to the status of the Dramatic Center of the West. The national government, the city of Rennes, and a collective of surrounding localities all cooperate in support of this theater. In its third season an association called *Friends of the Dramatic Center of the West* was founded to aid the further growth of the project in terms of public relations, ticket sales, etc. A trimester bulletin keeps the public informed about the repertory and propagandizes the various activities of the Center.

Aix-en-Provence

The enchanting capital of the Provence, serene and ancient Aix, is the seat of the Dramatic Center of the Southeast. The Center was created on January 15, 1952, as a result of an agreement with the Ministry of Education and the municipality of Aix. First called the *Comédie de Provence*, the group has so far performed in more than 30 cities of the Mediterranean region.

In addition to various governmental subsidies, the Center is also aided by the Friends of the Comédie de Provence. This association has organized classes in dramatic art as a pedagogical outlet of the theater. Producers and actors double as teachers. Thus continuity is established. Native talent finds supervision and opportunity for stage experience at the local Center.

In the past few years Aix-en-Provence has attained the prestige of sponsoring the most important summer festival held anywhere in the French provinces. During July an international and discriminating audience attends performances of opera and concert that are beginning to compete with those of Salzburg, Bayreuth, and Lucerne in distinction. The National Ministry of Cultural Affairs is also the patron of the Centre Français d'Humanisme Musical which offers courses in Aix during the festival season. Here André Jolivet, the eminent composer, holds a seminar in cooperation with other artists and scholars on the various aspects of contemporary music.

The forecast for Aix is decisively optimistic on all cultural issues. The old university town plays its role as a pivotal city of French art life on a year-round basis.

Intercommunal Dramatic Center of the East

Due to the grim succession of wars on its soil, eastern France is one of the most devastated lands of Europe. The results of rehabilitation are remarkable, if somewhat lagging behind the "economic miracle" achieved by West Germany. But on the French side of the Rhine River theater is played again and music is performed with an intensity and quality that does justice to the traditions of the art-conscious region.

The Dramatic Center of the East was founded in 1947 as an intercommunal enterprise. The city of Colmar took the initiative. This community of 47,500 has long been distinguished by its Museum Unterlinden — the art gallery housing such treasures as the "Isenheim Altar" by Matthias Grünewald.

Five communities participated in the establishment of this Center of the East: Colmar, Haguenau, Metz, Mulhouse, and Strasbourg. This marks a union of towns of different sizes and economic scope, ranging from the Alsatian capital Strasbourg (population 300,000) to the small historic town of Haguenau (population 20,000). The radius of the Center's activities is relatively small. These communities sharing their art life lie as close together as 30 and as far apart as 235 kilometers.

The first five years of this collaboration were a success. And to encourage its further growth and permanence, the French government committed itself to support the enterprise, offering it status as the Dramatic Center of the East. The procedure of support is as unusual in this Center as is its intercommunal setup. The governmental contract issued in December, 1952, called for the "concession" of the Center to an enterprising, experienced theatrical manager. He is appointed by a committee of representatives from the five municipalities. The mayor of Colmar is the president of this syndicate; he works in close contact with the national government in Paris.

The Dramatic Center of the East gives an average of approximately 300 performances per season. Meanwhile, many more communities wish to be included in the tours of the Center. To cope with these increased requests, the Center has divided its ensemble into two teams. The first group concentrates on large and medium-sized towns; the second, composed mainly of young actors, plays for small towns. Occasionally, these two teams join for large-scale representative performances.

Various activities of the Center are designed to deepen the appreciation of its ever-growing public for the theater. The audience is frequently invited to forum discussions on the scheduled plays, to lectures on various problems of the theater, interpreting its function in modern society.

Villefranche-sur-Saône
Theater Life in the Hinterland

For the purpose of our study, the modest beginnings of serious theater in towns and regions that had remained untouched by the national circuit of art life are as meaningful as the activities in capital cities with well-established performances of drama and music. For what interests us in the hinterland is the potential patronage, the methods by which individuals or small groups gradually succeed in the conquest of new territory for serious art. A great educational task still lies ahead in many parts of France, but encouraging lessons have been learned from the observation of grass-root cultural growth in small communities.

Villefranche-sur-Saône may serve as an illustration. This manufacturing town in east-central France has never had a theater. The lack of a proper hall was given as an excuse. Touring companies had to avoid Villefranche. When the Comedians of Saint-Étienne played in a cinema, the venture ended as a failure. And with this failure the hope for a theater in Villefranche might have been buried.

The enthusiasm and enterprising nature of one citizen, a government official, kept a theater alive. In 1957 he succeeded in forming the association Friends of the Theater, and he did not rest until he had persuaded a sufficient number of fellow citizens that Villefranche could no longer afford to be without a theater, that serious art was needed to counteract the rapidly deteriorating taste and morals. Religious and educational groups continued a campaign until 700 subscriptions were raised. One year later the Friends of the Theater numbered 1,600 members. About 400 pledges came from students, and an equal number from factory employees. This made a modest beginning possible. One could now invite some of the touring companies to play in Villefranche. These performances paid for themselves, mostly with subscriptions. The price for an individual ticket was fixed at less than 50 cents. In blocks of 100 subscribers it was only 40 cents. And one free performance was offered per season to all regular subscribers.

Impressed by the determination and success of a private group of its citizens, the municipality of Villefranche decided to offer the theater society a subvention of 200,000 new francs (approximately $40,000) for the year of 1959. The national government came forth with an additional grant of 60,000 new francs ($12,000). This joint patronage guarantees Villefranche its theater life. For the time being the city relies on the regular visits of the Dramatic Centers. Yet it might be possible, in the near future, to save sufficient funds to build a local playhouse for a permanent resident ensemble.

The story of Villefranche, related here in brevity, has its moral. The love for the theater of one single citizen (by no means an affluent man) proved strong enough to fire the idealism of a congenial group which in turn started a theater in a city seemingly indifferent to the arts. In the end, public patronage came to the aid of private initiative. Here is a town with a population of 20,000 — hitherto a desert culturally — which mobilized close to 2,000 subscribers for its regular dramatic season. Other communities could follow this example with equal success.

Today, certain regions of France still lack dramatic centers. Various departments on the Atlantic coast, particularly in Normandy, need organized forms of theatrical life. The same is true of many towns in the industrial North. At this writing the national government has a number of new centers under consideration. National interest is vested in the systematic cultivation of French repertory. Hence a stipulation accompanies all government contracts with the subsidized provincial centers, requesting that one-fourth of their total productions must represent premières of plays by French authors. At least one new production must be devoted to a classical drama. Altogether, the works of French dramatists must constitute two-thirds of the season's offering.

Lyrical Decentralization
Help for Provincial Opera Theaters

In addition to the Dramatic Decentralization, the French government has established an analogous, large-scale and long-term project aiming at the decentralization of the lyrical theater. For almost a decade after the Armistice of 1945 these plans remained in blueprint. The project of Lyrical Decentralization is more costly than its dramatic counterpart. The performance of opera requires a large apparatus: an orchestra, a chorus, often a ballet, in addition to the soloists. Customarily, salaries for singers are higher than those for actors. The scenery of most operas is more complex than that of drama. The French government was not in a position to embark upon an additional project of provincial art patronage, which would have obliged the treasury in the meager postwar years to increase its already strained art budget, at a time when a number of French cities were anxious to establish or reestablish resident lyrical theaters.

For years the situation seemed hopelessly deadlocked. Municipal theaters of France, depending on communal resources alone, could not pay even for the routine performances of the standard lyrical repertory. With the complete exclusion of performances of new works throughout the nation, the opera life of France faced the threat of being reduced to a lyrical museum. The only way found to avoid this stagnation was for the government to provide financial support. The following steps preceded its realization. The Director General of Arts and Letters, acting in accordance with the French Society of Authors and Composers, invited the representatives of various cities earmarked for the opera project to cooperate on a master plan of Lyrical Decentralization. The government offered to support tours of opera companies to key cities as well as to towns without a theater. Performances produced at Lyrical Centers were also to be presented in other communities by a system of circulation. To forestall partiality of government support to any community a committee of regional consultants was to aid the government office.

Certain municipalities accepted the offer with enthusiasm; a few were reluctant. With the approval of the Ministry of Finances, the government allocated subventions for the first two years (See Table IV.).

TABLE IV

Subventions for Opera Theaters (OF)

	Overhead, Salaries, Etc.	*Special Performances, Tours, Etc.*
1955	94,700,000 ($210,044)	67,000,000 ($160,867)
1956	97,300,000 ($215,555)	84,000,000 ($201,684)

Present allocations have risen in proportion to rise in costs. The subsidies for Lyrical Decentralization are derived from funds of the Ministry of National Education. The educational purpose is anchored in the aim of stimulating operatic life in the provinces. Civilized French life is enriched by the experience of the masterpieces of lyrical theater from Lully and Rameau, Gounod and Thomas, to Berlioz and Bizet. Important French operas of the twentieth century — the scores of Debussy, Ravel, Honegger, and Milhaud — are gradually to be absorbed by the provincial repertory. Yet the programs are not intended to be exclusively French.

In 1959 the Lyrical Decentralization received $420,000 from the national government.

Governmental Contract with Lyrical Centers

On March 3, 1947, the national government issued a decree defining the premises upon which French cities could apply for and receive subsidies for their opera houses. Contracts were drawn on a seasonal basis. Annual subventions of a minimum of $30,000 were available to qualifying municipal lyrical theaters. But governmental patronage aims at a diversification of support. State subsidy must not lead to a lessening of the financial support by the municipalities or the provinces. On the contrary, the Republic wishes it clearly understood that its help to the performing arts is to be matched by an increased regional effort.

The directors of each subsidized Lyrical Theater are chosen by the municipality from an approved list of candidates. Their names have been suggested by the National Minister of Education upon consultation with a committee whose members represent the cities chosen as Centers of Lyrical Decentralization. The regional committee prepares the artistic program and the budget for the oncoming season. Both are submitted to the National Ministry for approval. Yet the decision does not rest with the Minister alone. He consults with the committee whose task it is to evaluate the quality of the programs and to coordinate the most convincing of all suggestions that have reached the Ministry from various expert sources.

A few additional points of the contract may be noted. The supported Lyrical Center is expected to engage, for the full length of the season, a minimum staff of 2 conductors, 1 choral director, 1 accompanist, 1 vocal coach, 1 stage director, 2 assistant stage directors, 1 stage designer, and 1 dress designer. The theater orchestra is to have a minimum of 60, the chorus a minimum of 50. The ballet corps is to consist of at least 33 dancers. These 3 groups — orchestra, chorus and ballet — are engaged for the entire calendar year. The orchestra may be requested to give symphony concerts in its resident city as well as in surrounding towns.

The solo ensemble of the opera company comprises a minimum of 20 singers, none of whom may be associated with another theater during the tenure of the contract (except in special approved cases). These restrictions aim at preservation of a permanent ensemble — an ideal which has been lost, even at large theaters, in and outside France.

The Lyrical Theaters of the provinces assume simultaneously a variety of educational assignments. The maintenance of a music school for children may be included in the orbit of the Center. The organization of a ballet school is desirable, but optional. A choir school may be established, not only with the aim to train vocalists for the Center itself, but also to provide well-educated singers for the various artistic needs of the region — for church, concert, and social occasions. Similar goals might be realized by the members of the theater orchestra: they can organize classes teaching their respective instruments. These plans are designed to promote an indigenous art life in all of its ramifications. The provincial communities intend to train their own professional performers and to dispense with importations.

The blueprint for each Lyrical Center, then, simultaneously represents an organized educational program. It is designed to raise the standards of regional music-making to professional levels. This explains the proximity of Lyrical Decentralization to the national program of education. Each subsidized theater must guarantee, in addition to worthy performances of the general opera repertory, a defined minimum number of performances by contemporary French composers. Plans must include a new production of a French repertory work that has not been played in the city for eight years or longer. The season must also offer the performance of a French score that has never been performed on the local stage. Premières are to include the score of one or more contemporary composers that have never been heard anywhere in France.

Shared Sponsorship

The French government is prepared to cover approximately one-half the deficit of the Lyrical Theaters in the provinces. Their municipalities assume responsibility for the other half. In certain cases, the provinces (*départements*) likewise make contributions. Thus the support of local art patronage is one of shared responsibility. As the average deficit of a provincial opera theater is approximately $50,000 annually, the state pays $25,000 dollars, provided the regional sponsor matches this contribution.

A considerable number of cities have availed themselves of such governmental subsidies in accordance with the decree of March 3, 1947. These cities are Bordeaux, Lille, Lyon, Marseille, Metz, Montpellier, Mulhouse, Nancy, Nantes, Nice, Rouen, Strasbourg, Toulouse.

Some smaller theaters (such as Avignon) have participated, in a more limited way, in the government-sponsored circuit of lyrical performances.

Due to the inflationary spiral of expenses, the deficit of the Lyrical Theaters has been rising rapidly. A few municipalities (among them Lille and Nantes) declared themselves unable to cope with the unforeseen conditions and abandoned their operas, hoping to resume activities in the near future. The government immediately reallocated these available funds to other theaters in communities that had adjusted to the crisis.

Strasbourg

Changing Patrons

Of the cities included in the national program of Lyrical Decentralization, Strasbourg represents a special case. The handsome capital of Alsace has for centuries been exposed to a turbulent history. Yet the harmoniousness of its old architecture (like the rose-stone Gothic Cathedral from the eleventh century and a variety of other surviving monuments) seems to belie the city's past as a battleground. The location on the Rhine between French and German territories has involved Strasbourg in numerous conflicts; it has also endowed the city with some of the best cultural assets French and German civilizations have to offer. The province of Alsace alternately belonged to France or Germany, depending on the changing fortunes of wars and subsequent peace treaties. The old University of Strasbourg proudly claims Goethe as an alumnus.

The theater of Strasbourg for centuries was visited by French and German touring companies, giving both dramatic and musical performances which the educated bilingual part of the population patronized.

Thus the theater of Strasbourg has an unusual background, both in drama and opera. Unfortunately, it also has a tradition of devastating fires. During the severe winter of 1770, the announcement of the première of Molière's comedy *Tartuffe* promised that the theater would be well heated. Alas, this was not an idle pledge: after the fire that night, the theater was in ashes. Two more times, new halls of the Strasbourg theater were destroyed by flames.

The present building, attractively located on the Place Broglie, bears witness to the city's determination to have a representative municipal theater. In the decades following the defeat of France in 1871, German rule failed to Prussianize the province of Alsace. But 70 per cent of the population traditionally speak German, or a German dialect. Strasbourg has remained the seat of a provincial government. The theater blossomed. During the German interim, lasting to 1918, the Strasbourg opera attained great distinction. Such eminent German musicians as Hans Pfitzner, Wilhelm Furtwängler, and Otto Klemperer served as conductors. When the French reinherited the theater after World War I, they maintained its high standards. In 1940 the Germans overran eastern France, but they did not miss the opportunity to stress their role as art sponsors. They renovated the municipal theater at a cost of approximately $10,000,000.

The liberation came. Now it was the turn of the French government to prove its concern for the long-established tradition of Strasbourg as a cultural center. The national government in Paris assured the Alsatian capital of special treatment; but the municipality of Strasbourg assumed a large share of the financial responsibility.

Today, both the theater and the orchestra are under the tutelage of the city. After 1945 the French government began to contribute approximately $50,000 annually to the budget of the opera. Whenever the seasonal deficit proved to be higher than anticipated the city council came to the rescue.

The municipal theater gives both opera and operetta during the regular season, lasting from October 1 to May 31. The personnel of the theater is employed year-round with a one-month paid vacation. This provision pertains to the artistic directors, the orchestra, and the chorus. But the contracts with soloists fall outside of this arrangement: certain singers are engaged for specific performances, in keeping with recent procedures at the Paris Opéra.

The orchestra is completely maintained by the municipality. The musicians are city employees, entitled to pensions. Since 1958 the music director is likewise a municipal official (as far as his legal status is concerned). The musical staff of the opera consists of 3 conductors, 1 choral director, and 4 coaches. The orchestra derives supplementary income from its 10 subscription concerts. It also supplies the orchestral accompaniment for the concerts of the two largest choirs of Strasbourg — the Dom Chorus and the Wilhelmina Chorus. Strasbourg must be considered an orchestral town by comparison with other cities in the French provinces. In addition to the opera orchestra, there is the Orchestre Radio-Symphonique de Strasbourg, the second biggest radio orchestra of the nation; it has 80 members and is government-supported. There is also a semiprofessional orchestra, the Strasbourg Philharmonic.

The municipal theater is supervised by a committee of 16 to 20 members, chosen from the city council. The taste of these overseers is conservative: they represent a cross section of the population. Yet in 1959 these brave burghers approved their theater's production of *Wozzeck* by Alban Berg. Strasbourg claims the distinction of being the first French stage to have integrated into its regular repertory the epochal music-drama of the Austrian master. This happened because the municipal council accepted the judgment of artistic experts. In general, operas are performed in French, although exceptions are made. During June, 1958, Strasbourg was the seat of the World Festival of the International Society of Contemporary Music. Here too, the municipality cooperated generously.

Art patronage in Strasbourg illustrates a special point. It shows constancy of sponsorship in a city under different national rules. Whether France or Germany controlled Alsace, the arts fared well. It appears, in fact, that the one common denominator of the antagonistic neighbors was their care of culture in the coveted region.

Strasbourg commands today a leading position in art patronage, and other French cities make vigorous efforts to bring their cultural life up to comparable standards. From the national point of view, it would be untenable to favor indefinitely a few chosen communities primarily for historical or political reasons. Other cities of France are building up their art life in a systematic way. Parallel to the great national project of Lyrical Decentralization, there is a local resurgence in a large number of communities in every part of the country.

Théâtre des Nations
Rendezvous of World Theaters

A pioneering enterprise in the theatrical life of modern France is the *Théâtre des Nations* of Paris. This project was officially launched in 1954. But its inherent idea was tentatively formulated by Fermin Gremiere, who as director of the Trocadéro promulgated in the early twenties the formation of an "international theater." Gremiere's plan was considered by some as Utopian, by others as outright foolish. Who would listen to plays spoken in foreign languages? How many Frenchmen will want to attend Goethe's *Faust* performed in German, Chekhov's *Cherry Orchard* in Russian, or Pirandello's *Henry IV* in Italian? Was it not difficult enough to lure Parisians to serious French plays performed in French?

But after World War II the project of a Théâtre des Nations was revived and greatly extended by the directorial team of A. M. Julien and Claude Planson. The venture turned out to be a great success. Times had changed. The climate of the theater had become more cosmopolitan. It was no longer considered unrealistic to plan for the Paris production of plays in their original languages. The municipality was willing to support the plan (first with a subsidy of 70,000,000, old francs approximately $142,870). And so the *Festival d'Art Dramatique de la Ville de Paris* came into being. After its auspicious first season (1954) the Festival was repeated annually. The programs offered widely divergent fare. Bertolt Brecht's *Mother Courage* was given; Chinese opera came from Peking.

The warm response of the public to these first seasons prompted the Municipal Council of Paris and the Council of the Département Seine to enlarge the subvention as well as the scope of the project. For the third Festival (1956), lyrical and choreographic performances were added to those of the prose theater. Various foreign governments were eager to send their best theatrical companies as visitors to France. The Opera of East Berlin and the San Carlo Opera of Naples participated in this initial season of music drama.

Eventually, the idea of an international theater convinced the most die-hard skeptics. The national government decided to join the city of Paris and the Département Seine in the permanent support of the project. It now assumed a title expressing the global scope of its overall program: Théâtre des Nations. In 1957 this triple sponsorship on local, state, and federal levels made it possible to enlarge the program to three large cycles; it now offered a cycle of drama, 61 performances; a cycle of opera, 18 performances; a cycle of ballet, 12 performances. In the third season marionettes were added. By 1959 the total number of performances had risen to 129: the ratio of distribution within the overall program was 62 per cent prose theater, 38 per cent musical theater.

Cultural Exchange

Participation of important foreign theaters is annually assured by the following procedures: the Théâtre des Nations extends its invitations to companies abroad through diplomatic channels. The countries interested in guest appearance usually nominate their most representative theaters as candidates. The final selections, however, are made by the Théâtre des Nations; like all jury decisions, they are bound to cause occasional difficulties (some of them not without political implications). There is international competition for the prestige of participation in the Festival. The verdicts of large audiences and of knowing critics proved that the choices made by the Théâtre des Nations were convincing.

Neither the French sponsors nor the visitors are ever guided by commercial considerations. The prime motivation in all decisions is cultural exchange. The foreign nations financing tours of their best theaters to France are compensated by the gain of cultural prestige. The countries invited to send their theaters to Paris assume part of the financial responsibility. The foreign companies travel at their own expense, which might run very high (for example, when a large opera company transports its entire solo ensemble, chorus, orchestra, stage sets, etc.). The visitors keep the box-office receipts. The Théâtre des Nations provides the hall (plus maintenance, utilities, etc.), some of the technical personnel, and all forms of publicity in France. This arrangement works to the satisfaction of both partners.

The funds for the foreign tours to Paris are not raised exclusively by the governments of the visiting theaters. Thus the Paris appearance of the London Dramatic Workshop is subsidized by various townships on the outskirts of the English capital where this theater had regularly performed. In Malmö, Sweden, collections were held on the streets so that the municipal theater — the pride of this Scandinavian city — could afford to play in Paris.

Performing in Foreign Languages

The Théâtre des Nations has large and loyal audiences. Attendance figures are rising: in 1954 there were 25,000 spectators; in 1956, 75,000; in 1960, the figure passed 100,000. This growing public proves that the obvious handicaps which performances in foreign languages entail — even in the most cosmopolitan city of the Continent — can be overcome by various means. There is an extraordinary variety in the repertory. The 1959 season brought 26 foreign companies to Paris, speaking and singing 13 different languages within a total of 37 productions.

To reduce the language barrier, the visitor to the theater may rent a transistor radio which broadcasts a translation of the play in process. In addition to the modest rental fee for the radio, one's card of identity must be "pawned" for the duration of the play; this has proved sufficient insurance for the return of the radio. Traditional methods of information by means of program notes are likewise in use. *Rendezvous*, the program magazine of the Théâtre des Nations, always offers the synopsis of the play as well as pertinent commentary on its background and style.

At present the Théâtre des Nations is housed in the old Théâtre Sarah-Bernhardt, with a seating capacity of 1,200. But for the Paris première of Schoenberg's posthumous opera *Aron and Moses*, the Théâtre des Nations temporarily moved to the Théâtre des Champs-Élysées. Plans for a new home for the Théâtre des Nations are in blueprint.

Peace Corps of Theater

Today, the Théâtre des Nations offers a wide and fascinating panorama of global theater. It has brought national theater from Mexico City and the Japanese Noh Theater from Tokyo. A group of African Negro dancers, whose tribal folk art is on the verge of dying out, was imported to Paris. The indigenous ceremonial dances of African ballet made a deep impression, and the experience led to an important new theatrical project.

Approximately 100,000,000 Negroes live in Africa. They have a theater of their own which is obviously capable of modern development. The French have decided to assist the Africans in rebuilding and extending the scope of their indigenous theater. The Théâtre des Nations plays the main part in this project. It has sent French technicians to Africa for six months, to teach the Negroes contemporary Western stagecraft, and to help them in the preparation of new productions. As a result, a company of South African actors, subsidized by their own government, performed Shakespeare's *Romeo and Juliet* in Paris. Another Negro company from the Ivory Coast gave *Macbeth.* Thus the masterworks of English drama are becoming the property of the African Negro Theater. Primitive as African theater still is, its own productions have meaning for the West. Here is an additional and vital goal for cultural exchange. The French have formed here a peace corps of the theater. But their initiative transcends the limits of the stage. It is an interracial act of good will.

Théâtre National Populaire
Palais de Chaillot

The old Trocadèro, long a landmark of Paris, was demolished in 1937, the year of the World Exhibition. On the impressive site of the Trocadèro, overlooking Champs de Mars, rose the spacious and modern Palais de Chaillot, the home of the Théâtre National Populaire (TNP). The project, inaugurated by the Fourth Republic, established a permanent national theater on a broadly popular basis, yet with a repertory definitely serious in scope.

The Palais de Chaillot was built with the idea of accommodating large audiences. It has 2,800 seats, all of them comfortable and offering a good view of the stage. The circular access to the theater is spectacular and the interior of the building is attractive.

Affiliated with the TNP is the Théâtre Rècamier, suitable for performances in a more intimate style; it seats 600.

The Théâtre National Populaire performs in every medium: it offers drama and opera, classical operetta and ballet, instrumental and vocal concerts. The attribute "popular" in the title of the theater might suggest a conventional repertory offering light fare. This is definitely not the policy of the Théâtre National Populaire; rather it attempts to make great works of art popular — works that have wrongly been considered beyond the grasp of the masses. The TNP has been eminently successful in this educational program. Its French repertory contains works by Gide, Musset, Mérimée, Rolland, etc. World drama, in a wide range from Aristophanes and Sophocles to O'Casey and Brecht, is well represented. Jean Vilar, first director of the TNP, made good theater available to those who cannot afford to buy expensive tickets.

Classical masterworks are interpreted in a worthy manner. Modern performances have attained meritorious standards. The TNP also shows moving pictures. One series is devoted to "Classical Films." Another series runs "Masters of the Film."

The TNP, committed to the aim of public art education, has maintained a policy of low ticket prices. The basic price is at present 2.46 NF (fifty cents). In the ticket sale, priority is frequently given to schools and related educational organizations. Youth has taken full advantage of attending the dramatic and musical performances at the Palais de Chaillot. The adult audience of the TNP represents a cross section throughout the population of the capital. At greatly reduced prices, good seats are available to old people who, living on modest annuities, could otherwise not afford to attend performances at the Palais de Chaillot. These senior citizens form a characteristic segment of the audience. Their interest in the living stage has not been replaced by the domestic enjoyment of radio and television.

Concession of State Theater

The Théâtre National Populaire is managed on the basis of a concession; the French state owns the theater and remains its controlling authority. The government grants the concession to a theatrical expert who assumes charge of all aspects of administration. This method of "renting" a national theater to a director of semiprivate status involves specific problems. On the positive side — the opportunity to manage an officially endowed theater is a challenge for an enterprising and imaginative theater director. On the negative side — the financial and artistic responsibilities are considerable.

On August 20, 1951, the basic contract was signed between the state and the concessionaire of the TNP. According to Article 35, the state subvention is flexible. It is designed to meet annually the changing needs of the overall program which is submitted in advance. Article 3 obliges the concessionaire to deposit a modest security of 500,000 ($1,020 old francs) in return for the subsidy. Each season a number of performances must be given outside the Palais de Chaillot. On the tours of the TNP its basic policy of modest prices remains unchanged. Special reductions for students are available wherever the theater appears.

During the first decade of its existence (1951-1961) TNP played before 4,285,582 spectators. These performances were distributed as shown in Table V.

TABLE V

Distribution of Théâtre National Populaire Performances

Palais de Chaillot	1,384
Théâtre Récamier	384
Parisian Suburbs	80
Île de France	151
French Provinces	360
Avignon (festival, with an average of 2,204 spectators for each performance)	115
Foreign Countries	499

For the season 1960-61 the attendance at the Palais de Chaillot was 89.68 per cent of capacity.

The contract of the TNP also calls for the engagement, each season, of at least one young *régisseur* — a graduate of the National Conservatory of the Dramatic Arts. This stipulation aims at providing both employment and experience for young directors.

The government contract reminds TNP management and ensemble of their mission: always to be aware that their theater represents a national enterprise of France. Management and personnel are expected to collaborate in good faith. They must not "indulge in any religious or political propaganda which might prevent the steady good progress of their teamwork and harm the fraternal union of the company."

The Three Premières

The TNP reserves for certain cultural organizations a number of special performances that are closed to the general public. These performances are called "avant-premières" because they generally precede the presentation of new works to the invited press. These two performances ("avant-première" and "press première") are followed by the "official première" with open ticket sales for the general audience. Thus each première is offered three times, following in regular sequence.

For the avant-premières all seats are sold at the same low price (approximately fifty cents). These events have become very popular; no less than 20 cultural associations and youth groups regularly take advantage of them. The participating groups include Friends of the Théâtre National Populaire, the Committee of Students in Paris, the Center of International Exchange, Jeunesse Musical de France, and l'Alliance Française.

In addition to the regular performances, the TNP has introduced for the benefit of its public a series of "Dialogues." In these informal public discussions, the producers and actors of TNP participate, explaining various aspects of the scheduled plays. The TNP organizes special performances for children, concerts exclusively devoted to modern music, organ recitals, etc.

Informal Audience

What are some of the reasons for the signal success of the TNP? It is, admittedly, difficult to attract large popular audiences for regular attendance of the serious theater. But the TNP has accomplished just that. It would be an over-simplification to attribute this success only to stimulating productions and the artistry of the principal interpreters of the TNP.

Environmental factors have played a part in the conquest of the public: the audience feels at home at the Palais de Chaillot. An informal climate prevails in the foyer, in the ample social rooms, and in the auditorium itself. In the corridors of the TNP, one does not meet the chic, "exclusive" crowd of the Champs-Élysées. In fact, the title of the theater, *Palais de Chaillot*, is somewhat misleading. For the atmosphere of the Palais is as democratic as it is in the *faubourgs* of Paris. One may feel as appropriately dressed in a sport coat as in a tuxedo, in a sweater and skirt as in one of the latest creations of a fashionable Paris designer. Yet the informality at the Palais de Chaillot does not imply untidiness, but rather a simplicity of dress and behavior, which is an essential premise in France if a large young audience is to be attracted to the theater. As the TNP is often rented in advance to organizations for closed performances, the *milieu* suggests a theatrical club. The Palais also has a pleasant restaurant serving meals at reasonable prices. It is the first theater restaurant of its kind in Paris.

Recently there has been criticism of the modest size of the governmental subvention: it is argued that the state should make greater allowances for the TNP, in view of its proven ability to fulfill its principal assignment — namely, to create a new, popular audience for the serious theater. In the initial year, 1951, the annual support was $90,000. The subsidy has increased so that at its present rate a minimum of 150 performances can be given within a five-month period. In 1959 the personnel of the TNP numbered 137, of which 32 were actors. The ensemble is young, the average age is below 35. In 1960 the subvention of the TNP (approximately $330,000) amounted merely to one-third of the subvention allocated to the Comédie Française.

Avignon Festival as Antecedent

Certain basic concepts of the Théâtre National Populaire originated outside Paris. As Jean Vilar, founder-director of the TNP, explains: in Avignon a novel style of production explored new ways and means to present serious drama to large and popular audiences. In Avignon, at the medieval residence of the popes, the Festival of Dramatic Art opened on September 10, 1947. *Cid* by Corneille and *Prinz Friedrich von Homburg* by Kleist were the initial offerings in the Palais de Papes, which seats 3,000. As it happens, the Palais de Chaillot in Paris seats 2,800. The almost identical capacity of the theaters in the southern town and in the capital, as well as other crucial premises of dramatic production, suggested the transfer of the Avignon method to Paris. From the beginning Jean Vilar's principles of education guided the policy of the large theater in the old Papal Palace at Avignon: "I would rather play before empty benches than before an audience whose only qualification is the ability to pay high ticket prices." Vilar's approach to the solution of the dilemma proved also in Paris to be a moral as well as an artistic success. He continued to offer excellent theater at very modest prices. Government support made this possible.

The Fifth Republic has every reason to increase the subvention of this pioneering project inaugurated by the Fourth Republic; the public itself demands a raise for the TNP. But nothing dramatizes the impact of this theatrical experiment more than the fact that the national government intends, during the next decade, the establishment of no less than 20 stages modeled after the pattern of the TNP and distributed throughout France.

VIII. The Fifth Republic

State Ministry of Culture

Charles de Gaulle has been president of France since January 8, 1958. This is a long period for continuous rule in terms of recent French history. Prior to the Fifth Republic a major obstacle in the establishment of a consistent national art policy proved to be the rapid succession of different governments. Between the Franco-Prussian War (1870-1871) and Hitler's ominous ascent to power (1933) there were more than 88 changes of French government. The average duration of a cabinet was nine months. Every change inevitably had its impact on official art patronage, provided the change of cabinet meant also a transfer of power on the level of ministers, undersecretaries, and ministerial department heads. In France the Minister of Education (or Director of Fine Arts) frequently represents the wishes of a political majority. And it has happened that this majority was dispersed by the time a law or any other crucial decision on the national art policy could be put into reality. Certain pitfalls in the art life of the Third and Fourth Republics can, justifiably, be blamed on this lack of continuous government.

Other European countries have likewise had a relatively fast turnover of cabinets. But there is this difference: the government-supported art institutes (in Austria, for instance) are sufficiently removed from the direct impact of the political scene. They can continue their artistic course in spite of political crises. This is not so in France. Ever since the Golden Age, art patronage has been an exponent of the power in charge. The destiny of the performing arts depends today — as it did during the era of Louis XIV, the Revolution, or the Napoleonic reign — on the kind of official policy that the incoming power will adopt. While the very existence of the various national art institutes was never in jeopardy, continuity of planning was often handicapped by the inconstancy of government. Support is constant. Art policy is not.

The Fifth Republic has taken a very strong stand in favor of governmental art support and simultaneously has insisted on highest standards.

A crucial innovation is the establishment of a Ministry of State for Cultural Affairs (Ministère d'État chargé des Affaires Culturelles). President de Gaulle appointed André Malraux, the art philosopher and novelist, to this crucial post. In the reorganization of offices and redistribution of authorities, the Direction Générale des Arts et des Lettres is now a subsidiary of the Ministry of Culture. The national theaters, likewise, come under the control of the Ministry of Culture, which now functions independently of the Ministry of National Education. In the ultimate purpose, however, the aims of these government departments are closely related.

When assuming his post in the spring of 1959, André Malraux defined the cultural goal of the national art institutes: "the most noble works of humanity and before all, those of France, must be made available to the greatest number of Frenchmen." In regard to the national theaters, he emphasized again that the government was disinterested in financial returns but is most concerned that the large subsidies be put to best use.

Reforms concerning the national theaters are in France subject to governmental supervision. In November, 1959, the French Cabinet adopted the reorganizational measures proposed in April by the Ministry of Culture. Concerning the state theaters, Malraux epitomized his reforms in three words: *Programme*, *Salle*, *Époque*. He implied that the repertory would have to regain its cultural impact. Carefully chosen works would have to be given in the halls most suitable to their performances. More respect for the contemporary spirit was due in the performing arts. A renascence of classical drama was obligatory. Two experimental theaters were to be formed (one directed by Albert Camus,* the other by Jean Vilar). They were to present works by unknown and little-known authors, past and present.

Reforms at the Comédie Française

This study has traced the role of the Comédie Française from its inception under Louis XIV to its emergence as the stronghold of French dramatic tradition. Napoleon's Moscow Decree (1812) aimed at the permanent establishment of the art institute with national support. Certain ramifications of the Moscow Decree rule the Comédie Française to this very day.

During the Fourth Republic the theater, once envisioned as a shrine of French drama, lost sight of its mission to preserve the classical repertory. Shallow entertainment repressed the inherent educational values of the theater. Farce became more important than tragedy. The lack of genuinely artistic guideposts was blamed on the kind of management that guided the Comédie Française: the actors themselves were in charge. A committee of 6 senior actors ran the theater; 3 of them were elected by the actors; 3 were appointed by the government. For all practical purposes the actors alone decided the course of their theater. Their repertory favored lightweight nineteenth-century fare. And so comedies of Eugène Labiche and Georges Feydeau won out over the profound plays of Corneille, Racine, or Victor Hugo.

*The tragic, accidental death of the Nobel prize winning author has robbed the French art scene of his guidance.

The new Ministry of Culture set out to remedy the organization and repertory of the Comédie Française. Thus the decree of November, 1959, strengthened the power of the newly-appointed administrator of the theater, and the off-stage roles of the actors were sharply curtailed. Their administrative committee (composed of 6 senior actors) was to have only consultative function. The administrator of the Comédie Française and the consultants were all appointed by the Minister of Culture (the actors, however, upon recommendation of the administrator).

How does the Comédie Française select new plays for performances? The decisions are entrusted to an 11 member committee of readers including the administrator of the theater: 3 actors serving on the administrative committee and selected by their fellow actors; 3 actors not on the administrative committee; 4 representatives of the nation's literary life, 1 of whom must be a member of the French Academy. We take note, however, of a special premise: none of the 11 members may be a playwright. The fairness underlying the choice of personnel and carefully defined function of this committee is beyond reproach.

Subsidy and Cultural Responsibility

The annual subsidy to the Comédie Française is generous. There is, then, no excuse to build a repertory based on any other than purely artistic considerations. The government puts no financial pressure on the administration of the theater: it is not unduly concerned with the income from the box office. (See Table VI.)

TABLE VI

Budget of the Comédie Française for 1958 (OF)

	OF	($)
Total budget	812,000,000	($1,949,612)
Subvention	522,000,000	(1,065,402)
Income at box office	266,000,000	(542,906)
Income from various other sources	19,000,000	(38,779)
Income from outside contracts	4,100,000	(8,368)
Salaries for administrative personnel	50,000,000	(102,050)
Salaries for artistic personnel	194,000,000	(395,954)
Salaries for technicians	48,000,000	(97,968)
Operational costs	161,000,000	(328,601)
Stage maintenance	15,000,000	(30,615)
Social security	88,500,000	(180,628)
Equipment	132,000,000	(269,412)
Publicity	25,000,000	(51,025)
Production rights	46,000,000	(93,886)
Stage sets	45,000,000	(91,845)

In 1960 the subvention paid by the government to the Comédie Française was $940,000. The total personnel numbered 475. There were 32 senior actors (*sociétaires*) and 45 *pensionnaires*. The senior actors are normally under contract for twenty years and are eligible for pension. The remaining actors are employed on a seasonal basis.

Théâtre de France

Earlier in this chapter the background of the Odéon, the Left-Bank branch of the Comédie Française, was traced from its beginnings in 1781. At its post-revolutionary reopening in 1797, the theater assumed the name *Odéon* and in 1804, *Théâtre de l'Impératrice*.

"Make room for the young!" became the watchword for the Odéon during the Romantic era. Early in the twentieth century the directorship (1906-1914) of André Antoine brought a period of extravagant spectacles to this stage, which played havoc with its state-supported budget. But the government continued its subsidy none the less, as it had always done in the past. (See Table VII.)

TABLE VII

Subventions to the Odéon (OF)

Year	Amount
1794	100,000
1817	27,000
1824	60,000
1826	100,000
1829	160,000
1928	300,000
1930	400,000

TABLE VIII

Subventions, Comédie Française and the Odéon (OF)

Year	Amount
1953	343,000,000 ($ 700,063)
1956	406,000,000 ($ 828,646)
1957	460,000,000 ($1,104,460)

In 1946 reunion of the Odéon with the Comédie Française was attempted (in analogy to the *Réunion Lyrique* of the Opéra and the Opéra Comique). During the Third and Fourth Republics the two houses of the Comédie Française had been identified according to their halls and locations: La Salle Richelieu and La Salle du Luxembourg. But the Fifth Republic divorced these theaters once more. The Odéon became independent and was entrusted to the actor-director Jean-Louis Barrault. President de Gaulle appeared at the solemn rededication of the venerable theater. Now called *Théâtre de France*, it is committed to progress and experimentation. The Théâtre de France also houses the Domaine

Musicale, a series of concerts and related events devoted to modern music under the leadership of Pierre Boulez, the distinguished composer.

In 1960 the Odéon received a subvention of $336,000 as compared with $940,000 accorded to the Comédie Française.

Reforms at the Opéra and Opéra Comique

The Minister of Culture reaffirmed the Opéra's traditional task of presenting the masterpieces of the past. The performances were to be commensurate with the Opéra's prestige as the first lyrical stage of France. But, while maintaining its standard repertory, the Opéra must not fall into the stultified role of a musical museum. It is obliged to offer significant premières of contemporary music-drama.

The Opéra Comique must likewise assume new, additional assignments. It must serve, to an ever-increasing degree, as a testing stage. France has long lacked a forum for the young, and the Opéra Comique is to provide it. At the same time the neglected masterpieces of the seventeenth and eighteenth centuries, the lyrical scores of Lully and Rameau, of Monteverdi and Mozart, must be newly reintegrated into the repertory of the Opéra Comique.

In theory, the blueprint of the Ministry of Culture in behalf of the national opera theaters appears very convincing. Everyone interested in serious art hopes for its realization. In practice, the difficulties have proved to be like those in the Comédie Française. Differences of opinion in the relegation of authority and in the interpretation of the artistic task lead to a state of affairs in the national theaters that is far from peaceful.

Aid for the First Play

In its allocations of art subsidies the government of France is extremely conscious of the importance of youth. In the field of drama the so-called *Aid for the First Play* (*aide à la première pièce*) represents a significant procedure. It was created by the government to facilitate initial access to the stage for talented young authors. The original conditions attached to this aid, since modified, are that the play must have been originally written in French (translations are not considered), and that the play must never have been performed in public.

Aid for the First Play differs, in intent and scope, from other types of subventions available to authors and theaters which perform the plays. The anticipations are realistic. One does not expect masterworks. The emphasis is to encourage young talent showing promise.

The awards are made by the Minister of Education. He acts upon recommendation of a committee of writers, producers, and actors who have screened a multitude of manuscripts submitted from all over France. Aid for the First Play also entitles a reduction of taxes to the theater undertaking performance. The subsidies, which are modest, are forwarded to the management of the theater, which assumes all responsibility for the project. In this way the government helps both the young dramatist and the sponsoring theater. The gesture of help comes at the age when the young author needs this kind of encouragement, and it is certainly more constructive than singling out, again and again, firmly established authors for official awards.

The national government also offers awards to the best young theatrical companies throughout the country. In 1961 the budget for young companies (*Aide aux Jeunes Compagnies*) was 485,000 NF ($98,988). Hence the fraction distributed to each of about 50 contestants was small. Individual allocations fluctuate from 2,000 to 20,000 NF ($4,082).

Private Theaters Supported

Besides the national theaters, the Republic also helps certain private theaters and occasionally subsidizes interesting projects of the avant-garde. To qualify for such a subvention, the management of the theater must offer a "moral guarantee" that the production will live up to the concept of a cultural contribution and make a nominal down payment on the taxes which the government collects from tickets sold.

In 1960 Paris counted 52 theaters on the boulevards, with 17,449 seats. The municipality of Paris is the proprietor of five theaters; yet they are managed as private enterprises. These are Châtelet, Ambassadeurs, Gaieté-Lyrique, Marigny, and Sarah-Bernhardt. They receive nominal support. The total subvention granted them is 25,000,000 NF (approximately $1,000,000). Comparable sums are, in principle, allotted by the municipality to the other 47 theaters of which the city is not the owner.

Radiodiffusion Télévision Française

The French government supports 3 major radio programs within the framework *Radiodiffusion Télévision Française*. The first of these offers popular entertainment. The second concentrates on news service, national and international.

All cultural and scientific broadcasts originate on the third program, which is referred to as the *National Program* and is on the air for seventeen hours, from seven A.M. to midnight. Music, drama, and belles-lettres comprise the artistic portion of the National Program. The musical fare, serious and all-inclusive, offers opera and symphonic, chamber and choral music.

The state completely subsidizes all activities of the Radiodiffusion Télévision Française in Paris and in the provinces. The Ministry of Finance collects the listening fees and returns the moneys to the basic fund of the French broadcasting system. The annual listening tax is 25 NF ($5.00) per year for each radio. There are few French families without at least one radio. With ample means at its disposal, the French radio lives up to its cultural responsibility. It is one of the strongest patrons of the performing arts in Europe, and good music is available to all of France from early morning to late at night.

Radio Sponsors Serious Music

Radiodiffusion Télévision Française maintains no less than 4 orchestras in Paris and 6 in the provinces. The members of all 10 of these orchestras are engaged year-round. In Paris, the largest of these instrumental ensembles is the Orchestre National with 105 members. Radio Symphonique has 80 musicians; Radio Lyrique, which performs exclusively for opera, has 65 members. A small ensemble of 30 players is devoted to orchestral chamber music.

The 6 provincial orchestras are placed at strategic points throughout France: the government aims at the conquest of a broad public for serious music. Of these radio orchestras outside of Paris, 3 are of major size and scope (those in Lille, Lyon, and Strasbourg). The other 3 (those in Marseille, Nice, and Toulouse) are of medium size. All 6 orchestras not only perform regularly over the air, but give frequent public concerts in civic halls. These events are well attended and audiences continue to grow. Consequently, these radio orchestras are recognized as vital assets to their cities. The Republic supported these provincial radio orchestras with approximately $1,000,000 in 1959.

The national government no longer questions the legitimacy of permanent support of these strategic radio stations. It interprets this subsidy as "a moral obligation to the people of France," to quote Henri Barraud, the distinguished composer who has directed the Music Section of National Program since the liberation of France.

In addition to its very active orchestras, the Radiodiffusion Française maintains in Paris a permanent chorus of one hundred voices. This vocal group performs both *a cappella* or jointly with the orchestra in broadcasts of opera, oratorio, cantatas, etc. There is also a resident string quartet with a very busy schedule. Radiodiffusion Française regularly commissions new works, for the most part of French composers.

While the government officially supervises the financial policy of networks in regard to finances, the musical director has a free hand in the artistic policy. The concerts in Paris are noted for their interesting programs of old and new music. In contrast to the routine concert series given by the four principal orchestra associations of Paris, the radio stresses the significance of music itself, rather than that of prominent performers. In Paris a large broadcasting hall for public concerts is in the process of being completed.

The national television network operates on a basis that is analogous to that of radio. The Radiodiffusion Télévision Française is the nation's official and only telecasting system.*

The budget of the Radiodiffusion Télévision Française is calculated in advance, according to the income received from the license fees. One Frenchman out of three watches television every evening. In 1959, the combined budget for radio and television was 26 milliards, 3 million old francs ($53,072,123). The combined fee for radio and television is 85 new francs ($17.00), annually.

In 1963 the number of licenses issued for television sets had reached 4,000,000. Commercial advertising, as in other European countries, is limited. The government owns the company and controls all operations of Radiodiffusion Française.

The potentialities of educational television are regarded with great hope. *La télévision scolaire*, as it is called, is generally welcomed by the teachers. Considering the inherent conservatism of French pedagogy, particularly in the provinces, and its intellectual aloofness from all technical props, this is worthy of note. The variety of programs is impressive. Science programs rate high; "science fiction" is at home in the country of Jules Verne. New programs for the very young audience are constantly explored. The French are rightly famous for their tender, imaginative treatment of art addressed to children. The land of La Fontaine retells on the screen the heritage of fables with irresistible charm.

Almost every morning and afternoon children may enjoy special programs. But the young watchers present a problem. Many TV evening programs show films with the warning, *adults only.* To make certain that parents will know when this type of film is shown, a small white square appears on the lower right corner of the screen. This signal means, "Not for children!" The obvious trouble, however, is that the white square might attract rather than turn away the young patrons.

Self-Government of Concert Orchestras

This Chapter discusses the specifically French evolution of the performing arts and establishes significant points of priority in French patronage of the theater.

*A second channel is scheduled to begin operations in 1964.

Whether France can be claimed the birthplace of the orchestra depends on one's definition. The early growth of the orchestra as an organized ensemble of instruments belonging to different families can be traced to various events on French soil. The Frenchman Guillaume de Machaut (ca. 1300-1377), one of the towering composers of the fourteenth century, describes what might have been the initial orchestra: an ensemble of 36 instruments of different kinds, yet apparently assembled for unified performance. Groups of musicians played the same part. And in this embryonic phase of orchestral performance, the distribution of the instrumental parts lacked precise order. The method was one of improvisation, guided by the range rather than by the color of the instruments. In accordance with medieval practice of performance, an ensemble functioning in this manner can be considered an orchestra.

Likewise, in France the first orchestral score was printed: music for the *Ballet Comique de la Royne*, performed at Court in 1581. Ever since the Baroque era, crucial chapters of orchestral history have been written in France.

During the nineteenth century Hector Berlioz created a new concept of the Romantic orchestra: an ensemble of power and virtuosity, capable also of elfin lightness and tender expressiveness. Berlioz made an eminent contribution to the study of orchestral technique in his unique text, *Traité d'instrumentation et d'orchestration modernes* (1844). During his Paris period, Richard Wagner learned to admire not only the romantic orchestral witchcraft of Berlioz, but also the classical performances in the Concerts de Conservatoire directed by F. A. Habeneck, whose Beethoven interpretations "made the scales fall from my eyes," to quote Wagner's tribute to the French orchestra. French opera scoring was brought by Georges Bizet to supremacy of precision and textural finesse. At the century's end Claude Debussy created in his impressionistic orchestra new luminosity of timbres — the poetic record of a pioneering, typically French instrumental imagination.

This entire evolution of orchestral techniques and styles took place on the Parisian scene. French literature and painting can be traced to various regions of the country; but crucial musical developments in all media of performance remained closely tied to the capital.

Due to the long-established centralization of French art life in Paris, other French cities did not vitally participate in this remarkable growth. The consequences are apparent. Today only the orchestras of Paris are of a widely recognized quality. They make records internationally in demand and they are invited to tour throughout the world. The other large French cities — Lyon, Marseille, Bordeaux, even Strasbourg — have not yet trained and cultivated large orchestras of comparable standards. This is a point worthy of note, for provincial centers in various other countries have first-rate orchestras. The French government is conscious of this situation and is in the process of correcting it as an integral part of the national program of artistic decentralization.

As in the past, so today Paris is the nerve center of the nation's orchestral culture. There are the orchestras of the national theaters — those of the Opéra and Opéra Comique — which have maintained their fine reputations. There are the ensembles of the Radiodiffusion Française. There are 4 principal orchestral societies: Société des Concerts de Conservatoire; Concerts Pasdeloup; Concerts Colonne; Concerts Lamoureux. All but the first are named after the conductors who were responsible for their organization during the second part of the nineteenth century.

In Paris symphony concerts are held each Sunday at exactly the same hour: 5:45 P.M., which seems an impractical, competitive, arrangement. But many members of these symphonic orchestras are individually recruited from various other organizations (such as the Opéra, the Opéra Comique, or the band of the Garde Républicaine). During the week these musicians are scheduled for their regular assignments, and they must take advantage of available spare time to rehearse for Sunday symphony concerts.

The Parisian concert orchestras are managed as is the Vienna Philharmonic. As members of their concert orchestras, the French musicians are independent. They form their own organization; they choose their own manager and other executive officers; they elect their conductor; they share the income, which is a nominal addition to their salaries from their main employment.

Since the end of the Second World War, the radio orchestras have attained increased importance. These government sponsored ensembles give a limited number of public concerts free to the public. Contemporary music has a definite place at these concerts. The orchestras of the national theaters (such as the Opéra and the Opéra Comique) are supported in full by the government in compensation for their service in the pit of these stages. The musicians do not perform collectively outside of their theaters except for recordings. As state employees they have a fixed income with full pension.

Members of these theater orchestras, as stated before, have the right as individuals to join any concert orchestra of Paris. But the French government does not duplicate its support to the same group of performers. The concert organizations, however, receive modest aid from both the national government and the municipal council of Paris. These grants guarantee their overhead, the rental of halls, and the expenditures of administration. The subsidies protect the concert societies from deficits, but they do not cover salaries for the orchestra members who are fully employed by other state institutions.

French orchestra musicians belong to unions, which have done much to ameliorate their economic status. The union of French musicians has the reputation for being the strictest on the European continent. In 1959 a protracted strike lasting eight months resulted in much improvement. The living standard of the musicians in the state-supported organizations has become more than adequate.

From the viewpoint of progress, the most promising aspects of orchestral life in France are its recent decentralization and the conquest of new audiences in the capital as well as in the provinces. In grade and high schools musical classes are obligatory. And it is here that seeds for lifelong appreciation of good music are early and expertly planted. Regular attendance is a pedagogical goal.

In Paris large audiences for popular symphony concerts are taken for granted. The problem of bringing serious music to the French working class is handled realistically. Experience has shown the importance of choosing a proper hall. It is no secret that French workers do not feel comfortable in the elegant environment of the concerts given at the Théâtre des Champs-Élysées or other places of traditional formality. The workers show a preference for the Théâtre National Populaire. They feel at ease where they meet their own group. Everywhere, then, the problem is to find the proper hall along with an appropriate program to assure full receptivity of new audiences.

French Festivals

France has always had a special flair for celebrations that make even a serious occasion appear serene, and the serene a gay holiday. On great national celebrations, such as Bastille Day, France dances in the streets from early morning through the night into the next day.

Yet French theater and concert life — aside from the commemorations of special historic dates — has only recently joined the European upsurge of organized festivals in the performing arts. Before the Second World War there were very few such events in the entire nation. Today, no less than 70 festivals are scheduled regularly in France, and some have proved a creative potential that in the tempo of artistic achievement and international appeal surpassed even the expectations of their founders. Into this group belong, outside those in Paris, the summer festivals of Aix-en-Provence and Prades. But much progress (in different categories and on different levels) is being made in such large cities as Bordeaux and Strasbourg, as well as in a number of smaller towns. Some of these festivals aim at uncompromising artistic achievement. Others are regional attractions, distinguished by folkloristic spontaneity and by a display of local custom and tradition. The pioneer Festival of Dramatic Art in Avignon has been mentioned earlier in connection with its important progeny, the Théâtre National Populaire in Paris.

In Aix-en-Provence, the *ambiance*, a unique atmosphere and individual artistic climate, results from a communion between ancient local character and the specific style of performances developed at the Festival. The musical part of the program in Aix emphasizes both the old and the contemporary, with a propensity for the neglected. The rediscovery of an opera such as Haydn's *Il Mondo della Luna* (composed in 1777 on a libretto by Goldoni) delights the audience with its curiously timely subject — the extravagant interest in the world of the moon. Aix-en-Provence also plays a part in the renaissance of operas by Monteverdi. Within the modern repertory, the names of Berg, Hindemith, or Webern are prominent on the programs. The orchestra of the Südwestfunk of Baden-Baden, Germany, participates in this French festival and establishes teamwork and artistic comradeship across borders.

The French village of Prades, across the Pyrenees from Spain, offers remarkable performances of Baroque and classical chamber music. Prades exemplifies the founding of an important festival around the personality of one eminent interpreter: Pablo Casals, the legendary Spanish 'cellist, self-exiled from the Fascism in his native country, has proven in Prades that an obscure village can be rapidly transformed into an art center. Each summer audiences from all over the world come to this tiny border town to hear some of the best musicians of our time perform under the guidance of Casals. They play on a stage before the Baroque altar at the Cathedral of St. Pierre. Works by Bach have so far held first place.

The *Mai Musical de Bordeaux*, first held in 1949, is scheduled from May 17 to June 2. The Grand-Théâtre in this fourth largest city of France becomes the scene of drama, opera, ballet, and symphonic concerts. At the festival of 1963 the Comédie Française and the orchestra of the Paris Conservatoire participated. The Saint-André Cathedral accommodates performances of devotional music and solo recitals. The Château de la Brède and the Château d' Yquem likewise contribute concert rooms. The International Music Festival of Strasbourg (June 7-16) claims to be the oldest of its kind in France. The program of 1963 offered a multiformity of premières by such composers as Francis Poulenc and Franz Schmidt. The Strasbourg Ballet participated along with the vocal and instrumental forces of the Municipal Theater. The list of solo recitals brought to the Alsatian capital Rudolf Serkin and

Andres Segovia. The Rotterdam Philharmonic performed Mahler's *Song of the Earth* in a French translation.

In Besançon, birthplace of Victor Hugo, the summer festival is conservative: standard works are performed by renowned interpreters. Recently, however, the sponsors show interest in the contemporary scene and they have added a competition for young conductors.

Among other French towns that have successfully built up their festivals, one may mention Angers, Arles, Arras, Biarritz, Carcassonne, Épinal, Menton (specializing in chamber music), Metz (the most recently founded festival), Nice, Nîmes (with dramatic performances included), and Versailles (taking full advantage of the historic environment).

In 1961 the government accorded to 30 individual festivals the sum of 902,000 NF (approximately $180,400). Of this allocation the lion's share fell to the Popular Festival of Paris organized by the TNP. These government-supported festivals are regarded as a contribution to French culture. Many communities, however, finance their own festivals from various local or regional sources.

The growing list of French art festivals is no promise that every one of these events assures its audiences of a genuine cultural program. Some of the activities within this mushroom growth of "festive" performances have been hurriedly mounted for tourist traffic and commercial exploitation. It is deplorable — in France as elsewhere in Europe — when false folk product and ceremony are a mockery of authentic tradition and legitimate expression of folklore. At certain places performances of drama and music are advertised with the added lure of one or several guest artists from the Comédie Française, the Opéra, or Opéra Comique. But this guarantees neither a good ensemble nor a well-rehearsed production. In such cases, the tourist is not the only victim; the cultural prestige of France loses by such misrepresentation.

IX. L'État Mécène

Government in Support of Art

Whatever the analysis of the French art scene reveals in detail, the overall evaluation of a national art program, subject to parliamentary controls, cannot be detached from an examination of the country's political and economic picture. Generous spending for cultural causes by the most economy minded people on the European continent may be as surprising as it is eloquent. But it is no longer puzzling, once we realize that Frenchmen are taught to regard the cultural manifestations of their civilization as precious property.

The backbone of the French nation is still its workers and farmers. One-third of the workers of France are recruited from the rural population of 12,500,00. (In 1962 the total population of France was 45,750,0000.) The give and take of a pluralistic society obviously plays a flexible part in all official decisions ruling the art life of the country. As the budget is decided in the Chamber of Deputies, the voting record of each representative is closely watched by constituents at home: Frenchmen are not famous for their enthusiasm to pay taxes. Yet, the costly national art organizations are maintained from public moneys. No less than $3,500,000 are spent annually for the opera theaters in Paris alone! Will not such expenses appear prohibitive to the frugal French farmer in Provence, to the fisherman in Brittany, to the steelworker in the Department of Loire? Hard-working Frenchmen critically read about the national budget in their local papers. They discuss the finances of France in their favorite bistros with bold skepticism and Rabelaisian satire. They grumble and complain. What, then, makes them uphold their deputy who votes in Paris to support the arts?

Frenchmen of all classes have adopted and assimilated the basic concepts of French civilization, even if in their daily lives these concepts seem not to exist. For there are safety measures planted in the fertile system of French education. All children are early exposed to art appreciation in imaginative classes. The French high schools, with their tendency to emphasize the humanities, have a strongly art-minded curriculum. The children of uneducated parents may become, in maturity, staunch defenders of cultural issues because they have been taught, from elementary school on, to revere the traditional significance of their nation's art life. As patriotic Frenchmen they are sympathetic to the predicament of the arts. They understand why their support cannot be left to private initiative alone: today, the citizens of France are the patrons. They are prepared to vote for art at the polls.

And they do vote. The cultural budget is usually passed by Parliament — often with a considerable majority. In 1958 the budget of the governmental office of the Direction Générale des Arts et des Lettres was 50,048,680 NF (approximately $10,009,000). This amounted to 1.39 per cent of the total expenditure of the Ministry of Education. In 1960, when the Minister of Cultural Affairs asked for a substantial increase in his budget, all of his proposals were accepted by the Chamber of Deputies. This is remarkable. While Paris remains the nerve center of the nation, French policy is also decided in the market squares of Rouen or Orleans, in the old parks of Nice or Nancy, on the stairs of the *mairie* or the docks of Le Havre or Marseille — in thousands of places and homes where simple Frenchmen discuss the affairs of state with inherent rationalism.

The recent cultural program for Dramatic and Lyrical Decentralization, bringing the performing arts to the backward areas, to the mines and farms, to the factories and fishing ports, has already begun to bear fruit. As each year passes, the people at large become increasingly aware of the need for art. It is the new diffusion of the performing arts that holds the key to a vital future of cultural life.

Today, more than ever, Frenchmen seem resolved to maintain the high standards of their state-supported theaters, operas, and concert institutions, and to extend their educational mission in a long-range program to every corner of the Republic.

In 1959, the year of the inception of the Fifth Republic, the national budget for arts was as shown in Table IX.

TABLE IX

Art Budget (Beaux Arts et Lettres) 1959 (OF)

Direction Générale des Arts et des Lettres	
Art Instruction	791 million ($ 1,614,431)
Museums	590 million ($ 1,204,190)
National Theaters	2,369 million ($ 4,835,129)
Lyrical Theaters	1,576 million ($ 3,216,616)
Historical Monuments	2,200 million ($ 4,490,200)
Libraries	1,582 million ($ 3,228,862)
Cultural Relations	4,803 million ($ 9,802,923)

Controversy and Criticism

The Fifth Republic has, if anything, reinforced the role of governmental art support and, there can be no mistake about it, imposed a more rigid supervision of the national art institutes. The general conduct of artistic policy is now in the hands of the newly formed Ministry of Culture. Complaints about the state of affairs are widespread. But vehement public discussion and fierce criticism are traditional and probably necessary in France. There are deep-seated differences of opinion on major issues of civic life, and consequently of national art sponsorship.

It is too early to attempt a more comprehensive analysis of the achievements of the Fifth Republic as art patron.

Meanwhile, one hopes that the Ministry of Culture will gradually restrain its mode of operation. It is argued that the Ministry should primarily organize, advise, and persuade, but not command. The French government supports various scientific projects; here its function is clearly circumscribed. It supplies the financial means, but it does not administer scientific research. Many Frenchmen plead that the arts should be subsidized in a similar way.

But the important point in the the public reaction to a nation's art life is not that there should be no criticism. What matters is that the people should care. In any country a danger signal for the growth of cultural issues is indifference.

The lively participation of the French people on cultural issues may be observed on many fronts. A keen sense for traditional values applies to innumerable aspects of public life, and none is considered unimportant. The project of a new bridge to be built across the Seine River as a replacement of the old cast-iron Pont des Arts excites the entire city of Paris. "It is sheer vandalism," cry the conservatives, "to destroy the charming *passerelle!* The footbridge is a nostalgic reminder of old Paris." But there are the unsentimental ones who demand service and function. They insist that the overaged Pont des Arts has become unsafe. The footbridge, they say, must yield to modern traffic and give way to a structure equipped to accommodate motorized transportation. Further complications stem from conflicting administrative authority. The question is: what department has the final verdict to decide the fate of the small Pont des Arts, which has for a century and a half led Parisians from the National Institute to the Louvre, or back again to the Left Bank.

Sentiment or reason, conservative pride or progressive planning — these and countless other factors must be considered in official art policy throughout the nation. The government must aim at a balance that will be acceptable to an intelligently guided majority.

The fate of the Pont des Arts merely illustrates a typical and constant problem in the nation-wide struggle for the preservation of French cultural patrimony. Particularly the guardianship of architectural monuments remains a permanent task. As early as 1832 Victor Hugo published an essay entitled *Guerre aux démolisseurs*, and to the end of his life the great poet continued his vigorous campaign against ignorant or even willful destruction of art treasures.

More than a century later the Fifth Republic reinforces the war on vandalism and makes subsidies available for the conservation of irreplaceable masterpieces. But no less than 400 towns compete for governmental help. They need funds to maintain and restore a building, a street, or perhaps an entire historic quarter, threatened by deterioration or even razing. In some aspects, these problems of the French government compare with those facing the Republic of Italy.* Here, as there, the national program of conservation cuts deeply into funds that otherwise might be allocated to the performing arts.

*Cf. Chapter on Italy.

Test of Civilization
Permanence and Constancy of Patronage

The French chronicle, in a manner and frequency unparalleled in European history, reveals changes of government in rapid sequence. The overthrow of Bourbon Kings gave way to the Revolutionary Tribunal. The brief Consulate yielded to the Empires of the Napoleonic family, and the evolving nineteenth century witnesses further alternations of republican governments with monarchial episodes. But in all of these changes — somewhat bewildering to the foreign student of France — there remains the factor of constancy in the governmental art support of this thoroughly civilized nation.

French history also demonstrates the crises these social changes exerted on the patronage of the performing arts, and shows their frequent adjustments to new needs.

This Chapter has traced the beginnings of a permanent and organized patronage back to the Golden Age of French art, which radiated in the splendor of court life at Versailles. When a millennium of French kingdoms collapsed — and the Revolution of 1789 shook, within a single decade, the foundation of Europe's social structure — a new class, the citizenry, suddenly rose as the principal patron of the arts. Although insufficiently prepared for this new role, the Republic was eager to continue on its own terms the civilized duties of a seemingly liquidated aristocracy. The Revolution even invented new styles of performance — crude as they were — born from the first notions of a people's art. And the First Republic created patterns of sponsorship that have since been imitated by other nations, even in our own time. Where these efforts failed in eighteenth-century France, it was because of lack of experience, a dictatorial ruthlessness, and the general violence on the political scene to which the arts were so closely allied.

The turbulent alternation between the main phases of French government — between various monarchial and republican constitutions — did not harm the edifice of French art organizations, in spite of constant shifts in the governmental departments. This is a truly remarkable fact.

To this day, the national government of France has remained her most munificent art patron. This dominant role is more strikingly accentuated in France than in other European countries where the provinces and municipalities have long assumed important, and decidedly independent roles of regional art support.

The present, forceful turn of France toward Dramatic and Lyrical Decentralization merely stresses the deeply entrenched concentration of art patronage in Paris. It is primarily the national government which initiates and fosters French art life — at least for the time being — both in the capital and in the provinces. It is the Republic which subsidizes many of the dramatic and lyrical theaters, the orchestras, the radio, the television stations, etc. It is government that subsidizes art schools, aids youth organizations and even private enterprises, if they are serving a genuine cultural cause.

But neither private capital, industry, nor commerce can alone provide sufficient financial support of French art life. The people living in the 48 Départements of France pay the taxes from which official art support is derived. And the government of France is more than ever determined to bring art to all corners of the country. It is the momentous national project of decentralization that impresses us as the most decisive factor within the art policy of the Republic.

Important psychological effects of this decentralization may be detected in the minds of the French people and of the artists themselves. The Dramatic and Lyrical Centers create the feeling that other cities participate in the main current of national art life which the capital monopolized for centuries. The performers in the provinces no longer interpret their work as a mere steppingstone to a career in Paris — a crucial change of attitude. Work at the Centers has become an end in itself, and the provinces and municipalities are beginning to assume their own financial responsibilities.

Maisons de la Culture

Governmental plans for the future focus on a large-scale project allied, in its overall purpose, with the national program of decentralization. At this writing the Republic has inaugurated the first of a number of centers to be officially known as *Maisons de la Culture.* Each House of Culture will shelter the various media of the performing arts: drama, opera, classical operetta, and ballet. There will be symphonic concerts and chamber music. Films that have become "classical" will be shown. Original works of painting and sculpture, or even reproductions, will be seen in permanent or temporary exhibitions.

Three types of buildings are in the blueprint stage. The large centers will have two auditoriums, one exhibition hall, one permanent museum, a fine arts library, and the like. In short, the House of Culture will be the nucleus of communal art life. But in contrast to the workshops specializing in drama or opera, the new centers will unite — under one single roof — all cultural activities the citizens may hope to experience in their community. The government is confident that the Maisons de la Culture will be a means of educating, over the years, a large and faithful public.

Prior to 1965 cultural centers are to be built in the following cities: Amiens, Bordeaux, Bourges, Lille, Longwy, Nantes, Nevers, Rennes, Roubaix, Saint-Étienne, Strasbourg, Toulouse, Villeurbanne. In 1963 three halls were completed in Caen, Dunkerque, and Limoges. The setup in Caen, Normandy, shows how a town of 68,000 inhabitants devotes several theatrical projects to parallel cultural ends. Caen supports a Municipal Theater. There is the Compagnie de Théâtre de Caen, which is autonomous. Finally there is the Maison de la Culture of Caen, built and subsidized by the national Ministry of Culture. All art organizations use the same building, and its attractive hall seats 1,100. In the House of Culture designed for Villeurbanne (population 80,193) only a large glass wall separates the hall from the town. Thus there is no sharp break, but rather visual continuity between the daily city life and the art center.

In summary — the Maisons de la Culture have this dual function: on the national scene they are to achieve cultural decentralization; on the local scene, concentration of cultural experience.

The total expenditures of the Maisons de la Culture are very large; they will obviously increase in proportion to the continuous growth of the nation-wide enterprise. It is estimated that a minimum of $2,000,000 will be the cost of the smallest center. The maintenance of all centers, likewise, will be very expensive because their repertory and performances, their art exhibitions and libraries, etc., must be of distinguished quality, while the ticket prices are to be kept low. But regardless of the financial burden, the project of the Maisons de la Culture stands on firm ground within the overall budget of the Fifth Republic.

Debussy once called music "the most expensive noise after the cannon." Today, the bon mot of the great French composer takes on added meaning. National defense has not ceased for France with the Armistice of 1945. The cannons of World War I were cheap, compared with modern atomic weapons. But the strain of the defense budget has not meant a reduction of the art budget. The government still finds money for the arts — more money than ever before. *L'État Mécène: the state is the patron!*

Debt of the Present to the Past

In his *Memoirs* President de Gaulle envisions France "dedicated to an exalted and exceptional destiny . . . If, in spite of this, mediocrity shows in her acts and deeds, it strikes me as an absurd anomaly to be attributed to the faults of Frenchmen, not to the genius of the land. . . . To my mind, France cannot be France without greatness."

France, in the present twilight of her colonial realm and concurrent decrease of world power, is no longer great as an empire. This is a political fact France must face. Napoleon's dogma "God is on the side of the big battalions" can no longer lead the nation. Other concepts of greatness will carry the torch in the future. For France is not just another country. Her soil is the humus of a free civilization.

France has long reigned in the civilized world not by the sword but by the spirit of her thinkers and artists. In the realm of the performing arts French leadership is evident in every phase of history. From the profundity of sacred art life in medieval French cathedrals to the centuries-long munificence of secular art life sponsored by sovereigns and, finally, by the French people themselves, all patterns of patronage line up to form one single arch of cultural primacy.

The greater the past of a nation, the heavier is its obligation to the present. France is the guardian of an overwhelming cultural heritage, and thus her present government is charged with heavy responsibilities.

The world is conscious of French heritage and has acknowledged it in various tangible forms. When the Nazis occupied Paris and goose-stepped to the Arch of Triumph, a sharp pain was felt in every civilized country. When France was free again, the world had new hope for liberty.

WEST GERMANY

I. Dense Network of Art Life

To the art-conscious traveler a journey through West Germany reveals a phenomenon unique on the map of the world. Almost every German city of any consequence can take pride in its own theater, opera house, or concert hall. Even small towns which would be mere trading posts or railroad transfers in other countries, in Germany are art centers of no minor significance.

A resort town such as Baden-Baden (population 40,000) is the seat of a theater, a resident orchestra, a major radio network (the Südwestfunk) known internationally as a fortress of progressive art. An even smaller town, Donaueschingen (population 9,000), situated like Baden-Baden in the Black Forest, is host to one of the most important annual festivals of modern music. All over Germany, cities with populations well below 100,000 have capable orchestras and large choral societies devoted to serious music. And there are audiences to support them.

But the most remarkable aspect of the German art map is the close proximity of its centers to each other. In the Ruhr district, for instance, towns not even twenty miles apart boast their own independent municipal stages. These *Stadt Theater* usually accommodate a rotating repertory of drama and opera, of operetta and ballet. They engage their own company of actors, singers, dancers, professional choruses, and orchestras, year-round or for seasons long enough to provide adequate income for their personnel. The sum of German theaters performing opera surpasses the total number in the rest of Europe. Impressive playhouses equipped with most modern machinery have risen from the ashes of destruction. Other buildings are still in blueprint or not yet completed at this writing. Older ones are being reconstructed. Statistics are bound to be behind facts as the building program continues. Some of the former capital cities, such as Berlin or Munich, support more than one opera house.

A network of art organizations has been Germany's heritage for centuries. And Germany has rapidly resumed its tradition interrupted by World War II.

This Chapter is concerned only with the Federal Republic of Germany.* Yet the German Democratic Republic,** more commonly known as East Germany, reveals an art patronage that in extent and intensity is in no way second to that of Germany west of the Iron Curtain.†

In West Germany, and in East Germany, a wealth of art organizations has been inherited by the governments that have followed Hitler's Third

*Proclaimed May 23, 1949.

**Officially established October 7, 1949.

†For some statistics, cf. p. 275, footnote.

Reich. In both halves of the once-united nation the subsidies allocated to art institutes are very generous, and the only difference in the art life of the two is ideological. Governmental patronage directs the performing arts in East Germany toward a persistent support of its political doctrines. The West permits its art institutes a high degree of freedom.

Independence of Communal Centers

What lies behind this phenomenon of total art life and how could it blossom again so soon after massive destruction? Why do the individual cities of Germany insist on their independence? Obviously, neighboring communities could easily pool their performing forces, and thus multiply their artistic and economic strength. Patterns of modern living and the facile system of motorized transportation would suggest common enterprises, particularly as an aid for technically more demanding performances in small communities.

But the Germans resort to such methods of artistic partnership only occasionally. They collaborate in some of their many seasonal festivals, or in special cases such as the newly organized Opera-on-the-Rhine stationed in the city of Düsseldorf. Otherwise, the Germans follow their time-honored system of independent municipal art centers.

Since the Middle Ages, German towns have promoted the arts and crafts within their own specific communities and regions. Their pride in an indigenous communal art life is the chief factor in a consistently positive attitude toward art patronage. The impelling force behind German art support is today essentially the same as it was centuries ago. To trace motivations we have to turn back an entire millennium and examine various historic settings to which patronage has been inseparably tied. The mainsprings of German art sponsorship are viewed here chronologically, from the time when they began to nourish the art life of the nation.

The Reich
Illusion and Reality

For almost one thousand years various chroniclers have spoken admiringly or fearfully of a Teutonic Reich. Many of these references were made in poetic metaphor. Others, imbued with political meaning, gradually became part of the patriotic ideology of the German people.

Only in recent history did Germany emerge as a powerfully unified and politically homogeneous realm. In the maze of clichés, this fact has curiously escaped some German writers. Yet the idea that they could claim a "Reich of One Thousand Years" has haunted the Germans.

When Hitler came to power he immediately seized upon this favorite legend. He boastfully announced that the *second* German millennium, the Nazi Reich, had auspiciously begun.

The actual sovereignty of the German nation is linked to the rise of one of its constituent states, Prussia, which stems from the Peace of Westphalia in 1648. More than two centuries later, Prussia's dream was fulfilled: the kingdom became in 1871 the pivotal state of the new empire.

The Westphalian Peace had been preceded by bitter warfare of thirty years (1618-1648). Some causes of the conflict were religious, arising from a head-on clash between Catholicism and Protestantism. This protracted war, like other bloody contests for hegemony on German soil, left the country a shambles. But at least there was hope for a new principle that man would not be persecuted for his religious faith. Throughout the seventeenth and eighteenth centuries Germany was a loose union of small states under individual potentates. *This political structure had far-reaching effects on the patronage of the performing arts.*

The early nineteenth century marked the beginning of a new Teutonic national consciousness. The Congress of Vienna (1815), ending the Napoleonic warfare and trying to restore the political equilibrium on the disturbed Continent, assigned to Prussia leadership among the German *Länder* (states). But it was not until the third part of the nineteenth century that Otto Bismarck, the "Iron Chancellor," achieved the unification of Germany as the chief prize of victory in the Franco-Prussian war. Of approximately 360 territorial sovereignties that once were part of the Holy Roman Empire, only 39 survived. But the Reich had finally emerged as a political reality. Under the rule of the aggressive Hohenzollern it developed rapidly into the greatest political power in the heart of Europe. This Reich lasted forty-seven years and collapsed at the close of World War I.

During the hundreds of years in which Germany had lacked political unification, it maintained cultural unity. German people had in common a genuine love for the arts. They were always ready to foster art life generously, and they sponsored it in its multiple ramifications. Civic pride was frequently commensurate with the degree to which the performing arts flourished in the community.

The individual segments of the so-called Reich envisioned a common cultural entity. At the same time, however, they supported their art life on indigenous terms, with strong emphasis on different religious traditions, on age-old pageantry, often stressing folklore and regional customs. Their culture definitely did not spring from political strength or unity. It stemmed from the people themselves, from the citizenry, from the guilds, from the *Verein*, the small and often modest unit of art patronage.

All of this leads to a rather astonishing conclusion: Germany made towering spiritual contributions in times of political weakness. The periods of Germany's strongest political power did not produce her greatest achievements in the arts, letters, or philosophy. On the contrary, at the very height of her most brutal strength, the nation experienced the annihilation of cultural values.

Medieval Beginnings

On Christmas Day of the year 800, Pope Leo III crowned Charles, King of the Franks, at St. Peter's Cathedral in Rome. The Northern ruler, later known as Charlemagne, was hailed "Augustus, crowned of God, great and pacific Emperor of the Romans." It was fervently hoped that he would reawaken the Roman Empire of the Caesars. This dream did not materialize. But the event marked an epochal turning point in world history: the West gradually awakened to political as well as cultural identity.

The principal art patrons in Germany as elsewhere in medieval Europe were the bishoprics and the courts. Creative styles in art were clearly defined and divided between the sacred and secular. Yet the primacy of art patronage remained religious. Worldly traits in liturgy were as little tolerated by the Church Fathers in this northern Catholic domain as they were in Italy or France. But the courts were fast developing an art contrary in character to ecclesiastical concepts. Some of the German princes were eager to enjoy the arts in all of the earthly serenity they could convey.

The end of the Carolingian Renaissance in the ninth century witnessed a gradual beginning of the characteristics which we today call "German art," although many features still betray their roots in neighboring territories. A country in the center of Europe, Germany was always exposed to the impact of surrounding cultures. Foreign artists freely crossed the common borders to bring their finished craft to German land. German apprentices were quick to learn from these masters, at home as well as abroad. French architects taught their skill of design and their visionary technique of building to a new German generation. From the thirteenth century on, a French-inspired austere style developed, later to be known as German Gothic. In poetry a similar process of transference took place. Some of the epic poetry written in the Middle High German originated as a free translation from the French — a transference with poetic license.

The Minnesinger

Decisive impulses from Latin sources are likewise felt in early German music. An important example is the art of *Minnesang*, which blossomed on German soil from the twelfth to the fourteenth century. Knightly *Minnesinger* are the counterpart of the French troubadours and trouvères. The Minnesinger were lyric poets whose chief theme was love (for which "Minne" is the Middle High German word). Singing of Minne, the knights wrote both the poetry and the music for their romantic performances. A small harp, or fiddle, sufficed for the accompaniment of the Minnesang. The most distinguished Minnesänger was Walther von der Vogelweide (*ca.*1170-*ca.*1230). Equally revered among Walther's contemporaries was Wolfram von Eschenbach.* The Minnesinger's worship of womanhood marks complete emancipation from ecclesiastical control. It anticipates the *amour courtois* of the Renaissance. In 1184 Beatrix of Burgundy, wife of the legendary Emperor Frederick Barbarossa and patroness of the trouvère Guit de Proving, held an international song festival at Mainz.

Prominent among the patrons of the Minnesinger were the powerful Landgraves ruling the German Province of Thuringia. They organized song contests on a large scale, referred to as the *Sängerkriege*. These "wars of singers" were really public contests; they also mark the earliest antecedents of modern music festivals in Germany.

In 1207 Landgrave Hermann of Thuringia invited the most renowned Minnesinger of the time to the *Sängerkrieg* at the Wartburg, a spectacular song contest at his mountainous castle in the romantic vicinity of Eisenach. Both Wolfram von Eschenbach and Heinrich Tannhäuser were among the participants. Richard Wagner's opera *Tannhäuser* (first version 1845) blends authentic and legendary material surrounding this song contest at the Wartburg. Apart from its fictitious conflicts, the second act is a tonal monument to the patronage of Landgrave Hermann. He becomes a symbol of courtly sponsorship, which later developed to such great significance in German art life.

The Minnesinger fulfilled, from the sociological point of view, a crucial mission. They hastened the liquidation of the long-entrenched barriers between the two existing categories of music making: between the "high music" addressed to the aristocrats and the "low music" performed for the common people. This differentiation can be traced in and outside Germany. Thus the French scholar Johannes de Grocheo reports in his treatise, *Theoria* (*ca.*1300), that the *chanson de geste*, i.e., the epic narrative on heroic deeds, was sung before "old people,

*Wolfram's two epic legends, *Parzival* and *Titurel*, are the sources of Richard Wagner's final music-drama, *Parsifal*.

workers and laborers — before people of low caste." They were heard by "men when they rest from their toil, so that, when they learn about the misery of others, they can better endure their own burdens, and thus, with more cheer, return to their work. Such kind of singing helps to safeguard the state," de Grocheo observes.

This was no minor issue: certainly arts merited support, if they could perform in the interest of the state, even uplifting the spirit of men at work. Whatever the priority, the Minnesinger definitely formed the bridge from the exclusive circles of performing aristocrats to the open community of singing burghers. And here a new development set in: the people themselves soon assumed their role as patrons of the arts.

II. The Middle Class as Art Sponsor

The Wealthy Burghers

With the advent of modern times, the new middle class showed its recently won social status also by this concomitant aspect: its role as sponsor of civic art life began.

The wealthy burghers, a group of bankers and merchants, led the way. Some of these affluent men showed a high degree of communal conscience. They spontaneously embarked on art patronage which solidified their position of high esteem in the town.

The great representative figure of this phase in German art sponsorship was Jakob Fugger (1459-1525). (The West German Republic celebrated his five-hundredth birthday in 1959 with a special postal stamp.) This German merchant, known as the "banker to Popes and Emperors," extended his enterprises beyond the commercial world. Mindful of the social responsibility of his great wealth, he became the first great bourgeois patron of German urban life.

The Fugger family stemmed from the old cathedral town of Augsburg, where Jakob, in 1512, dedicated the organ in the church of St. Anne. From such ecclesiastical beginnings his patronage rapidly extended into far-reaching secular projects. He founded the *Musikkammer*, endowing it with a collection of rare instruments and a comprehensive library.[1] He organized a private orchestra in the manner of princely sponsors. The Fugger town mansion became the clearinghouse for artists and their activities from all over Europe. Maximilian I came to Augsburg for extended visits with Jakob Fugger, his financial advisor. The Emperor's entourage included his court orchestra, and thus began the exchange of instrumental ensembles between various cities that set a new pattern in Germany's art life. The sons and grandsons of Jakob Fugger added to the family fortune, which had its roots in trade and increased further through banking transactions. When Maximilian's grandson Charles V (Emperor from 1519 to 1556) was to be elected ruler of the Holy Roman Reich, a syndicate of European bankers led by the Fuggers decided the issue realistically by appropriate remuneration to the electors.

Germany's affluent burghers, who now found themselves at the wheel of political destinies, adopted aristocratic attitudes in terms of art support. The Fuggers eventually fostered international tours and an interchange of artists, which brought a cosmopolitan element into the German provinces. Orlando di Lasso (1532-1594) was introduced to the Munich court through the auspices of the Fugger family. This great contrapuntal master from The Netherlands had been conductor at the Church of the Lateran in Rome. In 1556 Orlando accepted the call to Munich, where he remained for thirty-eight years. He introduced to the Bavarian capital the significant art music of Europe. It was, in fact, during Orlando's tenure that Munich's historic role as an international music center began.

In 1575 Hans Jakob Fugger left his family's banking firm to become Intendant of Music at the court of Duke Albrecht V of Bavaria. Soon an exchange was arranged between the Munich Hofkapelle and the Fugger orchestra of Augsburg. The private instrumental ensemble of the wealthy burgher compared favorably with the established orchestra of the nobility.

Orlando di Lasso set a tonal monument to the enlightened art patrons when he dedicated his *Cantiones* (completed in 1573) to Hans Jakob Fugger and his family. An ingenious work, the *Cantiones*, was composed on texts in the four principal languages of the Renaissance — Latin, Italian, French, and German. This polylingual score is a token of an artistic community; it expresses supranationality, an ideal which is assuming new meaning today.

The Meistersinger

The burghers of Germany gradually established an art life of their own. They performed for their own social purposes. Their music making was organized within their crafts and professions.

This movement found its fullest expression in the unique organization of amateur musicians known as *Meistersinger*. The term may be translated "singing craftsmen."* The cobblers, the tailors, the bakers, and others united in guilds wherein the masters taught their trade to chosen apprentices. In the evenings, after arduous hours of work, the Meistersinger assembled not only for conviviality, but to pursue the art of poetry and music.

*The German word *Meister* does not only pertain to creative mastery; it may also refer to an artisan known for fine craftsmanship.

The Meistersinger thought of themselves as the legitimate heirs of the Minnesinger. Hence the Meistersinger stubbornly adhered to the traditional theory of the Minnesang: they taught the composition and performance of song according to a set of rules, watching pedantically over their strictest observance. The most productive period of the Meistersinger was the sixteenth century. But the beginnings of their guilds reach back much further; in Cologne and Mainz, they existed as early as the eleventh century. The Meistersinger appeared regularly at municipal festivities in and out of doors. They solemnly marched in colorful processions and were cheered by the entire population for their performances. The cultural importance of the Meistersinger lies in their wholehearted and long-lasting adoption of art patronage within the guilds, where vocal art grew on new and fertile soil.

The guilds created, developed, and performed their own kind of music. The Meistersinger met in the town hall or in church after Sunday service. Three times a year they held competitions for new members anxious to join their ranks. But these auditions were extremely rigid. The ever so strict *Merker* watched at these competitions that all rules of the *Tabulatur*, that ultraconservative compendium of musical and poetic laws, were conscientiously followed. The Merker is, in fact, the German ancestor of the professional music critic.

Richard Wagner, always preoccupied with Germany's cultural history, discovered in the traditions and procedures of these guilds the framework of his only serene opera, *Die Meistersinger von Nürnberg*. He treated in this work, once again, his favorite motives of patronage and song contest, which he had introduced in *Tannhäuser*. In the libretto of *Die Meistersinger*[2] the historic personality of the poet-shoemaker Hans Sachs represents the enlightened outlook: the wise and aging master symbolizes progressive judgment, opposing the jealously guarded, narrow rules of the guilds.

The real Hans Sachs (1494-1576) was not only a musician; he was also a dramatist in his own right, with a considerable number of comedies, carnival plays, and tragedies to his credit. In 1550 Sachs remodeled an abandoned church in Nürnberg into a theater, which marks, in fact, the first legitimate German playhouse on record.

Town Pipers
The Municipalities

In a typical pattern of musical evolution, vocal performance antedates instrumental performance. The musical activities of the guilds encompassed both: they sponsored singing groups in the manner of the Meistersinger and organized instrumental ensembles.

Even the smallest German towns took pride in their so-called *Stadtpfeifer*. These were guilds of instrumentalists who performed primarily on various woodwind and brass instruments, favoring trumpets and trombones of various kinds. Three times daily they played chorales from the steeples of a church, greeting morning, noon, and nightfall with music. The titles of such music were appropriately listed as *Turm-Musik*, music performed from the tower.

At least from the fifteenth century on the town bands would often employ woodwinds along with brass instruments. The woodwind players were called *Pfeifer* ("whistlers," "pipers"). Eventually the name *Stadtpfeifer*, town pipers, came to designate the entire band. On special occasions the municipal musicians would also play in the town hall. Their duties included performing for all official ceremonies, and for the weddings and funerals of prominent citizens. On holidays the town pipers marched in the processions of the guilds, sometimes preceding the formal parade of the Meistersinger. By the seventeenth century, important composers, among them Johann Petzel, contributed rather intricate scores for the Turm-Musiken. In the individual parts considerable technical demands were made on the performers. The bands of the old German cities must have been excellent, indeed, if the players were able to cope with such virtuoso writing.

The various municipalities themselves sponsored this kind of urban music making. And in this official town-patronage lie the roots of the broad support which German cities have offered ever since to their representative instrumental groups. Today, the pattern of orchestral subvention is deeply entrenched. Every German city of consequence subsidizes a resident orchestra.

Social Status of Performers

In the Middle Ages the treatment of performing artists — musicians, comedians, and theater folk of all kinds — lacked all fairness. Musicians were considered merely *fahrende Spielleute*, "wandering players" of whom the burghers had better be on guard. Excluded from church and community, these performers were practically unprotected by law.

But their status changed, though slowly, after the musicians had banded together in fraternities and similar organizations. They realized that in groups they could obtain modest bargaining power, and with it some clearly defined privileges. Progress was made when the municipalities began to employ the wandering instrumentalists as town musicians. Thus they became *verbürgert*, i.e., integrated into civic life. Their professional duties were now strictly circumscribed, and the musicians were quick to learn that they had to protect their newly-won rights. Thus they watched for "unfair labor practices." They tried to keep out of their ranks "ignorants, beer fiddlers and other kinds of unprofessional intruders." They fought what they called *Schwarzarbeit* ("black work") clandestinely done by incompetent players. Modern unionism comes to mind when we survey the statutes and procedures followed by these guilds of vigilant musicians centuries ago.

Trumpeters and drummers enjoyed special rights. They were regularly invited to perform at festivals in castles, at aristocratic tournaments. The learned court and field trumpeters earned their social acceptance early. Imperial documents, in fact, referred to their profession as a "noble and free art." Some trumpeters had the rank of officers.

Originally, only principalities and free cities were permitted to maintain this special class of musicians, and such privileges were envied. In the fifteenth century Emperor Sigismund shrewdly sold for large sums the rights of employing municipal trumpeters to the free southern German cities of Augsburg and Ulm. As late as 1608 the city council of Leipzig had to defend an "illegitimate" practice before the ruling Prince Elector: the municipal music director J. H. Schein[3] had dared to use trumpets at a patrician wedding. This was considered a breach of conduct.

Trumpet performance, then, was a matter of grave concern. In times of war the trumpeters were granted additional status. After all, an entire scale of fateful calls was in their hands. Their signals initiated attack and defense; they announced the time of awakening and rest; they called for prayer; they sounded taps. If taken prisoners, the trumpeters could be exchanged for officers. They even had the right of free movement as negotiators. Obviously, musicians entrusted with such tasks were not ordinary men. In peace or war their status was commensurate with their usefulness.

III. Patronage in Peace and War

The Lutheran Chorale

The country where Protestantism was born during the sixteenth century added a dimension of liturgical patronage. Martin Luther (1483-1546) gave much thought to the proper function of art within a newly envisioned form of worship. But music was his prime concern. The great reformer of the Church was himself a highly educated musician. According to his own statement, he was able "to write counterpoint fluently, and to compose all kinds of music." From 1523 on, Luther concentrated on revising the Protestant service. He was particularly concerned with the role of community singing in the church.

It was Luther's aim to give Protestant liturgy its own direction — in strict accordance with the newly-created confession. While he wished to preserve certain features of the old tradition, he insisted that the worshippers participate actively in the service. To such an end, preaching and praying, as well as singing, were to be in the native German language. The Latin text underlying the Catholic Mass did not communicate, in Luther's conviction, a sacred message to the people. Consequently, he banned the "dead" language from the service. Instead, the collective chorale of the Protestant congregation, with the text clearly understood in its native tongue, was to assume a decisive role: "I wish to make German psalms for the people," Luther promised, "that is to say, sacred hymns, so that the word of God may dwell among the people, also by means of song."

The Catholic Church had elevated the ancient *cantus choralis* — in the form of Gregorian chant — to the core of its liturgy. Luther realized that he needed a powerful replacement for Latin plainsong, for the solemn chanting in unison which the Christian Church had employed since early times. Hence, he shaped hymn tunes into a variety of chorales. As they were sung in eloquent, yet plain German, Luther made sure that the worshippers understood, to the fullest, the blended meaning of word and tone.

The congregations were not ready overnight for taking part in liturgical performance. And so, choirs made up of students from the newly founded *Gymnasia* (the high schools with strongly humanistic curricula) came to their support. These Gymnasia were sponsored by affluent citizens, and the carefully trained student choirs were paid at a fixed rate by the municipalities. Accordingly, the duties of these youthful choirs included both civic and ecclesiastical functions.

The Protestant congregation sang its chorales in simple harmony set for four voices (soprano, alto, tenor, and bass), so that the praying community of men, women, and children could perform as a mixed choir, usually accompanied by organ. The singing of these firm chorale melodies expressed symbolically the new Protestant Germany. In the bitter and long war that was to follow the new religious schism of Europe, some of the chorales were converted into battle hymns of the fighting Reformation.

But it was in times of peace that the Lutheran service proved to have far-reaching effects on the musical life of the people. In church everyone now actively participated in vocal performance. The singing of serious music inspired related experiences outside of liturgy. People began to make good music for their own enjoyment. They also became sponsors of professional performances of secular art music. Creatively, the chorale yielded the tone material and certain technical aspects in the treatment of some of the greatest German art music to come. In the God-abiding tone world of Johann Sebastian Bach (1685-1750) the chorale reached its greatest fulfillment. In addition to their influence on the nature of German music, Luther's reforms led directly to a new and vital concept of the professional musician.

It was also Martin Luther who in 1522 had first spoken of the concept of the *Beruf*. He referred to a man's calling, to a professional vocation aiming beyond earning one's livelihood. The true Beruf of the church musician implies a calling that presupposes ethical conduct, professional integrity, and fidelity toward one's chosen lifework in the sense of a joyfully accepted mission. The timeless patron of art, the Church, had always employed musicians who performed their task as part of their ecclesiastical duties. In the sense of Luther's definition, these performers could not be regarded on the same level as the monks. Luther's concept of Beruf gradually extended to both the sacred and secular categories of the musical profession. Johann Sebastian Bach, employed by the secular municipality, was of course paid for his services in the Protestant churches of Leipzig. The position was the source of his livelihood. But the master thought of himself as a professional, "pursuing a higher calling," and he interpreted music as a "divine art toward the recreation of the human soul."

Evening Music

The organ, principal instrument of church service, was soon regularly heard outside of liturgy. The newly flourishing keyboard music of the Baroque had created a fine repertory for hours of musical meditation. Small instrumental ensembles joined the organist in informal but always serious programs, usually taking place in the evening at church. Its dignitaries and congregation patronized these events under the simple title of *Abend Musik*. These musical evenings were open to the public.

Germany's most celebrated Evening Music was heard at St. Mary's Church in Lübeck, where Dietrich Buxtehude, the Swedish composer, had in 1668 assumed the post of church organist. In 1705, at the age of twenty, Johann Sebastian Bach made a pilgrimage on foot to the Hanseatic town to hear the then aged master perform and improvise on the organ of St. Mary's. Young Bach was deeply impressed, not only by the contrapuntal depth of Buxtehude's compositions, but by the earnest mood of the Abend Musik, and by the spiritual recreation it afforded the audience. Some of Bach's later activities as a performer and organizer of similar events were influenced by his youthful impressions in Lübeck.

Prior to the eighteenth century not many churches offered Evening Music as a regular fare. It was during the high Baroque that these hours of meditation spread all over Germany.

The so-called *Kantoreien* had a similar function; they were singing groups, with the church choir as their nucleus. The cantor was their conductor, and talented amateurs participated in informal choral concerts. In a general way, the newly established Protestant Kantoreien corresponded to the older Catholic church choirs. Yet the title Kantorei was not always used with clear definition. Thus a professional princely court Kapelle as well as a civic amateur group might have been called Kantorei. Luther's friend and helpmate, Johann Walther, founded a Kantorei in Torgau, with Prince Elector Johann as the chief patron. This Kantorei was made up of enthusiastic amateurs and professionals.

Collegium Musicum

Church, court, and city have so far emerged as the principal fountainheads of German art patronage. In due time, however, another important source arose — the schools of higher learning. The German universities, committed to the traditional quadruple division of their faculties — theology, philosophy, medicine, and law — gradually assumed a role in the sponsorship of the performing arts. This development was logical within the philosophy department: both music and drama were gradually included in the study of the humanities. To this day academic institutions have retained a certain initiative within Europe's art life.

From the sixteenth century on, musical activities at universities frequently centered around the so-called *Collegium Musicum*. This was in essence a performing group — yet it had different aspects at different times. The German antecedent of the Collegium Musicum was the so-called *Musik-Kränzchen* (or *Kränzlein*), first established in the city of Worms in 1561. The German diminutive Kränzchen reveals the sociable, somewhat jolly nature of a private musical circle. But the more severe Latin title, *Collegium Musicum*, justifiably suggests the gradual adoption of academic standards in procedure and performance.

Talented amateurs and professionals both joined in the performance of music in the lecture halls of the universities. During the sixteenth century most performances were vocal, and often held in the refectories of the churches. From the seventeenth century on, the steadily growing instrumental art of the Baroque manifested itself also in the repertory of the Collegia; in fact, a specific literature was written for these groups, and the public was invited to their performances. Composers were grateful for this new outlet for their works. A master of Georg Philipp Telemann's stature contributed works for the Collegia. Their educational purpose was stressed when teachers and students jointly performed the music which was also the subject of their theoretical discussion and analysis in class. Thus the Collegium Musicum became a part of the academic curriculum. Live performances offered the practical complement to the study of history and aesthetics. The most famous Collegia were at the universities of Hamburg and of Leipzig. (These Collegia were founded in 1660 by Matthias Weckmann and in 1701 by G. P. Telemann, respectively.)

Collegium Musicum, Abend Musik, and Kantorei, in a measure, were antecedents of the modern concert society. But it was not until the eighteenth century that formal concerts became established on German soil.[4] To this day a concert society of scholarly orientation is known as Collegium Musicum.[5]

Nucleus of Modern German Art Life

The era of the Thirty Years War (1618-1648) strangely forecasts some of the apocalyptical events which three centuries later were to destroy culture on German soil.

A fateful pattern emerges in the seventeenth century. The long war left the country a shambles. It also shattered the early hopes for a German Reich. With hundreds of courts destroyed and their sovereigns impoverished, most organizations devoted to the performing arts ceased to function in an orderly manner. But recovery after the war was swift, incredibly swift considering the contemporary limitations of economy, technology, and means of communication. The arts were high on the program of rehabilitation. Their claim to priority — which strikes us as significant within the redevelopment of West Germany today — is clearly evident in the seventeenth century. The Treaty of Westphalia (1648) created only a peaceful interim, but it lasted long enough to give new impulse to the art life of the country. No sooner were churches and courts rebuilt than the performing arts began to blossom anew.

The period of the Baroque, now approaching its first height, gradually brought new art media into focus. The opera asserted itself. Even theater and ballet — slower to unfold in Germany than in England or the Latin countries — began to make progress after the struggle on battlefields had ended. The symphony orchestra became established.

The Baroque era clearly reveals the nucleus of modern German art life. By the eighteenth century the number of art-supporting courts in Germany exceeded three hundred. The size of a principality was not necessarily an indication of the scope of its patronage; small residences compared favorably with the large in artistic achievement.

The continuous ascendance of the middle class to a firm and lasting role as art patron did not bring about a decline of aristocratic art support. If anything, the Baroque era reestablished and heightened the scope and splendor of performances at various German residences. The eighteenth century was a time when many rulers actively participated — as composers, poets, and performers — in the art life their capitals. They also competed in the search for creative talent in and outside their provinces. Some of the sovereign sponsors earned the true affection of their creative protégés and won the respect and gratitude of their people, the beneficiaries of art patronage.

What were some of the personal motivations of these patrons? What directed their artistic impulses to specific media? To what extent was the environment into which they were born responsible for their interest and direction?

Various premises determine the formation of positive attitudes toward art sponsorship. Whatever the inducement, only a personal history can provide us with essential clues, as the following section on Frederick the Great will illustrate.

IV. "Republic of the Arts"
Frederick the Great

Every rule has its exceptions. Not every German sovereign sponsored the arts. Some rejected them; some even hated them. No art life was tolerated at the Prussian court of Frederick William I.[6] The King, whose own education had been neglected, represents the archetype of a warmongering sergeant who has been elevated to absolute monarch by a twist of fate and political intrigue. At his court in Potsdam all manifestations of art life were *verboten* as of "no practical value." Music, in particular, seemed to epitomize everything that the King considered unmanly and harmful to the serious business of government.

His first son — also named Frederick and later known to the world as Frederick the Great — was raised under a program ruthless even by Prussian standards. The discipline of warfare and the doctrines of Machiavellian politics were to mold the character of this future soldier-king of Prussia. Studies in the humanities were cut to a minimum. Instead, the King ordered the tutors to drill his son in the harshest physical routine. Before long, young Frederick rebelled against his father's tyranny. His kindly mother offered solace. He also found sympathetic understanding in his governess, Madame de Roucoulle, and in one of his tutors, Monsieur Duhan, from France. The French language became dearer to young Frederick than his native German in which he heard so much sternness from his father. Frederick was eighteen when he decided to escape it all. He enlisted the help of two young officers, Katte and Keith, both lieutenants in the guard. The trio of friends plotted a joint flight. The attempt failed. Only Lieutenant Keith got across the border. Lieutenant Katte was caught, court-martialed by an officers' jury, and sentenced to hard labor. In a tantrum of sadism and tyranny the King changed the verdict to a death sentence. He ordered the execution of the young Lieutenant to take place in the very presence of the horrified Crown Prince. Frederick was sent to the forbidding fortress of Cüstrin as a prisoner. But perfect conduct earned him his freedom after fifteen months.

French Orientation at the Prussian Court

The King now ordered Frederick to marry Elisabeth Christine, Princess of Brunswick-Bevern. He assigned the royal couple the estate of Rheinsberg as their home, where Frederick remained until his ascent to the throne. Removed from Potsdam, he could, for the first time, express his own intellectual and artistic inclinations.

At Rheinsberg Frederick first attempted to inaugurate what he referred to as a "Republic of the Arts." He envisioned a free community of creative men in an environment liberal and congenial, and he began to build such a milieu conceived altogether in French taste and tradition. Thus the Rheinsberg Estate, palace, formal gardens, the entire mode of life in the residence became a manifestation of Frederick's aesthetics: his childhood love for all things French came to a first fruition here. At the age of twenty-four, in 1736, Frederick began his famous correspondence with Voltaire, whom he considered the greatest of all living men. Fourteen years later, after Voltaire had paid his fifth visit to Frederick (then King of Prussia), the philosopher reported to a friend in Paris: "I live here as in France. Only French is spoken here; German is for soldiers and horses."

Frederick's Rheinsberg library contained the philosophical and literary works of France. "I have read more books than all the Benedictine friars put together. . . . Without my books, I would have gone mad." Frederick collected paintings of the French school; in fact, he hoped to trace in his own gallery the development of French art from the Middle Ages to Poussin and Watteau. He acquired one of the three versions of Watteau's masterpiece, "The Embarkation for Cythera." The melancholy calm of this picture — evoking a voyage to the island of Venus where love never dies — seemed to assuage the harshness of the Prussian world in which Frederick was forced to live. He augmented his Watteau collection until it became the most important outside of France.[7]

The Crown Prince engaged for his residence a small orchestra with the Bohemian composer Franz Benda as concertmaster. Frederick himself spent much of his spare time performing on his favorite instrument, the flute. The most famous flute master of the era, Johann Joachim Quantz (1697-1773), had acquainted Frederick as early as 1728 with the technique of this instrument. The young prince was so delighted with Quantz's performance that he had decided to learn the flute himself, in spite of his father's violent objections.

On May 31, 1740, Frederick II became Prussia's King. The Rheinsberg years proved to be a mere rehearsal for the cultural performance the twenty-eight-year-old absolute monarch could now inaugurate in Berlin. What were, by comparison, diminutive plans for art life in the small residence now became large-scale projects in the capital. The arts and the sciences were immediate beneficiaries.

Berlin began to assume the appearance of a metropolis; the city already had 100,000 inhabitants. Frederick reinstated the Academy of Sciences at a level which made possible much brilliant and far-reaching research in the nineteenth century. He promoted elementary education and reorganized the school system on a progressive basis. Frederick assured religious freedom, protecting worshippers in faiths other than that of the official Protestantism. In retrospect, and judged by modern standards, his government still appears tainted with countless deplorable features of pre-revolutionary absolutism; Frederick's foreign policies were dominated by his will to build Prussia into a potential world power. In this, too, he succeeded. And so history records a great ruler on the Prussian throne — a thinker and artist who at the same time waged wars in the incessant struggle for power among the great European nations. Frederick was convinced that war was necessary if Prussia were to remain strong. Without this strength, he rationalized, he could never pursue the great spiritual aims which he had envisioned for his nation as a monumental "Republic of the Arts."

Different historians have given different answers to such a blatant paradox. Here is a ruler, cultured and martial; liberal yet fitfully intolerant; a scholar and an artist, and simultaneously a soldier with the lust to conquer. The cleavage of the German mind is incarnate in this great King. But the psychodynamics of Frederick's development are no longer puzzling: extreme parental hostility prompted in the sensitive and gifted son a way of life in opposition to the image of his father. And so the heir of an art-hating king lives in history as Prussia's greatest art patron. Frederick was an author, a composer of note, a virtuoso on the flute, a ruler of relative tolerance, a Francophile, a philosopher, altogether the antithesis of his father, the inhuman Frederick William I.

And his father's death was the official beginning of a brilliant era in the art sponsorship at the court of Potsdam, in the capital Berlin, and, finally, in the entire Prussian nation.

Opera Attendance as a Military Duty

One of Frederick's first acts of government was to commission his friend, the architect Knobelsdorff, to design plans for opera houses. Not one, but two opera theaters were to be built. Berlin was to have a large opera theater, open to the citizens, and the King a more intimate musical theater at his Potsdam residence.

On December 7, 1742, the Berlin Court Opera was opened with *Cleopatra e Cesare*, a work by its chief conductor, Karl Heinrich Graun. The opera was written and performed in Italian — as was the principal repertory of this German court theater. In Berlin, operas were given at least twice a week, on Mondays and Fridays. A minimum of two new works were produced each season, which normally began in December and lasted until March. Frederick paid for opera directly from the royal purse, not from taxes. It is true, all royal fortunes stem from the riches of a country — in Frederick's Prussia as well as in all other monarchies, past or present; but there was this difference: the King paid for serious art with sums that certain other rulers used for a variety of shallow and selfish amusement.

An incident following the termination of the Seven Years' War shows the duality of Frederick as art patron and supreme army commander. The opera house had been reopened following the signing of the Treaty of Hubertusburg on February 15, 1763. Yet the Prussians, fatigued and demoralized from the long war which Frederick finally won over Austria, were reluctant to listen to Italian opera. The Prussian public had become interested in a new genre, the comic opera based on simple plots, composed in a light musical vein, and sung in German. Reports of empty houses infuriated the King. He found a quick solution: he commanded that a company of royal grenadiers attend all performances of Italian *opera seria*.

Schedule in Sans Souci

Frederick's favorite residence in Potsdam, about thirty kilometers southwest of Berlin, was a small French rococo palace which he named *Sans Souci*, "without worry." At Sans Souci Frederick arose at five to have free time in his day always crowded with government business, audiences, and conferences — not to mention military inspections and parades. The early hours were used for reading and for his most favorite occupation, playing the flute.

In 1741 Frederick engaged J. J. Quantz with a high salary of 2,000 thaler as Court Composer and *Kammermusikus*. The King paid 100 ducats extra for each score he especially commissioned. Quantz remained to his death in the employ of the King, for whom he wrote close to 300 concertos and 200 smaller pieces. Quantz's treatise *Versuch einer Anweisung die Flöte traversière zu spielen* is dedicated to Frederick the Great. This famous textbook on "how to perform on the flute" is really an encyclopaedic study of interpretation and remains an important musicological document.

Among the composers serving on the King's musical staff was Karl Philipp Emanuel Bach, the second son of Johann Sebastian Bach. Karl Philipp remained in the King's service as harpsichord player and conductor for twenty-seven years, until 1767.

V. The Musical Offering
Secular and Liturgical Service

During the week of May 7, 1747, the elder Bach traveled from Leipzig to Berlin to make the acquaintance of a new daughter-in-law, the bride of Karl Philipp Emanuel. The visit proved to be of historic significance. In Potsdam, Bach was presented to the King, who received Johann Sebastian warmly. Frederick invited him to improvise on one of his seven Silbermann claviers, and finally asked the aging master to play extemporaneously a fugue, the theme of which the monarch himself had invented. On leaving Sans Souci, Bach promised to elaborate further on this contrapuntal subject. Soon after returning to his home in Leipzig, he sent a score entitled *Das Musikalische Opfer* to his royal host in Potsdam. In July, 1747, a part of *The Musical Offering* appeared in print with a long dedication to Frederick the Great. The inscription goes far beyond the customary politeness of a protégé to his patron. It shows Bach's genuine affection and professional admiration for the King. Bach referred to the fugal subject that Frederick had given him as a "truly royal theme," and addressed the King as "a true master, not only in the sciences of war and peace, but also in music."

The Potsdam episode and the subsequent publication of *The Musical Offering* mark the last bright events in Bach's humble creative life. Posterity views the legacy of Bach's art as one of its greatest possessions. It is well to remember that much of this immortal music was commissioned music: Bach's scores were currently written for church and court, for the needs of the community in which he lived. His professional career affords us a clear account of the function of patronage in the first part of the eighteenth century: Bach's appointments led from liturgical to courtly and civil positions. The circle closes as it began, in the service of the Protestant church. Some of Bach's most inspired scores were written in direct fulfillment of his contracts with various employers; others were commissioned by art patrons elsewhere. Thus the title of the *Brandenburg Concertos* recalls their sponsor and, indirectly, the occasion which gave rise to their existence. These six concertos mark the summit of Baroque orchestral music. Through his patronage of Bach, Duke Christian Ludwig of Brandenburg attains immortality to which his inconspicuous life would otherwise have no claim.

The Leipzig Years

In 1723 Bach exchanged the conductor's post for that of cantor. He made this step "in des Höchsten Namen"; he abandoned, "in the name of the Lord," court service in Cöthen for municipal service in Leipzig, where he hoped to compose, perform, and teach music within the orbit of the Lutheran church.

The Leipzig position caused Bach much disappointment. As early as September 14, 1725, he turned to his sovereign, the Prince Elector of Saxony,[8] for help in the struggle for his contractual rights as cantor and music director. As late as October 18, 1737, Bach again approached the royal patron in Dresden for protection[9]; disagreements with his employers had increased.

As music director of Leipzig's principal Protestant churches (St. Thomas and St. Nicolai), Bach was not satisfied with the vocal and instrumental forces at his disposal. On visits to Dresden, Saxony's capital, he observed the excellent orchestra of the Court Opera generously endowed by the King. "One only has to go there and see how his Royal Majesty's musicians are salaried; as they are free from worries and want, and as each has only one instrument to practise, it could not fail that one hears something truly excellent." Bach's comment is eloquent: the greatest Protestant church composer in history praises the secular patronage of opera, while he must deplore the limitations imposed by the sponsoring municipality on liturgical performance.

Meanwhile, on July 27, 1733, Bach had addressed a letter to Frederick Augustus, his Catholic sovereign; the letter accompanied a musical present which the master delivered in person to the Dresden court. With his characteristic frankness and sincerity Bach disclosed some of his motivations underlying the gift. He asked the King, ". . . if your Royal Highness would be good enough to appoint me to the court capelle, and to give directions to the proper authority for the issue of a patent. Such a gracious response to my petition will place me under the deepest obligation, and . . . in token of my humble duty and unwearied diligence, I am ready to compose both church and orchestral music whenever your Royal Highness may command . . . devoting all my powers to your service."* The gift was the *Mass in B Minor* bearing the dedication to King Frederick Augustus. In this only Catholic Mass composed by the Lutheran master, a supra-confessional element inherent in this devotional music reaches listeners of every faith.

VI. Opera, Ballet, Symphony

Jommelli in Stuttgart
Bayreuth Principles Anticipated

In the dukedom of Württemberg the years from 1753 to 1769 mark a great era of musical theater. Duke Karl Eugen underwrote the staggering expenses of opera and ballet in Stuttgart, Württemberg's capital. In 1750 he converted his garden chalet, the "Lusthaus," into a large "modern" theater. Its size was extraordinary: the *parterre* and the galleries accommodated an audience of several thousands.

Three factors stand out as the principal music-dramatic reforms at the Stuttgart Theater: operatic performances, prepared in many painstaking rehearsals, applying for the first time in a German theater the newly developed devices of musical dynamics; a ballet company of an excellence known hitherto only in France; the appointment of the best available artistic directors for both opera and ballet.

Duke Karl Eugen searched far to find performers who would raise the standard of the Stuttgart court theater. In Rome he met his future opera director, Niccolò Jommelli (1714-1774), then conductor at St. Peter's Church. Jommelli was a musician whose mind harbored equal gift for sacred and secular expression. Leaving the liturgical service in Rome, the *maestro di cappella* thus became an opera director in Stuttgart and inaugurated a new era in the performance of music-drama in Germany. Padre Martini, the illustrious teacher in Bologna, called Jommelli the "philosopher-musician." This characterization implied that deep aesthetic thought was at the root of Jommelli's art, of his conducting as well as of his composing. Having observed the maestro at work, the traveling British scholar Dr. Charles Burney claimed that Jommelli had caused a veritable revolution of taste in Germany. He was the first opera composer to integrate the elaborate, modern system of dynamics into the script of an opera score and its parts. As a result, the audiences heard in Stuttgart performances in highly differentiated scales of loudness and softness, a wealth of nuances, which we take for granted today, but which was new

*In 1736 Bach belatedly received the coveted appointment as court composer to the King of Saxony.

to the world of the Baroque. Jommelli's innovations in Stuttgart represented the operatic parallel to the symphonic style that emerged simultaneously at the nearby court of Mannheim.

French Ballet Style Adopted

The era of Karl Eugen forecasts a development that was to take place in Germany's opera life a century later: Stuttgart anticipates Bayreuth. Jommelli's reforms can be compared — in their interpretative purpose and uncompromising standards — with those of Richard Wagner. Both composers were great conductors; both were strongly motivated by the opportunity to perform their own operas in perfect settings. In eighteenth-century Stuttgart, as in nineteenth-century Bayreuth, music-drama was produced with utmost care and devotion, with indifference to cost and practicalities. Results were achieved in numerous and intense rehearsals which were made possible only by extraordinary sponsorship.

In 1760 Duke Karl Eugen appointed Jean-Georges Noverre (1727-1810) ballet master of the Stuttgart Opera. This was a crucial step. Noverre, extolled as the "Shakespeare of the Dance," was an eminent choreographer, scholar, and theorist.

In his *Lettres sur la danse et les ballets* Noverre clarified his aesthetic guideposts. Dance must reflect nature and character, he insisted. It must evoke artistic truth, genuine passion. Dance should be the mirror image of the soul, not empty court ceremonial nor mere popular entertainment. Noverre's *Letters on the Dance and the Ballets* rebuked, then, artificiality and superficial elegance which had crept into choreography at the French court.

Stuttgart was the first German town to witness Noverre's enlightened ballet style, a truly modern concept of dance which demanded the performers "to forget their feet and legs." They were to concentrate on the expression of face and body. A new art of gestures rose on the musical stage, a pantomine that was not a purpose in itself, but served the higher ideals of the music-dramatic art work. We cannot overlook the fact that Noverre was a contemporary of Gluck, the pioneer of the classical music-drama. Their reforms are related in spirit.

Duke Karl Eugen was well aware that Noverre's concepts were destined to revolutionize choreography throughout Europe. To induce the French ballet master and his wife, likewise a notable dancer, to move from metropolitan Paris to the provincial capital of Stuttgart, the Duke offered them a salary of 5,000 gulden, a large compensation for that time. But for Noverre, the promise of complete artistic freedom was decisive. He seized upon the opportunity to transform the Stuttgart court ballet into a perfect instrument for his choreographic visions.

Mannheim
Leading Eighteenth-Century Orchestra

The development of orchestral culture, as a result of the increased interest of the Baroque in the instrumental ensemble, soon reached a new height on German soil. The best orchestra of mid-eighteenth century was to be heard in Mannheim. The instrumental ensembles at the wealthy and powerful capitals Vienna, Paris, or London took second place when compared by contemporary experts with the Mannheim Hofkapelle, munificently sponsored by the Elector Palatine, Karl Theodor. Placed by power politics into this German residence on the middle Rhine, the prince, himself a notable 'cellist, lost no time in making his city a music center of first order.

Under Karl Theodor's patronage the Mannheim orchestra was enlarged to a maximum number of 50 players. It represented the first German orchestra employed in such strength on a permanent basis. From 1745, Johann Wenzel Stamitz, brought from Bohemia, officiated as "court-director of instrumental music." Creative initiative in Mannheim also stemmed from Franz Xavier Richter and, during the successive generation, from outstanding disciples of Stamitz, including his sons (Karl and Anton), Carlo Giuseppe Toëschi, Christian Cannabich, and others. After the death of J. W. Stamitz (1757) the direction of the orchestra fell to Cannabich.

A special feature in the performance of this famous ensemble was the new concept of instrumental dynamics. Mannheim accomplished for the symphony orchestra what Stuttgart had for opera: it created a novel type of performance, geared to a hitherto unknown scale of tonal intensities. Witnesses speak of "a *forte*-like thunder, a *crescendo* like a cataract, a *diminuendo* as gentle as a crystal brook rippling from afar, and a *piano* that recalled the soft breath of early spring." Such extraordinary variety of tonal nuances could result only from a unique ensemble of musicians. The report by Charles Burney, *The Present State of Music in Germany* (1773), relates that "there were more soloists and good composers in this orchestra than in any other in Europe. It is like an army of generals, everybody skillful to devise a plan like a battler, rather than to fight himself therein." The renowned historian showed himself to be a man of foresight with the following evaluation of the Mannheim performance:

"It has long seemed to me as if the variety, taste, spirit and new effect produced by contrast in the use of *crescendo* and *diminuendo* in these Mannheim symphonies had been of more service to instrumental music in a few years than all the dull and servile imitations in the styles of Corelli, Geminiani, and Handel had been in half a century."

The Mannheim school was, indeed, one of the most important factors in the establishment of the preclassical style; it marked the end of the Baroque orchestra.

VII. Classical Theater

The legitimate theater of Germany trailed behind the country's remarkable evolution of opera and other media of musical performance. This retard of German theater life can be ascribed to a variety of reasons; the most obvious is the lack of great German playwrights prior to the classical era in the last third of the eighteenth century. The sovereigns of the Baroque era had patronized mostly opera and concert. As shown earlier in this chapter, choral singing and instrumental performance had for centuries been the favorite musical activities of German burghers.

But the secondary role of the legitimate theater in Germany ended with swiftness when the giants of German drama, Lessing, Schiller, and Goethe, became associated closely with the living stage. The principal places of this new development were Hamburg, Mannheim, and Weimar. The curtain rose on one of the most extraordinary phases in the history and patronage of the legitimate theater.

Hamburg Dramaturgy
G. E. Lessing

In traditional German evaluation — temporarily upset only by the Nazi interim — Gotthold Ephraim Lessing (1729-1781) ranks closest in stature to the towering classical poets, Johann Wolfgang von Goethe (1749-1832) and Friedrich Schiller (1759-1805).

Lessing was a philosopher-poet, a scholar, a playwright, and a critic. He was the first master of the German theater who preached the ideals of a free humanity. Lessing met Voltaire as guest of his patron, Frederick the Great, and was inspired by the conversations and writings of this Frenchman considered Europe's foremost literary figure. Like Voltaire, Lessing became, on and off the stage, a protagonist of the new enlightenment.

In 1765 the actor-producer Conrad Ernst Ackermann inaugurated a large theater on Hamburg's Gänsemarkt, the site of the old opera house. He promised his public such welcome fare as extravagantly staged ballets, and serious drama interpreted by an ensemble of prominent actors. Soon the expenditures of the privately supported company exceeded its income. This prompted Johann Frederick Löwen, an ambitious writer, to form a theater society financed by twelve affluent Hamburg merchants. On October 24, 1766, Löwen rented the theater for ten years, taking over the Ackermann troupe. The new company ambitiously called itself the National Theater. Realizing that his own name lacked sufficient prestige, Löwen invited Lessing to join the National Theater: every significant German stage had by that time its poet in residence whose contractual task was to deliver a minimum number of plays for the season. Lessing, however, was not to be tied down in Hamburg to creative work on deadlines. He became, before all, the Konsulent of the theater society. On April 22, 1767, the National Theater opened and, concurrent with the event, Lessing published an optimistic *Ankündigung*, explaining to the Hamburg public the new theater's cultural plans.

In 1767 Lessing moved to Hamburg and observed: "I have signed a contract with the new theater and its concessionaires . . . a kind of agreement which promises me for several years a quiet life. . . . I want to complete here my stage works and hope to have them performed . . . such circumstances are necessary to rekindle my love for the theater." In September, 1767, the National Theater presented the première of Lessing's *Minna von Barnhelm*, the first German classical comedy.

But circumstances in Hamburg were not ideal. In spite of the theater's proud name the true concept of a "national theater" had not really crystallized outside of Austria and France. Nor was court patronage available in Hamburg: Emperor Maximilian I had made the north seaport a "Free City" as early as 1510. In Lessing's time the private and municipal art sponsors of Hamburg were often at cross purposes. The poet complained: "No one knows who is cook and who is waiter." But Hamburg offered Lessing considerable compensations. The theater was newly built. The stage had up-to-date equipment. The director, Conrad Eckhoff, was an enterprising and cultivated man. And the ensemble, for which Lessing was theater poet, was youthful and spirited.

Lessing published and edited a weekly journal, "a critical register of all plays performed; it is meant to accompany each step taken by the art of the poet as well as of the actor." These theatrical essays were later published under the title *Hamburgische Dramaturgie*. Beyond its literary significance, the *Dramaturgie* is one of the most important sources for our knowledge of the performing style of drama in the second part of the eighteenth century. Lessing emerges also as the pioneer of a new profession in the theater: he becomes the first so-called *Dramaturg*. This position, uniting scholarly research and criticism, and eventually editorial and administrative duties, has since become an integral part of German theater life, both at the playhouse and at the opera. The modern Dramaturg is the learned and experienced arbiter of all plays, or scores, submitted for production. He is the reader, a trusted artistic consultant of the administration. He may also be in charge of public and press relations. He is the editor of the Program Book. The scholarly and pleasantly informative nature of program magazines has contributed greatly to the educational mission of the German theater. Today, even small provincial stages provide their public with these attractive booklets, free of charge or sold for a nominal price.

Incidental Music Orchestra in the Prose Theater

Lessing's *Hamburgische Dramaturgie* reveals his attitude toward the function of music in the legitimate theater.[10] The poet considers music indispensable and assigns to the orchestra in contemporary drama a role related to that of the chorus in antiquity. By the second part of the eighteenth century incidental music had become a tradition in the German prose theater. Unfortunately, most of the original scores are lost. We know that music used for the changing dramatic repertory was often chosen at random, and by no means always carefully adjusted to the exigencies and aesthetics of the play. Many of the incidental scores represented early instances of *Gebraucshmusik*, i.e., music for practical use, functioning within the diversity of needs during a dramatic performance. Often such music was played with the curtain lowered (as overture, entr'acte, etc.). Much of this music was mediocre. Lessing demanded that only scores of high standards be chosen because "a great play requires music of genuine quality to surround it."[11]

The practice of incidental music developing in the eighteenth century was perfected to a new art in the first part of the nineteenth century. Scores like those contributed by Beethoven to Goethe's *Egmont*, and by Mendelssohn to Shakespeare's *A Midsummer Night's Dream* are unsurpassed within their category.

The performance of plays with incidental music had important sociological implications in an era when the attendance of opera at certain German principalities was still essentially the privilege of the court and enjoyed only by audiences invited by the patron.

The Stage as Pulpit

The patronage of the Hamburg theater was still unsettled when Lessing's activities in this city came to an end, and for several more decades the principal theater of the great seaport remained the testing ground of a theatrical culture struggling for wholehearted civic support.

In 1769 Lessing received a tempting proposal to come to Vienna. The Habsburg court, particularly the future Emperor Joseph II, planned to bring distinguished German scholars and artists to Austria. Lessing's interest is expressed in his letter to Christoph Friedrich Nicolai: "Whatever Vienna may be, more happens there for German art than in your Frenchicized Berlin. . . . Just try to speak there freely about certain questions, as Sonnenfels[12] does in Vienna. Just try to tell that aristocratic gang at court the truth as he does. Let him come out in Berlin for the rights of citizens, against despotism, and you shall find out which country is the most slave-like today in Europe."

But in spite of Lessing's sympathy for Austria and his apparent resentment of Prussia, life led him into an unexpected new direction. The poet exchanged the opportunity of settling in a world capital for the retired existence in a tiny residence. The Hereditary Prince of Brunswick (Braunschweig), a scholarly and benign man, offered Lessing the position of court librarian in Wolfenbüttel, and in the spring of 1770 Lessing accepted. Living alone in a large abandoned castle, he immediately buried himself in the treasures of the ducal library. In the remote environment Lessing created masterworks such as the drama *Emilia Galotti*, performed at the Brunswick Court Theater in 1772. It is probably the oldest German tragedy still in the repertory today.

In 1779 Lessing completed, in Wolfenbüttel, *Nathan der Weise.* It is this towering dramatic poem upon which the poet's world-wide fame as a playwright primarily rests. Lessing, the son of a Protestant pastor, referred to the theater as his favorite pulpit. And his *Nathan the Wise,* a deeply searching plea for religious tolerance, refers to the three great monotheistic religions, Judaism, Christianity, Mohammedanism, and their deeply rooted historic premises. In the symbolism of this drama, Nathan, a Jew, teaches tolerance, reconciliation, and forgiving love.

Lessing expected the storm of protest which his message created when the play appeared in print. The Faculty of Theology of Leipzig University set out to prevent the performance of the drama. The clerics of Frankfurt insisted that the council forbid the sale of the book because of "the scandalous content in regard to religion." The court-supported German theaters refused to produce *Nathan the Wise;* Lessing was no longer alive when the première was given on April 14, 1783 — in Berlin, of all places. The play was badly received. Yet the rest of Europe needed little time for the proper evaluation of *Nathan the Wise.* The dramatic poem was translated into many languages: into English as early as 1780, into French in 1783.

Meanwhile clear-thinking Germans comprehended the lesson of harmony and respect for all true religions which the German poet tried to teach his people one hundred fifty-four years before Hitler's mortal onslaught on freedom of religion. It was Goethe who appraised the fundamental message of *Nathan the Wise* with Utopian fervor: "May the fable, so fortunately told, remind the German public for eternal times . . . that it is called upon to listen, to understand. May the Divine feeling for tolerance and respect, expressed therein, remain sacred and worthy to the nation."

Friedrich Schiller
The Stage as a Moral Institution

In 1779 the Mannheim National Theater was opened under the direction of the dramatist August Wilhelm Iffland whose plays had attained nation-wide attention. The court of the Elector Palatine had concentrated, earlier in the century, on patronage of the virtuoso orchestra. Now Mannheim was ready to give the theater a large share of its support.

But a far greater poet than Iffland was to raise the National Theater to an early summit in the history of the German drama: it was in Mannheim that Friedrich Schiller's close alliance with the stage began. In 1781 the poet had published his youthful tragedy *Die Räuber*. The Mannheim Theater gave the first performance of *The Robbers*, destined to become the most crucial play of the generation. In 1783 Schiller was appointed poet-in-residence at the Mannheim Theater. Several of his subsequent tragedies, such as *The Conspiracy of Fiesco in Genoa*, and later in the same year, *Intrigue and Love*, were also first given at the National Theater.

In 1784 the poet published his famous address, *Die Schaubühne als eine moralische Anstalt betrachtet.*[13] This was a decisive turn in the ideology of the theater. Viewing the stage as a moral institution, Schiller pleaded for a new fusion of the pure dramatic essence of the play with an inherent moral purpose. Schiller rediscovered the proper function of the drama according to its Greek etymology, where it means "sacred action." Schiller's own plays are optimistic with his belief in the ultimate victory of moral forces. He shows how those who usurp power and mock at human rights are finally brought to justice. Vice and virtue, misery and happiness, foolishness and wisdom are portrayed in the plays of Schiller with an almost Utopian breakthrough of the good. Ultimately, the dramatic message must guide the audience toward a renewed sense of ethics. Schiller's theory is rooted in ancient Greek philosophy, as well as in the enlightenment of the eighteenth century of which he thus becomes the chief dramatic exponent in the German language.

Ambivalent Court Patronage

Schiller had written *The Robbers,* secretly, in the shadow of Stuttgart's military academy, under the sovereignty of Duke Karl Eugen. *The Robbers* is a dramatic declaration of war against convention, lies and hypocrisies, and all other evils of society. The principal message of *The Robbers* was defined in the revolutionary motto "In Tirannos," with which the second printed edition of the play was prefaced. Cautiously Count Dalberg, superintendent of the Mannheim Theater, accepted *The Robbers* for performance only under the condition that the time of action was to be moved back from the revolutionary eighteenth century to the ending Middle Ages. The premiére, January 13, 1782, was a sensational event. Contemporary reports are eloquent on the unique reaction of the first audience: "The theater was a mad house . . . clenched fists, stamping feet, hoarse cries; strange people falling into each other's arms and crying; women fainting . . . flames of enthusiasm!"

Schiller was a citizen of the dukedom of Württemberg. He had gone to Mannheim without permission of his sovereign and received upon his return to Stuttgart a sentence of fourteen days of "house arrest." When the news of the poet's second trip to Mannheim became known in Stuttgart, the Duke threatened Schiller with imprisonment in the fortress Hohenasperg and forbade the poet to have "anything literary" printed in the future. But in 1784 the Duke accepted *Die Räuber* for the repertory of the Stuttgart Court Theater. Apparently Karl Eugen did not identify himself with the "tyrants" who were the targets of *Die Räuber.* The Duke thought of himself as a liberal ruler and (as shown earlier) the Stuttgart court justly prided itself on an unflinching tradition of art support. Furthermore, Karl Eugen had become aware of the growing national fame of Schiller, his one-time protégé. But Schiller preferred to escape from the Duke's ambivalent patronage and searched for a more congenial environment. In the poet's own words, "*Die Räuber* cost me the loss of family and fatherland."

Schiller at Weimar

In 1784 Schiller visited the Duke of Weimar and read to him the first act of *Don Carlos.* Deeply moved by the tragedy, Karl August conferred upon the poet the title, *Counselor at Court.* At his next visit to Weimar, in 1787, Schiller was increasingly impressed by the intellectual climate and the spirit of patronage at this Saxon residence where Goethe had previously settled. In 1798 the Weimar Court Theater was rebuilt and redecorated. The first part of Schiller's monumental *Wallenstein Trilogy* was performed during September. The second and the last parts were produced in the following year.

In 1799 Schiller moved to Weimar, where he remained to the end of his life — near Goethe, his friend. In rapid sequence Schiller wrote within the final five years of his life *Maria Stuart* (1800), *Die Jungfrau von Orleans* (1801), *Die Braut von Messina* (1803), and *Wilhelm Tell* (1804).

In retrospect Schiller emerges as Germany's greatest dramatist. But the poet does not address merely his own nation; he speaks to Europe, to the entire world. His "Ode to Joy," which Beethoven adapted for the text of the choral finale in the *Ninth Symphony*, epitomizes the plea for the brotherhood of man.

The decrease of Schiller's popularity on the German stage, following the establishment of Bismarck's powerfully nationalistic Reich, is really a posthumous compliment to the poet whose philosophical idealism and world citizenship were bound to be a still greater embarrassment to Hitler's Fascist theater. We may observe in the humanistic message and fate of Schiller's lifework another curious instance in the dichotomy of German culture. The principal thoughts of this towering poet are truly prophetic; transcending their time, they soar high above the spiritual level of his contemporaries. This fact lends itself to a revealing comparison. In eighteenth-century France the thoughts of Voltaire are in perfect attunement with his own time. They clearly reflect the age of enlightenment. Schiller, in contrast, envisions a still unfulfilled tomorrow. Far ahead of epoch and nation, the German poet dreams of *one world:* "Alle Menschen werden Brüder," he exclaims in his "Ode to Joy" (1785).

Goethe as Theater Director

Eighteenth-century Weimar was a small town with a typically middle-class population. The court of Weimar, ruled by dukes, had assumed in the latter part of the century a role that was to remain fateful for the spiritual destiny of the entire German nation.

In December, 1774, the young heir to the Weimar dukedom, Karl August, on a journey to France stopped in Frankfurt and met Goethe. The Duke invited the poet, then twenty-five, to come to Weimar. When Karl August succeeded his father as regent, Goethe accepted the invitation. He arrived in Weimar on November 7, 1775, and stayed at this residence for the rest of his life.

During these years a unique chapter in the history of patronage was written in Weimar. In 1791 Goethe was appointed director of the Court Theater, a post he held for twenty-two years.

The role of this universal poet as director of a small provincial theater may appear paradoxical. A recognized leader in world literature, he shunned the large German-speaking capitals and preferred to settle in one of the country's diminutive residences. The Weimar Court Theater was by no means staffed with first-rate professional actors. Even in later years, Goethe only rarely succeeded in lifting the level of the Weimar productions above the provincial. But the great dramatist apparently could work well under very modest circumstances. He realized the challenge of building a company of actors and stage personnel from whatever forces were available. Goethe's preoccupation with the practise of dramatic performance is expressed in his *Ninety Rules*, which were intended as a specific textbook for his performers. The *Ninety Rules* deal with acting technique and diction and the proper behavior of actors. Outdated today, the *Rules* enable us to reconstruct the Weimar style of classical interpretation.

Weimar: Enlightened Patronage

The Duke's association with Goethe marks progress in the German chronicle of patronage: in classical Weimar the artist was no longer the servant or the mere employee of the prince. Goethe, as the friend of Karl August, became a member of the inner circle at court. The poet was even entrusted with certain responsibilities of government.

What a departure from earlier relationships between patron and artists! At the Cardinal's household in Salzburg, Mozart ranked as a servant. Haydn in Eszterhâza, although fully enjoying the benevolence of his sovereigns, had his meals with the domestics and remained at all times at a "proper distance" from the court. In Weimar, Baroque court etiquette forbade Goethe to be seated with the Duke and Duchess at their table, but Karl August frequently circumvented protocol and dined with Goethe alone.

Within his Court Theater, still in keeping with the German monarchial absolutism, the Duke was the omnipotent patron. And Goethe as theater director accepted the status quo. Significantly, two of Goethe's most personal plays, *Torquato Tasso* and *Iphigenie*, represent court poetry of a highly sophisticated kind and reflect the poet's personal experience of court life.

Goethe's attitude and behavior toward the patron are in striking contrast with that of his greatest musical contemporary, Beethoven, whose revolutionary independence of manner, and his publicly displayed contempt of royalty and aristocratic sponsors are notorious. The motivations of Goethe's conformity are clear. His output during the Weimar years bears testimony to an environment congenial to his productivity. In addition to his publications in the various literary categories, and to his philosophical and scientific studies, Goethe completed his *Faust* in Weimar, after having worked on the two parts of the tragedy for almost a lifetime. *Faust* is Germany's national drama.

Due to the patronage of Duke Karl August, Weimar had the two greatest poets of the nation in simultaneous residence. The circle was widened by the presence of Christoph Martin Wieland (1733-1813), whom Duchess Anna Amalie had appointed as tutor of her children. In 1773 the distinguished poet founded in Weimar the literary review *Der teutsche Merkur*, which emerged as the most important German publication of its kind. In 1776 Johann Gottfried von Herder (1744-1803), philosopher and poet, was assigned to the post of court preacher in Weimar, his home until his death. Enlightened patronage helped create the classical culture of Weimar. And the collaboration of Schiller and Goethe, two of the most profound thinkers of the Western World, established a fortress of supranational spirit in this small German town.

VIII. Court, National, Municipal Theaters

Education or Entertainment?

The Napoleonic wars disturbed the continuity of German theater life. Devastation on the battlefields, followed by civic turmoil, obviously interrupted artistic pursuits in many communities. But not every part of Germany had been directly involved in the warfare. Occasionally the French even helped the Germans to preserve their theater life, and soon an influx of French taste made itself felt. Napoleon was a constant patron of the arts: he arranged for tours of the Théâtre Français in occupied Germany, displaying his famous "Parterre of Kings."

The duchy of Weimar was repeatedly involved in the swiftly shifting events of European power politics. Napoleon imposed upon the Duke and his people heavy burdens in terms of payments, recruiting of manpower, delivery of food and various supplies. In 1808 the Emperor received Goethe in Erfurt and soon after made him a member of the Legion of Honor. On a visit to Weimar, Napoleon also showed respect to the aged Wieland and other significant representatives of German culture.

Weimar was by no means an isolated instance of theatrical achievement during these tempestuous times. In Königsberg, a royal Prussian decree of December 16, 1808, claimed the "theater as an art institute devoted to public education." In keeping with such ideology, this decree placed the theater, along with the Academy of Sciences and Arts, under the supervision of the Royal Ministry for Public Education. Such a step anticipated important developments.

On the other hand, some of the newly organized and privately financed stages hardly qualified for the status of genuine theater. They offered cheap entertainment, circus-like shows, and variety features. To keep some order in the theatrical chaos, the royal decree of September 11, 1810, stipulated that the right to operate a theater required a special license to be issued by the police department. This was a well-intended ruling, but it simultaneously placed police bureaucracy in charge of grave cultural decisions. And the police state interpreted the theater merely as a place of entertainment, designed for popular pleasure and amusement.

Following Napoleon's defeat, some of Germany's national or municipal theaters were reconverted into court theaters. This procedure was partly motivated by political considerations. The German sovereigns wanted to prevent the use of the stage as a forum for antimonarchial propaganda. Whatever their motivations, the support of the court theaters often remained impressive. In 1815 Prince Hardenberg, the Prussian Chancellor, instructed the Royal Theater intendant, Count Brühl: "It is your job to create for us the best theater in Germany! Later, you will tell us what it costs."

The cultural patterns set by the court theaters were in turn continued by a number of state and municipal theaters. Not rarely, the financial support was shared jointly: thus the provincial parliament, the *Landtag*, would allocate subsidies to a theater as expenditures on the "civil list" of the reigning prince. Whatever the various forms of support, the theater survived the upheavals besetting the country in the first part of the nineteenth century.

Concept of National Theater

Meanwhile the concept of a "national theater" had gained ground in Germany. Specifically it presupposes a stage supported not by an individual court, province or city, but by the entire country. The repertory represents the masterworks of the nation as well as the drama of world literature. Within the German-speaking countries, the Austrian Emperor Joseph II founded in Vienna's Burgtheater the first homestead of a National Theater in this universal sense. For its National Theater, the government does not merely pay the bill; it is equally concerned with the spiritual life of the theater.

The title *National Theater* was also applied to provincial, municipal, and even to privately supported stages. In Germany, Mannheim and Hamburg vie in their claim for priority in the establishment of the National Theater. The palm for this priority depends on definition. As we have shown, a new theater called National Theater opened in Hamburg as early as 1766. Between 1771 and 1812 Friedrich Schröder intermittently led this theater, bringing to it high standards of performance. Imbued with the idealism of Lessing and Schiller, with their belief in the educational mission of the living stage, Schröder fought in Hamburg for the best repertory conceivable. He tried to direct the taste of the public toward serious theater. He hoped for proper support from the press and the municipality. But the press, instead of helping, ridiculed Schröder's efforts. Discouraged by the ironical attitude of the city's nine newspapers, the Hamburg municipality vacillated, and postponed placing the theater on a sufficiently secure and permanent financial basis.

Meanwhile, Prince Elector Karl Theodor had in 1779 sponsored a National Theater in Mannheim. Due to an almost continuous patronage, theater life in Mannheim attained special significance: it is one of the first instances on German soil of sponsorship which passed smoothly from princely to communal patronage. The municipality assumed the financial burden in gradual steps; it correspondingly participated in certain aspects of theatrical administration.

The actual transformation of the Mannheim Theater into a municipal civic art institute did not materialize until 1830. But once the city had assumed full responsibility, it lived up to it under trying circumstances.* The extraordinary initiative of the city government in the rehabilitation of the National Theater after its destruction in World War II is best understood in terms of history.

Steps to Municipal Patronage

In spite of all difficulties in the establishment of civic patronage, progressive patterns of municipal theater support clearly emerged in Germany late in the eighteenth century. In an early phase the municipality let the theater rent free to a concessionaire. Various utilities, such as light and water, were likewise given free of cost. Stage equipment, machinery, decorations, and costumes were made available to the management gratuitously (or at a nominal fee). The concessionaire was at liberty to administer the theater according to his artistic judgment and financial calculation.

In an important step forward, the cities granted the use of their orchestras to their theaters. In return, the municipalities expected a certain number of evenings (or matinees) within the theater's regular schedule to be reserved for opera, *Singspiel*, and ballet. Obviously, this musical assignment somewhat curbed the emphasis on drama. Personnel, technical apparatus, rehearsals, and, of course, moneys had to be redirected to meet this varied repertory which is typical of the German Stadttheater to this day.

Table I shows subventions granted in the year 1851 to some of the principal theaters in Germany and Austria. In the German-speaking

*Cf. Mannheim after World War II, P. 290.

territory the highest support was received by the Vienna Court Theaters; within Germany, by the Prussian Court Theaters of Berlin. Outside of Prussia, the highest subsidy went to the Bavarian Court Theater.

TABLE I
Theater Support in Mid-Nineteenth Century[14]

City	*Theater*	*Subvention (DM)*
Vienna	Court Opera Burgtheater	498,000
Berlin	Court Opera Royal Playhouse	420,000
Munich	Court Theater	267,420
Dresden	Court Theater	240,000
Hanover	Court Theater	220,000
Kassel	Court Theater	180,000
Karlsruhe	Court Theater	171,430

To facilitate comparison, all subventions, including those allocated to art institutions outside of Germany, are listed in German marks.

In appraising the general benefits of patronage, the relationship of ticket prices to the buying power of the population must be examined. The impact of government support — or its very absence — is reflected in the cost of theater tickets.[15] (See Table II.)

In mid-nineteenth century, seats were most expensive in St. Petersburg and London, where the seasons were private enterprises. By contrast, the subsidized court and municipal theaters in Austria and Germany brought prices into the reach of the middle income class.

TABLE II
Ticket Prices in Mid-Nineteenth Century

City	*Theater*	*Cost of Ticket (DM)*
St. Petersburg	Italian Opera	25.60
London	Italian Opera	21.60
Paris	Italian Opera	9.60
Vienna	Court Opera	4.20
Berlin	Court Opera	3.00
Hamburg	Municipal Theater	2.70

IX. The Theater in the New Reich

The Stage as Political Forum

The political map of Germany underwent several major changes during the nineteenth century. Most crucial of these was the steady growth of Prussia, which gradually absorbed territory both in the northwest, toward the Lowlands, and in the German south. But the art map of Germany, i.e., the topography of cultural centers, remained essentially intact. These centers continued to be sponsored and controlled by individual sovereigns, by the Länder and the cities.

The various German Länder were eventually welded together, not only by jointly-undertaken warfare, but by a common cultural heritage. And although most German states were still concerned about saving their political independence, the performances of German drama and music actually stressed national oneness.

Before long the theater had become a forum of great political consequence. A new nationalistic literature played its role in the psychological preparation of the people for the unification of the Reich. The same German plays and the same German operas were performed in the subsidized court theaters of the various state capitals, such as Berlin, Hanover, Dresden, Munich, Stuttgart; in the Hanseatic cities, Hamburg, Bremen, and Lübeck; and in a host of provincial towns.

The smallest German town supported its *Schmiere*, which is the humorous, but hardly translatable German word for an insignificant provincial stage, where youthful daringness is enthusiastically substituted for lack of personnel, adequate rehearsal time, and proper equipment. These small theaters are still in every corner of the land. Nothing could stop them from producing, after one week's preparation, Goethe's *Goetz von Berlichingen* or Schiller's *Wallenstein*, with large casts and demanding roles. Nor did large-scale opera frighten these adventurous theatrical companies. Wagner's *Tannhäuser* or *Lohengrin* were tackled with equal gusto.

Ironically, Wagner served the cause of German unification during his many years of exile from his fatherland. Forced to flee Dresden as a revolutionary in 1848, he became an ardent nationalist abroad. Wagner's stage works, as well as his numerous and verbose prose writings, through myth and direct persuasion, cemented the notion of German greatness.

Everywhere in Germany stages played a significant role in the propaganda of patriotic sentiment; they spontaneously kept alive the plea for a common national culture. In the theaters, large or small, youth watched live performances of German works which they had read at home and learned to admire in school. They memorized poetry, from the Weimar classicists to the contemporary romanticists. And many verses assumed the status of proverbs, to be quoted in daily life at the slightest provocation. In the Gymnasium, the humanistic high school, medieval German was part of the curriculum. The *Nibelungen* epic was declaimed in the original language by youngsters all over the country. In short, education and theater were geared toward unification of the divided nation.

Road to Unification

The midway mark of the century came, but only to set back Germany's hope for the Reich — at least for the time being. Austria still succeeded in preventing Prussia from swallowing up more German states, such as Saxony and Hanover. But Prussia's struggle for European hegemony was only temporarily halted. It flared up with the rise of new *Führer* personalities which were to engrave their imprint upon history for the next hundred years.

In 1859 William I became regent of Prussia; two years later he was crowned King. He was a strong-willed man, determined to achieve unity of the German nation. Enormous scientific development and industrial progress in the German states favored these ambitions. Particularly in physics and chemistry great strides were made. German industry rapidly developed. It promoted an intense exchange of products among the Länder.

The interplay of cultural issues constantly emphasized the concept of German unity. Time and again the idea of undividedness was dramatized by the performing arts. In addition to the theater and opera, a dominant role was played by the nation-wide music festivals. They contributed their part to German unification by mass singing of all sorts, and by choral performances of patriotic scores, of cantatas, and ballads. The social components of these festivals — their trivial conviviality — added to the popularity of these events. It led to a wide awakening of nationalism, to a yearning for the common, yet divided fatherland.

The speedy victories of 1864 over Denmark, of 1866 over Austria, and of 1870-1871 over France produced an utterly Prussianized Germany. The nation had now become the strongest power on the Continent. In the Hall of Mirrors at Versailles, Prince Bismarck made a spectacular declaration of Prussian unity and power. The new Reich was pompously proclaimed under the leadership of William I of Prussia. On an elevated stage the Hohenzollern were declared to be the supreme dynasty of the Reich.

The empire represented a union of twenty-six states that lasted until the end of World War I. There were four kingdoms, Prussia, Bavaria, Saxony, and Württemberg; six grand-duchies, Baden, Hesse-Darmstadt, Oldenburg, Saxe-Weimar Eisenach, Mecklenburg-Schwerin, Mecklenburg-Strelitz; five duchies, Anhalt, Saxe-Altenburg, Saxe-Meiningen, Saxe-Coburg Gotha, Brunswick; and seven principalities, Waldeck, two Schwarzburgs, two Lippes, two Reusses. There were three city-states, the Hanseatic republics of Hamburg, Bremen, and Lübeck, and finally the "Reichsland" of Alsace-Lorraine (the token of the Prussian victory over France).

Patronage as Voluntary Deed

All of these sovereignties, courts, and cities, without exception, strongly supported the performing arts. The smaller of these principalities subsidized one representative theater. The larger courts maintained several stages. The Hohenzollern, in spite of their centralizing policies, did not attempt to interfere with the long-established traditions in the theaters of the various states. In certain cases, Prussia even helped to build new court theaters outside of her immediate domain. Their architecture displayed the pompous and ornate style of the Wilhelmian era. The total number of these representational stages approximately doubled the number of the sponsoring states. There were about fifty-five major theaters, gifts to the people from the sovereign, which were the principal scenes of cultural events and of all official representation.

There was no legislation of any kind to control the support of the theaters. Patronage remained a voluntary gesture of monarchial generosity. It was spontaneous, not yet subjected to any sort of social pressure. Yet there was never an interruption in the flow of subsidy. The continuity of this support was an accepted necessity. Without subsidy none of these theaters could survive, not even for a short time.

Meiningen
Significant Theater in a Small Town

Particularly the population of small towns could not possibly manage to maintain their theaters by the forms of public assessment then prevailing. This is illustrated by the theater life in Meiningen, a small town in Thuringia. Meiningen is a household word in any history of the theater. The drama company sponsored by the ducal court of Saxe-Meiningen achieved in the 1870's such an international reputation that it was repeatedly invited to visit other countries. The performances of the Court Theater from this diminutive German residence were eagerly awaited and studied in the large capitals of Europe, for the performing style of the Meiningers was challenging in its departure from hitherto-known techniques of acting and production. Their interpretation of Shakespeare's *Julius Caesar* (1874) is still considered a landmark; some scholars trace the beginning of the group style in acting to this very production.

In certain principles of its interpretations the Meiningen Theater corresponded to that of the famous Moscow Art Theater. Meiningen performances placed emphasis on the ensemble rather than on the individual actor. The concept of teamwork was decisive. The collective potential in the dramatic texture of the play was stressed. The director assumes increased authority and assures prominence for the entire group. He must cast minor parts with the same care as he casts the major parts, recognizing there are no minor roles in a real drama.

The Meiningen company was also an important stronghold of incidental music in the prose theater. Meiningen's theater created the post of the *Bühnen Musikdirektor*, who is responsible for the choice and proper performance of the scores used for the play. Another important member of the Meiningen staff was the stage painter; he was no longer considered a mere craftsman, busy backstage with his brush and pots of colors, but an artist, entrusted with the difficult task of creating, with the help of his sets, illusion and mood. The cooperation of producer, music director, painter, costume designer, and all other personnel was carefully geared to an overall concept of dramatic interpretation. Nothing was left to chance.

It is extraordinary that such spirited theatrical experimentation found its workshop in a provincial German town of only 15,000. But the art-consciousness of the ducal patrons had long been in evidence. The famous ducal palace was completed in 1680; by the eighteenth century theatrical activities at court were extensive. Some of the plays performed were published by the court printing office. In 1831 Meiningen established its first regular theatrical company. Communal participation in its support was invited. Stocks yielding 3.5 to 4 per cent were eagerly bought by the citizens. But 252 shareholders returned their interest regularly to the theater fund. Duke Karl August pledged an annual support of 3,000 gulden — sufficient to cover the deficit.

The most important patron in the history of the Meiningen Theater was Duke George. His interest was active and on a thoroughly professional level. He participated in many angles of dramatic production. He himself designed stage sets as well as costumes. Guided by a search for historical correctness, the Duke attained a high degree of realism: an "authentic" style of production, adopted by the Meiningen company, was a direct expression of its patron's scholarly approach to all problems of the stage. In 1862 the Duke wrote to the superintendent of the theater: "I regard art as something sacred. I pledge myself to employ my artistic judgment to the support of the best in the theater. The artist who truly serves art is entitled to the best; he needs full patronage."

On March 19, 1873, German newspapers carried an unprecedented headline. Duke George had married Ellen Franz, the leading actress of the Meiningen Theater. This "misalliance" bewildered aristocrats and burghers alike; but it obviously implied the final cadence of the Duke's identification with his company of actors.

The patronage of the Schauspiel in Meiningen did not mean a decrease in the status of music. On the contrary, the Meiningen Court Orchestra attained fame in its own right. Under the baton of Hans von Bülow, and temporarily under his deputy Richard Strauss, it rose to be one of the finest orchestras of Europe. Max Reger was the last master to head this ensemble before it dissolved into obscurity with the First World War.

The lesson of Meiningen restates the experience of Weimar earlier in German history. We realize that the significance of an art center may be in inverse proportion to the size of the town in which it is located. Both the generosity of patronage and the spirit of the community decide the fate of its art life.

Administration of Court Theaters

German theaters were run efficiently. Their management was usually in the hands of aristocrats. The professional experience of the chief administrator might have been in business or finance. Often he came from the privileged group of landowners and therefore, had knowledge in the supervision of various farm activities. This background created a somewhat ironical situation: the court appointed a count or baron, well versed in the handling of peasants and cattle, to control the cultural fate of its theater. If the superintendent had also a certain affinity with the theater, so much the better.

Every German Junker, as the noble landowners of small holdings, particularly in the north, were called, dreamed of being a general. And it was from the Junkers that theater superintendents were often selected. Each of the large stages added the prefix "General" to the title of its manager, who thus became a General Intendant. The chief of the opera was respectfully addressed as General Musikdirektor. This fulfilled the *wish-dream* of these leaders themselves, and of their staffs as well. Germans work best under strict command. There is no question that part of the German achievement in the performing arts is tied to the iron rule with which they also ran their theaters and concert organizations. They operate on the stage with the same thoroughness which is the earmark of the German civil service, always functioning with military discipline.

Free Theater
Conflicting Aims of Patronage

At various times throughout Germany's history the project of a serious theater with free admission was publicly discussed, but never fully realized. But theaters supported by court, state, or city inaugurated the so-called *Volksvorstellungen*, in which classical works were performed for the people at greatly reduced prices. There were also popular performances on Saturday or Sunday afternoons, with minimum admission charge. These and various related practices were motivated by the aim of offering popular education through the theater, with the government paying the deficit. Today, the German theater extends this educational policy into every possible direction, such as closed performances for children, for various youth groups, for workers, etc.

The report of the remarkable growth of the German theater must not overlook occasional setbacks. Throughout the entire nineteenth century conflicting trends were in evidence. There was an increasing demand for a free economic development of theater life. As the new economic concept of *Gewerbe Freiheit* ("freedom of trade") gained ground, the theater was viewed by some as a business, as a trade and occupation suitable for profit. The entrepreneur who took the financial risks of support demanded also his rewards from the box office. As a result, money-making projects determined the nature of the repertory. On the other hand, most court and certain municipal theaters continued to interpret their deficits as honorable losses, provided they resulted from a program distinguished by artistic integrity.

The impact of freedom of trade was not fully realized until the period following the formation of the German Empire. Threats to the serious theater arose in the confusion of economic, political, and cultural aims. To be sure, economic freedom was to be welcomed, and liberty, in all of its ramifications, was a precious goal; but the wholesale, indiscriminate application of certain "liberal" slogans and procedures to cultural issues played havoc with the arts. Hundreds of privately financed stages offered cheap fare to a naive public. But even in some government-supported theaters, profiteering concessionaires manipulated assignments for their own financial gains. All of this produced an untenable situation. One gradually lost sight of the original purpose of governmental subsidies to the theater. Under the pretext of Gewerbe Freiheit, a free-for-all in the commercialized theater developed.

But all of these conflicts, in the long run, were resolved by the prevailing cultural impulses and the inherent traditions of German art life. The dilemma led to an inevitable solution: complete governmental aid for serious theaters, and the expulsion of their money-grabbing managers. The people themselves came to realize that their cultural organizations were directly tied to subventions assuring a valuable art program. Wherever governmental support, or any support without a specified cultural purpose, was lacking for any length of time, speculation and commercialization ran rampant. Only temporarily could few exceptions to this rule survive.

Private Performances

This study does not include the commercial theater. But in exceptional cases certain of its aspects concern us, wherever the commercial theater made contributions to the nonprofit stage and to the conquest of a legitimate public for it. This interrelationship is illustrated by the Neues Deutsches Theater of Berlin, founded in 1883. Its sponsor, the successful playwright Adolf L'Arronge, disdained in this experimental venture the very kind of theater that had made him rich: continued performance of superficial comedies designed for box office appeal. But in the New German Theater, L'Arronge created a repertory stage offering classical tragedy and certain select modern drama. How was this venture financed? Profits from L'Arronge's commercial productions were converted into funds for his pioneering theater and for the education of a new public for earnest drama.

The New German Theater was not the only noteworthy experiment by the commercial stage. In 1889 the producer Otto Brahm opened a theater in Berlin which was conceived as a counterpart to the Paris Théâtre Libre. Both were private playhouses; performances were never open to the general public. Admission was only by season subscription. There was a need in Berlin for such a theater with a truly progressive repertory, unhampered by reactionary police censorship. In Bismarck's Germany the public theater had no chance of a frank treatment of certain social problems. Topics alluding to the plight of the poor and following the new trend toward a discussion of sexual themes were not tolerated in the theater.

The establishment of Berlin's Die Freie Bühne suggested a solution. It was to serve as a platform for the dramatization of the forbidden subjects. Some of the best actors, motivated by the artistic challenge of the new, contributed their services. And in an unexpected gesture of sponsorship, proprietors of commercial theaters offered to The Free Stage their halls for Sunday performances without a rental fee. The venture paid off to everybody's interest. For Die Freie Bühne helped to raise the standards of the commercial theater, and the new impetus of progressive German drama can be traced to these imaginative experiments in private patronage during the last decades of the past century.

In 1890 Die Freie Volksbühne was founded. The similarity of name suggests similarity of purpose with that of Die Freie Bühne. The Free People's Stage, as its title suggests, explored the possibilities of bringing progressive theater to large, popular audiences. For the opening season, Georg Büchner's pioneering drama, *Danton's Death,* was scheduled for performance. The censor forbade the production, and the editor of a social democratic newspaper, involved in the sponsorship of the drama, was sentenced to four months in prison.

The latest descendant of these free stages, the Neue Freie Volksbühne, purposefully moved away from Berlin's west, the fashionable theater district in and around the Kurfürstendamm, to the eastern sector of the city with its large districts inhabited by workers. After a difficult start, the Neue Freie Volksbühne became a huge success in terms of artistic achievement as well as of attendance.

The reawakened interest ushered in a new phase of the theater, encouraging a kind of social drama that was soon to conflict drastically with rigid measures of government censorship. The youthful works of Gerhart Hauptmann, such as *Tragedy Before Sunrise* and *The Weavers*, in their sympathetic treatment of the struggles of the working class, present a kind of social criticism that was directly fostered by the free stages. We shall see later how Hauptmann behaved under the stress of Nazi patronage. Dramatic expressionism, an important development in this new phase of theater, was notably represented by Frank Wedekind, a more complex thinker than Hauptmann, but one who did not live to be punished by Hitler for "decadence" in such plays as his *Lulu* and *Spring's Awakening*. Curiously enough, the early social drama celebrated its first triumphs in the self-complacent and affluent west end of Berlin.

X. First Third of the Twentieth Century

Four Phases of Patronage

German art life displays in our century four distinct phases of patronage. They correspond to the fundamental changes the nation underwent in its successive metamorphoses from the Imperial Hohenzollern Monarchy (1871-1918) to the Weimar Republic (1919-1933), and from the Nazi Reich (1933-1945) to the Federal Republic of West Germany established in 1949.

World War I marked Germany's first sweeping defeat after her swift and spectacular military victories in the nineteenth century. When the Hohenzollern Empire collapsed in 1918, Kaiser Wilhelm II went to Holland into exile, and the other sovereigns of the Empire were quickly dismissed, as Germany attained, for the first time in her troubled history, the hopeful status of a free democracy. The Federal Government moved from Berlin to Weimar, and the classical residence of Schiller and Goethe attained new meaning as the first capital of the new-born Republic.

But the patterns of the former monarchial art patronage did not change outwardly with the establishment of a democracy. A fast transition set in, analogous to that taking place simultaneously in Austria.

Here, as there, the monarchial art organizations remained intact. Some of their names had to be adjusted. The former court theaters became Staats Theater or Stadt Theater, depending upon the source of their support; there were changes in their administration. The Republic often promoted distinguished artists to the managerial posts formerly held by members of the aristocracy.

The new Republican patrons rarely took the trouble to make physical changes in or outside of the former court theaters, with their numerous architectural and decorative tokens of monarchial sponsorship. The golden eagles or lions, the coats of arms, the ornate royal boxes, and the plush princely interiors — all of these rather pleased the German bourgeoisie. The citizens felt that they now "owned" these theatrical palaces, just as they had become heirs to munificent art galleries, museums, libraries, and formal gardens. The court boxes, formerly occupied by brilliantly attired royal patrons with their families and guests, were now reserved for the leaders of the Republican government. Their appearance in these boxes was a welcome symbol: the people now participated, through their elected representatives, in the fate and administration of these state and municipal theaters.

The Weimar Republic Art Support and Crisis

A brief, dynamic phase in the history of the German theater and opera set in. Some of the new century's most significant works were written and produced during the twenties. The period witnessed the emergence of Bertolt Brecht as a leading dramatist; in 1922 he was awarded the important Kleist prize. During these years the policy of even the Prussian state theaters was liberal and progressive, in fact, outright daring for the time. On December 14, 1925, the Berlin *Staats Oper Unter den Linden* gave the historic première of Alban Berg's epochal opera *Wozzeck*. The following excerpts of some of the reviews tell how the right-wing press greeted the event:

> Splitting the convulsively inflated larynx of the Muse, Berg utters tortured mistuned cackling, a pandemonium of chopped-up orchestral sounds, mishandled men's throats, bestial outcries, bellowing, rattling, and all other noise . . . Berg is the poisoner of the well of German music. — *Germania*, Berlin, December 15, 1925.

> As I left the State Opera last night, I had a sensation not of coming out of a public institution, but out of an insane asylum. On the stage, in the orchestra, in the hall, plain madmen. Among them, in defiant squads, the shock troops of atonalists, the dervishes of Arnold Schoenberg. *Wozzeck* by Alban Berg was the battle slogan. I regard Alban Berg as a musical swindler and a musician dangerous to the com-

munity. One should go even further. Unprecedented events demand new methods. We must seriously pose the question as to what extent musical profession can be criminal. We deal here, in the realm of music, with a capital offense. — *Deutsche Zeitung*, Berlin, December 15, 1925.[16]

Such reviews were not to be taken lightly. The *Oper Unter den Linden* was a state institution entirely supported from taxes. The extreme political right began to command increasing strength. Inevitably, the reception of *Wozzeck* amounted to a violent threat to the progressive art policy prevailing in the Ministry of Education. These stupid reviews expressed the opinions of a sufficiently large, noisy, and dangerously militant sector of the German population. If such a tone greeted modern art in a state-supported theater of cosmopolitan Berlin, the reception in the hinterland was likely to be even more hostile.

But in spite of such intimidation, a considerable number of provincial theaters, all subsidized on different governmental levels, assumed the risk of spending tax money on the productions of highly controversial drama and opera. The government upheld to the very end of the Weimar Republic a patronage of the performing arts that was extraordinary by all standards. In Berlin three operas played nightly, two aided by the state, one by the city. Particularly, the *Staats Oper am Platz der Republik* under Otto Klemperer's direction distinguished itself by inspired interpretations. Challenging works of Stravinsky, Schoenberg, Milhaud, Janáček, and others were included in the repertory.

The state-supported Playhouse in Berlin brought, even to the performance of the classical repertory, a daring spirit of experimentation. All over Germany audience participation was lively and discussion centered around such questions as where one could enjoy the most sophisticated productions of the standard repertory. Where could one hear the best performance of *Tristan und Isolde?* Was it in Bayreuth during the Summer Festival, or perhaps in Munich where Wagner's opera was first performed in 1865? Did the Richard Strauss tradition at the Dresden State Opera really surpass in authenticity that of other opera theaters? Could Leipzig, conscious of its heritage, offer the most genuine performance of Bach's *St. Matthew Passion*?

Modern music could be heard in authoritative performances in Frankfurt, where William Steinberg created a challenging forum for the works of the avant-garde. Classical or contemporary drama, Kleist or Hebbel, Wedekind or Strindberg, the early works of Ernst Toller or Bertolt Brecht, were by no means excitingly produced only on metropolitan stages. Some of the theaters in the provinces, too, deserved a palm for their achievements.

The sum total of these enterprising theaters in Germany represented a vital organism; their activities were well integrated into the art life of the nation. Of such overall accomplishments the Weimar Republic was proud, and the result was indeed worthy of self-esteem.

To assess the record of unswerving governmental art patronage we must project it against its volcanic political background: during the fourteen years of the Weimar Republic (1919-1933) the Federal German Parliament (*Der Reichstag*) was dissolved no less than six times. This was a period that called for the most energetic and imaginative leadership from government. The Republic needed to dramatize the privilege of living in a free society. But Weimar was, as it is frequently called by the Germans themselves, a "false paradise."

The economic low of the early thirties, which rapidly led to catastrophic events, eventually had severe consequences for art support on all levels. Most German municipalities, hard pressed for funds, searched against odds for solutions to their financial dilemma. We will never know what the outcome might have been; for the Nazis took over. In their procedure to subjugate all the arts for political propaganda, large sums were suddenly made available for the art institutions of the nation.

XI. Perverted Patronage

The Third Reich

"The new millennium of the Third Reich" which Hitler claimed to have inaugurated, lasted twelve years, three months, and three days. Estimated in terms of destruction of all that civilized Germans had built up in preceding centuries, in terms of human lives and values annihilated, of tragedy unleashed, the Nazi era will remain immeasurable forever. We have no standards to gauge adequately the degree of human suffering. The sheer quantity of human slaughter prevents us from attempting to assess the apocalyptic tragedy.

"When I hear the word *Kultur*, I reach for my gun" was an often-quoted slogan of Nazi leadership. It describes well enough its familiar attitude toward civilization and intellect. But it fails to explain the numerous paradoxical actualities of Hitler's extensive art support. It tells us nothing about the far-reaching attempts of his propaganda machine to enlist the services of "Aryan" artists toward the "enlightenment" (*Aufklärung*) of the German people. Some of these measures concern us here. They are striking examples of a debased patronage. They expose the traps of a so-called "people's art" and its mortal dangers when it becomes tied to a totalitarian system.

Three vast and powerful experiments within our own time show the subordination of art to party lines as prescribed by dictators. The Soviet gradually insisted on the subjugation of art to politics. Mussolini and his underlings were next to formulate principles of a fascist art, without, however, realizing the total goal of their ruthless aspirations. It was not until the Nazis raped German culture that an enormous and systematic perverted art program rapidly rose before the world with all of its dreadful implications. In Hitler's Third Reich we can observe the relationship between dictatorship and art support in its most virulent form.

The Nazi reign began on January 30, 1933, when Reich President General Paul von Hindenburg appointed the former corporal to the all-powerful post of Reich Chancellor. This date may be regarded as the official beginning of a development that almost destroyed European civilization.

The Nazi government started immediately to undermine the sovereignty of the Länder and of their traditional state rights. Every form of Fascism aims at totalitarian control and Hitler accomplished this control quickly by an airtight centralization of power. The procedure immediately led to the silencing of local and regional self-expression throughout Germany. With the Federal Constitution of the Weimar Republic overthrown, its numerous art institutes were fast reduced to mere tools of the Third Reich. The same fate befell all provincial and municipal theaters, opera houses, and concert organizations. They were allowed to function only in relation to their usefulness to Nazi propaganda. In certain cases, former subsidies were increased and lavishly extended to all areas and media that could be safely lined up behind the political machinery, its racial laws, the concept of the "Führer principle." That art lost its innermost meaning under the deceitful tutelage of Joseph Paul Goebbels, the so-called *Minister of Propaganda and Enlightenment*, does not require amplification here.

The nightmare of totalitarian art life began with the rapid enforcement of racial laws in all cultural institutions. The "non-Aryans," along with politically-doubtful artists and teachers, were dismissed overnight. When these organizations were rid of directors and personnel "dangerous to the Nazi state," the art institutes themselves came under vigilant scrutiny and perpetual censorship. The first targets were works by Jewish authors and composers and works by so-called *cultural bolshevists*. In music this prompted a ban on past and contemporary masterworks, from Mendelssohn's incidental score for Shakespeare's *A Midsummer Night's Dream* to Hindemith's *Mathis der Maler*. In drama, it meant eliminating Lessing's *Nathan der Weise*, Goethe's *Iphigenie*, and other messages of classical humanism. The catalogue of twentieth-century stage works that were now "verboten" included a wide range of plays from Arthur Schnitzler to Bertolt Brecht. There is no need to list the trash which obedient Nazi scribblers hurriedly fabricated as ideological support for the Nazi theater and opera. A new "literature" came to life, also a flood of new scores for the concert stage (Hitler-inspired cantatas, etc.). Inevitably, the role of the performing arts under dictatorship is chained to the moral and intellectual level of its patrons.

The Sword at the Altar

The Nazis wasted no time abolishing freedom of worship. Thirty specific articles laid down the rules whereby the German people were to submit to a new barbaric "Church." The first of these summarily stated that "the Nazi Reich Church of Germany claims the exclusive right and the exclusive power to control all churches, Catholic or Protestant, within the borders of the Reich and declares them to be national churches of the German Reich." All members of the clergy were to be replaced by National Reich orators (Article No. 7).

The Bible was "verboten." Its circulation was to be stopped immediately. And thus for the first time since Johann Gutenberg's invention of printing in 1454 made possible the distribution of the Bible to the world, the Holy Book was banned by a government in a country inhabited by almost 70,000,000 Christians. But there was a replacement: Hitler's *Mein Kampf* now became the "Bible" of the Germans. This book of the Führer was pronounced by the National Reich Church as the "greatest of all documents." As Article 14 stated, "it embodies the purest and truest ethics for the present and future of our nation."

Hitler's blueprint for the new patterns of German life immediately caused a series of extraordinary events in the Länder and the capital, Berlin.

The Burning of Books

The principal avenue of old Berlin was Unter den Linden. Once a beautiful street with a row of large shady trees, it is still the location of some of the most formidable cultural organizations the German nation has created since the reign of Frederick the Great: the Humboldt University, the State Library, the handsome Court Opera, the Singakademie. All of these now belong to the Eastern sector of the divided city.

Three months after Hitler's ascension to power, Unter den Linden was the scene of one of the most extraordinary spectacles ever performed in a moribund civilization. On the avenue, during the night of May 10, 1933, a battalion of so-called "students," yelling Nazi tunes, marched to the square facing the University. They had stolen thousands of selected books from the library. These they threw into a large pile and set afire. A rhythmically shouting chorus screamed in wild tirade, announcing the names of the authors and the titles of the books burning in the flames.

Who were these writers whose works were condemned to the fire? They were identified by Propaganda Minister Goebbels and his illiterate underlings as spiritual enemies of the Hitler Reich. Of German-born authors, Albert Einstein and Thomas Mann were culprits; of the French, Proust and Gide; of the Austrians, Freud, Schnitzler, and Hofmannsthal; of the English, H. G. Wells. The list of Americans included, among others, Helen Keller.

In the twentieth century, on the avenue Unter den Linden, a performance out of the darkest ages of mankind took place — a dramatization of the Un-Geist, of the Anti-Christ, which no cinema director could have staged with more barbaric effectiveness.

Gleichschaltung
"Culture" Geared to Nazism

Having done away with these subversive books in this symbolic ceremony, which was repeated in other German cities, what did the leader offer instead? How were the German people to know what to think and what not to think, what to read and what to avoid, what to hear and what to see?

All answers were neatly provided by the law of September 22, 1933, which established the Kultur Kammer, the Chamber of Culture. In order to pursue a policy of German culture, the law said, "It is necessary to assemble the creative artists of all categories into a unified organization under the guidance of the Reich, which must not only decide all lines of progress, mental and spiritual, but also lead and organize the professions."

Seven departments were organized for the purpose of tightest controls over the fine arts, music, theater, literature, the press, radio, and motion pictures. It was a thorough organization of governmental supervision.

Everything that could conceivably occur in the field of arts and letters was rigged to serve Nazi politics. All procedures and performances were under party control, from the festivals on the largest national scale to the local band performances in the village, from the appointment of a metropolitan opera director to the hiring of a church singer in a remote mountain hamlet. It was impossible to obtain a menial job as a stagehand or extra at a provincial theater without having been admitted to the local cell of the official Nazi organization. The entire process of coordination was officially called *Gleichschaltung* — a term borrowed from physics, implying "placement into equal gear."

Totalitarian controls of civic life obviously had to begin with censorship of the press and radio. (Television was not yet functioning at that time.) These instruments of information were turned immediately into efficient means of Nazi propaganda. Editors were commanded "to eliminate from the newspapers anything which in any manner confuses the people, imposes selfish aims upon those of the community, tends to sap the strength of the German State (outwardly or inwardly), the common will of the German people, the defense of Germany, its culture and economy . . . or offends the honor and dignity of Germany."

The radio networks were transformed into unscrupulous tools of Nazi "enlightenment." The new law of October, 1933, also applied to the film industry, which soon became the pet project of Minister Goebbels. The state theaters, by contrast, were known to be the prime interest of Minister Goering. These two leaders, the Mephistophelian Goebbels and the bemedalled butcher Goering, were now the great official patrons of German art life. Fiercely competing with each other for power and popularity, they decided all important "cultural" issues. They made grand entrances at official performances and held court in the boxes.

Indoctrination

The Nazis knew well that they had to begin their *Gleichschaltung* at the earliest possible level. Nazification began in the kindergarten and ended nowhere. In secondary schools and colleges, learning for its own sake was rejected and all teaching was geared to the purposes of Nazi rule.

The newly-appointed Reich's Minister of Science, Education and People's Culture, Bernhard Rust, explained that the schools must cease to function as "institutions of intellectual acrobatics." In keeping with Hitler's precepts as laid down in *Mein Kampf*, education was to aim not merely at a stuffing with knowledge, but at building bodies physically healthy to the core.

The Nazis were quick to learn from other fascists, and adopted certain of Mussolini's demagogic techniques of indoctrination. As in Italy, the entire concept of education was revised. All textbooks were rewritten or newly written. As in Germany's churches, so in the schools, Hitler's *Mein Kampf* was interpreted as the supreme source of all guidance.

The centralized Reich government took over the long-established privileges of the Länder or municipalities in the supervision of schools on all levels. Self-government in the colleges ended. Violating European tradition, Nazis stipulated that rectors and deans of the universities were no longer to be elected by the academic body itself. Now all academic appointments were made by a Nazi *Obergruppenführer*. It would be gratifying to state that there were signs of an effective protest to all of this by the German professors. There was, in fact, a shocking degree of submission to the formal end of free search and thought at the universities.

"Decadent Art" and "Germanic Art"

In his youth Hitler had been a self-styled painter, but was rejected in his attempts to achieve the slightest degree of recognition. Throughout his life, as with Mussolini, the pretense of artistic creativity prevailed. Having achieved power, Hitler was ready to get even with his former critics and with those artists he considered "lunatics."

The key to Hitler's aesthetics was his concept of "Germanic art," which was now marked to take the place of "decadent art." In the process of "liberating the German people from the most poisonous art works" he arranged in 1937 for the now infamous Munich exhibition of *Entartete Kunst*. Subsequently he had 6,500 paintings removed from German museums. A comprehensive exhibition of these discarded works included such typical "lunatics" as Cézanne, van Gogh, Kandinsky, Klee, Kokoschka, Matisse, Nolde, Picasso, etc. Of German-born artists, Ernst Barlach, Franz Marc, Max Beckmann, and Max Liebermann were among the cursed.

On the other hand, what was generally shown as "Germanic art" turned out to be the most commonplace, reactionary *Machwerk*, mere makeshifts of painting and sculpture. It would be a waste of space to mention names; it would be a gross overstatement to grade such art "mediocre." The *locus topicus* of Hitler's "Germanic art" was somewhere between a pseudo-classicism and a false Biedermeier (that comfortable bourgeois style which he had admired in his Vienna days). The content of the new Nazi-sponsored art was, of course, highly representational. It was "propaganda art." There were paintings of goose-stepping storm troopers. There was fertility and pregnancy sculptured in all of its realistic manifestations, as the Nazis prepared for future manpower and cannon fodder. In countless German homes where, formerly, Adolph Menzel's famous painting of Frederick the Great playing the flute inevitably held the place of honor, there now hung prominently a portrait of Hitler on horseback, clad in shining armor, like a Wagnerian hero. All of this typical *Kitsch* was reproduced in millions of copies to decorate German homes, offices, and schools.

Hitler did not merely forbid "decadent art." He prescribed the true German art. And so he ordered what was to be concocted in the studios of the artists. It was he who directed all conceivable forms of

German art life, whether or not it was financially supported by the Nazi government. Before long Hitler had launched a totalitarian art program of a kind the world had never known.

In analogy to the Munich exhibition *Entartete Kunst*, the Nazis arranged for an exhibition *Entartete Musik*. The stated purpose of the event was to prevent the "decay of German music infested by Marxistic, Bolshevistic, Jewish and other un-German tendencies under the slogan of atonality and jazz." Represented among the "degenerate" composers were Schoenberg, Webern, Berg, Stravinsky, and Hindemith. When Bartók learned that he was not included in this index of decadence, he sent a letter of protest to official quarters insisting that he, too, be included among the list of "degenerates."

The performing arts functioned without curtailment. They were recognized as a powerful instrument of persuasion. The Nazis fully subsidized them where it suited their purposes. Undeniably, creditable acting and music-making continued, for the giant apparatus of the German theaters, operas, and symphony orchestras retained some of its traditional technical quality. Furthermore, the Nazis thought that the spectacle of art patronage could serve them as a claim to culture, as a strong alibi in the eyes of the world. Hitler displayed interest in the living stage. He was often seen in the theater, seated alone in his box. His musical taste ranged from Wagnerian opera to Viennese operetta. *Die Meistersinger* and *The Merry Widow* were two of his favorites.

How did some of Germany's famous artists fare under Hitler's personal patronage? The most celebrated German composer of the era was Richard Strauss. He was offered the presidency of the newly-founded Reichs Musik Kammer. Strauss accepted and thus helped to give this institution a semblance of prestige. The personal problems of Strauss became involved with the performance of his opera *The Silent Woman*, which he completed at the end of 1934. Both of Strauss' principal librettists were non-Aryans and consequently unacceptable to Nazi patronage. The poet Hugo von Hofmannsthal had died in 1929. Strauss subsequently enlisted the collaboration of Stefan Zweig. In spite of Zweig's Jewish faith, the Nazis permitted the première of *The Silent Woman* in Dresden on June 24, 1935. Two days before the event Strauss wrote to his new librettist: "If you could see our opera here and see how good it is, you would drop all worries about race and politics, and work as much as possible for me. The opera will make a sensation in London, where the whole Dresden ensemble is invited to perform. Dr. Goebbels will give Reichs support for the tour. So you see, the *bad* Third Reich has its own *good* sides!" But Strauss was too optimistic. *The Silent Woman* was banned "by high order" after the third performance. It is sometimes believed that Strauss gave lip service to Hitler in order to protect his own family: his daughter-in-law was Jewish, and thus his grandchildren were "racially impure." For whatever reasons Strauss accepted Nazi patronage, it all ended sadly: the aged master spent the final years of his long life as a lonely, disillusioned man in Swiss asylum. He returned to Germany only to die.

The role of Strauss as Germany's leading composer corresponds to that of Gerhart Hauptmann as the nation's most prominent dramatist. During the crucial years of their regime, Hauptmann permitted the Nazis to use his international fame for shabby political propaganda. And so the artist who had once contributed so nobly with his early plays to a more humane climate in his fatherland, abandoned the liberal role of his youth. Betraying his former ideals, Hauptmann was well rewarded. State-supported playhouses throughout the nation engaged in a systematic "rediscovery" of his many plays. Often, Hauptmann was on the scene acknowledging honors and sometimes appearing in the company of the most notorious Nazi leaders.

If figures of such world prestige set such precedents of behavior, what could be expected of the average German Kapellmeister or Dramaturg, and of the thousands of singers, instrumentalists, actors, and all kinds of theater folk who hoped to continue making their living in their fatherland? Innumerable composers and playwrights, painters, and architects did not allow any remnant of moral conviction to interfere with their jobs and opportunities.

Once more the Italian maestro, Arturo Toscanini, then at the very height of his popularity also in Germany, stands out as the lonely image of decency. He promptly cancelled his engagement to conduct at the Wagner Festival in Bayreuth, which had fallen under the personal patronage of Adolf Hitler. His eloquent gesture of protest was not in vain; Toscanini will be remembered for his solitary forthrightness.

XII. The West German Republic

West-East Division

After the overthrow of the Nazis, in 1945, German art life could not possibly resume the traditional course which the Weimar Republic had to abandon in 1933. Too much had happened in the intervening twelve years. The Hitler era was as destructive culturally as it was devastating in every other sphere. Never in history had there been less reverence for human life.

Responsible Germans are conscious of this. There are extraordinary tokens of remembrance. In Berlin, the one-time capital of the Reich, the authorities insisted with conviction and moral courage that the bomb-mutilated tower of the Emperor Wilhelm Memorial Church be preserved as it is. It is an ugly sight. Many Germans resent this constant and grim reminder of Hitler's world and wars. But there it is, and there it remains, on West Berlin's once elegant and still very busy main avenue, the Kurfürstendamm. The ruined spiral and portal of the great Lutheran church overlooks the unceasing traffic of the damaged city, which has regained its proverbial vitality even if it is no longer the center of a unified and free nation.

Through the center of old Berlin the boundaries of two worlds are arbitrarily drawn. Antagonistic ideologies clash head-on — a constant threat not only to the peace of the region but to that of Europe and the entire world. The very topography of Berlin is a strange symbol of the abyss.

At the end of World War II, German art life seemed to have reached its own dead end. Since the advent of Fascism in the heart of Europe, the focus of art life had shifted elsewhere: to France, England, and the United States. Switzerland, Holland, and Scandinavia likewise became important and liberal outposts of the performing arts.

Today, the stream of German culture, deflected by the Nazi horror, seeks to find that broad river bed which its free flow had cut across the ages. But the great postwar split — the division of Germany into East and West — created, also in the world of the performing arts, many problems without precedent.

A great deal of migration has occurred and continues daily as a consequence of the upheaval. Refugees, displaced persons, stateless, wandering human beings have added to Germany's ethnic variety. The total of displaced persons East and West is estimated at about 14,000,000. In some distant future something creatively new might emerge from this new melting pot on German soil. But, for the time being, the effect is confusing, disrupting.

Furthermore, Germany like Austria has been robbed of some of her greatest minds, due to Hitler's racial laws, but also due to voluntary emigration by those who refused to go along with Nazism and have decided never to return. The list of great emigrant scientists and artists does not require lengthy enumeration here. It suffices to recall that Albert Einstein, Sigmund Freud, Arnold Schoenberg, Paul Hindemith, and Thomas Mann left their native, Hitler-dominated countries and found peace for more creative work in the West. The names of the emigrant artists and scholars (Nobel prize winners among them) would amount to an impressive catalogue that will no doubt some day be compiled and studied in an effort to evaluate more definitely their contributions to their adopted countries. Their influence on American culture has been compared to that of the Greek scholars on the culture of western Europe, where they sought asylum after the fall of Constantinople in the mid-fifteenth century.

Consequences of Partition

The art life of the Weimar Republic, with all of its stimulating variety, presented a certain cultural unity. There prevailed a similarity of purpose in the performing arts. There was a productive interchange of artistic experience and achievement between the German states and their art centers, large or small.

Today, West Germany and East Germany oppose each other politically, and their political aims have deep-seated correlates in the arts. The West still adheres to creative freedom; the East holds to a directed art life in which the artists must clearly serve the political interests of the state. Due to the irreconcilable rift in political thought, there threatens a seemingly unfathomable gulf between the two worlds of art. German artists — on both sides of the Iron Curtain — feel the effects of this separation more strongly than their historic bonds.

It is a division which is bound to leave its imprint on the cultural future of the divided nation. Europe has often known a split between West and East and has often suffered from it. Ethnic differences have created marked borderlines of civilizations, and even wars. But the Iron Curtain cuts through a land long-united by cultural aspirations.

Behind the Iron Curtain lies German territory steeped in centuries-old artistic traditions which cannot be forgotten by the West. East Germany has absorbed the large regions of Saxony and Thuringia, the core of the Protestant Church and Church music almost since Luther's day. In the communistic sector lies Leipzig, where Bach spent the final twenty-seven years of his life as cantor at St. Thomas. Modern Leipzig is still a firmly established publication center of books and music. It is the seat of the *Gewandhaus* which, in the nineteenth century, was the home of Germany's most distinguished conservatory and orchestra, the school and the instrumental ensemble founded by Mendelssohn. They flourished to the day Nazi hordes smashed to bits the monument of the great Romantic composer.

Like St. Thomas in Leipzig, many old German churches with highly trained choruses and Baroque organs belong today to East Germany, which, ironically, has little use for organized religion and liturgical music. Dresden, like Leipzig, has become a communistic metropolis. In the history of the theater and music, this Saxon capital has been one of Europe's most important centers. The former province of Silesia has been absorbed by a Sovietized Poland. Within the performing arts this means the loss of Breslau, Silesia's capital, seat of a long established opera and of the university for which Brahms wrote his *Academic Festival Overture.* Chemnitz, one-time center of textile industries, a complete war victim, has been rebuilt from ashes. The theater-conscious city has been renamed *Karl Marx Stadt;* obviously the direction of its art life follows communistic ideology.

The dispossession of Weimar, the classical city of Schiller and Goethe, is painful to the West: we have observed the decisive role of this Saxonian residence in Germany's cultural and political history. In fact, both of Germany's one-time capitals, Weimar and Berlin, have ceased to function as nerve centers of the nation. The country's division has led to curious competition and duplication. In 1949, the bicentennial year of Goethe's birth, the West and the East competed in their claim to be the spiritual fatherland of the freethinking poet. A similar situation occurred in 1959 at the Schiller bicentennial and in 1950 at the bicentennial commemoration of Bach's death. There were two kinds of festivals for Goethe, two kinds for Schiller, and two kinds for Bach.[17]

In some of its ramifications, the German art scene presents a disquieting, though undeniably fascinating spectacle. Fundamental differences in political thought, West and East, cause far-reaching differences not only in the creative concept of new art, but even in the performing style of old art. This is inevitable. On either side of the Iron Curtain the style of interpretation reflects its ideological environment. Art is never created in a vacuum. Nor does it function in an abstract environment. All manifestations of its patronage are conditioned by its cultural, political, and economic premises.

Bund and Art Support

The Bundes Republik Deutschland, as this title indicates, represents a federative nation. The basic law of the West German Republic reflects its federalistic structure in terms of all institutions — political, educational, and artistic. The superior body is the Bundestag (Parliament) with the Bundespräsident as the head of the state. The representative body of the Länder (states) is the Bundesrat, headed by the Bundeskanzler (chancellor), who is politically the most powerful figure of the Republic. In a certain sense, the Bundesrat functions as a second chamber. Its members, appointed by the governments of their respective Länder, represent the individual interest of their home states.

In all financial questions, and consequently in all problems pertaining to art subsidies, the Bundesrat is decisive. The federal laws that determine taxes have to be confirmed by the Bundesrat. And moneys for art support stem from these taxes. Thus, important aspects of public patronage fall under the control of the Bundesrat. The two major political parties of West Germany are the Christian Democratic Union and the Social Democrats. In the Electoral College, the Christian Democratic Union holds (at this writing) a bare theoretical majority. An unwritten law divides West Germany's principal offices between Catholics and Protestants. West Germany's population is about equally divided between these two principal religions, but party affiliation does not necessarily correspond to religious faith. Many Catholics are Social Democrats; Protestants belong to the Christian Democratic Union. Nor does religious affiliation hold any firm clue to the kind of art favored for support. On the other hand, political ties are not irrelevant in this issue. In 76 West German cities with a population of more than 30,000, the Social Democrats elect the chief of the municipal government. The cities, the counties (Länderkreise), and the states (Länder) cooperate in the various forms of official art patronage. In many cases, the municipalities exercise the principal initiative. Thus the individual urban community remains, as it has for centuries, the center of gravity within modern German art support.

The Hitler rule had upset this pattern. When the Nazis came to power in 1933, they rapidly began to undermine the sovereignty of the member states. After the collapse of the Third Reich, the emerging Bonn Republic scrupulously restored the federalistic principles of government. Simultaneously, the patterns of regional patronage reappeared on the West German art scene.

The Länder as Patrons

The individual interests of the Länder are subject to debate and decision in the Bundesrat. All the states are determined to give full support to their art life. Each of the Länder competes for whatever help and privileges may be obtained from federal sources.

The specific character of its art life is conditioned by the nature, history, and economics of the Land. The level of art appreciation obviously differs from urban to rural regions, from the city-states (Stadt-Staaten like West Berlin or Hamburg) to the primarily agrarian Länder. Germany's vast mining and industrial districts (such as the Ruhr) have large populations of workers whose approach to art must be guided cautiously. Mountainous Bavaria, agrarian Hesse, the open farmland of the north, present different needs in terms of art education. Whatever their requirements, the Federal Republic leaves initiative and decisions to the state governments and the municipalities.

This procedure differs from earlier reviewed German methods that gradually led from complete independence of art-sponsoring principalities or kingdoms to tight centralization of all cultural centers. Bismarck was the first political leader to attempt such convergence, with Prussia as focus. The Iron Chancellor realized the dream of Frederick the Great to promote Berlin as the cultural center of the German nation.

With the collapse of the Third Reich, the pendulum was bound to swing in the opposite direction. All remnants of centralization were replaced by a new regionalism. Political exigencies made such a procedure the logical one. Again, art support was geared to the individual Länder. This particular concept of patronage corresponded to the history of the constituent member states.

The Federal Republic, viewed as an all-embracing political entity, allows for the individual self-expression of the Länder, for the preservation of their cultural identity in terms of indigenous background. Catholic and Protestant traditions are equally maintained.

Today, this is the only possible formula for Germany. Coexistence and tolerance must once more sound the keynote for civilized living. These premises were recognized by the postwar administration of the Allied Occupational Government: in helping the new Republic to rebuild its cultural organizations, the Western Allies coped with the diversified wishes of the German population. The Allies could undertake to support art projects with full conviction; this new patronage coincided with the political ideology and specific plans that the Allies had conceived for the new West German nation.

Under the circumstances, the Bonn constitution did not assign to the Bund (i.e., to the Federal Republic, with its seat in Bonn) a central supervision of national culture. This is a crucial point. It marks the intrinsic differences in the art patronage of West Germany and that of other European countries such as England, France, or Italy. Even Austria, in many aspects of her art support close to the German pattern, here seeks other solutions. The Swiss emphasis on cantonal sovereignty is close to the West German approach.

The Bonn Republic has what her citizens call a *Mischverfassung*, i.e., a constitution "mixing" certain aspects of federalism with specific methods of decentralizing authority. The Republic was conceived with the considerable inner variance of its population in mind. The founders of the new Germany carefully tried to reconcile disparities that had much too long disturbed the peaceful neighborliness of north and south, of Protestantism and Catholicism. To this day, latent tensions hinder the teamwork of certain regions, of groups of people that are different in terms of political thought, productive power, and economic status. The recent division of Germany and her consequent diminution has emphasized these differences of long historic standing.

The Germans admit that the present systems of art patronage are not ideal. One disadvantage in the present solution is a splintering of forces. There are projects where a collective federal effort instead of the division of funds could be more constructive. But as the choices of procedures remain free in the member states, the chance of federal interference in cultural issues is minimized. The various German states have arrived at definitions of their tasks through common declarations by their cultural ministers. According to official proclamation, they are determined to "create anew the spiritual unity of Germany and her inner freedom from within the Länder."

Overall German Interests

In spite of this recognition of regional sovereignty, the need for an overall clearing house for national cultural issues soon became apparent. As a result, a *Bundes Ministerium für gesamtdeutsche Fragen* was established, i.e., a federal office for the solution of cultural questions that concern the entire West German Republic. This special ministry deals most particularly with specific problems which arise as a consequence of the partition of Germany. In the procedures of this office, national sovereignty is recognized. The Länder are willing to cooperate in the higher interests of their nation. By and large, such collective work has proved to be successful. Yet there has been criticism, even heated arguments, because of rivalry between the individual members of the Federal Republic. It is difficult, often impossible, to adjust cultural policies of the entire nation to regional thinking and planning. This would be true of any federal government anywhere in the world. In postwar Germany the atmosphere is highly charged.

Permanent Conference

The need to solve cultural problems that pertain to the entire West German Republic through collective effort, and to arrive at a generally acceptable interpretation of relevant issues, led in 1949 to the foundation of another body closely related to the Bundes Ministerium für gesamtdeutsche Fragen, i.e., Conference of Cultural Ministers of the States. The new group has as its purpose insuring the welfare of national cultural interest, at the same time safeguarding the independence of the Länder in whatever decisions are taken on a national level. Notwithstanding the careful theoretical definition of the spheres of competence, the relationship between the Bund and its individual states remains in delicate balance, which is known to have been disturbed on certain occasions. It became necessary for the Federal Ministry to insist that the authority of the national government be recognized in issues clearly above the subjective interests of the member states.

The underlying philosophy recognizes in the Bund not only the indispensable instrument of total national government, controlling the political, economic, social interests of West Germany, but a spiritual organism of its own. It is the "clearing house" of national culture.

The Federal Republic has so far been in the position to administer cultural activities with a minimum of jurisdiction. Bonn, as the capital of the Bund, merely supervises the purposeful distribution of federal moneys for the arts. They are forwarded to organizations and places that are entitled to receive federal financial assistance, only after such allocation has been mutually agreed upon. The aid must serve clearly defined and generally approved artistic ends. The subsidized institutions in the different states of the Republic are free to proceed on their own terms, unhampered by federal bureaucracy. No red tape is allowed to slow down the procedure of allocating funds. The men in charge of the art institutes are usually administrators of proven ability who assert their judgment without undue influence from federal sources.

National Projects

What are some of the cultural projects considered worthy of national support?

Within the performing arts the federal government recognizes its duty to preserve those institutions distinguished in the past and retaining strong cultural significance in the present. This category is illustrated by the Bayreuth Festival, one of the first musical organizations to receive subsidies from the Republic.* Unlike such operatic projects of international prestige, there are various German festivals of a modest scope that qualify for federal patronage. An example is that held in Bad Hersfeld, Hesse, which devotes its festival program mostly to drama. The deficit is covered by a modest federal subvention of approximately $20,000 annually. The reason for the special treatment of this small festival is that Bad Hersfeld lies close to the Iron Curtain. Thus, the theater is endowed with a special mission: to exhibit a free stage unfettered by political ideology. The Hersfeld program is intended to dramatize the differences of theater in the open Western society and of theater under communistic rule. Hersfeld welcomes visitors from East Germany and offers them free tickets.

Whether Hersfeld or Bayreuth — an unpretentious or a highly esteemed theater project — the federal subsidies are determined by the

*For details on the support of the Bayreuth Festival see pages 297, 298.

evaluation of cultural function. The final decision is always made in consultation with the participating member states.

Another focal point of federal interest is the theater in Recklinghausen, a small industrial town in the Ruhr district. During the poverty-stricken years, from 1945 to 1948, a group of unemployed actors came from Hamburg into this industrial core of the nation. Here, in the Ruhr, the artists traded food, shelter, and fuel for performance. From barter for the dire needs of daily life, a modest theater project originated. Today it has grown into a characteristic outpost of German art life: the theater of Recklinghausen is strongly supported by the unions of workers (Gewerkschaften). The federal government, impressed by the success of the theater and its cultural implications in a mining district, decided to lend firm support to the Recklinghausen art project.

Another small town patronized by the Republic is Donaueschingen. Its cultural significance is in inverse proportion to its diminutive size. The Republic helps to support Donaueschingen, an old art center, which in 1922 was transformed into a progressive enterprise devoted to modern music.*

The Bonn Republic also helps the Institute for Modern Music in the southwestern city of Darmstadt. In the nearby castle, Kranichstein, seminars and concerts are held during the late summer. They present a significant forum on contemporary music.

In contrast to Donaueschingen or Darmstadt as outposts of modern music, such towns as Ansbach in Bavaria devote their art programs exclusively to old music. In Ansbach, as in other comparable instances, the federal subvention is modest, but it suffices to cover minimal expenses. Without federal aid, activities could not continue. The patronage on the part of the Republic also has psychological value: if the Bund lends its stamp of approval, the local forces and Länder are inclined to cooperate.

The federal government aids a number of orchestras, provided such encouragement is warranted. Among the supported ensembles is the Bamberg Symphony, an organization of unusual background. This group consists of fugitives from Prague. When Czechoslovakia was seized, instrumentalists from the Bohemian capital found a temporary haven across the German border in the Bavarian town of Bamberg. Reorganizing themselves and assuming the name of the Bamberg Symphony Orchestra, the Prague musicians over the years established a fine reputation, particularly with their recordings conducted by important interpreters. The federal subsidy to Bamberg represents special acknowledgement: here refugee artists have not only been offered political

*For background of Donaueschingen Festival see pp. 298-300.

asylum, but they have been given an unusual opportunity to continue their chosen vocation as performers.*

The orchestra of Radio Berlin likewise receives federal support; its function is crucial, within the artificial island, West Berlin, encircled by Soviet territory. The annual subsidy of $70,000 supplements the orchestra's budget, which is partly covered by listening fees.**

In the capital city of Bonn itself, the Bund aids the municipality in support of the theater and its resident orchestra with approximately $40,000 per year. The construction of the new concert hall of Bonn, the Beethoven auditorium, was made possible through the help of the Bund.†

The Federal Republic participates in many other artistic projects, some of them on the periphery of the performing arts, and of a scholarly nature. Thus the government contributed $20,000 toward the purchase of the Beethoven collection, formerly owned by the Swiss art patron Dr. Bodmer. This valuable acquisition is now housed in the Beethoven Museum of Bonn.

Germany has always been a country of large and efficient choruses. The federal government occasionally supplements the basic subsidies which these vocal groups receive from their respective communities. Special acknowledgement is accorded to choral societies with a minimum of one hundred years of continued existence, provided they represent genuine artistic achievement. The token of federal appreciation is the "Zelter Plaque," donated each year by the President of the German Federal Republic.‡

In accordance with the officially defined "overall German interests," the Bund also assures the preservation or reconstruction of cultural shrines and various national monuments. Into this category belong such projects as the rebuilding and maintenance of the destroyed birthplaces of Goethe in Frankfurt and of Schiller in Marbach. Likewise included in this federal custody are various objects of religious veneration, architectural monuments such as the domes of the age-old cities of Aachen and Speyer, the Church of St. Mary in Lübeck, the Sebalduskirche in Nürnberg. A special task was the reconstruction of the medieval synagogue in Worms, the oldest Jewish building on German soil.

*The city of Marl in the Ruhr district has offered a permanent home to the orchestra known as *Philharmonica Hungarica*, made up of musicians who fled Budapest at the time of the civil upheaval in 1956. In Marl, however, the support is primarily municipal rather than federal.

**Cf. sections on German Radio and on the city of Berlin.

†Cf. p. 281 for details.

‡The Plaque is named after the founder of the Berlin Singakademie, Carl Friedrich Zelter (1758-1832). The composer-conductor was a close friend and principal musical advisor of Goethe and a teacher of Mendelssohn.

XIII. Art Within "The Economic Miracle"

The reconstruction of West Germany after World War II has been generally recognized as a remarkable phenomenon, not only on the political and economic fronts but on the art scene as well.

The economic recovery has been interpreted as *Wirtschaftswunder* ("economic miracle"). Of all the Continental countries west of the Iron Curtain, the Bonn Republic shows, indeed, such striking development and progress that describing it as an "economic miracle" is not a mere figure of speech. The sheer quantity of new structures immediately convinces the observer of the enormous physical rehabilitation: new industrial plants, railroad stations, airports, vast housing complexes designed for advanced conveniences of living, modern secondary schools, and new universities.

There are many handsome new buildings devoted to the performing arts: new theaters, operas, concert halls, in large and small German cities. Ingeniously planned radio and television stations house the latest experimental devices known in the field of the electrical media.

Statistics bring the background of this reconstruction into sharper focus. In the area now covered by the West German Republic nearly 3,000,000 apartments were destroyed. This represents almost 25 per cent of total living quarters. An additional 2,500,000 dwellings showed such intense damage that they required major repairs. The comparison of these figures with those of other Continental countries is informative: Holland and Italy lost 4 per cent, France 3 per cent, Belgium and Great Britain each 2 per cent of prewar housing. In short, the destruction in Germany far exceeded that in other countries. Under the circumstances, it would have been understandable if the Bonn Republic, within its reconstruction program, had given precedence to such absolute necessities as hospitals, railroad stations, schools, bridges, roads, etc. *Yet theaters and concert halls were immediately included in the governmental rebuilding program.* Today, almost every German city of consequence has at least one theater reopened or even newly built.* The reconstruction program began in 1948. Much assistance came from the United States, notably through the Marshall Plan.

The immediate emphasis on art is the logical result of an historically founded evaluation. It is the consequence of an educational philosophy shared, as we have shown, by successive German governments. They all have given priority to art and have tried to maintain standards of art life even in times of utter desolation.

*Cf. P 294; the story of the theater in Münster is a typical illustration of priority within the communal program of reconstruction.

Theaters
Old, Rebuilt, New

By 1945 many German theaters, concert halls, libraries, and museums were in rubble and ashes. Among the victims were theaters of historic significance. While Germany's oldest theater, the Ottoneum of Kassel, opened in 1605, curiously survived the air attacks of war, the opera houses of Frankfurt and Cologne, the Mannheim National Theater, the Münster Stadt Theater, and many others were demolished beyond repair.

Yet the rebuilding from within was the most immediate task: the reestablishment of genuine leadership and the reorganization of lost ensembles. Slowly Germany remobilized competent producers and conductors. Recruiting actors and singers of quality, orchestras, choirs, and ballet ensembles was difficult. Some of the active personnel had been killed in the war and its aftermath; others were still imprisoned or had disappeared altogether; some had left Germany never to return. But gradually, performers were mustered, and organizations capable of interpreting great art works were ready once more.

With a minimum personnel for productions assured, the next problem was to find space for performances. A few representative theaters were still fit to use (for instance, the Prinz Regenten Theater in Munich and the principal theaters in Stuttgart and Nürnberg). But a number of usable theaters had been requisitioned by the occupying forces for other purposes. In the immediate postwar years, this complicated matters. The Germans were not yet in a position to rebuild their destroyed halls. They had to utilize whatever qualified as substitute stages; the most primitive solutions were welcome. Cellars and dilapidated cabarets became "theaters." Stages were set up in hotels and schools. Moving picture halls and ballrooms were considered more than adequate. These ersatz stages served temporarily until the Allied Occupational Government decided to help West Germany in the rehabilitation of her theater life. Finally, with the first approaching phase of economic prosperity, the foundations for new modern theaters were laid in an ever-increasing number of cities.

At this writing, theaters have been reconstructed and are in full use in such cities as Aachen, Augsburg, Bielefeld, Bochum, Bremen, Braunschweig, Düsseldorf, Duisburg, Giessen, Hagen, Hanover, Krefeld, Mainz, Oberhausen, etc. (Some of the architecturally most significant newly-built theaters, such as the National Theater in Mannheim or the Opera in Cologne, are discussed elsewhere in more detail.) On the other hand, some theaters still perform in makeshift arrangements, often under conditions that restrict the potential of production and the size of the audience. The Frankfurt Opera plays in the former Schauspielhaus, which has been equipped with a large revolving stage to accommodate modern productions. The Munich Opera has been reopened in its regal historic setting, the National Theater.

Significance of Repertory Theater Subsidies and Statistics

Since the classical era, the theater, in order of cultural rank, has held first place in Germany. It might be compared in intellectual prestige with belles-lettres in France; in popular acclaim, with opera in Italy; in traditional impact, with the colleges of England. The decentralization of the German theater was always, and still is, one of its notable achievements; it is a sociological factor of considerable significance.

In the United States, the success of an author, a play, or any theatrical talent is before all decided in New York City. Paris determines the fate of art issues of France. London arbitrates British drama. In Germany, the pulse of her theater life can be clearly felt in independent art centers throughout the nation.

Today, Germany's legitimate theater throughout the nation is even better supported than it was in the past. It has not suffered the competition of radio and television to the same extent that is evident in other countries. On the contrary, it appears that the electrical media have not only promoted public interest in attending live performances in the theater, but have created new opportunities for authors, actors, producers, and everybody connected with the living stage. Twenty million people (out of West Germany's population of fifty-five million) visit the theaters every year. The total subsidy for the repertory theaters amounted in 1961 to 150,000,000 DM ($37,500,000) annually.* This figure includes the support for opera houses, which customarily take the largest slice.

Of Germany's 148 theaters, 118 are fully subsidized.** The Bund supports 20 theaters. The Länder support 18 theaters. The municipalities support 80 theaters. Private funds support 30 theaters.

The upsurge of the German theater reflects the full support of the population which foots the bill in terms of taxes and attendance. The public goes to the theater. West Germany and Austria are the most "theater-happy" countries on the European continent. No comparable

*4DM = $1.00 (There have been fluctuations in exchange).

**East Germany (German Democratic Republic), with a population of 17,200,000 inhabitants, has 88 theaters and opera houses performing for an annual audience of 16,000,000. There are new theaters in East Berlin, Potsdam, Halle, Magdeburg, Karl Marx Stadt, Dresden, and Erfurt, and also in such small towns as Neustrelitz and Anklam. Thirty-five theaters were completely renovated, rebuilt, extended, or modernized in the past fourteen years, and fifteen destroyed buildings were rebuilt.

situation exists in the Mediterranean countries where, as previously indicated, the support of the serious theater leaves something to be desired.

Some observers are distrustful of mere statistics; they wonder whether the high attendance results from organizational machinery which makes of the visit to the theater a social virtue, and casts shadows on "delinquents." The organizational factor is undeniable; it is, as a matter of fact, stronger in Germany than anywhere else on the Continent. But there is really nothing wrong with organizational tactics propagandizing good theater. Such a method can work everywhere. It certainly is not objectionable, if it eventually produces tangible results in shaping a more civilized society through systematic education in art.

Statistics show that in the *average* West German city every fifth inhabitant goes to the theater at least once a year. This figure, of course, is multiplied by that of the regular subscribers. They attend the theater more frequently, either individually or collectively, by joining one of the various clubs (Theater Ringe, Theatergemeinden) that insure the continuity of large audiences. Members of these groups average 7 to 10 visits to the theater per year. Because of these established patterns, attendance does not present a problem to the German theater.

A major factor in the direct support of the living stage is the theater clubs. In its present setup the *Volksbühne* has an enrollment of 410,000 members, distributed throughout 98 local centers. It is estimated that each member of the People's Stage attends approximately 10 performances during the season. As the average ticket price, in subscription, is 3 DM (75 cents), the Volksbühne has a considerable income, approaching 12,000,000 DM ($3,000,000) annually.

Creative Predicament

With all of its achievements and advantages, one grave problem plagues the German theater: the lack of genuine creativity. With the exception of Bertolt Brecht, Germany has failed to produce, during the past two generations, a dramatic author of world stature. To be sure, a number of gifted playwrights are at work in Germany today, and some of them have won much national acclaim. But objective observers are concerned with the obvious dearth of redeeming productive forces. The theater cannot grow without the vitality of challenging new messages.[18]

The situation has necessitated the importation to Germany of significant foreign plays in very large numbers. This is good. The reorientation of German taste along cosmopolitan viewpoints was overdue, and might still bear fruit. Furthermore, the systematic reemphasis upon the best German drama of the past, particularly the revival of the great classics, serves to restore the spiritual equilibrium of the national repertory.

The German government, on all levels, shows its awareness of the inherent problems. Prizes and awards are offered as part of a systematic search for real gift and promise among the new generation of German authors. Of prizes offered through various channels, one should mention the Dramatist Prize of the German Theater Union, the Gerhart Hauptmann Prize, the Prize of the Free People's Stage of West Berlin, the Prize of the Mannheim National Theater.

XIV. Cities and Their Culture

Decentralized Art Life

The decentralization of government in the West German Republic terminated some of the nation's proudest institutions in the field of the performing arts. There are no longer the Bundes or Reichs Theaters as they existed under the Hohenzollern monarchy. The Weimar Republic had continued the federal support of these organizations — of the former court operas and the royal playhouses — under their new titles of *Staats Theater*. After the collapse of the Nazi Reich, the emphasis of patronage shifted again to the Länder and municipalities.

Today the art life of West Germany is decentralized. Thus cultural activities are close to the very source of their sponsorship. The citizens who pay the taxes for their art life have the gratification of ownership; for they can say: it is *our* theater, *our* opera, *our* orchestra.

Within the dense network of German art centers, some stand out for their special achievements: for the preservation of tradition or for their courage of experimentation. The following cross section focuses on a limited number of cities and organizations for a brief survey of their art life in relationship to sponsorship. The choice in no way suggests that the communities and institutions singled out here constitute isolated phenomena. On the contrary, they illustrate something typical in German art life. They are instances of an unflinching civic patronage, often of a long-standing and apparently unshakable tradition.

What matters here is to show characteristic examples within the great variety of form that German art support has assumed in different regions. The performing arts, in particular, depend on a multitude of contributions that stem from the people themselves.

To feel the pulse of the musical life of Germany, one must not limit oneself to a visit of the festivals in Berlin, Munich, or Bayreuth, or to attendance at performances during the winter season in the various state capitals. For the art life of a nation is created and recreated every day at many places and on many levels. It is maintained in the village and in the metropolis. To keep the performing arts alive on a high level, the craft of the theater and of music must be thoroughly taught and learned and practiced, nation-wide. Behind the spectacular achievements of the performing organizations in the cities are their anonymous helpmates, schools and conservatories, the endeavors of innumerable groups from whose ranks the great performers emerge. There are the professional and amateur groups, the *Vereine*, some of them modest in scope, but serious in purpose. There are dramatic clubs, formerly mentioned, *Kreise* or *Ringe*. There are the societies devoted to the organized attendance and support of the theater within their respective communities. Some of these organizations also engage in unpretentious performances within their own memberships. It is active participation by thousands of organizations which plays a dominant role in the full-fledged support of the national art life.

The Choirs

There are about 30,000 organized choirs in West Germany. In sheer numbers they represent a vital factor in the country's art life.

Choral activities are characterized by a maximum of variety. They span every conceivable type and cast from ecclesiastical choirs to the singing groups of workers, from fully employed professional theater choruses to amateurs who cannot read notes.

The two principal religions of the Bonn Republic, Catholic and Protestant, maintain their traditional roles as sponsors of liturgical music. Since the Middle Ages, *a cappella* choirs have sung in the Catholic cathedrals of Bavaria and the Rhineland, of Franconia and most of Germany's large cities from the Baltic to the Alps.

The land which gave birth to Martin Luther and Heinrich Schütz, to Bach and Handel, has remained the seat of great Protestant church choruses, although their very cradle — Saxony and Thuringia — now belongs to the East.

The West sponsors numerous municipal oratorio choirs and their serious programs, frequently offering liturgical scores. In many German cities, particularly of smaller or medium size, the theater chorus is the versatile nucleus of municipal choral life. The same opera choir that performs with appropriate dramatic action in *Fidelio*, *Freischütz*, or *Lohengrin* may convincingly sing, on another occasion and with the necessary stylistic adjustment, in the *High Mass* of Bach or the *Requiem* of Brahms.

Every German town has its secular mixed choirs. There are the typical Männergesangvereine, and there are independent women's choruses. Male choirs are organized in every trade, business, and profession. There are children's choirs and youth choirs of all grades. The Jugend Musik Bewegung (the Music Movement of Youth) grew out of the Romantic youth movement. To this day it sponsors "Open Singing Lessons" to counteract the spread of cheap and commercial music. The leader of this movement, the pedagogue Fritz Jöde, attempted in the early twenties the integration of music into kindergarten, settlement houses, recreation centers, and other organizations devoted to the education of youth.

Germany was the first country to support workers' choruses, known as *Arbeiter Gesangvereine*. Originally their background was political: meetings, rehearsals, and performances served as a cover for party rallies, particularly around the middle of the nineteenth century, when the persecution of the working class reached new heights. Later, under the reign of Chancellor Bismarck, such "musical" meetings of workers decidedly contributed to the survival of the labor movement. But in the long run, rehearsals and performances given by the Arbeiter Gesangvereine were by no means mere pretext. The workers eagerly learned how to read music; their groups developed, over the coming decades, remarkable standards of repertory and performance. Their proficiency reached a height during the Weimar Republic. The music-making of the workers stimulated a new literature specifically written for their concerts and heard within their own social circle. A poet of the stature of Bertolt Brecht wrote his cantata, *Die Massnahme* (The Measures Taken) for the workers' chorus, *Gross Berlin*. And Hanns Eisler contributed the score for Brecht's work.

Today, choral ensembles from liturgical cathedral choirs to politically oriented workers' choruses perform in every German town. Legions of choral ensembles are held together by social purposes only. Others function on the high professional level. But whatever their background and aim, the blossoming of choral life in Germany would be impossible without adequate subsidy. Within the German patterns of diversified patronage, there have always been ways and means to maintain the choruses which contribute to the life of the community.

The Orchestras

Since the middle of the sixteenth century, as we have shown, the Germans maintained competent bands in every town. By the middle of the eighteenth century certain courts supported symphony orchestras of virtuoso standards.

Today the symphony orchestra is a prime factor of communal culture. It is no exaggeration to say that a catalogue of German orchestras would be tantamount to a list of German cities. In the majority of cases, the service of the orchestra in the pit of the Stadt Theater solves the problem of subsidizing the civic symphony. But many communities maintain symphony orchestras independent of the organizational framework of their theaters. In certain cities there are "competing" concert cycles where the opera orchestra and the symphony orchestra both give subscription concerts independently. The radio orchestras have extended the scope of this vast program even further.

The Berlin Philharmonic, the Munich Philharmonic, the Bamberg Symphony are well known examples of orchestras exclusively performing in concerts. The most famous German orchestra is the Berlin Philharmonic. Two of the oldest German orchestras now belong to the East: the Leipzig Gewandhaus and the Dresden Staats Kapelle. The best-known orchestras of the West are, in addition to those mentioned, are the Bavarian State Orchestra, the Hamburg State Orchestra, the Cologne Gürzenich Orchestra, the Frankfurt Opera Orchestra, and the orchestras of the large radio networks. Their titles usually indicate the basic kind of subsidies which these organizations receive. Whatever the form of subsidy, in every city the choir, the orchestra, and the theater are the foundations of cultural life.

Bonn
Capital of the Republic

The capital of the West German Republic is Bonn on the Rhine. It is Beethoven's birthplace. This fact gives the old cathedral city a timeless distinction. With the choice of Bonn as the seat of government, the Second Republic followed an earlier pattern; Weimar, the "classical" town of Goethe and Schiller, had served as the capital of the First German Republic from 1919 to 1933. The meaning of these choices is eloquent: both Bonn and Weimar are cultural shrines.

In Bonn each citizen is called upon to do his share toward supporting the art life of his town. When the municipality, shortly after the collapse of the Nazi Reich, requested new taxes for the subsidy of its cultural enterprises, a city referendum to decide the issue proved completely successful. The vote was not influenced by political platforms or party affiliations. The citizens of Bonn were, in fact, among the first in West Germany to commit themselves on the renewed question of a tax-supported art life, and on this crucial issue Bonn served as a test case. Funds for the theater and concerts were considered a necessity, even at a time when food and housing were scarce and other staples of daily living were at a premium. In these early postwar years the municipality raised for its cultural program, exclusively through city taxes, close to $8,000,000. This is a remarkable achievement for a city of 145,000.

Art patronage in Bonn is diversified: the federal government, the province of Nordrhein-Westphalia, and the municipality of Bonn join forces. Benefiting from this triple subvention are several projects devoted to Beethoven.

The handsome narrow house at Bonnergasse 20 where Beethoven was born on December 16, 1770, and where he spent the first years of his childhood, is collectively maintained. Now a museum, the three-story wooden structure in downtown Bonn contains invaluable relics of Beethoven and his family — a large number of his manuscripts, letters, other documents, instruments, furniture, and pictures.

In 1899, Beethoven's "Geburtshaus" was to be torn down to make room for a "modern" building. But twelve enraged citizens of Bonn jointly founded the "Verein Beethovenhaus" to forestall such vandalism and they raised the funds necessary to buy the house. Money for its continued maintenance was to be appropriated from the proceeds of a festival held every second year. The programs are devoted exclusively to the performance of chamber music; Bonn claims that this is the first festival of chamber music in history.

The Third Beethoven Hall

In 1845, eighteen years after Beethoven's death, the city of Bonn erected a monument for its greatest son on the Münster square. The city needed a hall for the festive musical performances connected with the inauguration of the monument. And so Bonn's first Beethoven Hall, entirely made of wood, was built. In 1870 the centennial of Beethoven's birth inspired the second hall. The fever of the Franco-Prussian War was not allowed to interfere with plans for the construction. In fact, the contractor of the project could proudly boast: "I shall build the Beethoven Hall entirely out of 'violin wood.'" The actual use of this fine lumber was believed to have contributed to the excellent acoustics of the hall. It fell victim to an air attack in 1943.

The third Beethoven Hall was inaugurated on September 8, 1959, with a festival of eleven days. The concert house is situated near the Rhine, overlooking the scene of the master's youth — the landscape of the Seven Hills and the ruins of the ancient castle "Drachenfels." The new hall cost 9,500,000 DM ($2,375,000). It was planned as a Mehrzweckhalle, i.e., a hall designed for several purposes. Thus it may function as a representative concert house, equipped with a large and small hall, and also as a theater and a place for conventions, exhibits, lectures, social evenings, and even for the carnival which in the Rhineland is an age-old folk custom. Throughout the year the Beethoven Hall serves as a cultural center where children as well as adults can find various forms of recreation.

The investment has already paid off: the hall is fully subscribed and has a long waiting list.

Theater of the City

The very title of Bonn's theater, where Beethoven once sat in the pit as a viola player, indicates the principal source of its subsidy. Not even in its national capital does the West German government wish to lead in art support; it limits itself to a contributing role. Thus, in a typical procedure, the municipality emerges as the main patron of the Bonn Stadt Theater.

The total cost of maintaining the operation of the theater (not including the support of the orchestra) amounted during the season 1960-61 to 2,496,710 DM ($624,177). Out of this total, 892,050 DM ($223,012) were paid for salaries to the artistic personnel (31 in Schauspiel, 25 in opera, 8 solo dancers, 32 choral singers).

The orchestra (68 members) has its own budget (with special income derived from symphony concerts). The theater contributes 319,000 DM annually to compensate the orchestra for its services. The concert activities of the orchestra require an additional subsidy of 782,876 DM ($195,719) annually. The Bund pays 56,390 DM ($14,097), the Land Nordrhein-Westphalia 20,000 DM ($5,000), the city the remainder.

After deducting its own income (from box office, etc.) the theater needs an annual subsidy of 1,646,800 DM ($411,700). Toward this the Bund contributes 123,610 DM ($30,902); the Land Nordrhein-Westphalia, 115,000 DM ($28,750); Westdeutscher Rundfunk Cologne, 150,000 DM ($37,500); and the city contributes the balance, 1,258,190 DM ($314,547). The theater gives most of its performances in a temporary home, Bonn's Bürgerverein, which has been remodeled into a hall. Performances also take place in the Kammertheater of the University and in the new Studio of the Beethoven Hall.

In 1964 the new Bonn Stadt Theater will be completed. It will cost 16,000,000 DM ($4,000,000), for which the Bund, the Land Nordrhein-Westphalia, and the city of Bonn will each raise one-third.

During the season of 1959-60 the theater gave 427 performances in Bonn, 59 on tour. Single ticket prices in the Bonn Theater are typical for the price range in the municipal stages of middle-sized cities. (See Table III)

TABLE III

Ticket Prices for the Bonn Stadt Theater (1959-60)

Opera	2.20 to 9.10 DM	($ .55 to $ 2.28)
Schauspiel	1.80 to 8.00 DM	($ .45 to $ 2.00)
Kammerspiele	3.50 to 6.20 DM	($ .88 to $ 1.55)
Beethovenhalle Studio	3.00 to 6.50 DM	($ .75 to $ 1.63)
Subscription A (10 plays, 8 operas, 2 operettas)	65.00 to 153.00 DM	($16.25 to $38.25)
Subscription B (12 plays)	28.00 to 74.00 DM	($ 7.00 to $18.50)

Subscriptions are payable in 3 installments over a period of 18 months.

Since the season of 1960-61, a small tax of 0.10 DM (2½¢) is added to each ticket: this deduction is for the benefit of old-age pensions for retired artists. Subscribers are entitled to the advanced ticket sale for all special performances with guest artists, or for other events scheduled outside of the regular series.

A Smaller Berlin

In 1939 the population of the former Reich's capital was 4,300,000. At the war's end (1945) it had dwindled to 3,300,000. Due to the division of the metropolis into the West and East sectors, West Berlin now has a population of 2,200,000 (approximately the size of Philadelphia). But Berlin is still West Germany's largest city.

The abnormal political topography has caused severe consequences for the city's art life. The cultural development of Berlin was in proportion to the city's growth as the nerve center of the Reich. Today, surrounded by a Soviet belt, Berlin has lost its function as the center of the German nation. This does not imply that Berlin has become a provincial city. But one no longer travels to and from Berlin as the capital; one does not traverse the city from the south to the north, from the west to the east. Because of the Soviet circle, one normally makes a detour around Berlin.

Such revitalized cities as Munich, Hamburg, Düsseldorf, or Frankfurt are sharing Berlin's former role as arbiter and principal sponsor of the performing arts. The centuries-long diffusion of German art life prepared these cities for such a task. Meanwhile, Berlin continues to be the site of art events of international scope, in spite of the city's relative isolation.

No other city in the Western World has become a more obvious victim of power politics than Berlin. As a direct result, art life in the one-time capital has assumed strange aspects of cultural division.

The conquest of Berlin was completed on April 2, 1945, and the Soviet Army entered the destroyed Reich's capital. Moscow time was introduced to Berlin. All clocks were adjusted to those in the Russian capital, as the initial symbol of submission and penetrating changes that were to come. During July, 1945, regiments of the Western Allies moved into carefully defined sections of the city, as agreed upon by the Allies. Thus Berlin became a four-power city. The one-time center of the Reich is today a frontier town with the Wall dividing West and East.

Rapid Rehabilitation of Art Life

There are various ways and means to measure destruction. We learn that in 1945 there were 75,000,000 cubic meters of debris in Germany. But this figure takes on more meaning if we know that more than one-sixth of the total amount of debris in Germany covered central districts of Berlin where once stood theaters and operas, concert halls and museums, churches, schools, hospitals, and apartment houses. Almost two-thirds of the entire housing space, one-fourth of the 438 schools, and nearly half of the 208 churches and 174 bridges were destroyed or heavily damaged. No wonder there was a move to abandon Berlin altogether; the damage was considered beyond repair.

In 1949 the Russian blockade was lifted. The United States had a decisive share in the vast and rapid rebuilding program that was now under way. Funds made available through the Marshall Plan, as well as through private American donors, helped to construct various edifices devoted to education and art. The Congress Hall, the Memorial Library, and the Free University are among the buildings that are permanent tokens of American generosity. The United States government has contributed $7,800,000 to the Free University. The Ford Foundation was the principal private patron of this educational project.

The Memorial Library, likewise completed with American aid, is one of the largest lending libraries in Europe. It contains an innovation for Germany: soundproof booths for those interested in listening to serious music. Another important new building is the Concert Hall of the Hochschule für Musik, a modern glass structure. It housed the concerts of the Berlin Philharmonic prior to the inauguration of the orchestra's own home, scheduled for the season 1963-64. The new Philharmonic auditorium (capacity of about 2,000) is circular in design: the audience is seated around the stage, partly on different levels of the main floor, partly in galleries. Thus the orchestra can be heard and seen from every angle of the hall with equal advantage. The cost of the auditorium is estimated at $3,500,000.

West Berlin's new opera house, the Deutsche Oper, was inaugurated on September 24, 1961, with a performance of Mozart's *Don Giovanni*. The modern structure, located on the spacious Bismarck Strasse, cost almost $7,000,000. It replaces, in terms of the music-dramatic repertory, the older Städtische Oper, which will be used primarily for light opera, Singspiel, and operetta.

In 1962 the Council of the city-state West Berlin voted an extraordinary subvention of $60,000 so that a high artistic level of performance could be maintained. This sum supplements the regular subsidy of the theater.

Indestructible Theater

Before World War II more than 40 theaters played nightly in Berlin; most of them were destroyed by the war's end. No one who knew Berlin at that time — devastated, paralyzed, and plundered — could envision anything distantly resembling theatrical performances. Life itself was a tragedy with which no dramatic fiction could compete. But as soon as the city assumed some semblance of functioning, thoughts of a theater came back into the minds of Berliners; it was, in a measure, their theater that restored the beginnings of civic life. Goethe's *Faust* was the first play to be staged within the city limits, in a dance hall left undestroyed. As time went on, other substitute stages were found. Today, theater in Berlin is not only a regularly established institution but once again a hotly contested battleground of ideology.

City-State in Support of Art

The one-time capital of the Reich is now a Stadtstaat (a city-state like Hamburg or Bremen) officially called *Stadt und Land Berlin.* Regardless of political nomenclature, the municipality is the principal patron of art in Berlin. Thus the city supports the Philharmonic Orchestra, paying for all expenditures. The members are municipal employees. Their special privileges include pensions at retirement, amounting to 75 per cent of their final salary.

Berlin also played its part in the support of RIAS (Rundfunk in the American Sector). Originally, the United States supported this radio station which had a specific mission as an outpost of Western culture. A fine orchestra was built, absorbing 40 experienced musicians who had come from the Eastern zone. The statutes of the RIAS orchestra corresponded generally to those of the Berlin Philharmonic. After the withdrawal of American subsidy Berlin could not support this radio station alone. Hence, the orchestra formed a corporation (Gesellschaft mit beschränkter Haftung). Both the city-state Berlin and the federal government in Bonn helped in this transformation; Berlin with $50,000 and the Bund with $35,000. The RIAS orchestra gives 20 to 30 public concerts and performs some popular music. In general, the maintenance of high quality in the orchestras of Berlin is difficult; there is strong competition for first-rate players throughout Germany. Other radio networks are financially better off than Radio Berlin. Some of the young musicians leave Berlin and settle elsewhere in West Germany. In other professions, too, similar uncertainties prevail. Unless this trend is checked, Berlin will become a city of middle-aged and old people.

The principal secular choirs of Berlin are all subsidized. So are the important liturgical choirs. The Choir of St. Hedwig's Cathedral, founded at the time of Frederick the Great, receives 30,000 DM for its services. The Domchor, once paid for out of the private purse of the king, is supported with 55,000 DM.

City in the Landscape

By 1963 West Berlin had rebuilt 23,900,000 square meters within the destroyed territory. The program of reconstruction is officially under the sponsorship and supervision of the Municipal Senator for Building and Housing. His task is not only to watch over the orderly development of all plans, but to insure their realization commensurate with modern aesthetic concepts of city planning. This is an all important point in its cultural implication. The vision of a "city in the landscape" has been adopted as a guide for the general blueprint of reconstructing West Berlin. In addition to German architects, renowned builders from abroad have been engaged to help toward this goal.

Prior to officially established municipal supervision of city planning, anyone who had the necessary funds could build as he pleased, wherever he purchased land. From such laxity and noninterference, innumerable tasteless structures played havoc with the appearance of German cities. By contrast, organic building in keeping with aesthetic legalities is an axiom today. In West Berlin the new Hansa district is an outstanding instance of imaginative architecture planned by a municipality. The importance of expertly guided patronage in civic building is here dramatized by the realization of a city in the landscape.

New Role of Munich

With Berlin eliminated as the political and intellectual Reich Center, Munich has once more assumed a decisive cultural role. The population of the Bavarian capital has risen from 826,000 in 1938 to 1,045,000 in 1959. Today, it is the largest university city within the Federal Republic; there are 24,000 students enrolled. Two thousand painters and sculptors live there. The Bavarian metropolis once known as the "Florence of the North" became the cradle of Nazism in the 1920's. Hitler lived in Munich during the formative years of the movement.

Today, the citizens of Munich fight a withdrawing battle from these memories. And Munich's prestige as an ancient art capital proved its practical as well as psychological value. The Land of Bavaria and the Municipal Council of Munich were quick to seize the argument of art in the task of moral rehabilitation. Munich's traditional reputation as an important theater center has been successfully recultivated. Thus it was convenient to suggest an aura of unbroken continuity by stressing the tradition of the Bavarian State Opera in terms of its time-proved repertory with emphasis on Mozart, Wagner, and Richard Strauss.

The home of the Opera, the National Theater, had its public reopening, in November 23, 1963. This theater, historic forum of German music-drama, had been the scene of a series of Wagner premières: *Tristan und*

Isolde (1865), *Die Meistersinger* (1868), *Das Rheingold* (1869), *Die Walküre* (1870). The "private" première of *Parsifal* took place in the year following Wagner's death (1884), with the general public excluded, and only for the benefit of the King himself:* Ludwig II, the patron of the theater, believed that he had also the right, at chosen occasions, to be its audience of one.

After World War II the State Opera has found temporary quarters in the Prinz Regenten Theater (reopened in November 1945 with Beethoven's *Fidelio*). The old Residenz Theater — that jewel of rococo architecture where Mozart once stood on the conductor's podium — has again assumed important assignments. (Curiously, the old theater was the first in Germany to introduce electric lights, in 1883, and the revolving stage, in 1896.) In the early phases of its history the Residenz Theater epitomized the exclusiveness of royal patronage. It was specially decorated to please King Ludwig; here, too, he enjoyed performances given for him alone. The royal dreamer (his extravagance and passion for music and drama, for creative and performing artists, for building theaters and palaces) was accused of depleting the national treasury. Ludwig II was finally declared insane. He committed suicide in June, 1886.

The most significant playhouse of Munich is the Kammerspiele. It was originally privately managed, but later taken over by the municipality. The small theater claims distinction as the forum of an international dramatic repertory. Reopened in November, 1945, the theater has resumed its cosmopolitan role. The State Playhouse moved from temporary quarters in the Theater am Brunnen Hof into the new Residenz Theater, now considerably modernized. It is before all the stage of classical tradition.

Munich is the home of three symphony orchestras. The best of these belongs to the Bavarian Rundfunk and is entirely supported by income from radio listening fees. Public concerts take place in the Herkules-Saal. During the war Munich lost both of its traditional concert halls, the Odeon and the Tonhalle.

Munich's impressive art life is to a large extent subsidized by various forms of taxation. The average city tax per person is 180 DM (about $45) annually. In the amount of its taxed income, Munich holds ninth place among West German cities. But it yields to none in the scope of its present art life. And once more the municipal department for cultural affairs is imaginatively guided.

---

*Wagner's final work was to be reserved for Bayreuth. Thirty years after Wagner's death, *Parsifal* was first performed there for the general public during the festival season of 1913.

Frankfurt
Conservative and Progressive Sponsorship

In the Roemer, the Town Hall of the Free City of Frankfurt, the electors and their plenipotentiaries chose for almost five hundred years the German rulers. In the Emperor's Hall the solemn ceremonies of the coronation itself were held. Near the Roemer stands the venerable Goethe House where the poet lived from his birth in 1749 until 1775 when he left for Weimar. In Goethe's time Frankfurt's population had become one of Europe's most art-minded. The community witnessed much cultural progress during the nineteenth century.

In the years of the Weimar Republic the characteristic and colorful city with its ancient Dom and churches, its synagogues and tasteful patrician houses, displayed a curious blend between the old and the new, the decidedly conservative and the daringly progressive. The *Frankfurter Zeitung* was one of Europe's most respected dailies. Its coverage of the arts was exemplary within Continental journalism.

Today the municipal theaters are trying to regain their prewar prestige. Their activities are supervised by a theater deputation which consists of representatives of the Magistrat (the Municipal Council). The procedure of management is typical for most of Germany's city-sponsored theaters. The chief of the municipal theaters (of the Opera and the Playhouse) is the Intendant, who is appointed by the Magistrat. The artistic directors — the Opera chief and the director of the Playhouse — are likewise responsible to the Municipal Council. All plans, the budget as well as the repertory, are submitted to the Magistrat in advance. These projects have to be approved by the theater deputation whose attitude, by and large, is liberal. The theater deputation is usually willing to support the artistic directors in their belief that significant modern works must be presented, even if their appeal is limited to a small minority.

The annual budget of the municipal theaters is about $2,000,000. A subsidy of $1,250,000 is required. The rest of the expenditures is recovered by the income from the box office and other related revenues (broadcasts, tours, etc.). Attendance is very satisfactory, but not always 100 per cent. In the Opera, ticket prices range from 70 cents to $3.50; in the Playhouse, from 50 cents to $2.40.

Of the Opera, completed in 1881 in the ornate style of the Italian Renaissance, only a shell is left. It stands as a forbidding reminder of events which, in March, 1944, led to its destruction. But one still reads the motto on the façade of the ruins: "To the true, the beautiful, the good." A large group of citizens, sentimentally attached to the historic building, has founded the "Committee to Save the Opera House." Another group feels that it would be preferable to invest the $5,000,000, which the reconstruction would approximately cost, in a new theater. The Schauspielhaus has temporarily become the home of the Opera. As the concert hall of Frankfurt is likewise destroyed, plans for a large representative auditorium are in blueprint.

Today Frankfurt no longer gives the appearance which Goethe so vividly evokes in his autobiography *Dichtung und Wahrheit*, and which at least part of the ancient city had retained prior to World War II. Newly-built because of extensive war damage, many of Frankfurt's novel structures show the influence of American architecture. The city has regained its commercial importance. It is prosperous and can afford an extensive building program to house the arts.

Hamburg
Repertory Opera Versus Stagione

Theatrical performances have been flourishing in Hamburg since the seventeenth century. The city built its first opera house in 1678. Some of the performances matched the brilliance of court opera. And it was in Hamburg that German opera reached, creatively, its first height; Reinhard Keiser (1674-1739) was its principal director and widely acclaimed resident composer.

Drama flourished early in Hamburg. Dutch companies were regular visitors with performances of plays of Vondel or Hooft. English comedians came and performed in their original language. This Chapter has traced the growth of Hamburg's National Theater, with Lessing serving as Dramaturg. The great poets Klopstock and Heine also lived in Hamburg; it is the birthplace of Mendelssohn and Brahms. Hans von Bülow and Gustav Mahler were conductors at the Opera. An art tradition of consequence developed in the Hanseatic city.

Today, Hamburg is the capital of the city-state (Stadt-Staat) of the same name. The new Hamburg State Opera, completely tax-supported, is daring in its architecture as well as in its artistic leadership. One of the structural innovations introduced at the Opera is the type of box: the design blends the historic aristocratic, private compartment with the democratic opera balcony. Within a few years this musical stage has developed an uncompromisingly modern repertory under its Intendant, the composer Rolf Liebermann. In postwar Europe numerous opera theaters outside of Italy have adopted the Italian *stagione* pattern of operation: a limited number of masterpieces is chosen for performance during the season, or for part of it. By contrast, Germany's and Austria's large theaters are traditionally inclined toward a very comprehensive repertory of classical, romantic, and contemporary works. But the postwar era has shattered this procedure and substituted the limited *stagione* schedule even in theaters that have been long devoted to a varied and frequently changing program.

The Hamburg Opera stands out in maintaining a diversified repertory, which reaches from old masterworks such as Monteverdi's *Coronation of Poppea* to the première of the "electronic" opera *Aniara*, by the Swedish composer Karl-Birger Blomdahl. Hamburg was first to produce in the very same season the two operas of Alban Berg: *Wozzeck* and *Lulu*. For here in this Hanseatic city the conviction prevails that contemporary music-drama must be integrated and firmly maintained in the general repertory, if it is to become part of our cultural experience.

Mannheim
A City Around a Theater

"Before a Mannheimer gives up his theater, he gives up his life," declared the Lord Mayor of the city, speaking in September, 1946, to inaugurate the campaign for funds to rebuild the destroyed National Theater. Mannheim's Ober-Bürgermeister (a man with a strong anti-Nazi record), making this extreme statement in behalf of his city's culture, attempted to dramatize an attitude of traditional devotion, which need not be weighed against the full impact of its formulation. It sufficed to emphasize the historical meaning of theater in the life of Mannheim.

This southwest German city of 245,000, industrial center and large inland port, was heavily damaged by war. We have identified Mannheim earlier in this Chapter as the nerve center of Europe's orchestral culture during the middle of the eighteenth century; in its last decades Mannheim became a theatrical outpost of lasting consequence. From such traditions stems the attitude of the population toward the theater.

Following Mannheim's war devastation the citizens found ways and means to build a new National Theater. In June, 1953, the foundation National Theaterbau Mannheim was created to raise funds for the structure. Two lotteries yielded, in 1953 and 1956, 1,000,000 DM ($250,000), approximately $1.00 per inhabitant. Additional moneys were collected at various social events. Soon it became clear that much greater returns were required and that the city, burdened with general postwar rehabilitation, could not carry the financial burden of the new theater alone. Finally, National Theaterbau Mannheim raised close to $1,000,000 (in addition to returns from the lottery). The financial department of the city announced that all donations to the theater fund were eligible for income tax deductions.

The original cost of the theater was estimated at 6,000,000 DM. Before long it appeared that twice this amount was necessary: 12,000,000 DM (approximately $3,000,000). At this point the Land Baden-Württemberg joined with a subsidy of 3,000,000 DM ($750,000). Encouraged by the success of the campaign, Mannheim decided to start building on June 18, 1954. The National Theater was completed in 1957. Its design is often claimed by experts to be the most convincing of its kind in Germany. The blueprint of the new structure combined under one single roof two theaters: the "Large Hall" (seating 1,200) is primarily devoted to opera; the "Small Hall" with an adjustable seating capacity of 600 to 800 serves the performance of drama. Both theaters join in a single operational setup. Their common administration and machinery are of obvious practicality.

Variability of stage was one of the main premises of design. Certain features can be changed to suit individual productions. The traditional separation of the auditorium from the stage is eliminated. There is no fire curtain. The Mannheim plan marks the first instance in Germany of a theater built without this equipment, long considered indispensable. With its simple, streamlined structure and single-tracked spatial effect, the "Small Hall" gives the illusion of being much larger.

The theater is administered by the board of directors: the Lord Mayor as chairman, and a maximum of thirteen members. Seven of these belong to Municipal Council; three represent the largest financial donors to the theater. The remaining members, including the Intendant of the theater, are artists.

Stuttgart Liederhalle

During the night of October 8, 1943, the concert hall of Stuttgart was destroyed in the strongest air attack of the war on this city. Since 1864 this hall had been the property of the Liederkranz (the Singing Society) of Stuttgart. In October, 1945, Stuttgart held its first postwar concert in the Markus Kirche, which proved to be much too small to accommodate the overflowing audience. From this date on the municipality has concentrated on plans to build a new Liederhalle. It was unthinkable that the capital city of Württemberg be without a center for its cultural and social life. The municipality and the Stuttgart Liederkranz signed a contract in which the Liederkranz sold to the city the site of its razed building. Yet the Singing Society's contract permanently reserved the right of free use of certain rooms in the future Konzerthaus for its own cultural purposes.

Just as the new Beethoven auditorium of Bonn, so Stuttgart's Liederhalle was designed as a multipurpose building. There are three halls with a capacity of 2,000, 750, and 350, respectively. The building includes a restaurant accommodating 500, and a garage for 500 cars. The great hall is intended primarily for large orchestral and choral concerts, but can be adjusted for conventions and even banquets. The middle-sized hall is best suited for chamber music. The small hall serves well for lectures and solo recitals.

The design of the large hall is asymmetric. The lines flow contrapuntally toward each other. The architect strove not only for acoustic perfection, but aimed at an auditorium which would create a festive "musical" mood. The balcony is not raised in the rear of the hall but gradually ascends on the left wall, near the stage, and thus swings itself in a wide curve over to the right wall. When the seats are removed for banquets a real fountain spouts forth in the center. Such Baroque playfulness is part of the Liederhalle at various places.

Cologne
Rhenish Traditions

Cologne, envisioned in the Middle Ages as the "German Rome," has for centuries been a fortress of sacred and secular art. The University of Cologne was founded in 1389 by the sole efforts of a group of enlightened citizens. Self-reliance in cultural issues remained a leading motive through the history of the Rhenish cathedral city — in times of prosperity as well as distress.

During World War II the bombardment of the city miraculously spared Cologne's Dom, one of the pure monuments of German Gothic architecture. But it laid flat a large section of the inner town and, along with it, the Opera and other buildings housing the arts. In 1945, Cologne attempted to play theater again, even though stage equipment, costumes, etc. were inadequate. It was decided to try, even under the most primitive circumstances. A hall in the old University of Cologne offered at least a wooden platform, but no heat or light was available. While there were neither streetcars nor buses to bring the people to the performances, furniture trucks served as transportation. But the audience came, sitting in coats and under blankets, and there was theater again in Cologne.

Eventually, it became possible to acquire some lumber to build an ersatz stage. And in the Aula of the university, the first postwar opera performances, *Lohengrin* and *Tannhäuser*, played to capacity audiences. The public was not happy in this makeshift theater and dubbed it the *Zigarrenkiste*. None the less, the "cigar box" sufficed to accommodate

200 different works in more than 4,000 performances. And when the small hall of the Kammerspiele was rebuilt, additional space for the performance of drama became available.

The main task confronting theater-conscious Cologne was the rebuilding of the Opera. Should the ruined shell, with its still firm foundation, be salvaged or should one start completely anew? On June 7, 1951, the Municipal Council decided in favor of a new, radically modern opera house. The verdict was not unanimous (27 voices voted for and 16 voted against this plan). The site was to be close to the inner city, where Cologne's Dom, the Rathaus, the Gürzenich, the old concert house, and the new Westfunk are located.

The choice of a medium-sized hall for an opera theater is worthy of note. Cologne is by European standards a large city (population 770,715). It might have seemed more appropriate to provide the Rhenish capital with a larger opera theater. But the decision against it was dictated by artistic, as well as acoustical considerations. The style of Mozart's operas, for instance, and of other intimate works of the lyrical repertory is not well served in a large theater. And so, after lengthy arguments, pro and contra, the municipality decided in 1953 to limit the seating capacity to 1,360 for the Opera. The construction of an additional smaller hall, to seat 800, is under consideration.

The original design of the Opera's exterior with its unusual architectural rhythm and towers is somewhat reminiscent of Babylonian or perhaps Mexican styles. Between concrete pillars rise several terraces. The large glass walls and the airy balconies are set in effective contrast to the compactness of the overall structure. Lighted in the evening, ready to receive its audience, the total impression of the Cologne Opera is festive and convincingly contemporary.

Kassel
Medium-sized State Theater

Kassel, the capital of the state of Hesse, opened its first theater, the Ottoneum, as early as 1605; it was, in fact, the first public stage on German soil. This venerable seventeenth-century theater survived the bombardment of World War II. But Kassel's Opera, built in 1909, was destroyed beyond the possibility of reconstruction.

The Opera has been replaced by an attractive, medium-sized municipal auditorium well equipped for the needs of dramatic and musical performances. From a technical point of view the Kassel State Theater (primarily paid for and supported by the state of Hesse) is as modern as it can be. The inside is a curved amphitheater. The orchestra pit is sunk, as in Bayreuth.*

The Court Opera of Kassel attained great prestige early in the nineteenth century when the noted composer Ludwig Spohr (1784-1859) was its guiding spirit. In 1821, the year of Spohr's appointment, the Opera received a subvention of 180,000 gulden, a very large grant for that time. The new Kassel State Theater recently honored the centenary of Spohr in 1959 with a festival performance of his music drama *Jessonda*. The event is worth recording. In 1933 Hitler forbade the performance of this work on "racial grounds": a white man and a colored woman are happily united as the opera ends. *Jessonda* also commands special attention in the evolution of music-drama: the score represents the first "through-composed" German opera, i.e., there are no spoken dialogues and the music is continuous.

Münster
Priority of Theater Support

Münster, capital of Westphalia, brings to mind a great decision in European history. The Treaty of Westphalia, on October 24, 1648, terminating the Thirty Years War, promised freedom of worship along with the other stipulations aiming at lasting peace. Three centuries later, awakening from the Nazi trauma, Münster lived up to a civilized role in the midst of the shambles left of the old town.

The Municipal Council, besieged with the most pressing problems in the field of communications, of public welfare, and general reconstruction, immediately examined the possibilities for building a new theater. The first step was made when a group of actors built a makeshift stage, surrounded by rubble. The older citizens wanted their theater rebuilt as soon as feasible, but a young generation had grown up under the Nazis with different "ideals." Sports and physical training were their primary interests. Münster had no stadium for the masses interested in sports. Nor did the city own a public bathhouse and swimming pool. Would not many more people benefit from such facilities than from a new theater?

The municipality of Münster, however, took a firm stand. Faced with the question of priority — whether to build first the stadium, the bathhouse, or the theater — the decision was in favor of the theater, and a group of local architects was commissioned to design it.

Today Münster has a handsome, circular-shaped multipurpose Stadt Theater. It is built with extensive use of glass, near the original site

*But in contrast to Bayreuth, the conductor in the Kassel Opera remains visible not only to the musicians in the pit and to the singers on the stage, but to the audience as well.

of the destroyed Opera. The annual subsidy of the Münster theater exceeds 3,000,000 DM. Thus the equivalent of approximately $750,000 is regularly available for the theater alone in a city of 160,000. How is this goal reached? Joint patronage is the answer. The state of Nordrhein-Westphalia shares the deficit with the city of Münster.

In the Municipal Council there are traditionally a number of men who love art and who are ready to fight for it, if necessary. As in every German city, the Council represents a cross section of the population — members of the professions, merchants, workers, etc. That the Council does not interfere with the artistic policy is readily shown by the repertory of the theater. Münster is predominantly a Catholic city. This does not prevent the regular performances of plays upholding heterogeneous beliefs. A drama of Paul Claudel, inspired by Catholic mysticism, may be followed the next evening by an existentialist play of Jean-Paul Sartre.

XV. German Festivals

Art festivals in various forms reach back almost a thousand years on German soil. The contests of the Minnesinger, the folk festivals of the Meistersinger, the brilliant Baroque performances at court are all stations on the road to the contemporary German festivals of drama and music.

These Festspiele are of a highly diversified nature. They cover every medium of performance. They rank from the revival of medieval scores and mystery plays to the premières of experimental works by the young generation.

According to location, two categories of festivals are evident. Either they may take place in small communities (Bayreuth, Baden-Baden, Donaueschingen) which for a limited time assume a cosmopolitan atmosphere and where all, or some, of the performers are imported. Or they may revolve around the resident companies of large cities (Munich, Berlin) where seasons are extended for extraordinary events and schedules. The Berlin Festival in spite of all political and geographical handicaps commands international significance.

Like Bayreuth, other towns have specialized in festivals devoted to one great master. There are the Beethoven Festival of Bonn, the Richard Strauss Festival of Munich. The small town of Eutin in Oldenburg has a festival for Weber, its great son.

A group of German cities dedicate their festivals to the universal genius of the Austrian Mozart. Thus the amiable architecture of Würzburg, one of Germany's oldest municipalities on the Main River, blends naturally with the scenery of eighteenth-century opera. Other Mozart festivals take place in Munich; in the rococo theater of the castle in Ludwigsburg; and in Augsburg, birthplace of Mozart's father, Leopold, a composer in his own right.

Some events scheduled at historic sites establish an intimate relationship with artistic tradition, such as the Bach Festival at Ansbach, where the master served as organist in 1703. The town of Göttingen is distinguished by its Handel Festival. During the Weimar Republic the music department of the University of Göttingen sponsored the systematic reawakening of Handel's neglected operas.

The Bayreuth Festival grew from the vision of one artist, Richard Wagner, and gradually assumed world stature. Other festivals, like those of Donaueschingen or Darmstadt, are joint efforts of an enterprising team of founders or of entire communities.

All German festivals have in common public financial support. Subsidies, as always, come from municipal, state, or federal sources; in certain cases, there is a confluence of additional private or semiprivate funds.

Numerous large festivals have a tradition dating back at least one century. There is the Niederrheinisches Musik Fest, taking place alternately in such Rhenish centers as Cologne, Düsseldorf, etc. This institution has sponsored much important music over the past century.

Bayreuth

In 1834 the twenty-one-year-old Richard Wagner was music director of the Bethmannsche Truppe, a small theatrical company resident in the town of Lauchstädt. On a tour of this group Wagner saw Bayreuth for the first time. It was not until 1851 that he communicated his plan to build a theater in Bayreuth: "In a beautiful quiet landscape, away from the factory smoke and stench of our civilization, a rude theater is to be erected from boards and beams, and to be equipped only with such scenery and machinery as is deemed vital to performance. Singers and orchestra are to be invited. Neither they nor the author are to have financial benefits from the performances. All true enthusiasts are to be admitted free of charge." Some aspects of this dream became reality; some of its idealistic elements fell by the wayside.

In 1870 Wagner read in an encyclopedia of the large stage with which the court theater of the Margrave in Bayreuth was equipped. On the spur of the moment Wagner planned to produce his *Ring* in the Bavarian town; he took clever advantage of the national upsurge accompanying the Prussian victory over France and the subsequent formation of the Reich. Wagner, hoping to enlist the patronage of the Reich's first chancellor, Prince Bismarck, went to Berlin to pursue further the Bayreuth project. Emperor Wilhelm I attended a concert conducted by Wagner in the capital of the new German Reich. But nothing came from the Prussian patrons. Meanwhile, the town council of Bayreuth had offered the composer the site for a new festival house. The year 1872 witnessed the foundation of the Bayreuth Society of Patrons, and on May 22 ground was broken for the opera theater which was to be devoted solely to German masterworks. At this solemn occasion Wagner conducted Beethoven's *Ninth Symphony* in the Margrave's court theater.

But funds for the Festspiel were not raised fast enough and Wagner became very impatient. When Friedrich Nietzsche visited Wagner in Bayreuth, the composer bitterly complained about the lack of genuine patronage on the part of the German public. Wagner's outburst prompted Nietzsche's attack on the German Philistines: "They confuse culture with learning; they lack true enthusiasm and resort to empty historicism."

But Wagner was a controversial figure; the notoriously unlovable qualities of his personality disturbed many of his potential sponsors. One single patron, however, compensated for them all. In 1874 King Ludwig II of Bavaria offered Wagner the munificent credit of 100,000 thaler for Bayreuth. In addition to royal sponsorship, Wagner succeeded in enlisting the help of the newly-founded Wagner Vereine that were springing up in a number of German cities. The Bayreuth Society of Patrons sold 1,000 shares for 300 thaler each. Finally, the accumulation of funds from various sources made possible the opening of the Bayreuth Festival.

On August 13, 1876, the first *Ring* cycle was produced within the framework of the Festival. The first audiences were amazed by the ground plan of the Festspielhaus. With the help of the architect Gottfried Semper, Wagner had designed an amphitheater, breaking with the class-conscious blueprint of court theaters. In Bayreuth every visitor had a clear view of the stage, and the acoustics were good in every part of the hall. This was an important step toward the democratization of the audience. But the influence of the Bayreuth blueprint on theatrical architecture did not manifest itself until the present gigantic building program sponsored by the German Länder and cities following World War II. In Wagner's Munich only the Prinz Regenten Theater had utilized the principle of the Bayreuth ground plan.

The initial deficit of the Festspiel amounted to 147,851 DM. Wagner decided to propagandize his national festival of music-drama in a magazine appropriately called the *Bayreuther Blätter*. The first issue of the journal was devoted to an interpretation of the festival concept as something set apart from the routine of city life: "In Germany, only the remote village proves to be productive, never the great capital city. Thus it was in small corners of our fatherland where my work was supported and encouraged most, whereas in the large markets and capitals one only poked fun at it. This seems to me a beautiful proof of my cause, as I clearly recognize that my work can prosper only on a soil far removed from the traffic of the great world, and from the powers that control it."

Wagner's vision of a small town festival prevails today in many variations and in various countries. But Wagner's sociological differentiation no longer holds true because some of the "small corners" have been turned into "large markets."

The Bayreuth Festival, beginning in the final week of July and lasting until August 25, is supported by collective patronage of the Bonn Federal Republic, the state of Bavaria (to which Bayreuth belongs), the municipality of Bayreuth, and a society called *Friends and Sponsors of Bayreuth.* They all share the deficit. While the Bayreuth Festival can rely on a 100 per cent ticket sale, the deficit is substantial, because of the extraordinary expenses involved.

Munich

In 1901 Munich inaugurated the first of its summer seasons of music-drama. Here, too, the works of Wagner gave the initial impulse. But the opera tradition of the Bavarian capital is also close to Mozart (who conducted here, in 1781, the première of his opera *Idomeneo*) and to Richard Strauss, Munich's favorite son. Of living Munich composers, Carl Orff is often represented on the programs. The works of Wagner are temporarily performed in the Prinz Regenten Theater, and those of Mozart in the delightful rococo theater built by the architect François Cuvilliés in 1753.

Bayreuth and Salzburg are powerful competitors for Munich. At the box office the rivalry is not felt; tickets for all events are at a premium.

With Berlin, Munich offers the most comprehensive festival program in Germany. It includes not only opera, theater, and concerts, but exhibitions, lectures, and indigenous pageantry.

Donaueschingen

Twenty-one-hundred feet high in the Black Forest lies Donaueschingen, at the spot where two small rivers join, the Brege and the Brigach, and form the Donau (the Danube). At their confluence is Donaueschingen — a county seat and popular resort. Most of its 9,000 inhabitants make a modest but secure living from cattle breeding and beer brewing. There is also some domestic textile industry. Located on the age-old crossroads from Germany to Switzerland and France, Donaueschingen is a delightful sight. The main church, built in 1724, betrays with its

Austrian Baroque architecture some of the cultural background of the town. For it was from the old Austrian province of Bohemia that the art-loving rulers of Donaueschingen, the Fürstenbergs, came to this southern part of Germany. Before long, they made their small residence large in terms of art patronage. Subsequent generations of the Fürstenberg dynasty maintained a sponsorship far superior to that of principalities many times the size of Donaueschingen.

By the eighteenth century the Fürstenbergs had established an important art collection. The gallery in their tasteful castle contains treasures of first rank, among them major paintings of Matthias Grünewald, Lucas Cranach, and both Holbeins.

But music was the favorite art of the Fürstenbergs. Their friendly patronage is recorded in a letter written by Mozart's father: "In Donaueschingen, his Highness the Prince received us very friendly. We did not have to be announced. We had been expected with eagerness, and the councilor, music director Martelli, came immediately to bring us compliments and to invite us. In short, we stayed here twelve days. For nine days there was music from five to nine in the evening. We always played something special."

In this account by Leopold Mozart, dated November 10, 1766, from Salzburg, we also learn that Prince Fürstenberg gave him 25 *Louis d'or* and 2 diamond rings for his prodigious children, Wolfgang, age 10, and Marianne, age 12. The Prince and his musical guests "parted with tears."

In 1817 a renowned opera composer, Konradin Kreutzer, was appointed Kapellmeister at the Donaueschingen residence. During the nineteenth century, opera performance predominated at the princely estate.

In 1921 Heinrich Burkhardt, then music director of Donaueschingen, suggested to the Prince a festival of chamber music. In the summer of the same year the Kammer Musik Tage became a reality. Ever since, this institution remained decisive in the patronage of modern chamber music. The festivals were annually repeated from 1922 to 1926. From the very beginning the programs were uncompromising in choice. In fact, their orientation would have to be called ultramodern for their day. Here, in Donaueschingen, one heard the newest chamber music of Paul Hindemith, Alban Berg, Ernst Krenek, young composers then, who were slowly becoming known outside avant-garde circles. In the years that followed, chamber music by Bartók, Schoenberg, Stravinsky, Webern was first performed here. The mere list of names indicates that the choice of the Donaueschingen committee was prophetic.

The Nazis obviously had no use for the Donaueschingen Festival and the spirit of its patrons. But in the postwar years the collaboration between the French military government of occupation, the municipal council of Donaueschingen, and the state of Baden-Württemberg proved productive. The Musik Tage were resumed, and once again are a vital factor in Europe's musical life. The death in 1959 of the generous sponsor Prince Max Egon Fürstenberg was mourned by artists the world over.

XVI. The Rundfunk

Networks and Their Background

The Rundfunk (radio) is decidedly one of the great patrons of the performing arts throughout Germany. Music is the prime beneficiary. We can only envy the enterprising and affluent organizations of the German Rundfunk and its various networks: they represent a substantial contribution to the art life of modern Europe. Through the radio networks, Germany after the liberation was assured the continuity of her musical life and theaters.

In the postwar collapse the Rundfunk has served as the corrective in a desperate situation. By bringing the best available music and plays into every home, the radio offsets the decline of taste and counteracts the low standards set by the Nazis: it has continued to offer chamber music and Lieder to the people at a time when the interest in these noble, intimate forms of music was rapidly waning. In the crucial years, when the theater was struggling for its rehabilitation, the radio sent classical drama to the homes and schools of the devastated land.

The rich financial means, which the German radio has today at its continuous disposal, permit artistic activities of considerable width and depth. The stations compete with each other in the quality of their extremely varied programs. In the category of drama (Hörspiel) the repertory reaches from ancient tragedy and comedy to the controversial plays of the avant-garde; in music, from Gregorian chant to twelve-tone scores and electronic experiments. Some stations have become known for their sponsorship of highly specialized enterprises: Cologne, for example, for its electronic studio.

The Rundfunk offers liturgical music of the principal denominations. One may listen to orchestral concerts of symphonic scope, or music which is outright entertainment. American jazz is now regularly added to the performance of European dance. The large radio stations employ their own orchestras and choruses year-round; performances are conducted by staff or guest conductors.

German listeners buy their radio sets commercially; they remain their private property. Each owner of a set pays 24 DM per year (approximately $6) for his license. On November 1, 1960, the total number of radio licenses paid for in West Germany was 15,796,000. Thus the revenues collected from listening fees are large. There are more than 4,000,000 registered listeners in the area served by the Westfunk Cologne alone. The networks spend their resources in convincing ways.

The reorganization of West Germany's postwar radio networks originated in conformity with the subdivision of the country into the zones of occupation: after the Allied administration of the West German Länder had been established, the American military government permitted each of the four Länder within its zones to set up Rundfunk stations. Yet these radio networks were to remain independent of their respective home states. Political considerations opposed their close association. The networks were formed by grouping regions and cities, sometimes across state lines, into large, strictly nonpolitical units. The Federal Republic of West Germany had not yet come into existence at this transitional time.

In the British zone of occupation the organization of the Rundfunk remained centralized, patterned after the model of the British Broadcasting Corporation. The British military government helped to establish the Nordwest Deutscher Rundfunk, as a joint project of the four Länder in the British zone.

The French military government followed the British pattern. It founded, on the outskirts of Baden-Baden, the so-called *Südwestfunk*. The progressive activities of this modern network — one of the most advanced in Europe — seem curiously out of step with the leisurely life of this conservative spa.

During the later years of Allied occupation these various networks were gradually turned over to the Germans themselves. In 1949 Germany assumed control of the Westfunk and, in the spring of 1954, the Sender Berlin was established. Other networks gradually came into existence.

Today the major stations producing individual programs are the following: the Norddeutscher Rundfunk (now subdivided into the independent stations, Hamburg and the Westfunk Cologne); the Hessen Rundfunk, Frankfurt; the Südwestfunk, Baden-Baden; the Süddeutscher Rundfunk, Stuttgart; and the Bayrischer Rundfunk, Munich. In addition, there are smaller stations such as RIAS Berlin, the Sender Freies Berlin, the Sender Saarbrücken, and Radio Bremen.

The major radio networks are legally defined as *Anstalten des öffentlichen Rechts*, i.e., institutions of public right. The tasks and problems which these networks have in common are regularly discussed by a cooperative to which all radio stations in the Federal Republic of West Germany report. The chief administration rotates annually from one Rundfunk to another, to secure impartiality of policy and of common interest.

The income of each of these stations is in proportion to the number of subscribers living under its carefully defined territory. As listeners' fees are the principal financial means of operating the networks, some of the small stations collect an "Ausgleichsbeitrag," a contribution from financially stronger stations to equalize the differences in income.

The present setup of the mass media throughout the Bonn Republic is by no means considered ideal by the Germans themselves. The overall national interests, it is felt, are not sufficiently represented because of the subdivision and independence of the networks. West Germany lacks, at present, a national outlet.

Whatever its general shortcomings, the German radio remains a generous art patron. Examples from the program and operation of two German networks will suffice here to suggest the extent of this responsible patronage. But any one of the other large West German stations could be chosen with conviction to illustrate the largess of sponsorship within the mass media.

Südwestfunk
Patron of Modern Music

Since its foundation in 1946 the Südwestfunk Baden-Baden has considered it one of its principal tasks to offer its listeners a comprehensive survey of music, with a strong emphasis on modern scores. The programs are spread throughout the day, evening, and night. A weekly minimum of fifty hours is devoted to serious music. Contemporary aesthetics and techniques are analyzed and explained. There are constant and comprehensive reports about musical developments throughout the world. As a matter of policy, all public concerts given by the Südwestfunk offer, in addition to the classical and romantic repertory, at least one modern work. As a generous patron of contemporary music, the Südwestfunk has offered since its inauguration more than 100 commissions, equally divided between German and foreign artists. These commissions are extended not only to well-established composers, but to relatively unknown talent, as well.[19] Frequently these commissions are offered for performances at special festive occasions (such as the Donaueschingen Musik Tage). In 1955 the Südwestfunk was host to the International Society for Contemporary Music. During the summer the activities of the Südwestfunk extend into France, where its forces participate at the Festival in Aix-en-Provence.

Hörspiel

The German theater was long known for its stimulating international repertory. Hitler called a halt to such a program. But after 1945 the German Rundfunk revived the tradition of presenting world theater to the Germans. The first play broadcast by the Südwestfunk was Cocteau's *The Human Voice.* In 1956 the plays performed were by 3 Americans, 3 Austrians, 4 British, 6 French, 1 Israeli, 3 Italians, 1 Swede, and 2 Swiss, in addition to works by 20 German authors. Today the representation of foreign drama retains parity with German productions.

Under the title *Hörspiel* the radio has successfully inaugurated its own kind of "play for listening," appropriately conceived for the aural medium without the visual dimension. The German radio insists in continuing this development of the Hörspiel in spite of the inevitable inroads of television. Comparative statistics show that the German radio is firmly maintaining its hold on its audiences. Programs of high standards, imaginatively conceived, still unite a large circle of listeners before the loud-speaker. And German experts predict that the Hörspiel will continue to have its faithful followers. In an average season the Südwestfunk performs approximately 30 original Hörspiele by German and foreign authors, in addition to radio adaptations of numerous stage plays.

The program of the Schulfunk complements education in the classroom. Radio for Schools devotes more than 200 broadcasts annually to various pedagogical goals, in a wide range from biblical themes to recent German history. Somewhat belatedly, the truth about the Nazi past is being exposed to young audiences. The Youth Radio is an extension of the Schulfunk. Problems of our time have priority.

Westfunk

While the Südwestfunk operates its diversified and vital program from widespread studios on the slopes of the Black Forest, the Westfunk Cologne functions from a large compact structure in the busy center of the Rhenish metropolis. The streamlined Funkhaus was completed in 1952. It has a large concert hall for public performances; a hall for chamber music; 8 studios; and numerous additional work and rehearsal rooms. Cologne has attained international attention as Germany's experimental center of electronic music. The composer Karlheinz Stockhausen has his workshop here. The Westfunk sponsors this pioneering research.

Topographically, the three programs of the Westfunk aim at Cologne and vicinity, Westphalia and overseas. The Westfunk serves 4,000,000 listeners with 4 orchestras, including the symphony orchestra of 107 players; an orchestra of 52, playing popular music; a dance orchestra of 37; a small instrumental ensemble of 14; a chorus of 50. All of the instrumentalists and vocalists are employed permanently on a twelve-month contract. A special ensemble, the Cappella Colonensis, performs old music on historic instruments.

The symphony orchestra of the Westfunk gives regular public concerts; at least one contemporary work is performed in each of them. A special series, Musik der Zeit (Music of our Time), is devoted to a survey of the contemporary scene and offers public concerts.

Not all of the large concerts given by the Westfunk are free; for some there is a modest admission charge, to avoid unfair competition to the traditional, regular series of public orchestral concerts (such as the distinguished Gürzenich series) which otherwise would be at a disadvantage. The Westfunk offers commissions. Some notable contributions to modern music have been made in this way. Luigi Nono's *Canto Sospeso* may be cited as an example.

One must not speak of the German radio orchestras without paying tribute to the achievements of such internationally known groups as the orchestra of the Norddeutscher Rundfunk, a seasoned ensemble of 110 members. The repertory of its regular concerts in Hamburg (and other North German communities) comprises a wide range of old and new music. The activities of the RIAS Symphony Orchestra were discussed earlier in conjunction with art support in West Berlin. In Munich the orchestra of the Bavarian Rundfunk has emerged since World War II as the best in the Bavarian capital. The quality of all radio orchestras — in Hamburg, as in Baden-Baden, Cologne, Berlin, or Munich — is obviously maintained by the largess of subvention. The members of these orchestras enjoy the security of annual contracts which include four weeks' paid vacation. Continuity of working conditions permits long-range planning which, in turn, is conducive to rehearsing and performing without undue pressures.

Television

Germany's television networks operate analogously to the radio. The networks are "institutions of public right." The cooperative of all television services is managed by an administration which rotates annually among the participating groups. At first, the public was offered one single channel, with six hours of daily programs produced by the cooperation of seven networks. In the meantime, demands for a second channel have been voiced throughout the nation.

Channel Two, controlled and supervised by German Television, marks a departure from established procedures. The new channel is intended as a semicommercial venture. Yet in spite of their financial interest, the advertisers are not to exert any influence on the content of the programs. This new policy is being sharply criticized. There is widespread fear that it will open the door to far-reaching commercialization of German television, and eventually lead to a lowering of cultural standards. The issue of Channel Two has created a curious partnership determined to fight the proposal of the government. Only rarely have Christian Democrats and Socialists, Protestant and Catholic leaders, churchmen, and spokesmen of the labor movement, etc., formed a common front against a proposal personally advocated by the Chancellor of the Republic. Bavaria, a predominantly Catholic state, for the time being has refused to become a part of the new enterprise.

As late as 1963 the general policy throughout West Germany permitted only limited advertising: a maximum of 20 minutes per day is allowed. No advertising of any kind is broadcast on Sundays.

Television licenses are issued by the governments of the Länder. This has caused complexities in regard to censorship. The West German constitution guarantees, in principle, freedom of expression for all public media. But this liberty does not imply an unqualified admission of all subject matter over the air waves. A reasonable degree of self-censorship was anticipated in the warning: "All content offensive to public morals is considered inadmissible." An example of general controversy concerning a television show was the production of *Lysistrata*, a modernized version of the ancient play by Aristophanes. The Christian Democratic Union banned the show on the television networks in six states which are controlled by this party. On the other hand, the networks in the states governed by Social Democrats were willing to show the film.

The listening tax for television is 5 DM per month ($1.25). But an increasing number of subscribers pay the annual combined license fee of $21 for both radio and television. In 1953 there were only 1,524 television licenses issued in West Germany (exclusive of Saarland and West Berlin); in 1960, there were 4,384,077. This number has almost doubled during 1963. The figures indicate the meteoric increase of participation and of the growing capital available for the operation of the networks.

XVII. Social and Cultural Security

This Chapter devoted to West Germany shows the unequivocally positive evaluation the Bonn Republic gives to all aspects of art subsidy. The patronage of the performing arts, as we have shown in various instances, has been given priority with the government program of reconstruction. The federal government, the Länder, and the municipalities are always ready to subsidize the performing arts generously.

How does such costly art support affect other obligations of the German government? Does the plus in terms of art subsidy cause a minus in crucial areas of public spending within the domain of governmental responsibility?

To find answers to these questions one may examine crucial issues which at present are much debated in the United States, such as the entire complex of public health insurance and other aspects of social security. These issues have divided public opinion. How does Germany approach their solution?

As early as 1884 Germany instituted the first mandatory social legislation.* It was partly the work of Bismarck, whose innate conservatism was flexible enough to accept certain inevitable patterns of change. The "Iron Chancellor" yielded to the demands of the people for an increase of their social protection, and received credit for its realization.

Today, West Germans have what they consider a very adequate program of combined social and health insurances, and the resulting benefits are considerable; they are a political and psychological necessity in a country which borders on the Iron Curtain. For the West German Republic must maintain standards of social welfare that not only successfully compete with Soviet procedures, but clearly establish the superiority of an open society based upon confidence that freedom from want is assured to all.

The German Cleavage

The German tale is one of extremes. For one thousand years a thread of cultural achievement illuminates the texture of the nation's history. But inhumanity disgraced the very earth from which a proud culture had gradually grown. The war ruins, which at this writing still clutter some of Germany's sites and cities, grimly dramatize a paradox wherein civilization and barbarism can alternate in such proximity of time and sameness of place.

How can one account for this tragic absurdity? A clear answer may never be obtainable, because the all-important question — where the deeper blame and guilt must be fixed — is infinitely complex and ultimately not without global ramifications. Whatever explanations future historians will offer, how can one avoid a second skeptical look at the blessings of a cultural wealth which failed to insure a spirit of man's humanity to man?

The riddle of the German paradox must not be by-passed in an honest inquiry. We have established the fact that Germany was unified cul-

*In 1884 the bill for insurance against injury became law; in 1887 the bill for old-age insurance and sickness was adopted by the Reichstag.

turally in the many centuries in which she lacked political unification. As a politically splintered nation Germany was capable of great civilized deeds. Her small principalities became notable art centers; her communities emerged as generous patrons.

By contrast, decline set in as the physical strength of the unified Reich increased. The nation sunk to a cultural zero at the height of her savage force.

There must, then, have been something basically wrong for some time in the living organism of German culture. And it is not too difficult to arrive at least at a partial diagnosis of the spiritual illness. It is one of betrayal from within. There is no doubt that German civilization has been betrayed by those who were first pledged to its loyal defense — the professors, the intellectuals, and the artists themselves. One cannot evaluate this German cleavage without recalling the damaging part played by the nation's universities, which are, obviously, the exponent and measure of intellectual life. It is true, Schiller and Kant once stood as teachers before students in the classrooms of German colleges, which for centuries were also significant defenders of spiritual life and peace. But from the nineteenth century on, another kind of teaching began to assert itself. The classical spirit of humanism was replaced by the instructions of ardent nationalism. Reason yielded to passion, love to hatred, logic to muddled thinking. Academic authority lent the stamp of approval to a variety of anticultural concepts.

The moral and intellectual paralysis of the German universities temporarily succeeded in reducing their spirit of search and enlightenment to sheer absurdity. They did this so well that the rest of the world now looks at the concept of German culture as something obscured by diabolical shadows. The German theater and literature — in fact, all the arts in all their branches — enthusiastically endorsed this aggressive nationalism and dangerous arrogance.

So-called *philosophy* plainly extolled war: "It is mere illusion and pretty sentiment to expect much (even anything at all) from mankind if it forgets how to make war. As yet no means are known which call so much into action as a great war, that rough energy born of the camp, that deep impersonality born of hatred, that conscience born of murder and cold-bloodedness, that fervor born of effort in the annihilation of the enemy, that proud indifference to loss, to one's own existence, to that of one's fellows, that earthquake-like shaking which a people needs when it is losing its vitality." Thus spoke Nietzsche. The intensity and sweep of the poet's language intoxicated his countrymen. In his first book Nietzsche explored in Wagner's sense "the birth of tragedy out of the spirit of music." But with his discovery of the *Übermensch* the poet turned philosopher and his concept of the Superman trapped the German mind. He taught his compatriots that will for power was will for mastery. Triumphant mastery was that of man over man.

The echo of Nietzsche's teachings in Germany was a loud roar. But his success was a failure, for he did not heal the illness of his age — he mortally aggravated it. Enthusiastically acknowledged as the leader of educated Germans, Nietzsche became the idol of legions of artists and intellectuals. The people at large accepted his doctrines in simplified versions and, with them, the glorification of war and its gruesome realities. In the twentieth century Germany's will to culture yielded to total war, destruction, and genocide.

There is a Faustian schism in the soul of Germany as she plays her antithetical roles. The nation which had so greatly contributed to Western civilization missed its chance of continued cultural leadership.

Disaster was prepared during the short-lived interims of peace when large segments of the nation were swept by racial demagoguery and by anticivilized slogans shouted by fascist gangs. Gradually, democratic Germany was conquered by its enemies from within.

At odds with the immediate past, the generation of fathers who were partners of the Nazi scheme find it difficult to answer the questions of their sons: "How was it all possible? Why did you not prevent it?" The fathers cannot escape these questions which are a threat to the image of paternity they must create and preserve for their children. They have only the option of restitution on the few roads that lead toward a rehabilitation of shattered human and cultural values.

Thus a peculiar reaction to a national guilt has contributed to the powerful attempt to restore high cultural ideals. From the consciousness of their old civilization spring new deeds that have helped the Germans transform a period of utter disillusionment into a new cultural development. And thus one sees new glass-encased opera houses and streamlined theaters, garden cities and imaginatively modern architecture on new squares where a few years earlier only rubble and ashes were visible. This priority in the build-up of her cultural life marks a convincing road for Germany's return to an old order which honored the dignity of life.

The German Lesson

One might feel that the German experience presents us, in its complex overall patterns, with more questions than answers. This might be so. But in spite of this, we have much to learn from the German lesson, for the clinical picture of the nation's grave illness during the Nazi years is sufficiently clear. And we can gain insight into the normal from the pathological.

We are faced here, before all, with the fact that art is never an antidote against man's aggressiveness. Why does culture not serve as counteractive? This is the sad part of the story: an old civilization has never served as a preventative against barbarism gradually rising from within a country. Other forces overwhelmingly shape a nation's destiny. Economic factors are preeminent in determining the direction a country will take. And political demagoguery always finds fertile ground in times of crisis and economic distress. We also see magnified in the German example how fast spiritual achievement may be destroyed by the tools of advanced technology, once they fall into the hands of evil government.

It is unfortunately true that the spirit of Bach and Schiller did not prevent Hitler and Goebbels from assuming power in Germany. But we do not yet have all the answers for the *causes* of the tragedy. We do know: flowers do not stop bullets.

We can learn further from the German experience that those who attack the freedom of the arts, in whatever form, are suspect. We must always be apprehensive of those who are hostile to free intellectual expression. We must also distrust those who withhold support from a free art life. The rejection of art, or the assault on its progress, are unmistakable symptoms of the fascist disease. From their earliest sabre-rattling beginnings in the 1920's, the Nazis attempted the systematic sabotage of every manifestation of the progressive spirit in Germany's cultural life. They kept up their onslaught to the bitter end. We should conclude, then, that attacks on the arts are symptomatic of a more serious illness. A totalitarian tyranny always usurps the arts and forces the artist into a yoke. A liberal democracy, by contrast, should help the arts in every form. For a free and flourishing art life is a sign of a sane society.

We are faced here, before all, with the fact that art is never an antidote against man's aggressiveness. Why does culture not serve as counter-action? This is the sad part of the story: an old civilization has never served as a preventative against barbarism gradually rising from within a country. Other factors [illegible] Economic factors are [illegible] will take? And political [illegible] in times of crisis and [illegible] example [illegible] the lack of [illegible] in the hands of evil governments. It is [illegible] that [illegible] Goethe and Schiller did not [illegible] after any [illegible] that [illegible] We do [illegible]

[illegible]

THE LOW COUNTRIES

The Netherlands - Belgium - Luxembourg

Political historians and modern economists recognize the fundamental unity which has long determined the destiny of three Western European countries — today known as Holland, Belgium, and Luxembourg. Whatever the changing geopolitical names and governments of these countries, their coexistence leads back many centuries. The Low Countries, as they have long been called, were once part of the old Carolingian Empire, founded in the seventh century and absorbed in the tenth century by the Holy Roman Empire. A long succession of French, Spanish, Austrian, and Dutch sovereigns alternated wholeness or division for these three bordering states. They were for centuries part of that larger parallelogram of forces drawn by the power politics of the Old World.

Today, a new concord of the three countries is expressed by their own economic agreement. This union has assumed the name *Benelux*, a word contrived by adding the first syllables of Belgium, Netherlands, Luxembourg. This name indicates a new vision of partnership in the politics of Europe, where so many lives, natural resources, and energies are constantly wasted on atavistic rivalry, fabricated hatred, and rekindled nationalism.

Benelux symbolizes an initial attempt of a European group of states to cooperate economically, as well as politically, for the common good of the people.

In each of these countries — today all hereditary monarchies — the arts play decisive roles. Luxembourg, the smallest of the three, maintains an art life of a significance out of proportion to its diminutive size and its total population of only 314,000. The Netherlands, with a population of 11,702,239, and Belgium, with 9,153,000, tenaciously guard their age-old artistic legacies. The governments of both nations participate increasingly in the development and financial support of their cultural organizations. The performing arts fare well under such auspices.

THE NETHERLANDS

I. Independence, Survival, Art Patronage

The Netherlands is an international crossroads. For its cultural growth as Europe's most densely populated country, geographical position has proved a marked advantage. Politically, the topography of The Netherlands has turned out to be a tragic detriment. For the peace-loving Dutch — whose heroic energies built much of their land out of the sea and transformed their watery, wind-swept countryside into a continuous garden — have been persecuted by wave after wave of invasions from hostile nations. In most of these wars the Dutch have defended their freedom with a courage and persistence that have inspired glorification in great works of arts and letters.

Thus, Goethe's tragedy *Egmont* (1787) pays tribute to the heroism of the Dutch uprising against Spanish despots in the sixteenth century.[1] Beethoven, too, inspired by Egmont, the noble leader of Dutch resistance, contributed magnificent incidental music to Goethe's drama.[2] Schiller devoted his epochal monograph, *The History of the Revolt of the Netherlands Against the Spanish Government* (1788), to an analysis of the desperate struggle of this small and valiant nation against the tyranny of world powers.[3] Thus these classical German artists have immortalized the fight for freedom of their Dutch neighbors — of the very people whom the Nazi hordes tormented during World War II, devastating cities like Rotterdam, and turning other Holland communities into places of terror.

In Rotterdam, near the water front of the once-again bustling harbor, stands a grim and moving memorial by Ossip Zadkine. His sculpture recalls the horror to which Hitler's bombers exposed the Dutch during the tulip season of 1940, when they killed 30,000 innocent inhabitants and left Rotterdam a flaming hell. Lament and triumph blend in this statue of a tortured giant. His arms raised to the sky, he stands projected against the reborn port city of peaceful energies.

In 1949, four years after the War's end, The Netherlands lost its prize colonies, the Dutch East Indies, and with them the rich resources of the Indonesian archipelago. Again, four years later, in 1953, Holland suffered the kind of catastrophe which has plagued the Dutch through the ages — a new reminder of the constant and still unconquered enemy, the sea! This struggle has kept the Dutch in harness even during peaceful interludes. But today, as yesterday, the recovery of their land from the recurring aggression of the water becomes the background of industrial life. The Dutch are engaged in enormous projects to combat destructive floods, and to change marshes into fertile soil. Eight hundred people live on each square mile of land, and the Dutch need every single bit of land as living space for a population of more than 11,000,000. Hence tremendous hydraulic projects were bound to become the principal enterprise of the nation: the closing of the Zuyder Zee and the new Delta Plan, designed to control permanently the estuaries of the rivers emptying into the North Sea on Dutch territory. Such mammoth operations are by no means only preventive of destruction; they are building new life and industry for Holland. Future projects include the building of what is designed to become the largest harbor on the Continent, which will be called *Europort.* These enterprises not only keep the Low Countries above water; they make an ally of a hostile element.

Priority of Art Patronage

The gigantic efforts of modern technology and their staggering costs have not detracted the Dutch from the support of their art life. Considering the major blows which The Netherlands has suffered in the past two decades alone, it would not be surprising if bitterness, hard-boiled economic realism, even cynicism, had directed the Dutch exclusively to technological and scientific pursuits, to the most urgent aspects of life in terms of national rehabilitation, and perhaps even to extreme defensive measures in pessimistic anticipation of history's repeating patterns.

But the Dutch people have relinquished their art life as little as they have yielded to the attacks of human hordes or elemental catastrophes. It is a tribute to the nation that it has upheld the priority of art in spite of all calamities, and that it has found satisfactory formulas to balance in its economy the needs of physical and spiritual rehabilitation. This model attitude is obviously a manifestation of a collective national psychology, and in the history of The Netherlands we find the clues to its understanding and attitude.

Land of Many Names and Changes

The history of Holland, even by European standards, is a very involved tale of political changes. Its multiform chapters account for the various names that are still used synonymously, and somewhat loosely, to denote the nation and its people. The names are helpful as cultural references: they are passports to historical phases in the making of modern Holland.

In the year 500, Clovis, founder of the Frankish Monarchy, became the first ruler of what we know today as the territory of the Low Countries. It eventually became part of the realm of Charlemagne (*ca.* 742-814), which was divided among Charlemagne's three grandsons by the Treaty of Verdun in 843. The northern portion of Charlemagne's realm, including the Low Countries, was absorbed by the Holy Roman Empire in 925.

In the southwest of the Low Countries the people already spoke Dutch. But the word *Dutch* — which today signifies the people as well as their language, national unity, and culture — had then not assumed its modern meaning. Etymologically, the Middle German word *Dutch* simply means *people.* The Dutch in the south were Franks, those in the north were Frisians. In the east Saxons predominated. Eventually all the people of The Netherlands adopted the West Germanic idiom of speech known as *Dutch.* Their cultural connection with their eastern neighbor, Germany, is thus also linguistically established. But it was particularly from the south and across the sea from the west that this country on the crossroads greatly profited from a variety of national associations.

The growth of Dutch art life naturally coincides with the development of many urban centers during the Middle Ages. The Low Countries (comprising as they did both Holland and Belgium) had gradually become a territory of many towns. In 1500 it counted more than 200 fortified cities and 150 important towns which, although without walls, had the civic life of full-grown cities.

During the fifteenth century the ruling House of Burgundy absorbed under its sovereignty the feudal states of Brabant, Gelderland, Holland, and Zeeland. From 1515, Emperor Charles V, heir of the Austrian Habsburgs, reigned over the provinces of the Low Countries. He belonged to an extremely art-loving family. Charles's grandfather Maximilian I had been an enlightened art patron in his Austrian residences.

Era of Music and Painting

The reign of the Burgundian and the Habsburg dynasties marked an era of tremendous creative achievement in the Low Countries. Art patronage had been a long-established tradition at the courts of these rulers before they assumed control in The Netherlands.

Today the entire world pays tribute to the significance of Dutch painting. But universal consciousness and full recognition of music written by composers of the Lowlands from the fourteenth to the sixteenth centuries is yet to come.

Some of the great painters and composers were born and reared within the political territory of the modern kingdom of The Netherlands. Other famous Dutch musicians, like so many painters of The Netherlands Schools, came from Burgundy, from Flanders, from Hainault, and still more distant parts which in modern geopolitical terms are called Belgium or France. Ethnological identification and precise terminology is made difficult by the ambiguous concept of "The Netherlands Schools," although accepted in various studies devoted to painting and music.

For the purpose of this study, it suffices to recall the grandeur of creativity and art patronage then prevailing in The Lowlands. Certain composers of this era emerge as towering figures in history; they were in demand in every Western country. Cathedral choirs and vocal and instrumental ensembles at courts all over Europe were under the direction of composer-conductors who had come from The Netherlands. Their biographies reveal important insight into the nature and scope of sacred and secular patronage. The activities of Heinrich Isaak (b. Brabant, *ca.* 1450; d. Florence, 1517) and Orlando di Lasso (b. Mons, 1532; d. Munich, 1594) have been considered earlier in this study. The Burgundian Josquin des Prez (b. Hainault, 1450; d. Condé-sur-l'Escaut, 1521), called *princeps musicorum*, traveled widely and left his spiritual imprint wherever he went.

Burgundian masters of the preceding period were Binchois and Dufay. Gilles Binchois (b. Mons, 1400; d. Soignies, 1460) became choir master for the Duke of Burgundy. Guillaume Dufay (b. Hainault 1400; d. Cambrai, 1474) served at the cathedrals of Cambrai and Mons as well as at the Papal Chapel. Philip the Good entrusted Dufay with the musical education of his son Charles.

Johannes Ockeghem (b. prob. Flanders, 1430; d. Tours, 1495),* unmatched master of medieval polyphony, worked the greatest part of his life under French sponsorship. A Dutchman in the more narrow sense was Jacob Obrecht (b. Berg-op-Zoom, 1452; d. Ferrara, 1505), who counted Erasmus of Rotterdam among his pupils. Adrian Willaert (b. Roulers or Bruges, *ca.* 1490; d. Venice, 1562) carried contrapuntal concepts of Netherlandish music into Italy when he became choir master at St. Mark's Cathedral in Venice.

From the fifteenth to the seventeenth century an almost bewildering number of masterpieces of painting originated in Holland-Flanders. There was Jan Van Eyck (1385-1440), portrait painter of visionary insight; Pieter Brueghel the elder (1525-1569) with his dramatic portrayal of peasant life; Hieronymus Bosch (1460-1516) with his phantom-haunted world and apocalyptic scenes; Frans Hals (1580-1666), the first great artist of liberated Holland; Peter Paul Rubens (1577-1640), who ranks as the most flamboyant and internationally admired of Flemish painters; Jan Vermeer (1632-1675), who recreated the calm intimacy of Dutch life. And seventeenth-century Holland enriched the world with Rembrandt van Rijn (1606-1669), whose art is a record of the fundamental experiences of a groping humanity.

---

*Neither the places nor dates of birth of Ockeghem and a considerable number of other masters from the Lowlands have been recorded with certainty.

The sovereignty of The Netherlands in music and painting came to its inevitable end: artistic evolution is subservient to large cycles that rule the patterns of creative achievement. We observe throughout history how artistic supremacy reigns only temporarily and is subject to strong reversals. And so great national Schools, sometimes spanning several generations, finally yield to decline in eternal patterns of sinuosity that are more readily detected than explained.

Thus we observe that the Low Countries eventually surpassed even Italy in the art of painting. The paintings of Rembrandt, Rubens, and Vermeer followed hitherto uninterrupted triumphs of the Italian Renaissance. In music this pattern of primacy was reversed. The last of the great masters born in the territory of The Netherlands moved away to various European churches and courts. Orlando di Lasso ended his wanderings with decades of achievement at the Munich court. Adrian Willaert settled in Italy, where such future masters as Andrea Gabrieli and Cipriano de Rore became his apprentices. In the composition and performance of music, Italy eventually assumed the leadership which The Netherlands could not indefinitely maintain.

Proximity of Crafts and Arts
Double Occupation

During the era of great creative achievement in The Netherlands there was a curious evaluation of the artist and his product. This was a period of perfection in Dutch craftsmanship. Works of craftsmen bordered on real art in concept and order, in the precision and imaginative treatment of materials. On the other hand, most of the great artists were regarded by contemporaries as only skilled craftsmen. Many artists did not earn their living as artists; double occupation was frequent for musicians or painters. Creative artists served in menial jobs absurdly unrelated to their vocation. The great composer Jacob Obrecht was employed as a butler; Jan Steen, ingenious painter of Dutch manners, was a brewer in Delft; Pieter de Hooch, delightful genre painter of intimate Dutch middle-class domesticity, was a servant attending a wealthy burgher. The sober Dutchmen found it impossible to be in awe of Frans Hals; they observed this remarkable painter working on his canvases when visibly under the influence of his favorite liquid refreshment. But whatever the sources of inspiration, many artists made their living outside their calling. The interpretation of the creative process in a "romantic" manner belonged to a still distant future. The image of the artist creating in a spell of inspiration, transforming on canvas or note paper "heaven-sent ideas" into works of art, was completely outside the old practical

Dutch way of thinking. Hence the artist was not considered essentially different, neither better nor worse than any other Dutch citizen or soldier. The artist was just another worker, and so his product was "handled" as a matter of business. A typical Dutch market offered its buyers herring and cheese, meat and flowers, along with works of craft and of art. If the buyers liked the paintings, the dealer would order more from the artist. If his "wares" did not find favor, he was forced to change his style, or to seek other sources of income.

Musicians obviously did not have these practical advantages. They could not sell their products on the stalls of the market place. If they were not skillful performers or commissioned composers, they had to find jobs outside the musical profession so that they and their families could eat.

All of this is by no means only of historic interest. The entire complex regarding the social status of the artist merits reexamination in the light of our own attitude toward related problems. Have the centuries that separate us from old Holland brought such progress that we can afford to ridicule the lack of esteem and the circumstances under which the artist lived? The hard fact is that double occupation prevails in modern America as it did in The Netherlands of the obedient valet-composer Obrecht or the footman-painter de Hooch. Today, thousands of talented American artists must resort to part-time employment, often in menial jobs. And seemingly responsible Americans see nothing wrong with such a state of affairs.[4]

Charles V
Music in Dutch Churches

Art patronage in the Low Countries was long the privilege of foreign princes. Both the Burgundian and Habsburg sovereigns avoided living in the north, favoring such cities as Brussels or Ghent as their residences. Charles V, Emperor of the Holy Roman Empire, was born in Ghent; he also held court in Mechlin, a Catholic stronghold, and in other places. The general preference for the southern part of the country inevitably expressed itself in various patterns of courtly art support. Church and State still functioned in close proximity. Charles V was a Catholic zealot. Son of a Spanish mother, he dreaded and fought the infiltration of Protestantism. Like many others of the Habsburg dynasty, Charles V was an art patron of consequence. He was a musical connoisseur, and he sponsored Catholic music over his vast realm. To his immediate protectorate, among other institutions, belonged the *capilla flamenca*, as the famous Burgundian chapel was called in Spain (then a pivotal state of the Habsburg Empire). The Emperor loved the singing of the *capilla flamenca*, and he took the choir with him on various journeys about his Empire.

Charles V had the talent, but only temporarily the strength, to enforce the imperial power of a unified Holy Roman Empire upon his inherited Habsburg realm. His dream of an undivided Europe did not become a reality. As Emperor, he never learned to speak well the German language and he never identified himself closely with the interests of The Netherlands. His political commitments were too scattered over Europe's map to allow concentration on any regional culture. Thus, what might have developed into art patronage on a true imperial scope materialized only in fragments and episodes.

In addition to his love of music, Charles V was a noted bibliophile and became known as an author. He was a patron of painters. While having his portrait painted, the Emperor stooped to lift from the floor the brush which had fallen from the hand of Titian. "It is only right," Charles observed, "that an artist of Titian's rank should be served by his emperor." The incident was unprecedented in the annals of art patronage. Charles V appointed the Venetian master a lifelong member of the imperial court and raised his status to that of hereditary nobility.

In 1558 Charles V formally abdicated. A large part of his immense realm fell to his son Philip II, whose reign of suppression caused the Dutch revolt and the eventual separation of The Netherlands from the Habsburg Empire. Freedom came to The Netherlands during the last third of the sixteenth century when the Low Countries were united under William the Silent. In 1579 the Union of Utrecht created a federation of the seven northern provinces which in 1581 declared their independence from Spain.

Meanwhile the Reformation had been on the march. Protestantism, in fact, was one of the powerful impulses in the struggle against the Spanish rulers. In 1568 the assembly of Dutch Church delegates, meeting in Wesel, formally accepted the Presbyterian polity of Calvin. The austerity in both ritual and living demanded by Calvin also affected the arts. Calvin envisioned the entire world as a convent; the ritual should offer no opportunity for appreciation of the beautiful art works which adorned Christian churches. The doctrine of Calvin had far-reaching consequences for the performance of music, in and outside of liturgy. Calvin was, for instance, notoriously opposed to organ playing. The Dutch ministers, too, remained for a long time critical of all instrumental participation in church music. They admitted the organ within the ecclesiastical frame only as discreet accompaniment to singing the Psalms. Such strictness recalls the attitude of Roman Popes who insisted on *a cappella* performance (the unaccompanied choral style) for the liturgical service.

Burgomaster as Art Sponsor

The ministers of the Dutch Reformed Church were equally skeptical of secular art. Under the circumstances, the beginning of organized art life in the northern part of The Netherlands was the achievement of the citizenry. The burgomasters (the mayors) of the towns often assumed the initiative. The city of Leyden employed in 1593 the organist Cornelius Schmit as municipal musician. At regularly scheduled hours he was to play the organ in church "for the edification of the burghers." The performances were to deter the citizens from cheap musical entertainment at inns of ill repute. But in spite of such moral purpose, civic patronage of music was challenged, and at times the municipality had to fight clerical opposition for the right to sponsor secular performances. The ministers of the Reformed Church went so far as to forbid organ recitals in the evening, although the burgomasters argued their worthiness.

The clergy protested in vain. Secular organ performances during the seventeenth century became the nucleus of public recitals under the patronage of the Dutch cities.

The Early Theater of Holland

Chambers of Rhetoric

The Burgundian era witnessed what may be considered the beginning of indigenous theater in The Netherlands. Like their neighbors, the Dutch had their own Mystery plays. Some Dutch folk plays of the late Middle Ages reached beyond their national borders.

Of this early theater, the Morality play *Elckerlijc*, attributed to the late fifteenth century, assumed lasting significance; it tells the original story of *Everyman*, that universal folk drama of man and his good and bad deeds on earth. In modern adaptations *Elckerlijc* has maintained lasting interest. The *Nederlandse Comedie* (under the auspices of the Holland Festival) annually offers *Elckerlijc* in open-air performances in the historic city of Delft. The German version of *Elckerlijc*, known as *Jedermann*, is annually given at the Salzburg Festival on the Cathedral Square.

Another centuries-old Dutch theatrical tradition lives on with the annual New Year's performance in Amsterdam of *Gijsbreght van Aemstel;* this is one of the many plays by Joost van den Vondel (1587-1679), whom the Dutch consider their greatest poet. Some of his works evoke the national glory of the Dutch Republic; others defend his Catholic faith.

An early significant expression of the Dutch theater was the Chambers of Rhetoric. They were dramatic guilds which can be traced to the Middle Ages, and they functioned as cells of civic art life in various communities. In the north, the town of Middleburg boasts of having been the seat of the oldest Chamber, dating from 1430. The late sixteenth and the early seventeenth centuries marked the height in the role of the Chambers, which were usually sponsored by a group of prominent, affluent citizens, although occasionally a single individual assumed full patronage. The members of the Chambers of Rhetoric were referred to as the *Rederijkers*. The Chamber known as De Eglantier emerged as a center of literary culture in Amsterdam. Eventually, De Eglantier joined forces with members of the Duytsche Academic, which had hitherto offered a stage for dramatic performances. The merger of the two groups led to the founding of the Amsterdamsche Schouwburg in 1637. This City Theater of Amsterdam still flourishes after more than 300 years.

Jewel of the Land

The Dutch towns were always proud of their theatrical companies. The best ensembles participated in public festivals. They marched with the guilds in festive processions to competitions where the best performance reaped a coveted award. Before long, these Dutch art festivals became the joyous battleground on which the cities vied with each other in pageantry and folkloristic performances of all kinds. Civic pride was a strong motivation. Communities tried to surpass each other in elaborate décor and colorful processionals. The festival itself was called the *Landjuweel*. It was the Jewel of the Land because it displayed the most precious possessions of each region — its culture, its traditions, and the shining quality of its performers. In a narrower sense, *Landjuweel* also referred to the prize given at the festival.

These communal or regional meetings, with all of their theatrical presentations, had still another function to fulfill beyond their pageantry. Through the popular theater of the Chambers the new faith of Martin Luther reached large audiences. And various messages of the Reformation, often carefully camouflaged but sufficiently understood, were passed on to the people. Thus the theater of the Dutch burghers functioned, as it were, as a second pulpit. To the foreign rulers of The Netherlands, the Chambers seemed to be a fifth column. One thing is certain: when Dutch unification finally became a political reality, the popular stages of the nation had played their contributing role, and had played it well.

The Jewel of the Land is the important antecedent of the typically regional festivals which the national government of The Netherlands annually supports in each province as a survival of old Dutch culture.

In retrospect we realize that the beginning of Dutch theatrical life — like secular musical activities — must be credited to the citizenry. Here again, the municipalities had to face clerical opposition; the members of the Dutch Reformed Church objected to secular art on principle. They attempted to forbid, or at least to restrict, the theater, even in cosmopolitan Amsterdam with its large and partly transient population.

II. The Citizens Support the Arts

Middle-Class Culture

In the many prosperous towns of The Netherlands the citizenry has fostered domestic and communal art. An autonomous spirit of civic patronage, which developed independent of the church and independent of the court, is one of the distinctive features of the country's cultural history; herein lie the fundamental differences between art patronage in The Netherlands and in its neighboring countries. We have seen why the Dutch Reformed Church was primarily not an art-minded denomination and why the temporary eclipse of indigenous court life in the Low Countries and the subsequent emergence of the republic were greatly responsible for a growth of self-reliance among the Dutch bourgeoisie. As a result, there rose in Holland a significant middle-class culture which has asserted itself for almost half a millennium — regardless of the changing political fate of the nation.

The main stream in the performing arts, however, by-passed The Netherlands from the early seventeenth century to the late nineteenth century. Thus opera, orphaned without adequate court sponsorship, made a retarded entrance on the stages of Holland. Even the drama temporarily lacked the proper forum, which other Continental nations maintained at theaters generously supported by the court. But Holland created patterns of patronage suitable to her own needs and conditions, and never ceased to function as a large market for the visual arts. From the late eighteenth century on, Holland was prominent in the printing and publication of music. Gradually the nation grew into a land of concerts. The theater and the opera were first established in Amsterdam and in the royal residence of The Hague. Other cities followed suit.

This retarded development of art centers for the performing arts is closely tied to the political history of Holland. In spite of its republican interregnum, the country was slow to achieve the level of democratic freedom that was won by other nations much earlier. Only during the second part of the nineteenth century did The Netherlands establish fairly stable parliamentary institutions. Europe's revolutionary climate around the flaming year of 1848 had its consequences also in The Netherlands; for the first time, the Dutch were able to secure a constitution expressing full-fledged democracy. Although the Crown retained large slices of absolute reign, it did not assume responsibility in art support. In 1898 further steps toward democratic progress were made by the Dutch people. But it was not until 1914, the initial year of World War I, that The Netherlands actually gained the status of a true democracy — not only in name, but in the working reality of political procedures. Under the reign of the late Queen Wilhelmina, Holland developed into the solid organism of a free nation. It is no coincidence that the blossoming of the great Dutch musical organizations concurs with this political evolution.

Art in a Constitutional Monarchy

The constitution of The Netherlands claims (in Article 192) education as an "object of the government's continuous care." This concept is being extended in an ever-increasing degree to the performing arts. Today their support is closely integrated with the educational program of the nation. Subsidies are allocated, as elsewhere in Europe, on national, provincial, and municipal levels.

Certain aspects of Dutch art patronage are complicated because of the structure of government. The Netherlands lacks religious homogeneity and an inherently common denominator of cultural experience of the kind we encounter in such Continental countries as Austria, Italy, and, to a large degree, France. Holland compares with Switzerland or Germany in duality of religious structure. Here, as there, heterogeneous groups underwent a slow process of mutual assimilation while safeguarding their respective religious and cultural traditions. In modern Holland men of different creed and background live in harmony which has stood the strictest conceivable tests of national emergencies and wars. But the exigencies of old established cultural differences must also be taken into account in the national patronage of Dutch art life in times of peace. After all, the art program is supported by all the people and in parliamentary manner.

The Netherlands has curiously reversed that pattern by which Europe's recent history converted most of its former monarchies into republics. In Holland the opposite sequence occurred. A republic was dissolved in 1795. A kingdom was proclaimed by the Congress of Vienna in 1815; The Netherlands became a constitutional monarchy ruled by the House of Orange; and the House of Habsburg relinquished its last segment of The Netherlands.

A chief political problem in the new kingdom was the claim for independence within the framework of a constitutional monarchy by the once-sovereign states. Should sovereignty be abandoned for the sake of a higher national unity? Or should the state rights — in tangible unmistakably defined terms — be preserved in the new government? The ultimate decision was that of a compromise, of a give and take, which is logically reflected in the governmental support of contemporary Dutch art life.

Central Administration of Art Subsidy

It is no coincidence that in contrast to most other hereditary kingdoms on the Continent the Dutch monarchy has survived both world wars. The exemplary behavior of the late Queen Wilhelmina, as well as the uncompromising attitude of her government on the side of democracies, has fortified also in times of peace the rule of the House of Orange.

In the musical life of Holland the "Mengelberg episode" is remembered as a test case. William Mengelberg, world-famous veteran conductor of the *Concertgebouw*, and for decades the most popular and powerful artist of the kingdom, was dismissed following the liberation of Holland because of his openly expressed sympathies with the Nazis. The dishonorable discharge was a lesson. National patronage is bestowed only upon artists who deserve such distinction as citizens, and not only as experts in their fields.

Today, as in the past, the executive power belongs to the Crown: to the Queen and her personally appointed ministers. Yet the legislative powers are exercised jointly by the Crown and the Dutch Parliament, called States-General. Parliament consists of two chambers. The first chamber is elected by the provincial legislatures; the second chamber is elected by all citizens of voting age. The Crown exerts its executive authority through the Council of Ministers; its chairman functions as Prime Minister. The sovereign appoints and presides also over the State Council, which is consulted on all legislative and some executive issues.

Within this setup the Crown has considerable influence on all aspects of the national art life. Often this amounts merely to theoretical rights, to honorary functions (such as appearances at representational performances), to honorary chairmanships, and the like. The proud announcement "under the patronage of her Majesty the Queen" is a status symbol, a promise of quality rather than an implication that the royal purse has largely contributed to the enterprise.

The Dutch government supports the national art life through three major offices: the Ministry of Education, Arts, and Sciences; the

Ministry of Foeign Affairs; the Ministry of Social Affairs and Public Health.

The relative concern of these ministries with the performing arts obviously changes according to specific circumstances, but the prime responsibility rests with the Ministry of Education. An equation is clearly anchored in this trust: "Art is the property of education." But the government in no way interferes with the artistic management of any organization selected for support. The procedure of subvention is a simple one. The art institutes submit their tentative budgets in advance. They are examined by the Minister of Education, Arts, and Sciences, who makes his recommendations on the strength of his evaluation of the project. The Minister of Finance also has his say about budgets as they relate to the national expenditure. But the ultimate decision rests with the States-General. Thus the will of the people — through Parliament — is the prime and controlling factor of art patronage. The monarchial framework lends to it a kind of pageantry and royal glamour. It would be a mistake to underestimate the psychological value of this plan for the majority of the Dutch people.

The Government Encourages the Arts

Holland established the Ministry of Education, Arts, and Sciences relatively late, namely, in 1918, at the end of World War I. Yet we encounter, much earlier, documentary recognition of the philosophy that education and art should become spiritual partners. The word "encouragement" stands out in these documents. It epitomizes the basic attitude the Dutch government has adopted and maintained as the keynote of its assistance to the arts. The aid is financial, implying no undue controls or interference. There is no meddling with artistic leadership and expert decision.

The procedure is aboveboard. There are no appointments by improper political machinations, for the Dutch are quick to demand open inquiries if their suspicions are aroused. The States-General jealously guards democratic standards. Thus the role of governmental art patronage is clearly defined in its purpose and carefully restricted in its procedures.

The positive attitude toward the governmental encouragement of the arts is manifest in the steady increase of allocations. The amounts granted to the Music and Dance Section of the national Ministry of Education, Arts, and Sciences during four consecutive years show this trend. (See Table I.)

TABLE I

Ministry of Education, Arts, and Sciences
Grants to Music and Dance

1956	F.* 4,906,720 ($1,373,881)
1957	5,768,700 ($1,615,236)
1958	6,148,120 ($1,721,473)
1959	6,737,500 ($1,887,255)

TABLE II

Budget for Ministry of Education, Arts, and Sciences (1959)

Elementary Education	F.	577,786,000 ($161,780,080)
Secondary Education		131,318,270 ($ 36,769,115)
Technical Education		180,971,000 ($ 50,671,880)
Higher Education		167,292,651 ($ 46,841,942)
	Total F.	1,057,367,921 ($296,063,017)

*F.—florin or guilder—one florin=approximately 28 cents.

In 1959 the total budget for all the arts was F. 11,000,000 ($3,080,000). Of this amount, Music and Dance received F. 6,737,500 ($1,887,255). The greater expense involved in the performance of music is recognized by the larger allocation.

The Arts Council

The law of March 30, 1955, created a National Arts Council "to advise the Minister of Education, Arts, and Sciences about the task of government in regard to the arts." The Arts Council either acts upon consultation, or takes the initiative itself, to suggest and advise the government office. The Council is divided into several sections which correspond to the various branches of the arts. The setup of the music section characterizes the procedure. The board consists of prominent representatives of the national musical life.[5]

For its general activities, during 1959, the Arts Council was allotted F. 99,550 ($27,874). In addition to the National Arts Council of the Netherlands, there are a number of regional and municipal arts councils, all serving related purposes in the provinces.

Provinces and Patronage

The Kingdom of The Netherlands is divided into eleven provinces: North Holland, South Holland, Utrecht, Gelderland, Friesland, Groningen, Drente, Limburg, Overijssel, North Brabant, and Zeeland. These provinces function as independent political units yet retain their allegiance to the Kingdom.

The direct representative of the electorate is the Provincial Council. The Council has the authority to make — under royal approval — ordinances and regulations concerning all public interests which, for whatever reasons, have not been taken care of by an act of state. The

Provincial Council deals with all issues beyond local rights and concerns within the framework of the province. In this category belong various problems of the economic and social life in the provinces for which the municipalities fail to provide, either because the issue exceeds primary local importance or because the cities are financially unable to accept the responsibility. Provincial supervision pertains to public utilities (such as electricity, water, and gas); the care for parks and landscape; and the maintenance of recreational areas. *Significantly, the public care for the arts falls into the category of public utilities.* We take special note of this association: the arts are utilities. The arts are interpreted as *needs of daily life*—just as light and water are! They must be cared for, as public gardens and places of public recreation are cared for and maintained.

National Council for Regional Culture

The Dutch provinces have only in recent years begun to make regular contributions to the performing arts. The budgets show steadily increasing subsidies throughout the last decade.

In Holland certain aspects of municipal administration are also the concern of the provinces. At the helm of the province is the Royal Governor who presides over the meetings of both the Provincial Council and Provincial Executive. His appointment is for an unlimited tenure. And while the Royal Governor holds ex officio a post of implied significance for art patronage, the important decisions have consistently rested with thc arts councils, i.e., with consulted experts and, essentially, with the artists themselves. Government does not interfere with artistic policies.

Art life in the provinces is aided by the National Council for Regional Culture. This organization is the central body of all regional councils. Eight of the Dutch provinces are directly associated with the Council: North Holland, South Holland, Utrecht, Gelderland, Friesland, Groningen, Drente, and Limburg. Three provinces keep their contact by way of a representative: Overijssel, North Brabant, and Zeeland. The councils founded in the eleven Dutch provinces are financed by the provincial governments.

The overall purpose of the National Council, as its name implies, is to preserve and stimulate regional culture. The National Council is the master organization which coordinates the specific efforts of the provinces and promotes annual regional conventions and festivals. In the field of music, the individual regional councils support choral festivals, competitions for wind and brass bands, amateur organizations of all kinds. Obviously, the preservation of folklore and folk tradition is important within the regional program.

III. Municipal Patronage, The Hague

The city of The Hague, the royal residence, is an impressive example of municipal art patronage in The Netherlands. The total scope of cultural subsidies from the city purse and their relative benefits show in the following list of the city's supported organizations in all the arts. To appreciate the increase of subsidies over a five-year period, allocations for both 1958 and 1963 are quoted whenever possible.

Three Kinds of Subsidy from the Town Clerk's Office

In the Town Clerk's office a special department of eleven officers administers the municipal art program. Subsidies fall into three divisions: municipal art institutes administered only by the city; municipal art institutes created by the city with representatives of both the municipality and private institutes on the governing board; private art institutes subsidized by the city.

1. Municipal Art Institutes Administered Only by the City

Within the performing arts the Royal Theater is subsidized. Its support equals the estimated deficit of the theater's expenditures. Both its manager and entire staff are employed by the local government. The city also subsidizes the Open-Air Theater Zuyderpark (which is a branch of the Royal Theater) which performs during the summer season.

The Royal Theater

1958	*1963*
F. 294,744 ($82,528)	F. 396,844 ($111,116)

The Municipal Museum, the Bredius Museum, and the Dutch Costume Museum are subsidized by the city of The Hague. All employees are in local government service. The Municipal Museum houses a collection of exotic musical instruments which is unique on the Continent.

The Municipal, Bredius, and Dutch Costume Museums

1958	*1963*
F. 1,512,520 ($423,505)	F. 1,761,533 ($493,229)

2. Municipal Art Institutes Created by the City with Representatives of City and Private Institutes on the Board

In this category belongs support for the visual arts and literature and for the performing arts.

On each of the boards of these various organizations are members of the City Council as well as artists (active in the respective field of interest). The head of the Municipal Art Department serves as secretary-treasurer.

The Jacob Maris Foundation

The Jacob Maris Foundation sponsors painters, sculptors, and graphic artists who are residents of The Hague.

1958	*1963*
F. 7,000 ($1,960)	F. 7,000 ($1,960)

The Johann Wagenaar Foundation

The Johann Wagenaar Foundation is designed to promote music by Dutch composers and to award commissions and prizes.

1958	*1963*
F. 5,000 ($1,400)	F. 10,000 ($2,800)

The Hague's Art Foundation

The Hague's Art Foundation is given permission by the Town Council to have a certain number of performances in the Royal Theater. This foundation sponsors a repertory company under the name of *De Haagsche Comedie*. Until 1953, the city of The Hague and the central government shared the defraying of any deficit on an equal basis. The ratio has now changed: the city has assumed 60 per cent, the state 40 per cent. (Theatrical repertory companies at Amsterdam, Rotterdam, and the provincial theatrical group at Arnhem are likewise state supported.)

1958	*1963*
F. 294,900 ($82,572)	F. 440,100 ($123,228)

The Jan-Campert Foundation

The Jan-Campert Foundation devotes itself to the promotion of Dutch literature.

1958	*1963*
F. 7,500 ($2,100)	F. 7,500 ($2,100)

The Hague's Art Institution for Youth

The Hague's Art Institution for Youth stimulates children's interest in the arts by organizing performances in concert and theater especially designed for school children.

1958	*1963*
F. 30,000 ($8,400)	F. 42,500 ($11,900)

The Dr. H. P. Berlage Foundation

The Dr. H. P. Berlage Foundation aims at the promotion of architecture and architectural interest in the city.

1958	*1963*
F. 100 to start the fund ($28)	F. 4,000 ($1,120)

3. Private Art Institutes Supported by the City

The Hague Philharmonic Orchestra

	1958	*1963*
Subsidy Guarantee for Salaries	F. 360,600 ($100,968)	F. 453,360 ($126,940)
Special Subsidy (to be refunded from revenues)	F. 218,500 ($ 61,180)	F. 248,682 ($ 69,630)
Subsidy Toward the Pension Fund	F. 80,335 ($ 22,493)	F. 150,618 ($ 42,173)
Total	F. 659,435 ($184,641)	F. 852,660 ($238,703)

Besides its support from the municipality, The Hague Philharmonic is also state-endowed. The national government pays the same amount as the city.

In addition, the municipality grants subsidies of F. 75,460 in behalf of a former pension fund for the retired members, for widows and orphans, and for retired members of the society, the Residence Orchestra.*

Other state-endowed municipal orchestras are the Amsterdam Concertgebouw Orchestra, the Rotterdam Philharmonic, the North Holland Philharmonic, the Utrecht Municipal Orchestra, the Guelders Orchestra at Arnhem, the Brabant Orchestra, the Overijssel Philharmonic, the Frisian Orchestra, the Groningen Orchestra, and the Limburg Symphony Orchestra.

The Netherlands Opera

The principal lyrical theater of Holland has its seat in Amsterdam, but The Hague shares in its support on the condition that the Opera give a minimum of twenty-five performances in The Hague. Additional subsidies are given by other municipalities, such as Amsterdam, Rotterdam, Utrecht, where the Opera performs, and by the central government in recognition of the theater's contribution to the nation.

1958	*1963*
F. 135,000 ($37,800)	F. 162,500 ($45,500)

The Holland Festival

The Hague contributes to the support of this yearly summer event; headquarters are in The Hague and in Amsterdam. Other cities which participate in the rotating scheme of the Festival also contribute to its subsidy.

*Cf. Page 334 ff. for further details.

The Holland Festival

1958		1963
F. 115,000 ($32,200)	[F. 25,000 ($7,000) is included to insure a number of performances at moderate prices.]	F. 175,000 ($49,000)

The National Ballet

1963
F. 45,000
($12,600)

The Dutch Dance Theater

1963
F. 165,000
($46,200)

Dutch Literary Museum and Document Center

The object of the Museum is to obtain and preserve a central documentary collection on Dutch literature from the middle of the eighteenth century on; only manuscripts of Dutch writers are included.

	1958	*1963*
City	F. 15,000 (plus housing) ($4,200)	F. 44,000 (plus housing) ($12,320)
State	F. 34,600 ($9,688)	F. 75,000 ($21,000)
Provinces	F. 2,000 ($ 560)	F. 2,000 ($ 560)

The Hague's Cultural Center

The act of March 25, 1948, established the Cultural Center to coordinate and to stimulate all local organizations and activities pertaining to arts and sciences.

1958	*1963*
F. 20,000 ($5,600)	discontinued

Netherlands Chamber Orchestra

(This orchestra has its seat in the Hague.)

1958	*1963*
F. 33,995 ($9,518)	F. 45,000 ($12,600)

Society Orange-Nassau Museum

1958	*1963*
F. 8,330 ($2,332)	discontinued

Free Academy for Plastic Arts in The Hague

1958	*1963*
F. 30,000 ($8,400)	F. 46,300 ($12,964)

Academy for Plastic Arts

1958	*1963*
F. 264,427 ($74,039)	(taken over by national government)

Royal Conservatory of Music

1958	*1963*
F. 18,130 ($5,076)	F. 25,773 ($7,216) (now largely subsidized by state)

Dutch Orchestral Society

1958	*1963*
F. 6,500 ($1,820)	discontinued

West Netherlands Symphony Orchestra

1958	*1963*
F. 6,500 ($1,820)	F. 9,200 ($2,576)

Hofwijck Society

1958	*1963*
F. 2,000 ($560)	F. 3,000 ($840)

School for Popular Music

1958	*1963*
F. 25,260 ($7,072)	F. 28,625 ($8,015)

Other Subsidies from The Hague

The Hague pays subsidies to a considerable number of other organizations devoted to the arts.

Fund for the Arts and Science Collection

Commissions are granted to artists, and works of plastic arts are purchased.

1958	*1963*
F. 40,000 ($11,200)	F. 40,000 ($11,200)

Amateur Symphony Orchestra

1958	*1963*
F. 3,500 ($980)	F. 3,500 ($980)

Choral Societies

1958	*1963*
F. 15,000 ($4,200)	F. 28,750 ($8,050)

Wind, Brass, and Accordion Bands

1958	*1963*
F. 18,000 ($5,040)	F. 30,000 ($8,400)

Special Performances of Artistic Value

1958	*1963*
F. 10,000 ($2,800)	F. 12,500 ($3,500)

Miscellaneous Expenses for Cultural Purposes

1958	*1963*
F. 6,000 ($1,680)	F. 7,500 ($2,100)

Summary

The municipality of The Hague voted in 1958 F. 3,676,466 ($1,029,410) for cultural purposes; this sum for art support (not including allocations to general educational projects) amounted to 1.84 per cent of the total annual budget of the city. In 1963 the city of The Hague voted a total of F. 5,633,565 ($1,577,398) for cultural purposes. This represents 2.29 per cent of the entire annual budget of F. 245,479,325 ($68,734,211).

IV. A Land of Concerts

In The Netherlands 11,000,000 people support 11 large orchestras. Each of the provinces subsidizes its own symphony orchestra, full time.

Holland is a country of concerts. Statistics indicate that this nation gives, in proportion to its population and size,* more concerts than most other European countries. In addition to 11 major concert orchestras (aided by government on various levels) are other groups of symphonic scope. The Netherlands Radio employs 2 symphony orchestras and 1 chamber orchestra.

Each of the 11 government-supported orchestras gives a minimum of 100 concerts per season. These events take place in the home cities of the ensembles, as well as in neighboring communities which regularly sponsor their visits. In 1960 the sum total of live performances given by all Dutch orchestras (including chamber ensembles) exceeded 2,100. During the main season, from September to July, no fewer than 100 symphony concerts are scheduled throughout The Netherlands every month. To this must be added the numerous choral and chamber music concerts, Lieder recitals, and the like. In sheer quantity of performances, this makes for an impressive record.

*According to the government estimate of 1960 the population of Holland was 11,702,239; the territory comprises 12,850 square miles.

Modern Holland counts 998 municipalities of various sizes. We have noted the paramount role the citizens of these towns have played as art sponsors throughout the centuries. Individual patronage of prominent burghers developed into collective patronage of communities. Municipal patronage is at the root of Holland's musical life.

Middle-class culture, so characteristic of Holland, naturally expressed itself in various domestic forms of music-making, in singing and instrumental playing of small ensembles, suitable to "house music." The establishment and sponsorship of larger performing groups in Holland's musical life must be credited to civic patronage which blossomed independently of church and court. Clearly, the cultural strength of The Netherlands is to the highest degree rooted in the private initiative of its middle class. Civic pride and unswerving devotion to public duty eventually stimulated governmental aid to cultural projects where self-help proved inadequate.

In its primarily civic ties, the evolution of musical culture in The Netherlands differs from patterns of patronage in other countries. The Dutch orchestras were not anchored at princely courts. Unlike the German orchestras, they did not normally serve as accompaniment for opera. Holland became predominantly a country of concerts; neither the prose theater nor the opera played here the early and decisive roles they assumed in neighboring Germany.

Eleven Concert Orchestras

The Concertgebouw

Around 1880 a group of music-loving citizens in Amsterdam began to raise funds for the construction of a proper concert hall. The dignified Concertgebouw was built on the street now called in honor of Jacob Obrecht, Dutch master of music. The Concertgebouw accommodates about 2,300 people. The inauguration on April 11, 1888, symbolizes the beginning of a cultural renaissance in the other cities of Holland. It was another manifestation of middle-class patronage and of neighboring communities vieing with each other in civic achievement. The Concertgebouw Orchestra (deriving its name from the building that is its home) is of recent origin compared with other great symphonic organizations in Europe. It was founded as a limited liability company. Its activities started out in an extremely informal way, somewhat in the manner of pop concerts: coffee, tea, or beer was served to the audience as the music was played. At times, the concerts were identified as *matinée musicale* or as *soirée musicale.*

On July 29, 1910, the mayor of Amsterdam proposed to the city council the granting of a subsidy of 5,000 florins to the Concertgebouw

Orchestra for the oncoming season. The proposal was accepted without a single dissenting vote. The Dutch capital thus became the first city in the nation to receive a governmental subsidy for its orchestra. The Concertgebouw was managed privately until 1952, when it was recognized as a foundation to be permanently supported by three sources: the national government, the province of Northern Holland, and the municipality of Amsterdam.

For the season 1962-63 the following subsidies were granted to the Concertgebouw:

Government	F. 600,000 ($168,000)
Province of North Holland	F. 50,000 ($ 14,000)
Municipality	F. 1,180,000 ($330,400)
Total	F. 1,830,000 ($512,400)

Salaries for members of symphony orchestras are fixed by the government. For this purpose the various Dutch orchestras are grouped into three different classes. The Concertgebouw belongs to Class I. The members of each orchestra are also divided into groups according to their position (first chairmen, section men, etc.). For each group there are a fixed minimum and maximum salary. The maximum is reached after fourteen years of service. For the Concertgebouw the figures range from F.7,020 ($1,965) to F.13,090 ($3,665). A further source of income for all members of the orchestra is recordings and radio and television engagements. The Concertgebouw limits its public performances to 155 per season. All orchestra members are entitled to a six-week vacation during the months of July and August; they receive their monthly salary during this period and a special vacation allowance of 4 per cent of their yearly salary. All members participate in the pension plan for government employees. They receive a pension at the age of sixty-five. The amount depends on the years of service; after forty years of service they are entitled to 70 per cent of their last earned salary. All orchestra members pay a premium of 6.7 per cent; 14 per cent is paid by the Concertgebouw Foundation.

The Hague Philharmonic

In 1912 the municipality of The Hague followed the procedure set by Amsterdam two years earlier in assisting its resident orchestra. Founded in 1904 by private initiatives, The Hague Philharmonic was to be aided by an annual sum of F.10,000($2,800), thus doubling the initial subsidy of the Amsterdam Concertgebouw. Within fifty years this figure has multiplied sixty-six times to F.659,435 ($184,641).* This large grant for The Hague Philharmonic is noteworthy, particularly in view of the fact that The Hague is only fifty-six kilometers from Amsterdam. But The Hague is proud of its independent art life.

The Rotterdam Philharmonic

The merit of indigenous culture is equally upheld by other Dutch cities. Thus Rotterdam is the home of a fine and enterprising orchestra; yet this seaport city is only about sixteen miles from The Hague. The Rotterdam Philharmonic originated through the self-help of its players. A group of musicians engaged in the entertainment industry sought escape from the drudgery of their jobs in cinemas, cafés, and night clubs by playing for their own recreation orchestral music of serious quality. These informal sessions gained momentum; more musicians wished to join. An art-minded nucleus of the Rotterdam public became interested in these performances. In June, 1918, the players formed the Society of Professional Musicians for the Mutual Cultivation of Art. Concerts were scheduled on Saturday afternoons (to allow the professionals to earn their living at night). Tickets were sold at a nominal fee; the musicians were not concerned about financial gain. Eventually, the Rotterdam authorities realized the value and potential of the Society of Professional Musicians. The municipality decided to endorse the orchestra, which in due time assumed its present title, the Rotterdam Philharmonic. From 1930 on, the orchestra claimed a regular playing strength of 60 and the repertory was enlarged to include significant contemporary music.

In May 1940, the Nazi air attack on Rotterdam destroyed — along with large sections of the city and port — the Philharmonic rehearsal hall, the library, and most of the orchestral instruments. Good fellowship among Dutch artists immediately asserted itself: instruments and other gifts from their colleagues throughout the nation made it possible for the Rotterdam musicians to resume playing.

Today, the Rotterdam Philharmonic has a seasonal minimum assignment of 100 symphony concerts. To this are added engagements in the pit of the Nederlandse Opera as well as the accompaniment of various oratorios and other choral performances.

Utrecht Municipal Orchestra

The origins of organized concert life in Utrecht, ancient imperial residence, are traceable to 1631. In this year the Collegium Musicum Ultrajectinum was founded and sponsored by the University of Utrecht.

*As previously mentioned, the national government likewise contributes to the maintenance of this orchestra; it guarantees 50 per cent of the salaries.

The dual role of Dutch colleges as centers of scientific research and of the performing arts recalls an analogous development in neighboring Germany.

In spite of this early auspicious start, it was not until two centuries later that Utrecht resumed civic initiative in terms of a more extended orchestral life. But the community made up for time lost. It sponsored what was temporarily considered the most progressive orchestra of the nation. The spirit and earnestness of the Utrecht ensemble is assessed by its repertory. French music ranks high, but Schoenberg and Webern, Bartók and Hindemith were introduced to Holland by the Utrecht Municipal Orchestra, and it shares with related Dutch organizations the cult of Bruckner and Mahler. Utrecht continues its orchestral activities into the summer, when this historic city of 250,000 becomes host to an annual music festival.

Limburg Symphony Orchestra

Maastricht is the capital of Limburg, one of the small provinces in the southeast of The Netherlands. The cultural commitment of the city is rooted in history. Maastricht is the seat of the oldest church in Holland, St. Servatius. Today, an industrial frontier town with a population of 86,000, Maastricht is a mere hour's ride from Liège, ancient Belgian music center, and also close to the German city of Aachen with its long-established art life. The Dutch government is concerned that the cultural level of Maastricht should not be permitted to remain below the standards set by these neighboring Belgian and German communities.

Maastricht originally undertook the support of its orchestra from municipal resources alone. The development, so typical of Dutch orchestras, began in 1863 when a municipal conservatory was founded. Some of the instructors became the first-desk-men of the orchestra. Having achieved sufficient technical ability, the most promising young students eventually joined their teachers in the sections. With an orchestral nucleus established, the road to sufficient support was uphill, none the less. The period following the Armistice of 1945 witnessed many concerts given by the Maastricht Orchestra in various Limburg communities. The response to these tours was encouraging, and demands for guest appearances increased. At this point the provincial government of Limburg adopted the Maastricht players. In the change of name in 1955 from Maastricht Municipal Orchestra to Limburg Symphony, the adjustment in the type of support is reflected. Most of the smaller towns benefiting from the orchestra's tours now share the cost of its maintenance. During a typical season (1960) 70 concerts were given outside and 35 inside Maastricht. Some of the events scheduled outside the capital aim at the musical education of the Limburg coal mining districts. These concerts for workers and their families are an unqualified success; new audiences are conquered for good art.

Haarlem, Groningen, Arnhem

The city of Haarlem has long taken as much pride in its organ performances as in the cultivation of its tulips and hyacinths. In 1579 the principal organist of Haarlem was employed as a civil servant. Simultaneously, the city assumed the responsibility for the care of the historic organ in the Church of St. Bavo.

The transfer of public interest from organ recitals to symphony concerts was a natural though slow process. Eventually, Haarlem emerged as the seat of a fine symphonic orchestra, known as the North Holland Philharmonic. (Haarlem is the capital of the province by this name.) Both the city and the province support the orchestra. The final solution of its costly subsidy was sought and found by transforming the municipal ensemble into a provincial one. In addition to the combined subsidies obtained from these main sources, a considerable number of smaller towns in the province of North Holland (where the orchestra performs) assume a share of the cost of the concerts.

The growth of the Haarlem orchestra reveals patterns similar to those of the Arnhem and Groningen orchestras. In all three cities the first step was the conversion of a band into a symphonic ensemble. Much of the initial aid came from private sponsors. In each case, the municipality lent a helping hand as soon as the proficiency of the musicians and the interest of the public reached a promising level. In a final step the provincial government sponsored the orchestra in return for concerts given in various cities of the state.

The university city of Groningen vies with Utrecht in claiming to be the home of the oldest symphony orchestra in Holland. In their later development both are typical products of Dutch middle-class society.

The beginnings of the Groningen Orchestra are traceable to the unpretentious society, *De Harmonie.* In a building acquired by some of the society's affluent members the band of the home guard gave concerts on Sunday evenings. Some private donors contributed money for the training of young musicians who would eventually become competent performers of classical music. In 1861 the society was ready to announce the debut of its own professional orchestra of 24 players. In return for the private financial support, the orchestra was pledged to perform at certain social events sponsored by De Harmonie.

The next crucial development coincided also in Groningen with the national postwar rehabilitation. The government had to step in to assure sufficient financial support on an annual basis. As a result of such regular support the orchestra could extend beyond the provincial capital.

The Orchestral Society of Arnhem, capital of Gelderland, was founded in 1889. A considerable number of nearby Rhenish cities in West Germany were flourishing art centers. Arnhem was determined to reach for a similar level; the city succeeded in shortening the various transitional phases of orchestral growth. In 1949, the status of the municipal Arnhem Orchestra changed into that of the Gelderland Orchestra, so-called after the name of the sponsoring state. In 1960 the orchestra played 125 concerts in Arnhem and in the various towns of Gelderland.

Brabant, Overijssel, Friesland

Holland is vitally concerned with sponsoring art in urban areas as well as in the vast farm lands and industrial regions. As a result, all eleven provincial governments of The Netherlands assume ever-increasing shares in the subsidy of art organizations. A manifestation of recent enterprise of provincial patronage is the support of three new orchestras, all founded within three years. These young symphonic organizations are the Brabant Orchestra (1950), the Overijssel Orchestra (1951), and the Frisian Orchestra (1952). Located in the largest cities of their respective states, the orchestras receive official and permanent subsidies. The methods of support are almost identical; the assignments are analogous for all three. Dutch middle-class culture has created a wide field of artistic receptivity even in the many smaller towns of these three provinces.

From its inception in 1950 the sponsors of the Brabant Orchestra planned to use the city of Hertogenbosch, capital of North Brabant, as the pivotal place of service to the province. This orchestra skipped the otherwise typical development from band and amateur status to a symphonic professional level. It never depended exclusively on municipal subsidy. The Brabant Orchestra is regularly invited for guest appearances in other Dutch provinces. A system of exchange visits has been inaugurated by which the orchestras of Rotterdam or Maastricht come to Hertogenbosch whenever the Brabant Orchestra appears in these cities. The Brabant musicians play even at Amsterdam's Concertgebouw and are invited to give concerts beyond the national Dutch border, performing in such cities as Antwerp. All of this amounts to healthy artistic competition, insuring mutual standards, challenging the pride of the orchestra members and of their patrons at home.

The Brabant Orchestra is subsidized by the national and provincial authorities, who underwrite the anticipated deficit. In addition, the towns covered by the tours guarantee an annual minimum support.

The contribution of each city is proportionate to the size of the population. The number of municipalities presently contributing to the orchestra surpasses 100. Finally, a number of large industries, based in North Brabant, share the financial encouragement of the orchestra. The combined subsidies make it possible to engage on a year-round contract 72 musicians who play close to 200 concerts annually. Four cities of the province of North Brabant are the prime patrons: Hertogenbosch, Breda, Eindhoven, and Tilburg (a city which has recently built a modern theater).

The province of Overijssel, in the southeast of Holland, is not a region of large-scale industries, but of smaller manufacturing centers and low-lying pastures, abounding with the dairy products of the country. The problem of providing a population of workers and farmers with good music is being solved here in an exemplary fashion.

The middle-class population of the towns of Overijssel was the first target of the cultural program. In the beginning, concerts were offered in Enschede (population 90,000), the largest city in Overijssel. The orchestra had started unpretentiously as an amateur group. Following the Armistice the Twents Philharmonic Orchestra was formed. The county of Twente, in the southeast part of the province of Overijssel, financed the efforts of the players. The concerts were so well-liked that other regions of Overijssel requested guest appearance of the Twents Philharmonic and underwrote its expense. In 1951 the provincial government of Overijssel guaranteed the maintenance of the orchestra. Accordingly, the Twents Philharmonic assumed the title Overijssel Philharmonic as its newly won status symbol. During the last decade, only professional instrumentalists fill the chairs of this orchestra. Sixty musicians are employed on an annual basis. Since 1955 the Overijssel Philharmonic also serves as the permanent orchestra of the Forum Opera Company in Enschede. Here, then, is systematic growth of an orchestra in what was long considered the cultural hinterland of a nation: a small county group of amateurs climbed with determination up the steps of a ladder to professional achievement, and reached the level where the granting of governmental support is artistically justified.

Leeuwarden is the home city of the Frisian Orchestra. The provincial capital of Friesland is the seat of fine craftsmanship in gold and silver, and a trading center for cattle. For many years the citizens subscribed to a small number of concerts in Leeuwarden, but the limited support did not permit expansion.

In 1952 the orchestra's patrons decided on a campaign throughout their province. They were not disappointed; adequate state subsidy resulted from their appeal. Again, we note the intent and independence of the effort. Leeuwarden is only 40 miles from Groningen, the seat of one of the oldest orchestras of the nation. But the Dutch are determined to spin their orchestral networks all over the country, aiming at a density of music centers to compare with Germany's. Today, the national government, the provincial Frisian authority, and no less than 44 municipalities are pledged to aid the orchestra on a regular annual basis.

Details of the subsidization are worthy of study. Twenty-five larger cities made provision to aid the Frisian Orchestra with twelve cents annually per inhabitant. Seventeen smaller municipalities contribute from 4 to 10 cents per inhabitant. Leeuwarden (population 80,000) offers 35 cents per inhabitant. The sum total of these contributions results in the permanent maintenance of an orchestra of 50.

Chamber Orchestra

Dutch orchestral patronage not only pertains to large-scale symphonic ensembles. The chamber orchestra, too, receives its share of official support appropriate to the importance of great music created for this medium since the Baroque era. Holland maintains several such ensembles. Outstanding among them is The Netherlands Chamber Orchestra, founded in 1955. A group of twenty string players, experienced in chamber music, formed the ensemble to give a number of performances during the Holland Festival. But The Netherlands Chamber Orchestra (augmented with wind or percussion players for the execution of certain works) now performs throughout the country as well as abroad. The government covers the deficit. In 1962 the state subsidy was F.220,500 ($61,740). The Hague paid F.45,000 ($12,600).

In 1959 the section Music and Dance of the national Ministry of Education, Arts, and Sciences allocated the eleven symphonies and The Netherlands Chamber Orchestra a total of F. 3,027,000 ($847,560).

Tomorrow's Audience

The curricula of Holland's secondary schools devote much time to music. This penetration of music education into Holland's elementary and high schools is of recent date. Public schools have organized a special music curriculum and they maintain their own choirs and orchestras. A great deal of music is specifically written for performances by young people in the schools.

The Netherlands Student Orchestra, founded in 1952, recruits its players from the 11 Dutch universities and technological institutes. The first of this kind in Europe, the orchestra adopted a policy of commissioning established composers to write scores, conceived with the particular abilities of the young performers in mind. But such works are not intended as light fare; most of them call for intense rehearsing. The policy has proven an unquestioned success. Discussions among the composers, conductors, and players contribute to the growing interest in the technical and aesthetic aspects of music making.

One of the principal methods in the support of the performing arts is the systematic encouragement of what the Dutch refer to as "healthy amateurism." This implies a nation-wide governmental program helping organizations of nonprofessionals who are engaged in serious music. Again, special emphasis is on the young. Youth orchestras have been formed not only in large cities (such as Amsterdam, The Hague, or Rotterdam) with their long-established conservatories, but also in many smaller provincial towns (such as Leeuwarden and Zeist). From all individual youth groups in the 11 provinces of The Netherlands a competent team has been chosen for the National Youth Orchestra. In 1957 it gave its first widely-hailed concert in Arnhem.

V. Opera and Ballet

Belated Opera

The early evolution of opera, as we have shown, is allied with numerous music-loving courts and their art-sponsoring sovereigns in such countries as Italy, Austria, Germany, and France. The lack of comparable opportunities delayed opera in Holland until the early part of the nineteenth century.

The first Dutch homestead of opera was Théâtre Français in The Hague. Since 1830, the crucial year of the Belgian uprising, the Théâtre Français in The Hague began to offer what was then standard repertory in Paris and in Brussels, with emphasis on the operas of Auber, Grétry, and some Italian composers, sung in French. The next generation continued the private sponsorship of the lyrical theater with the establishment of the Hoogduitse Opera in Rotterdam (1860). A privately managed enterprise, like the Théâtre Français in The Hague, the Rotterdam Opera courageously played the new works of Wagner before many music centers of Europe had attempted these difficult productions.

Between the years 1886 and 1894 Amsterdam supported the so-called Hollandse Opera. This marked an important step forward. The management believed that the production of music drama in the native Dutch language would stimulate sufficient interest in the French, German, and Italian operatic masterworks. About the same time, in the late nineteenth century, original Dutch opera came to the fore. The initial works were not of enduring quality, but the combined efforts paved the way toward the foundation of a national Dutch opera. This was a slow road, without either court or public support. The few enterprising companies struggled valiantly, only to find that opera will never pay its way and that someone has to underwrite the ever-mounting deficits. While Dutch audiences gradually learned to appreciate the serious musical theater, the climate had not yet warmed up for governmental subsidy. The alternative solution (if opera was to continue under the prevailing system of private management) was to save on artists' fees, on rehearsals, and on all other production costs. These savings were tantamount to inferior performances.

Nederlandse Opera

The year the Dutch government changed its attitude and gave financial aid to opera is significant. In 1945, following the liberation, a new upsurge of national culture benefited the cause of music drama. The government decided, jointly with the municipalities of Amsterdam and The Hague, on the financial support of a national opera company. Amsterdam, the national capital, was to be the basis of the new theater, known as the *Nederlandse Opera.* Following its opening with Puccini's *La Bohème* in 1946, the management prudently integrated into the standard repertory a considerable number of contemporary works, including scores by Britten, de Falla, Janáček, Milhaud, and Stravinsky. Between 1950 and 1958 two operas by Dutch composers were given their premiéres: *Philomela* by Hendrik Andriessen and *François Villon* by Sam Dresden. (The latter production was simultaneously offered as part of the Holland Festival of 1958.)

The headquarters of the Nederlandse Opera is the Stadsschouwburg of Amsterdam (Amsterdam City Theater). In 1960 the ensemble consisted of 30 singers, all engaged with annual contracts. The ballet has 20 members, the chorus 45, and the orchestra 70. The Nederlandse Opera performs not only in Amsterdam, but in various other key cities of the nation. During the season 1960-61, 22 different operas (offered either as matinées or in the evening) showed the following distribution according to cities: Amsterdam 130; The Hague 30; Rotterdam 20; Utrecht 10. To these figures must be added a few performances in smaller Dutch towns.

The Nederlandse Opera regularly appears at the annual Holland Festival,* sometimes with visiting artists in the vocal parts and with guest conductors or producers. An unconventional attitude was shown in the works chosen for the first recording of the Nederlandse Opera: Janáček's poignant music drama, *From the House of the Dead*, based on Dostoyevsky's novel.

*Cf. page 345

Two Young Opera Companies

The impulse for music drama in Holland, once ignited, is gaining momentum. In 1955 an enterprising young group founded the Forum, an opera company designed to fill the geographic gap in the north and east of the country not reached by the Nederlandse Opera. The Forum was originally anchored in Utrecht. From this old music center the Forum tours hitherto neglected territory, offering the kind of productions that can be mounted even on makeshift stages. Today, the Forum bases its operation in the city of Enschede, in the nerve center of the cotton, mining, and weaving industries near the Westphalian border. Enschede is the most practical starting point for touring these crucial workers' districts.

Holland supports a third regular company concentrating on music drama, the Zuid-Nederlandse Opera with headquarters in Maastricht. The company was founded in 1953. It tours primarily the southern towns of the country. In keeping with Dutch policy aiming at indigenous art life, the ensemble of the opera is made up of young singers and instrumentalists mostly recruited in the southern provinces. The Limburg Symphony Orchestra serves in the pit for the accompaniment of the performances. During the warm season the Zuid-Nederlandse Opera moves into open-air theaters in such towns as Bussum and Valkenburg. From the viewpoint of attendance, the venture is considered a great success, both in Maastricht and throughout the various towns of Limburg.

Concluding our glimpses of Holland's opera life, we note that within a time of less than 8 years — between 1946 and 1953 — 3 companies of different scope and size but with identical cultural purpose have been founded and continue their activities with promising success. The brief interval has proved sufficient to arouse more than satisfactory public participation. Holland was long regarded as hopelessly indifferent to opera. Today, the country is the scene of several well-functioning musical theaters.

In 1959 the Ministry of Education, Arts, and Sciences supported these 3 opera companies with F. 1,288,000 ($360,640).

Ballet

Along with opera, The Netherlands supports a number of ballet companies. The National Ballet (the former Dutch Ballet) has its seat in Amsterdam, and its main purpose is the training and upkeep of an indigenous Dutch dance group maintaining high standards. It also administers a ballet academy which is independent of the Royal Conservatory. The National Ballet receives subsidies from the following sources:

National Government	F. 718,500 ($201,180)
City of Amsterdam	F. 403,000 ($112,840)
City of The Hague	F. 45,000 ($ 12,600)

The Dutch Dance Theater, which has its seat in The Hague, was founded in 1959 by a group of solo dancers originally associated with the Dutch Ballet. Subsidies are as follows:

National Government	F. 40,000 ($11,200)
City of Amsterdam	F. 40,000 ($11,200)
City of The Hague	F. 165,000 ($46,200)

VI. Diversified Patronage

The Holland Festival

The Netherlands annually holds a series of festivals. The Holland Festival, normally scheduled from June 15 to July 15, is the only European festival not confined to one locality: it has three centers — Amsterdam, The Hague, and Scheveningen (the seaside resort near The Hague). And performances are regularly scheduled in such cities as Rotterdam, Utrecht, Delft, Haarlem, Arnhem, Leyden, and Hilversum (the seat of Holland's principal radio network).

The Holland Festival proves how an enterprise may grow in a few years from modest regional beginnings to a project commanding international attention. In 1947, the "Society Sea-Bath," at Scheveningen, organized a summer festival with programs scheduled also in Amsterdam and The Hague. For the next summer, events were coordinated under a newly created organization which became the first Holland Festival. Its program now offers significant drama, opera, and ballet. These include performances given by such Dutch music organizations as the Concertgebouw, The Hague Philharmonic, The Netherlands Opera, The Netherlands Bach Society, The Netherlands Chamber Orchestra, The Netherlands National Ballet — and there are dramatic performances by The Netherlands Comedie and The Netherlands Drama Company.

The Festival achieves an international aspect through the guest performances of some of Europe's most noted organizations in the field of the performing arts. The list of visiting companies at the fifteenth Festival (1962) included the Old Vic Theatre (London), The Royal Shakespeare Theatre (Stratford-on-Avon), Piraikon Theatron (Athens), Burgtheater (Vienna). In earlier seasons the state operas from Vienna and Munich appeared. In the field of choreography, the Ballet du XXè Siècle and the American Ballet Company participated.

Administration and Subventions of the Holland Festival

The Holland Festival is administered by a foundation governed by a small board of 6 members. Their chairman is the director of the art department in the Ministry of Education, Arts, and Sciences. Again the typical Continental alliance of an art project with education is evident. The procedure of programming is as follows: the secretary of the Festival submits his plans to the board, and the board members (who are not professional artists, but men of broad culture and knowledge) make the final decisions. The record shows their overall attitude is progressive.

The Festival is supported by several sources: the national government, the cities of Amsterdam, Rotterdam, Utrecht, and The Hague, and private donors. Contributions are obtained from certain industrialists who pledge to aid the Festival in case of a deficit. But in general, the estimated budget is carefully observed. In 1962 The Hague contributed F. 175,000 ($49,000); Amsterdam, the same amount; the state, F. 190,000 ($53,200); and the municipalities of Rotterdam and Utrecht, smaller amounts.

On certain occasions expenditures have been shared by the Holland Festival and the invited organizations. The performances of Richard Strauss' *Ariadne auf Naxos*, given by the Düsseldorf Opera, were jointly underwritten by the West German government and the Holland Festival. Productions of such demanding works as Schoenberg's opera *Aron und Moses*, Hindemith's *Cardillac*, or Berlioz' *Benvenuto Cellini* were, from a financial point of view, calculated risks. These events compensated in cultural prestige for monetary losses. It is hoped that the subvention of the Festival will be further increased in the near future, particularly to make the continuation of a moderate price policy possible. At present, tickets range from 5 to 7 florins, but good seats would have to cost at least 15 florins, if no subsidy were forthcoming. Tickets for the Holland Festival are inexpensive, however, in comparison with those of Salzburg, Bayreuth, or Munich.

Donemus: Semiprivate Foundation

Dutch art patronage occasionally relies upon a combination of private patronage with public support. An interesting example of an organization originally based on private initiative, but today receiving official subsidy, is the foundation Donemus in Amsterdam. The Latin formula, from which the name is cleverly derived, means: *Do*cumentation in The *Ne*therlands for *Mus*ic. The original purpose of Donemus was to provide performers, in and outside of Holland, with scores and records of contemporary Dutch music, and with documentation in every conceivable form. A small country, Holland has a very limited home market. The printing of new Dutch music involves high financial risk which publishers can rarely afford to take. The task clearly calls for subsidies in the framework of a nonprofit organization.

Donemus is a direct consequence of the devastation caused by World War II. When the Nazis destroyed Rotterdam most of the manuscripts of Willem Pijper (1894-1947), the noted Dutch composer, were burned with his house and the rest of his belongings. Some of Pijper's friends and admirers, in an effort to avoid similar losses, began to make microfilms of whatever was left of his unpublished music and of any new works that he wrote after the catastrophe. This led to an obvious next step: to make microfilm copies of music by other living Dutch composers. Thus it was from a general plan of preserving contemporary Dutch art that Donemus originated. It performs its multiple self-assignments free of charge. Today, this foundation fills a vastly enlarged peacetime function: it is intended to bridge the road from the completed score to its performance, and eventually to the publication of the music.

In addition to printing the manuscripts of promising Dutch composers, Donemus also furnishes documentation and analytical material on the scores. The procedure is usually as follows: first, the composer's manuscript is reproduced in microfilm. From the film a limited number of pocket scores are manufactured by one of the various duplicating techniques. The scores are advertised in a systematic, dignified manner. The chief source of information is the magazine *Sonorum Speculum*, which the foundation regularly publishes. Through these combined ways the composer's work reaches the attention of interpreters, scholars, critics, and the public at large.

Doneto: Propaganda for Dutch Plays

An organization related in purpose to Donemus, but geared to the sponsorship of drama in The Netherlands, was established in 1950. The name of the foundation Doneto means Documentation in The Netherlands for Drama. It was the Foundation for the Utilization and Protection of Copyright (SEBA) that originally suggested Doneto and undertook its support. The scope of drama is interpreted in a wide sense; music dramatic works are included in the propaganda.

Doneto currently publishes a catalogue offering information about the present state of Dutch drama, thus serving as a clearinghouse for various dramatic organizations. What is written by Dutch authors, even of young unknown talent, may in this way reach those who can produce it on the stage.

VII. Governmental Support of Dutch Theater

The scope and nature of Dutch theater are relatively unknown abroad. The indigenous theater of The Netherlands does not have the advantage of a language universally known. It still lacks significant translations. As a result the original Dutch repertory is not familiar in other countries.

In The Netherlands, however, the present state of theater life is prosperous. The Dutch theater follows the Continental pattern of engaging a regular ensemble for one or several seasons. Actors, producers, and the technical staff thus work as a team in association that is not limited by the run of an individual play.

The Dutch theater enjoys governmental subsidy on three levels according to changing local circumstances.

The following professional theater companies are subsidized by the government: (1) De Nederlandse Comedie, Amsterdam; (2) De Haagsche Comedie, The Hague; (3) Rotterdams Toneel, Rotterdam; (4) Toneelgroep Theater, Arnhem; (5) Het Zuidelijk Toneel "Ensemble," Eindhoven (Amsterdam); (6) Toneelgroep Centrum, Amsterdam; (7) Stichting Nieuw Jeugdtoneel, The Hague, and its subsidiaries (Toneelgroep "Arena" and De Nieuwe Komedie); (8) Toneelgroep Studio, Amsterdam.

The first 3 are local companies, but they are required to give a number of performances in towns other than their own.

The Toneelgroep Theater and Het Zuidelijk Toneel "Ensemble" are regional companies. The former serves the east and the latter serves the south. And both companies perform outside their respective areas.

Toneelgroep Centrum and Toneelgroep Studio are touring companies that give performances all over the country, even in the smaller towns, and in towns with very modest facilities for theatrical productions.

Toneelgroep "Arena" performs for children and elementary schools throughout the country. De Nieuwe Komedie plays to children in preparatory and secondary schools and to adult audiences in the provinces.

All of these activities are subsidized according to a total budget approved in advance by the government, which guarantees that the operating deficits will be met. The first 5 listed receive 40 per cent of the operating deficit from the national government and 60 per cent from the town or region in which they are established.

The last 3 companies are subsidized largely by the national government, but not on a percentage basis. In addition, various provincial and municipal authorities subsidize the theater either by making a direct grant to a company or by participating in a national organization called the *Stichting Toneelfonds*, which divides all contributions received among the companies according to certain criteria. The Nederlandse Televisie

Stichting also helps the theater companies, indirectly, to meet their costs, since it regularly engages their actors to play in television productions.

Table III and Table IV survey the most important aspects in the operation of the Dutch theater. Table III lists the total subsidies allocated to theater companies throughout the nation for the season 1961-62. Table IV indicates the number of performances given by the theater companies in the eleven provinces of The Netherlands during the three successive seasons from 1958 to 1961.

TABLE III

Total Subsidies to Dutch Theater Companies for the Season 1961-62.

Company	*Government*	*Local or Regional*	*Provincial and Municipal*	*Theater Fund*	*Total*
Nederlandse Comedie	F. 308,000 ($86,240)	F. 463,200 ($129,696)		F. 29,460 ($8,248)	F. 800,660 ($298,417)
Haagsche Comedie	F. 273,400 ($76,552)	F. 410,100 ($114,828)	F. 4,200 ($1,176)	F. 17,950 ($ 5,026)	F. 705,650 ($197,582)
Rotterdams Toneel	F. 276,400 ($77,392)	F. 414,600 ($116,088)		F. 21,130 ($ 5,916)	F. 712,130 ($199,396)
Toneelgroep Theater	F. 262,800 ($73,584)	F. 394,200 ($110,376)		F. 19,470 ($ 5,451)	F. 676,470 ($189,411)
H.Z.T. "Ensemble"	F. 140,000 ($39,200)	F. 210,000 ($ 58,800)		F. 14,730 ($ 4,124)	F. 364,730 ($102,124)
Toneelgroep Centrum	F. 313,600 ($87,808)		F. 67,000 ($18,760)	F. 7,410 ($ 2,074)	F. 388,010 ($108,642)
Toneelgroep "Arena" Nwe. Komedie	F. 289,400 ($81,032)		F. 62,500 ($17,500)	F. 8,010 ($ 2,242)	F. 359,910 ($100,774)
Toneelgroep Studio	F. 213,000 ($59,640)		F. 21,000 ($ 5,880)	F. 1,840 ($ 515)	F. 235,840 ($ 66,035)

The Het Zuidelijk Toneel "Ensemble" also acts as a television drama group and receives on that account a contribution of F. 125,000 ($35,000) from the Nederlandse Televisie Stichting. The N. T. S. has also placed a sum of F.100,000 ($28,000) at the disposal of The Netherlands theaters in general.

In the subsidies of theaters the government makes sure that the distribution of allocations is fair. Thus the division of Holland into two major religious groups, Catholic and Protestant, is carefully observed. For instance, the provinces of North Brabant and Limburg are predominantly Catholic. Aid to their theaters is balanced by equal support in Protestant regions.

The first new theater which Holland inaugurated after World War II is in Tilburg. This rising industrial center in the south of Holland now has reached a population exceeding 100,000. The seat of Tilburg's theater is in the municipal Schouwburg, a modern glass palace with a

TABLE IV

Number of Performances by Companies in Various Provinces (1958/1959, 1959/1960, 1960/1961)

	Nederlandse Comedie			Haagsche Comedie			Rotterdams Toneel			Toneelgroep Theater			H.Z.T. "Ensemble"			Toneelgroep Centrum			"Arena/" Nwe. Komedie			Toneelgroep Studio		
	1958/ 1959	1959/ 1960	1960/ 1961	1958/ 1959	1959/ 1960	1960/ 1961	1958/ 1959	1959/ 1960	1960/ 1961	1958/ 1959	1959/ 1960	1960/ 1961	1958/ 1959	1959/ 1960	1960/ 1961	1958/ 1959	1959/ 1960	1960/ 1961	1958/ 1959	1959/ 1960	1960/ 1961	1958/ 1959	1959/ 1960	1960/ 1961
Groningen	13	14	14	12	10	9	14	16	16	24	23	22	20	13	16	18	12	14	14	3	6	13	11	11
Friesland	3	3	3	2	2	2	3	3	3	5	5	4	10	6	7	19	14	14	2	—	8	11	11	12
Drente	1	2	—	—	—	—	3	1	2	7	8	6	8	5	5	12	14	8	31	17	19	7	7	33
Overijssel	23	29	22	13	12	12	17	14	13	55	56	50	17	18	23	30	19	16	23	28	37	17	24	27
Gelderland	39	37	36	22	19	14	28	23	27	79	74	64	15	7	13	24	15	14	11	22	13	23	30	27
Utrecht	47	47	43	30	29	25	42	32	38	52	53	45	11	25	21	22	11	19	19	32	17	7	11	15
North Holland	294	298	274	78	71	69	80	110	122	133	112	117	77	77	158	152	144	135	116	151	122	43	46	78
South Holland	108	104	98	273	270	265	239	215	190	60	57	64	8	4	17	24	22	23	152	112	128	9	12	24
Zeeland	2	2	—	3	2	2	6	5	6	3	3	3	9	6	7	30	8	18	2	26	20	17	12	7
North Brabant	29	28	24	21	20	22	23	22	27	27	21	31	53	43	66	39	38	33	16	28	47	26	50	38
Limburg	6	12	6	6	9	9	9	8	8	7	14	12	9	6	16	14	27	15	12	11	13	2	8	19
Total	565	576	520	460	444	429	464	449	452	452	426	418	237	210	349	384	324	309	398	430	430	175	222	291
At home	216	217	201	226	223	230	168	141	138	48	44	38	21	16	16	87	109	98	38	28	41	21	29	54

beautifully decorated interior. Other towns of the size and importance of Tilburg are likewise earmarked for new playhouses. At present, the theaters with the best facilities are in the following cities: Groningen, Leeuwarden, Emmen, Deventer, Enschede, Arnhem, Baarn, Utrecht, Amsterdam (City Theater), Haarlem, Hilversum, Velsen, Dordrecht, The Hague, Rotterdam (2), Vlaardingen, Breda, Bois-le-Duc, Roosendaal, Maastricht, Sittard, Heerlen, Oss, Gorkum.[6]

VIII. Radio and Television
Five Broadcasting Companies

Regular radio broadcasts began in The Netherlands shortly after the Armistice of World War I. By 1923 various groups of listeners had established a number of independent broadcasting companies. They were organized in accordance with the religious affiliation and political orientation of their members. Thus 5 groups originated, which are identified as follows: A.V.R.O. (Neutral); K.R.O. (Catholic); N.C.R.V. (Protestant); V.A.R.A. (Socialist); V.P.R.O. (Liberal Protestant).

In 1947 a permanent cooperative group was formed — The Netherlands Radio Union (N.R.U.). It began its activities on March 1 from its studios in Hilversum, near Amsterdam. The teamwork was designed to coordinate the activities of the 5 groups and to facilitate the common use of studios and all technical equipment, libraries, etc. The N.R.U. also served as a clearinghouse of all national Dutch programs, and allocated available air time (over the two Hilversum transmitters) on the basis of fairness and political equality.

On February 6, 1959, the Broadcasting Act was introduced to Parliament; its second chamber, directly elected by the people, represents the authoritative body deciding also the issues relevant to the mass media. The government appoints a commissioner for broadcasting who, in turn, reports to the Dutch Ministry of Education, Arts, and Sciences. A commission has authority over the programs; he is regularly invited to the meetings of the N.R.U. A board of trustees, called the *Radio Council*, works closely with the Minister of Education. At present, the board has 15 members. They are appointed by the Crown and serve for four years. The commissioner has the right to veto questionable programs or individual personnel engaged by the radio. The technical apparatus of the Dutch radio, however, remains outside the commissioner's administration and is under the supervision of the national post office.

Television Act of 1956

The Netherlands began experimenting with television in 1935. In 1951 after the interruption due to the Nazi occupation and war, private industry in collaboration with the Dutch radio companies established a television studio in Bussum. The Netherlands Television Foundation (Nederlandse Televisie Stichting) was organized in 1951. It corresponds in organization and legal status to the N.R.U.

The royal decree of December 24, 1955, prepared the way for the Television Act of 1956. In essence, it entitles the existing broadcasting companies to extend the scope of their activities into telecasting. Both the radio and television programs of Holland are 40 per cent communal and 60 per cent national in origin and scope.

The main source of income for both the radio and television networks is license fees, which the post office collects. The Dutch pay 12 florins annually for each radio set. Television costs 30 florins annually per set. In 1960 there were 2,538,717 radios and 465,504 television licenses on record. From this income, 40 per cent is deducted for various purposes: by the post office, chiefly as remuneration for expenses in collecting the fees and as compensation for services rendered by organizations such as The Netherlands Radio Transmitting Company (Nozema), Government Information Service (R.V.D.), Interreligious Council for Radio Matters (I.K.O.R.), Popular Radio University (R.V.U.), and Radio Nederlandse.

The balance of the total collected listening fees, 60 per cent, belongs to the N.R.U. and to the 5 broadcasting companies previously listed. The board supervising Dutch television consists of representatives of the 5 companies. The interest of the government is watched by the official Delegate for Television.

We have previously referred to the support which the Dutch radio and television give to music and theater.

The degree of public participation in the fate of the mass media was indicated by the fact that the proposal to introduce commercial television was a widely debated issue during the election campaign of 1963. The project of a second Dutch network on a commercial basis was launched by a syndicate of financiers and businessmen, and backed by part of the press. A rare coalition of Catholic and Protestant groups, with added support from the political left, defeated the crucial part of the plan. A second network was ratified, but like the first it will be operated on a noncommercial basis.

IX. Role of Regionalism

The background and structure of radio and television in Holland illustrate how carefully the Dutch gear these mass media to the individual needs and specific interests of the population. Nowhere in Europe is the national diffusion of performances in any given medium so closely associated with group spirit. But we understand the reasons for such cautious procedure. We have characterized the growth of culture on Dutch soil as an essential achievement of the middle class, rather than of church and court. The transmutation of individual and private art patronage into governmental channels was slow in Holland — slower than elsewhere on the Continent. Today individual initiative gives way to all kinds of group sponsorship through societies, foundations, semi-governmental bodies, art-sponsoring industrial and business organizations.

To this day, marked particularism and regionalism are entrenched throughout the eleven provinces of the nation, for each of these is the successor to an old state and each maintains its own culture and traditions. Different idioms or dialects are spoken in the different regions. How stubbornly the Dutch adhere to their inherent regionalism can be illustrated by countless examples from their daily lives and their manner of speaking. Some people in Friesland say, when planning a visit to Amsterdam: "We are going to Holland." When a girl from the provinces marries an Amsterdammer, she is apt to announce: "I am going to marry a Dutchman!" Obviously, particularism and regionalism assume varying degrees in the different provinces. But the government remains conscious of the great importance the Dutch burghers attach to their individual traditions. And in all aspects of official art patronage in Holland, individuality of specifically regional thinking and feeling is respected.

But there is another side to this picture. The common fate and suffering of The Netherlands in two world wars have united the Dutch in times of peace. In contrast to neighboring Belgium, there was no collaboration of the Dutch royal family with the invading enemy. There was no division within, no fifth column. The Dutch people of all classes magnificently stood up to the grave test. And this has promoted a new kind of unity which is bound to express itself, if not today, in the near future. Progressive Dutchmen predict that their new unity will promote more unified patterns of art support.

BELGIUM

I. Toward Independence

Art life in Belgium since the emergence of this country as an autonomous kingdom concerns us in this section of the book. We have called attention to the long, intense interrelationship of Belgium and The Netherlands. Today, these two nations are politically and culturally independent. Since their official separation in the fall of 1830 the ancient name *Belgium* has been officially used to designate the newly created monarchy. A few facts and events of Belgian history are recalled here, because they affect the patterns of art support. The Belgian constitution stems from February 1831, but many features in the political organism of the country precede this date.

In 1795 Napoleon united Belgium with the Republic of France. His downfall ended this union; the Treaty of Paris (1814) separated France and Belgium. The interim sufficed to reinforce in Belgium the strong traces of French civilization, particularly of Napoleonic administration. Some of the unwise decisions made at the Congress of Vienna resulted, on May 31, 1815, in the union of Belgium with Holland; and under the Dutch Crown, Belgium became part of the United Kingdom of The Netherlands. Belgians deeply resented this annexation of their country by the stronger, primarily Protestant state. During the long period when their fate was tied to that of their northern neighbor the Belgians assumed the psychological attitudes and anxieties typical of minority groups. As Catholics, they feared for their freedom of religious expression and for the integrity of cherished traditions. They were also determined to keep French as the language of their land. But the Dutch rulers quickly superimposed their language not only in schools and courts, but in all manifestations of official life.

When, in 1830, William I of Orange, the unpopular King of the Dutch, formally proclaimed the *Fundamental Law*, many of its paragraphs alarmed the Belgians. The Archbishop of Brussels, Belgium's capital, publicly disapproved this royal edict; he forbade his diocese to take the oath of allegiance to the King. The Belgian Liberal Party feared that the independent press might lose its freedom. The new powers, usurped by the Dutch King, spelled absolutism. The ultraconservative Belgian Catholics and the revolutionary liberals (strange bedfellows of a kind frequently found in European politics) in 1828, had formed a common front, the so-called *Union.* Its purpose was to rid Belgium of the Dutch rulers. In a sad reversal of time-honored aspirations as defenders of liberty, The United Netherlands was involved in bitter civil strife, suppressing the self-expression of a constituent member. Thus are the changing tides of history, when free people pay dearly for the blunders of ruthless power politics.

Europe's upheavals had made of Brussels a city of refugees. Liberal politicians, artists, and intellectuals from various corners of Europe, particularly from neighboring France, found asylum here, hoping for a turn of events in their home countries.

An Opera Ignites a Revolution

History is frequently reflected in works of art, but this causality can be reversible. Works of art have inspired historic events.

In one of the curious episodes of European annals, the performance of an opera kindled the spark that set off a revolution. It happened in Brussels on August 25, 1830. On the anniversary of the King's ascension, a gala performance of *La Muette de Portici* was scheduled in the Opéra. That the management chose this work by the French master Daniel-François Auber for the festive occasion was remarkable: the libretto and the fiery music abound with the spirit of revolution. The story of *La Muette* centers on the historic uprising of Neapolitan fishermen in the summer of 1647 against the cruel Viceroy of Naples. Auber's opera culminates in a powerful call to freedom.

When the Brussels performance in midsummer of 1830 reached the climactic moment of the music-drama, the audience took its theme to heart. Excited, the people rushed out of the theater onto the boulevards. "Let us imitate the Parisians!" was their battle cry, recalling the French Revolution. The Belgians set fire to official buildings; they threatened the houses of the Dutch members of the government. Civil war broke out. As the police and militia showed only passive resistance, the Brussels revolution eventually spread throughout the country, and succeeded.

Belgium was free. It was a logical separation. In 1831, when the Treaty of London recognized Belgium as an independent nation, Prince Leopold of Saxe-Coburg-Gotha, a naturalized Englishman, was elected King.

II. Flemish and Walloon Coexistence
Linguistic Duality

Throughout the remaining nineteenth century the two large ethnic groups that constitute contemporary Belgium — the Flemings and the Walloons — continued a shaky political coexistence. Because of this duality, two languages prevail in Belgium — Flemish and French — which have their idiomatic derivatives.[1] There are two Belgian literatures: one in Flemish, the other in French.

Within the performing arts this dichotomy is strongly reflected. There is a Flemish and a French stage; there is a French opera in Brussels and a Flemish opera in Antwerp. The consequences of this schism for the mass media radio and television are self-explanatory.

The law of August 21, 1921, divided Belgium into two parts according to ethnic and linguistic borderlines. The Flemish segment is concentrated in the provinces of Antwerp, West and East Flanders, Limburg, the *arrondissements* of Louvain and Brussels and in the province of Brabant. The French segment includes the provinces of Liège, Luxembourg, Namur, and the *arrondissements* of Nivelles in the province of Brabant.

Approximately 3,500,000 Belgians speak Flemish, approximately 3,000,000, French, and of these only about 1,000,000 speak both languages fluently. Flemish, then, has a plurality of about half a million over French. The Flemings represent 50 per cent of the Belgian population; the Walloons, 33.61 per cent. In 1932 another law declared the full equality of Flemish with French: both were to be fully recognized as the official languages of the country. According to the new decree, corrections should be made every ten years to adjust to the fluctuation of language borders which still occur as the consequence of various factors. These modifications are to be followed by appropriate adjustments in administration, in the educational system, and correspondingly, in all aspects of Belgian public life.[2] Governmental art support obviously belongs in this category.

Monarchial and State Patronage

The political structure of Belgium is rooted in her free towns, the communes. The nine provinces mark the next level of administration. But the Belgian constitution of 1831 failed to explain in detail the issues that are the specific concern of these provinces or the communes, respectively. Whatever the present interpretation of the law, the national government is now taking ever-increasing responsibility in the support of the arts.

Belgium is one of the most densely populated countries in Europe. In an area of 11,775 square miles, approximately 9,153,000 people live. The geographical position and natural wealth of Belgium has repeatedly tempted invaders, particularly the Germans. During the Second World War, on May 28, 1940, King Leopold III surrendered to Hitler. Ten years later the Belgians voted (with an uncomfortably small majority of only 7 per cent) to recall their exiled sovereign. The Socialist Party continued a stern opposition to Leopold, who abdicated on July 16, 1951, in favor of his eldest son Baudouin, who is the present King.

In contrast to Holland, Belgium emerged from World War II in relatively stable condition. The Nazis had saved Belgian industries for their own use. A few years after the Armistice, Belgium was well on the road to economic recovery, even prosperity. The early resumption of seemingly peaceful conditions created a favorable climate for the growth of Belgian art life. Many facets of national art support are, in fact, the result of postwar developments.

The Crown is the official source of all art patronage emanating from various governmental offices. The executive power rests with the monarch, and the Belgian constitution does not divorce the executive from the legislative power, which is jointly held by the King, the Senate, and the Chamber of Representatives.

Europe's history repeatedly shows how enthusiastically crown rulers have participated in the art life of their countries. In modern Europe, however, this tradition is rapidly fading.

Belgium's exception to this deterioration of royal privileges is due to Queen Elisabeth, King Baudouin's grandmother. The aged Queen is revered for her distinguished record of encouragement to art. A recent Belgian postal stamp showing her portrait bears the inscription, *Artium Patrona.* This claim is no exaggeration. The Queen has, indeed, devoted much of her time and remarkable energy to the patronage of the arts, and she lends specific support to music. She is herself a violinist, and studied in her youth with the Belgian virtuoso Eugenè Ysaye. Throughout her long life the Queen has enjoyed performing at informal evenings of chamber music. Practically all major musical institutions of Belgium have benefited, directly or indirectly, from her royal sponsorship and initiative.

In 1937 the Queen Elisabeth International Music Competition was established. This contest is well-endowed and of international consequence. The jury is made up of famous musicians. In 1959 Darius Milhaud wrote a new work, *Concert Royal*, specifically for performances by the competing musicians; they all studied and played this music as their "modern" number in the contest repertory.

The Queen has also sponsored the formation of the fine Orchestre de la Chapelle de la Reine Elisabeth. And the country's first concert organization, the Orchestre National de Belgique, owes its existence to the joint enterprise of Queen Elisabeth and the Ministry of Education.

Today, the reigning King Baudouin is Belgium's chief official patron. All laws pertaining to national art support are published in the form of royal ordinances. But along with the name of the King, the signatures of two cabinet members directly concerned with this issue appear on the decrees: the Minister of Education and the Minister of Finance.

All documents are published both in French and Flemish. If the personal impact of the King's art sponsorship is limited, it is matched by highly efficient organization of governmental and private agencies that permanently take charge of Belgian art life.

III. Belgian Opera Houses

Théâtre Royal de la Monnaie

Approximately one-tenth of the entire population of Belgium lives in Brussels. Being the royal residence as well as the seat of government, modern Brussels has also emerged as the principal art center of the country. In its governmental support of the theater, Belgium leans strongly toward the Latin affinity with the lyrical stage. Just as Italy or France, so Belgium devotes the lion's share of its art subsidies to opera theaters.

The changing pattern of public art support in Belgium is illustrated by the nation's principal opera house, the Théâtre Royal de la Monnaie of Brussels. Prior to the season 1963-64 it was sponsored jointly by the royal government, the municipality of Brussels, and the province of Brabant. Meanwhile this distinguished theater has become the Belgian National Opera. Building and grounds belong to the city of Brussels, which also owns all equipment, the stage machinery, costumes, and other effects. The municipality entrusts the management of the opera to a concessionaire and signs with him a contract for several years, subject to renewal. The share of support assumed for the year 1960 by the municipality was F.8,000,000 ($160,000)* and by the national government F.17,260,000 ($345,000). At this writing the Théâtre Royal de la Monnaie operates as a communal institution, generously subsidized by the state, which more than doubles the municipal subvention. For the season, 1962-63, the royal government supported the theater with a grant of $348,000. The municipality of Brussels paid $200,000; the province of Brabant added $60,000.

The Théâtre Royal de la Monnaie leans toward the typically French repertory as it is cultivated in Paris, 180 miles away. Yet the Brussels Opéra does not eschew Italian and German works. It has, in fact, the distinction of having offered the first performance in French of Wagner's *Ring*. The opera's choreographic forces, known as the *Ballet du XXè Siècle*, live up to the implication of the name in the modern aspects of performance as well as in the choice of repertory.

Since 1960 the management has favored fewer performances for the sake of quality, which implies sufficient rehearsal time. The minus in

* $1.00=50 francs

new productions is made up by a practical solution. Three other opera companies of Belgium — resident in Antwerp, Ghent, and Liège — visit Brussels in a regular circuit. This exchange assures the best available opera performances in Belgium.

Operas in the Provinces

A number of other lyrical theaters receive considerable assistance from the Belgian government. (See Table I.)

The Opéra Royal Flamand is a municipal theater important in its own right. Located in the ancient port city of Antwerp (near the tri-state corner of Belgium, The Netherlands, and Germany), the Royal Flemish Opera is distinguished by a spirit of experimentation. This may seem surprising, considering the notoriously conservative orientation of the Flemish. But their metropolis has never lacked progressiveness and sophistication. Antwerp's art life maintains spirited rivalry with that of the French-orientated national capital of Brussels. The Flemish Opera is a theater to be reckoned with on the contemporary art scene; it is not merely another lyrical outpost in the provinces. The relatively high national subsidy bespeaks the recognition the government accords this particular theater; it also indicates a political consideration: equal distribution of moneys between French and Flemish cities.

Ghent, capital of East Flanders, has been known since the Middle Ages as a cultural center. Today a city of 217,000, it supports in the Opéra Royal de Gand a theater with a stimulating repertory. At the same time, the municipality of Ghent is mindful of its role as sponsor of the visual arts.

The city of Liège had achieved musical distinction before the establishment of the Belgian monarchy. Liège gave to the world two famous composers: André Grétry (1741-1813) and César Franck (1822-1890).

The town of Verviers (population 42,537), situated on the main line from Liège to Cologne, and thus close to the West German network of good musical theaters, likewise receives a national subvention for its opera.

Mons (population 26,058), capital of Hainault, qualifies for the same allocation as Verviers. It is noteworthy that even such small cities as Verviers and Mons maintain theaters and have their place in the national scheme of art support. The cities chosen for subsidies do not necessarily represent a fixed pattern of governmental aid. As the following excerpts from a recent royal decree in support of the lyrical theaters will show, subventions are presently granted to six opera theaters; but their choice is subject to change. (See Table I.)

TABLE I

Subventions from the National Government to the Lyrical Theaters

	1959	1960
Théâtre Royal de la Monnaie (Brussels)	*F. 17,270,000 ($345,400)	F. 17,260,000 ($345,200)
Opéra Royal flamand d'Anvers (Antwerp)	F. 13,260,000 ($265,200)	13,260,000
Opéra Royal de Gand (Ghent)	F. 4,535,000 ($ 90,700)	4,535,000
Opéra Royal de Liège	F. 4,535,000 ($ 90,700)	4,535,000
Théâtre de Verviers	F. 1,350,000 ($ 27,000)	1,350,000
Théâtre Royal de Mons	F. 1,350,000 ($ 27,000)	1,350,000

*Belgian franc = 2 cents.

IV. Royal Decree in Support of Lyrical Theaters

Article 67 of the Belgian Constitution is the legal basis of royal edicts directing financial assistance to the arts. At the proposal of the Ministry of Public Instruction, King Baudouin, on December 17, 1951, signed the law relative to the support of Belgium's lyrical theaters. The decree shows the high measure of vigilance the government exercises over the use of the moneys allocated. But these far-reaching controls of the subsidies need not be interpreted as bureaucratic. As they concern tax-raised funds, their spending is jealously watched in a country of ethnological dichotomy. The decrees in behalf of art support are issued, like all other governmental documents of Belgium, both in French and Flemish.

ARTICLE 1.

Within the limits of the national budget, subventions are granted to recognized lyrical theaters under specified conditions.

ARTICLE 2.

Six lyrical theaters can be selected for support.

ARTICLE 3.

The municipalities which are the seats of the lyrical theaters selected for support must individually, or jointly with the grantee (provided the theater is managed by a concessionaire) annually submit the budgets of receipts and expenses to the Minister of Public Instruction. The budget should be reasonably balanced. The community must assume the deficit of the accrued operational costs.

All provisions are made for the duration of the season. An estimate of the overall deficit is submitted to the Minister of Public Instruction for preliminary approval.

ARTICLE 4.

The bookkeeping of the supported lyrical theaters must cope with a form determined by the Minister of Public Instruction and the Inspector of Finance. The accounting is supervised by the Minister of Public Instruction (or by his delegate) as well as by the Inspector of Finance.

The budget and the bills of expenditures are submitted no later than March 30th of each year to the Ministry of Public Instruction. Each theater must submit to the Minister of Public Instruction, in the form determined by him, all further requested information.

ARTICLE 5.

A detailed list of all supplies needed for the lyrical theater must be submitted for approval to the Minister of Public Instruction.

ARTICLE 6.

The communal administrators of the lyrical theaters submit, upon request of the Minister of Public Instruction, the candidacies for concessionaires (or directors) of lyrical theaters prior to their appointments on the part of the Municipal Council.

The appointment of a grantee (or the nomination of a director) not agreed upon by the Minister could result in a withdrawal of the subsidy. The appointment of the concessionaire, and the nomination of a director, must not take place without proper information of the public. The concessions are for five years or more. The employment of an artistic director will not be conferred for more than five years.

ARTICLE 7.

Each theater must employ a minimum staff of artistic personnel. The names of the members of this staff are submitted for approval to the Minister of Public Instruction. The artists on this staff, whether they are foreigners or not, can be engaged only in accordance with the salaries determined in the submitted budget. The engagement concluded in these contracts, or by private agreement, must be communicated monthly to the Minister of Public Instruction.

ARTICLE 8.

Each season the officially recognized lyrical theater must, if so requested by the Ministry of Public Instruction,

1. perform at least one work that has not been published in Belgium;
2. produce one work (corresponding to a minimum of two acts*) by a Belgian composer;
3. offer new productions of at least three repertory works.

ARTICLE 9.

The lyrical theater must not give more than seven performances during one week. One free day per week must be granted to the entire artistic personnel.

ARTICLE 10.

The municipalities (or their concessionaires) operating lyrical theaters must put aside each month the tax assessment for the national office of social security. This money must be forwarded every three months to the office of social security.

ARTICLE 11.

The subventions are granted in accordance with the scope of production. The number of annual subsidized performances and the amount of the subsidy for each of these are fixed by the government. The productions qualifying for the benefit of subventions are determined by the Ministry of Public Instruction. The subsidy for each performance is determined in proportion to the minimum staff of artistic personnel of each theater.

*Obviously such a score could also be an opera that is not subdivided into different acts but is of comparable duration.

ARTICLE 12.

Any violation of the conditions of the agreement may result in the withdrawal of the subsidy; yet warning must be given prior to the first of June.

Recognition may be withdrawn, if the artistic quality of the performances is not up to expectation.

ARTICLE 13.

The payment of the subvention is made to the communities in four installments: February 1, April 1, September 1, and December 1.

ARTICLE 14.

The Ministry of Public Instruction is charged with the supervision of the present order.

V. National Support of Theater and Concert

The lack of a National Belgian Theater had long been felt, particularly in view of the remarkable literature created by Belgian authors for the stage. Soon after World War II the plan for a government supported playhouse came to fulfillment. In September, 1945, it was decided to establish two permanent national companies: one in Brussels, performing in French; the other in Antwerp, performing in Flemish. The parallel setup of these national playhouses with Belgium's two principal opera theaters is evident.

The National Theater also maintains a number of touring groups which perform during the season in the major cities of the country. It is hoped, however, that Belgian cities, long distinguished by cultural traditions, will eventually establish their own resident companies. For the time being a preference for the opera prevails in the taste of the population and in government support.

The total public subsidy for prose theaters in Belgium is still small. In 1960 it amounted to 17,000,000 Belgian francs (about $340,000). This is somewhat more than 11 per cent of the grand total of governmental aid to the performing arts (exclusive of the national radio and television, which are self-supporting).

During the year 1960 the entire governmental subvention of the theaters, operas, orchestras, and public libraries amounted to 149,399,000 francs, which is approximately $3,000,000.

Limited State Supervision

The Belgian government supports three of the nation's large concert orchestras. There is limited state supervision of the finances and complete artistic freedom.

TABLE II

Government Support to Three Orchestras (1960)

Belgian National Orchestra	F. 9,400,000 ($188,000)
Orchestra of the City of Antwerp	1,250,000 ($25,000)
Orchestra of the City of Liège	1,250,000 ($25,000)

The leading concert organization of Belgium is the Orchestre National de Belgiue, established in 1936 at the initiative of the Ministry of Public Instruction. But the organization is not directly controlled by the government, which merely underwrites the deficit and appoints the manager of the orchestra. The Minister of Public Instruction is represented on the council of the orchestra and has the right of veto in all major decisions. The chairman of the orchestra's board is the president of the Commission of the Royal Conservatory. The board is composed of delegates from each of the associations which regularly employ the Orchestre National. In the season 1960-61 twelve million Belgian francs ($240,000) were required for the running expenses of the orchestra. But the orchestra earns part of its deficit through various outside engagements. For certain official occasions the orchestra donates its services: festivities under the patronage of the King, expositions, national holidays, governmental representations, etc.

The Belgian National Orchestra consists of 62 musicians who receive their appointments by strict competitive auditions. Supplementary performers are chosen according to the changing needs of the repertory and always subject to the approval of the conductor in charge. The management proposes to the Ministry of Public Instruction the names of conductors and soloists. The number of concerts given by the orchestra has increased each year. At present there are more than 100 concerts each season. The orchestra is frequently sent on tour throughout Belgium, and occasionally abroad.

Royal Decree in Support of Concerts

In addition to the previously listed orchestras of Antwerp and Liège, the Belgian government offers financial aid to certain concert organizations which apply for grants and are eligible under specified conditions. The following excerpts from the royal decree No. 8559 of December 6, 1954 concerning these subsidies show a somewhat nationalistic point of view. But the extent to which Belgium protects her native artists is not unreasonable. Belgium is a small country. It competes in the performing media with stronger neighbors. And Belgian artists are in a disadvantageous position because of the relative lack of opportunities, for which the national government wishes to compensate. The royal decree comprises six articles.

ARTICLE 1.

Within the limits of budgetary credits, and within conditions determined below, subventions may be granted to concert societies in order to cover, totally or partly, the deficit of their past seasons, or to help them realize the program of the coming seasons.

ARTICLE 2.

Subsidies can be requested by

1.) concert associations of the five Royal Conservatories of Music in Belgium;
2.) other concert societies that are unquestioned nonprofit organizations.

ARTICLE 3.

The conditions attached to subventions for the concert associations of the Royal Conservatories are determined by the Ministry of Public Instruction.

ARTICLE 4.

Concert associations defined in Article 2, second paragraph, may receive subventions, provided they comply with the following conditions:

1. Concerts must fall into one of the four categories listed below to be eligible:
   a. large-scale symphony concerts
   b. concerts of chamber orchestras
   c. concerts of small ensembles of chamber music
   d. solo recitals.
2. With the exception of exchange concerts (organized within intercultural agreements), the great symphony concerts, or the concerts of chamber music must be given by Belgian organizations. Fifty per cent of the soloists must be Belgians.

   The concerts of small chamber music groups and the solo recitals (with the exception of the exchange concerts) must be given by Belgian artists.
3. One tenth of the total concert programs must be devoted to the performance of works by Belgian composers.
4. The ticket price for subsidized concerts (with the exception of large symphonic concerts) must not exceed thirty francs (about sixty cents) per ticket.
5. The concerts must always be of sufficient artistic quality.

ARTICLE 5.

Requests for subventions must be submitted to the Ministry of Public Instruction prior to July 1.

Each request is to be accompanied by the budget of the past season.

The concert societies are required to include in their first applications copies of their statutes, and to communicate all facts relative to their organizational structure.

Detailed programs as well as the accounts of receipts and expenses must be submitted by September 15.

ARTICLE 6.

The amount of subvention allowed for each concert is determined by the Ministry of Public Instruction on the basis of individual circumstances which, in turn, are evaluated in regard to the category of performances, their quality, and the prices charged for admission. The prices are fixed by the Ministry of Public Instruction.

Hiring Government Supported Orchestras

The government requests that all organizations receiving public support be hired only under a scale decided upon by the Ministry of Public Instruction. The amount of the fee changes according to the status of the hiring organization.

The following categories are differentiated according to the nature of control, purpose, and financial ability: regular employers of the orchestra; occasional employers; school concerts, popular concerts, and concerts of the *Jeunesses Musicales;* concerts organized by the Service of Popular Education in Brussels; concerts organized in the provinces; concerts played for Radiodiffusion and National Television. For each of these categories the fees are adapted to the cultural purpose. The government assumes the responsibility for deficits.

Jeunesses Musicales

Music for Youth is an important international movement founded in the midst of World War II by Marcel Cuvelier, a Belgian pedagogue. It was hoped that youth could unite after the tragedy in a spirit of fraternity. In essence, the Jeunesses Musicales represents a blend of the international youth movement with music education; the members, in the best sense, are the Boy and Girl Scouts of Music. There are classes, concerts, and competitions. Meetings are held in- and out-of-doors.

In 1956 the First World Congress of the Jeunesses Musicales was held in Madrid. Yearly conventions shift from one participating nation to another. Today, more than twenty countries belong to the organization. In 1960 instrumentalists and singers from five continents made up the forces which performed Beethoven's *Ninth Symphony* at Berlin. Wherever the annual convocations are held, performances alternate with lectures, forum discussions, and social meetings.

The heightened attention paid to youth is one of the most convincing aspects of Belgian art sponsorship. Recognizing that youth is the audience and the patron of tomorrow, the Belgian government undertakes the support of the Jeunesses Musicales and related organizations in various local branches. Allocations to the Jeunesses Musicales are distributed by the Administration of Arts, Letters, and Education (an adjunct of the Ministry of Public Instruction).

In the cultural budget of the Belgian government, the support of the Jeunesses Musicales and of various art centers organizing music recitals appears as modest items. Thus, for the year 1961 the total allocation to the Jeunesses Musicales and to art circles was F.188,000 ($3,760). But the subvention was enough to keep the project alive.

TABLE III

Government Grants to Music for Youth (1961)

Jeunesses Musicales (Verviers)	F. 20,000
Centre Culturelle d'Uccle (Brussels)	17,000
Jeunesses Musicales (Termonde)	17,000
Centre d'Art (Brussels)	15,000
Jeugd en Muzick (Antwerp)	15,000
Jeunesses Musicales (Eupen)	15,000
Jeunesses Musicales (Ghent)	15,000
Jeunesses Musicales (Namur)	15,000

Governmental subsidies include numerous other smaller grants, usually around F.5,000 ($100). All of these allocations may be renewed annually. They are given on the basis of the royal decree of January 20, 1956, pertaining to subventions for concert associations. Table III indicates that large and small cities alike are the beneficiaries of governmental support.

Concerts at Noon

In Belgium, as in France, most working people and students enjoy a midday pause between twelve and two o'clock. This long intermission suggested the establishment of a concert organization, designed to make special use of this pause by offering recitals of fine music. In January, 1948, an organization of originality and practicality was founded in Brussels: the so-called *Concerts de Midi.* They offer recitals of chamber music, of art songs, and related programs of an intimate artistic nature. In Brussels, the Concerts at Noon take place in the Royal Museum of Painting and Sculpture (where the capacity of the hall is about 850).

The Concerts at Noon operate in association with the Ministry of Public Instruction; the various institutes where the concerts take place (in Brussels as well as in the provinces) are under the supervision of this national ministry.

The entrance fee to these concerts is nominal, a mere 5 francs (10 cents). But attracting capacity audiences for midday concerts is somewhat complicated. The listeners for whom these concerts are primarily intended — working people and students — have to return to their jobs and schools at a fixed hour. Hence they must be given the opportunity to have a meal at the Museum, either before or after the concert. This, in turn, necessitates a fast-moving cafeteria service of a kind Europeans are just beginning to adopt.

Today the Concerts at Noon unite faithful audiences in several cities. In 1949 Liège followed Brussels with its Concerts de Midi under the auspices of the municipality. In the same year, Antwerp inaugurated an analogous series in the heart of the city. Next in line to establish Concerts at Noon were Mons, Ghent, Namur, and Charleroi. Most of these concerts take place on Wednesdays.

The Concerts at Noon have to be subsidized to operate on a broad, popular basis. Tickets, programs, meals must be available at a minimum price to the public. On the other hand, performers must receive compensations that are adequate by professional standards.

The officially defined aims of these concerts may be summarized as follows: to promote chamber music (which is neglected in Belgium); to aid performers who devote themselves to chamber music; to make it possible for the artists to give recitals for an adequate fee; to make good music available to the working public, to youth, and to all those who cannot afford to pay expensive ticket prices; to offer, in the middle of the working day, an hour of relaxation in a cultivated environment.

The success of this venture has been unqualified. Additional concerts must now be scheduled. In Brussels alone artists have to be engaged for about 70 concerts annually. Since their inception, the Concerts at Noon have given close to 700 concerts attended by 500,000 people, and about 3,000 artists have been engaged as performers.

VI. Bilingual Broadcasts

The administration of the Belgian Broadcasting System (Radiodiffusion Belgique) is under the jurisdiction of the Royal Ministry of Communications. The entire radio program is supervised by the government. Belgian law, as previously explained, guarantees the right to use the country's two principal languages in all official communications. Hence French and Flemish are employed over the Belgian stations. The national radio offers, in fact, two simultaneous broadcasts: one is referred to as the French Network and the other as the Flemish Network. All major programs of national and international scope are heard in both languages. Television follows analogous patterns.

The government supported radio excludes commercials. Before the Second World War they were limited, but they were banned after the War. A few private stations still profit from advertising.

The basic income of the state broadcasting networks is derived from listeners' fees. Belgians pay 240 francs annually (approximately $5) for the radio and 840 francs (approximately $16) for television. There is hardly a family within the population of 9,000,000 that does not own at least one radio. Consequently, the Radiodiffusion Télévision Belgique has sufficient income from its license fees. Television sets are not yet as popular as in America, but the income from the accumulated license fees suffices to defray basic expenses.

Considering the ethnological division and political tension within the country, how does governmental control influence the programs of the mass media? Radio and television reap the benefits of the freedoms promised by the Belgian constitution. This implies freedom of expression in every medium, except where such privilege is misused "in offending concepts of decency and public morals."

The Belgian record of the mass media indicates that no political party is favored. Each of the major parties is assured equal time for political expression and ideological comment. The equality pertains to religious programs, too. As a matter of democratic principle, even the atheists are allowed air time in this overwhelmingly Catholic nation. For the Belgian constitution contains no law enforcing religious expression or combating the lack of it. The law guarantees freedom of education, freedom of the press, as well as all the other liberties inherent in the concept of democracy.

In keeping with current European policies and procedures, the Belgian radio is a generous sponsor of the performing arts; it particularly supports serious offerings that involve heavy financial risks. Radiodiffusion Télévision Belgique has at its disposal three good orchestras: a large symphony orchestra of 80 men (which is augmented for works requiring larger casts) and 2 smaller instrumental ensembles. The state radio sponsors chamber music groups and permanently engages a large professional choir.

VII. Art Support
Crystallization of National Pride

Of Western Europe's smaller nations, none has been more plagued than Belgium by the recent combination of domestic and international upheavals. Belgium's rapid postwar rehabilitation is partly offset by the loss of her African empire. And the chaos in the Congo inevitably has upset, at least temporarily, Belgian equilibrium at home; it has brought to the boiling point the old antagonism of political factions. The Flemish-Walloon dichotomy has caused renewed civil strife. Demonstrations have led to violence in the capital and provinces.

The mere fact that Belgian art life aspires today to new heights — in spite of struggle on various fronts — is in itself worthy of admiration. Curiously enough, that permanent ethnological schism within the Belgian nation has proven to be an actual gain from the viewpoint of governmental art patronage. For what is lost in uniformity of purpose and linguistic representation within the performing media is gained by the keen spiritual rivalry between the two main segments of the Belgian nation and its respective art centers.

A good opera in Brussels implies a good one in Antwerp. National subsidies for an orchestra or theater in Flanders require an equal allocation for similar organizations in the Walloon part of the country. As previously shown, even small cities, on both sides of the linguistic frontier, become the beneficiaries of governmental art support.

Progress on the Belgian art scene is favored by still other circumstances. The World's Fair held during 1958 in Brussels dramatized the meaning of international standards through the guest performances of numerous companies visiting Belgium at that time. The Belgians were quick to realize that some of their national organizations did not measure up to some of the visiting ones. And this recognition triggered crucial reforms.

In the cultural shadow of her more powerful neighbors, art life in contemporary Belgium was slow to develop its own resources in a systematic and concerted manner. The various patterns of diversified, private patronage proved inadequate to promote Belgium's theaters, operas, orchestras, ballets to levels comparable with those attained by the principal art organizations of France, Germany, or Holland.

But the Belgian government is making great strides and has come up with a series of convincing and original solutions. During the summer of 1963 the transformation of the Théâtre Royal de la Monnaie into the National Belgian Opera was accomplished. This long-expected conversion places the historic opera house in Brussels on a secure financial basis, equal to that accorded the state-supported theaters on the Continent. Belgium also plans the establishment of new cultural centers in both Walloon and Flemish territories. Decentralization of cultural activities is a logical goal as well as a political necessity in view of the Belgian dichotomy. Projects such as the Jeunesses Musicales or the Concerts de Midi aim in the right direction: it is the activation of youth and the conquest of new audiences that matter in a systematic and forward-looking national art program.

From the bitter competition between the Walloons and the Flemish, common interests rather than old jealousies may slowly emerge and finally win out. For example, it is to the credit of the entire Belgian nation that the historic glory of Flanders should not be forgotten by the rest of the world. Were not the Burgundian sovereigns, ruling their realm from Flemish residences, once extolled as the leaders of the West? During the thirteenth and fourteenth centuries the city of Bruges was not only the principal harbor and trading place of the Northwest; Bruges was also an art center equal to any of the most civilized cities of the Renaissance. The growth of French-speaking Brussels into a world capital marks a relatively recent and equally important development.

Imaginative leadership in modern Belgium is conscious of the fact that at a time of duress and loss of world power the *reprise du contact* with a great cultural past is a convincing form of global propaganda. In 1960, when the Museum of Bruges exhibited a large collection of "Belgian" masterpieces of the fifteenth century, visitors from over the world stood in awe before the timeless achievement of the Flemish School of painters. The success of this art event shows a way. For a nation that can unite in its pride of a great cultural past can put this past to new uses in the future.

LUXEMBOURG

I. Art Support in Diminutive Nation

Cultural Affinities

On the map of the world the grand duchy of Luxembourg appears only as a dot. This miniature nation, none the less, has made its impression on the art scene of Europe.

With a population of 314,000 and measuring about 999 square miles, Luxembourg is bound on the north and west by Belgium, on the east and southeast by Germany, and on the south by France. The history of Luxembourg has been for centuries a part of the history of other nations. Luxembourg was once a strategic fief of the Holy Roman Empire, and members of the Luxembourg dynasty ascended to the imperial throne. At times, Luxembourg was alternately ruled by Burgundian, Austrian, and Spanish sovereigns. Twice Luxembourg has been integrated with France, with which it has remained culturally akin.

In 1815 the Congress of Vienna divided Luxembourg between Dutch and Prussian sovereignty. In 1830, when Belgium broke loose from Holland, Luxembourg was adopted by the new Belgian state; yet Prussia retained its garrison in Luxembourg City. European power politics created further diplomatic transactions and border changes. Eventually the dissolution of the German Confederation newly established Luxembourg's neutrality. The House of Nassau assumed the reigns of the grand duchy. In 1890 Luxembourg fell to Adolphus, Duke of Nassau-Weilburg, and the successors of this dynasty are the rulers of Luxembourg to the present day. In August 1914 the Kaiser's troops occupied the grand duchy, and from 1940 to 1944, Hitler held it. Then the Nazis were driven out by the liberating American army, and Luxembourg welcomed Grand Duchess Charlotte back from exile.

The multi-national aspects of Luxembourg's history are logically reflected in the facets of her civilization. Today the dominant language is French; most citizens also speak their own Luxembourg idiom and a German dialect. The architecture in the small capital likewise reveals the variegated chapters in Luxembourg's chronicle. Thus the grand ducal palace, a relic of Spanish occupation, recalls the elaborate style of the Iberian Renaissance. New residential quarters disclose French affinity, and older middle-class dwellings, a German influence.

The support of the performing arts in Luxembourg likewise represents a curious blend of factors that are explained by the country's background. There are remnants of aristocratic patronage, for Luxembourg is still a country with a ducal sovereign. There is a considerable amount of private initiative, in fact, proportionately more than in other countries included in this book.

Governmental interest in the performing arts in Luxembourg dates back more than a century. In 1842 the Luxembourg government founded a music corps. Recruited as an army band, this group was also capable of playing music on the serious art level.

In 1844 the Municipal Conservatory of Luxembourg was established and soon became the nucleus of musical activities in the grand duchy. Today this institute is maintained by the city of Luxembourg with some support by the state. The municipal council appoints the faculty. The Conservatory has a long tradition as a sponsor of public performances. In 1886 Franz Liszt gave the last solo recital of his life in the Conservatory. In 1906 the institute was reorganized under the supervision of Belgian artists and the military band was augmented to sixty musicians. To qualify, the members were required to play additional orchestra instruments, notably strings. This procedure makes it possible for a military band to double as a symphony orchestra. The example is typical: it shows how Luxembourg makes the most of her limited resources. For the performance of large symphonic works, the orchestra is increased. Today Luxembourgers are proud that they do not, as in former years, have to import instrumentalists from music centers in neighboring countries. In 1923 a conservatory was founded in Esch, the second city in the state of Luxembourg.

The only theater of the duchy is in Luxembourg City. It has a small but pleasant hall. Plans for its modernization or even for a new theater are under way.

Radio Luxembourg

The radio station of Luxembourg, privately owned, has attained international attention. French capital is invested in this network and, curiously enough, all news broadcasts originate in Paris and are relayed to Luxembourg.

The symphony orchestra of this radio station is a well-established ensemble, numbering 60 regular members, increased to 80 when necessary. The orchestra frequently offers significant programs, and often sponsors contemporary works.

The commercial factor in this unusual private patronage of an expensive orchestra is undeniable. The sponsor has at these concerts the chance of extensive advertising. The Luxembourg broadcasts reach an audience far beyond the border of the grand duchy. They are regularly heard in Belgium, Holland, France, West Germany, and even in England where the state-owned networks avoid advertising (or limit it to a minimum). And so, the commercials of Radio Luxembourg make large profits for the sponsors.

Many Luxembourgers are critical of this state of affairs. They resent that their radio station is owned by a private company with headquarters outside their country. But the broadcasts are enjoyed at home and abroad, none the less. Programs are not limited to symphony concerts; there are also chamber music and solo recitals and other serious performances. Some of the broadcasts are played for the public, which is admitted free of charge.

The grand duchy receives royalties from the radio station and does not intend to abandon this source of revenue, at least at present. Some observers express hope that in due time income from the network will be channeled into the patronage of an independent art program, sponsored by the state and produced exclusively within the sovereignty of Luxembourg.

II. Belated Art Consciousness

We see, then, that certain patterns of art support in Luxembourg differ from those in other European nations, for organized public art life developed late in Luxembourg.

It is surprising to learn — in view of the rich natural resources of the country — that Luxembourg has long been a very poor land. Only after the systematic industrial exploitation of iron ore did wealth come to the country. Primarily restricted to a military function, Luxembourg did not, even as late as the first part of the nineteenth century, experience the kind of cultural impetus which in the surrounding nations had prevailed for centuries. In modern Luxembourg a great part of industry and capital is owned by foreign companies. To this day there is a certain transient quality in the civic life of the country, and controlling industries take no active part in art life. Only few of those who earn large profits in Luxembourg are inclined to spend money on civic improvements there. In spite of this situation, there has developed a small indigenous culture in Luxembourg, where art has grown in a kind of closed milieu. In principle, both the state and the municipal governments of Luxembourg are now ready to lend their support to the performing arts. But in this small country opinion is strongly divided as to what represents the best interests of its people. That infamous cry that the man on the street does not care for "highbrow" art is frequently heard. Luxembourg lacks the cultural traditions that have set standards for the people in her neighboring countries. But, convincingly, the present government seeks to improve public taste through systematic art education.

In short, there are many signs of cultural progress in Luxembourg. The grand duchy makes no pretense of being a power. Yet the fact that its capital has been chosen as the seat of the European community of coal and steel has promoted city and state to an important center. The iron and steel industry is the very lifeblood of Luxembourg: it represents 80 per cent of the country's economy, and Luxembourg ranks high among steel producing countries. Furthermore, Luxembourg belongs to the economic community familiar under the concept of the Common Market. These advantages and improvements in agricultural life are promoting the country's prosperity. The state can now support many cultural projects. It stresses art education in the public schools and the training of expert teachers. There are no less than three art museums in the capital of this diminutive nation. Luxembourg is also the center for a small but vigorous art colony and the home of an intelligentsia whose voice is more often heard. These are good omens for a cultural future. With its unique combination of a history limited in artistic traditions, a government and a people newly awakening to the greater need for a worthy art life, and an industrial force both wealthy and foreign, Luxembourg may work out for itself a system of art patronage that would follow more closely the patterns set by neighboring nations.

ENGLAND

I. Spirit of British Art Patronage

Ideological Premises

Of all European nations England is closest to the United States in spirit and tradition. The two nations hold to a common ideal, which Alfred North Whitehead defined as "the belief in the plain good sense of well-meaning people, freely organizing themselves." The carefully defined role of British government in support of the arts is consistent with this spirit and with British parliamentary tradition; it dramatizes the role of the state as the servant of its citizens.

The United Kingdom represents one of the few constitutional monarchies to survive the apocalyptic events of two World Wars. Considering the proverbial conservatism of the nation, one might expect vestiges of old methods of patronage to survive; but contemporary British art support represents a truly modern solution of the problem. Viewed from the point of art patronage, England is and is not "Europe." Britain's splendid isolation has created in her cultural sphere ways distinctly her own. The contemporary British approach is thoroughly European insofar as it firmly upholds the conviction that art is a public necessity for which the government is responsible. Although many aspects of British art life differ from historically established Continental patterns, England presents one of the most convincing examples of diversified art support. Just as in most European countries, patronage in England is the sum total of private plus governmental subsidies on local and national levels. Private aid to the arts runs the whole gamut from individual initiative to subsidies granted by trusts and foundations. Municipal corporations participate to an ever-increasing degree in art support, although the tempo is slow by comparison with that on the Continent.

National patronage is vested in the so-called *Arts Council of Great Britain.* In intent and structure the Council is a model of democratic support of the arts. Perhaps its greatest virtue is the successful separation of government support from government control. The important developments, which ultimately led to the charter of the Arts Council, will always be remembered as a noble chapter in England's recent history, in which the cultural needs of the British people were dramatically projected against a background of war.

Art — Solace and Strength

The period between the two World Wars witnessed a remarkable blossoming of private patronage. Many organizations contributed to the spread of music and drama in each stratum of the British population.

Noteworthy is the part played by amateur groups, aided by the Carnegie United Kingdom Trust. At this time the appreciation of art extended significantly beyond the limits of the upper and middle classes: labor unions became increasingly interested through such organizations as the Workers' Educational Association.

During the bitter war winter of 1939 the blackout of London and of other English communities threatened to cancel all semblance of organized performances of music and drama for an unknown duration. But life under constant pressure and misery could not obliterate the need of the population for the enjoyment and solace of the arts. On the contrary, the arts promised escape from the terror of bombings during night and day. No more sweeping testimony to the strength of the arts under utmost duress is conceivable.

Circumstances called for emergency action. A committee was formed, which became known as CEMA, the Committee for the Encouragement of Music and the Arts. The new group was privately sponsored. The initial subvention came from the Pilgrim Trust, and Lord Ernest MacMillan was elected chairman. Soon the Committee's endeavors were crowned by success. The positive response of the public-at-large was no coincidence. Much credit goes to the British Broadcasting Company (BBC), which developed new methods of educational radio. Through its efforts the best in music and drama reached the most remote mountain hamlet and mining village of the United Kingdom.

The spark that ignited the founding of CEMA originated from a modest organization not concerned primarily with the performing arts. This was a venture known as *Art for the People*, and it proved to be an important forerunner of procedures which, at a later time, led to the country-wide spread and propagation of serious music and drama.

The underlying thought was that many people in England never have a chance to visit a museum. There are many fine galleries in Britain, but they are not readily accessible, even in urban regions, for the underprivileged and the working population. Obviously, art galleries are far removed from the rural districts. Thus, the idea presented itself to bring art directly to the people. In England (as elsewhere) a considerable number of old and new masterworks are in private collections. Many of the owners were willing to lend their pictures for a touring exhibit. The itinerary favored small and distant communities, particularly the farming regions.

This was the beginning of the movement, Art for the People. It was not a costly project. The Carnegie United Kingdom Trust paid one-third of the bill; the rest was met by private donors.

War came. Art for the People held its first wartime exhibition at the City Literary Institute of London. But would anybody attend an art show with air raid sirens shrieking their warnings and the city getting a foretaste of the Nazi blitz? Londoners flocked to the exhibit, in spite of the turmoil, and perhaps even because of it. Dr. Thomas Jones, Secretary of the Pilgrim Trust, was deeply moved by this spectacle of courage and appreciation. Shortly after, the Trust was approached for a grant to sponsor a wartime extension of Art for the People. The project was now to include the performing arts. Dr. Jones realized the challenge and the merits of the new idea: it aimed at a union between private and civic patronage. Thus, at the outset of World War II, CEMA was born.

CEMA — Early Activities

The primary task of CEMA was, in the words of its chairman Lord Ernest MacMillan, "to fortify national morale in the grievous trials of war, especially among those communities which, evacuated from the cities, would find themselves without occupation for their enforced leisure."

From its very beginning the founders of CEMA envisioned a wide scope of activities. Before all, a helping hand was extended to already established organizations in the field of music and drama, so that they could carry on in spite of war. But CEMA also began to support new projects with the dual task of helping the artist as well as the art-hungry country. Many artists had lost their source of income because of the War. Even renowned performers could not earn enough to make ends meet.

In the musical field CEMA engaged performers (vocalists as well as instrumentalists) and sent them on tour throughout the country. Even the smallest communities were considered for their visits, if there was reason to expect at least a modest audience. Concerts were started in factories. Performers played during lunch and midnight breaks. Such concerts afforded the first opportunities for young, unknown artists (i.e., Kathleen Ferrier, who became one of the greatest singers of her time). But internationally famous performers also participated in concerts for factory workers and for the armed forces.

The role of music as therapy was explored. It proved to be a means of tranquilizing bomb-shocked people and other patients convalescent from various kinds of illnesses. In its initial year CEMA gave the extraordinary number of 400 concerts a month.

Drama on the Road

The approach of CEMA to the almost hopeless situation of the theater in wartime England was analogous. As in music, professional groups were reorganized and new companies were formed. Amateur ensembles were encouraged. As the result of the imaginative diffusion of the theater, new audiences were created throughout the nation. Rural populations saw their first live performances of fine plays interpreted by professionals. Old Vic, a fugitive from its hall in blitzed London, arranged for three companies to meet the great demand for its performances in the provinces. By 1943 there were 16 mobile theatrical companies under the direction of CEMA. These did not include opera and ballet groups which were also touring England.

The Captive Audience

Performances were held in all possible and seemingly impossible places. A new term — *captive audience* — attained meaning in these years of emergency. The tragic circumstances exposed new audiences to great art. People watched and listened in air raid shelters and rest centers, in churches and hospitals, in military camps and in factories of all sizes. The audiences, frankly, were not always ready or eager for the experience of serious art. They were, for better or worse, captive audiences. Men and women who formerly would not have cared to listen to anything but cheap entertainment found themselves for the first time exposed to great art.

But the repeated experience worked wonders. Collective listening under trying circumstances intensified the receptivity of an untrained public. After the war had ended, large sections of the captive audience remained faithful to serious art, and a new public began to pay its way into the theater and concert.

Government Assumes Responsibility

The Pilgrim Trust had financed CEMA's initial efforts by a grant of £25,000. Impressed by the first signs of success, the British government, through its Board of Education, decided after four months to match the grant of the Trust, pound for pound, up to a total of £50,000.

This marked a departure of lasting consequence. *For the first time the British government assumed responsibility for the performing arts.* By the third year of the War, the Pilgrim Trust had contributed a grand total of £62,500 to the project. At this point the Trust withdrew, and the destiny of CEMA was left in the hands of the Board of Education.

CEMA Becomes Arts Council

At War's end CEMA had won a victory that had far exceeded its originally stated purpose and the expectations of its sponsors.

On June 12, 1945, the Chancellor of the Exchequer declared in the House of Commons that there was a permanent need — even in peacetime — for an organization entrusted with the encouragement and diffusion of the arts. He announced on this occasion that the government had decided to incorporate CEMA into an officially sponsored organization to be known as the Arts Council of Great Britain. The Treasury would be in charge of its finances. The Council, like its predecessor CEMA, would not report to the Ministry of Education.

The difference is not negligible. Most Continental nations relegate the patronage of the performing arts to their ministries of education. But, in postwar England the government added a gesture of aloofness from any kind of control. The tie-up of the Arts Council with the government was to be financial only.

Policies of the Arts Council

The official birthday of the Arts Council of Great Britain is August 9, 1946. On this date a royal decree incorporated its charter, entrusting it with manifold responsibilities for the art life of the nation.

The principal policies of the Arts Council can be summarized along the following lines: the pursuit of quality is a primary aim; there can be no compromise on the question of standards. Consequently, specific organizations of exemplary attainments have to be supported, which will serve as models to which the nation can look for guidance.

To make the arts accessible throughout the country is another all-important aim of the Arts Council. British art life, still concentrated in a few large centers, must be gradually decentralized. Rural as well as urban populations are to share the enjoyment of live performances.

Adequate housing for the performing arts is of preeminent concern to the Council. In this respect, Britain still trails far behind Continental achievements. Even in the postwar period other European countries have given high priority to the building program of representative operas, theaters, and community centers. England had long needed suitable theaters and halls. Since the War, many old theaters in London and the provinces have closed their doors.

Yet there is a strong countercurrent, and new shelters for the performing arts have been built, or are in the blueprint stage. Most important: the impulse for this program stems from the communities themselves; they realize that they must shoulder this cultural assignment.

Coventry has built a new theater, and so has Nottingham. In Bristol, the Theatre Royal, built in 1766, has been modernized. The Arts Council made in its second year (1946-47) a grant to the trustees of the Theatre Royal toward the reduction of the outstanding debt of the theater, and appropriated money for the cost of alterations, renovations, and modernization of equipment.

Quality of offering, accessibility of good live performances, decentralization, and adequate housing are basic points of policy that continue to direct the program of the Arts Council. To a certain degree, these guideposts are interrelated. And they lend themselves to an interpretation which is flexible with the changing needs of England's cultural life.

The Arts Council aids a large number of amateur performers, among them approximately 500 choral and orchestral societies as well as music clubs throughout the country. Annual allocations are either forwarded directly, or distributed through the National Federation of Music Societies. These grants are slight, but they suffice to defray basic expenses. A helping hand is also extended to such groups as the Rural Music Schools Association and the Society for the Promotion of New Music.

Structure of the Arts Council

The Arts Council is strictly nonpolitical. It is not a government department. It does not correspond to offices in other European countries, such as the Ministry of Culture or the Ministry of Education. The chairman of the Arts Council presides at all official meetings, but he is not the chief who can insist on specific artistic policies. The artistic direction of the Arts Council stems from its individual panels, devoted to music, drama, poetry, and the visual arts. There is a subcommittee for opera and ballet. These panels function on a rotating system; every three years the membership changes. The total membership of the panels is about 70. The system of rotation makes possible fresh viewpoints.

The administration of the Arts Council has undergone changes. During the war years one kind of administration was needed for CEMA; in peacetime, another kind for the Arts Council. In 1946 the Arts Council inherited 9 regional offices that had been installed by CEMA for its war activities. By 1955 the Council had closed all regional offices. Instead, 3 mobile officers were put in charge of the provinces. These men were chosen for their knowledge of the regions, as well as for their specialization in the arts. To compensate for the closing of regional offices and to redirect the funds thus freed the Council increased its subsidies to various national organizations, among them the National Federation of Music Societies, which covers the territory of the provinces.

Local Government Act

Until the postwar era the power of local governments was cautiously defined and restricted in regard to art subsidy. The Local Government Act of 1948 authorized, for the first time, expenditures for the benefit of the performing arts.

Specifically, the Local Government Act encourages the annual allocation of "up to 6*d.* rate on the arts," either as direct subsidy or for buildings. The local authorities may also spend for the performing arts "one half of one per cent of the net cost which the Ministry fixes for schools and colleges." According to a recent study on this subject, the overall response of British communities has not been satisfactory. We learn from the report to the Gulbenkian Foundation that "local authority expenditure over the country as a whole does not exceed the equivalent of a three-fourths pence rate for museums and galleries and one-fifth pence rate for music and drama. Even county boroughs spend less than a two pence and one-half pence rate, respectively, on cultural projects. As long as local authorities as a whole spend less than a twentieth of the six pence rate permitted, then they can be regarded as only marginal instead of major patrons of the arts."[1]

Funds and Finances

A staff of specialists helps the Council in all matters pertaining to management. This staff consists of a secretary general, a deputy, a secretary and finance officer, and of the directors for art, music, and drama. The total personnel numbers around 100 (including all employees, drivers, and aides in the art department).

A Treasury official assists the Council as an assessor. His assignment is to guide the Council in all financial problems. The Council also includes a representative of the Scottish Office and of the Ministry of Education. They serve as principal observers for their respective offices. At all times the books of the Council are subject to strict examination by the Committee of Public Accounts and the Select Committee of Estimates.

The following course determines the grants which Parliament allocates to the Arts Council. Each year the Council submits to the Chancellor of the Exchequer an itemized request for money, representing the budget which the Council anticipates for the tentative programs of the various organizations it intends to support. The figures are carefully checked in the Treasury, prior to public debate in Parliament, whose members ultimately vote the yearly grant to the Arts Council. The Council's hopes for a quinquennial grant have so far not materialized. A five-year allocation would enable the Council to plan on a long-range basis, instead of being tied down to what is considered "a hand-to-mouth policy." The subsidies to the Council are for strictly defined projects. There is never a block grant. If a specified sum for Old Vic or Sadler's Wells, for example, has been withdrawn by the Council, this amount would not be automatically available for another organization.

The value and role of the Arts Council are no longer questioned by Parliament. They are not issues hotly debated along party lines, as are other problems of national or international affairs. The Council is supported by both the Conservative and Labor parties.

The Arts Council also receives grants from private sources. It is incorporated as a charitable trust and it can never extend its subsidies to any institution that aims at profit. In its initial year (1946) the Council received from the Exchequer a total grant of £235,000 ($658,000); in 10 years it increased to £820,000 ($2,296,000). For the year ending March 31, 1961, the Council obtained £1,225,434 ($3,431,215).*

Art from the Grass Roots

The categories of organizations which are the benefactors of yearly grants from Parliament by recommendation of the Arts Council include operas, ballets, orchestras, repertory theaters, arts festivals, art centers, art clubs, etc. It is the function of the Arts Council to aid and keep alive a limited, carefully chosen group of organizations devoted to the performing and visual arts throughout Britain.

Of the total income received by the Council, 78.5 per cent is transferred directly to the selected institutions. In its initial phase CEMA completely managed all of its enterprises. It delivered theatrical and musical performances to the very doorsteps of the places visited. Today, however, the Arts Council aims to make the institutions independent in all aspects of its activities, including management; it hopes to promote new growth from the grass roots all over the country. In every town, there is a nucleus of talent out of which an indigenous art life can be created. At certain places there already exist modest organizations which can be sufficiently activated. Such encouragement is characteristic of the Council's present policies; ultimately, it expects to limit its role to the allocation of subsidies.

Some of the early investments are now paying the expected dividends. Thus, theaters which hitherto depended on provision and supervision of the Council have become independent. Several theaters in cities of medium size, such as Bristol and Salisbury, fall into this group. The new civic theater in Coventry, one of the outstanding postwar projects, is directed by an independent trust. In general it is hoped that all organizations devoted to drama and music will be individually managed at the place of their origin.

*£ = $2.80.

II. The Orchestras

First Public Concerts

The history of public concerts in England spans three centuries. In 1672 John Banister, a violinist in the King's Band, announced in London a series of afternoon concerts. "Music performed by excellent masters" was his promise.

In 1713 the first adequate quarters, Hickford's Room, were adopted for public performances. Subsequently, Handel and Mozart appeared in this "hall." Between 1775 and 1874 important orchestral concerts took place in the Hanover Square Rooms.

A crucial phase in the chronicle of orchestral history in England was the subscription concerts organized by J. P. Salomon. This imaginative entrepreneur brought Haydn to London, when his services as music director at the princely estate of Eszterháza had ended. For his two visits to London (1791-92 and 1794-95) Haydn wrote the twelve "London Symphonies" and conducted them at the Salomon concerts. These events were the result of private enterprise; the scores conceived for the occasion have remained an integral part of the symphonic repertory.

In 1813 the Philharmonic Society of London was founded to sponsor the creation and performance of significant orchestral and instrumental music. Through friends living in England, Beethoven soon made contact with this institution, which invited him to come to London in 1818 and to compose two symphonies for the Society's exclusive use. Beethoven's ill health prevented the project from materializing. But the British Society performed various of his works, and proved generous when it learned of his fatal illness. In his final weeks the dying master sketched some music for his intended *Tenth Symphony* to be dedicated to his English sponsors.

During the entire nineteenth century Britain maintained a considerable patronage of orchestral music. Today, the overall problems of supporting first-class symphony orchestras are no different in the United Kingdom from those in the rest of the world. In general, however, British orchestras are not as financially secure as those on the Continent. And yet, most British cities possess at least one hall suitable for large-scale orchestral and choral performances; sometimes it is the Town Hall or Trade Hall.

Financing Concerts

Throughout the United Kingdom concerts are normally supported from the sale of individual tickets and subscriptions, grants from local authorities, subsidies by the National Treasury (distributed through the Arts Council), and private contributions.

British managers report a sizeable increase of their audiences. Yet the resulting plus at the box office is offset by the inflationary trend. All costs connected with the financing of first-class symphony orchestras have increased. At the same time, it is felt that the ticket prices cannot be raised in proportion, provided one wishes to adhere to one of the basic policies of the Arts Council: to make live performances accessible to wide circles of the population.

In important instances the cooperation of local authorities has proved to be adequate for supplementing the income of the orchestras. During the season 1957-58, for example, concerts given by 9 major symphony orchestras of Britain were attended by 2,500,000 people. These orchestras earned a total of £720,000 from box office receipts and other sources. The total costs of these concerts were £943,000. The Arts Council contributed £79,800 toward meeting the deficits. Local authorities assisted with £143,000; only a very small deficit remained.

TABLE I

Typical Budget of the London Philharmonic, Subventions and Their Sources

Arts Council	£ 14,500	
London County Council	2,000	
Local Authorities	4,600	
British Council	7,500	
	£ 28,600	($80,080)
Annual Deficit	£ 17,400	($48,720)

TABLE II

Five Permanent Symphony Orchestras Aided by the Arts Council (1960-61)

	Number of Concerts
Birmingham Orchestra	204
Bournemouth Symphony	221
Hallé Orchestra	244
Liverpool Philharmonic	186
Scottish National Orchestra	180

In association with specific assignments for the Arts Council, the London Philharmonic and the London Symphony Orchestra gave 63 and 18 concerts respectively.

Manchester: Hallé Orchestra

For more than one hundred years Britain has maintained *permanent* orchestras. The oldest of these is the Hallé Orchestra of Manchester. It serves a community comparable to Pittsburgh, Pennsylvania in its role as a large industrial and educational center.

The story of the Hallé Orchestra is originally one of private initiative. The ensemble developed from the Gentlemen's Concert Orchestra, which began its activities in this British manufacturing city in 1848. In the following year the Westphalian conductor Charles Hallé reorganized the group. He assumed complete financial responsibility. For all practical purposes this orchestra, then numbering 40 players, was a one-man enterprise. In 1858 the organization became known as the Hallé Orchestra. The title suggested that the concerts were undertaken at the sole financial risk of the conductor-manager. He imported his first chairmen from London. Under Hallé's initiative the entire music life of the city took on momentum. He founded the Royal Conservatory of Music in Manchester. He took his orchestra on successful tours, which, in turn, encouraged greater civic patronage at home. At the time of its founder's death (1895) the Hallé Orchestra had become a widely esteemed institution. In 1898 one of the great interpreters of the era, the Austrian conductor Hans Richter, was appointed music director. Yet with all of its new artistic achievements, the security of the Hallé Orchestra left much to be desired. From the founding of the orchestra in 1848, until 1943, the musicians were paid on a fee-per-concert basis. In good years, when the orchestra was much in demand and toured extensively, this remuneration was adequate.

The tragic years of World War II — as shown before — heightened rather than decreased British art life. Musical activities continued during breathing spells from the Nazi blitz. The Hallé Orchestra received many new invitations, playing about 200 concerts yearly. Under these circumstances, the executive committee, long anxious for a general rehabilitation of the group, judged the time ripe to put the orchestra on a permanent basis. Curiously, the decisive impulse for this step did not come from the city of Manchester itself, but from the nearby industrial town of Sheffield. In 1942 the Sheffield Philharmonic Society, lacking an orchestra of its own, offered to engage the Hallé Orchestra for a series of regular symphony concerts. This promised the Manchester musicians a sound financial future; and in the following year (1943) the Hallé Orchestra was reorganized. All of its men were now given full-time contracts.

The various changes of support which the Hallé Orchestra underwent from its inception as a private organization are worthy of study. After a century of private subsidy the public has taken over. The Arts Council, in accord with its policy of aiding established organizations of unquestioned standards, has offered financial assistance. Today various local authorities throughout Britain sponsor the Hallé Orchestra. Here, again, the procedure of assistance varies. A number of municipalities offer annual grants. In return, the Manchester Orchestra gives a certain number of guest concerts. For these, however, the Hallé Concert Society promotes the concerts and takes the financial risks. Other communities engage the orchestra for individual concerts, guarantee a fee, and are committed to meet the losses. With a third group of sponsoring municipalities the aid is indirect: here local authorities subsidize their own musical societies, which are thus in financial position to engage the Manchester group. In Lancashire and Cheshire a number of localities join forces to provide visiting orchestras (from Manchester and Liverpool) with a fixed annual grant, which amounted to £20,000 ($56,000) in 1958. In addition to year-round commitments there are seasonal engagements of short duration. These are the bookings of the orchestra by music festivals. Such events are normally supported by the local authorities as well as by the Arts Council. The Hallé Orchestra also has an income from records and broadcasts, for which the engaging parties assume full financial responsibility. In 1951 the deficit was still about £17,000 ($47,600). In 1952 the Manchester Corporation came forth with a promise of £9,000 ($25,200) for the years 1953 to 1956. Only the sum total derived from all the quoted bookings, and the subsidies received from the Arts Council, from the Manchester Corporation, and from other municipalities, represents sufficient income to guarantee the existence of the orchestra and the welfare of the players.

In 1959 the orchestra received £12,000 ($33,600) from the Arts Council and £18,000 ($50,400) from the Manchester City Council. For the year ending March 31, 1961, the Hallé Concerts Society received £25,767 ($72,147) from the Arts Council. The Hallé Orchestra gives approximately 250 public concerts a year. At the regular series in the Free Trade Hall, the concerts attracted a 90 per cent attendance.

Liverpool Philharmonic

Like industrial Manchester, the ancient port city of Liverpool prides itself on maintaining one of the oldest orchestral organizations in the Kingdom. In fact, both the Liverpool Orchestra Society and its first supported orchestra were founded as early as 1840, eight years prior to the Manchester Symphony. But the Manchester Symphony claims permanence since 1848.

Liverpool is one of the few English cities with the advantage of an adequate symphony hall. Liverpool has attained the distinction of having first inaugurated industrial concerts, an enterprise that has since been copied all over the world. Each season, about 30 such concerts are given in Liverpool. The attendance record is excellent, averaging 91 per cent. Liverpool is in a densely populated industrial region: 2,000,000 people live in the Merseyside area. Within the city limits of

Liverpool alone, 80 concerts are played during the year. There are 3 main series, totaling some 60 concerts. The subscription concerts are attended well even though the prices are rather high for English standards. For the Tuesday subscription concerts, the average ticket is 7*s*9*d*. ($1.07) per seat.

The orchestra must give a minimum of 100 concerts out-of-town in order to earn additional income and to maintain its members on full-time salaries. Among the organizations that regularly engage the Liverpool Philharmonic and thus contribute to its regular income are the British Broadcasting Company (with 30 engagements) and various civic groups and choral societies (which account for 35 additional concerts each season). But the remaining 35 to 40 concerts are given in relatively distant cities (such as Newcastle or Cardiff). The audience potential in these communities has not yet reached optimal figures. In spite of the losses incurred, the Liverpool Philharmonic continues to make these tours. It is expected that the Arts Council of Great Britain will eventually be able to increase subsidy to the orchestra, particularly in view of its educational mission in the hinterland.

In 1959 the Liverpool Philharmonic received £20,000 from the Arts Council and £29,000 from local civic authorities. For the year ending March 31, 1961, the orchestra received £27,000 from the Arts Council.

Birmingham Symphony Orchestra

In 1920 — late even by English chronology — the city of Birmingham established a municipal orchestra. Regular subsidies were pledged by the Municipal Council of this industrial city of 1,117,000 inhabitants. More recently, several local authorities in the Midlands have shared in this support. The orchestra now plays regularly for the Birmingham Education Committee, and frequently serves other local educational authorities. Today, the society maintaining the orchestra has a large membership. A capital fund for the benefit of the orchestra was initiated in 1951 and has steadily grown by public subscription.

The Arts Council of Great Britain has become a regular patron of the Birmingham Orchestra, which now has full symphonic strength of 83 players. For the year ending March 31, 1961, the orchestra received £22,000 from the Arts Council. But diversified sponsorship on local and regional levels has contributed to the security of the players: the orchestra also received from the City Corporation of Birmingham £28,000, and from other local authorities £2,000. The new Summer Promenade Concerts attracted capacity audiences.

Private Patronage in London

Royal Philharmonic Orchestra

From its title one could assume that the Royal Philharmonic Orchestra is in some form supported by the Crown. In reality, the renowned ensemble has been an entirely private organization since its founding and apparently will continue on this basis in the future. The Royal Philharmonic is, in essence, the creation of Thomas Beecham. The late Sir Thomas exemplified, like Charles Hallé of Manchester before him, the type of conductor who from the start assumed complete charge of all artistic and financial matters connected with the management of the orchestra. But in contrast to the Manchester conductor, who was an immigrant to England and a self-made man, Sir Thomas Beecham was born into a British millionaire family. His father, a manufacturer of pills, was willing — after long resistance — to finance various ambitious and very costly productions of ballet and opera to be directed by Thomas Beecham at Drury Lane. The enterprising young conductor moved on to further more ambitious projects. In 1910 he offered at Covent Garden the English première of *Elektra* by Richard Strauss. In 1911 he brought Diaghilev's Russian Ballet to England. During World War I Thomas Beecham financed opera and concert performances throughout the United Kingdom. In 1932 he founded the London Philharmonic Orchestra, which subsequently performed also for concerts of the Royal Philharmonic Society and Covent Garden. The formation of the Royal Philharmonic Orchestra in 1947 marks Beecham's lasting achievement. Constantly meeting the deficits, he could afford to keep the orchestra independent of any governmental subsidy. After the death of Sir Thomas in March, 1961, the trustees of the orchestra decided to continue its maintenance on a private basis as a tribute to the memory of this rugged exponent of private patronage.

Public Subsidy of Orchestras

In addition to the Royal Philharmonic, London is also home to a number of other concert orchestras devoted exclusively to public performance, broadcasting, and recording of serious music. The previously mentioned London Philharmonic is annually engaged by the home counties for numerous concerts. Eleven local municipalities outside of London share in the subsidy. As to the London County Council, rental rebates constitute its main support to the London Philharmonic. In 1961 the Arts Council contributed £9,000 to this orchestra.

The London Symphony Orchestra receives £5,000 from the Arts Council. This well-established orchestra dates back to 1904. The orchestra controls its own affairs and the members participate in the management. In 1945 the London Symphony reorganized itself as a "nonprofit distribution company" under the presidency of Sir William Walton. The Arts Council lent a helping hand.

The orchestras of the British Broadcasting Company enjoy security of regular year-round employment, which this government supported radio network provides, not only for its London musicians, but also for other symphonic ensembles anchored at various radio stations throughout the country.

A few smaller instrumental groups have been, or still are, recipients of Arts Council grants, such as the Philomusica, the Boyd Neel Orchestra, and the English Chamber Orchestra.

The Philharmonia Orchestra of London (well known through its records) has no support from the Arts Council. This London group is entirely self-supporting and (at this writing) self-governing.

Scotland participates to an ever-increasing degree in the evolution of British orchestral life. The Scottish National Orchestra, in typical procedure, derives its annual subsidies from the Arts Council Committee in Scotland and from a number of Scottish local authorities. Eighty-seven localities raised £40,000 during the season of 1957-58. For the year ending March 31, 1961, the Scottish National Orchestra received £28,500 from the Arts Council Committee in Scotland.

A relatively high subsidy of £30,000 was cxtended to the Western Orchestral Society, Limited. The Bournemouth Symphony Orchestra, which is associated with this society, also received from the Bournemouth Corporation £12,500. The orchestra of this southwestern city of 145,000 gives concerts in Wales where numerous small communities cooperate to make these visits financially possible. Some of the towns in South Wales have attained an admirably high rate of concert attendance.

Wages and Benefits

The salaries of British orchestra musicians are still below Continental standards. At the outset of the season 1962-63 wages fell into 3 categories. Approximately 50 per cent of the orchestra members earned $42 weekly. The first chairmen commanded the top fees of $56 weekly. A middle group earned $48 weekly.

This represents an unfavorable, not to say untenable situation, even considering the familiar differences in standards of living, English and American. On the other hand, the contracts for the provincial orchestras provide for continued fifty-two weeks employment, and allow for a month's vacation (of which three weeks are paid in full).

The situation in London is different. At this writing only the BBC Orchestra enjoys the security of a permanent contract. Other London concert orchestras operate on limited agreements — for individual concerts, for the length of varied specific engagements, etc. Here, the average wage is $8.40 per concert, including one rehearsal.

Table II indicates the average number of concerts given by some of the leading provincial orchestras of England. But, in their present demands, the musicians seek a limit of 200 concerts per year (with full wages guaranteed). One of the main goals in this drive for improved working conditions is the establishment of old-age pensions. They are not a novelty in England, for 3 of the provincial orchestras have inaugurated benefits which are now sought by all British musicians.

It is worthy of note that the Orchestral Employers' Association (representing all national societies engaging orchestra players in the United Kingdom) and the Musicians' Union are in full accord; they both agree that help from the government is the only possible solution. The National Treasury is expected to increase its subsidies to the orchestras. Any raise of ticket prices and subscriptions is considered unrealistic: it would most likely result in curtailment of attendance and thus nullify the purpose of the raise. The union is aware that the Employers' Association, for the time being, is in no position to pay higher fees.

The Arts Council of Great Britain, as the administrator of government funds for the arts, is in full sympathy with the combined requests of the union and employers, and represents these demands in the discussions with the government. The added costs to the Treasury would be relatively modest. For the next two seasons (1963-64, 1964-65) it would amount to approximately $800,000. This would make it possible to augment the average income of each orchestra musician by £5 per week ($14 per week) to a minimum of $56 per week on a yearly basis.

Children's Concerts, Privately Sponsored

Private patronage has produced on the London scene a remarkable concert series of orchestral music. In 1922 Sir Robert and Lady Mayer attended New York youth concerts directed by Walter Damrosch. Deeply impressed with the mission to introduce children to symphonic art, the British visitors decided to transplant the idea to England. They underwrote a similar project in London, offering their young audiences programs of masterworks with explanatory comments spoken from the stage by the conductor himself. Due to the rapidly increasing success of these, similar concerts were soon in demand throughout the Kingdom. Before the advent of World War II almost 30 centers provided fine orchestral music for more than 1,000,000 children. Today, the London Young People's Concerts are spread over seven months of the year.

In a typical British pattern the success of private initiative stimulated official patronage: today the London County Council and a number of provincial authorities offer children free admission to orchestral concerts, which are scheduled during school hours as part of the educational program. The Ministry of Education has established an Advisory Council for the Encouragement of Music for the Young. The project offering good music to young audiences has grown in geometric proportion. In London alone the number of annual orchestral concerts designed specifically for the young approaches 300. All of these concerts are performed by professionals.

A musical magazine for the young called *Crescendo*, costing a mere 6*d*. (edited by Sir Robert and Lady Mayer), offers information on the lives of the composers and on the music to be heard. London has also another series related in spirit and success: the Ernest Read Concerts for Children, inaugurated in 1926.

III. Opera and Ballet

English National Opera

The absence of a regularly supported national opera theater in the capital of the United Kingdom has long appeared as a blemish on the English art scene. This deficiency seems strange, particularly in view of England's historic contribution to operatic development.

Henry Purcell (1659-1695), the great English master of the early Baroque, complained in the preface to *The Fairy Queen* about the unfavorable position of English opera — in contrast to national opera in Italy and France. Purcell raised, in fact, what appears to be the first significant plea for support of opera in Great Britain. This extraordinary document, dated from 1692, has lost nothing of its impact.* Georg Frideric Handel, German born and widely traveled, decisively aided, during the first half of the eighteenth century, the establishment of music dramatic traditions in England. British light opera found a perennial model in *The Beggar's Opera*, first performed in 1728.

Even these few examples show that the deeply entrenched English coolness toward opera cannot be blamed on the paucity of significant works created on British soil. Some seek the culprit in Anglo-Saxon Puritanism, which views opera and ballet as wicked. Or did the supremacy of English drama overshadow all other forms of theatrical expression? Whatever the reason for its backward state, to this day British

*Quoted on pages 431, 432.

opera life is limited to a few key centers. Few theaters outside London can accommodate the large apparatus of a touring full-sized opera company. And so it happened that opera, the most unlikely medium to succeed under private patronage, until recent developments has depended upon it in England. While private sponsors of opera are still to be reckoned with on the British art scene, the scope of music drama is too vast and financially demanding to be left to individual patronage, if large audiences are to enjoy this art form throughout the United Kingdom.

Covent Garden

Fortunately, the Arts Council of Great Britain recognizes the cultural significance of opera. One of the early objects for the Council's support was Covent Garden, London's old opera house on a flower and vegetable market.

Covent Garden is the third theater erected on this place. The original house, on the Bow Street site, had been built by John Rich in 1732 out of the profits of *The Beggar's Opera*. For over one hundred fifteen years, Covent Garden was one of London's two "Royal Patent Theatres." In 1847 Covent Garden became known as the "Royal Italian Opera." But opera was regularly performed here under *private* management. There was also the Italian Opera playing at "Her Majesty's Theatre in the Haymarket." And so, a typically Continental pattern of rivalry between competing opera companies reached the British capital. This might have worked to improve quality of performance. But the Haymarket Theatre was favored neither by fate nor by the public. Fire burned the building to ashes in 1867, and Covent Garden became the principal scene of opera life in Great Britain. With its absorption of French and German works into its repertory, the theater accordingly dropped "Italian" from its title. It was now the "Royal Opera, Covent Garden." But in spite of the fact that its name never excluded the attribute "Royal," no substantial support was forthcoming from the royal purse, from the Treasury, or from other official sources.

Toward the end of the nineteenth century Sir Augustus Harris offered at Covent Garden brief seasons of international opera. He imported famous singers and conductors from the Continent. Until the beginning of World War II, Covent Garden Opera was managed and paid for by private syndicates, which continued a policy of short, international seasons based on standard works. These productions had few, if any, inner ties with indigenous English musical life. They certainly provided no stimulus for either British composers or interpreters.

Postwar Policy

In the fall of 1945 a new, overdue orientation was sought by Covent Garden. The initial impulse stemmed from a music publishing house in London which was willing to undertake the risk of leasing the theater and underwriting its maintenance. Covent Garden Opera Trust was established. Before long the newly formed Arts Council was ready to help. The first chairman of the Arts Council became also the chairman of the Opera Trust. Its clearly defined aim was to promote Covent Garden as a permanent and continuous home for opera and ballet. This, then, marks the belated start of national opera in England — centuries after organizations of similar design had become firmly entrenched on the continent.

The annual report of the Arts Council, published for the year ending March 31, 1961, lists the grant allocated to Covent Garden as £500,737. This is the lion's share of the Council's general expenditures of £1,004,387. But, according to the management of the Royal Opera House, such subsidy based upon 43 per cent of the theater's costs is no longer sufficient. All expenses have risen, and maintenance is still a major burden. To date, the building which houses Covent Garden is still in private possession. The Ministry of Works has taken a lease on it until 1991. In turn, the Covent Garden Trust is charged by the Ministry £49,000 annually for rent (including taxes and insurance). Thus a rather curiour *quid pro quo* of ownership and patronage results. Art-minded Englishmen are annoyed by the unwarranted discrimination against the Royal Opera. Other British art institutes maintained by the government (such as the Tate Gallery or the National Gallery) are exempt from similar payments of rent.

Table III indicates attendance and receipts of the Royal Opera House for 1960-61. Table IV indicates the Opera's income and expenditure for the seasons 1959-60 and 1960-61.

TABLE III

House Attendances

	Performances £	*Attendances*	*Receipts* £	*Average Attendance*	*Average Receipts* £
Opera—Ordinary prices	92	174,473	139,119	1,896	1,512
” —Special ”	64	126,029	173,584	1,969	2,712
” —Gala ”	1	1,586	4,009		
” —Visiting Co. ”	12	17,543	19,152	1,462	1,596
Ballet—Ordinary ”	92	156,945	125,249	1,706	1,361
” —Special ”	18	38,263	45,829	2,126	2,546
” —Gala ”	1	1,625	4,228		

During the period from April 1960 to March 1961, 157 performances of opera were given at Covent Garden.[2]

TABLE IV

*Royal Opera House Income and Expenses (1959-60 and 1960-61)**

Year	*Expenditure (Excluding Overseas Tours)* £	*Expenditure of Overseas Tours* £	*Total* £	*House & Tour Receipts (Excluding Overseas Tours)* £	*Receipts of Overseas Tours* £	*Sundry Income* £	*Arts Council Grant* £	*Net Surplus* £
1959-60	1,049,447	78,560	1,128,007	589,622	90,537	41,051	473,000	66,203
1960-61	1,152,512	257,491	1,410,003	576,108	313,063	51,121	500,737	31,026

Salaries and Wages

Year	*Artists & Management* £	*Orchestra* £	*Stage & Staff* £	*Administration & Front of House* £	*Others* £	*Total* £
**1959-60	340,756	155,984	186,739	61,840	67,512	812,831
***1960-61	388,628	146,756	213,601	70,880	72,159	892,024

**Includes New Zealand and South Africa Tours
***Includes South Africa and U.S.A./Canada Tours

Numbers of Employees on Payroll

Year	*Artists & Management*	*Orchestra*	*Stage & Staff*	*Administration & Front of House*	*Others*	*Total*
1959–60	224	123	179	124	147	797
1960–61	229	124	202	134	149	838

*Cf. The Fifteenth and Sixteenth Annual Reports of Royal Opera House

Present Policy of Royal Opera

The guideposts that govern the present policy of Covent Garden are officially stated as follows:[2]

Presentation of established masterpieces

Revival of interesting and beautiful works outside of the regular repertory

Performance of new works with special attention to our native composers

Discovery and development of British artists

Appearances before the London public of artists of international fame and achievements, whether singers, conductors, producers, or designers.

These five points represent a policy which is difficult to balance; for these guideposts are, admittedly, not always compatible.

Covent Garden still depends, to a large degree, on the star system and the standard repertory. The general public expects the Royal Opera House to import to London as many famous singers as possible. Certain devotees are attracted only by celebrated interpreters presenting the familiar fare. A progressive minority realizes, howcver, that opera must grow from within. This is believed to be true not only of new music-dramatic works, but also of the productions themselves. A national operatic culture is expected gradually to supplant the expensive international star system with a competent, highly-trained native ensemble.

New Role of Covent Garden

For the first time in its history the Royal Opera House plays in the cultural life of the nation a role corresponding to that of analogous representative theaters on the Continent. Since 1946 Covent Garden has offered performances of opera and ballet for ten or eleven months of the year. This new schedule is in contrast to the brief seasons of a few months given by the Royal Opera prior to World War II.

Covent Garden now sends its performing forces on regular tours throughout the United Kingdom. This is considered part of its regular assignment. The opera provides such festivals as those at Edinburgh and Leeds with special offerings.

The nature of Covent Garden as a principal scene of festive national representation is always manifest when visiting foreign royalty or heads of state are entertained in the Opera by the Queen and her court.

Private Aid, Friends of Covent Garden

Consecutive budgets of Covent Garden show that the Treasury has repeatedly increased annual allocations to the Royal Opera House; and as indicated before, the Arts Council of Great Britain administers these public subsidies. But by comparison with government subsidies of principal opera houses in France, Germany, Austria, and Italy, the English subvention is still small. Hence, aid from private sources is welcome, either in terms of financial contribution or in various forms of direct and indirect propaganda for the Royal Opera.

An organization known as The Friends of Covent Garden solicits annual subscriptions at a minimum contribution of 5 guineas ($14.70) for full membership or 3 guineas ($8.80) for associate membership. The funds are used for purposes defined by a 5 point program:

To buy tickets for students

To arrange auditions and offer prizes and scholarships for opera and ballet

To assist new composers, choreographers, and stage designers

To make possible the production of new ballets and operas which may not be certain of immediate commercial success

To provide improved equipment and additional facilities which cannot be made available within the present budget.

The priority given this program toward the appreciation of opera by students, as well as the offering of scholarships, deserve special attention. The logical road is taken to integrate the musical theater deep into British life. Emphasis is placed on the future.

The Friends of Covent Garden is an organization recognized as a "charity." Hence it is possible to contribute to it by "Deed of Covenant"; it costs no more to pay in this way, for the organization can recover income tax, and thus the value of the contributions increases.

English Opera Group

During the season 1960-61 the Royal Opera House, Covent Garden, assumed responsibility for the management of the English Opera Group. Benjamin Britten had formed an indigenous British opera company after World War II. It was difficult to keep alive such a group in a country where opera, even with a conventional repertory, had found so little support. But the group survived, attaining noted success abroad as well as at home. In its new association with Covent Garden, Mr. Britten continues to play an active part. The governing board of the English Opera Group now consists of 10 members (5 of whom are nominated by Covent Garden).[3] During the season 1960-61 the group appeared at festivals, among them Aldeburgh, Leeds, and Schwetzingen (Germany).

Opera for Youth

In 1959 the deficit of Covent Garden had reached a crucial state. At that time the British government stepped in with increased subsidies. But repeated payments of high deficits are not the answer. The attempt to make opera popular in England must pursue the natural path: it must start with children. If symphonic music could be brought close to English youth by systematic exposure, why could not the musical theater be approached by a parallel road? The patron of youth concerts, Sir Robert Mayer, decided to sponsor a series of opera nights for young people. The Sadler's Wells Company was engaged for this project, and performances were offered at nominal prices. The success of the venture surpassed the expectations of its private patrons. Before the initial season had ended, a very large audience of young opera fans had been won. This is interpreted as one of the most optimistic signs on the English opera scene. And it is now generally conceded that the future of opera in England depends on the sustained interest of young people who come to the theater because they have learned to love opera, and not because it is fashionable to be seen at gala performances.

Royal Ballet

An opera theater needs a ballet corps. In 1945, as part of its general reforms, Covent Garden invited the Sadler's Wells Ballet to become the opera's resident dance company. It was a natural solution and has worked well and to mutual advantage.

This ballet group had traveled an uphill road to success. Following its transformation from an amateur to a professional ensemble, the dancers had only their talent and perseverance to count on. There was no encouragement of any kind by city or state. The young group was kept going by the interest of the general public in the ballet — at the Old Vic on Waterloo Road, or at Sadler's Wells on Roseburg Avenue, Islington, where the young company gave its first, imaginatively produced performances. But within less than twenty-five years this troupe had become a national institution. The most crucial steps in its career were these: the reopening of Sadler's Wells Theatre in 1931, which lent itself to the reorganization of the ballet company, now called the Sadler's Wells Theatre Ballet; and the opening of a ballet school. On January 16, 1957, Queen Elizabeth granted a Charter of Incorporation which fused the Sadler's Wells Ballet, the Sadler's Wells Theatre Ballet, and the Sadler's Wells School in a corporation under the title *Royal Ballet.*

In connection with its present assignment as the ballet of the Royal Opera House, the subsidy of the dance group is covered by the overall budget of Covent Garden. But a special grant by the Arts Council of

Great Britain for the year ending March 31, 1961, allocated £15,000 to the Royal Ballet School. The budget of the ballet alone is approximately £100,000 ($280,000) annually.

During the season 1960-61 the company of 118 dancers was divided into 2 groups. The one undertook tours of the U.S.A., Canada, South Africa, and the English provinces. These tours, rewarding both artistically and financially, amounted to forty-five working weeks of 8 performances a week in 80 cities and towns. The "home group," in addition to the usual repertory, put on 3 new productions (2 forty-five minute one-act ballets and 1 ballet in two acts and three scenes).

Sadler's Wells

In addition to Covent Garden, the Arts Council considers two other historic London theaters as national institutions requiring continuous support. These — Sadler's Wells and Old Vic — are committed to maintain high uncompromising standards within their respective cultural assignments.

The history of Sadler's Wells leads back to the seventeenth century. In 1683 a well in the garden of the tavern keeper Sadler was found to contain curative waters. Next to his inn the enterprising owner built a place of entertainment and, along with it, advertised his medicinal well. In 1765 a small theater was built at Sadler's Wells, which was to experience many changes. It was a music hall, a playhouse, and an opera.

Today, Sadler's Wells may be described as a people's opera. It corresponds in certain ways to the Opéra Comique in Paris, or to the Volksoper in Vienna. The repertory of Sadler's Wells includes masterworks in the lighter genre such as *The Barber of Seville*, *Don Pasquale*, or *The Bat* (*Die Fledermaus*). From the repertory of tragic opera, *La Traviata* or *Tosca* may be included. Sadler's Wells does not duplicate the function of Covent Garden, but rather attempts to complement it. During the season 1962-63 the repertory was extended to include significant contemporary works (among these, *Rise and Fall of the City of Mahagonny* by Kurt Weill and Bertolt Brecht). The policy of presenting opera from the end of September until April, followed by operetta during the summer months, has proved successful. The attendance has risen.

Sadler's Wells has tried at various times to join forces with Covent Garden, or with the popular Carl Rosa Opera Company, founded by a German violinist in 1875. The Carl Rosa Company has for three-quarters of a century done much spadework for opera in England. But the attempted amalgamation of the various opera companies did not prove to be feasible.

The story of the private management of Sadler's Wells ends between the two World Wars. In 1925 public funds for the theater were solicited by a committee of distinguished citizens. Sadler's Wells was to become a home for both dramatic and musical performances. But is was not until January 6, 1931, that the new theater, with a seating capacity of 1650, opened its doors to the public. Shakespeare's *Twelfth Night* and Bizet's *Carmen* were the first offerings in their respective genres. With the season 1934-35, Sadler's Wells established itself as a center of opera in English. And Sadler's Wells has retained this function in a double sense: it sponsors works of British composers, and it regularly performs the foreign repertory in English.

From its very beginnings, in 1946, the Arts Council of Great Britain has taken Sadler's Wells under its wing. The original grant was a mere £15,000. The Council has multiplied this subsidy, recognizing that Sadler's Wells Opera and the Theatre Ballet Company offer a vital program, both in the capital and in the provinces. Part of the policy is to keep prices as low as circumstances will permit. For the year ending March 31, 1961, the Sadler's Wells Trust Limited received £275,000 ($770,000) from the Arts Council. The London County Council provides a grant of £25,000 ($70,000) and an additional £10,000 for capital expenditures. Thus the total allocations for the year ending March 31, 1961 amounted to £310,000 ($868,000). (See Table V.)

The considerable increase of subsidies is necessary: Sadler's Wells maintains 3 companies with a personnel of 400; 2 companies perform opera and 1, operetta — providing London and certain key centers in the provinces with seasons of musical theater; the tours comprise over forty weeks. Most recent plans envision new housing for Sadler's Wells at the South Bank Art Center. The joint sponsors will be the London County Council and the national government.

The city of London, then, has in Sadler's Wells and Covent Garden 2 permanently supported opera theaters performing throughout the year. The gradually changing attitude toward opera throughout England is reflected in the activities of a number of smaller companies, all engaged in the performance of music drama. Among those supported by public funds are the Welsh National Opera, which received from the Arts Council a subsidy of £25,228 ($70,638) for the year ending March 31, 1961; the Handel Opera Society, subsidy £1,000 ($2,800) for the same year; the New Opera Company, subsidy £2,000 ($5,600) for the same year.

TABLE V

Sadler's Wells Trust Limited

*Accounts 1960-61**

DEFICITS	£
The accumulated Deficit — brought forward from the preceding year	75,822
Deficit for period to the end of March, 1961	17,613
Total Deficit	93,435
GRANTS	
The Trust received an increase in grant from the Arts Council of £ 75,000, bringing the total Arts Council grant for the year to	275,000
The London County Council provided the Trust with a grant of	25,000
Total	300,000
In addition to the above, the London County Council provided a grant for capital expenditure of	10,000
Total	310,000

	1959–60 £	1960–61 £
Salaries:		
Principals	69,051	58,725
Chorus	61,724	63,415
Management	5,273	6,895
Music Staff	10,350	11,362
Guests	12,781	17,307
Royalties	16,568	9,783
Fees	5,923	5,245
Overtime	3,486	4,387
Touring Allowances	9,822	13,680
Traveling	5,917	10,636
Cartage	7,801	11,584
Incidentals	3,422	4,644
Tuition	139	61
Opera Ballet	14,610	12,753
	226,867	230,477
BROADCASTS AND TELEVISION		
Opera Company, Guests, Orchestra, Wardrobe, Stage, Theatre, and Administration Expenses	5,945	997
ORCHESTRA		
Salaries	94,360	102,755
Extra Payments	4,888	2,673
Touring Allowances	5,461	8,511
Library	4,539	5,299
	109,248	119,238

*Annual Report of Sadler's Wells Trust Limited (1960-61)

TABLE V (continued)

OPERA

Receipts at Sadler's Wells	68,155	118,277
Share of Receipts at London Coliseum	92,238	—
Share of Receipts on Provincial Tours	61,952	88,314
Net Receipts from Foreign Tours	—	18,958
Receipts from Broadcasts,	9.753	—
Television and Recordings	—	2,476
	232,098	228,025

IV. The Theater

Patronage of Drama

On the strength of its unique dramatic traditions, England obviously ranks supreme in the history of the theater. In spite of a spectacular past, it was not until the end of World War II that national patronage of drama began aiming at a scope worthy its rich heritage. Hitherto, public support was primarily given to the visual arts. Museums and galleries were the favored objects of subsidy from official or private sources. The performing arts were neglected. But the policy has decidedly changed. For the year ending March 31, 1961, the Arts Council allocated a total grant of £154,341 ($432,154) to the support of drama throughout the Kingdom.

The Standard Drama Agreement carefully defines the prerequisites for public subsidy. In brief, the conditions of official support for theatrical companies are these:

> The seriousness of artistic purpose must be clearly established
>
> High standards must be maintained in the overall repertory, and in all individual productions
>
> The management of the theater must be efficient
>
> The operation must be nonprofit (if there are financial gains, they are to be reinvested in the theater and its productions).

The Arts Council believes in the systematic diffusion of national art life. To achieve such decentralization in the category of drama, the support of repertory theaters in the provinces must follow, in order of priority, the perpetual maintenance of "the established powerhouses of opera, music and drama" in England's key cities. This recent British art policy corresponds to traditional European patterns.

Table VI indicates the support given by the Arts Council of Great Britain to theaters in London and the provinces, 1960-61.

TABLE VI

Drama Theaters Supported by Arts Council

(1960-61)*

	£	
Birmingham Repertory Theatre Limited	10,000	($ 28,000)
Bristol: Old Vic Trust Limited	8,000	($ 22,400)
Cambridge Arts Theatre Trust	1,000	($ 2,800)
Canterbury Theatre Trust Limited	2,400	($ 6,720)
Carlisle Theatre Trust Limited	2,300	($ 6,440)
Cheltenham Everyman Theatre Company Limited	1,650	($ 4,620)
Chesterfield Civic Theatre Limited	1,000	($ 2,800)
Colchester Repertory Company Limited	2,000	($ 5,600)
Coventry: Belgrade Theatre Trust Limited	9,000	($ 25,200)
Derby Playhouse Limited	1,300	($ 3,640)
Farnham Repertory Company Limited	500	($ 1,400)
Guildford Theatre Club Limited	4,000	($ 11,200)
Harrogate (White Rose) Theatre Trust Limited	11	($ 31)
Hornchurch Theatre Trust Limited	2,000	($ 5,600)
Ipswich Arts Theatre Trust	4,000	($ 11,200)
Leatherhead Repertory Company Limited	2,000	($ 5,600)
Lincoln Theatre Association Limited	7,350	($ 20,580)
London:		
English Stage Company Limited	8,000	($ 22,400)
Mermaid Theatre Trust	5,000	($ 14,000)
Old Vic Trust Limited	40,000	($112,000)
Pioneer Theatres (Theatre Workshop) Limited	2,000	($ 5,600)
Loughborough and District Theatre Association (Stanford Hall) Limited	1,500	($ 4,200)
Margate Theatre Trust Limited	945	($ 2,646)
Newcastle Playhouse Trust Limited	950	($ 2,660)
Northampton Repertory Players Limited	3,632	($ 10,170)
Nottingham Theatre Trust Limited	10,350	($ 28,980)
Oxford: Meadow Players Limited	6,000	($ 16,800)
Salisbury Arts Theatre Limited	2,700	($ 7,560)

*Based on The Sixteenth Annual Report of the Arts Council of Great Britain.

Manchester, Repertory Theatre

The history of English repertory theaters begins in Manchester: on September 7, 1908, Miss Annie E. F. Horniman opened the Gaiety Theatre with her own company in her native city. Manchester had earlier achieved cultural distinction with its fine orchestra. Now the industrial center was home to a theater as well. This started a new trend. In other British communities repertory theaters were founded and maintained by private sponsorship. Birmingham and Liverpool are important examples. Private contributions have since been widely replaced by local funds, and in selected cases national allocations have joined the support.

Experience shows that the most successful theaters were independent centers within their communities; they did not rely on regular importations from without. Most of these new repertory theaters gave young authors, actors, and producers their first chances. Acknowledging the varied roles of these stages — maintaining tradition as well as serving as a contemporary forum — the Arts Council had helped about 30 of these repertory theaters by 1962.

Bristol, the Theatre Royal

For its first enterprise in the management of a stage in the provinces, the Arts Council turned to the Theatre Royal in Bristol. The Old Vic Company became anchored in this theater as its regional subsidiary. A drama school was subsequently founded with the backing of the Arts Council. The City Council of Bristol helped the Bristol Old Vic in the financial support of its productions. In the spring of 1950 the municipality voted a modest annual grant of £1,500 ($4,200) to be paid for at least three seasons toward operating the Theatre Royal, Bristol. In addition, £5,000 ($14,000) were allocated for expenditures toward the building. This marks an early example of cooperation between a local Authority and the Arts Council of Great Britain, a joint enterprise which has worked out to best advantage. The City Council appointed a management committee for the theater under the chairmanship of the Vice-Chancellor of the University of Bristol. The proximity of theater and education is reflected in this tie. The board of the theater is made up of 2 representatives of the Corporation, 2 of the old Vic, and 2 of the Arts Council. Independence of artistic management is assured, and the directors have no responsibility in the maintenance of the building.

The Belgrade Theatre of Coventry
Local Authorities and Housing of the Arts

The Arts Council has repeatedly stressed its conviction that the responsibilities and the financial burden of art support should be shared by the local authorities. The previously mentioned Local Government Act of 1948 encourages regular annual allocations to the arts by British municipalities. Specifically, expenditures up to a 6*d.* rate are authorized in England and Wales, and to a 4⅘*d.* rate in Scotland.[4] But the extent to which local authorities have taken advantage of the opportunities offered by the Local Government Act varies greatly. Certain communities stand out by their model attitude. The ancient yet remarkably progressive city of Coventry appears to be the first local authority in England to build a new civic theater after the massive destruction by the second World War. Other cities, such as Canterbury, resorted to adaptations of older buildings to house their theatrical companies. But Coventry decided to provide new "bricks and mortar" for its art life. A new municipal theater was designed and financed by the Corporation. A commemorative gift of £12,000 was received from the city of Belgrade for the timber needed to build the theater.

The question of priority in Coventry's building program merits our attention. The city had faced since the Armistice a series of urgent tasks of reconstruction. In 1940 the Luftwaffe completely destroyed the five-hundred-year-old Cathedral. The shopping center and civic district were likewise flattened. But in the past two decades the city and the symbol of its inner strength, the Cathedral, have risen again from the ruins. On May 25, 1962, the new Cathedral was consecrated.

Four years earlier, on March 27, 1958, the new Belgrade Theatre of Coventry, seating 910, had opened its doors to an enthusiastic public. This theater is recognized as one of the most satisfying in Europe. The foyer, the neat shops, and the restaurants of the building add to the amenities. The modern architecture of the handsome theater, set within a park-like environment, embellishes the ancient city.

The Coventry Corporation has appointed 15 persons (10 of whom are members of the City Council) to form the nonprofit, distributing theater trust. This group appoints the artistic and administrative personnel and is responsible for the business management of the theater. But the artistic directors enjoy liberty of action, once the budget and the overall policy have been agreed upon with the trustees.

Three Patterns of Theater Support

Various other municipalities have successively decided to participate in the subsidy of their local repertory theaters. During the season 1948-49 playhouses were opened in Chesterfield, Nottingham, and Swansea; all found ready support in their respective communities. The management of these 3 theaters shows different patterns.

The playhouse of Chesterfield corresponds to the Continental type of civic theater. The building is the property of the municipality, which paid for the equipment of the stage and the refurbishing of the hall. But the company is managed independently by its artistic and business directors. The governing board, which appoints the management, includes representatives of the Town Council and of local art societies.

The funds which enabled the Chesterfield Theatre to begin its work were raised within the community by public subscription. The citizens contributed generously, and so the role of the Arts Council of Great Britain could be limited to offering a guarantee against loss.

In contrast to the civic playhouse of Chesterfield, the theater of Nottingham is privately owned. The management remains independent. The trustees of the theater, however, include representatives of the Corporation and other local interests. In 1949 the Vice-Chancellor of Nottingham University succeeded the Lord Mayor of the city as chairman. Nottingham, like Bristol, is conscious of the interdependence between schools of higher learning and the serious theater. The city's educational authorities have joined the country in the subsidization of the Nottingham Theatre. This educational fiber within British art life corresponds to Continental ideology.

The Swansea Theatre has retained, among these 3 examples, the highest degree of independence. The enterprise is entirely private. The Arts Council of Great Britain lends its support none the less; its goal is the establishment of a center for professional theater in this strategic region of Wales.

In England the task of spreading theatrical culture to the hinterland is urgent. Many towns in Wales, in the North, the East, and still other regions, are to this day without theaters. But experience has taught how to mount plays with small casts on makeshift stages. The Arts Council has not been deterred by adverse environment. It continues to support drama with minimum staging, not rarely performing in faroff villages to new audiences. Such tenacity has paid off. Statistics indicate the constantly increasing interest of the provinces in serious drama.

Touring Companies

One of the obvious methods to realize the Arts Council's aim of a nation-wide diffusion of drama is the organization of country-wide tours. These visits to the hinterland have become regular features. They provide performances of classical as well as contemporary works. Regional guest appearances are normally concentrated in a few weeks. Thus, in the fall of 1958 the Arts Council's company was sent on a seven-week tour of Wales. The company remained for a week in Swansea, where it participated in the October Festival of Music and the Arts. Next, the group traveled throughout the rest of Wales, playing to a total audience of 19,537, i.e., to a 66 per cent capacity. This is considered very promising in view of the limited educational background of the population.

Theater Circuit

The interchange of productions between repertory theaters — or the *Theatre Grid*, in the neat phrase of the Arts Council — has proven an excellent means of enriching the programs of individual dramatic centers.

In 1955 the theaters in Nottingham and in Sheffield decided on a trial exchange of certain productions; and so did the playhouses of Salisbury and Guildford. During the following seasons more repertory interchanges took place successfully between Nottingham and Sheffield; Guildford and Colchester; Northampton and Salisbury; Leatherhead and Bromley. During recent years more theaters have learned how to overcome the difficulties inherent in this Theatre Grid and how to take additional advantage of its obvious practicality. Normally, the Arts Council pays for the costs of this circuit. So far, the public has supported these ventures,[5] showing appreciation for the extension of the local repertory.

Audiences on Wheels

The Arts Council has introduced to England a scheme of mobile audiences. The idea is to make it cheaper, easier, and more comfortable for visitors within reasonable distances "to attend their nearest theater."[6] The audience is taken in comfortable buses to the hall. After the performance they are returned as close as feasible to their homes. The cost of the theatrical visit is thus lowered. Again, the Arts Council pays for this project, by direct grants to the organizing theater managements (See Table VII.)

TABLE VII

Audience on Wheels

Theater	*Subsidy* £	*Number in the Parties*	*Box Office Earnings*
Cambridge	410	8,342	£1,960
Canterbury	113	2,340	340
Colchester	276	6,677	1,150
Margate	306	6,156	781
Northampton	751	15,024	3,077
Nottingham	307	4,913	860
	2,163 ($6,056)	43,452	£8,168 ($22,870)

We see from Table VII how this investment more than pays off. It succeeds not only in introducing new audiences to serious drama but realizes a clear gain at the box offices of the participating theaters.

Repertory Theaters

In certain localities support for drama is offered for the first time; in others, former support is extended; and aid is also forthcoming for new housing of dramatic companies.

An interesting instance of regenerating a theater is provided by the town of Barrow-in-Furness. The Renaissance Players at Her Majesty's Theatre have managed to keep their stage alive in this isolated but important industrial region. Struggling with rising costs, the community finally sponsored a reorganization of the theater on a nonprofit basis. The local authorities decided to support the company with £1,000 annually. The Arts Council matches this amount. And a shipbuilding firm, Vickers-Armstrong (resident in Barrow-in-Furness), adds an equal sum. With an annual subsidy of £3,000 ($8,400) a repertory theater can be modestly maintained for a brief season.

Analogous circumstances of combined national, local, and private subsidy may be observed in other small towns, such as Bromley, Carlisle, Harrogate, Lincoln, etc. The Arts Council and the local Corporations have increased their support to existing theaters in Birmingham, Cheltenham, Colchester, Coventry, Derby, Northampton, cities with established traditions. During the season 1960-61 a number of Corporations decided to provide new housing for the Birmingham Repertory Theatre, as well as for the theaters in Chichester, Croydon, Eastbourne, Guildford, Leicester, Manchester.

Aid for New Dramatists

A living stage is inconceivable without young talent supplying the theater with new challenging plays. The support of a community theater is incomplete without aiding new authors of promise. The British have no illusions that "subsidies will ever make a Shakespeare." Admittedly, all the stipends, prizes, and practical opportunities offered so far through the Arts Council may not have delivered a genius.[7] On the other hand, according to the Arts Council Report, past encouragement of new dramatists has vitalized the British stage. It is, once more, in contact with contemporary thought.

The Arts Council has outlined the following ways in which young dramatists may be helped:

1. Officially supported repertory theaters are expected to produce new works. Toward this goal, the Arts Council, during the season 1958-59, aided such theaters as the Meadow Players at the Oxford Playhouse with a grant of £3,000. The Theatre Workshop Company at the Stratford Theatre Royal received £1,000. And the English Stage Company at the Royal Court Theatre was allocated £5,000.*

2. The Arts Council financially aids repertory theaters in the production of works by unknown or little-known authors. The procedure is this: the management of a nonprofit repertory theater submits to the Council a play marked for production and requests a limited guarantee against loss at the box office. By 1959, 27 managements had availed themselves of 78 such guarantees from the Council.

* Among the playwrights, John Arden, Brendan Behan, and John Osborne had their start with these theaters.

3. The third method is direct aid to the young dramatist who receives from the Arts Council a stipend enabling him to devote full time to his creative work. A committee of actors, producers, and authors makes tentative suggestions, but the final decisions, both for guarantees to the theaters as well as for the individual bursaries, are made by the Drama Panel of the Arts Council. This committee consists of 19 members, all experts in the theater.

Toward a British National Theater

The project of a British National Theater, which at this writing has not materialized, is more than a century old. In 1860 Thomas Taylor, a journalist with a flair for the stage, founded the first committee to establish a national theater; since then, periodic attempts have been made, all failures for lack of funds. George Bernard Shaw became the protagonist of this idea. Today, one of the great writer's favorite projects is close to fulfillment: London is marked as the logical place for a British National Theater, not only because of the city's role as the capital of the United Kingdom, but also in view of its brilliant tradition as a center of world theater. Today, there are about 45 theaters in London.

As early as 1949 the National Theatre Act granted the Treasury the right to allocate £1,000,000 ($2,800,000) toward establishment of a national theater in London. Its operation was to be under the public auspices. In 1961 the London County Council was ready to further the support of the project with £1,300,000 ($3,640,000). But, to the dismay of large groups of art lovers throughout the Kingdom, this plan was shelved by the Chancellor of Exchequer. A compromise solution was offered. The Treasury would increase its annual grant on 2 government supported theaters of great prestige — namely, the Old Vic and the Royal Shakespeare Theatre (with headquarters in Stratford-on-Avon and a London branch).

The Chancellor was widely critized for "lack of cultural idealism"; he was also called impractical. Both playhouses, the Old Vic and the Royal Shakespeare Theatre, have been severely handicapped by their present inadequate quarters. Public protests brought results. In April 1962 the Chief Secretary to the Treasury informed the House of Commons that the government had received the recommendation to build 2 theaters — a theater in the round and an opera house — both on the South Bank near the Royal Festival Hall. These plans have been duly referred to the Arts Council of Great Britain.

Old Vic

Of English theaters, the time-honored Old Vic comes closest to the Continental concept of a national theater. In the early part of the nineteenth century the masterworks of Shakespeare were staged here alongside inferior plays and entertainment in various genres, from farces to fireworks. But such were the customs of that period. Nearby Covent Garden did not hesitate to perform classical operas in the most outrageous arrangements, in which Mozart was "improved" with additional airs composed by amateurs listed in large letters on the bill. In 1880, when private management (under Emma Cons) assumed the reins of the Old Vic, the purpose was, in part, to provide London with large-scale but quality entertainment. The people were to enjoy the theater, rather than cheap amusement and taverns. To this day the Old Vic has retained aspects of its function as a people's theater. Large blocks of inexpensive seats are available for workers, organizations, and the like.

The course of the Old Vic as a serious theater was not marked by smooth sailing. Lillian Baylis, who established at the Old Vic in 1914 a permanent Shakespeare repertory under private patronage, battled with the London County Council when certain of its requirements threatened the survival of the theater. In retrospect, the status of the Old Vic as the nation's leading dramatic stage is reflected in the catalogue of its performers and directors, which includes, in successive generations, most names of consequence on the English stage. It was long considered an honor as well as a contribution to play at the Old Vic at financial sacrifices; London's West End theaters offer much better salaries. But the state of affairs, wherein the actors, producers, and other theater people are expected to support the country's first "powerhouse of drama," could not continue very long.

The prestige of Old Vic and the scope of its activities remained limited, prior to the Armistice of 1945. The slow rise of the theater to international fame and internal security followed an unblessed interregnum, hampered by intrigue, bureaucratism, and financial chaos. The governing board of private patrons could not alleviate the burden of support nor clarify the artistic direction.

In 1950 the original home of the Old Vic — badly damaged by the Nazi blitz — solemnly reopened its doors. The Arts Council of Great Britain had become a new patron of the theater. It was decided that the Old Vic would operate with 2 companies of equal rank, and after their run in London, certain productions would be taken to the provinces. But the success of the new arrangement was only partial; public support outside of London left much to be desired. In 1953 it was decided to produce Shakespeare's entire "First Folio" during five successive seasons.

The performances attained 85 per cent capacity. The intake for the initial season was £90,000, or three times the amount of the Arts Council subsidy. The prices were kept low. Of the 1,004 seats at the Old Vic, two-thirds were kept at 2*s*.6*d*. Children under sixteen were admitted to all matinees at half price. The season 1959-60 brought further success. New plays stimulated general audience interest. A considerable number of additional affiliations placed Old Vic on a sound basis. Invitations and tours throughout England and overseas increased.

Royal Shakespeare Theatre

In Stratford-on-Avon, Shakespeare's birthplace, a now world-famous playhouse is devoted to preserve in performance the artistic integrity of the poet's lifework. Known as the Royal Shakespeare Theatre, the organization has its headquarters in Stratford, but maintains two branches in London, housed at the Aldwych Theatre and at the Arts Theatre.

Stratford does not aim at the kind of traditionalism that might be compared with the essentially historical adherence to Molière's style at the Comédie Française. In Stratford the productions of a few imaginative directors have made possible a considerable variety of interpretations, suggesting the vast possibilities in the recreation of the Shakespearean drama. But the Stratford performances are distinguished by textualism: Shakespeare's word remains sacrosanct.

During the season 1961-62 the Royal Shakespeare Theatre earned more than £500,000 ($1,400,000). Attendance figures at the 3 theaters (in Stratford and London) reached almost 700,000, which is tantamount to an average of better than 80 per cent capacity of these theaters.

The National Treasury, for the season 1963-64, granted the Shakespeare Theatre a subsidy of £30,000 ($84,000). The Arts Council, administering this fund, will also support the company's tour through the provinces with £10,000 ($28,000). This aid represents the necessary minimum to cover the deficit of the Royal Shakespeare Theatre. The grant does not allow for experimentation or substantial increases of salaries.

V. Festivals

At least three centuries of continuous activities are traceable in the history of British public festivals in the performing arts, not counting events of a more exclusive and spectacular nature that date back much earlier: the courtly tournaments and command performances at the royal or aristocratic courts of England.

The British variant of public music festivals came into being through a series of ecclesiastical enterprises. In 1655 the first Festival of the Sons of the Clergy was held in St. Paul's Cathedral in London. This occasion, devoted to liturgical music, simultaneously served a philanthropic purpose, and was to be perpetuated annually. In 1724 the Gloucester Cathedral became the scene of large-scale choral performances with orchestral accompaniment. This, too, was of charitable intent: the widows and orphans of clergymen in three cathedral cities — Gloucester, Hereford, and Worcester — were the beneficiaries of the box office receipts. From the church performances alternating in these towns, the Three Choirs Festival developed. After an interruption during World War I the Festival resumed in 1920. Today, it is large in scope; guest interpreters of national stature are now in charge, rather than local musicians.

But not all English festivals proved to have the longevity of the Three Choirs Festival. Some were given up; others were held at irregular intervals. Many sprang from unpretentious beginnings. The so-called *Competition Festival Movement*, in its first stages, was limited to contests for brass bands and later extended to other media. By 1882 the festivals of the movement comprised choral competitions. Today, hundreds of organizations belong to the British Federation of Musical Competition Festivals, with headquarters in London.

The festival idea has generally gained new momentum in England since the Second World War. As on the Continent, festivals range from internationally famous performances of music and drama to specifically regional events, designed to maintain folk custom and sometimes folk idiom. The mere listing of events upholding the festival tradition in England shows great variety in scope and purpose. There are the festivals in the medieval coronation town of York. There are the festivals in Wales, which for nearly seven hundred years has belonged to the Kingdom of England but has retained ethnological characteristics of the old Celtic language and a literature dating back to the early Middle Ages. The Welsh love of indigenous poetry, drama, and music finds expression in their annual National Eisteddfod. By contrast, the Cheltenham Festival, held annually in July, is a forum of British contemporary music. In the same month the Haslemere Festival stresses music of early periods performed on authentic old instruments.

The Leeds, Norwich, and York festivals are scheduled triennially. The Leeds Festival, originally limited to choral works, now offers programs of diversified and challenging music in various media. This is all the more remarkable, for Leeds Festival is not, like similar European events, an international meeting-ground. The Festival takes place in October, after the traveling season. In the words of its director, Lord

Harewood, the Leeds Festival offers "opportunities where the local population and art-lovers within driving distance can enjoy a concentrated week of serious musical programs."

TABLE VIII

*British Festivals Supported by Arts Council (1960-61)**

Festival	£	$
England:		
Aldeburgh Festival of Music and the Arts	£ 1,000	($ 2,800)
Cheltenham Arts Festivals Limited:		
Cheltenham Festival of British Contemporary Music	1,750	($ 4,900)
Cheltenham Festival of Art and Literature	350	($ 980)
Dolmetsch Foundation (Haslemere Festival)	350	($ 980)
Ludlow Festival Society	350	($ 980)
Orchestral Concerts Society Limited (Bath Festival)	1,500	($ 4,200)
St. George's Guildhall Limited (King's Lynn Festival)	750	($ 2,100)
Three Choirs Festival Association Limited (Three Choirs)	750	($ 2,100)
York Festival Society Limited	3,500	($ 9,800)
Scotland:		
Edinburgh Festival Society Limited	15,000	($42,000)
Wales:		
Anglesey Welsh Drama Festival	400	($ 1,120)
Brecknock County Music Festival	150	($ 420)
Dee and Clwyd Festival	200	($ 560)
Denbighshire and Flintshire Drama Festival	25	($ 70)
Drama Council for Wales	50	($ 140)
Garthewin Welsh Drama Festival	128	($ 358)
Llandaff Festival	848	($ 2,374)
Montgomery County Music Festival	600	($ 1,680)
Swansea Festival of Music and the Arts	1,250	($ 3,500)

*Cf. The Sixteenth Annual Report of Great Britain

* * * * *

The following pages review the festival receiving the strongest public support (Edinburgh), contrast it with one that functions on a *private* basis (Glyndebourne), and in more detail describe the operation of an artistically significant music festival organized around a very small community (Aldeburgh).

Edinburgh: International Meeting-ground

The Edinburgh Festival Society finds its mission in the performance of "the world's great masterpieces in a manner befitting their stature." When the Earl of Harewood assumed the directorship of the Edinburgh Festival in its fifteenth season, the program took on progressive momentum. Today, the Edinburgh offerings are distinguished by originality and courage. In 1961 chamber music of Arnold Schoenberg and some of the master's last choral works were heard within the hitherto more conventional framework of the Edinburgh concerts. At the 1962 Festival the participating organizations included, in addition to English companies, the Belgrade Opera Company from Yugoslavia and the Belgian Ballet du XXè Siècle.

In 1963 Martha Graham and her Dance Company appeared at Edinburgh, as did the Stuttgart State Theater Ballet.

In recent festival seasons, productions in the field of drama attracted considerable attention. In 1963 the participating groups included the Chichester Festival Theatre, the English Stage Company, and the 59 Theatre Company.

Following the International Writers' Conference on the Novel (in 1962) a Drama Conference devoted to the discussion of the contemporary theater was held — open to the public — during the Festival of 1963.

The season begins around the middle of August and lasts until the second week of September.

The support of the Edinburgh Festival is derived from various sources. For the year ending March 31, 1961, the Arts Council of Great Britain contributed £15,000 to the Edinburgh Festival Society. But the Edinburgh City Council has tripled its initial subsidy, increasing it from £25,000 to £75,000. There is also support from private donors, and all of it is needed. Unlike the sold-out performances of Salzburg or Bayreuth, the Edinburgh Festival has an attendance of approximately 75 per cent. Geography plays its part: while the central European festival sites are the summer attractions of art-minded travelers from all over the world, Edinburgh obviously depends only on a much smaller potential of visitors from Great Britain and abroad. But in 1961 subsidies sufficed to raise approximately 72 per cent of the total Festival costs. Ticket sales and additional revenue from broadcasts, program books, and advertising have proved sufficient to maintain the income of the Festival Society at a necessary minimum.

Glyndebourne: Opera Privately Sponsored

The Glyndebourne Festival of Opera originated, in its entirety, as the work of private initiative and patronage. Inaugurated in 1934 with 6 performances (over a period of two weeks), the Glyndebourne season now lasts three months, with all performances sold out in advance. From May to August opera lovers may take an afternoon train to Glyndebourne, the Sussex country seat of the late Mr. John Christie, industrialist and art patron. A two hour ride south-bound from Victoria Station reaches the four-hundred-year-old Elizabethan estate and mansion, where Mr. Christie has added a modern opera house, seating approximately 700. The theater is a memorial to his wife, the singer Audrey

Mildmay. The Glyndebourne Opera, situated in a lovely environment of parks and ponds, retains the quiet charm of an old English country place. During the intermission of performances the visitors may enjoy the country gardens and may picnic near the lake. But Glyndebourne is an expensive affair. A fifty dollar bill for two (the tickets are $15 each) will just cover the visit and most of its amenities. This delightful experience of opera, painstakingly rehearsed and often brilliantly performed on a beautiful estate, takes opera back where it originated early in the seventeenth century — to lordly sites and privileges enjoyed by a fortunate few. It is aristocratic entertainment, anachronistically laid in the twentieth century. But Glyndebourne stands for quality and impeccable style. Out of the impulse of private patronage an artistic ideal is realized here in the very country that has such a disappointingly indifferent record for the support of opera. Glyndebourne favors the supreme works of a period: Monteverdi's *L'incoronazione di Poppea*, Mozart's *Marriage of Figaro*, Beethoven's *Fidelio*, Debussy's *Pelléas et Mélisande*. Contemporary operas have also been staged (Benjamin Britten's *The Rape of Lucretia*, and *Albert Herring;* Stravinsky's *The Rake's Progress;* Hans Werner Henze's *Elegy for Young Lovers*).

Glyndebourne has remained aloof from the issues and advantages of public art subsidy. Only once, in 1951 during the Festival of Great Britain, was a state subsidy offered and received. At that time the contribution was sizeable, amounting to £25,000 ($70,000). Yet a recent departure from the exclusiveness of Glyndebourne policy must be greeted as a step in the right direction. On August 21, 1961, the Glyndebourne Opera offered Mozart's *Don Giovanni* at a concert performance in London's Albert Hall.* The sponsor of this extension was the British Broadcasting Company. The temporary transfer of the Sussex Opera to the capital is noteworthy as a democratic development of operatic patronage in England.

Aldeburgh: Festival in a Fishing Village

Since Roman times Aldeburgh in Suffolk has been known as a fishing village. Today, the North Sea village, some 90 miles northeast of London, has become a small but important outpost of art. The festival of Aldeburgh was conceived after World War II by Benjamin Britten, the distinguished English composer who is also a noted interpreter. With his English Opera Group, Britten had undertaken tours to the Continent. He looked for a place to anchor this group and augment an opera festival with other kinds of music. Aldeburgh answers this need. A brief but concentrated festival was organized for the first time in 1948. In

*The Glyndebourne Opera has also appeared at the Edinburgh Festival.

a typical season it is scheduled for about ten days, usually beginning in the middle of June. The program offers opera, choral and orchestral concerts, chamber music, Lieder recitals, lectures, and exhibitions.

The subsidy of the Aldeburgh Festival is diversified. There are about 450 "Friends of the Festival" — a group of private donors who make annual contributions. There is a modest grant from the Arts Council of Great Britain, £1,000 for the year ending March 31, 1961. The participation of the BBC assures further income. Some compensation is derived from recordings. The performing forces of Aldeburgh consist of the Festival Orchestra (about 35 players) and the Festival Chorus, and Benjamin Britten is the principal organizer and producer, the pianist, accompanist, conductor, and editor of old music. He is particularly interested in youth and education, and many aspects of the Festival are geared to the activation of young people.

Aldeburgh dramatizes the idea that culture springs from within the community. The citizens of the quaint North Sea village participate in every feasible way: the chorus, the youth groups, the extras in the opera, and whenever possible, vocal and instrumental soloists are selected from the Aldeburgh area. This is a communal enterprise for which all regional facilities are put into action. Performances take place in the churches at Aldeburgh, Blythburgh, Framlingham, and Oxford. The East Suffolk Education Committee lends a hand; the staff of the Suffolk Rural Music School helps in the preparation of the chorus and orchestra. Local committees take care of the attractive decorations in buildings and exhibitions. The programs offer old and new music. The orchestral works of Bach, classical sonatas, and Lieder by Schubert are on the list.

Aldeburgh is distinguished by the absence of commercialism. There is no advertising, and none is needed. Only 500 people can be accommodated and the Festival is always sold out.

London Festival
From Mercantile to Municipal Patronage

Some of the merchants who over the years assembled wealth in the city of London have been generous to the arts and aided them in good times. Today a group of business leaders in the capital join in cooperative art sponsorship under the guidance of the London municipality. In 1961 the City Corporation took the initiative to underwrite the London Festival, scheduled for twelve days in July at an estimated cost of £30,000. The City Corporation was ready to spend £7,500 if this sum would be matched by similar donations from London merchants and the Arts Council of Great Britain. It was estimated that there would be a return of about £15,500, and so the deficit would not exceed £14,500.

The initial programs also aided creative artists with commissions offered by the Festival Committee. Performances were given in some of the historic buildings in London. The *Yeoman of the Guard* by Gilbert and Sullivan was scheduled at its original site, the Tower of London. Historic landmarks available for Festival performances are St. Paul's Cathedral, Guildhall, Apothecaries' Hall, and others.

St. Pancras: A Borough as Art Sponsor

In 1955 the Borough Council of St. Pancras (within the metropolitan area of London) embarked for the first time on the venture of a festival of its own, offering performances of drama and music. In both fields young artists have had their start in these performances patronized by the Borough of St. Pancras. In 1961 the Borough allocated about £20,000 for the festival. The attendance was so satisfactory that only £6,000 had to be spent by the Borough to cover the deficit.

St. Pancras takes advantage of the provisions made by the Local Government Act. As it happens, the deficit of £6,000 equals only one half-penny for each pound of the taxes. This implies that St. Pancras could go further in spending the allotted limit (sixpence per pound) for local art support, and the Borough might well do so in the near future. But at least a progressive pattern was set, first by St. Pancras,* and successively by the City Corporation of London.

It is hoped that many more cities and boroughs throughout the country will follow this pattern of a new productive relationship between local authorities and art sponsorship on the basis of the Local Government Act.

VI. Radio and Television

Organizational Structure

In 1922 a Conservative government helped in the formation of the British Broadcasting Company (BBC), setting it up as a private organization. In 1927 a royal charter transformed the BBC into a public corporation. The governors (the board of trustees) supervise the permanently employed administrative staff. The board includes the chairman, vice-chairman, and three national governors for Scotland, Wales, and Northern Ireland.

The maximum tenure for the governors is five years. The chief executive is known as director-general. The trustees supervise the management, all programs, and the technical aspects of operation.

The board of trustees is appointed by the national government. These trustees are not executives; they merely deal with the overall policy.

*For performance in 1963 the St. Pancras Libraries and Arts Committee, which is responsible for the program, selected such works as Verdi's *Ernani* and Britten's *Noye's Fludde.*

The director-general appoints the chiefs of the individual departments (including the heads of the drama and music sections).

The top control of the British broadcasting and television authority by Parliament is almost theoretical in nature. Practically, BBC remains independent in all matters of policy. This, of course, is crucial. Responsible judgment within Great Britain agrees that the BBC is free of political misuse; it has successfully rebuked lobbying for specific interests.

Nature of Programs

BBC divides its services into the following three categories: Home Service, Light Programme, and Third Programme (justifiably considered the most meritorious innovation of the BBC).

In 1957 these three services were replanned. Their new design is mindful of the extreme differences in taste and cultural need of British audiences.

Home Service: this program is of widest range. All religious and school broadcasts are concentrated in the Home Service, which occupies seventeen hours each day and offers both information and entertainment. It also broadcasts various musical programs. The principal news services originate here. There are important discussions on current affairs and political broadcasts.

Light Programme: likewise assigned seventeen hours a day, it is geared to those "who wish to enjoy relaxation and distraction in the least demanding form." There are variety programs of all kinds. The music department, appropriately, broadcasts light fare, particularly dance music. In all departments the emphasis is on popular appeal.

Third Programme: occupying three hours a day, it is designed for the intellectual audience, for listeners of cultivated taste and interests. The Third Programme is the prime sponsor of serious music and drama, of lectures and related educational features. In the field of drama the *avant-garde* is often favored. In opera and concert high standards are maintained. Events abroad are frequently transmitted. Cultural issues overseas are regularly discussed.

In addition to these three listed programs, there is Network Three, which uses the frequencies and transmitters of the Third Programme at a time when they are not employed by this service. Network Three can be heard from Monday to Friday between 6 and 8 P.M. and on Sundays from 2:30 to 5:00 P.M. On Saturday afternoons when the Home Service and the Light Programme are occupied with sports, Network Three regularly broadcasts orchestral concerts, offering a discriminating repertory of masterworks. Network Three is essentially at the service of a minority audience: its interests range from the arts to the sciences, from gardening to chess.

Licenses and Financing

Legally, broadcasting and television within the United Kingdom are controlled by the Wireless Telegraph Acts (revised several times between 1949 and 1955). The right of supervision is conferred upon the Postmaster-General. Sending or receiving of radio communications is prohibited except under license. Owners of radio and television sets must obtain annual licenses which can be purchased at the post office. The license costs £1 for radio; £2 for television — plus an excise duty of £1 — a total of $11.20 annually for radio and television.

The financial support of the BBC stems from three principal sources: an annual grant from the Exchequer (this revenue is derived from receiving licenses); an annual grant-in-aid from the Exchequer, in compensation for various services (such as the European services, the overseas service, and the monitoring service); and profits from BBC publications.*

The biggest share of these funds used for the operation of the domestic services is derived in income from licenses for both radio and television. The BBC's share is governed by a financial agreement with the Postmaster-General (dated February 1, 1957).

TABLE IX

Overall Figures for BBC (1959-60)[8]

	Radio £	*Television* £	*Total* £	
Gross License Revenue	15,060,464	21,149,216	36,209,680	($101,387,104)
Less: Post Office Expense	999,262	1,394,798	2,394,060	($6,703,368)
Treasury Retention	1,051,459	1,478,008	2,529,467	($ 7,082,508)
Income Forwarded from Postmaster-General	13,009,743	18,276,410	31,286,153	($ 87,601,228)
Other Income, Publications, Interest, etc.	644,868	588,920	12,333,788	($ 34,534,606)
Total	13,654,611	18,865,330	43,619,941	($122,135,834)
Revenue Expenditure				
Programs	6,584,581	8,194,751		
Engineering	2,769,206	5,021,084		
Other	2,548,232	2,600,069		
Total Operating Expense	11,902,019	15,815,904		
Depreciation	580,676	911,535		
Income Tax	440,107	720,000		
Total Expenditure	12,922,802	17,447,439	(£30,370,241)	($85,036,675)
Balance Available for Capital Expenditure	731,809	1,417,891		
Net Capital Expenditure	30,716	1,790,147		
Net Variation in Reserves	701,093	—372,256		

**Radio Times* with a weekly sale of over 8,000,000 copies produces a large advertising revenue.

TABLE X

Analysis of BBC Radio Program Output (1959-60)[9]

	Home Service		*Light Programme*		*Third Programme*		*Network Three*		*Total*	
	Hours	%	*Hours*	%	*Hours*	%	*Hours*	%	*Hours*	%
Serious Music	1,305	20.9	67	1.0	774	54.7	147	23.7	2,293	16
Light Music	614	9.9	2,703	41.6	5	.3	8	1.3	3,330	23
Features and Drama	650	10.4	465	7.1	402	28.4			1,517	10
Variety	219	3.5	575	8.8					794	5
Dance Music	142	2.3	1,164	17.9			27	4.4	1,333	9
Talks and Discussions	995	16.0	486	7.5	187	13.2	274	44.1	1,942	13
News	887	14.2	588	9.0			31	5.0	1,506	10
Schools	409	6.6							409	3
Children's Hours	349	5.6	66	1.0					415	3
Religion	300	4.8	96	1.5	8	.6	26	4.2	430	3
Outside Broadcasts	100	1.6	260	4.0			96	15.5	456	3
Miscellaneous	259	4.2	36	.6	40	2.8	11	1.8	346	2
	6,229	100.0	6,506	100.0	1,416	100.0	620	100.0	14,771	100
Presented by										
London	5,290	84.9	5,337	82.0	1,364	96.3	451	72.7	12,442	84
Regions	939	15.1	1,169	18.0	52	3.7	169	27.3	2,329	16

Television on BBC and ITA

Inaugurating European television as a public service, the British laid the conceptual groundwork for the large Continental networks in regard to their cultural assignment. The British were first to insist on ethical standards at the government supervised radio and television networks. The British government also reserved the right to veto all offensive programs. There is a policy to educate as well as to entertain, to guide rather than to be led by questionable mass taste.

From its inception in 1936, England depended exclusively on the single television channel of BBC which, according to the charter, operated on a noncommercial basis. The Television Act of 1954 made possible the establishment of what is known as the Independent Television Authority (ITA); it operates a second channel on a commercial basis.

The ITA is directed by a board set up like that of the BBC. There are a chairman, a vice-chairman, and 8 members (of whom 3 are charged with the supervision of television in Scotland, Wales, and Northern Ireland). The Postmaster-General appoints this board on a part-time salaried basis. The members chosen are experts in their respective fields.

The transmitting system is the property of the ITA, and so are all studios and technical equipment. But the telecasts are produced by individual program companies, which in turn remunerate the ITA for these privileges. The program companies have the right to limited advertising, from which some of their own income accrues. Advertising occurs between — *never during* — the programs. It may last from two to three minutes. The programs are never sponsored; merely the brief time allotted for the advertising may be bought. But the Television Act charges the ITA with the responsibility of "safeguarding good taste or decency." The programs must provide proper balance in content. Time must be accorded impartially for political telecasts.

Both networks, BBC and ITA, are each allotted a total air time of approximately 50 hours a week (which does not include time for religious and educational services). Neither of the channels operate in the morning. Both BBC and ITA telecast from 2:30 P.M. to 11:30 P.M. Time and programs are appropriately adjusted to children, youth and adult audiences.

On July 5, 1962, the government, following a recommendation by the Committee for Broadcasting and Televising, consented to the establishment of a third television channel under the supervision of BBC. Operation is scheduled for 1964. ITA will likewise be permitted to have a second channel which, however, is not expected to be ready until 1966.

The status of commercial networks and their advertising has become a highly controversial issue in England. The Committee, under the chairmanship of the noted industrialist Sir Harry Pilkington, published a White Paper condemning the planned nationalization of the commercial network, and calling for less violence and triviality on television. Only if, and when, commercial TV has demonstrated its capacity "to realize the purposes of broadcasting," the Paper stated, should the Independent Television Authority be given the privilege to operate the second channel.

The present majority within British government is less adverse to commercial television, because it has made definite contributions in certain fields, including the arts. The British people will have the opportunity to express their preference. The final verdict of the issue will be cast by Parliament.

Independent Television has on earlier occasions made direct grants to the arts. Thus the 4 major companies,* for the year ending April 30, 1959, have allocated £100,000 ($280,000) to arts and sciences, and extended this aid into 1960. Where the recipients of the TV grants were also the beneficiaries of Arts Council support, the TV moneys were earmarked to supplement and not to relieve the Council's contribution. A Committee of Review[10] decided on the distribution of television grants. Two advisors of the Arts Council are in attendance. In music, the largest of these TV grants has gone so far to the Sadler's Wells, £5,000 ($14,000), and to the Hallé Orchestra, £2,414 ($6,759). Within patronage for drama, the Old Vic and a considerable number of repertory theaters throughout the country were favored.

In summary, it must be emphasized that the BBC, in sound as well as in sight, has emerged as a generous patron of art. The BBC is England's principal sponsor of serious music. Just as the German Rundfunk or the Radiodiffusion Télévision Française, the BBC offers permanent employment to hundreds of musicians in the vocal and instrumental media of performance. The ideal of live music has been upheld in an era of increasing mechanization. In terms of its programs, of commissions and sheer quantity of good music performed, the BBC deserves undivided admiration.

VII. Summary and Evaluation

The British art program is one of high quality. But if measured in terms of moneys allocated to the arts, most of the Continental nations are decidedly ahead of England. For the year ending March 31, 1961, the total allocation of the Arts Council of Great Britain was £1,500,000 ($4,200,000). This is less than half of Austria's annual art support; yet the population figure of Austria is approximately one-seventh that

*ABC Television Limited, Associated-Rediffusion Limited, Associated Television Limited and Granada TV Network Limited.

of Great Britain. Other small Continental countries, such as Switzerland or Holland, likewise surpass England in the generosity of subsidies. Compared with the art budgets of West Germany, France, or Italy, British expenditures for the performing arts can only be characterized as meager.

In the present estimate of the Arts Council of Great Britain, £2,500,000 per year would be adequate to aid the performing arts on a nation-wide basis. At this writing, about one-half of the Arts Council's total grant is assigned to London's Royal Opera House, a fact widely criticized in certain quarters of the country.

But in spite of these obvious limitations, the Arts Council has won irrefutable points of merit. It has succeeded in building up considerable new audiences that enjoy serious art, and support from the public has greatly increased. In many cities the audiences now pay two-thirds of the total cost. These facts are encouraging; they exceed comparable figures even in countries that otherwise surpass England in important aspects of their art patronage. Under the circumstances, the Arts Council of Great Britain is justified in interpreting the statistics with confidence for the future. Experts predict that the present audiences will be doubled within a decade — barring another war.

What Does the Arts Program Cost the Taxpayer?

In 1959-60 the government grant to the Arts Council of Great Britain was £1,218,000 ($3,410,400). In terms of taxes this amounts to slightly less than 6*d.* a head. The allocation in 1960-61 increased to £1,500,000 ($4,200,000); it meant a little more than 7*d.* a head (8.2 cents). This, in turn, is "almost equal to the cost of making four miles of the new motorway."[11]

Considering the meaning of this equation, what is the complaining about? It seems absurd that there should be a serious argument about costs of public art support. As a further point of comparing public funds spent on educational projects, the expenditures of England's public libraries may be cited. Their cost is £16,000,000 ($44,800,000) per year, although their facilities are used by only one-fourth of the total population. Is it fair, then, that the performing arts receive not even one-tenth of the libraries' share?

It has taken fifteen years for the public art grants to rise from a mere £235,000 ($658,000) in 1946 to its 1961 level of £1,500,000 ($4,200,000). England is slow to change, but progress may be seen in the fact that the common objection to art support — "let those who want it, pay for it" — has become less vociferous. It was violent in certain quarters when the Arts Council started its pioneering task.

Aid from Local Authorities

At this writing one can report progress, but not yet full utilization of the opportunities afforded by the Local Government Act of 1948. This point is crucial. The hope for intense and widespread national diffusion of the arts is anchored with the local authorities. At present, their participation in the program of the Arts Council is not at all indicated by the size of British communities. Thus, Hornchurch (population 122,600) supports a playhouse with an annual allocation of £6,500 ($18,200),[12] but there are cities four or five times as large which contribute as little as £250 to their resident theaters. Only widespread propaganda will change this Philistine attitude. If the 1948 Act were fully applied, local authorities would be contributing nearly £15,000,000 ($42,000,000) a year to the performing arts. Arithmetic bears out the deplorable fact that in 1960 their support amounted to a miserly £250,000 ($700,000), or to only one-sixtieth of what the localities could be spending.

The Arts Council is frank in expressing disappointment about this state of affairs. On principle the Council appreciates every form of diversified patronage. The English realize that patronage works best when it has many springs of initiative. But the English art scene demonstrates the pitfalls of isolated and uncoordinated sponsorship. Occasional donations cannot substitute for continuous subsidies.

The British Council

In addition to the Arts Council of Great Britain, another institution of large scope plays a vital part within England's scheme of public art support. This organization is the British Council. It was founded in 1934 with the primary function to encourage a better appreciation of Great Britain abroad, and to maintain a closer cultural relationship between England and other countries. British ministers and trade missions on all continents had repeatedly advised the government to establish a central body for diffusion of British culture on a global scale, and to coordinate the work of all organizations with similar goals.

The work of the British Council will be readily appreciated in the United States. For in our cultural program abroad our government is willing to spend limited appropriations for the arts. On both sides of the Atlantic it is understood that the arts are unique means of propaganda and that they can be effectively applied in a working partnership with a nation's foreign policy.

In 1940 the British Council was granted a royal charter which defined its aims to be the promotion of a wider knowledge of the English language and of the United Kingdom abroad.

How is the work of the British Council financed and managed? Most of its funds are grants voted by Parliament. The Council is directed by an executive committee of 30, whose members come from both sides of the House of Commons, from the universities, the trades union movement, and other fields of British life. Nine members are nominated by the government as experts in their respective professions.

In the field of the performing arts the program of the British Council consists for the most part in foreign tours: individual artists as well as organizations are sent abroad. In drama and in music the companies from London and from the provinces are chosen for this distinction of British representation. Thus the program serves as an incentive at home, and as a means of propaganda overseas.

The Shakespeare Memorial Theatre Company appeared at such events as the Holland and Berlin festivals; it performed in Vienna and Zurich, Copenhagen and Oslo. The City of Birmingham Symphony Orchestra played in The Netherlands during British Week, May, 1955. Numerous other groups and individuals travel abroad to represent England at various official occasions. The British Council arranges for transportation and frequently underwrites losses at these ventures.

The arts budget of the British Council is small. For all the arts, including visual arts, drama, and music, the expenditure for 1955 was £48,325 ($135,310). In fact, direct expenditure for the arts accounted for only about 1.6 per cent of the Council's parliamentary grants for the year.

The total grant allocated to the British Council for the same year was £2,587,757 ($7,245,719).

British Opinion and Public Support

The English solutions of art support are bound to come under close scrutiny in the United States. We cannot remain indifferent to the convincing answers England has found in terms of her parliamentary supervision and democratic management of public art patronage.

This is not to imply that the British themselves evaluate the past record and the present state of their official art patronage with complete unanimity. Debates in Parliament and frequent public discussions take issue with current practices. Differences of opinion prevail everywhere. The Philistine part of the national press complains about additional burdens in times of financial crises, and financial crises seem a perennial state today in England. By contrast, progressive as well as responsible conservative British opinion wholeheartedly supports an increase of subsidies. And in spite of all differences, it appears that the Arts Council, in its present structure, is generally interpreted as the logical method of national art support.

It is generally agreed that one cannot bring an art program of large scope and distinction — like that sponsored by the Arts Council of Great Britain — on a common denominator aiming at wide popularity. Equalization of a governmental art program can be accomplished only in totalitarian states. By contrast, democratic procedures must always provide discriminating leadership, and not merely aim at popularization. There must be respect for the needs of the cultural minority. Artistic policy must remain free, and judgment be left in the hands of the experts. The British definitely live up to these premises. They offer, within their pluralistic society, opportunities to experience the arts on different levels. They also insist in sponsorship of modern art, even if it does not appeal to the man on the street.

Some criticism pertains to the distribution of public subsidies for regional needs. To be sure, such complaints repeat themselves in almost every European country where government is the arbiter in the allocation of funds. In most European countries the national capital has emerged as the country's primary art center. These cities were — and in certain nations still are — the residences of royal courts. Traditionally, the principal dramatic and musical institutes are housed in these cities.

In England the charge is occasionally heard that the administration of the Arts Council, with its headquarters in London, favors unduly the British capital. A certain amount of centralization in London must be conceded. But from its start the Arts Council has maintained offices in other key cities of the provinces, such as in Edinburgh (Scotland) or in Cardiff (Wales), in addition to the headquarters in London. The Council has no intention of decreasing any aid to the provinces. The opposite is true. The publicly stated policies point to an augmentation of these provincial subsidies as soon as and wherever feasible. On the other hand, the Arts Council is committed to aid already established organizations. Hence, the choice of certain London theaters and orchestras as immediate beneficiaries of public support is inevitable. Thus it was obligatory to guarantee the financial continuity of the Old Vic or Sadler's Wells, of Covent Garden or the Royal Ballet; for the Council could not allow these established organizations to deteriorate for lack of funds.

In 1960-61, of the total grants made by the Arts Council, 60 per cent was distributed to art organizations in London; 40 per cent went to the provinces. But some of the London companies visit the provinces; and if this contribution is taken into account, then the division of allocations between the capital and the provinces is approximately equal. The Council hopes, however, that in the near future an increasing number of provincial cities will organize and maintain with local funds their theaters and concert societies. A notable start in this direction has taken place. The Council is prepared to help any such communal undertaking, circumstances permitting.

The loudest and most frequently heard complaint against present governmental policy concerns the limited amount of subsidies.[13] The charge is justified as the tables in this chapter suggest. The government does not make enough moneys available for distribution through the Arts Council, as the following table indicates.

TABLE XI

Grants of the Arts Council to Musical Organizations (1960-61)[14]

Opera and Ballet	£	
Royal Opera House, Covent Garden Limited	500,737	
Sadler's Wells Trust Limited	275,000	
Royal Ballet School Limited (Grant for Capital Expenditure)	15,000	
Mercury Theatre Trust Limited (Ballet Rambert)	16,000	
*English Opera Group Limited	5,000	
*Intimate Opera Society Limited	1,500	
Western Theatre Ballet Limited	3,000	
New Opera Company Limited	2,000	
Handel Opera Society	1,000	
Youth and Music (Opera Performances for Young People)	350	
*Amateur Operatic Societies	2,039	
		£821,626 ($2,300,552)

Symphony Orchestras	£	
City of Birmingham Symphony Orchestra	22,000	
*Hallé Concerts Society	25,767	
*London Philharmonic Orchestra Limited	9,000	
London Philharmonic Society Limited	6,000	
London Symphony Orchestra Limited	5,000	
*Royal Liverpool Philharmonic Society	27,000	
*Western Orchestral Society Limited (Bournemouth Symphony Orchestra)	30,000	
*Northern Sinfonia Concert Society	1,500	
		£126,267 ($ 353,547)

England

TABLE XI (continued)

Other activities		£
*Brighton Philharmonic Society Limited		1,500
British Institute of Recorded Sound:		
Administration	L750	
Central Gramophone Library	1,500	2,250
Institute of Contemporary Arts (Music Section)		1,000
Jacques Orchestra Limited		250
Philomusica of London Limited		2,000
Royal Musical Association		2,000
Royal Philharmonic Society		1,750
Rural Music Schools Association		500
Society for the Promotion of New Music		1,250
Finsbury Pageant Committee		250
*Payments to Music Societies and Clubs affiliated with National Federation of Music Societies in Respect of Guarantees (Including Federation Administration) 1959/60 and 1960/61		28,924
Direct Grants and Guarantees to Other Musical Organizations		6,385
		£ 48,059 ($ 134,565)

*Maximum commitments are given, not necessarily the amounts paid.

Cultural Independence

The respect for the cultural independence of Scotland and Wales is organizationally expressed in the functioning of individual committees working within the frame of the Arts Council. (See Table XII.)

TABLE XII

*Expenditures of Arts Council Committees for Scotland and Wales (1960-61)**

	£	$
Scotland		
General Expenditures (1960-61)	£ 93,932	($263,009)
Music (with the Scottish National Orchestra Receiving £32,000)	43,522	($121,861)
Drama (Including 6,570 for Tours)	27,683	($ 77,512)
Typical Figures for Repertory Theaters		
Perth Repertory Theatre	4,000	($ 11,200)
Dundee Repertory Theatre	4,000	($ 11,200)
Glasgow Citizen's Theatre	5,250	($ 14,700)
Wales		
General Expenditures	52,187	($146,123)
Opera	26,951	($ 75,462)
Other Musical Programs (Orchestra, Music and Arts Clubs, etc.)	7,635	($ 21,378)
Drama	10,114	($ 28,319)

*Some figures represent maximum commitments, and not necessarily amounts paid.

We recognize that these budgets represent an enormous progress since the initial grants of the Arts Council. In the first year (1945-46) the Exchequer's grant to the Council was £235,000 ($658,000). The growth of the project in sixteen years is evident from the figures in Table XII.

"St. Paul's does not pay its way."

Whatever dissatisfaction exists regarding present allocations, the charges must be addressed to Parliament. The Arts Council is not, in the strict sense, a governmental agency, but rather the distributing center of public funds which the government granted to the Council for the year ending March 31, 1963. A typical situation arose in 1958 in regard to the problem of housing the performing arts. The Arts Council submitted to the Chancellor of the Exchequer the first installment of an inquiry into this crucial issue. But the Chancellor made it known that "he had no objection to the Arts Council publishing this section of its report, provided it was understood that publication did not imply government approval."[15] Such independent positions are characteristic of British procedures. In general the government and the Council are not at cross purposes. In this connection, we become aware of an interesting coincidence: certain members of government (on different levels) who persistently object to raising allocations for the Arts Council are apt to be inimical to other indirectly related issues, such as salary increases to England's underpaid schoolteachers. The psychological parallel is revealing; it marks serious deficiencies on the cultural scene of Great Britain.

Be this as it may, we appraise the British achievement primarily for its intent and nobility of direction; here is a national art patronage, carried by parliamentary procedures and executed with intransigent fairness in the democratic spirit. The scheme is not perfect; it is presently hampered by deplorable economic weakness. It will have to be modified and adjusted in the crucible of daily experience. The English are meeting the challenge.

In 1958, when the British Broadcasting Company had to fight curtailment of its famous Third Programme, a storm of protest broke loose throughout the country. In his eighty-fifth year, the late dean of British composers, Ralph Vaughan Williams, made his final public statement in behalf of this exemplary radio program, which has justifiably become the pride of English broadcasting and serves as the model for analogous programs on the Continent.

In an essay, "Hands Off the Third," Vaughan Williams wrote: "To all of us, audiences and performers alike, the Third Programme has been of inestimable benefit. Let me repeat, it has been the envy of the world. It is something worthwhile, something splendid, something which we should be proud to claim as unique in the world. Is it to be sacrificed for the sake of the kind of standardized entertainment which is already being mass-produced in every country? We are told that broadcast must pay its way — but does St. Paul's Cathedral pay its way? Do the Court of Justice and our Council Schools pay their way? Music is a symbol of spiritual experience fully equal to that of St. Paul's. Must it be fettered to a balance sheet?"

Addendum

Henry Purcell, *The Fairy Queen* (*The Preface*) 1692[16]

Tis known to all who have been any considerable time in Italy, or France, how Opera's are esteem'd among 'em. That France borrowed what she has from Italy, is evident from the Andromede and Toison D'or, of Monsieur Corneille, which are the first in the kind they ever had, on their publick Theaters; they being not perfect Opera's, but Tragedies, with Singing, Dancing, and Machines interwoven with 'em, after the manner of the Opera. They gave 'em a tast first, to try their Palats, that they might the better Judge whether in time they would be able to digest an entire Opera. And Cardinal Richelieu (that great encourager of Arts and Learning) introduced 'em first at his own expense, as I have been informed, amongst 'em.

What encouragement Seignoir Baptist Luly had from the present King of France, is well known; they being first set out at his own Expense; and all the Ornaments given by the King, for the Entertainment of the People. In Italy, especially at Venice, where Opera's have the greatest Reputation, and where they have 'em every Carnival, the Noble Venetians set 'em out at their own cost. And what a Confluence of People, the fame of 'em draw from all parts of Italy to the great profit of that City, is well known to everyone who has spent a Carnival there. And many of the English Gentry are sensible what advantages Paris receives, by the great number of Strangers which frequent the Opera's three days in a Week, throughout the Year. If therefore an Opera were established here, by the Favour of the Nobility and Gentry of England; I may modestly conclude it would be some advantage to London, considering what a Sum we must Yearly lay out among Tradesmen for the fitting out so great a work.

That Sir William Davenant's Siege of Rhodes was the first Opera we ever had in England, no Man can deny; and is indeed a perfect Opera:

that being this difference only between an Opera and a Tragedy; that the one is a story sung with proper Action, the other spoken.

That a few private Persons should venture on so expensive a Work as an Opera, when none but Princes, or States exhibit 'em abroad, I hope is no Dishonour to our Nation: And I dare affirm if we had half the encouragement in England, that they have in other Countries, you might in a short time have as good Dancers in England as they have in France, though I despair of ever having as good voices among us, as they have in Italy. These are the two great things which Travellers say we are most deficient in. If this happens to please, we cannot reasonably propose to our selves any great advantage, considering the mighty charge in setting it out, and the extraordinary expense that attends it every day 'tis represented. If it deserves their Favour? if they are satisfied we venture boldly, doing all we can to please 'em? We hope the English are too generous not to encourage so great an undertaking.

EPILOGUE

THE EUROPEAN PERSPECTIVE IN SUMMARY

I. Persistent Patronage

The inquiry into European art patronage has enabled us to observe in a minimum of space a maximum of diversity. As the preceding Chapters have shown, this patronage is not limited by time: from antiquity to the present, European civilization has been distinguished by munificent sponsorship of art. In the era of early Christianity the sovereign domain of patronage was the Church, and for centuries the arts remained within the ecclesiastical orbit. Art, then, was interpreted as *ancilla religionis*, the "humble handmaiden of religion." There always coexisted, however, the secular forms of art and the worldly forms of their support. On European soil Greek and Roman civilizations clearly showed the way. By the Middle Ages the patronage of secular art blossomed at numerous royal and princely courts throughout Europe. Side by side, the sacred and the secular emphasized the enrichment of worship and life, although their inherent differences of purpose and aesthetics led to serious conflict.

The Renaissance challenged the patronage of ecclesiastical authority and developed many new patterns of art patronage. From the Low Countries to the Apennine Peninsula thousands of new towns arose whose citizens eventually assumed a proper share in the indigenous art life of their municipalities.

But the new middle-class culture did not eradicate the older forms of art support. On the contrary, subsequent eras, notably the Baroque, witnessed the powerful revitalization of patronage by churches and courts all over Europe. The Baroque marks, in fact, a climax of ostentation in the performance of drama and music. Church celebrations adopted worldly elements of the grandiose and the spectacular. Secular rulers participated actively in a vital art life as poets, composers, and performers. The aristocracy emulated and competed with royal patronage. Handsome new theaters and opera houses were built. Italy promoted opera as a public spectacle. England, soon after France, witnessed the beginning of a regular public concert life. By the nineteenth century the concept of a democratic audience was firmly established in many European countries. Everywhere in Europe the people emerged as art patrons. To this day they have not abandoned their privilege.

European history, in spite of its many recorded changes in boundaries and rules and types of government, confirms the persistence of aid to the arts. The people, even to the point of sacrifice, support the art organizations of their native land. A cultural continuity has provided unchanging unity in the individual histories — support for the things which endure in spite of crucial changes.

At the outbreak of World War I, Europe still had eighteen monarchies. In 1914 there were only two republics — France and Switzerland. Then, the disintegration of European imperialism overturned many thrones. Only Great Britain and a group of smaller nations have retained their old monarchies. Today, fifteen republics exist on the Continent. Whatever the form of government — monarchy or republic — European countries have always managed to make large funds available for the arts. When royal patronage ended, the people adopted public patronage. They voted moneys to assist the arts through federal and state parliaments and through municipal councils. Parliamentary action in behalf of the arts expresses a popular mandate. The passing of laws, the acceptance of budgets, and other items pertaining to official art support require majority agreement by the political parties in control. Ways and means differ, as we have seen, from country to country: there are the "Cultural Penny" of Austria, directly earmarked for art support, or the tax derived from "Spectacles and Sporting Events" in Italy, or subsidies appropriated in other countries directly from the treasury without resort to special taxation. Conservative and progressive factions, although otherwise politically opposed, agree on a common cultural cause.

Motivation of Sponsorship

What generates such warmth of Europe's art climate? Can a similar set of circumstances, attitudes, judgments, and sentiments be successfully cultivated in our country?

In this concluding part of our study we focus on certain aspects of European patronage that are relevant to American art life at a crucial stage of its cultural evolution. As private art sponsorship reaches a precarious state in our country, alternatives must come under fresh and unprejudiced examination.

All patronage, the world over, stems from motivation. To give, one must have reasons to give. One gives if one believes in the worthiness and particularly in the necessity of giving. In this sense, patronage is a matter of belief and trust. Without proper motivation, permanent support of any cause is inconceivable.

We have shown in many instances chosen from Europe's past and present how art patronage has resulted directly from traditions nourished over long periods of time. Motivation for supporting the arts, as we have seen, has been instilled individually and collectively. As psychologists indicate, attitudes begin at home. Education inculcates love for art in the young: it can be developed in the kindergarten, in the elementary and high school, and in the college. But motivation can also be instilled and fostered successfully in the adult. Systematic planning can direct popular will toward the support of art. In their propaganda for art, Europeans have long applied a variety of psychological techniques — on the largest conceivable denominator of education and through every medium of public information.

The different attitudes toward art in Europe and America are definitely not the result of differences in the nature and endowment of the respective populations. People are not more "gifted" abroad. Any pedagogue with sufficient teaching experience in both American and European schools knows that American youth is capable of as much response to art as youth in the oldest civilizations of Europe. But the methods by which European children and adults are made aware of the significance of art range from an obvious to a more subtle and imaginative persuasion. Respect for the arts is nurtured as early as possible, and continuously. Children grow up with consciousness of a great artistic heritage. On streets and squares of their cities they see venerable churches and monuments, beautiful public buildings, handsome operas, theaters, and concert halls, and they see visitors coming from other lands to study and enjoy these monuments to artistic achievement. Even if the children lack innate sensitivity to these architectural masterpieces, they cannot escape the systematic teaching of art appreciation in the schools. The child learns to respect art and to develop a set of values that condition his later attitudes and give an art-conscious direction to his mature life.

Prestige and Security

Young Europeans are aware that their government is closely identified with the art life of the nation. Some of the great theaters are called state theaters. A state opera, a state playhouse, a state orchestra, or an art institute may have the name of the province or of the municipality. The young grow up knowing that these institutions are officially supported. The government, watching over these organizations, lends them prestige, even glamour. To support them is patriotic.

There is no feeling of economic insecurity for those who work within such organizations. On the contrary, anybody connected with them holds a coveted appointment — from the director down to the last stagehand. Positions carry tenure, annuity, and privileges. All of this influences young Europeans ready to decide on a career. In our country youth is quick to discern the Cinderella role of the artist. And ours is a realistic youth, attuned to high American living standards, to the material comforts of life provided by an affluent technological society and a job with adequate wages.

II. Dramatization of Art Values

Art Is News

In Europe art is always news. Often it is front-page news. Significant art events receive as prominent a place and sometimes as much space in the daily newspapers as politics, business, and finance, as national and international developments that spell high news value and priority to the editors. On the most crucial day of the Korean crisis, which might have set off a third world war, the front pages of Viennese newspapers broadly covered the appointment of a new director for a state theater.

Thus the man on the street, even the most indifferent one, becomes accustomed to seeing art news printed alongside world events. A specific and continuous publicity conditions the reader. He is prepared to accept art as a matter of general importance.

Positive publicity prevails not only with newspapers in large cities. The press of smaller communities, proud of indigenous achievement, follows the metropolitan pattern. Much crucial support of the arts stems from the constructive attitude of the publishers and editors of the daily newspapers and of magazines and journals. They follow a rule unwritten but long-established of placing strong emphasis on reporting art life. Not rarely do reviews of concerts, of opera, of theatrical performances begin on the first page. They might even appear as *feuilleton*, marked off, and prominently placed on the page. This routine pertains not only to premières and other gala performances that might be classified as outstanding social events; it applies to the general repertory as well. That art is news is a generally accepted pattern in European journalism, and the public estimate of the arts is reflected in the kind of press it is given. Radio and television also give prominent coverage to serious art. They provide voluntary publicity on the municipal, provincial, and national networks. Art events beyond the border of the country also are under frequent discussion. International broadcasts of performances are exchanged as a matter of routine.

It is encouraging to observe that there are American newspapers which have adopted a policy of knowledgeable and often scholarly coverage of art life. On the other hand, many newspaper publishers, even in large cities, do not consider art worthy of learned reportage.

Stamps, Bills, Coins

The imagination and response of the people to art can be engaged to good advantage by simple methods in which the government communicates with the citizens outside the legislative sphere. In Europe civic receptivity is instilled by government on all levels, often with simple down-to-earth methods.

Postal stamps, money bills and coins, street names, even the names of trains, planes, and ships — things properly related and others perhaps far-fetched — all line up in a teamwork of indirect propaganda for the arts. Viewed singly, they might not be important; some of them might seem playful, whimsical. But their effect is cumulative. We find throughout Europe many instances of this kind of art support, which might be classified as peripheral encouragement of the performing arts. Their influence is unmistakable.

A postage stamp can be more than a receipt for the cost of mailing a letter. It can be a small homage, a stimulant for thought in many fields. It can even be a miniature introduction to art. All European countries regularly use stamps as a means to propagandize culture. Postal stamps from The Netherlands promote art appreciation with a wide pictorial range of reproductions, from etchings of the seventeenth-century giant Rembrandt to a small portrait of the modern Dutch composer Willem Pijper (1894-1947). In West Germany the inauguration of the third Beethoven Hall in Bonn* suggested to the post office various tokens of commemoration, including a souvenir sheet with a facsimile quote from Beethoven's *Ninth Symphony*. The world tour of the Vienna Philharmonic in 1959 was celebrated by issuing an Austrian stamp, 2 schillings 40, with pictures of a harp and violins in the foreground of the design. The centenary of Gustav Mahler (1960) brought a profile of the composer on the 1 schilling 5 stamp. The cancellation mark of the post office shows the symbolic curtain of the Salzburg Festival.

France issues stamps in honor of her composers from the early Baroque to the twentieth century: Lully and Rameau, Berlioz and Bizet, Gounod and Thomas, Ravel and Debussy. In 1940 philatelists as well as the general public were charmed by a stamp projecting the portrait of Debussy against a picture illustrating his orchestral prelude *Afternoon of a Faun*.

The European salute to great artists through stamps transcends narrow patriotic borderlines. Belgium, for example, issued a series of Mozart stamps during the bicentennial of 1956. The 4.2 franc stamp showed one of Mozart's manuscripts beside the picture of Queen Elisabeth, with the Latin inscription, "Elisabeth Artium Patrona."

What could be more appropriate picture material for Italian postal stamps than scenes from operas? For the Puccini centenary in 1958, the garret scene of Act I of *La Bohème* decorated a stamp. The universal genius of Verdi has been commemorated on various occasions by individual stamps tracing the composer's life from the humble country church at his birthplace, Le Roncole, to the place of many of his triumphs in maturity, La Scala in Milan.

*Cf P. 281.

The United States has portrayed famous men on stamps, bills, or coins, but has restricted subjects, for the most part, to figures of political history and commemorative occasions. In recent years, however, the post office issued a series of stamps which included portraits of Stephen Foster, John Philip Sousa, Victor Herbert, Edward MacDowell, and Ethelbert Nevin.

Currency in the form of coins and bills provides another means to familiarize the population with pictures of great artists and scientists. In Austria the 100 schilling bill shows the portrait of Franz Grillparzer, the classical poet. Anton Bruckner, the composer, appears on the higher bill of 1,000 schilling as well as on the newly released 25 schilling coin. The 500 schilling note shows the University of Vienna and, on the reverse side, one of its Nobel prize winning teachers, the psychiatrist Dr. Wagner-Jauregg. Austrian silver coins bear the profiles of Haydn, Mozart, Schubert, Johann Strauss.

Street Names

What could be a simpler reminder of art for the "man on the street" than the very names of streets themselves? In Europe the names of many squares, avenues, parks, and the like are marked with the names of great figures in art history. The map of almost any Continental town— small, medium, or large — provides examples. There are few, if any, Italian cities without their Piazza Verdi or Via Manzoni. Painters' names like those of Rembrandt or Vermeer naturally prevail in Holland. France honors similarly the memory of Molière and Victor Hugo, of Berlioz and Debussy. Even French chauvinism does not begrudge the Austrian Mozart a prominent Parisian avenue named in his honor. Every German town has its Goethe or Schiller Strasse, Beethoven or Wagner Platz.

Homage is not limited to creative artists; it is extended to performers. Thus Salzburg has its Max Reinhardt Platz, Toscanini Hof, and Furtwängler Park, to honor these interpreters whose work, in the conviction of the city council and the art world at large, contributed much to the formation and growth of the Salzburg Festival. The entire district around the Festspiel Haus is called the "Festspiel Bezirk."

The practice of naming streets, boulevards, and avenues after great artists is not neglected in the United States. But the rapid growth of many of our cities has favored a more practical system of identification, such as numbers or letters. Where names are used, the honor is more frequently awarded to presidents, generals, or prominent political figures. The renaming of old streets is rarely practical. But as new districts rise and as art and civic centers are built, more consideration could be paid to our own artists and to those of other countries.

III. Housing the Arts

Victor Hugo observed about Notre Dame Cathedral, "Mankind has not had an important thought that has not been written in stone."

Civilizations are, certainly, recognized and remembered, even after thousands of years, by their buildings. In places such as Delphi or Syracuse, the past glory of Greece lives on through the ruins of spectacular amphitheaters. To this day the Arena of Verona, Italy, which dates from the first century, is effectively used for opera performances during the summer season. The town of Vicenza has a playhouse in ancient style; Andrea Palladio, the Renaissance architect, achieved in the simple wooden structure of the Teatro Olimpico* a marvel of harmonious design and theatrical perspective. Many other structures in the Old World remind us that the arts have always been magnificently housed. Some of the theaters are art works in themselves; they bear testimony to a proud cultural concept of patronage.

Today this tradition is kept alive throughout Europe as it was in antiquity, in the Renaissance or in the Baroque. Luxurious operas and theaters, concert halls and palatial museums have been placed with architectural vision in the centers of old towns.

Some of these buildings stand in the neighborhood of venerable cathedrals, on spacious squares hallowed by history. Such planning has meaning. For these theaters were conceived as *temples of art*, designed to receive devoted as well as festive audiences. Some of the works of art heard and seen in these handsome halls command a response not unrelated to religious veneration. Some are meant to cheer and to delight. But whatever the opera or play, the very building in which it is presented is part of the theatrical experience; the buildings themselves have been assigned a leading role.

Good theaters reveal their backgrounds in terms of architectural styles. If the style is authentic, it conveys certain aspects of patronage: royal, aristocratic, or democratic sponsorship is appropriately reflected in the façade as well as in the interior of the building. The styles of the older theaters bespeak the lordly manner of patrons who invited their guests into noble surroundings as the proper setting for the appreciation and enjoyment of great art. Theaters were built close to courtly palaces, sometimes directly connected with them. Often the very access to these theaters is a promise, an anticipation of festive things to come. Vienna's Burgtheater stands in dignity on a large square, surrounded by three lovely gardens. It faces the neo-Gothic Rathaus and is approached with ease from every direction, normally by way of Vienna's circular boule-

*In 1583, after the death of Palladio, the theater was completed by his pupil Scamozzi.

vard, The Ring, where the access to the opera house is equally impressive. Even the theaters in Austria's smaller cities, in Graz, Linz, or Innsbruck, and of course, the Festspielhaus of Salzburg, have been planned and built with generosity and with much consideration for the beauty of their location.

The Paris Opéra rises, elegant and aloof, above metropolitan traffic and turmoil which the builders of this theater could hardly have foreseen in the second part of the nineteenth century. In Bordeaux, the inner city houses the handsome Grand Théâtre, dating from 1773, on the spectacular Place de la Comédie. The theaters of Italy are set in their environment with naturalness and equipoise. In specific cases like that of the rococo opera house La Fenice in Venice the site of the theater is as unique as the Lagoon City to which it belongs. In downtown Naples quarters are crowded, but the Neapolitans have kept their decorative opera theater San Carlo free of modern congestion. The charming park of the regal palace romantically shields the theater from the Mediterranean; and even the busy access from the Galleria Umberto has retained the feeling of Baroque ceremoniousness.

Munificence of Planning

Most court theaters built in the seventeenth, eighteenth, or nineteenth centuries belong to a past when it was almost a rule to endow them with decorative wealth and physical expansiveness. But today, many theaters or concert halls are designed with spaciousness and elegance dictated by modern concepts of architecture. Contemporary sponsors and architects face radically different problems of design. They build for democratic audiences. The stages must accommodate modern productions.

The builders in Europe's old towns with narrow streets for pedestrians and horse-drawn carriages must now also cope with the exigencies and agonies of motorized traffic. The centers of some European cities no longer yield sufficient "living space" for the requirements of large theaters and concert halls. They must be planned in areas of new development or redevelopment where free approach and parking space are available and where urban traffic can freely flow back and forth from and to the hall. In addition, the new districts permit the expression of contemporary authoritative styles, unburdened by dated architectural environment, and builders can really start afresh.

Even England, slow to follow Continental trends, gradually has awakened to this challenge. The outstanding examples of British postwar search for a suitable location of a new large-scale art center are the Royal Festival Hall of London and the planned extension of two additional halls on the South Bank of the Thames in a slum area earmarked for rehabilitation. Built at a cost of £2,500,000, the Festival Hall was not expected to be self-supporting: it is interpreted as a civic expenditure for public service, and the annual deficit was estimated to reach £90,000.*

The study of the Royal Festival Hall leads to important observations, particularly because far-reaching changes on this vast London project are still being made long after the completion of the principal structure. The very access to the Hall has come under criticism and the entire complex of buildings is being reappraised. At present, one approaches it from the Waterloo Bridge. Aesthetically, this leaves much to be desired. A new entrance will be built directly facing the Thames, and the front of the main building will be brought closer to the embankment. A large glass façade on two levels will overlook the river and the city. Day and night there will be an impressive view from all floors of the building.

The principal hall — two others are in the blueprint stage — was completed for the inauguration of the Festival of Britain in 1951. In addition to the large auditorium (seating 3,000) one of the foyers was adapted for solo concerts and became known as the *Festival Hall Recital Room.* Among other shortcomings, the acoustics were found to be unsatisfactory. Hence the London City Council, one of the main sponsors of the Royal Festival Hall, has approved the structure of two new small halls,[1] planned by a team of experts in architecture, engineering, and acoustics; and obviously musicians and managers are being consulted for the best advice.

Making space available for art centers by planned demolition of old districts in the manner of British or American slum clearance has become unnecessary in many European towns. During World War II, in many cities one block after another was laid flat by air bombardment. Consequently, building anew within the belts of the inner towns has become possible in various regions, for instance in the Rhineland and Westphalia. But German municipalities throughout the nation seized the opportunities to build in harmony with new city planning. The new opera houses of Cologne or Hamburg, the theater in Münster, the National Theater in Mannheim, all are examples of theaters that could be newly built fairly close to the sites of the buildings they replaced. And each building stands uncrowded, sovereign, on open squares, unchallenged by other edifices in the town.

*Although the deficit has never reached this amount and has stayed as low as £30,000, it is anticipated that when repairs are necessary the losses will eventually mount to £60,000. These figures refer to difference between the actual income and all expenses of running the Hall.

Special cases of rebuilding old, regal theaters at their historic locations are represented by La Scala in Milan, the Vienna State Opera, or the National Theater in Munich — all war victims which were reconstructed with scrupulous restoration of their original appearance, for the general feeling was that the emotional experience created by these old theaters could not be successfully transferred to changed sites and structures. Hence, these three historic opera houses were reconstructed not only with their familiar façades, but with the essential aspects of their elegant interiors. The stage equipment was brought up to newest standards. It would have been possible to construct completely new opera houses for the same cost, perhaps even for less, but public sentiment overwhelmingly opposed this plan. In each of these cities the opera is the heart, and without its familiar, regular beat, cultural life seemed inconceivable.

Patrons' Pleasure

Europeans traditionally aim at transforming the visit to the theater into an aesthetic experience even in terms of the environment. The English have a neat phrase for providing amenities for their audiences: they speak of "patrons' pleasure," which they realize in their new theater by blending formal attractiveness with comfort. Thus the new Royal Festival Hall in London is both an auditorium and a social center. It houses exhibitions; there is a substantial library; there are attractive rooms for meetings allied with cultural causes; there are several restaurants and reception halls. Recent plans envision also a national theater and opera house as part of this metropolitan center, and both buildings are to provide appropriate amenities.

In general, Europe's new cultural centers provide modern solutions in terms of topography, media, and amenities. They aim to conquer new audiences from every stratum of the population.

Not only metropolitan cities of Europe have adopted the axiom of aesthetically appealing halls. Middle-sized municipalities build theaters with the added delight of socially harmonious environments. In Upper Austria, for instance, the new Kammerspiele of Linz is a small theater, modestly gracious and without ornate décor, but the interior displays indigenous art, particularly painting and sculpture. Murals depict scenes from the theatrical history of the Danubian town and the province.

Patterns of integrating, not separating, the arts have long been followed in Austrian theaters. The loggia of the Vienna State Opera is decorated with beautiful frescoes by Moritz Schwind, which miraculously survived war destruction. In the foyer of the Opera stands the striking bronze portrait of Mahler sculptured by Rodin. The new Salzburg Festspielhaus merits a visit, were it only to see the murals by Oskar Kokoschka. All over Europe, a parallel display of visual and performing arts in handsome buildings offers added incentive for visiting the theater. This is no minor point. Nothing is unimportant in the conquest of audiences, particularly of the young. The theater is inherently a social factor in the life of our communities. In an era of increasing depersonalization, the theater must function, as it did in the past, as a counter-force.

Variety of Design

On the European art scene West Germany provides the student of theatrical architecture with the best available objects for research. The scene is almost all-inclusive. He will find here all types, from the ancient and hopelessly outdated architecture to the ultramodern and outright experimental.

Some of the new theaters are decidedly elegant; but theirs is an elegance in harmony with modern concepts. Materials are applied and blended in a contemporary manner. Glass façades, panelled wood, pure stone and marble, or sculptured effects of broken light and the modern color palette create a holiday atmosphere for the theatrical visit.

Other theaters are sober. Their appearance does not intend to stress escape from reality. On the contrary, such halls are reminders that the theater is also a teacher, a guide. Some of the plays are performed as "Lehrstücke" (in the sense of Bertolt Brecht). They instruct the audience. But whatever their specific architectural style, Germany's theaters express a new order. They represent the reality of a new audience, the spirit of a "classless" patronage. A "democratic" prerequisite fulfilled in the new German theaters is equal comfort for all visitors. This means not only a comfortable seat but the chance to have a good view of the stage and its action from every place in the house. In this respect, the design of many old theaters was guilty of flagrant discrimination.

Today, audience participation is also heightened by the link of the stage with the auditorium. There is no break, no borderline. There are neither "Guckkasten," nor "fishbowl," as the Germans humorously refer to the old types of stage. The front rows and the proscenium are continuous. Utmost attention is paid to good acoustics. Architects are eager to avail themselves of the accumulated knowledge of the past and to apply it to new structures. Consultation with both scientific and artistic experts is always taken for granted. The enumeration of the technical equipment in the new German theaters would be tantamount to a catalogue of newest inventions: electronic switchboards, television circuits, cycloramas. No sooner are these and other devices available than they are adopted by the German theaters.

In spite of so much achievement in theatrical architecture, there is much criticism. Not all of the German burghers are happy with modern design, which they find in conflict with their conservative sense of beauty. On the other hand, many progressive citizens complain that some architects do not go far enough, that they compromise with questionable middle-class taste, and that the governmental sponsors sacrifice genuinely modern concept to majority will.

Other European countries, as we have shown in the preceding Chapters, are likewise engaged in a considerable building program devoted to the performing arts.

The Maisons de la Culture of France are providing useful suggestions for art centers in middle-sized communities. At this writing some of the most interesting theater designs have not yet become reality.

Of European opera projects still in blueprint the new Opera House in Amsterdam warrants special attention. The opportunity to beautify the ancient city with a new large-scale musical theater is part of the total design. The Opera House will be in Amsterdam South, along the North Amsterdam Canal. This site, close to the center of the town, affords ample space for building and parking. A square will be formed in front of the Opera House; the nearby Amstel Canal is to be widened, and the appearance of the entire district will be beautified. The Amsterdam Opera will seat 1,400 and cost approximately $6,000,000. All visitors approach their seats by way of the handsome main foyer. The horizontal organization of the Opera House accommodates three levels on which all activities involved in the operation of the theater will take place.

Because the Europeans have built or are building many challenging theaters, their accumulated experiences can be utilized to good advantage in America. Halls individually conceived for specific media of performance are found to be best. Large multipurpose halls, in spite of their practicality, and sometimes remarkable permutability, do not represent the most satisfactory solutions. The best acoustics prevail in halls originally designed to meet the definite exigencies of a medium: a repertory theater, an opera house, a symphony hall, a chamber music room. European halls, famous for their good acoustics and fine atmosphere, are not large. And experts do not consider an auditorium with a seating capacity of more than 2,800 suitable for an opera or symphony hall. The desirable figures for repertory theaters are correspondingly lower, frequently below 1,000.

Many European theaters are impressive examples of architecture imaginatively placed within the town plan. They greatly contribute to the appeal and fame of their cities. There is something personal, sometimes unique, about the best of them. The people are proud of their theaters. The patrons of the past are gone, but their heirs, the citizens, care for this legacy with devotion. They have inherited a commitment to sponsorship, and they live up to it spontaneously.

The Need for New Theaters and Concert Halls

America has been slow to accept the idea that proper housing is a basis for the healthy functioning of the performing arts. But times are changing. Curiously enough, many citizens opposing government support of the arts are not aware that the Lincoln Center for the Performing Arts represents the cooperation of private patrons, the City of New York, the State of New York, and the Federal Government. In addition to individual philanthropists, foundations such as Ford, Rockefeller, Avalon, have contributed their part to the $150,000,000 project, which proves the feasibility of collaboration between private initiative and governmental sponsorship on different levels.

Why has adequate shelter for the arts been so long and so grimly neglected throughout our country? Various answers come to mind; but it is self-evident that the people at large have not sufficiently cared for the arts to endow them with dignified settings. While the achievements of American architecture in so many forms amaze the entire world, we have to apologize for the scarcity of theaters and symphony halls or for the inadequacy of those that exist. There are, of course, the few familiar exceptions. But in too many cities, unattractive and technically unsatisfactory halls — war memorials, high school auditoriums, mosques, even moving picture theaters — have been and still are widely accepted as places for presenting concerts, operas, plays, and ballets. Visiting companies have found it difficult, sometimes impossible, to perform even in our principal cities because of the lack of adequate stages. Ironically, satisfactory halls are sometimes torn down to make room for office buildings or for parking lots and garages.

In 1960 it became known that the Garrick Theatre in Chicago, a work of the American pioneer architect Louis Sullivan, was to be destroyed to make room for a parking garage. There was civic indignation, and protest against the impending demolition of the Garrick Theatre found support even in Europe. The theater was torn down, but the shocking event had its compensations. On August 7, 1963, Governor Otto Kerner of Illinois signed a law to preserve "areas, places, buildings, structures, works of art and other objects having special historical, community or aesthetic interest or value."

Another example of impending vandalism was the threatened demolition of New York's venerable Carnegie Hall. If it had not been for the cultural conscience of Isaac Stern and a group of public-spirited citizens whom he frantically mobilized, Manhattan would have lost its fine concert auditorium, ennobled by the patina of musical history.

Within the last generation not a single stage devoted to legitimate theater was built in metropolitan New York. The Lincoln Center Repertory Theater is the first theater devoted to spoken drama built in the nation's largest city since 1927. And this is the record in a metropolis world-famous for its perpetual new building program and for daring architectural achievement.

But America is awakening to the need and challenge of building art centers in our cities. Some have been completed; others are, at this writing, still only in blueprint. Belatedly, Washington, like the European capitals, will be beautified by an art center worthy of national representation. The twin cities, Minneapolis and St. Paul, have through diversified patronage made a repertory playhouse possible — the Tyrone Guthrie Theater — and have thus embarked on a project which may well set a pattern for the rest of the nation.

The "Acropolis of Pittsburgh" is to be built in the Lower Hill district; this cultural center will include a permanent rent-free home for the Pittsburgh Symphony Orchestra, and other facilities for the arts. The $40,000,000 project has been inaugurated by three Pittsburgh foundations.*

Decentralization — an Axiom

Creating shelters for the performing arts requires multiplication in hundreds of municipalities from coast to coast. If our aspirations for a worthy cultural program are to succeed, the arts will have to be given the priority in housing which they have enjoyed in Europe for centuries.

The preceding chapters surveyed the vital aspects of decentralization on the European art scene. Whether we study the art map of Holland or Belgium, of France or Italy, decentralization emerges as the answer given by Continental nations in search of an art life to be shared by all the people. Today, as in the past, Germany leads in this trend. The government of France is spending large sums on projects of dramatic and lyrical decentralization. Austria has been building fine theaters in small towns, even in Alpine hamlets, where conditions warrant such an enterprise. We also note that the communistic part of Germany does not concede priority to the West German Republic in munificent housing of the performing arts.

*The A. W. Mellon Educational and Charitable Trust has reserved the 9.2 acre site, and this Trust, the Howard Heinz Endowment, and the Buhl Foundation have given the Urban Redevelopment Authority $200,000 to finance planning and design studies.

In the United States such a pattern is a self-evident proposition; the special circumstances of art life in such a large and young country demand a far-reaching national program of diffusion in every medium of performance. American art life must no longer be allowed to cluster around metropolitan centers. It has to spread to all areas, including the hinterland, so that the radius of cultural opportunities can grow organically.

Combining Beauty and Function

Recent studies have investigated the best plans for future theaters in our country. Thus the Ford Foundation commissioned "eight selected teams of architects and stage designers" to propose "eight ideal solutions to the designs of different theaters, without cost limitations or design restrictions."* Such studies provide important guides: their suggestions should be profitably applied as new halls are being planned.

Not all European theaters are designed for a clearly defined representation of patronage and purpose. Some of them could be anything from temple to bank, from moving picture theater to office building. We can learn from the best solutions of the Europeans and also, negatively, from their mistakes. The sober new Teatro Communale of Florence is an example of cheerless functionalism. Perhaps the most businesslike among the large costly postwar theaters has risen east of the Iron Curtain: Leipzig's $10,000,000 opera house fails to convey, with its sleek functional appearance, the aura of a festive theater. But this East German opera has acquired a reputation for its highly efficient stage and satisfactory auditorium. Other new European theaters feature a grim utilitarianism that is not congruent with the world of the performing arts.

The American theater of tomorrow must be spared this kind of dullness. The point is crucial: after the technical requirements of a modern stage and of the auditorium have been fulfilled, the planners of new halls must not forget that beauty and dignity are assets to any public building. They are obligatory in those devoted to the arts. Was it Puritan tradition, economy, poor design, and outright bad taste (or an unlucky combination of all) that played havoc with too many of our older theaters and concert halls in the United States? Whatever the answer, we hope that tomorrow's builders will pay sufficient consideration to both function and beauty. The needs of the public, the amenities, will have to be

*Among the participants in this theater design program were such distinguished teams as Eldon Elder (stage designer) and Edward Durell Stone (architect); George C. Izenour (designer-engineer) and Paul Schweikher (architect); Jo Mielziner (stage designer) and Edward L. Barnes (architect).

taken into full account: agreeable access to the hall (so that energies and tempers are not spent before the curtain rises or the downbeat falls), adequate cloakrooms, comfortable seats that afford clear visibility of the stage, and good acoustics. A theater requires the sum total of conveniences on which human beings depend for comfort and pleasure.

Every American community should be proud to have an appropriate art center conceived with aesthetic validity as well as practicality. Under no circumstances should these centers be prosaic and cheerless; nor should their functionalism be like that of streamlined clinics, factories, or banks. The American theater of tomorrow must be beautiful, even though we know that the concept of beauty is as elusive in architecture as in any other art. Judgment of beauty is deeply rooted in subjective experience. Background and learning, taste and other psychological factors enter into one's judgment of what is beautiful.

Who is to decide the issue? America has created an architecture which in pioneering spirit and striking imagination has influenced the world. Yet in many public buildings conformity and poor taste confront us.

The architects should not be the exclusive targets of the blame. The fault lies also with the public sponsor in charge of the commission. Under no circumstances must the decision on public commissions be left to inexperienced, mediocre minds. Political bureaucracy often placates "the man on the street," who is not necessarily a competent judge of the buildings he sees in his community. Popular realism (as the Soviets call it), which seeks standards of beauty in criteria pleasing to the masses, has produced under all European dictatorships a hybrid architecture. In democracies, where the artistic expression remains free, the people's comprehension of beauty needs expert guidance. In architecture, as in the sister arts, aesthetic concepts are in constant flux. The imagination of prophetic artists forecasts today the aesthetic laws of tomorrow. The American scene is distinguished by buildings which anticipated future trends; yet their architecture was at first derided publicly. During successive decades, however, these imaginative structures assumed the stature of masterpieces in the public mind.

In our plans for art centers, theaters, and symphony halls we must rely on architects who will not compromise their standards with an hypothetical, common denominator of prejudicial mass taste.

It is most gratifying to know that many art centers are in blueprint from coast to coast. But the sponsors must be mindful that even the most beautiful building will not fulfill its purpose if the community does not fully support the arts which the building is designed to shelter.

IV. Cultural Assignment of Mass Media

Radio: Concept of Third Program

Fundamental differences between Europe and America characterize the artistic policies and business procedures operating the mass media. In Europe governments supervise radio and television; in America the networks are privately owned and managed.

Europeans pay for radio and television. In the countries under study the government charges the owner a modest license fee for each receiving set.

The sets are bought commercially and remain private property. The sum total of the fees constitutes the basic capital for the expenditures of the networks. In countries or regions with large populations the license fees accumulate large funds which enable the networks to offer ambitious cultural programs; they can afford to lose money on expensive but worthwhile projects. "I am a Croesus; I do not know what to do with all of my wealth," the director of one of the large West German stations smilingly confessed. But he knows very well what to do. His music division, for instance, has commissioned an impressive number of valuable and provocative new scores. The radio station maintains an imaginative program, devoted to the education of its audiences on carefully differentiated levels. Old and new music, some of it requiring many painstaking rehearsals, is regularly heard in live performance. The programs range from Gregorian chant to electronic experiments. Some stations have won fame in a highly specialized field (Cologne, for example, in electronic music).

The major networks of Europe employ good orchestras of their own, full-time professional choruses, able staff conductors, and musicologists supervising the programs with scholarly competence.

In the category of drama analogous artistic policies prevail. Ancient drama, tragedy and comedy of the world theater of all periods, and experiments of modern theater are represented. The networks offer commissions to playwrights and poets. A new genre, the Hörspiel, has been created to cope with the exigencies of drama for radio broadcasting.

In countries where the networks incur deficits (as in Austria) the loss is always underwritten by the government. For the principal motive underlying the officially stated policies concerning the mass media is that of public service without any financial profit. In many programs the educational aspect is emphasized; stress is laid on high standards. Certain European programs bar commercial advertising. The best stations compete with each other in the quality of their broadcasts.

It would be inaccurate, however, to describe the European radio as being exclusively devoted to high caliber offerings. Actually, the Continental stations present their programs to suit their different audiences. Thus, tuning in at various hours of the day or evening we can hear popular and "middle brow," in addition to intellectually satisfying and avant-garde programs. The musical performances include popular songs, marches, jazz, and operettas.

The educated segment of the audience is served by what the British Broadcasting Company was first to name the *Third Program*, designed as a regular offering for an audience of cultivated taste and sustained interest in serious art. A similar triple division defines also the overall programming of the Radiodiffusion Télévision Française. In both countries there are three networks: the First Program (variety shows, musical comedies, etc.) is intended only to entertain; the Second Program (locally or internationally) deals exclusively with news broadcasts; but the Third Program, which the French call the *National Program*, is entirely devoted to what might be termed "cultural" in the true sense; it includes theatrical programs of high standard and poetry and prose readings. The main division of serious music offers operas, symphonies, chamber music. Science, likewise, belongs to the Third (National) Program: both art and science are coordinated within the cultural category.

The general organizational policy of most European networks is analogous to that observed in England or France. A tripartite division of assignments is planned to safeguard cultural standards. The networks make popular adjustments in their First and Second programs. The Third program remains free of compromises in its service to culture.

"Canned" Music versus Live Performance

From the viewpoint of art patronage the cultural role of radio in the United States does not compare favorably with that in Europe. We are confronted with an unquestionable decline: the major networks have given up some of their earlier endeavors in the field of serious art. The abandonment of the famous NBC Symphony Orchestra, Toscanini's creation, and of other valuable symphonic programs points to a lamentable retrogression of sponsorship. Recorded music supplants live performance in every medium, including chamber music, so ideally suited to radio broadcasting.

The announcement, in May, 1963, that CBS would discontinue the concert broadcasts of the New York Philharmonic Orchestra (which had been carried nation-wide for thirty-three years) is a recent example of this regressive trend. The subsequent announcement by the Mayor of New York City to make available the "full facilities of the city-owned radio and television station to the New York Philharmonic" is a step toward municipal patronage — a step in the right direction toward diversified art sponsorship.

It would be unfair to overlook the fine efforts that some commercial radio stations are offering their listeners, particularly in New York and a few other cities. Valuable programs of old and new music are maintained; occasionally live performances are included. But the overall national picture of radio's contribution remains disappointing. In large sections of the country, even programs of recorded music fall below acceptable standards. Furthermore, the concentration on "canned" music will never qualify as a substitute for real patronage, for the employment of musicians and actors, for commissions to composers and poets, for the establishment of independent music and drama divisions — all of which are customary in Europe's radio networks.

There are, of course, various reasons for the present state of radio programs. Before all, television has encroached upon radio's mass appeal. But the specific function of radio as the unique mass medium of sound-without-sight could still be a vital factor in our culture as it is in Europe.

Television: Issues and Procedures

European television follows, generally, patterns similar to those of European radio. From the point of view of governmental supervision, television appears as radio's adjunct; and there are analogous business procedures.

Television sets, like radio sets, are privately purchased. But the licenses for television, because of the higher production costs, are more expensive than those for radio. Many Europeans cannot yet afford to purchase television sets for their homes. In its programs European television seeks a course parallel to that of radio; it reserves sufficient time for cultural hours.

In the preamble of the royal charter granted the British Broadcasting Company, the function of the mass media is assessed as the "means of disseminating information, education, and entertainment." The original license given to BBC contained a clause to the effect that the company "must not receive money or other valuable consideration from any person in respect of the transmission of messages."[2] Recent concessions in the form of spot commercials placed between television programs, but never during programs, are the target of widespread attacks in and out of government circles.

On the Continent, the various national, state, or municipal networks function on analogous principles of public service. The European concept of the mass media assumes that it is the people who "own" the air waves of a nation. Those entrusted with their management are merely the guardians of a public assignment, appointed by and responsible to the people. Financial profit is not a goal. For the time being most European governments guard against encroachment of advertising interests. But there are increasing pressures. And it remains to be seen which governments will resist commercial inroads.

Europeans have not always enjoyed the role of the mass media as a public service. The older generation has not forgotten the ominous function of radio in times of political disaster. The Nazis, for instance, made their conquests almost as much by way of propaganda and threats through the mass media as they did by brutal armed force. Such memories contribute to the determination of European democracies to maintain government supervision of the mass media through their freely elected governments. This procedure seems to them necessary for safeguarding the democratic way of life.

In America radio and television are commercially controlled enterprises, in fact gigantic private industry. Under the prevailing circumstances, we face the basic question which Europeans have answered negatively: can a method using the airways extensively for advertising be truly beneficial to the people?

What are the achievements of American commercial television in terms of the quoted three fundamental categories — information, education, and entertainment?

In the field of information the results are often truly remarkable. The news on a great variety of subjects is communicated well, often with ingenuity. Documentaries with extraordinary photography offer the kind of insight into public issues never obtainable before.

The specific educational task of television — in the sense of systematic instruction or planned promotion of knowledge, taste, and other cultural values — is for the most part left to that specific group of stations identified as Educational Television. None the less, commercial radio and television sponsor distinguished programs also in the cultural category. For these opportunities one is always grateful. But in proportion to the income of the networks and their complete command of air time there are not enough of these valuable programs.

In the field of entertainment, programs of so-called mass appeal crowd out the few telecasts presenting diversion of discriminating quality. Furthermore, the good programs in any of the three categories are splintered by frequent and crudely inserted commercials that sorely test the viewer's patience. They break in at the most inappropriate time, disturbing sequence and mood. Too much entertainment on our networks falls below desirable levels; this claim no longer needs extensive argument. This issue is now publicly debated, with increased insight in the stakes involved. We are becoming critical of existing standards. Alarming practices on certain television programs have been subject to analysis and widespread controversy. Formidable numbers of religious leaders, educators, artists, as well as responsible civic groups, insist that the intolerable practices of television be corrected without delay. Congressional committees are examining, among other aspects, the alleged self-censorship of the networks.

It is estimated that television is watched in no less than 50,000,000 American homes sometime during every day and night of the week. What could be a more magnificent opportunity than to use this most popular mass medium constructively? Why are so many of our so-called television "sponsors" guided by what Freud identified as the *Drang nach unten*, the "pull downward," in the human personality? They evaluate the standards of their audience as "subterranean," as one of the best known television producers privately admitted.

What the People Want

At present there are only three major networks serving more than 190,000,000 people. These few channels do not provide us with adequate choice at any given time. Obviously, those who financially control and technically administer these networks have been granted great privileges within our free, competitive society. They have received the licenses to operate a public service and they must live up to standards to which they are committed in their voluntary contracts with the Federal Communications Commission.

The basic question confronting American television is this: are the networks to accept and to follow an alleged popular common denominator of bad taste, as reflected in so many of their shows, or are the networks to lead by setting proper standards and by gradually working for the acceptance of discriminating programs? The objection is often heard that it is dangerous to permit a cultural minority to set directions for the multitude. Is it not more dangerous to reverse the procedure; namely, to encourage "low-brow" taste (inevitably found in large segments of the people all over the world) and make inferior standards a basic measure of service to Americans?

In defense of the enormous part occupied by reprehensible entertainment on the air waves, it is often asserted that television must be geared to mass appeal. We are told in defense of inferior shows: "This is what the people want." Do all of them really want it? Have Americans been given a systematic and continuous choice of something better? The fallacy of the formula — "give the people what they want" — has been indicted and exposed by various studies. It can never be right to give all the people something bad because some of the people want it. In this attempted oversimplification of supply and demand on television we detect, without difficulty, an invalid form of rationalization. Here is an attempt to promote half-truths to aid selfish financial interest. Furthermore, the American people are infinitely more intelligent than some television producers assume.

The image of America created in the rest of the world is of ever-increasing concern to us. Our government has sponsored numerous projects abroad and still spends vast sums of money to protect the integrity of this image. Under the circumstances, we are shocked by the report of Dr. Truman B. Douglas, Executive Vice President of the Board for Homeland Ministries for the United Church of Christ, who returned from a world-wide trip with this comment: "I have come to regard the misrepresentation of American life and purpose by the movies and television as a subtler and more disastrous form of treason than the activities of a hundred professional spies and saboteurs. . . ."

Government Aid to Educational Television

In the United States the strongest antidote to commercial television is a type of station and programming known as Educational Television. In its substance and general intent, it corresponds to the cultural role of Europe's Third Program. The total contribution of Educational Television to America is inestimable.

Pittsburgh, an industrial metropolis, first showed the road to the educational approach with its station WQED — a veritable oasis on the television scene. This station in Pennsylvania prepared the way for the establishment of similar stations throughout the country. By 1963 their number had reached 73, and 5 more are in the process of construction. Yet the need is estimated at a minimum of 1,000.

Educational Television has so far been supported by a typically American pattern of diversified patronage. At present approximately one-third of the stations are financed by state or local funds. The Station KRMA in Denver, Colorado, is supported entirely by the public school system.

Another third of the educational stations are subsidized by universities. Among the academic sponsors are the universities of Maine, Nebraska, and North Carolina. The remaining third depend on a combination of local funds and private patronage (foundations, industry, and regional campaigns). Station WQED in Pittsburgh belongs in this category of diversified support. But without the generosity of foundations as well as the initiative of individual patrons, this pioneer station could not have survived. Today, 25 per cent of WQED's subsidies are from city and county schools; approximately 30 per cent, from special projects. The remainder is derived from foundations, local corporations, local government, and the annual campaign. Throughout the country, however, the total income of educational stations remains far below the support needed to expand technically and to fulfill their cultural assignment. On all levels of government, aid to Educational Television is imperative. For most educational stations do not have the funds to command costly professional services. Performers and directors, engineers, photographers, and technicians of all sorts are offered salaries by commercial networks which Educational Television stations can normally not afford. Considering all financial and technical limitations, Educational Television has established admirable superiority in many of its cultural programs and proved beyond doubt its lasting value to the country.

This value so far has tended to be in the quality of content rather than in the production technique, which does not always attain the standards set by the commercial networks.

Fortunately, this contribution is being increasingly recognized. The attitude of the federal government has changed. As late as May 13, 1960, the House Rules Committee killed a proposal to authorize federal grants for the building of Educational Television stations. The vote was 5-5; the bill was not cleared for action on the House floor. But the effort toward progress went on. A milestone was reached on May 1, 1962, when President Kennedy signed a bill to commit federal funds on a matching basis with state and private funds to aid Educational Television over a five-year period. Thirty-two million dollars was authorized to "provide vitally needed federal support in the construction of educational television stations, while assuring at the same time, state and local cooperation." The President recalled at this occasion that the 1862 Morrill Land-Grant Act reduced "old barriers to education and offered new opportunities for learning." More than a century has passed since that important departure committing federal moneys for educational projects.

On December 12, 1963, Anthony J. Celebrezze, Secretary of Health, Education, and Welfare, announced five federal grants amounting to $693,342 to help establish and expand Educational Television stations.

Duality of Television Circuits

The present duality of our television circuits might provide a workable formula for the future. This would entail generously supported educational stations and higher standards for the commercial networks. Such a development no longer seems Utopian, since the role and purpose of television are being reappraised from various viewpoints. The Federal Communications Commission is examining the procedures of national networks and local stations. In essence, more public service is demanded. But a breakthrough of greater responsibility by the networks is in sight. Corrective measures have been proposed by official spokesmen of the commercial stations.

The establishment of advisory committees may be among the methods that could assure proper aims and higher standards. Such committees for radio and television (as well as for other organizations devoted to the performing arts) are customary in Europe. They traditionally include educators, ministers, members of the professions, in addition to artists of proven integrity and judgment. The advisory bodies do not duplicate the job of censors, but work jointly in democratic procedure, hoping to find appropriate solutions for the issues at hand. Obviously, the effectiveness of any committee is commensurate to the quality of guidance and authority the members command.

Europe has so far shown little interest in paid television. It is being introduced as "Choiceview" in England. The Continental countries prefer improvement and adjustment from within the established networks supervised by their governments. In the United States paid television, a logical protest against inadequate program selection, obviously merits study as soon as sufficient data from various sections of the country are available for objective appraisal.

This brief comparison of certain aspects of the mass media on both sides of the Atlantic may conclude on a reassuring note. In the United States the recognition and government aid to Educational Television, its increasing support by foundations and local authorities, as well as the gradual awakening of the citizenry to the enormous cultural significance of radio and television, suggest an optimistic prognosis.

Our country's gigantic industries provide certain productive clues for the mass media. The scientific laboratories of the nation and the campuses of our universities and colleges are among the places where the industries sponsor extensive basic research. Today's theoretics are the applied research of tomorrow. The large-scale support of fundamental scientific investigation by corporations with primarily commercial aims is a generally accepted pattern in the United States as it is abroad.

A related interaction could prevail between the inventive strength inherent in the performing arts and their wholehearted employment by America's affluent networks. For radio and television will always have to depend on the feedback of living art. Even the entertainment industry cannot continue to survive, let alone to prosper, without recharging the grid circuit in terms of new ideas and techniques that stem from the creative sources of living art. Patronage is more than a civilized duty. It is common sense.

Europeans are aware of this mutual relationship; they believe in the process of regeneration derived from living art in all of its ramifications. Otherwise the Continental networks would not be the permanent employers of costly drama and opera groups, of orchestras, choirs, chamber music ensembles, and the like. Nor would the stations commission playwrights and composers. New works explore the mass media in terms of their creative exigencies. There is room for experimentation. The truism that no harvest is possible from a dried-out soil is reflected in such imaginative sponsorship. The gathering of crops requires — with radio and television as well as with any other medium — a wholehearted and long-range investment in their cultivation.

IN SEARCH OF AN AMERICAN FORMULA

I. Defining the Goal

Democracy has been explained in many ways. It has been interpreted in part as a fact, in part as a dream. The conclusions of our study pertain to both of these components. We are faced with the reality of a basically private patronage which has already been established in our country. But we also envision a more abundant art life in keeping with our rich resources and the spirit of a free society. Whatever conclusions we may draw, they cannot be independent of this image of our way of life.

The solution of the problem involves its definition. We must first decide on our cultural goals. It would be futile to discuss ways and means of art support before knowing the aims involved. Our goals have been stated on different levels, often merely in general terms. We seem to be agreed on the aim of American leadership in a free world which we fervently hope to maintain. But we must remember that our claims to this leading role are judged by our cultural achievements as well as by our technological strength, armed power, and material wealth.

We cannot escape the question which the rest of the world is asking: does American civilization, if measured in terms of its national art life and educational potential, entitle the United States to global leadership?

Other countries claim leadership with ever-increasing forcefulness and considerable success.

We have been most generous abroad in providing ample means for Europe's cultural reconstruction. Traveling from country to country, one sees the gifts of American munificence and the structural tokens of this help: universities, concert halls, theaters, palaces, newly built or rebuilt with American money. In the meantime, many of our own communities go begging for similar gifts and support. As previously observed, even major cities of our country lack proper housing for the arts; they have no theater or symphony hall; their art organizations are in a constant state of crisis and struggle for survival. Many museums are inadequately supported. Public libraries lack sufficient funds. All these shortcomings do injustice to our self-concept of a great nation.

The Luxurious and the Necessary

The core of our problem may be framed in these basic questions: do we consider art an indispensable element of our lives? Do we see in art a property of humanity without which the American way of life is unthinkable? Are we willing to cultivate the growth of a flourishing art life with the generous care it requires, so that it can enrich the lives of all of our people? Or is the present state of art support to be continued with all of its insecurities and inadequacies?

These are rhetorical questions, for this study is motivated by a firm belief in the arts and their primary role as a civilizing force in democracy, and its conclusions are founded upon the conviction, which has been confirmed by observing European patronage, that we can find acceptable ways of giving support to the performing arts. We have shown in numerous examples how passionately Europeans cling to the tenet that art is a necessity, even through wars, destruction, and poverty. There are unassailable reasons to conclude that American art life could in scope and generosity equal, if not greatly surpass, that of European countries which are very much smaller and economically weaker than the United States. But we must first abandon the widespread notion that the arts are a luxury. We must accept the view that they are a prerequisite of civilized life in a free democracy.

Diversified Patronage

Americans have for generations enjoyed the fruits of a private patronage which has generously and valiantly tried to meet the needs of her cultural growth. Individual donors and, more recently, foundations have supported our art life with a munificence worthy and, at times, surpassing that of European royalty.

We hope to preserve all forms of American private patronage, and are optimistic in the belief that these contributions of private initiative will indefinitely continue. But too many Americans regard private patronage as a bottomless well. They are not concerned with what would happen if and when the foundations would exhaust the fortunes they are still allocating to the arts. Some people see in a foundation a substitute for a great father figure who cares, provides, pays all bills, and will do so *ad infinitum*.

At this point, three questions confront us:

1. Are our foundations, individual donors, and all other private sources of patronage able to support the rapidly growing and widely expanding art life in the United States?

2. Can these combined sources assume the enormous task of a perpetual underwriting of this art support in all its various ramifications?

3. If such an assignment should prove to be unacceptable, what are the alternatives? If the first and second of these questions can be answered positively, then our problems are obviously solved. The time-honored American principle of private sponsorship would continue to prevail in the future. The task would then be one of practical organization, of a new overall planning. We would have to set up an apparatus that could serve the people.

But if the third question, which implies that private patronage alone cannot carry the burden, is relevant, we have to face new possibilities. We have to find new ways of supplanting private funds for the support of our art life. This implicitly would mean governmental assistance to the performing arts. Government aid would have to assume the deficit between the income from private subsidy and services of our art organizations and the total cost of their operation.

Obviously, governmental allocations to the arts should be on all levels. In Europe, as we have seen, the various national governments interpret art support as a traditional obligation. But the European example shows that federal aid to the arts does not imply substitution of federal moneys for state, local, or private funds. On the contrary, federal encouragement serves everywhere as an incentive for state and local efforts. In certain countries (such as Switzerland) the total emphasis is on regional efforts. In West Germany the wide circle of national patronage encompasses numerous and greatly diversified projects. Federal art support is geared to a program supra-regional in character, to issues of general significance for the entire West German nation; frequently, the federal government acts only in a complementary capacity and expects local patronage to be the principal agent.

In no European country west of the Iron Curtain has governmental aid to the arts meant the end of private sponsorship.

Diversified patronage, then, is a formula that is working well in Europe. Can it not be equally or perhaps even more successful in America for carrying on the great artistic gains of the past and for insuring their successful development in the future?

But the obvious deficiencies in our present art program will have to be corrected. There will have to be long-range national planning as well as unprejudiced and imaginative strategy to solve immediate communal problems. We will have to develop on all levels our own organic structure of art patronage with government participation. "Government subsidy is not a right, but a privilege," observed John D. Rockefeller III, chairman of New York's Lincoln Center for the Performing Arts, in an address made at the annual convention of the American Symphony Orchestra League in San Francisco (1963).

Liberty under Government Patronage

The principal objections to all forms of governmental art support stem from deeply-rooted and long-held doubts. Many Americans wonder if a congenial partnership between government and culture is possible in our country. Suspicious of politicians, they forget that there are many devoted and outstanding men and women in the field of public service. Still, it is maintained, among other objections, that certain politicians will attempt to misuse their power and try to influence the administrators of government-supported art institutions for selfish ends.

Meanwhile, cooperation between government and private patronage has taken on some initial forms in our country and has proved successful. Thirteen states of the nation have established Arts Councils or are planning to do so in the near future.* We have previously referred to the diversified patronage which made the Lincoln Center for the Performing Arts a reality.

What is the European record in the all-important issue of liberty under governmental art patronage? Do the European governments guarantee freedom of action to officially subsidized organizations? What degree of freedom is available to the individual artist under government sponsorship? There is no question that European totalitarianism has compromised the arts. The record of art under dictatorships is intolerable. But so was life itself under these dictatorships. Our nation is concerned with art support by a free democratic government.

*As this study goes to press, the following states (listed in alphabetical order) are involved in projects of Arts Councils: California, Connecticut, Michigan, Minnesota, Missouri, Nebraska, Nevada, New Jersey, New York, North Carolina, Ohio, Virginia, Washington.

In the countries under study we found no cause for concern. Government supported organizations enjoy artistic independence. The conduct of the British Arts Council may serve as an example, because the democratic traditions of England are fundamentally related to our own. We learn that no British Minister or member of Parliament directs the policies of the Arts Council nor decides how and to whom its grants shall be made. There is not a single instance on record of a Chancellor of the Exchequer requiring or directing, or even advising, the Arts Council to do this or not to do that. And while, as a matter of routine, the procedures of the Arts Council are discussed and criticized in the House of Commons, successive Chancellors have invariably declared that they will under no circumstances interfere with the decisions of the Council.

As all European governments are committed to analogous principles, interference does not appear as a serious threat to subsidized organizations of the performing arts. In each country the Minister of Education (or Culture)* and the government-appointed administrators of art institutes are obliged to work within long and securely established democratic frameworks. The ministers receive and adhere to the recommendations of committees of experts and authoritative consultants. We have previously described how the selection of artistic directors is marked by cautious teamwork.

Pitfalls, Criticism, Vigilance

This study does not claim that ideal conditions exist in all government-sponsored art organizations in every city of Europe. The pretense that instances of impropriety (or other difficulties caused by a multitude of interpersonal conflicts) never occur would be tantamount to alleging that human nature has miraculously changed on the other side of the Atlantic. One would have to announce solemnly that, of all people, those connected with the theater and music are noble, good, and virtuous. They are not. There are and always have been pitfalls in Europe's public art life. And the sharpest critics are the Europeans themselves, because issues of art life deeply concern them.

Various safety valves, however, protect the integrity of art life. In France, for instance, the consulting role of government committees of experts reaches deep into the educational system, of which the arts are a vital part. Thus the professors of the art academies (or conservatories, etc.), who receive their appointment by the Minister of Education, are always chosen from a small list of candidates proposed by the Superior Council of the organizations concerned. The art institutes themselves participate directly on crucial decisions made by the Minister.

*The titles of these governmental offices vary slightly in different countries.

Similar methods control appointments in the official art life of Switzerland, Holland, Belgium. The governmental committees or arts councils traditionally include the most trustworthy experts available. With good will, it is not difficult to determine which artists or scholars within a community or country have risen to authority and reliability of judgment.

Other factors guard liberty of action within the European system of art support. There is the pressure of quality. Theaters, operas, orchestras, radio and television networks must produce, and produce well. They are the pride of their nations, their provinces, their cities. Their standards are guarded jealously from within. There is always open competition from the outside. And the management of an art institute survives in office by success, not by mediocrity or failure. As radio and television bring important performances into every home, the national theaters and orchestras are inevitably exposed to general criticism, both in and out of the country. The borders of European nations are no barriers for participation. London listens to Paris, Paris to Brussels, Brussels to Amsterdam, Amsterdam to Cologne. Constant international exchange leads to vigilance of national and even regional standards. We have referred to the provision in Belgium whereby the managers of state supported theaters are appointed only after the public has been duly informed of the potential candidates and thus had time to express a critical opinion. Such measures exist to counteract provincialism and the choice of "favorite sons."

There is keen competition for recognition and, therefore, for achievement not only between musical organizations, but also among the repertory theaters of Europe's different nations. French is spoken not only in France; it is the principal language of Belgium, Luxembourg, and Western Switzerland. English is taught as the second language in most schools of West European countries. German is the native language of Austria and of large parts of Switzerland. In short, language is not a major barrier: for example, transcontinental tours, such as those of the Comédie Française or of Vienna's Burgtheater, are events appraised at many places outside of their homelands. While the qualities of these famous government supported theaters are thus judged internationally, lesser known art organizations in Europe's provincial cities are the favorite objects of regional pride. Hence the self-interest of all art administrators, from the federal Minister of Education down to the playhouse manager or opera chief in a distant provincial town, is to offer good theater and good music.

Every system has its advantages and disadvantages. We cannot forget that the private support of American art life holds no guarantee for paradisaic innocence in procedure. In June, 1963, it became known that the Office of the Attorney General of the State of New York was preparing an investigation of the procedures of financing the theater, both on and off Broadway. A preliminary report charged that "the practices found to be thriving in this important area of the arts have created a situation fraught with danger both to the play-acting community and the investing public." The conclusion is inevitable: in the arts, as well as in government, industry, commerce, or the professions, the question of morality is not primarily a matter of the controlling system; the success of all collective enterprise depends ultimately on the nature of its leadership as well as on the cooperation of individuals working toward a common goal.

II. Integrating Art and Education

A Classical Concept

European art patronage stresses its affinity with education. Federal ministries of education and culture — or corresponding provincial and municipal departments — are permanently in charge of public art support.

There is no exception to this principle in the Continental countries covered by this study. Different procedures merely relegate responsibilities to different levels of government. Thus the supervision of the performing arts is primarily federal in Austria, France, or Italy. It is chiefly on the provincial (state or cantonal) level in The Netherlands, Switzerland, or West Germany. In England support originates with the Arts Council of Great Britain, which in turn depends on Parliament for its money. In all of these countries, municipalities participate in the patronage. As a result of such diversified aid, the art institutes of Europe enjoy continuous care, in fact, a financial security comparable to that granted to the government supported institutions of learning.

The procedure is no coincidence. It springs from the deep-seated conviction that art is a property of education. The great monuments of art are viewed as gifts to humanity. The task of imparting this artistic heritage to the people is interpreted by the Europeans as a responsibility of education, as is the teaching of the various other branches of human knowledge. Since antiquity, Europeans have interpreted the people's education as a primary responsibility of government.

Let us, at least for the sake of the argument, accept this philosophy which is the product of Europe's age-old humanistic traditions. The modern belief in this affinity is supported by the history of great human ideas. The concepts of art and education were closely allied in classical Greek civilization. Aristotle expected education to lead man, with the help of the noble arts, out of his rude state of nature to an ethical and intellectual culture. Plato subordinated art to the good of the state. He interpreted art as a tool of social enlightenment and believed that true teaching reveals which forms of art serve best and which ones are inimical to the morale of the citizens and must therefore be excluded from the ideal state.

In the medieval curriculum secular education embraced philosophy and the seven liberal arts, which were taught along with sacred doctrines of the scriptures. The great thinkers of the Renaissance interpreted education in the etymological sense of the Latin word *educere* (to lead forth). The scope of education comprised not only the formal methods of teaching, the training within school walls, but it implied the extra-mural dissemination of universal knowledge and culture. Analogous thinking may be traced through the different chapters of educational philosophy from the great humanists to our time.

Once the aggregate of these classical ideas and their influence on the relationship of art and education is understood, their equivalence in the modern ideology of European art patronage becomes convincing. These historic premises help to clarify why European governments continue to make art a main concern of education. This cultural philosophy has abundantly borne fruit.

Art: Education and Entertainment

Admittedly, this traditional ideology does not correspond to the outlook of numerous Americans. There are those who claim art to be only entertainment. There are many others with a variety of reasons for opposing the traditional attitude. Most arguments on this issue are wasted: because they result from a vague usage of terms; their meaning is obscured by a reliance on clichés and their reiteration.

We have in America a gigantic entertainment industry. It has an interest in convincing audiences that art serves merely to relax, to divert, to amuse. This is an easy, readily accepted formula that spells effortless pleasure. Naturally there can be no serious quarrel about the entertainment factor in art; it would be as absurd to repudiate this factor as it would be to challenge the very pleasure principle itself.

To settle a futile dispute of semantics in advance, we would like to recall that it was Plato who observed that "the excellence of music is to be measured by pleasure. But the pleasure must not be that of chance persons; the fairest music is that which delights the best and best educated, and especially that which delights the one man who is preeminent in virtue and education."[3]

In a related sense, we should like to distinguish between what Mozart so handsomely called "delight" in music and the kind of "entertainment" which certain commercial interests sell to the people at the expense of legitimate art. Furthermore, we must revise a widespread skeptical notion concerning the manner in which education may function. It has assumed in the minds of many a grim image — one of Puritanical bleakness, of a strict schooling that kills the very joy of learning on mere contact. Those who have such assumptions are understandably antagonistic to a tie between education and art.

But true teaching is an art in itself. It gives light — communicating experience. It creates aesthetic pleasure and enchantment. Horace expressed this thought gracefully by his phrase "teaching while delighting." Once the idea of education is freed from burdensome and uninviting associations, the fear of its alliance with art should be lessened.

When European governments accept responsibility for the arts through their ministries of education and culture, the obligation is all-inclusive. Its scope is not limited to schools. It pervades, as we have shown, the daily lives of the people. It naturally culminates in the task of creating the proper climate and congenial environment for the performing arts.

The European governments do not think of art as a luxury, as an entertaining adjunct to their lives. They interpret it as a necessity, as an indispensable segment in the living organism of a civilized society. And so they are willing to pay for art — not only as education in the schools, but also as performance in the theaters, concert halls, on radio and television networks. In short, the basic concept of art education is extended to a nation-wide task—in and out of schools. This assignment is motivated by the conviction that every child and adult should benefit from the experience of art in its enriching aspects.

Only under generous systematic and permanent care can the performing arts serve in harmony with the profound visions of the masters. In the theater, in the concert, the audience is the silent choir attuned to the thoughts of a great creative mind and to the revelation of a communicating heart. Obviously such messages do not aim at entertainment in the sense of mere distraction or passive diversion. Art may offer serene repose, but no idleness; a spiritual delight, but not easy amusement; a festive mood, but not untidy contentment.

Such are the thoughts which underlie the philosophy prompting the European nations to establish ministries of culture and education and to entrust these offices with the permanent care of the performing arts.

Correcting Halfway Measures

In the United States the Federal Office of Education has so far insufficiently concerned itself with the arts. There is no legitimate reason why this all-important office should not be endowed with wider powers and adequate funds to encourage our national art life. As in countless other aspects of public education and public affairs, patronage presently favors the sciences over the arts. Hence the agencies entrusted with scientific projects have all the advantages, financially as well as in their operational procedures. But we hope the Federal Office of Education will be given an independence of status and importance commensurate with the leading role it must assume in encouraging the whole culture of our country.

The United States pays very large sums for education. About one-fourth of the American population — 46,000,000 — is at present registered for education, full-time. Art is finding its rightful place on every level of the school system. Elementary schools encourage active participation in the performing as well as the visual arts. Progressive curricula offer scientists, engineers, and various other groups of college students (who have earlier been excluded from organized education in the humanities) valid courses in art appreciation. As a result, American youth, exposed to such learning, is becoming more art-conscious than previous generations.

Throughout the nation, elementary and high schools present live music to their pupils in valuable programs. Symphony orchestras resident in the communities give programs prepared specifically for audiences of different age groups, presenting concerts for young adults and grade school children, and even "tiny tot" concerts. Chamber music groups likewise perform within the framework of the schools. Demonstrations of the various instruments and stimulating discussions of musical topics are an informal part of the general program. A creative task is undertaken: the audience of the future is being molded.

Classroom education is no longer limited to the young. Statistics show that adult education in America has reached an enrollment of 10,000,000; within this group large numbers study art.

It is in the public schools that America makes its largest investment in the performing arts. Let us take music as the outstanding example. Our extensive blueprints for musical studies in the public schools are justifiably imitated in other parts of the world. In the United States more than 40,000 full- and part-time music teachers are employed in tax-supported schools. The catalogue of their musical activities is expanding annually. In 1960, 9,000,000 American children received instrumental instruction in schools, compared to 2,500,000 one decade earlier.[4] But with all this growth and impressive quantity of music education in our country, we should be concerned with what happens outside the school walls.

There certainly is an enormous gulf between what we teach as music in the schools and what one hears after classes under the title of music. Everywhere in our daily lives bad music surrounds us. In the schools we teach the young to appreciate serious music, good drama, fine poetry and painting. But these impressions must compete with a flood of illiterate "entertainment" out of school. We complain about the superficiality of the young and forget that we are surrounding them with everything that creates it. These early years are the very ones which psychologists identify as decisive for the subsequent development of the individual personality. Senator Abraham Ribicoff, during his tenure as Secretary of Health, Education, and Welfare, invited experts in the field of sociology and child guidance to a conference with the purpose of freshly appraising the interrelationship between certain television shows and juvenile delinquency.

The core of Europe's art life is entrusted to government supported art institutes which perform regularly, and on a year-round basis, the very masterworks which are subjects of study and appreciation in the schools. The actual experience of the art work in live performance — for which there is no substitute — thus becomes the natural complement of learning within school walls. The two programs are interconnected; they are harmonious. Instead of pulling in opposite directions, they create a cumulative cultural experience.

Eliminating Waste of Talent

The advantages of European art patronage become self-evident if we turn to the urgent problem of the young artist and his future in America. We lack what certain European countries have in such abundance: sufficient media of performance in the field of serious art to absorb the flow of talented youth graduating annually from our schools.

Ironically, foreign visitors to our campuses are amazed by the drama and opera departments in our universities and praise the technical equipment of the best of these workshops and the quality of their performances, which at certain schools attain professional standards. These college theaters fulfill, at least in part, the historic function of the European court, state, and city theaters.

In many American towns the legitimate theater has found its sole refuge in the drama workshops of our colleges, a fact which provides partial answer to the American need for decentralization. Yet with all of these distinguished efforts on academic soil, where are our talented graduates— actors and singers, producers and conductors, designers and stage technicians — to turn for professional employment after commencement?

In addition to theaters where students learn, we need many professional theaters where mature artists perform for the benefit of our communities.

No nation anywhere in the world can afford to waste its talent. The artistic and intellectual endowment of our youth represents the kind of capital that can never be replaced. By building and maintaining theaters and opera houses throughout the nation, we not only could give employment and opportunities to scores of gifted young artists, but could simultaneously expand performances all over the country and offer millions of Americans the chance to see and hear masterworks in live performance of professional standards. Just as in the case of radio and television, those objecting to cultural programs will say: "The masses do not want this kind of art; they enjoy only light entertainment." The fact is that the American people, at large, have not really been given a choice. They have not yet had the same opportunities as Europeans for developing a taste for first-rate art. In the few cases and places where they did have this chance the decision was in favor of good art. For example, the Shakespeare Festival, which offers free performances in New York's Central Park during the summer, is a huge popular success. When the project was in jeopardy during 1961, a storm of protest broke. The Festival continued, and in 1962 it was voted an appropriation of $100,000 by the Board of Estimate. A $400,000 amphitheater was dedicated on June 18, 1962. Youth is prominently represented on the stage as well as in the audience. Other successful Shakespeare festivals in the United States are held in Akron, Ohio; Ashland, Oregon; San Diego, California; Stratford, Connecticut.

From coast to coast youth greets musical projects with similar enthusiasm. Stimulated by the preparatory art education in schools, demands for youth concerts designed for various age levels have greatly increased. They have, in fact, doubled, or in certain places, tripled, during the past few seasons. The success of these events forecasts even larger audiences for the near future.

Another trend indicating the existence of a public educated in the arts and willing to support them is that listening to records and building record libraries of fine music, poetry, or drama are no longer hobbies of the few. They have become an integral part of the lives of countless art-loving Americans in every age group. There are numerous other positive signs, proving beyond doubt that America is ready for an art life equalling the scope of the performing arts in Europe.

American music festivals, for example, have grown in numbers and have attained quality and stature. The high level of achievement in the performing arts coincides with the marked increase of foreign visitors to our country. This is of consequence at a time when tourism is becoming an important factor in the American economy. Foreign currency must come in as the dollar flows out.

Europeans have long recognized their cultural assets as sources of income, and their public art support takes this into consideration. Visitors to the United States do not come only to see the Grand Canyon, the Lincoln Memorial, or the United Nations. They are also attracted by cultural events: they attend the theaters, concerts, art exhibitions, and festivals. One can not overlook this contribution of American art life to the domestic income.

Particularly during the summer season America offers musical events of great strength, such as the Tanglewood Festival under the direction of Erich Leinsdorf. In Marlboro, Vermont, Rudolf Serkin has created a shrine of chamber music with strong accent on the young performer. It is doubtful that this specific experience in one of the most noble forms of music-making can be matched today anywhere in the world.

Plans are in blueprint for a large-scale summer festival in Saratoga Springs, New York. Eugene Ormandy envisions here a center for the performing arts which will also provide the permanent summer home of the Philadelphia Orchestra.

III. Art Support as Public Service

Granted, there will always be those who will never care for any form of serious art. And even many more who will be incensed if they are asked to pay for it. They are the ones who will continue to ask why they should pay for the kind of drama and music which they do not enjoy. The answer is that with our taxes all of us support many institutions and projects, local, state, and federal, from which we as individuals never derive direct benefit. People without children pay school taxes. The tax-supported public libraries contain a multitude of books which we personally might not wish to read, but we pay for the maintenance of all departments in the library so that each citizen may borrow the books that suit his taste or needs. Some people do not journey to the national parks; others do not ride on turnpikes. But everybody pays for them as public services. In a great democracy we have the privilege of not availing ourselves of services; but we should never deprive fellow citizens of them.

The European scene clearly shows how well the art institutes function when they are treated as public service. We have also observed that the "services" may chronologically precede the general demands and needs of the people at a particular time. When Emperor Joseph II of Austria created Vienna's Burgtheater in 1778, he intended it to be a "gift to the nation." As years went by, this gift became the coveted property of the people; they care for the theater with devotion. If the French government today embarks on a long-range program of dramatic and lyrical decentralization, the purpose is to promote future as well as present interest in the performing arts throughout the Republic. In each case of such national patronage, the issue is not merely to meet an already existing need. Enlightened sponsorship may create the demand. The Arts Council of Great Britain acts on this principle with marked success. The motivation of national patronage is an investment in the future of the British people.

In our country there is some unclear thinking on the sequence of procedures which cultural leadership must pursue. The first step must be to create the opportunities for the people, to have the media of performance available. The second step, participation of the people, will follow, as the European experience shows in every period and country.

Orchestras in the United States

We like to think of America primarily as a land of orchestras, and with full justification; we can rightly claim to have some of the finest orchestras in the world, directed by the best conductors. We also boast that we have more than 1,000 symphony orchestras. But this high number is misleading: it suggests a deceptive view of symphonic life in our country. Most of these ensembles are amateur groups. This is not to imply that the amateur orchestras are not desirable. On the contrary, they are essential in the scheme of our art life. They might in the future develop into competent ensembles, and obviously deserve today the full encouragement of their communities.

The American Symphony Orchestra League differentiates between "Major" and "Metropolitan" orchestras on the basis of their annual budget.[5] Fewer than 30 of our orchestras can be considered professional if judged by proper criteria of performance and operation. Most of our orchestras are part-time organizations. For many of their players music is merely a hobby; they earn their living in a great variety of other professions. Significantly, such conditions prevail by no means only in small communities. Many American orchestras import the nucleus of their players from nearby professional organizations in large cities. Thus, the Pittsburgh Symphony supplies not only a number of first players, but a complement of "section men" for several small orchestras in a radius of eighty miles from the Steel City. This is a necessary procedure for the time being. Without such a makeshift, it would simply not be possible to give concerts with any degree of competence in the following towns: Wheeling, West Virginia; Youngstown, Ohio;

Altoona, Butler, and McKeesport, Pennsylvania. But in the long run, this procedure of importations is inimical to indigenour music-making, which has been recognized in Europe's autonomous art centers for centuries.

We are casually accepting in American art life the phenomenon of the "semiprofessional." And semiprofessional orchestras are considered good enough to serve the cultural life in many of our large communities. One of America's metropolitan areas with a population exceeding 1,000,000 must be satisfied to listen to Beethoven's *Ninth Symphony* performed by an orchestra that is supplemented by part-time musicians. As the conductor of this orchestra in the midwestern city stated: "My piccolo player is a bartender; we have a mail carrier, a hotel bellhop, a gardener, a taxi driver, and a door-to-door salesman. From the latter, my wife bought a vacuum cleaner."[6]

The part-time musician, admirable as his enthusiasm is, divides his time between his profession and his hobby. The professional musician's study and training never ends. His is an altogether different assignment. After a day's work he must practice at home for his next rehearsal or performance.

Each sizeable American community needs a professional orchestra and should not settle for less. It is true, the contributions of amateurism to the art life of a country are apparent and appreciated all over Europe. But there is a clear distinction between dilettantism and professionalism. The amateur does not take the place of the professional.

In America there are by far not enough professional orchestras to make full-time use of our promising instrumentalists. The few who succeed in finding positions are often discouraged by the unfavorable economic outlook. Many give up. They are not strong enough to brave the hardships and disappointments. Others are lured into the commercial field. Students find ready money playing in jazz bands over the weekends; often they abandon serious music and become commercial entertainers for the rest of their lives.

The American Federation of Musicians published a survey[7] of economic conditions under which the members of symphony orchestras live and work. The report concentrates on 26 orchestras which in 1960 maintained "integrated managerial personnel, continuing organization and regular seasonal schedules of twenty weeks or more." We learn from the report that only 9 of these major symphonies could offer musicians regular seasonal employment of thirty weeks or more. In 1960 the seasons of the remaining 17 ranged from twenty to twenty-eight weeks of the year. The average annual income in America from symphony performances earned by symphony musicians was less than $4,000 before taxes, or about $75 per week when spread throughout the year. This is an average figure which exceeds what is actually earned by more than half of the players in these 26 major orchestras. The average annual income which instrumentalists derive from service in most of our major orchestras is not an adequate wage for the living standards in the United States. Moreover, in only 12 of these 26 major orchestras were musicians eligible for employment insurance. Only 4 of these orchestras provided hospitalization benefits. And only 10 of these leading orchestras had a pension fund.

In comparing the European with the American situation, not the orchestra member's actual income but its relative buying power must be considered. But the all-decisive factor favoring the European instrumentalist is the security of his employment, the long-term contracts and pensions. Only in a few top orchestras of the United States do the players enjoy a comparable security. The majority of our orchestra members are at a great disadvantage because of the brevity of seasonal engagements, the absence of tenure and pensions, and the modesty of the average income.

The Pittsburgh Story

In this unsettled phase of diversified American art patronage, recent developments in Pittsburgh show a reaffirming trend. From its very beginning the Pittsburgh Symphony Orchestra was supported from private sources. Only recently local government, city and county, came to its aid on a modest basis.

For the Orchestra's 1958-59 season, the city contributed $50,000. For the following four seasons, these subsidies were cut to $35,000. In 1963 the subsidy was cancelled altogether. It was asserted that "luxury" had to give way to "necessity." The streets of the city needed costly repairs. The budget did not permit luxury items such as contributions to the Pittsburgh Symphony. In 1964 the city restored its contribution to the extent of $15,000.

Allegheny County began its donations to the Orchestra with a contribution of $25,000 in the 1960-61 season and increased its share to $50,000 the following season. For 1963-64 the county's contribution reached $70,000. The subsidies of both the city and county are earmarked for concerts free to the people.

But the funds raised by the Pittsburgh Symphony Society through annual campaigns within the community at large have been insufficient to meet the Orchestra's growing deficit. The residual deficits, i.e., that part of the total operating deficit of the season which exceeds the amount received from all regular money-raising efforts, were covered, year after year, almost entirely through special gifts from the Howard Heinz Endowment and from the A. W. Mellon Educational and Charitable Trust. As such gifts could not have continued indefinitely, the situation gave cause for great concern.

Fortunately, the upward course of cultural development was not halted. Pittsburgh foundations responded generously to the Orchestra's call for help. An endowment of $5,000,000 was established. Of this sum, $3,000,000 was pledged by the Howard Heinz Endowment; $1,000,000 by the Richard King Mellon Charitable Trust; $500,000 each by the A. W. Mellon Educational and Charitable Trust and Mr. Paul Mellon, individually.

As Mr. Charles Denby, President of the Pittsburgh Symphony Society, explained: "The gift of this endowment constitutes a tribute by the donors to the growing musical spirit of the community and to the hard work, devotion, and determination of many hundreds of people over many years to maintain a great symphony orchestra in Pittsburgh. I hope that establishment of the endowment will give to members of the orchestra a sense of permanence and security, and to the rest of us new enthusiasm and an inspiration to greater efforts."

Mr. Denby also explained that "these gifts have been made on two conditions: First, that the Society proceed at once to embark on an organized campaign to endeavor to double the principal of the endowment over the next five years. Second, that the Society continue to enlist regular annual financial support from the community at large. By action of its board of directors the Society has willingly accepted these conditions. The Society will before the end of this calendar year receive income from the endowment in the amount of $160,000. For the next few years the income should amount to close to $200,000 per year. The income will literally save the life of the orchestra."[8]

If the Pittsburgh trend were conclusive for the entire nation, the general outlook for art patronage would be encouraging. The United States, however, does not consist only of metropolitan areas with potential to support their orchestras, theaters, operas, and all the other cultural organizations. From coast to coast there are thousands of communities in urgent need of art subsidies, and without foundations (resident or otherwise) to come to the rescue. The economics of smaller communities rarely permit adequate support of the performing arts.

Culture must be promoted everywhere, not only in metropolitan areas. Middle-sized towns, the hinterland, too, must be included in the experience of great art. The previous chapters have shown that European governments have long recognized this postulate and that the art maps even of small countries are dotted with cultural centers from which all sections of the nations can benefit.

The Pittsburgh story demonstrates the accumulative patterns of American art support and its concomitant cultural growth. "A climate of optimism" as to the ability to raise the matching fund prevails in Pittsburgh. The receipt of $500,000 toward the matching fund was announced by the Pittsburgh Symphony Society, a gift from the Claude Worthington Benedum Foundation. Through its endowment fund the Pittsburgh Orchestra is assured of survival, a deserved reward for having valiantly upheld, through its concerts, broadcasts, records, and tours, the prestige of the Steel City as a cultural center.

The quality of the Orchestra has been recognized by the State Department, which selected the Pittsburgh Symphony and William Steinberg, its distinguished director, for a tour to Europe and the Near East, in the late summer and fall of 1964. The achievements of the American musicians raise the cultural prestige not only of their resident city, but also of the United States. Clearly, the Pittsburgh story spells potential victory for the collective venture of diversified patronage on the cultural front of our country.

The Opera

For opera companies, too, statistics paint a hopeful picture. According to the magazine *Opera News* there are no less than 750 opera-producing organizations in America; they gave approximately 4,000 opera performances during the 1958-59 season. Their number has since increased, but again these statistics are illusory. Only a few of these organizations maintain resident ensembles. The prevailing practice is to import the principal singers, sometimes also conductors and producers, etc. The total "seasons," haphazardly spread over the year, rarely amount to more than a few performances; some of these so-called "seasons" offer one single opera per year.

There are, however, numerous opera workshops functioning year-round in our colleges. And just as in the collegiate drama workshops, some creditable productions of opera can be heard on campuses from coast to coast. As to the many local opera companies (no matter how amateurish some of their serious efforts are), they at least establish America's interest in music drama.

There are other hopeful signs. On November 8, 1959, the Rhode Island Opera Guild performed Verdi's *Aida* in cooperation with the Rhode Island Department of Education. The venture seems to mark the first state-supported opera performance in our country. The state appropriated $7,000 through the channels of its Department of Education. According to the *Providence Sunday Journal*, the Veterans' Memorial Auditorium of this city could have been filled to capacity four or five times, so strong was the demand for tickets. No matter how modest their initial support and the present setting, these operatic efforts must be taken seriously and encouraged wherever they take root. It would be foolish and outright snobbish to subsidize only the established powerhouses of opera in New York City, San Francisco, or Chicago.

The sum total of all opera groups in our country is far from providing sufficient professional opportunities for our operatic talent. America is a land of beautiful voices. European opera directors will corroborate this fact. They ought to know: they annually engage hundreds of our singers for their opera seasons. Most of these young Americans must remain abroad if they want to continue their operatic careers.[9]

Complaint is widespread about the lack of experience of young American conductors. The charge is justified. But how could it be otherwise when we do not offer these young musicians the time-tested training ground for directing vocal and instrumental forces, namely, the orchestra pit of the musical theater. Here, in the theater, apprentices learn their craft, conducting not only operas, but operettas, ballets, and incidental music (in addition to gaining preliminary experience as coaches with their innumerable practical assignments). Europe, particularly Germany, Austria, and Italy, abounds in these opportunities. Middle-sized and even small cities have their municipal theaters where young conductors start their careers. The smaller towns frequently offer them the best chances to undergo diversified training. Many important conductors have served such internship on provincial stages.

The lack of opera theaters in our country sharply curtails the outlet of American composers for music-dramatic productions. The current project of the Ford Foundation, allocating $950,000 for the performance of 18 new operas composed by Americans, is a big step forward at a time when no government subsidies are available. Four leading opera theaters were chosen for this project: the Metropolitan Opera, the New York City Opera, the San Francisco Opera, and the Chicago Lyric Opera. They are to produce over a span of eight years the commissioned scores. These opera companies are free to engage creative artists (composers and librettists) according to their own judgment.

If opera is to have a rightful place in our country, we must be in a position to offer American talent seeking an operatic career a future at home. This obviously means more than the haphazard support of opera companies which occasionally play in makeshift halls and import from New York or Europe expensive stars for box office attraction. It means the patronage of indigenous opera companies maintaining professional standards and varied repertories. Such opera theaters would offer opportunities indispensable to the development of American talent. The theaters would be the homes of orchestras, choirs, and ballets. They are always the training grounds for solo singers, conductors, producers, stage designers. They might be seats of schools. In Europe the opera theaters are also the favorite scenes of official representation and festivity. Opera houses are communal centers. The hearts of their cities pulsate in these theaters.

Educational Paradox

In contrast to the discouraging outlook for the young American performer, the future is secure and bright for the graduating scientist and engineer. Frequently, he is offered a good position even before he has received his diploma. He can choose a job according to a variety of personal preferences, locations, etc. The medical student, too, knows he will be badly needed. Every graduate in the various professional fields is assured of an economically safe future. But the young American artist faces struggle and uncertainty.

We are confronted here with another disconcerting example of a puzzling paradox in American civilization. On the one hand, we are willing to pay large sums for art education in schools. There is a constantly increasing need for more art teachers. A young musician can make a modest but secure living as an instructor in the elementary or high schools. On the other hand, we have little to offer the young aspiring performer in professional life. The official *Handbook* (1960 edition) of the United States Bureau of Statistics in the Department of Labor warns young people not to choose the performing arts if their aim is a lucrative profession. "There is no money in making music," the *New York Times* in its edition of February 2, 1962, informed its readers. The *Handbook* specifically recommends that music students enter the field of teaching rather than that of performing.

Surely there is something wrong with our logic: we are preparing youth in our schools for a future that does not exist in professional reality. Obviously music in school should be in a vital relationship to music out of school. But our young talent cannot find sufficient opportunities, because we have failed to organize the support of the arts in professional life in any secure and permanent manner.

At the Crossroads of Patronage

We must not accept this situation as final. We can have a hopeful point of view. The American people are always ready to accept a challenge once its urgency has been properly explained to them.

In the past it was convenient to leave the responsibility for art subsidy to the rich. But the paternalistic role of the wealthy patrons may not last forever. Even foundations might reach the end of the well. Consequently, a mature citizenry must today share the burden of art sponsorship.

The community is the traditional springboard of American culture. But continued realization of local patronage is often handicapped by lack of funds. If private support likewise fails, help can come only from the state and federal governments.

The crisis of the Metropolitan Opera Company (to which we previously referred) proves that one must plan anew in changing situations. Only the intervention of the United States government and the personal initiative of the former Secretary of Labor Arthur Goldberg prevented the imminent cancellation of the Opera's season 1961-62. This was a test case: the Metropolitan is the principal opera theater of a city inhabited by 7,781,984 — a figure exceeding the total population of the entire country of Austria, which supports the Vienna state theaters with $6,000,000 annually. In Europe the closing of a musical theater comparable in scope to the Metropolitan is almost inconceivable. Actually, cancelling the season of a government-supported theater would require parliamentary procedure. A new law would have to be passed.*

But the New York crisis was not without compensation. It dramatized the fact that the form of private patronage which saw America through the nineteenth century and the first half of the twentieth century cannot be fully relied upon today. Demands for public art support were heard and reappraised. We have shown that the Metropolitan Opera is not the only American art organization to reach an impasse under the present form of its support. Its difficulties brought the entire complex of American patronage into renewed and sharp focus. It is now clear that we cannot sacrifice our art life on the altar of outdated methods, if they prove insufficient to cope with the complexities of operation, the inflationary high costs of maintenance, and the growing artistic needs of our art organizations.

We must ask ourselves if there is, in the long run, another alternative to our problem in America. Is it likely that private capital can continue to pay for a vital and constantly expanding art life? An affirmative answer seems unrealistic, particularly in view of the rather alarming results of the studies investigating the present state of theater and music in our country. It will be difficult to cling to conservative and anxiety-

*Strikes by government-employed stagehands are on record in France (and elsewhere). They have resulted in cancellations of a series of performances. These difficulties were always resolved by intervention of the federal ministers supervising these theaters.

laden methods at a time when millions of young Americans — better prepared than the preceding generations to enjoy art and to share in its performance — will make their needs increasingly felt.

But one thing is certain: if the Europeans can support their art life with so much liberality, Americans can do it, too. And we can find our own formula for a diversified patronage that could be second to none in efficiency as well as generosity. We possess all the resources required for this task. We have the talent. We have more than a nucleus in terms of the performing media. We have imaginative and unselfish civic leadership in many of our communities.

A specifically American pattern can emerge from the analysis of the positive experiences abroad and the opportunities at home. We should rely on the helping hand of government at every level and without interference. This aid must not in any way stifle our traditional way of local initiative, nor should it inhibit the private impulse. On the contrary, American patronage must rise from the time-tested, democratic equilibrium of united civic forces.

We have previously examined the relationship of government support and freedom of action granted to subsidized art institutes in Europe. We have come to the conclusion that there is no basis for apprehension. Americans are likely to overlook the large catalogue of government participation in our own public services such as the mails, highways, bridges, dams, national parks, etc. Europeans, as we have shown, interpret the arts as comparable public utilities offered for the good of all the people.

Abraham Lincoln explained that "the legitimate object of government is to do for a community of people whatever they need to have done, but cannot do at all, or cannot so well do for themselves, in their separate and individual capacities."[10] The history of federal assistance to educational projects — and we consider the arts in this domain — dates back a century to the land-grant provision for schools (1862), which coincides with Lincoln's presidency. As pointed out earlier, there followed many other and more extensive instances of government help to education and to its multiple aspects of research and scholarship. American schools of higher learning accept federal, state, and private aid. There is no troublesome overall record of government interference in education when funds were obtained from the government. If the method works in education, we should be able to make it work also in art. Particularly in the performing arts, subsidies from the national treasury may have to supplement the traditional support from private sources and local government.

Those who cry "wolf" every time the term *government subsidy* is mentioned merely prove that they are the ones who lack confidence in the freedom obtained through our elected democratic processes, our democratic constitution, and the democratic evolution of our common cultural property in a free country.

The repudiation of a nationally supported art program is also rooted in other kinds of doubt. Insincere argument (by lobbyists for various interests, by demagogues, and by ignorants-at-large) has almost succeeded in convincing many Americans that the serious arts do not merit public spending, as though the theater, opera, or concert would be something frivolous — the "plaything of the rich" — and therefore not worthy of taxpayers' money. It is quite true, every European country uses, directly or indirectly, public funds for its art projects. Does this mean that the Europeans are spendthrifts? Can such proverbially parsimonious people as the Swiss, the French, the Italians, the Dutch really be called squanderers?

Europeans consider art support a sane investment. They are well aware of the costs. But they are determined that their citizens should enjoy the benefits of a flourishing culture. To be sure, the performing arts rarely pay their way. But they do pay on the broad cultural front of national life, on educational and spiritual issues which are interpreted as moral issues. It was such conviction that led Switzerland to form an Office of Spiritual Defense (1938); Great Britain, at a time of national crisis to found its Arts Council (1946); France, coincident with the inauguration of the Fifth Republic, to organize Ministry of Culture (1958). "In regard to art, the state is here to spend money not to save it," was the way a high official in the Austrian Ministry of Education expressed the underlying philosophy of generous cultural appropriations.[11]

IV. Proposed Legislation

European traditions have, over the centuries, created the right climate for the blossoming of the performing arts. They have established the proper kind of environment, which takes will, planning, and a long concerted effort to maintain at a productive level. Successive European governments have accepted these cultural aims and realized them in terms of educational procedures.

In any nation of the world a suitable art climate depends on a sympathetic philosophy on the part of government. We have observed remarkable progress in the art life of the United States; we note a change in the general psychological premises, which seems to favor increased support of the arts at the present time.

The Eighty-Seventh Congress (1961-1962) had thirteen bills under consideration which specifically relate to the encouragement, growth, and development of the arts in the United States. Seven of these provided "for the establishment of a Federal Advisory Council on the Arts." They are listed here in the order in which they are in the official pamphlet "Aid to Fine Arts" (printed for the use of the Committee on Education and Labor by the United States Government Printing Office, 1961):

H. R. 4172	introduced by	Mr. Frank Thompson, Jr., of New Jersey
H. R. 413	" "	Mr. Carroll D. Kearns of Pennsylvania
H. R. 3250	" "	Mr. Dominick V. Daniels of New Jersey
H. R. 5408	" "	Mr. John V. Lindsay of New York
H. R. 6484	" "	Mr. Seymour Halpern of New York
H. R. 3640	" "	Mrs. Frances P. Bolton of Ohio
S. 741	" "	Mr. Hubert H. Humphrey of Minnesota and co-sponsored by Mr. Joseph S. Clark, Jr., ofPennsylvania, Mr. Paul H. Douglas of Illinois, Mr. Wayne Morse of Oregon, Mr. H. A. Williams of New Jersey, Mr. John Sherman Cooper of Kentucky, Mr. Jacob Javits of New York and Mr. Edward V. Long of Missouri.

Six of these proposed bills were "to establish a program of grants to states for the development of programs and projects in the arts and for other purposes:"

H. R. 4174	introduced by	Mr. Frank Thompson, Jr., of New Jersey
H. R. 1942	" "	Mr. Carroll D. Kearns of Pennsylvania
H. R. 2227	" "	Mr. Frank Chelf of Kentucky
H. R. 2275	" "	Mr. Adam C. Powell of New York
H. R. 3509	" "	Mr. Emanuel Celler of New York
S. 785	" "	Mr. Joseph S. Clark, Jr., of Pennsylvania and co-sponsored by Mr. Hubert H. Humphrey and Mr. Claiborne Pell.

During the Eighty-Eighth Congress (1963-1964), still in session as this book goes to press, various bills for the encouragement of the nation's art life were again introduced. Some of these bills (for example, H.9587, H.5494, H.5496, S.1316, S.2379, H.6364, and H.7196) are designed to establish a "National Council for the Arts and a National Arts Foundation." Among the sponsors of these bills are Mr. Joseph S. Clark, Jr. of Pennsylvania, Mr. John Sherman Cooper of Kentucky, Mr. Hubert H. Humphrey of Minnesota, Mr. Jacob Javits of New York, Mr. Edward M. Kennedy of Massachusetts, Mr. John V. Lindsay of New York, Mr. Edward V. Long of Missouri, Mr. Lee Metcalf of Montana, Mr. Claiborne Pell of Rhode Island, Mr. Jennings Randolph of West Virginia, Mr. Abraham A. Ribicoff of Connecticut, Mr. Hugh Scott of Pennsylvania, Mr. Frank Thompson, Jr. of New Jersey, Mr. H. A. Williams, Jr. of New Jersey. Other bills before the Eighty-Eighth Congress aim at establishing a "National Institute of the Arts and Humanities and authorizing programs of information, education, advisory services and financial assistance for the encouragement and advancement of artistic and cultural activities and for the development of a more widespread appreciation of America's cultural heritage and accomplishments." These bills are identified as H.324, H.1155, H.1895, H.4629, and H.5140. Among the sponsors of these bills are Mr. John H. Dent of Pennsylvania, Mr. John E. Fogarty of Rhode Island, Mr. Edward Boland of Massachusetts, Mr. William Beck Widnall of New Jersey.*

All these bills proposed in support of a national art life amount to an impressive record. Certain members of Congress have publicly expressed their conviction that the time is now ripe to gain sufficient strength for the passing of such laws. In this connection it is well to remember that legislation in Congress is not determined by the urban vote alone, but that a large ballot is cast by members from the rural areas. Would the vote representing the farmlands tend to endanger art legislation? The analogous situation in Europe does not restrict aid to the arts on national or regional levels. Strong rural majorities in large sections of France, Switzerland, Holland, Belgium, or Austria do not jeopardize parliamentary decision in favor of art support. On the contrary, efforts in these countries to decentralize national art life are paying off also in terms of a voting record for the arts. In England, where the national art program is still in the formative years, the systematic conquest of the hinterland has high priority and is likewise expected to bring fast results.

V. Commitment to Culture

Budget for "Spiritual Defense"

President John F. Kennedy recognized the consonance of a free democratic life with a free art life. He claimed the White House as a citadel of American art life and thus created a new image of cultural leadership in our government. He aimed at the formation of a National Council for the Arts and eventually at legislation from which the nation itself would emerge as America's chief patron. But the efforts of the martyred President in behalf of the arts and the artists in America remained an unfinished symphony. Its principal themes, however, were clearly stated, and their final integration into the texture of American culture is a commitment for successive governments. President Lyndon B. Johnson has already expressed his intent to maintain enthusiasm and support for the arts.

On December 20, 1963, the Senate passed the bill (S 2379) providing for the establishment of a National Arts Foundation and authorizing

*Cf. Congressional Record of Eighty-Eighth Congress.

grants up to $5,000,000 in the fiscal year ending July 30 and of $1,000,000 in each following fiscal year. Like European arts councils, the Foundation will offer matching grants to nonprofit professional art organizations and will help in the development of new groups. The catalogue of projects to be sponsored is not limited to the performing arts. In addition to music, theater, and ballet, the Foundation will assist literature, painting, sculpture, architecture, radio, television, motion pictures, and other art projects. The bill has still to be approved by the House of Representatives.

This is a beginning. The bill creating the National Arts Foundation would certainly mark a most welcome turn of events; but much larger sums would eventually have to be approved by Congress to aid the arts.

The late President Kennedy observed, "An industrial civilization brought to the highest point of development has still to prove that it can nourish and sustain a rich cultural life." This, indeed, is our immediate task, and one that cannot be postponed any longer as the world faces the basic choice between two social orders, between an open or a totalitarian society. The superiority of our free way of life must be demonstrated beyond doubt. In this contest of civilizations, a properly functioning cultural life is a fundamental necessity. The pitfalls of our art life have, in fact, become a main target of our critics abroad, and not without justification. Why should not the free and wealthy United States sponsor an art life which would fully reflect the spiritual benefits of liberty and affluence, of free thought and unfettered aesthetic expression?

Many of our citizens object to the high cost which such a large-scale art life supported on various levels of local, state, and federal government would present in terms of taxation. The objectors say that the United States cannot afford the high price of culture. Yet the American people can afford the highest living standards as well as the highest national budget in the contemporary world. The correction of a situation in which vast spending does not include an adequate appropriation for our cultural life is obligatory in the ideological struggle with the East: the "materialistic" Soviet bloc abundantly supports the performing arts from its national treasuries. The price tag of a fully supported American art life would be very low by comparison with the lasting benefits.

We are ready to spend billions of dollars for arms to defend freedom. We entrust this task, as we must, to our government. Ironically, we are reluctant to spend tax pennies for the enriching beauty of a free life which the arms are supposed to defend. If our free lives are essential to us, then let us donate a small fraction of the vast national spending to make this freedom spiritually worthwhile. "Spiritual defense!" We should like to borrow this succinct term, coined by the Swiss at a time of totalitarian threat to their federation; and in this sense we would like to plead for some money for support of the cultural life in our country.

Hierarchy of Values

Throughout the ages science and art have coexisted. The two domains of human search have not only been compatible, but a source of mutual inspiration. In Europe science and art are both given strong financial support by government. In America technology is the prime beneficiary of enormous public and private subsidies. Today, of course the main motivation for this technological spending is defense. The budget for the fiscal year 1963 allocated for national defense, $52,690,000,000; for education, $1,470,000,000; for space research and study, $2,400,000,000. The total budget, $92,500,000,000, marks an increase of $3,400,000,000 over the preceding year. National security and space activities account for more than three-fourths of the increase.

The arts are neglected in this budget. There is no reason that scientific advances should crowd out our art life. While the growing mechanization of our age cannot be halted, we can relegate technology to its proper place where it can develop all of its marvelous resources without devouring the spiritual in our lives. Technology can make possible not only mass destruction, but also peaceful mass communication. We cannot turn back the clock that has marked for us an age of growing dehumanization of man; we can, however, hope to build a strong bulwark of the spirit, and in this task we should rely on the timeless strength inherent in great art.

We need art — today more than ever before. We need art as an antidote against automation. We need the aesthetic enchantment of art, its creative illumination, to counteract the push-button emptiness of our mechanized life. We need art as an armor against the disillusionment and anxiety of our times, as an added defense against the destructive forces inherent in man, before it is too late and they assume the dimensions of total slaughter.

The patronage of art, America's most urgent problem in the cultural sphere, requires fresh, objective consideration in all of its alternatives. The plain fact is that we have not yet begun to explore the possibilities of total art patronage; we have only rejected them. All the resources of high cultural attainment are available to us. If our art life is to keep pace with those aspects of American civilization in which we lead the world, we cannot without grave risk postpone our commitment to culture.

NOTES AND BIBLIOGRAPHIES

This is largely a book of facts. As stated in the Prologue, personal investigation is at the root of the contemporary data. The author visited most of the places and art institutions surveyed in this study, and many others not mentioned by name. Data were assembled by conferring directly with government officials, with administrators and directors of the European art organizations surveyed in the preceding Chapters. Normally no special reference is made here to materials and statistics obtained by personal interview.

A Selective Bibliography for each Chapter has been added to the Notes. There is also a General Bibliography. It includes not only books and source material the author has consulted but many others which might guide reader and student toward additional information on the basic themes and issues discussed in the Chapters.

Much of the history of music and the theater implicitly yields significant aspects in the chronicle of art patronage. The systematic study of the performing arts in regard to their liturgical and secular support throughout the ages emerges to a certain extent from an abstraction of general histories of music and the theater.

There exists to the author's knowledge no comprehensive treatment in book form of the patronage of the performing arts in Europe. On the other hand, many publications are devoted to the history of the theater and music. It may suffice here to direct the reader to some established sources, to histories, dictionaries, monographs, and periodicals to facilitate further study.

As to the support of the performing arts in the United States, a systematic account has still to be written.* But numerous articles and essays have appeared in print. The fight for adequate support of the performing arts in America, in fact, is being fought on various fronts. In recent years particularly, many accounts have appeared in newspaper columns in the *New York Times*, the *New York Herald Tribune* and other art-conscious dailies from coast to coast. Anyone attempting to trace this development will also have to consult the *Saturday Review*, *International Musician*, *Musical America*, and other journals and magazines earnestly concerned with the safeguarding of American art life. A few radio and television programs have made time available for the debate of public art subsidy.

*Comprehensive studies covering the development and support of the performing arts in the United States are in progress as this book goes to press. These studies are supported by the Rockefeller Brothers Fund and the 20th Century Fund.

The Rockefeller study will focus on the development of institutions of art and suggest possible solutions for the principal problems. The study sponsored by the 20th Century Fund will concentrate on an economic analysis of the performing arts. There will be coordination and exchange of information to avoid duplication.

The all-important report "The Arts and the National Government" submitted to the President by August Heckscher was published after this manuscript was completed.

AUTHOR'S NOTES

There are two kinds of notes in this book. Footnotes on the page with asterisk references — one asterisk for first reference; two asterisks for the second reference; a dagger for the third (per page). Notes here, at back of book, with Arabic number references, are in sequence within chapters.

PROLOGUE

pp. 1–7

1. O. Glenn Saxton, Professor of Economics, Yale University, *The Plight of the Living Theater in the United States.*

2. Cf. Frank Emerson Andrews and Ann D. Walton, *The Foundation Directory.* (*Russell Sage Foundation,* New York, 1960). According to this report, the humanities received (in a typical year) $33,922,000 out of a total of $625,000,000 dispensed by 4,685 foundations. The report includes in the category of the humanities: "fine arts, communications, music, recreation, and history."

AUSTRIA

pp. 9–49

1. A selection of compositions by the emperors Ferdinand III, Leopold I, and Joseph I, edited by Professor Guido Adler, was published in 1893.

2. Prince Paul Anton Eszterházy engaged Haydn as court conductor in 1761; in 1762 Prince Nicholas became the sovereign of Eisenstadt and Eszterháza.

3. The first reference to this offer occurs in Beethoven's letter of November 1, 1808.

4. In 1812 young Prince Kinsky was fatally injured by a fall from his horse. In the same year, at the height of the Napoleonic wars, Prince Lobkowitz went bankrupt. Inflation further reduced Beethoven's annuity.

5. Cf. Alma Mahler, *Gustav Mahler; Erinnerungen und Briefe* (Bermann-Fischer Verlag, 1949).

6. The parliamentary election of 1962 gave the Clerical party 81 seats, the Socialists 76. The Communists lost all seats, but a new right-wing party gained 8 seats.

7. Salzburg's distinguished Music Academy functions year round.

8. We note the choice of works in one single summer season (1958): *Wozzeck* by Alban Berg; *Mathis der Maler* by Paul Hindemith; *Palestrina* by Hans Pfitzner; *Notre Dame* by Franz Schmidt; *Salome, Ariadne auf Naxos,* and *Der Rosenkavalier* by Richard Strauss.

9. The capital of Vorarlberg is Bregenz, seat of a summer festival.

10. Thespis, the Greek poet, sixth century B. C., is considered by some scholars to have inaugurated the performance of tragedy. According to Horace, Thespis traveled around the country in a cart on which his plays were acted.

SELECTED BIBLIOGRAPHY

Adler, Guido (ed.) *Denkmäler der Tonkunst in Österreich* Vienna.
Austrian Information (Published by Austrian Information Service, New York)

Austrian Year Books (Published by State Printing Office, Vienna)

Budget and Operational Plans of Theaters in Austrian Provinces

Budgets of City of Vienna (Published by the Magistrate of the City of Vienna)

Budgets of Federal Republic (Published by State Printing Office, Vienna)

Die Stadt Wien als Mäzen Vienna, 1932

Geiringer, Karl *Haydn A Creative Life in Music* New York, 1946

Griesinger, G. A. *Biographische Notizen über Joseph Haydn* Leipzig, 1810

Huber, Alfons, and Redlich, Oswald *Geschichte Österreichs* Vienna, 1939

Kralik, Heinrich von *Die Wiener Philharmoniker* Vienna, 1937

Kraus, Karl *Die Fackel* Vienna, 1899-1934

Kulturarbeit der Stadt Wien (Published by Municipal Office for Culture and Popular Education) Vienna, 1955

Laube, Heinrich *Das Burgtheater Wien* Vienna, 1868

Mandyczewski, Eusebius *Geschichte der K. K. Gesellschaft der Musikfreunde in Wien;* 2 volumes Vienna, 1912

Marboe, Ernst *The Book of Austria* Vienna, 1948

Mayer, Franz Martin *Geschichte Österreichs* Vienna, 1901

Nowak, Leopold *Joseph Haydn* Vienna, 1951

Österreichisches Jahrbuch (Published by Federal Press Office) Vienna 1962

Redlich, Joseph *Kaiser Franz Joseph von Österreich* Berlin, 1928

Riehl, Hans *Barocke Baukunst in Österreich* Vienna, 1930

Schenk, Erich *Mozart* Vienna, 1955

Stefan, Paul *Geschichte der Wiener Oper* Vienna, 1932

Steiner, Hugo *950 Jahre Österreich* Vienna, 1946

Thayer, A. *The Life of Ludwig van Beethoven,* (tr. and ed H. Krehbiel); 3 Vol. New York, 1921

Wiener Stadthalle Vienna, 1958

Wiener Theater Jahrbücher ed. by Friedrich Langer 1952-1958

Winkler, Arnold *Geschichte Österreichs 1918-1945* Vienna, 1946

Wlassack, Ernst *Chronik des K. K. Hofburgtheaters* Vienna, 1876

Year Books: *Landestheater Graz*
Landestheater Innbruck
Landestheater Klagenfurt
Landestheater Linz
Landestheater Salzburg

Zweig, Stefan *The World of Yesterday* New York, 1933

ITALY

pp. 51–108

1. *Cf. Georgics* III.
2. Novalis was the pen name of Friedrich Freiherr von Hardenberg, German poet and novelist (1772-1801).
3. Pope Leo X was the son of Lorenzo, and Clement VII was his nephew.
4. Such expedients were normally of a contrapuntal nature; for instance, the doubling or diminution of the note values tried to hide the secular building stones of the music.
5. In its twenty-second general session, adopting the canon proposed by the musical experts one week earlier.
6. Contrary to legend, Palestrina had written the *Mass*, named in honor of his principal sponsor, Pope Marcellus II, prior to 1545, the initial year of the Council of Trent. This fact merely proves the composer's anticipation of the Tridentine directions.
7. The *Giovinezza* was written in 1909, thirteen years before the advent of fascism, by the operetta composer Giuseppe Blanc. The indistinguished tune was adopted by the Fascisti as their official hymn. They were confident that they could promote it to the popularity of a hit song by constant repetition. They did.
8. Cf. Slonimsky, Nicolas *Music Since 1900* Coleman-Ross Co., Inc. New York. [Used by permission of Publisher]
9. Rome had been declared an open city, and so was spared the destruction of Nazi barbarism.
10. In the municipal elections of 1960 the Communist Party received 27.9 per cent of the total vote.
11. In 1898 Toscanini was appointed musical director of La Scala. He abandoned and resumed this post several times throughout his brilliant and stormy career.
12. Cf. Dr. Antonio Ghiringhelli, Edizioni della Scala, 1956. *Appunti Sul Teatro Lirico.*
13. After the death of his brother, Joseph II, Peter Leopold became Emperor of Austria, assuming the name Leopold II.
14. Altogether, the musicians receive thirteen salaries — an extra check at Christmas, in typical European procedure.

15. For the so-called "gala nights" (special premiéres) tickets cost $16.00. At these social occasions evening dress is required in stalls and boxes.
16. Cf. *Verdi: The Man and His Letters*, edited by Franz Werfel and Paul Stefan, tr. by Edward Downes.
17. The principal composers of the early Neapolitan school were Francesco Provenzale (1627-1704), Alessandro Stradella (1642-1682), and Alessandro Scarlatti (1660-1725).
18. Ferdinand had been engaged to another daughter of Maria Theresia, the Princess Marie Josefine; she died. The Austrian Empress was quick to arrange the marriage of Maria Carolina with Ferdinand.
19. The names reach from Palestrina, Frescobaldi, Monteverdi, Corelli, and Scarlatti to Mendelssohn, Wagner, Mahler, Schoenberg, Stravinsky, Hindemith, and other masters.
20. Among these were the Filarmonica (founded in 1821) and the Società Musicale Romana (founded in 1874).
21. In the official communication issued by the Council of Ministers and the General Direction of Spectacles, Rome, July 23, 1958, addressed to all prefects of the Republic.

SELECTED BIBLIOGRAPHY

Biennale di Venezia *Revista Trimestrale*

Burckhardt, Jacob *Civilization of the Renaissance in Italy* (tr. S. G. C. Middlemore) London, 1929

Croce, Benedetto *A History of Italy* Oxford, England, 1929. tr. by Cecilia M. Ady

Duchartre, Pierre Louis *The Italian Comedy, the Improvisation, Scenarios, Lives, Attributes, Portraits and Masks of the Illustrious Characters of the Commedia dell'Arte* tr. from the French by R. T. Weaver London and New York, 1929

Fellerer, Karl Gustav *Palestrina* Regensburg, 1930

Gatti, Guido *Verdi* 2 Vol. Milan, 1930-1933

Ghiringhelli, Antonio *Apunti Sul Teatro Lirico;* Edizioni della Scala 1956

Hay, Denys *The Italian Renaissance* Cambridge, England 1961

Hazlitt, W. C. *The Venetian Republic* London, 1915

Il Ponte: Lo Spettacolo Oggi in Italia Florence, 1957

Il Teatro di San Carlo; Dell'ente autonomo del Teatro; Naples, 1951

Kennard, Joseph Spencer *The Italian Theatre*, 2 vols. New York, 1932

La Scala 1946-1956 Edizioni della Scala Milan, 1956

Martin, George *Verdi His Music, Life and Times* New York, 1963

Piccolo Teatro; 1947-1958 Milan, 1958

Rome — Teatro dell Opera Rome, 1958

Salvatorelli, Luigi *Sommario della Storia d'Italia;* 4 vol. Turin, 1938

Santa Cecilia *Revista Bimestrale* Rome, 1958

Schrade, Leo *Monteverdi* New York, 1950

SWITZERLAND

pp. 109–131

1. *Kulturpolitik in der Schweiz; Schweizer Spiegel Verlag* (Zurich, 1954).
2. Cf. *Tonhallegesellschaft*, for organizational status of orchestra.
3. To this day the Zurich Opera is managed under its original title, Stadt Theater Aktiengesellschaft — a name which indicates the private element in the setup of the theater. Cf. *Vertrag zwischen der Stadt Zürich und der Theater Aktiengesellschaft* Zürich.
4. Annual Reports, Rechenschaftsberrichte des Verwaltungsrates der Theater Aktiengesellschaft Zürich.
5. Such a policy is by no means generally adhered to throughout Europe. Ticket prices for festivals and special performances in West Germany, Italy, France, or Austria are very high. Management aims at maximum income which is obtainable during the tourist season. Scalpers often sell tickets at exorbitant commissions for festival performances.
6. Berichte des Vorstandes der Tonhallegesellschaft Zürich.
7. In 1962 serious disagreement occurred when the orchestra refused

to rehearse Beethoven's *Fidelio* for a scheduled festival performance under a distinguished guest conductor, following arguments during previous rehearsals. This episode, involving questions of artistic discipline and procedure, led to deplorable consequences which in turn shed light on the status of an independent orchestra within an opera theater.

8. Basler Orchester-Gesellschaft; Jahresbericht; Jahresrechnung.
9. Cf. The original Zurich Collegium Musicum was founded in 1613.
10. The present subsidy is earmarked for a substantial raise.

SELECTED BIBLIOGRAPHY

Basler Orchester-Gesellschaft Dienstvertrag

Burckhardt, Jacob *Reflections on History* London, 1943

Die Berufsbühnen in der Schweiz Zürich, 1931-32

Die Schweiz Herausgegeben von der Neuen Helvetischen Gesellschaft Zürich, 1919-1954

Erneuerung des Schweizerischen Theaters 1934

Giterman, Valentin *Geschichte der Schweiz* Thaygen-Schaffhausen, 1949

Huber, Hans *How Switzerland is Governed* Zurich, 1946

Mitteilungen der Schweizerischen Gesellschaft für Theaterkultur 1949-1956

Sacher, Paul Alte und Neue Musik; Das Basler Kammerorchester 1926-1951 Basel, 1952

Soloveytchik, George *Switzerland in Perspective* London, 1954

Stadtheater Basel; Jahrbücher

Stadtheater Zürich; Jahrbücher

Statistisches Jahrbuch der Schweiz Basel, 1900-1962

Theater Aktiengesellschaft Rechenschaftsberichte Zürich

Tonhalle Gesellschaft Berichte des Vorstandes Zürich

Vertrag zwischen der Stadt Zürich und der Theater Aktiengesellschaft Zürich

Vertrag zwischen der Stadt Zürich und der Tonhallegesellschaft Zürich

Weiss, Fritz *Schweizerische Gesellschaft für der Theaterkulture* Thalwil, 1953

FRANCE

pp. 133–210

1. Quoted in Jacques Barzun's preface to his translation of *Figaro's Marriage.* As Dr. Barzun explains, "Figaro's ideas about society were hardly new, except on the stage, when they appeared there in 1784. Thanks to the 'liberals' of a century before, to Montesquieu and Voltaire, to Diderot and the Encyclopedists, thanks above all to Rousseau's writing and personality, the enlightened aristocracy and high bourgeoisie of the eighteenth century were quite convinced that birth was worthless compared to talents and that established authority cloaked incompetence and injustice. A theatrical audience could respond to Figaro's indignation because it seemed not so much subversive as appropriate."
2. Cf. Louis Véron *Mémoires d'un bourgeois de Paris* (1856-57).
3. Significantly, the two other dramatic scores of Berlioz experienced their first important productions outside of France. In 1862 *Béatrice et Bénédict* (after Shakespeare's *Much Ado About Nothing*) was heard in Baden-Baden, Germany. In 1890 the first part of *Les Troyens* was produced, posthumously, at Karlsruhe (in a German translation); the second part of this work, *Les Troyens à Carthage*, was given at the Paris Théâtre-Lyrique in 1863.
4. "At the time of the *Fronde*, Paris was the largest city of France; in 1789, it was France herself."

SELECTED BIBLIOGRAPHY

Antoine *Le Théâtre* Paris, 1932

Barzun, Jacques *Berlioz and the Romantic Century* New York, 1950

Belloc, Hilaire *The French Revolution* London, 1960

Bourgeois, Emile *History of Modern France;* 2 volumes Cambridge, England, 1919

Brunetiere, F. *Les Epoques du Théâtre français* Paris, 1906

Chouquet, Adolphe-Gustave *Histoire de la Musique dramatique en France* Paris, 1873

Crosten, William L. *French Grand Opera; An Art and a Business*, New York, 1948

Davis, William Stearns *A History of France* New York, 1919

Duruy, Jean Victor *Histoire de France* Paris, 1891

Gautier, Théophile *Histoire de l'art dramatique en France* Paris, 1858

Histoire du Romantisme en France Paris, 1874

Hawkins, Frederick *The French Stage in the Eighteenth Century*, 2 volumes 1888

Lancaster, Henry Carrington *A History of French Dramatic Literature*, 9 volumes Baltimore and Paris, 1929-1942

Lavignac, A. J. Albert *Encyclopédie de la Musique et Dictionnaire du Conservatoire* Paris

Lintilhac, E. *Histoire Générale du Théâtre en France* Paris, 1904-1911

Maurois, André *A History of France* New York, 1956

Matthews, Brander *The Theaters of Paris* London and New York, 1880

Molière, Jean Baptiste *Oeuvres Complètes* Paris, 1904

Park, Julian *The Culture of France in Our Time* Cornell, New York, 1954

Pincherle, Marc *L'Opéra-comique française* Paris, 1951

Pruniéres, Henri *A New History of Music* tr. and ed. by Edward Lockspeiser New York, 1943

Rambaud, Alfred *Histoire de la Civilization française* Paris, 1898

Reunion des Théâtres Lyriques Nationaux Réglement Général Paris, 1942

Rolland, Romain *Histoire de l'Opéra en Europe avant Lully et Scarlatti*, 3rd ed. Paris, 1931

WEST GERMANY

pp. 211–309

1. Part of the Fugger Library, now housed in the Vienna National Library, represents an outstanding collection of source material.
2. In contrast to the licentious treatment of historic facts in *Tannhäuser*, Wagner relied on careful research for his *Meistersinger;* he realized in the first and third acts of the opera an authoritative evocation of their traditions.
3. Johann Hermann Schein (1586-1630), one of the most significant composers of the seventeenth century. During his Leipzig tenure he held the proud title: "General-Director der Musik."
4. England must be considered the pioneer country of "modern" concert life. Public performances for the benefit of a paying audience were presented in London as early as 1672. John Banister, member of the band of King Charles II, is credited with the innovation.
5. Cf. developments in Basel, Zurich, Winterthur etc. Chapter on Switzerland.
6. By the treaty of Utrecht, Elector Frederick III of Brandenburg became King Frederick William I of Prussia. He acceded to the throne on May 15, 1713; European powers acknowledged the emergence of Prussia as a new kingdom.
7. Today, there are some 40 tableaux by Watteau in existence; 9 of them can be seen where one would least expect to find them — in Berlin.
8. Augustus II; Elector of Saxony (1694-1733); King of Poland (1697-1704; 1709-1733).
9. Frederick August III (1696-1763); Elector of Saxony (1733-1763); as Frederick Augustus II, King of Poland.
10. Cf. Hamburgische Dramaturgie, No. 26.
11. Ibid.
12. Joseph von Sonnenfels, writer and poet, future director of the Burgtheater in Vienna.
13. Originally delivered as a lecture before the *Kurpfälzische deutsche Gesellschaft* in Mannheim.
14. Max Martersteig, *Das deutsche Theater im neunzehnten Jahrhundert* (Breitkopf und Härtel; Leipzig; 1924).
15. Ibid.
16. Nicolas Slonimsky, *Lexicon of Musical Invective* (Used by permisson of Coleman-Ross Company, Inc. New York, 1953).
17. The birthplaces of Goethe (Frankfurt) and Schiller (Marbach) are both in the Western zone. Bach's Thuringian birthplace, the town of Eisenach, belongs to the Eastern

zone, as do the principal stations of his lifework.

18. Since the completion of this book, *The Deputy* by Rolf Hochhuth has attracted international attention.
19. The list of recipients of these commissions includes Boulez, Dallapiccola, Honegger, Liebermann, Messiaen, Milhaud, Nono, Petrassi, Stockhausen, Wildberger, Zimmermann, etc.

SELECTED BIBLIOGRAPHY

Benz, Richard *Die Zeit der deutschen Klassik* Stuttgart, 1953

Brinkmann, H. *Entstehungsgeschichte des Minnesangs* Halle, 1926

Brachvogel, A. E. *Geschichte des Königlichen Theaters zu Berlin* 1878

Bulthaupt, Heinrich *Dramaturgie des Schauspiels;* Vol. 1-10 Oldenburg, 1902

Dickinson, Robert E. *Germany, A General and Regional Geography* New York, 1953

Drese, Claus Helmut *Das Neue Nationaltheater* Mannheim, 1957

Deutschland Heute (Official Statistics) Bonn, 1955

Eisenberg, Ludwig *Grosses Biographisches Lexikon der deutschen Bühne im 19 Jahrhundert* Leipzig, 1903

Gurlitt, Willibald *Johann Walter und die Musik der Reformationszeit* Lutherjahrbuch, 1933

Herrig, Hans *Die Meininger und ihre Gastspiele* 1879

Hinkel, Hans *Handbuch der Reichskulturkammer* Berlin, 1937

Hitler, Adolf *Mein Kampf* Munich, 1925, 1927

Konzerthaus; Stuttgarter Liederhalle Stuttgart, 1956

Kohn, Hans *The Mind of Germany* New York, 1960

Kraus, C. von *Walther von der Vogelweide* Berlin, 1935

L'Arronge A. *Deutsches Theater und deutsche Schauspielkunst* Berlin, 1896

Lehmann-Haupt, Hellmut *Art under Dictatorship* New York, 1954

Martersteig, Max *Das deutsche Theater im neunzehnten Jahrhundert* Leipzig, 1924

Moser, H. J. *Die Musikgenossenschaften im deutschen Mittelalter* Rostock, 1910

Müller, E. H. *Heinrich Schütz* Leipzig, 1925

Neumann, Angelo *Erinnerungen an Richard Wagner* Leipzig, 1907

Pichler, Anton *Chronik des Grossherzoglichen Hof und Nationaltheaters in Mannheim* Mannheim, 1879

Pinson, Koppel S. *Modern Germany; its History and Civilization* New York, 1954

Quantz, Johann Joachim *Versuch einer Anweisung die Flöte Traversière zu spielen* Kassel and Basel, 1953

Schlenther, Paul *Genesis der Freien Bühne* Berlin, 1889

Schuh, Willi (ed.) *Richard Strauss — Stefan Zweig Briefwechsel* Frankfurt, 1957

Shirer, William L. *The Rise and Fall of the Third Reich* New York, 1960

Snyder, Louis L. *Documents of German History* New Brunswick, N. J., 1958

Stuckenschmidt, Hans Heinz *Musik unter Hitler* Forum, *Vienna, 1963*

Uhde, Hermann *Das Stadttheater in Hamburg* 1879

Valentin, Veit *The German People; Their History and Civilization from the Holy Roman Empire to the Third Reich* New York, 1946

Weber, E. W. *Zur Geschichte des Weimarischen Theaters* Weimar, 1865

UNITY OF THE LOW COUNTRIES

p. 311

SELECTED BIBLIOGRAPHY

Eyck, F. Gunther *The Benelux Countries; An Historical Survey* Princeton, 1959

Geyl, Pieter *Holland and Belgium; Their Common History and their Relations* Leyden, 1920

Meade, James E. *Negotiations for Benelux; An Annotated Chronicle* Princeton, 1957

THE NETHERLANDS

pp. 313–353

1. Count Egmont (commander of the revolutionary forces that rose against Philip II, King of Spain, and his brutal governor-general, the Duke of Alba) was executed in Brussels on June 5, 1568.
2. For the Vienna première of Goethe's play in 1810.
3. *Geschichte des Abfalls der Vereinigten Niederlande von der Spanischen Regierung.*
4. Cf. P. 470ff.
5. In 1960 the board included 1 music educator, 1 musicologist, 1 conductor (or manager) of a symphony orchestra, 1 singer, and 1 instrumentalist (active as soloist on the concert stage), 1 choral conductor, 3 composers, 2 orchestra musicians, and 2 musicians representing government sponsored and private art organizations.
6. Cf. *Theatre;* Amsterdam; commissioned by the Ministry of Education, Arts and Sciences.

SELECTED BIBLIOGRAPHY

Barnow, A. J. *The Making of Modern Holland* London, 1948

Landheer, Bartholomew *The Netherlands* Berkeley, Cal., 1946

Reeser, Eduard (ed.) *Music in Holland* Amsterdam

Renier, G. J. *The Dutch Nation* Amsterdam, 1947

Sonorum Speculum (Periodical published by the Donemus Foundation with the support of the Ministry of Education, Arts and Sciences) Amsterdam

BELGIUM

pp. 355–371

1. Flemish is a variant of the Dutch language and its West Germanic-Netherlandish roots. The Walloons speak, in addition to French, their own Romance dialect, which exists in contemporary Belgium in four different varieties.
2. Cf. *Belgium*, edited by Jan-Albert Goris. Berkeley, California, 1945.

SELECTED BIBLIOGRAPHY

Borren, Charles van den *Orlando di Lassus* Paris, 1920

Brenet, M. *Grétry, sa vie et ses oeuvres* Paris, 1884

Coussemaker, E. H. de *Histoire de l'harmonie au moyen-âge* Paris, 1852

Fierens-Gevaert, H. *Histoire de la peinture flamande des origines à la fin du XVè siècle* Brussels, 1927

Goris, Jan Albert (ed.) *Belgium* Berkeley, California, 1945

Hamelius, P. *Introduction à la littérature française et flamande de Belgique* Brussels, 1921

Hymans, Louis *Histoire parlementaire de la Belgique de 1830 a 1890;* 8 vol. Brussels, 1877-1901

Pirenne, Henri *Histoire de Belgique;* 6 vol. Brussels, 1900-1926

LUXEMBOURG

pp. 373–376

SELECTED BIBLIOGRAPHY

Herchen, Charles Joseph *History of the Grand Duchy of Luxembourg* Luxembourg, 1947

Tudor, Edwards *Belgium and Luxembourg* London and New York, 1951

Weber, Paul *Geschichte des Luxemburger Landes* Luxembourg, 1948

Notes and Bibliography

ENGLAND

pp. 377–432

1. Cf. *Help for the Arts* (A report to the Calouste Gulbenkian Foundation, 1959).
2. Cf. Annual Report of the Royal Opera House, Covent Garden, 1960-61.
3. Ibid.
4. Cf. Eleventh Annual Report of the Arts Council of Great Britain.
5. Cf. Ninth, Tenth, and Twelfth Annual Report of the Arts Council of Great Britain.
6. Cf. Fourteenth Annual Report of the Arts Council of Great Britain.
7. Ibid.
8. Cf. BBC Handbook 1960 London.
9. Ibid.
10. Cf. BBC Handbook 1961 London.
11. Cf. Fourteenth Annual Report of the Arts Council of Great Britain.
12. Ibid.
13. A special problem which still remains to be solved concerns the support of the Royal Shakespeare Theatre. Late in 1960 the Royal Theatre in Stratford-on-Avon, the poet's birthplace, established an extension of its activities in London; its Shakespearean productions in the capital have justly won international distinction by their stylistic validity. But recently the management of the Theatre disappointed its many admirers by the announcement that it could not continue its London performances for 1963-64 unless a contribution of £50,000 from the Arts Council was forthcoming. Actually, the Arts Council is not at fault; the government, at different times, has issued ambivalent and even conflicting plans. And the government's costly project for a national theater on the South Bank of the Thames has diminished the hope of the Royal Shakespeare Theatre for a substantial subsidy in the near future.
14. Cf. Fifteenth Annual Report of the Arts Council of Great Britain.
15. Cf. Sixteenth Annual Report of the Arts Council of Great Britain.
16. Cf. *Works of Henry Purcell* Vol XII Novello and Company, Limited London, 1903.

SELECTED BIBLIOGRAPHY

Arts Council of Great Britain Annual Reports London

BBC Handbooks (British Broadcasting Corporation) London

Britain An Official Handbook; prepared by the Central Office of Information, London, 1958

British Council Annual Reports London

British Federation of Music Festivals Year Books London 1957

Facing the Music (A Memorandum submitted to the Arts Council of Great Britain by the Orchestral Employers' Association) London, 1958

Haley, Sir William *The Responsibilities of Broadcasting:* The Lewis Fry Memorial Lectures 1948

Maitland, James A. F. *English Music in the Nineteenth Century* London, 1902

Paulu, Burton *British Broadcasting: Radio and Television in the United Kingdom* 1956

Royal Festival Hall The Official Record; ed. Max Parrish, London; Published in Association with the London County Council, 1951

Royal Opera House Annual Reports London

Sadler's Wells Annual Reports London

Shaw, Watkins *The Three Choirs Festival: The Official History* 1713-1953

Walker, Ernest *A History of Music in England* 3rd ed. London, 1952-1954

EPILOGUE

pp. 433–483

1. One, known as the *Small Hall*, is designed for performances by chamber orchestras, small choirs, and related ensembles of reduced size. The other will be the *Recital Hall* accommodating approximately 400 people; it will be appropriate for the performance of Lieder, sonatas, and the like.
2. Cf. *BBC Handbook, 1961* (British Broadcasting Corporation, London).
3. Cf. Plato, *Laws* II, 658e.
4. Based on statistics published by Broadcast Music, Inc. in *Twenty Years of Service to Music* (1940-1960).
5. "Major" orchestras operate on annual minimum budgets of $250,000. The budget of the "Metropolitan" orchestra ranges from $100,000 to $250,000.
6. Cf. *International Musician* (May, 1961).
7. Ibid.
8. Cf. *Announcing Establishment of the Pittsburgh Symphony Endowment*, November 18, 1963.
9. Thus, the Zürich Stadt Theater, under its former Intendant Herbert Graf, has set a remarkable record in creating opportunities of stage experience for young American singers in Switzerland. In 1960 about 160 American-born singers were engaged in the opera theaters of West Germany. The procedure, however, is being severely contested by the German Theater Union which contends that the United States should provide its own opportunities in this initial phase in the careers of her young artists.
10. *Complete Works of Abraham Lincoln* (Vol II, p 186) Edited by John G. Nicolay and John Hay New York, 1905.
11. In a debate on the budget of the Salzburg Landestheater, members of the Council expressed dissatisfaction with the proposed budget of the management because it did not, in the opinion of the Council, ask for adequate appropriations for the season 1962-63.

GENERAL BIBLIOGRAPHY

Abraham, Gerald *A Hundred Years of Music* New York, 1938

Adler, Guido (ed.) *Handbuch der Musikgeschichte;* 2 vol. Berlin, 1930

Aid to Fine Arts Hearing before the Select Subcommittee on Education and Labor, House of Representatives Eighty-seventh Congress Washington, 1961

Baker's Biographical Dictionary of Musicians, revised by Nicolas Slonimsky New York, 1958

Barzun, Jacques *The House of Intellect* New York, 1959

Beaumarchais, Pierre *Oeuvres Complètes* (ed. Fournier) Paris, 1875

Boas, George *The Heaven of Invention* Baltimore, 1962

Bücken, Ernst (ed.) *Handbuch der Musikwissenschaft Potsdam*, 1927-1936

Bukofzer, Manfred *Music in the Baroque Era* New York, 1947

Burney, Charles *A General History of Music from the Earliest Ages to the Present Period:* London 1776-1789

The Present State of Music in France and Italy London, 1771-1773

The Present State of Music in Germany, The Netherlands and the United Provinces; 2 volumes London, 1773-1775

Chailley, Jacques *La Musique médiévale* Paris, 1951

Cheney, Sheldon *The Theatre* New York, London, Toronto, 1951

Collins, R. W. *A History of Medieval Civilization in Europe* Boston, 1936

Congressional Records (U.S.A.)

Coussemaker, Edmond Henri de *Histoire de l'harmonie au moyen-âge* Paris

David, Hans T. and Arthur Mendel *The Bach Reader* New York, 1945

Dorian, Frederick *The History of Music in Performance* New York, 1942

Della Corte, Andrea *L'Opera comica italiana del Settecento* 2 volumes Bari, 1923

Dumont, G. M. *Parallele des plus belles salles de spectacle d'Italie et de France* Paris, 1763

Einstein, Alfred *Music in the Romantic Era* New York, 1947

Eitner, Robert *Quellen Lexicon der Musiker und Musikgelehrten der Christlichen Zeitrechnung bis zur Mitte des XIX Jahrhunderts.* 10 volumes Leipzig, 1899-1904

Engel, Hans *Musik und Gesellschaft* Berlin-Halensee, 1960

Ferguson, D. N. *A History of Musical Thought* New York, 1935

Florimo, Francesco *La scuola musicale di Napoli e i suoi Conservatori* Naples republished 1880-1884

Goethe, Johann Wolfgang *Sämtliche Werke.* 16 volumes Stuttgart, 1904

Grove, George *Dictionary of Music and Musicians* 5th ed., ed. by Eric Blom New York, 1955

Hauser, Arnold *The Social History of Art:* 2 volumes; Translated in Collaboration with the author by Stanley Godman) London, 1952

Heckscher, August *The Public Happiness* New York, 1962

The Arts and the National Government Report to the President Washington, 1963

Landon, Robbins H. C. *The Collected Correspondence and London Notebooks of Joseph Haydn* Fairlawn, N. J., 1959

Lang, Paul Henry *Music in Western Civilization* New York, 1941

Lessing, Gottfried Ephraim *Sämtliche Werke* Leipzig and Vienna, 1911

Knepler, Georg *Musikgeschichte des XIX Jahrhunderts* Berlin, 1961

Macgowan, Kenneth, and William Melnitz *The Living Stage* Englewood Cliffs, N. J., 1955

Mantzius, Karl *A History of Theatrical Art in Ancient and Modern Times* (Tr. by Louise von Cossel and C. Archer), 6 volumes London, 1903-1921

Mumford, Lewis *The City in History* New York, 1961

Nicoll, Allardyce *World Drama from Aeschylus to Anouilh* New York, 1950

Nietzsche, Friedrich *Sämtliche Werke;* 7 volumes Leipzig, 1930-1931

Preussner, Eberhard *Die bürgerliche Musikkultur* Hamburg, 1935

Reese, Gustave *Music in the Middle Ages* New York, 1940

Music in the Renaissance New York, 1954

Riemann, Hugo *Musik Lexikon, 12th* ed., edited by Willbald Gurlitt Mainz, Germany, 1959-1961

Rouché, J. *L'art théâtrical moderne* Paris, 1910

Sachs, Curt *Our Musical Heritage* New York, 1948
The Commonwealth of Art New York, 1946

Sachs, E. O. and E. A. Woodward, *Modern Opera Houses and Theatres* London, 1896-1898

Schering, Arnold *Studien zur Musikgeschichte der Frührenaissance* Leipzig, 1914

Schweitzer, Albert *J. S. Bach* (tr. by Ernest Newman) London, 1935

Schiller, Friedrich *Sämtliche Werke.* 16 volumes Stuttgart, 1904

Sittard, J. *Zur Geschichte der Musik und des Theaters am Württembergischen Hofe* Stuttgart, 1891

Slonimsky, Nicolas *Lexicon of Musical Invective* New York, 1953
Music Since 1900 New York, 1949

Spitta, Philipp *J. S. Bach* (tr. by Clara Bell and J. A. Fuller-Maitland) New York, 1899

Theatre in the Twentieth Century (ed. by Robert W. Corrigan) New York, 1963

Works of Aristotle (tr. under editorship of W. D. Ross) London, 1955

Works of Plato (trans. by B. Jowett) 4 volumes New York, 1937

Wagner, Richard *Gesammelte Schriften* 14 volumes Leipzig, 1914

Windelband, Wilhelm *A History of Philosophy* New York, 1958

The periodicals, scholarly journals and magazines listed below are valuable for further research; many of them have been consulted for this study.

Acta Musicologica
Archiv für Musikwissenschaft
Arts (L'hebdomadire de l'intelligence française)
Drama
International Musician
Journal of the American Musicological Society
Melos
Monatshefte für Musikgeschichte
Music and Letters
Musical America
Neue Zeitschrift für Musik
New Theatre Magazine
Notes
Opera
Opera News
Players Magazine
Recherches Théâtrales
Revista Musicale Italiana
Revue Musicale
Sammelbände der Internationalen Musikgesellschaft
Saturday Review
Studien zur Musikwissenschaft
Theatre Arts
Theater der Zeit
The Musical Quarterly
The Music Review
Vierteljahrschrift für Musikwissenschaft
World Theatre
Zeitschrift für Musikwissenschaft

INDEX

T

U